International Standard Library of Chinese Medicine

Tui Na

Project Editors: Huang Lei, Liu Shui
Copy Editor: Xu Qian-qian
Book Designer: Guo Miao
Cover Designer: Guo Miao
Typesetter: He Mei-ling

International Standard Library of Chinese Medicine

Tui Na

Jin Hong-zhu (金宏柱)

Professor of Acupuncture & Tui Na,
Nanjing University of TCM,
Nanjing, China

Secondo Scarsella, MD, DDS

Attending Maxillofacial Surgeon,
Department of Maxillofacial Surgery, San Salvatore Hospital,
L'Aquila, Italy
Visiting Professor of Nanjing University of TCM,
China

Ding Xiao-hong (丁晓红)

Professor of International Education College,
Nanjing University of TCM,
Nanjing, China

PMPH 人民卫生出版社
PEOPLE'S MEDICAL PUBLISHING HOUSE

人民卫生出版社
PMPH PEOPLE'S MEDICAL PUBLISHING HOUSE

Website: http://www.pmph.com/en

Book Title: Tui Na (International Standard Library of Chinese Medicine)(DVD Included)
推拿学（国际标准化英文版中医教材）（含光盘）

Contact address: No. 19, Pan Jia Yuan Nan Li, Chaoyang District, Beijing 100021, P.R. China, phone/fax: 8610 5978 7338, E-mail: pmph@pmph.com

For text and trade sales, as well as review copy enquiries, please contact PMPH at pmphsales@gmail.com

Disclaimer

This book is for educational and reference purposes only. In view of the possibility of human error or changes in medical science, the author, editor, publisher and any other party involved in the publication of this work do not guarantee that the information contained herein is in any respect accurate or complete. The medicinal therapies and treatment techniques presented in this book are provided for the purpose of reference only. If readers wish to attempt any of the techniques or utilize any of the medicinal therapies contained in this book, the publisher assumes no responsibility for any such actions. It is the responsibility of the readers to understand and adhere to local laws and regulations concerning the practice of these techniques and methods. The authors, editors and publisher disclaim all responsibility for any liability, loss, injury, or damage incurred as a consequence, directly or indirectly, of the use and application of any of the contents of this book.

First published: 2011
ISBN: 978-7-117-14291-5/R·14292

Cataloguing in Publication Data:
A catalogue record for this book is available from the CIP-Database China.

ISBN 978-7-117-14291-5

Printed in The People's Republic of China

Editorial Board

Authors

Jin Hong-zhu (金宏柱)
Professor, Acupuncture & Tui Na, Nanjing University of TCM, Nanjing, China

Secondo Scarsella, MD, DDS
Attending Maxillofacial Surgeon, Department of Maxillofacial Surgery, San Salvatore Hospital, L'Aquila, Italy
Visiting Professor of Nanjing University of TCM, China

Ding Xiao-hong (丁晓红)
Associate Professor, International Education College, Nanjing University of TCM, Nanjing, China

DVD Authors

Wu Yun-chuan (吴云川)
Associate Professor, Second Clinical College, Nanjing University of TCM, Nanjing, China

Gu Yi-huang (顾一煌)
Professor, Second Clinical College, Nanjing University of TCM, Nanjing, China

Fan Jing (范静)
Lecturer, Second Clinical College, Nanjing University of TCM, Nanjing, China

Contributors (Listed alphabetically by last name)

Chen Hong-gen (陈红根)
Associate Senior Physician, Jiangsu Provincial Hospital of TCM, Nanjing, China

Fan Jing (范静)
Lecturer, Second Clinical College, Nanjing University of TCM, Nanjing, China

Geng Tao (耿涛)
Associate Senior Physician, Jiangsu Provincial Hospital of TCM, Nanjing, China

Gu Yi-huang(顾一煌)
Professor, Second Clinical College, Nanjing University of TCM, Nanjing, China

Guo Ai-song (郭爱松)
Senior Physician, Affiliated Hospital of Nantong Medical College, Jiangsu, China

Hu Bin (胡斌)
Associate Senior Physician, Henan Provincial Hospital of TCM, Henan, China

Li Shou-dong (李守栋)
Associate Professor, Second Clinical College, Nanjing University of TCM, Nanjing, China

Li Yi (李怡)
Lecturer, Second Clinical College, Nanjing University of TCM, Nanjing, China

Liu Xiao-dan(刘晓丹)
Lecturer, Second Clinical College, Nanjing University of TCM, Nanjing, China

Ma Rong-lian (马荣连)
Senior Physician, Jiangsu Provincial Government Hospital, Nanjing, China

Pan Hua-ping (潘化平)
Senior Physician, Nan Hua Hospital, Nanjing, China

Wu Yun-chuan (吴云川)
Associate Professor, Second Clinical College, Nanjing University of TCM, Nanjing, China

Xue Ming-xin (薛明新)
Senior Physician, Jiangsu Provincial Hospital of TCM, Nanjing, China

Yang Xiao-xian (杨晓仙)
Associate Senior Physician, Jiangsu Provincial Hospital of TCM, Nanjing, China

Zhang Hong-ru (张宏如)
Lecturer, Second Clinical College, Nanjing University of TCM, Nanjing, China

Zhang Shi-nian (张仕年)
Senior Physician, Jiangsu Provincial Hospital of TCM, Nanjing, China

Zhu Yi (朱毅)
Lecturer, Second Clinical College, Nanjing University of TCM, Nanjing, China

Translators (Listed alphabetically by last name)

Brendan Costello
Brendan Costello, BA. MA.
Lecturer in English Philology and Translation Studies at the University of the Basque Country, Spain

Chen Yan (陈滟)
Lecturer of International Education College, Nanjing University of TCM, Nanjing, China

Ferlisi Vincenza Ma.D
English Translator, Florence, Italy

Gu Zhen-yu (顾震宇)
Lecturer, International Education College, Nanjing University of TCM, Nanjing, China

Guan Yan- ting (关燕婷)
Assistant, International Education College, Nanjing University of TCM, Nanjing, China

Shen Tian (沈甜)
Lecturer, International Education College, Nanjing University of TCM, Nanjing, China

Xiong Ying (熊英)
Lecturer, Second Clinical College, Nanjing University of TCM, Nanjing, China

Yi Su-mei (衣素梅)
Associate Professor, International Education College, Nanjing University of TCM, Nanjing, China

Zhang Xu (张旭)
Professor, International Education College, Nanjing University of TCM, Nanjing, China

About the Authors

Jin Hong-zhu

Prof. Jin Hong-zhu served as Director of the Second Clinical College of Acupuncture and Tuina and as Department Head of the Acupuncture and Qi Gong Institute of Nanjing University of Traditional Chinese Medicine, where he now serves as a Doctoral Supervisor. Prof. Jin is also a part-time Professor at the Anhui College of Chinese Medicine and Chairman of the Executive Council for the Tui Na Association of Jiangsu Province.

Prof. Jin has provided profound theoretical research and distinctive clinical experiences in tui na massage over the last 40 years, while at the same time possessing great skill in the treatment of intractable and refractory diseases with Chinese medicinals, acupuncture and qi gong therapies.

He has acted as editor of more than ten textbooks for undergraduate and post-graduate students, and has participated in the compilation and editing of hundreds of professional publications.

Through the 1990's Prof. Jin has lectured in many countries, including Great Britain, Holland, Ireland, Italy, Japan, Korea and Portugal. His brilliant lectures and effective treatment methods continue to inspire worldwide interest in the study of Chinese medicine.

Dr. Secondo Scarsella, MD, DDS

Dr. Secondo Scarsella, MD, DDS is a Specialist of Odontostomatology and Maxillofacial Surgery now practicing at the San Salvatore Regional Hospital in L'Aquila, Italy. He graduated In 1989 from the 81st International Advanced Acupuncture Course run jointly by Nanjing University of Chinese Medicine and the WHO Cooperative Training Center; he studied Chinese Pharmacology and Tui Na at the Nanjing University of Chinese Medicine from 1993-1995.

Dr. Scarsella is currently a Visiting Professor at the Nanjing University of Chinese Medicine and Board Member of the Italian Federation of Tui Na and Qigong Schools. He is also President of Italian Academy of Chinese Medicine, and Chief Editor of *Yi Dao Zha Zhi*, an Italian journal of Chinese medicine.

Ding Xiao-hong

Prof. Ding Xiao-hong is employed at the International Education College of Nanjing University of Chinese Medicine, and has been engaged in international TCM education for 31 years. She has lectured in many countries including Australia, Great Britain, Denmark, Italy, Norway, Papua New Guinea, Portugal and Sweden. Prof. Ding's many TCM translation projects have played a great role in the popularization and growth of Chinese medicine worldwide.

Editorial Board for *International Standard Library of Chinese Medicine*

Sponsored by
World Federation of Chinese Medical Societies

Preface

Chinese tui na massage was known in ancient times as "*an qiao* (pressing and treading)". With a history in China spanning thousands of years, this traditional therapy remains a most effective method for both treating diseases and maintaining general health. In primitive society, so-called medical treatment for pain was mainly limited to "pressing and rubbing the local area with the hand"; that is to say, when one was sick or in pain he or she would instinctively press, tap or palpate the areas of tenderness in order to relieve the pain or discomfort. Through the improvement of the illness and disappearance of pain, such treatments were gradually recognized and developed systematically along with the birth of channel theory and acupuncture point location.

The earliest extant Chinese medical classic, the *Huáng Dì Nèi Jīng (The Yellow Emperor's Inner Classic 黄帝内经*) states: "In central areas, since the terrain is flat and wet, products in nature are abundant and rich. The people who live there have a variety of foods, so it is not as necessary to work hard to keep a comfortable life. The diseases affecting people there usually involve weakness of the vessels, tendons, muscles and bones, accompanied by cold and heat. Regarding treatment, *Dao Yin* (conduction exercises) and *An Mo* (massage) are recommended". This statement implies that many diseases are related to the environment and diet, and also that both internal and external disorders can treated with qi gong, tui na and massage. Throughout the developing history of China over thousands of years, tui na and massage were not only put to use but were also welcomed by the people. In the Tang Dynasty, the most flourishing period in Chinese history, tui na and massage were applied broadly and regarded greatly by the government of the day; these methods were taken as formal medical therapies with education and professional training. The indications for tui na were also extended to cover a variety of internal and external conditions including gynecology, pediatrics and general healthcare.

In the Ming and Qing Dynasties, Chinese tui na developed in a time of great prosperity, and there were two successes deserving mention: one was the popularization and rapid expansion of pediatric tui na; the other was the establishment of tui na nomenclature which originated from the former name "*An qiao* (pressing and treading) and *an mo* (massage). However, because of the vast territory of China, both names are still used to describe this therapy. The difference between the two terms is that tui na mostly refers to medical treatment, whereas *an mo* (massage) mainly refers to massage for general healthcare.

Along with the evolution of the global society, medical measures have inevitably undergone many changes. Nowadays, people are seeking non-invasive treatments without side-effects, and many also pay great attention to the numerous approaches to holistic health; this viewpoint follows the inexorable trend of cultural development. For this reason, tui na and massage have become widely respected therapies.

As the understanding of tui na and massage continues to spread outward from China, it has become more and more popular. Overseas students who wish to study this traditional therapy will find this textbook to be clear and accurate with equal emphases on theory and practice.

Chapters 1 and 2 briefly introduce the history, actions, methods and principles of Chinese tui na while introducing the basic knowledge of channels and acupoints, thus laying a foundation for further study in Chinese medicine.

Chapters 3 and 4 focus on developing the skills required to diagnose disease and practice tui na exercises.

Chapter 5 mainly discusses 28 simple and complex manipulations for treating adult patients.

On the basis of previous chapters, Chapter 6 illustrates tui na treatments applicable to 33 frequently seen diseases from the categories of internal medicine, gynecology, EENT and so on.

Chapter 7 is a comprehensive overview of pediatric tui na techniques with specific manipulations, points, and the methods applicable for the treatment of children.

Chapter 8 is a refined introduction to 5 self-care exercises that involve movements choreographed according to the theory of 5 *zang* organs.

In a word, this book on tui na covers the traditional features of Chinese medicine in an easy to study format that is also practical as a reference for clinical work. We sincerely hope that our efforts in compiling this book will benefit both patients and practitioners.

Authors
May 2011, Nanjing

Table of Contents

Chapter 1 General Introduction 1

Section 1 Brief History of Tui Na Therapy........1

Pre-Qin Period (2070 B.C. – 221 B.C.)........1

Qin - Han Period (221 B.C. – 265 A.D.)........2

Wei-Jin-Sui-Tang Period (265 A.D.– 960 A.D.)........4

Song-Jin-Yuan Period (960 A.D.– 1368A.D.)........4

Ming-Qing Period (1368 A.D. – 1911 A.D.)........5

Modern Period (1911 A.D. ------)........6

Section 2 How to Study Tui Na........6

Section 3 Functions of Tui Na........7

Regulating Yin and Yang........7

Reinforcing Deficiency and Reducing Excess........8

Invigorating Blood and Dissolving Stasis........9

Relaxing the Sinews and Removing Channel Obstructions........11

Correcting Sinews and Adjusting Joints........12

Section 4 Principles and Methods........13

Principles of Tui Na Treatment........13

Common Manipulations........17

Reinforcement and Reduction in Tui Na Therapy........22

Chapter 2 Channels, Collaterals & Acupuncture Points 27

Section 1 Basic Theory of Channels, Collaterals & Acupuncture Points........27

Twelve Channels........28

Eight Extraordinary Vessels........30

Section 2 Commonly Used Acupuncture Points........32

Chapter 3 Common Diagnostic Methods Used in Tui Na Therapy 47

Section 1 Examinations with the Four Diagnostic Methods........47

Inquiry........47

Inspection........48

Auscultation and Olfaction........52

Palpation........53

Section 2 Special Examinations 58
Section 3 Joint Motor Function Examinations........ 71

Chapter 4 Basic Practicing Methods of Tui Na Exercises 83

Section 1 Characteristics and Actions 83
Clear Movement and Comprehensive Training........ 83
Focusing on Mental Qi and Emphasizing Internal Energy 83
Combining Medical Treatment with Exercise and Practice to Strengthen Therapeutic Effects 84
Section 2 Practicing Method for *The Classic of Sinew Transformation* (*Yì Jīn Jīng*, 易筋经)........ 84
Wéi Tuó Presenting Pestle (*Wéi Tuó Xiàn Chǔ*, 韦驮献杵)........ 85
Monster Controlling Magic Pestle (*Héng Dán Xiáng Mó Chǔ*, 横胆降魔杵) 86
Supporting Heaven Gate with Palm (*Zhǎng Tuō Tiān Mén*, 掌托天门)........ 87
Picking Star and Changing Constellation (*Zhāi Xīng Huàn Dǒu*, 摘星换斗)........ 88
Pulling Nine Oxen by Their Tails (*Dào Zhuài Jiǔ Niú Wěi*, 倒拽九牛尾) 89
Displaying Paw and Spreading Wings (*Chū Zhǎo Liàng Chì*, 出爪亮翅) 90
Nine Ghosts Pulling Sabre (*Jiǔ Guǐ Bá Mǎ Dāo*, 九鬼拔马刀) 91
Three Plates Falling on Ground (*Sān Pán Luò Dì*, 三盘落地)........ 92
Blue Dragon Displaying its Claws (*Qīng Lóng Tàn Zhuǎ*, 青龙探爪)........ 93
Hungry Tiger Pouncing on Its Prey (*È Hǔ Pū Shí*, 饿虎扑食) 94
Bowing Down to Beat the Drum (*Dǎ Gōng Jī Gǔ*, 打躬击鼓)........ 95
Shaking the Head and Tail (*Diào Wěi Yáo Tóu*, 掉尾摇头) 95
Section 3 Practicing Method for *Shào Lín* Internal Exercise (*Shào Lín Nèi Gōng*, 少林内功)........ 96
Standing Stance (*Zhàn Dāng Shì*, 站裆势) 97
Horse Stance (*Mǎ Dāng Shì*, 马裆势)........ 98
Bow Stance (*Gōng Jiàn Dāng Shì*, 弓箭裆势) 98
Close Stance (*Bìng Dāng Shì*, 并裆势) 99
Big Stance (*Dà Dāng Shì*, 大裆势)........ 99
Suspending Stance (*Xuán Dāng Shì*, 悬裆势) 99
Pushing Eight Horses Forward (*Qián Tuī Bā Pǐ Mǎ*, 前推八匹马) 100
Pulling Nine Oxen Backward (*Dào Lā Jiǔ Tóu Niú*, 倒拉九头牛) 100
Pulling Golden Ring with One Hand (*Dān Zhǎng Lā Jīn Huán*, 单掌拉金环) 101
Phoenix Spreading Its Wings (*Fèng Huáng Zhǎn Chì*, 凤凰展翅) 101
Conqueror Supporting Tripot (*Bà Wáng Jǔ Dǐng*, 霸王举鼎)........ 102
Pushing the Boat Along the Water Flow (*Shùn Shuǐ Tuī Zhōu*, 顺水推舟) 103
Embracing the Moon (*Huái Zhōng Bào Yuè*, 怀中抱月) 103
Immortals Guiding the Way (*Xiān Rén Zhǐ Lù*, 仙人指路) 104
Holding Tower with Flat Hand (*Píng Shǒu Tuō Tǎ*, 平手托塔)........ 105
Turning Palm to Fold Tile (*Yùn Zhǎng Hé Wǎ*, 运掌合瓦)........ 105
Wind Blowing Lotus Leaf (*Fēng Bǎi Hé Yè*, 风摆荷叶) 106

Supporting the Sky with Two Hands (*Liǎng Shǒu Tuō Tiān*, 两手托天) 106
Single Phoenix Facing the Sun (*Dān Fèng Cháo Yáng*, 单凤朝阳) 107
Scooping the Moon from the Sea Bottom (*Hǎi Dǐ Lāo Yuè*, 海底捞月) 108
Supporting the Sky and Embracing the Earth (*Dǐng Tiān Bào Dì*, 顶天抱地) 108
Splitting Hua Mountain with Vigorous Efforts (*Lì Pī Huà Shān*, 力劈华山) 109

Chapter 5 Tui Na Manipulations 111

Section 1 Basic Tui Na Manipulations for Adults 112

One-finger Pushing(*Yì Zhǐ Chán Tuī Fǎ*, 一指禅推法) 112
Rolling (*Gǔn Fǎ*, 滚法) 114
Kneading (*Róu Fǎ*, 揉法) 115
Rubbing (*Mó Fǎ*, 摩法) 116
Scrubbing (*Cā Fǎ*, 擦法) 117
Pushing (*Tuī Fǎ*, 推法) 118
Mopping (*Mā Fǎ*, 抹法) 120
Scattering Manipulation (*Sǎo Sàn Fǎ*, 扫散法) 120
Foulage (*Cuō Fǎ*, 搓法) 121
Vibrating (*Zhèn Fǎ*, 振法) 122
Shaking (*Dǒu Fǎ*, 抖法) 123
Pressing (*Àn Fǎ*, 按法) 123
Continuous Pressing Manipulation (*Yā Fǎ*, 压法) 124
Pointing (*Diǎn Fǎ*, 点法) 125
Pinching (*Niē Fǎ*, 捏法) 125
Grasping (*Ná Fǎ*, 拿法) 126
Twiddling Manipulation (*Niǎn Fǎ*, 捻法) 127
Plucking (*Bō Fǎ*, 拨法) 127
Patting Manipulation (*Pāi Fǎ*, 拍法) 128
Striking Manipulation (*Jī Fǎ*, 击法) 128
Flicking (*Tán Fǎ*, 弹法) 129
Rotation (*Yáo Fǎ*, 摇法) 130
Pulling-Stretching Manipulation (*Bá Shēn Fǎ*, 拔伸法) 132
Back-Carrying (*Bēi Fǎ*, 背法) 134
Pulling (*Bān Fǎ*, 扳法) 135

Section 2 Compound Tui Na Manipulations for Adults 139

Pressing-Kneading Manipulation (*Àn Róu Fǎ*, 按揉法) 139
Grasping-Kneading Manipulation (*Ná Róu Fǎ*, 拿揉法) 140
Pushing-Rubbing Manipulation (*Tuī Mó Fǎ*, 推摩法) 141

Chapter 6 Tui Na Treatment for Adult Diseases 143

Section 1 Orthopedic Diseases 143

Stiff Neck 143
Cervical Spondylopathy 146
Acute Lumbar Sprain 153
Chronic Lumbar Strain 155
Degenerative Spondylitis 157
Third Lumbar Transverse Process Syndrome 160
Lumbar Disc Herniation 162
Closed Injury of Chest and Hypochondrium 166
Subluxation of Sacroiliac Joint 169
Piriformis Syndrome 171
Myofascitis of the Back 173
External Humeral Epicondylitis 176
Wrist Sprain 179
Strain of the Iliotibial Tract 181
Osteoarthritis of the Knee Joint 183
Ankle Sprain 186
Temporomandibular Joint Dysfunction 189

Section 2 Treatment for Disorders of Internal Medicine, Gynecology and the Five Sense Organs 192

Epigastric Pain 192
Diarrhea 196
Constipation 199
Hypertension 202
Coronary Heart Disease 207
Headache 211
Insomnia 216
Sequelae of Wind Stroke 219
Dysmenorrhea 222
Climacteric Syndrome 226
Impotence 229
Toothache 232
Tinnitus and Deafness 235
Depression Syndrome 237
Irregular Menstruation 240

Chapter 7 Tui Na Treatment for Common Pediatric Diseases 247

Section 1 Basic Tui Na Manipulations for Children 247
Pushing 247
Kneading 249
Pressing 250
Rubbing 251
Nipping 251
Pinching 252
Transporting Manipulation (*yùn fǎ*, 运法) 253
Pounding Manipulation (*dǎo fǎ*, 捣法) 254
Section 2 Compound Manipulations of Pediatric Tui Na Therapy 254
Wasps Going into the Honeycomb (*Huáng Fēng Rù Dòng*, 黄蜂入洞) 254
Scrubbing and Rubbing like Pressing String (*Àn Xián Zǒu Cuō Mó*, 按弦走搓摩) 255
Scooping the Moon up from The Water (*Shuǐ Dǐ Lāo Yuè*, 水底捞月) 255
Crossing the Heaven River On Horseback (*Dǎ mǎ Guò Tiān Hé*, 打马过天河) 256
Transporting Earth into Water (*Yùn Tǔ Rù Shuǐ*, 运土入水) 256
Transporting Water into Earth (*Yùn Shuǐ Rù Tǔ*, 运水入土) 256
Section 3 Specific Points for Infants 257
Kǎn gōng (坎宫) 257
Tiān mén (天门) 258
Tài yáng (太阳) 258
Ěr hòu gāo gǔ (耳后高骨) 259
Tiān zhù gǔ (天柱骨) 260
Rǔ páng (乳旁) 260
Rǔ gēn (乳根) 261
Xié lèi (胁肋) 261
Fù (腹) 262
Qí (脐) 262
Dān tián (丹田) 263
Dù jiǎo (肚角) 264
Fèi shù (肺俞) 264
Jǐ zhù (脊柱) 265
Qī jié gǔ (七节骨) 266
Guī wěi (龟尾) 267
Pí jīng (脾经) 267
Gān jīng (肝经) 268
Xīn jīng (心经) 269
Fèi jīng (肺经) 269
Shèn jīng (肾经) 270
Xiǎo cháng (小肠) 271
Dà cháng (大肠) 272

Shèn dǐng (肾顶) 273
Sì héng wén (四横纹) 273
Xiǎo héng wén (小横纹) 274
Zhǎng xiǎo héng wén (掌小横纹) 275
Wèi jīng (胃经) 275
Bǎn mén (板门) 276
Nèi láo gōng (内劳宫) 277
Xiǎo tiān xīn (小天心) 278
Nèi bā guà (内八卦) 278
Zǒng jīn (总筋) 279
Dà héng wén (大横纹) 279
Duān zhèng (端正) 280
Wǔ zhǐ jié (五指节) 281
Èr shàn mén (二扇门) 282
Èr rén shàng mǎ (二人上马) 282
Wēi líng (威灵) 283
Jīng nìng (精宁) 283
Bó yáng chí (膊阳池) 284
Yī wō fēng (一窝蜂) 285
Sān guān (三关) 285
Liù fǔ (六腑) 286
Tiān hé shuǐ (天河水) 287
RN 22 (*tiān tū*, 天突) 288
RN 17 (*dàn zhōng*, 膻中) 289

Section 4 Common Pediatric Diseases 290

Cough 292
Fever 294
Asthma 296
Vomiting 299
Diarrhea 301
Anorexia 303
Constipation 305
Night Crying 307
Enuresis 309
Infantile Myogenic Torticollis 311
Infantile Subluxation of Radius Head 312

Chapter 8 Self-Healthcare Tui Na Therapy 315

Section 1 Functions of Self-Healthcare Tui Na therapy 315

Section 2 Approaches to the Manipulations 315

Soothing Liver Regulating Qi 315

Soothing Heart and Tranquilizing Mind Method 317
Strengthening Spleen and Harmonizing Stomach Method 319
Ventilating Lung and Releasing Exterior Method 321
Stabilizing Kidney Increasing Essence 323
Appendix 1 Glossary of Tui Na Manipulations for Adults 325
Appendix 2 Glossary of *Shào Lín* Internal Practicing Methods 327
Index of Point Names—Numerical Codes **329**
Index of Point Names—*Pin Yin* **333**
Index of Tui Na Manipulations for Adults **337**
General Index **339**

Chapter 1 General Introduction

In the earliest Chinese historical documents from three thousand years ago, tui na was referred to as pressing and treading (*àn qiāo,* 按跷) and massage (*àn mó*, 按摩). The name "tui na" is first seen in *Elaboration on Pediatrics* (*Yòu Kē Fā Huī*, 幼科发挥) written in 1549 by Wan Quan, the famous pediatric specialist from the Ming dynasty. From that time onwards, the term "tui na" has been used in the texts about this topic. The evolution of the name reflects improvements to the theoretical content of tui na therapy, which was enriched and gradually became more scientific and rational, along with the development and changes in the practice of tui na therapy. Also from the time of the adoption of this name, there is a substantial leap in the history of tui na therapy.

Taking the basic theory of traditional Chinese medicine (TCM) as its guidance, tui na is a kind of therapy in which the tui na doctor treats disease by applying manipulations or certain instruments to stimulate the patient's body surface in some special areas or points. As such, it may be classified as an external treatment within TCM practices. Tui na is a scientific system focused on researching how to treat diseases with tui na therapy and studying the mechanism, method and scope of tui na therapy.

Tui na therapy is one of the most important components of traditional Chinese medicine since it provides abundant information that contributes to the theoretic system of TCM. For thousands of years, tui na therapy has played an extremely important role in human health care.

Section 1
Brief History of Tui Na Therapy

Tui na originates from physical labor. In prehistoric times, human beings hunted and gathered to obtain food, collected branches and rocks to build dwellings and huts, sewed animal skins to make clothes to keep warm, and went trekking to survive. All these activities and struggles could cause damage to the body, muscles, soft tissues and bones. Prehistoric humans instinctively tried to stop bleeding by pressing the wound, or to get rid of swelling and pain by rubbing the local area. After many years of using these rudimentary practices, they created some naive manipulations, i.e. the primitive tui na method, which became one of the most frequently used methods in relieving diseases.

Pre-Qin Period (2070 B.C. – 221 B.C.)

The period after the dynasties of Xia, Shang and Zhou and up to the time that Emperor Qin united China is called the pre-Qin period. According to historical records, many medical books achieved widespread circulation during the Warring States Period, but later, most of them were destroyed in the war. The medical classics written by various ideologists and thinkers of that period survive in fragmentary form only. Thus, evidence of the success of tui na in this period is mainly based on two major archeological discoveries of last century: oracle inscription bones unearthed from ruins of the Shang dynasty and recordings from a medical book found in Mawangdui Han Tomb, Changsha.

In the Shang Dynasty, people held superstitious beliefs in ghosts and spirits, and praying or offering sacrifices to gods would have been the main method to cure illness. A record of many disorders can be found on oracle inscription bones, but as yet no references to treatment with acupuncture and moxibustion or with medicinal material, nor names of therapists working with such methods, have been found amongst the records. In contrast, many records on the oracle inscription bones include references to tui na treatment given by a masseur, and many characters in the oracle inscriptions are connected with tui na therapy. This proves that, in addition to sacrifices to gods, the main therapeutic method was tui na, which was in use much earlier and more extensively than acupuncture and medicinal materials. Among the medical books unearthed from the Mawangdui Han Tomb, *Formulas for Fifty-two Diseases* (*Wǔ Shí Èr Bìng Fāng, 五十二病方*) is mainly concerned with tui na. Two special features of tui na therapy are introduced in this book. The first is the use of massage with medicinal material and ointment, considered to be the earliest application in the history of tui na. Judging from the process of manufacture described, such medicinal ointment was at the initial stage of its development. The other feature is the use of specific tools during tui na treatment, such as a wooden cone for treating hernia. The most characteristic tool is the "medicinal towel", used to treat some sexual disorders or to promote wellbeing, which should be recognized as a great contribution to medicine from the history of tui na health care. In fact, the earliest primitive tool used in tui na therapy was the Bian stone and there were various Bian stones for different disorders, not only those used in acupuncture. The use of these tools in tui na therapy provides more effective results for the treatment.

Qin - Han Period (221 B.C. – 265 A.D.)

The Qin – Han Period was the most important stage in the development of tui na. According to *Han History* (*Hàn Shū, 汉书*), the first treatise on tui na, *Ten Volumes Of Massage Of Yellow Emperor and Qi Bo (Huáng Dì Qí Bó Àn Mó Shí Juàn, 黄帝歧伯按摩十卷)*, came out together with *The Yellow Emperor's Inner Classic (Huáng Dì Nèi Jīng, 黄帝内经)*. In terms of content, the book was a treatise on health care and tui na; in terms of medicine, the book possibly came out of the same medicinal school as *The Yellow Emperor's Inner Classic*. It is probable that while *The Yellow Emperor's Inner Classic* focused on discussion of diseases and took acupuncture and moxibustion as the main approaches for treating diseases, *Ten Volumes Of Massage Of Yellow Emperor and Qi Bo* stressed health preservation and adopted tui na as the main method of health care. Regrettably, this ten-volume masterpiece of tui na was lost in wars. As a result, it is impossible to construct a complete picture of the development of tui na before the Western Han Dynasty. Nevertheless, in *The Yellow Emperor's Inner Classic* numerous references to tui na appear, which provide some insight and make it clear that the unique therapeutic system of tui na had been formed in the Qin – Han Period, and many sections of this masterpiece are theoretic summaries of tui na since the Shang Dynasty. *The Yellow Emperor's Inner Classic* points out that tui na originated in the central region of China, equivalent to the vicinity of present-day Luoyang (Henan province), where the boundaries of the Shang Dynasty lay, thus confirming the evidence for the existence of tui na from the oracle inscriptions on bones.

Observation, inspection, auscultation and olfaction, inquiring and palpation are the most important diagnostic methods in tui na therapy. References to performing palpation with tui na manipulation to improve accuracy of diagnosis abound in *The Yellow Emperor's Inner Classic* and the book fully affirmed the role of tui na therapy, attributing it with functions of moving qi, invigorating the blood, dissipating cold, relieving pain, dredging the channels and collaterals, eliminating heat and calming the mind. At the same time, the book stressed that tui na should be applied together with acupuncture, moxibustion and medicinal materials, etc. Many tui na manipulations are illustrated in *The Yellow Emperor's Inner Classic*, such as pressing, rubbing, palpating, flicking, pushing, grasping, flexing, stretching and rotating. Among these manipulations, pressing and rubbing are used most, and for this reason massage *(àn mó, 按摩)* was the name of tui na at that time. *The Yellow Emperor's Inner Classic* also sets forth the requirements for the training of a tui na therapist: anyone engaged in tui na must have a healthy body and strong hands. The tools used in tui na therapy mentioned in *The Yellow Emperor's Inner Classic* are Round Needle *(Yuán Zhēn, 圆针)* and Spoon Needle *(Dī Zhēn, 堤针)*. Round Needle is used in the reducing method and Spoon Needle in the reinforcing method. In short, the contribution and impact of *The Yellow Emperor's Inner Classic* to tui na therapy go beyond what has been mentioned here. Most importantly, *The Yellow Emperor's Inner Classic* lays down the basic theory of TCM. The main content such as the theories of *zang-fu* organs, yin-yang, five phases, qi, blood and body fluids, diagnostic methods, principles of treatment, all become the most important guiding rules.

In *Essentials from the Golden Cabinet (Jīn Guì Yào Lüè, 金匮要略)* written by the renowned doctor Zhang Zhong-jing of the Han Dynasty, for the first time ointment rubbing was taken as one of the methods of preventing disease and promoting health. In addition, the book also recommends a kind of herbal powder by mixing *fù zǐ* (Radix Aconiti Lateralis Praeparata) and salt for a tui na treatment of headache. The ointment-like *Rubbing Vertex Cream (Mó Dǐng Gāo, 摩顶膏)* was later derived from this. The eminent doctor Hua Tuo advocated *Five Animal's Game (Wǔ Qín Xì, 五禽戏)*, which provided a set of effective health care methods for future generations. Hua Tuo made the best use of rubbing with ointment, and he was the first to broadly apply rubbing with ointment clinically.

Generally speaking, from instinctive self massage to the time of *Ten Volumes Of Massage Of Yellow Emperor and Qi Bo* and *The Yellow Emperor's Inner Classic*, through constant refinement over many years, tui na at last developed into a clinical discipline with a unique therapeutic system. Not only was the theory synthesized and improved, but also its clinical application was more complete, broader and better defined, and was advocated and used by notable doctors of the period, such as Bian Que, Zhang Zhong-jing and Hua Tuo, among others. Therefore, the Qin-Han Period was the time that tui na became a unique therapeutic system, and also represents a zenith which links the earlier and later history of tui na.

Wei-Jin-Sui-Tang Period (265 A.D.– 960 A.D.)

In the Jin and Tang Dynasties, the feudal monarchy gradually gave more importance to tui na therapy. During the Sui Dynasty, the imperial medical Bureau first established the title of massage doctor. Building on this development, the Tang Dynasty established a larger imperial hospital with more complete equipment. The hospital had a massage department and the staff were given the titles of massage doctor, massage therapist and massage worker. The massage doctors taught the students conduction exercises and tui na with the aid of massage therapists and workers, thus starting formal tui na teaching. Self-administered tui na was given wide attention during this period. *Emergency Formulas to Keep Up One's Sleeve (Zhǒu Hòu Bèi Jí Fāng, 肘后备急方)* by Ge Hong and *Important Formulas Worth a Thousand Gold Pieces (Qiān Jīn Yào Fāng, 千金要方)* by Sun Si-miao records many methods of self-administered tui na; the massage method created by Lao Zi is one of them. Chao Yuan-fang included methods of health preservation and conductive exercises in every chapter of his book *Treatise on the Origins and Manifestations of Various Diseases (Zhū Bìng Yuán Hòu Lùn, 诸病源候论)* and paid particular attention to health preservation by rubbing the abdomen. The exent of self-administered tui na demonstrates that tui na therapy in this period began to focus attention on preventing diseases and health care, and to consider the active role of the patient in fighting disease. The combination of medicinal materials and manipulations resulted in great developments for tui na therapy. Ge Hong thought highly of the application of massage with cream, and he was the first doctor to explicate massage systematically with syndrome, method, prescription and medicine. *Emergency Formulas to Keep Up One's Sleeve* records 8 formulas of massage with cream, all of which were prescribed by distinguished doctors. On the basis of the method for inducing labour recorded in *Liu Juan-zi's Ghost-Bequeathed Formulas (Liú Juān Zǐ Guǐ Yí Fāng, 刘涓子鬼遗方)*, Arcane Essentials from the Imperial Library *(Wài Tái Mì Yào, 外台秘要)*added two more methods of inducing labour by massage with salt and decoction. The book lists lots of well-known formulas of massage with cream, and most of them cite their sources. During this period, the scope of tui na therapy gradually increased, for example, Six Classics of the *Tang Dynasty (Táng Liù Diǎn, 唐六典)* said tui na could eliminate 8 kinds of diseases relating to wind, cold, summer heat, damp, hunger, over-eating, stress or strain and lack of exercise. *Arcane Essentials from the Imperial Library* indicates: "If attacked by wind-cold just one day, manifesting headache and rigidity of back, massage is the best method." Tui na was also introduced into Korea, Japan, India, Arabia and Europe during this period.

Song-Jin-Yuan Period (960 A.D.– 1368A.D.)

During the Song-Jin-Yuan Period, tui na was applied even more widely and greater attention was given to analyzing the manipulations employed. *Comprehensive Recording of Divine Assistance (Shèng Jì Zǒng Lù, 圣济总录)* was the first book to contain monographs on massage *(àn mó, 按摩)* and is the earliest and the most complete monograph existing today. The author first offers a detailed explanation of the significance of tui na therapy and the difference between pressing manipulation and rubbing manipulation. He expresses the need to separate massage and conductive exercises and, at the same time, he provides a brilliant overview of the mechanism of massage. Taking the original articles of *The Yellow Emperor's Inner Classic* as a basis, the author elaborates in detail on the scope of application of tui na therapy, pointing out under what kinds of condition the result would be "pain relieved after pressing, no effect after pressing, pain aggravated after pressing, comfort after pressing." This distinction was of great significance to the clinical application of tui na therapy. The writings on tui na therapy in *Comprehensive Recording of Divine Assistance* are not long, but the analysis of several important questions is thorough with accurate conclusions, making an important theoretic contribution to the development of tui na therapy. During this period, ointment rubbing underwent new developments. *Formulas from Benevolent Sages Compiled during the Taiping Era (Tài Píng Shèng Huì Fāng, 太平圣惠方)* recorded six prescriptions of Mo Ding Gao for treating eye disorders. These are the earliest recordings about Rubbing Vertex Cream (*Mó Dǐng Gāo, 摩顶膏*) used for eye disorders, and produced profound influences on the future development of ointment rubbing. Among four major schools in the Jin-Yuan Period, Zhang Cong-zheng was considered number one in the work of introducing tui na. He listed massage as one of the methods to induce sweating in his book *Confucians' Duties to Their Parents (Rú Mén Shì Qīn, 儒门事亲)*. The reduction methods of putting the arms on a ladder in sitting position for dislocation of the shoulder joint, hanging upside down for dislocation of the hip joint and hanging reduction for spinal vertebral fracture mentioned in *Effective Formulas from Generations of Physicians (Shì Yī Dé Xiào Fāng, 世医得效方)* could be used to replace pulling and extending manipulation. As such, they are important advances in tui na history, opening up a new chapter in treating orthopedic disorders by traction with equipment in the history of Chinese medicine.

Ming-Qing Period (1368 A.D. – 1911 A.D.)

The Ming-Qing Period is another heyday in the development of tui na. First of all, there was a breakthrough in the compilation of tui na texts; the pediatric tui na books were available one after another. For example, Chen's book *Mystic Art of Infant Care (Bǎo Yīng Shén Shù, 保婴神术)* written in the Ming Dynasty is the earliest tui na text still in existence, and later was compiled into Yang Ji-zhou's *The Great Compendium of Acupuncture and Moxibustion (Zhēn Jiǔ Dà Chéng, 针灸大成)*; the imperial doctor Gong Yun-lin's *Complete Book of Pediatric Tui Na Secrets with infantile pulse and formulas (Xiǎo Ér Tuī Ná Fāng Mài Huó Yīng Mì Zhǐ Quán Shū, 小儿推拿方脉活婴秘旨全书)*, also named as *Complete Book of Pediatric Tui Na (Xiǎo Ér Tuī Ná Quán Shū, 小儿推拿全书)* was the first offprint; the description of eight methods of pediatric tui na in Zhou Yu-fan's *The Secrets of Pediatric Tui Na (Xiǎo Ér Tuī Ná Mì Jué, 小儿推拿秘诀)* was the most brilliant; Xiong Ying-xiong's *The Principles of Pediatric Tui Na (Xiǎo Ér Tuī Ná Guǎng Yì, 小儿推拿广意)* was honored as the best book in the Qing Dynasty since it had appendix of frequently-used infantile formulas and drugs; Luo Ru-long's *Secret Booklet of Pediatric Tui Na (Yòu Kē Tuī Ná Mì Shū, 幼科推拿秘书)* was the most comprehensive and coherent, considered as a shortcut for studying pediatric tui na; Xu Qian-guang's *Three Character Classic of Tui Na (Tuī Ná Sān Zì Jīng, 推拿三字经)* was written clearly with rhythm, easy to read and memorize, so as to benefit clinical practice; Zhang Zhen-jun brought together the positive aspects of other schools to set up his own special style in his book *Modified Important Technique of Tui Na (Lí Zhèng Tuī Ná Yào Shù, 厘正推拿要术)*, which became a compendium that collected the most important successes of pediatric tui na before the 14th year of Kuang-Hsu and was reprinted many times. This book was the first to set out eight methods of pediatric tui na, i.e. "pressing, rubbing, pinching, kneading, pushing, moving, twisting and rotating." It represented the formation of special system of pediatric tui na. Secondly, adult tui na also developed greatly during this period. The situation could be described as a hundred schools of thought contending like a hundred blossoming flowers; many tui na techniques came into being, such as tui na with bone setting, pointing acupoint, one-finger pushing, tui na for eye disorders, surgical tui na, tui na with inner strength, tui na for health care and many others too numerous to mention. Thus, in the history of tui na, the Ming-Qing Period was an era with comprehensive development, creation and advances.

Modern Period (1911 A.D. ------)

Many schools of traditional Chinese medicine appeared in this period. These schools include one-finger pushing tui na, tui na based on channels and collaterals, tui na by pointing acupoint, tui na based on abdominal diagnosis, tui na with internal energy, tui na with rolling manipulations, tui na for stomach disorders, etc. These tui na schools expanded by way of "master teaching apprentice face to face" to carry on the past and create original new opinions. The academic publications in this period are excellent both in pictures and language, making them easy to understand. Huang Han-ru's book *Huang's Medical Discourse (Huáng Shì Yī Huà, 黄氏医话)*, published in 1933, is the first medical text on tui na from this period. In his book, the author records his clinical experience and the cases he treated during decades of clinical practice of tui na therapy, and he also introduced the origins and features of one-finger pushing tui na. Unfortunately, no mention is made of manipulation techniques, with the effect that the later tui na scholars were not able to gain an understanding of this aspect of his work.

Section 2
How to Study Tui Na

Tui na is a clinical discipline of TCM characterized by both theory and practice. A tui na therapist should be proficient in basic knowledge of both traditional Chinese medicine and western medicine, as well as diagnosis, pattern differentiation and treatment, and professional tui na skills. In addition, practitioners must possess a level of physical fitness which can adapt to tui na clinical practice and permits skillful manipulations and techniques. Conseuqently, tui na students should study the basic precepts of traditional Chinese medicine and western medicine, but also acquire systematic professional skills and receive rigorous training on the body and manipulation techniques.

As far as a grounding in medical theory is concerned, basic knowledge of TCM includes the theory of yin-yang, five phases, channels, collaterals, wei-blood and wei-qi, etiology, pathology, the four examinations, eight-principle syndrome differentiation and treatment. Aspects of western medicine to be studied include anatomy, physiology, pathophysiology, pathological anatomy and physical diagnosis. Particularly important for tui na clinical practice is familiarity with the anatomic structure of the human body, sports physiology, ganglion, circulation of fourteen channels, and the location and action of frequently used points.

To acquire professional skills, the exercises should be carried out step by step as described in the chapter on Exercises Practiced in Study of tui na. When doing the exercises, attention should be paid not only to acquiring strength, endurance and flexibility, but also to fostering psychological qualities, namely developing stamina and a persistent attitude, with a view to laying down the foundations for future clinical tui na work. Secondly, the study and practice of the various manipulations mentioned in this textbook should be under the guidance of teachers. The instructions for the manipulations must be followed strictly and in order so that progress is made step by step, as a result of continual effort. Techniques should be practiced by going through each of the three basic stages: practice on a rice bag, practice on a human body and practice by treating frequently seen diseases. Thirdly, the information about tui na therapy in this textbook should be carefully studied, and the student should make use of every possible opportunity to acquire the skill of treating disease. In this way, a combination of theory and practice will greatly enhance the result of study.

In short, for a person with certain medical knowledge, after a period of earnest study and practice, it is not difficult to learn the rudiments of tui na, but prolonged professional training is unquestionably necessary in order to grasp those difficult manipulation techniques which demand high-level technology, and to be able to apply them in a clinical context.

Section 3
Functions of Tui Na

Regulating Yin and Yang

All disorders of the human body can be generalized in terms of yin and yang. Pathologic changes, such as disharmony of qi and blood, dysfunction of *ying* qi and ***wei*** qi, are related to an imbalance between yin and yang. This is considered to be the inner root of diseases and may exist in the emergence, the development or the whole process of a disease. Various pathologic changes may appear in the disease process. Whether a disease be exogenous or internal, the resulting pathologic changes are always caused by a preponderance or weakness of yin and yang. Tui na aims to regulate the condition of yin and yang according to the nature of the symptoms or syndromes, to return the body to a state of equilibrium of yin and yang and to restore normal physical function, so as to treat disease. This goal of regulating yin and yang is mainly based on the action of channels, collaterals, qi and blood, because the channels and collaterals are distributed in the various parts of the body, they pertain to *zang-fu* organs internally and connect with limbs and joints externally. Since qi and blood circulate in the channels and collaterals, they link all the *zang-fu* organs, orifices, skin, sinews, muscles and bones up into an organic whole. Tui na manipulations work on a local area and may remove obstructions from the channels and collaterals, promote qi and blood, nourish sinews and bones. As a consequence, the effects may reach the internal organs and other areas via qi, blood, channels and collaterals. For example, the proper manipulations on the abdomen and back may inhibit intestinal hyperperistalsis to a normal condition. Conversely, the manipulations may also turn bradystalsis to euperistalsis. Observations of the movement of stomach during tui na on acupoints have shown that, after massage on BL 20 (*pí shù*) and BL 21 (*wèi shù*) stomach movement increased, while massage on ST 36 (*zú sān lǐ*) inhibited stomach movement. Further research has illustrated that after tui na the movement of the stomach often decreases in the case of hyperactivity, and increases if tui na is applied for hypoactivity.

Reinforcing Deficiency and Reducing Excess

Generally speaking, substance insufficiency in the human body and hypofunction of the organs are considered to be a deficiency. Conversely, excessive pathogenic qi or hyperfunction of the organs is excess. Clinical practice has shown that qi, blood, body fluids, *zang-fu* organs, channels and collaterals undergo corresponding changes with the result that deficient conditions may be supplemented and excessive conditions reduced by applying tui na manipulations on certain areas of the body, thus curing the disease. Though no substance is introduced directly into the body, tui na manipulations on the body surface create stimulation that can promote or inhibit physiological function and thus reinforce deficiency or reduce excess.

Modern physiological research shows that for an organ, weak stimulation may activate and excite its physiological function, while strong stimulation usually inhibits physiological function. Clinically, for patients with weak spleen and stomach, applying soft and gentle manipulations such as one-finger pushing on BL 20 (*pí shù*), BL 21 (*wèi shù*), RN 12 (*zhōng wǎn*) and RN 6 (*qì hǎi*) as prolonged, rhythmical stimulation would give good results. For patients with gastrointestinal spasms, strong manipulations such as pointing and pressing on the corresponding points of the back may relieve the spasm in a short time.

Of course, a manipulation of a given strength may cause different effects depending on the individual and other related factors such as constitution, the site of the manipulation and threshold of endurance. Clinically, the strength of a manipulation is usually measured in terms of the patient's reaction: manipulations which cause severe soreness and distention are considered strong, while those causing mild soreness and distention are considered gentle.

Furthermore, the effect of reinforcing deficiency and reducing excess also depends on the frequency and direction of the tui na manipulation. Changes to the frequency of a manipulation within certain limits are no more than quantitative, but if the change goes beyond these limits, the manipulation changes qualitatively. For example, one-finger pushing with normal frequency can remove obstructions from the channels and collaterals, and harmonize *ying qi* and *wei qi*. However, the same manipulation with a high frequency is used to invigorate blood, eliminate swelling, push pus outward and drain toxins, and is often used to treat carbuncles and furuncles. High frequency manipulations, since the strength is more focused, penetrate deeply into the organs and tissues to function effectively as "clearing, resolving and promoting", and they are referred to as reducing methods. Conversely, manipulations with the opposite effect are known as reinforcing methods. The direction of a manipulation on a specific area may also condition the reinforcing or reducing effect. Taking the manipulation of rubbing on the abdomen as an example, rubbing clockwise results in dissipation, whereas counterclockwise rubbing on the abdomen increases gastrointestinal digestion and counts as a reinforcing method.

Invigorating Blood and Dissolving Stasis

Blood stasis is a kind of pathogenic product caused by blood stagnation in certain areas of the body due to abnormal blood circulation. This product subsequently becomes the causative factor for certain diseases, and tui na may eliminate stasis by applying adequate manipulations.

1. Promoting Blood Circulation

Modern medical research has shown that the disorder of microcirculation is one of the main factors in blood stasis. Certain pressure differences between the artery and vein is a major factor for promoting blood circulation. If the pressure difference is less than a certain value, the blood flow may slow down and even stop, thus causing blood stasis. Though tui na manipulation is applied only on the surface of the body, the pressure of the manipulation can be delivered to the vessel wall, so that the vessel wall is pressed down and then rebounds up in a rhythmic manner. When the vessel is pressed down, the pressure from the heart and the flexibility of the vessel wall cause the local pressure at the proximal site to increase sharply. By rapidly removing the pressure, the blood then flows to the remote end as a vigorous short-term impact. Given that the artery is not easily deflated (as the pressure in the artery is comparatively high) and also that the venous valves in the veins prevent blood flowing backwards, this actually pushes blood flow in microcirculation from the small artery to the small vein. The material exchange in the blood completes the process of microcirculation, so tui na manipulation is of great significance for promoting blood circulation in microcirculation. Experimental evidence shows that when tui na manipulations are carried out on the shoulder, microcirculation at the finger nail fold speeds up. The enhanced flow rate increases vascular volume at the fingertips, and the effect lasts for a period of time after the manipulation. This is one aspect of the action of invigorating blood and dissolving blood stasis.

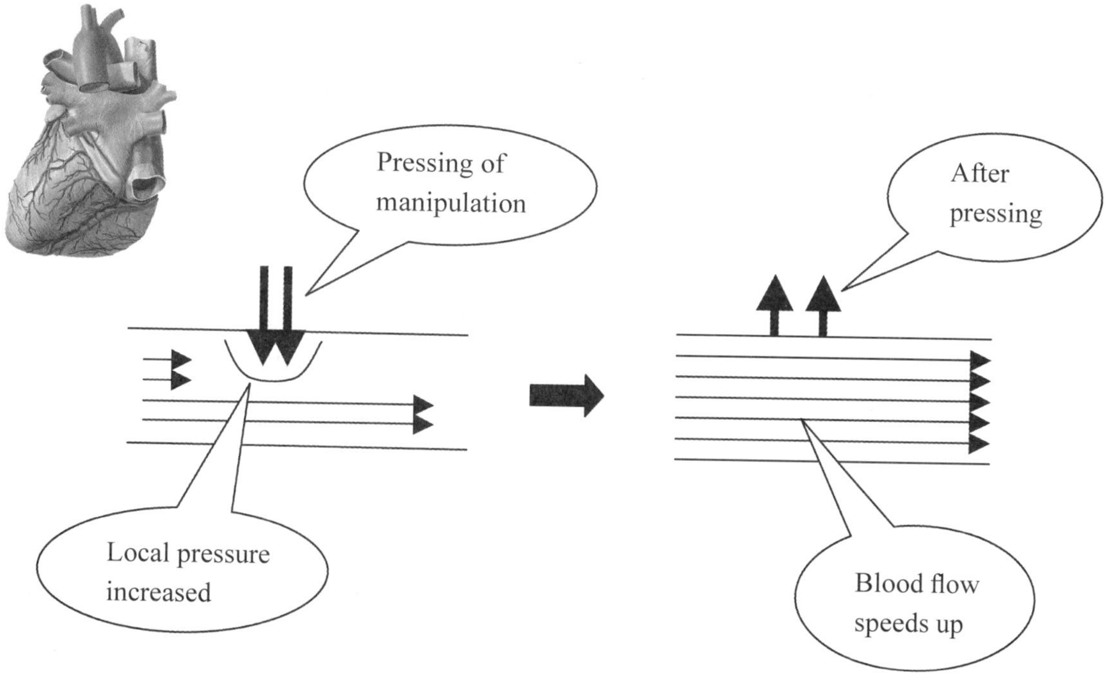

2. Improving Blood Rheology

Blood stasis and blood rheology are closely related. The higher the blood viscosity is, the more difficult the blood flow. Blood viscosity is not fixed, and it is correlated to the speed of blood flow. The faster the blood flows, the lower the viscosity is, and vise versa. When the flow rate lowers to a certain level, the blood will be stagnant and coagulated. By means of tui na manipulations such as squeezing and pressing, the flow rate is enhanced and blood rheology is improved. Modern experimental studies have demonstrated that tui na has a certain influence on blood rheology in patients with blood stasis. Regardless of the conditions of high or low shear, whole blood viscosity ratio decreased to some extent, and it is worth noting that the deformability of red blood cells also increased and blood rate markedly improved. Because changes in the blood components will have a certain impact on blood rheology, studies have shown that after tui na treatment the total number of leukocytes in healthy people increases, the proportion of lymphocytes increases and the phagocytic ability of leukocytes is greatly enhanced. Tui na treatment on patients with anemia gives rise to an increase in both the number of red blood cells and hemoglobin.

3. Reducing Resistance of Blood Flow

Resistance of blood flow is an important factor for blood circulation, and is closely related to the diameter of small vessel. According to fluid mechanics, vascular resistance is inversely proportional to the fourth power of vascular diameter, with the result that even minor change of vascular diameter can greatly reduce the resistance of blood flow.

A direct effect of tui na manipulation may be to relax the smooth muscle of blood vessels to expand their diameter. In addition, studies have shown that manipulation can reduce sympathetic excitability on the one hand, and promote decomposition and excretion of free adrenalin and noradrenalin in blood on the other hand, thus contributing to the expansion of small artery diameter and the reduction of blood flow resistance. Furthermore, the pressure and friction produced by the application of manipulations on the body surface can consume and remove lipid material in large quantities from the vascular wall to restore flexibility, thus keeping vessels unobstructed and reducing blood flow resistance.

4. Improving Heart Function

Rhythmic pulsation is a chief factor responsible for blood circulation, and the cardiac output for every pulsation is the main indicator to measure circulatory function. Studies have shown that tui na applied on the appropriate area can improve cardiac function. It has been shown that tui na applied to PC 6 (*nèi guān*) and BL 15 (*xīn shù*) slows down the heart rate, extends the diastolic phase of the cardiac muscle, increases blood perfusion thereby enhancing the oxygen supply to the cardiac muscle, decreases the pressure at the late diastolic phase of the left ventricle, and markedly increases the systolic function of the left ventricle.

5. Promoting the Establishment of Microcirculation

In the body, tiny vessels like a mesh of tubes form the vascular network. This is the major site for the substance exchange between blood and tissues and blood circulation in these small vessels is known as microcirculation. In a situation of rest, an average of only 8%~16% of the capillaries are open. Comparison before and after tui na treatment shows that the opening of capillaries in the local area increases. Accordingly, further experiments on animals have been carried out by cutting rabbits' Achilles tendons, suturing and then applying tui na treatment to the leg. It was found that the number of open capillaries on the site where tui na was applied rose to as much as 32% and a large number of small vessels appeared at the severed end of the Achilles tendon to form a new vascular network. In contrast, in the animals in the control group, the tissues around the Achilles tendon showed only some small depressed vessels with thickened walls, and thrombosis was widespread throughout the vessels, manifesting the state of congestion. As a result of the new vascular network, the ruptured tendon in the tui na group was healed faster than that in the control group. The study also showed that the number of capillaries in the local area was 50 times greater than the situation before tui na treatment.

Relaxing the Sinews and Removing Channel Obstructions

Muscular contraction, tension or even spasm, local numbness and pain are frequently seen symptoms in tui na clinical practice. Tui na therapy can eliminate these symptoms by relaxing tendons and removing obstructions from the channels to obtain a certain therapeutic effect.

After injury, the damaged tissues send out pain stimuli to put associated tissues in state of alert by means of the body's normal reflex function. Muscular contraction, tension and convulsion are just a reaction to this state of alert, with the aim of reducing the body's activities and avoiding excessive

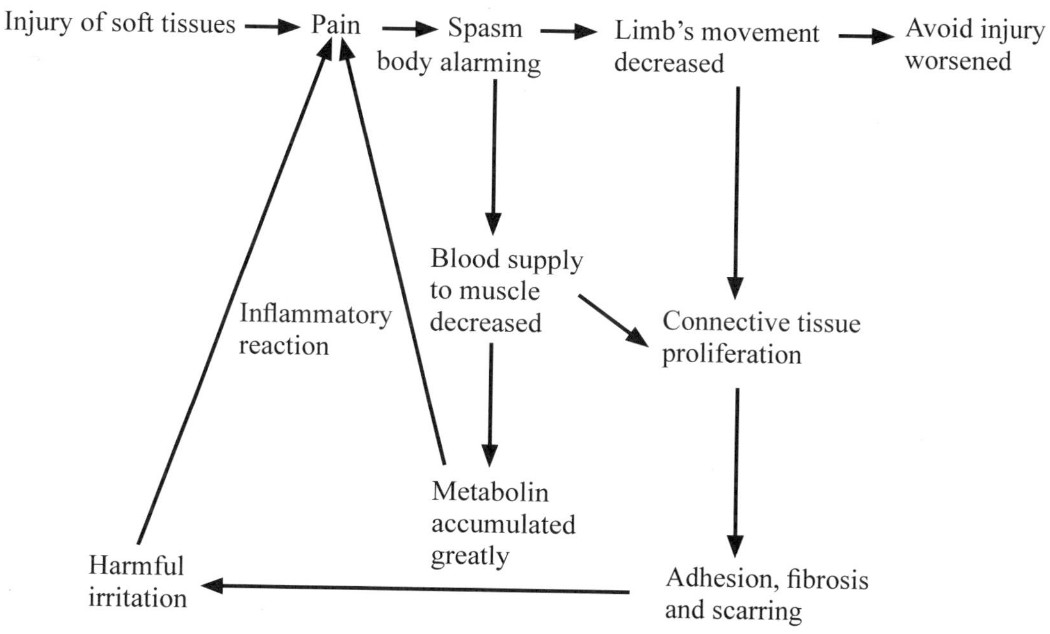

movement which may cause more pain or injury. At this point, if treatment is not administered in time or is incomplete, muscular tension and spasm is not effectively relieved, and the cramping muscle may constrict blood vessels which go through it, thus reducing blood supply. This is aggravated by the fact that a cramping muscle needs much more blood than a relaxed muscle. The result is that a large quantity of metabolites accumulates to cause inflammatory pain. Chronic and prolonged lack of blood and oxygen in the damaged muscle or tissues gives rise to various degrees of connective tissue proliferation or even adhesion, fibrosis and scarring. In turn, this creates harmful long-term stimuli, thereby aggravating pain, muscular tension and spasm to form a vicious circle. Tui na can break this vicious circle to speed up the repair and recovery of damaged muscle.

How is soft tissue spasm dealt with? Ⅰ. Tui na can stretch the damaged soft tissues by means of manipulations which move joints to eliminate tension and spasm. Ⅱ. By raise the temperature of local tissues with tui na manipulations to relieve tension and spasm of soft tissues. Experimental evidence shows that after tui na treatment, the local temperature is greatly raised in the local area and is also higher in other associated parts of the body. Ⅲ. Tui na has an excellent sedative and analgesic effect: it can ease muscular tension and spasm due to pain to relax tendons and remove obstructions from the channel. Pain is a kind of special sensation and any stimulus which exceeds the body's threshold may result in a painful feeling. Tui na can keep pain in check by enhancing the body's pain threshold and reducing the severity of the stimuli. Tui na manipulation can inhibit the transmission of the pain signal conducted by thick nerve fiber, just like closing the gate to stop the pain signal, so as to relieve pain. The stimulation of inflammatory mediators is the main factor causing pain. These inflammatory mediators, such as bradykinin, 5-HT prostaglandins, platelet degradation products and P material, are produced in large quantities around the lesions as a result of the inflammatory reaction, and they are strong algogenic substances. Tui na manipulations on the local area speed up the contact of the inflammatory mediators with enzymes that cause their destruction, thus reducing the local concentration and so creating an analgesic effect.

Modern research into tui na demonstrates that the effect of relaxing tendons and removing obstruction from the channels also influences EMG. After tui na treatment, patients with neck, back and leg pain show reduced or null tonic myoelectric activity, as evidenced by ECG readings.

Correcting Sinews and Adjusting Joints

All disorders resulting from abnormal anatomical position, which may be brought about by a variety of reasons, can be corrected by the direct effect of external manipulations.

For the dislocation of joints, manipulations to move joints can take the joints back to the normal anatomical position. In sacroiliac subluxation, pain appears due to pressure on trapped joint synovium and the stretching of local soft tissues; oblique pulling manipulation and passive movement by extending and flexing hip and knee joints can be applied to adjust dislocation, with the result that pain is lessened and even disappears. In the case of an extruding intervertebral disc, which is very common in clinical practice, the extruding part presses on the nerve root causing lumbago and radiating pain in the lower legs; application of enforced straight leg raising, oblique pulling manipulation and traction can change the positions of the extruded part and the nerve root so as to free the nerve root and relieve pain.

Tui na can also correct malposition of soft tissues through the effect of external manipulation. For example, in the case of a slipped tendon, a cord-like tubercle is often touched at the slipped site with severely limited joint movement; flicking, pushing and pulling manipulations may return slipped tissue to its normal position. Articular cartilage injuries often cause locking joints, making certain physical activities difficult; tui na can unlock the joints with appropriate manipulations. In short, tui na can correct tendons and sinews and adjust joints through the direct effect of manipulations to put various tissues in position, free the channels and joints, and achieve a therapeutic effect.

Section 4 Principles and Methods

Principles of Tui Na Treatment

The principles of tui na are principles of treatment, determined in accordance with the concept of holism and the philosophy of giving treatment based on pattern differentiation. Clinically, these principles determine the methods, prescription and medication used. Diseases manifest various syndromes with complex pathological changes and the process of pathological change shows up in different ways; furthermore, time and place also influence the pathologic changes in an individual to produce diverse results. Therefore, in the course of clinical treatment, one should be good at identifying the root of the disease on the basis of complicated and changing symptoms. Only then can the root of the disease be treated by: supplementing healthy qi and eliminating pathogens in accordance with the conditions of deficiency and excess resulting from the conflict between healthy qi and pathogens; regulating yin-yang in accordance with pathological changes due to disharmony of yin-yang; normalizing *zang-fu* functions and rectifying qi and blood in accordance with pathogenesis of *zang-fu* dysfunction and disorders of qi and blood; and giving treatment in accordance with time, place and individuals.

1. Treating the Root of Diseases

Treating diseases should focus on the root, which is to say finding the fundamental cause of disease and then treating that cause. This is a basic principle in tui na clinical treatment.

The emergence and development of any disease is always displayed through a number of symptoms, but those symptoms do not always reflect the nature of disease, and some may even be misleading. Only through comprehensive analysis can the nature and causative factors of diseases be found in order to determine the appropriate methods of treatment. For example, sciatica is a frequently seen disease in tui na clinical work and may be caused by a variety of reasons, such as prolapse of a lumbar intervertebral disc, piriformis syndrome, pelvic tumor, hip arthritis, hip injury, an improperly positioned gluteal injection, diabetes, vertebral arthritis, lumbosacral fascitis, lumbar spinal stenosis, spinal tuberculosis, spinal metastasis, spinal cord tumor and so on. During treatment, tui na cannot be a simple method just for relieving pain and diagnosis should aim to obtain a clear conclusion: a combination of clinical observation and results from physical and chemical examination is required to identify the real cause of disease. If the disease can be treated by tui na therapy, the methods of relaxing tendons, activating collaterals, eliminating swelling and stopping pain can be applied to really "treat the root of disease".

Routine treatment and contrary treatment are keys to treating the root of disease in tui na clinical practice. Routine treatment is the method of identifying the nature of disease – cold, heat, deficiency or excess – by analyzing clinical manifestations in order to apply the appropriate principles of treatment, namely "treat cold with heat", "treat heat with cold", "treat deficiency with reinforcement", "treat excess with reduction", "treat blood stasis and blood pathogens with the expelling method". Routine treatment is the most common method in tui na clinic. Taking peripheral arthritis of the shoulder as an example, pain and dysfunction in the shoulder joint are its main symptoms, usually caused by deficiency of qi and blood, invasion of exogenous pathogenic cold and damp, or trauma and injury. When the causative factors are clear, the routine treatment methods are reinforcing qi, generating blood, eliminating wind-cold, resolving damp, and removing obstruction from the channels and collaterals to improve blood circulation in the shoulder joint, to speed up the absorption of exudates, to promote restoration of disordered sinew and ligaments, and to relax adhesion.

Contrary treatment, a method which is no less important in tui na clinical practice, is usually used for false or pseudo symptoms manifested in complicated and severe diseases with a mismatch between the symptoms and the nature of the disease. The contrary method includes principles that are applied in accordance with the pseudo-symptoms and which appear to be contrary to the principles of routine treatment. Examples of principles of contrary treatment include "treat an obstructive syndrome with tonics" and "treat an incontinent syndrome with the dredging method". Since the symptoms in this case are false signs, contrary treatment is still essentially the same as routine treatment as both methods aim to identify and treat the root of disease.

"Treating the root of disease" does not exclude "treating the root and branches simultaneously" and "treating branches for acute syndrome". This is because symptoms and causative factors may vary in the changeable syndromes and so treatment should be given accordingly. In tui na clinical practice, acute pain syndromes, such as acute lumbago, are often encountered. In such cases, pain is often the primary symptom due to various factors. Treatment may not immediately tackle the root or ultimate causative factor of the disease, but may rather try to stop pain with appropriate tui na methods. Only when pain has been significantly relieved, can the root of the disease be treated by means of diagnosis and syndrome differentiation. As can be seen, treating symptoms directly may sometimes be required in emergency situations or to create the necessary conditions for identifying and treating the underlying causative factors. However, treating the root is still taken as the basis for treating diseases, and the principle of "finding the root in treating disease" is upheld.

2. Reinforcing Healthy qi and Eliminating Pathogens

The emergence of disease is just the process of the struggle between healthy qi and pathogens.

Tui na treatment applies a series of manipulations to strengthen healthy qi and eliminate pathogens in order to change the balance of power between healthy qi and pathogens. By gradually increasing healthy qi and gradually decreasing pathogens, the disease is transformed to a normal state. Strengthening healthy qi and eliminating pathogens is also a basic principle in tui na clinical practice.

This principle is a specific application of the more general tui na principle to "treat deficiency with reinforcing methods; treat excess with reducing methods". Strengthening healthy qi is a reinforcing method, involving manipulations which are done along the channels and towards the heart with gentle strength and even speed, usually employed for deficiency syndromes. Eliminating pathogens means a draining method, indicating that manipulations are done against the channels and away from the heart with greater strength and speed, usually applied for excess syndromes.

3. Regulating Yin-Yang

The human body is a system with an equilibrium of yin-yang, and disease may arise if this balance is disturbed, i.e. a preponderance or a weakness of either yin or yang replaces the normal dynamic balance between yin and yang. Regulating yin-yang is also one of the basic principles in tui na clinic.

Yin disease occurs when yang is preponderant and yang disease when yin is preponderant, and the body may manifest symptoms of hypoactivity or hyperactivity, respectively. For hypoactivity, it is better to apply excitory manipulations with low frequency and light pressure; for hyperactivity, inhibiting manipulations with high frequency and heavy pressure to inhibit hyperactivity. Weakness of yin-yang may occur as yin deficiency, yang deficiency, deficiency of both yin and yang, yin deficiency with yang hyperactivity, and yang deficiency with yin hyperactivity. During tui na treatment, the methods of reinforcing yin, benefiting yang, reinforcing both yin and yang, and enriching yin while controlling yang can be selected to suit the specific conditions to regulate yin and yang. Since yin and yang depend on each other, when syndromes due to deficiency of yin-yang are treated, it is important to "treat yin for yang" or "treat yang for yin", that is, yang should be reinforced whenever yin is, and yin should be enriched whenever yang is, so that "yang can be generated endlessly with the help of yin, while yin will rise up to find an unending source".

4. Regulating the Functions of *Zang-fu*

The human body is an organic whole, *zang* organ and *zang* organ, *zang* organ and *fu* organ, *fu* organ and *fu* organ. These organs coordinate and promote each other physiologically, and influence each other pathologically. A disorder in any *zang-fu* organ may influence the functioning of other organs. For example, a lung disorder may be a disorder of the lung itself, or caused by disorders of the heart, liver, spleen and kidney. The following cases illustrate this point:

— Asthmatic cough due to deficiency of heart qi and blood stasis of the heart vessel caused by dysfunction of lung qi in descending, which should be treated with the principle of warming heart yang;

— Hemoptysis due to excessive liver fire resulting in upward attack of qi-fire, which should be treated by reducing liver fire;

- Cough with profuse sputum caused by dysfunction of the lung in ascending and descending due to phlegm resulting from weak spleen producing damp and phlegm, which should be treated with the principle of strengthening the spleen and drying dampness;
- Dry cough, dry throat and mouth caused by kidney yin deficiency failing to reinforce and moisten the lung, which should be treated with the principle of warming the kidney to accept qi.

Therefore, in treating disorders of *zang-fu* organs with tui na, it is essential not to think of one organ, but to pay attention to regulating the relationship between various organs and coordinating their functions to achieve a satisfactory therapeutic result.

5. Regulating the Relationship between Qi and Blood

Qi and blood are the main material basis for various *zang-fu* organs and their tissues and functional activities. Qi and blood have their own functions, but also rely on each other. Physiologically, qi can produce blood, move blood and control blood, and it is said that "qi is the commander of blood." While blood provides the material basis for the activities of qi and carrying qi, it is said that "blood is the mother of qi." If the relationship between qi and blood is abnormal so that they fail to support and promote each other, there will be a variety of blood disorders. The principle of rectifying qi and blood is "reduce when excessive, reinforce when deficient" in order to restore and coordinate the relationship between qi and blood. Just as qi can promote blood, qi deficiency or qi stagnation may slow down blood circulation resulting in stagnant blood circulation. This is referred to as blood stasis due to qi deficiency or stagnation of qi and blood, and should be treated by supplementing qi and moving the blood or rectifing qi, invigorating the blood and eliminating blood stasis.

6. Giving Treatment in Accordance with Time, Place and Individual

During treatment, the therapeutic method used ought to be selected according to time, place, body constitution and age.

The notion of time encompasses the season and time of day. For instance, winter is dominated by cold, which may be combined with dampness, and aged people typically have liver and kidney deficiency: therefore, they often have joint pain and ought to be treated with tui na manipulations which will warm the body. In contrast, summer is dominated by summer heat, which often combines with dampness to disturb the spleen and stomach: therefore, it is better to apply manipulations aimed at eliminating summer-damp and benefiting the spleen and stomach. With respect to the time of day, if the treatment is given in the morning, manipulations should be gentle and not too strong to prevent fainting; if the treatment is given in the evening, manipulations which may invigorate the mind should be avoided because the body starts to regulate its rhythm in the evening in preparation for sleep.

Different geographical conditions can also influence tui na treatment because different geographical environments give rise to dissimilar living habits in the population, and those living habits may affect the functions of various organs. For example, people living in the northern high-latitude cold regions usually like spicy food, and they have to take active exercise in order to acclimatize themselves to the cold. These two factors make the northern people healthy and robust, and only strong and heavy tui na manipulations are effective for them. Conversely, people who live at low-latitude warm northern regions with a mild climate and sweetish diet are not so hearty as the northern people in body metabolism, and their build is comparatively shorter and thinner. As a result, it is better to apply gentle manipulations to them as otherwise treatment may no be effective or could even cause more injury.

Giving treatment in accordance with the individual is particularly important in tui na clinical practice. This is because tui na acts upon the body surface with direct external force, and the characteristics of each body should be considered. The relevant factors to be taken into account are usually age, sex, profession, body constitution, past history and family history. Manipulations appropriate for young and middle-aged people are probably beyond the tolerance of elderly people and children. For patients with a tendency towards malignant bleeding and with a family history of tuberculosis, the strength of manipulations should be increased gradually to avoid adverse consequences. A patient's occupation also has a close bearing on the treatment, especially for those people working long-term in the environment of radiation and chemical reagents, as they must never be subject to rough and forceful manipulations.

Common Manipulations

Fundamental tui na treatment is based on the core theory of traditional Chinese medicine, which is nothing more than reinforcing deficiency, reducing excess, strengthening right qi, eliminating pathogens, regulating yin-yang to restore the balance between qi and blood and obtain results. Tui na therapy involves applying manipulations on special areas or points of the body. Thus, the action of a manipulation is based on two factors: firstly, the nature and quantity of the manipulation and secondly, the specific area and points stimulated. Stimulating different areas and points with manipulations of the same nature and quantity may produce different effects. By the same token, stimulating the same area or points with manipulations differing in nature and quantity may also produce different effects. Therefore, therapeutic effect cannot be defined simply in terms of the nature and quantity of the manipulations, nor can it be judged from just the stimulated areas and points. To study the effect of tui na treatment, both aspects must be taken into account.

Following this classification of manipulations according to their nature and quantity, combined with the area/point of application, tui na therapy has ten methods: warming, dredging, reinforcing, reducing, sweating, harmonizing, dissipating, clearing, emetic and resolving. Each will be described in turn.

1. Warming Method

The warming method is employed for the deficiency-cold syndrome, and is carried out with manipulations that are slow and gentle in rhythm. The manipulations ought to be applied continuously for a long period time on every area and point of application until the patient has a feeling of warmth and irritation deep in the body. This reaction can supplement yang qi and is suitable for yin-cold or the deficiency-cold syndrome.

In a clinical context, the manipulations of pressing, rubbing and kneading are often applied on RN 12 (*zhōng wǎn*), RN 6 (*qì hǎi*) and RN 4 (*guān yuán*), as well as a scrubbing manipulation on BL 23 (*shèn shù*) and DU 4 (*mìng mén*) to warm and supplement kidney yang, strengthen the spleen, normalize the stomach, benefit healthy qi, disperse cold and stop pain.

2. Dredging Method

The dredging Method is the most frequently applied method in tui na therapy. Tui na therapy takes the theory of channels and collaterals as its theoretic basis. The channels and collaterals are distributed over the entire body. They are the main passages for the circulation of qi, blood and body fluids, and form a network which links the whole body into an organic whole. They also represent one of the ways that the exogenous pathogens attack the internal organs. The main mechanism responsible for disorders of the channels and collaterals is blockage resulting in unsmooth circulation of qi and blood. "Where there is an obstruction, there is pain," the obstruction of the channels often manifests itself in the form of pain, swelling, blood stasis and numbness. Only when the channels and collaterals are free from obstruction, do qi and blood flow smoothly and body fluids circulate ordinarily, thus "reinforcing yin-yang, moistening tendons and bones, and benefiting joints." Tui na is ideal for removing obstruction from the channels and collaterals and physicians of various dynasties paid great attention to the dredging effect of tui na therapy.

The dredging method involves a large group of therapeutic methods. Based on its therapeutic action, the method is subdivided as follows: dredging by opening, dredging by dispersing, dredging by clearing, dredging by warming, dredging by rectifying, dredging by scattering, dredging by benefiting, dredging by subduing, dredging a joint, dredging an orifice, dredging the block, dredging a channel, dredging a collateral, dredging a blood vessel, dredging *zang-fu*. The dredging method in tui na therapy, except the application for supplementing Eight Methods like sweating method, emetic method, purgative method, harmonizing method, warming method, clearing method, reinforcing method, resolving method, is also used widely to dredge the channels for stopping pain, dredge the collaterals for resolving swelling, benefit the joints, and readjust the sinew and bone.

3. Reinforcing Method

Reinforcing implies nourishing and tonifying qi, blood and body fluids, as well as the weak functions of *zang-fu*. "Reinforcing healthy qi and eliminating pathogens" is a clinical guiding principle. The reinforcing method is widely applied and can be used in the following cases: for deficiency of qi and blood, weakness of spleen and stomach, deficiency of kidney yin, night sweating due to yin deficiency, nocturnal emissions. Usually, the reinforcing method involves rolling, rubbing, scrubbing and so on, namely, gentle and soft manipulations without strong stimulation.

The following examples demonstrate the use of the reinforcing method in a clinical context:

— One-finger pushing, rubbing and kneading are applied clockwise on the abdomen, particularly on RN 12 (*zhōng wǎn*), ST 25 (*tiān shū*), RN 6 (*qì hǎi*) and RN 4 (*guān yuán*);

— Pressing and scrubbing are used on the urinary bladder channel, particularly on BL 21 (*wèi shù*) and BL 20 (*pí shù*) to regulate spleen and stomach function, with the effect of invigorating the spleen, harmonizing the stomach, supplementing the middle jiao and replenishing qi;

— One-finger pushing or scrubbing on DU 4 (*mìng mén*), BL 23 (*shèn shù*) and BL 52 (*zhì shì*), followed by rubbing, kneading and pressing on abdominal points, such as RN 4 (*guān yuán*) and RN 6 (*qì hǎi*), serves to build up and supplement original qi and to strengthen *ming men* fire.

4. Reducing Method

The reducing method is usually used for excess syndrome to lower energy. The reducing method can be used to treat abdominal distention and fullness or distending abdominal pain accompanied by constipation and retention of urine resulting from a build up of excessive heat and fire and food accumulation. However, the reducing method of tui na therapy is not as strong as the reducing effect of medicines: it can be used for a weak patient with constipation caused by insufficient body fluid, and this is precisely when the tui na reducing method is more appropriate.

Clinically, it is possible to apply relatively strong manipulations to obtain the necessary reducing effect, and manipulation frequency is gradually increased from slow to fast. Though the reducing method is strong, there are no side effects because tui na therapy reduces excess by regulating the functions of internal organs using external manipulations. Taking food accumulation and constipation as an example:

— One-finger pushing and rubbing can be applied on RN 8 (*shén què*) and ST 25 (*tiān shū*), followed by kneading manipulation on DU 1 (*cháng qiáng*) to drain excess from *fu* organs;

— For constipation due to excessive fire and insufficiency of body fluid caused by yin deficiency resulting, rubbing clockwise on the abdomen is good for promoting bowel movement without damaging yin.

5. Sweating Method

The sweating method involves inducing sweat and a dispersion effect to remove pathogens from the body surface. The sweating method is usually used for external contraction caused by wind-cold or wind-heat. For external contraction due to wind-cold, grasping is applied, first gently and then with strength, increasing the stimulation gradually to let the force penetrate deeply into the body. Strong manipulations may relieve external contraction and induce sweating of the whole body, which achieves the aim of dispelling wind and dispersing cold. For external contraction due to wind-heat, a light grasping manipulation which is gentler and quicker is applied to relax the muscle and flesh; during the treatment, the patient feels comfortable all over the body and sweats slightly. Along with sweating, pathogens are dispersed automatically and the body recovers.

The sweating method is usually done with pressing manipulations and one-finger pushing manipulations, as the following cases show:

— Applying one-finger pushing and grasping on GB 20 (*fēng chí*) and DU 16 (*fēng fǔ*) can dispel and disperse wind;

— Pressing and grasping on LI 4 (*hé gǔ*) and SJ 5 (*wài guān*) can eliminate all kinds of external pathogens;

— DU 14 (*dà zhuī*) is the meeting place of all kinds of yang and applying one-finger pushing, pressing and kneading there can disperse heat and remove obstructions from three yang channels;

— Applying pushing, pressing and grasping on BL 12 (*fēng mén*) and BL 13 (*fèi shù*) may dispel wind and disperse lung qi.

Any syndrome relating to external obstruction due to wind-cold and wind-heat can be helped with grasping, pressing and one-finger pushing since these manipulations are effective in dispelling wind, dissipating cold, relaxing muscle and relieving the exterior syndrome. For this reason, Zhang

Cong-zheng of the Jin Dynasty listed tui na as a sweating method.

6. Harmonizing Method

The harmonizing method involves reconciliation and regulation. It is not advisable to treat the half-exterior half-interior syndrome with sweating, vomiting or purgative methods, but it can be treated with the harmonizing method. The manipulations of the harmonizing method should be even, soft and slow, and they usually include manipulations such as vibrating and rubbing. The method can rectify channel qi and normalize blood circulation. It is of use for pain caused by qi stagnation of the liver and stomach, irregular menstruation, disharmony of the spleen and stomach and general distending pain resulting from disorder of qi and blood, and obstruction of the channels and collaterals. With the effects of these manipulations, the channels and points regulate qi and blood, relieve both exterior and interior syndromes and balance yin and yang, so as to restore normal physical state to the body.

Clinically, the harmonizing method is used for three purposes: to normalize qi and blood, to harmonize the spleen and stomach, and to soothe liver qi. The method of normalizing qi and blood includes rolling, one-finger pushing, pressing, kneading and twisting on the four limbs and the back, or gentle grasping on GB 21 (*jiān jǐng*). As for harmonizing the spleen and stomach and soothing liver qi, one-finger pushing, rubbing and twisting are applied on bilateral LV 13 (*zhāng mén*) and LV 14 (*qī mén*), RN 13 (*shàng wǎn*), RN 12 (*zhōng wǎn*), BL 18 (*gān shù*), BL 20 (*pí shù*) and BL 21 (*wèi shù*).

7. Dissipating Method

The dissipating method involves scattering and dispersing. The distinctive feature of the dissipating method in tui na is that it can dissipate retention and stagnation, whether it be substantial or non-substantial. For the accumulation of pathogens in *zang-fu*, the stagnation of qi and blood and the retention of phlegm and food, the dissipating method can be used to free the circulation of qi and blood free and to disperse accumulation. Dysfunction of the spleen in transportation and transformation due to over-eating may cause fullness and distention in the chest and abdomen, and can be treated with the dissipation method.

The dissipating method in tui na is usually with soft, rapid and gentle manipulations, particularly waving and rubbing manipulations. The following examples demonstrate the uses of the dissipating method:

— Swelling in surgery can be treated with rapid vibrating;
— Fullness due to qi stagnation is treated with gentle one-finger pushing and rubbing;
— Accumulation of substantial pathogens may be treated with one-finger pushing, rubbing, kneading and twisting.

The frequency of these manipulations goes from slow to fast in order to overcome binding constraints and to dissipate stasis.

8. Clearing Method

The clearing method, made up of the manipulations which are firm but gentle, is applied on selected areas and points to clear heat and calm down restlessness. This is the main method for common febrile disorders.

The following cases:

- For excessive heat at qi level, pushing along the *du mai* from DU 14 (*dà zhuī*) to caudal clears the heat;
- For deficient heat at qi level, rubbing on the lumbar region gently nourishes yin and clears fire;
- For excessive heat at blood level, rubbing forcefully along the *du mai* from DU 14 (*dà zhuī*) to caudal clears heat and cools blood;
- For excessive heat in qi level, pushing gently along the courses of the Urinary Bladder Channel on the back (from the lower part to upper part) is suitable;
- For deficient exterior heat, pushing gently along the courses of Urinary Bladder Channel on the back (from upper part to lower part) to clear heat and relieve the exterior syndrome.

9. Emetic Method

The emetic method is also known as the inducing emetic method and provokes vomiting to expel pathogens, thus treating any internal accumulation and constraint. In tui na, the emetic method is used for the retention of phlegm and food which cannot be treated with the sweating method and purgation.

In addition to inducing vomiting by putting fingers into the throat, the emetic method can be also achieved by putting two fingers over RN 10 (*xià wǎn*) and then pushing the fingers upward to RN 22 (*tiān tū*). This method is suitable for food retention which results in abdominal fullness, a gurgling sound in the throat and short breath, or acute food poisoning which remains in the stomach. Such pushing may bring a substantial mass in the stomach out through the mouth.

10. Resolving Method

The resolving method deals with resolving and removing stagnation, and it eliminates stagnation, blood stasis and accumulation and build up. In tui na, the resolving method is often used to treat the retention of food, blood stasis, qi mass, painful swelling, phlegm mass and stubborn arthralgia. It is also used to disperse accumulation-gathering, invigorate blood and eliminate blood stasis, move qi and dispel distention, dissipate stagnation and resolve swelling, soften nodules and transform phlegm, and remove obstructions from the channels. The resolving method involves the principles of rectifying qi, uplifting sinking, promoting digestion and draining dampness.

Method of rectifying qi: the manipulations used for treating disease by rectifying qi, moving qi, adjusting qi and freeing qi circulation are subsumed under the method of rectifying qi. For example, applying pressing and kneading manipulations on BL 18 (*gān shù*), BL19 (*dǎn shù*), RN 6 (*qì hǎi*) and SP 10 (*xuè hǎi*), and twisting and rubbing manipulations at the hypochondriac regions treats disorders due to a binding constraint on liver qi, such as hypochondriac and distending pain in the epigastric region, distending pain in the breast or lower abdominal pain in women, and dysmenorrheal.

Method of raising sinking: this method is a kind of manipulation for lifting and raising yang qi. The method is advisable for diarrhea, poor appetite and stomach prolapse due to failure of spleen yang in ascending.

Method of lowering qi: qi counterflow implies an upward attack of qi due to a disorder of qi circulation in *zang-fu*, and so qi must be lowered in order to counteract this anomaly. For example, separating pushing on RN 17 (*dàn zhōng*) is used to treat coughing and shortness of breath; and pressing and rubbing on PC 6 (*nèi guān*) and ST 36 (*zú sān lǐ*) to descend qi and stop vomiting for treating nausea, vomiting, belching and hiccups due to an upward attack of stomach qi.

Method of promoting digestion: this method resolves the retention of food by promoting digestion. For belching and vomiting due to retained food from the previous day, rubbing and kneading on the abdomen are advisable to aid digestion and stop vomiting.

Method of draining dampness: manipulations which can expel water and dampness from the body by increasing urine or dispelling phlegm and dampness all fall under the method of draining dampness. For insufficient urine, rubbing on the abdomen and scrubbing on BL 31 (*shàng liáo*), BL 32 (*cì liáo*), BL 33 (*zhōng liáo*) and BL 34 (*xià liáo*) are suitable; for coughing and asthma due to profuse sputum in the throat, pressing and kneading manipulations on RN 22 (*tiān tū*), RN 12 (*zhōng wǎn*), PC 6 (*nèi guān*) and BL 13 (*fèi shù*) are effective.

Reinforcement and Reduction in Tui Na Therapy

Reinforcing deficiency and reducing excess is one of the basic principles of TCM therapy and is a fundamental concept in all areas, whether that be making formulas and prescribing drugs, acupuncture or tui na. Within the reinforcing and reducing methods employed by TCM, tui na plays an important role and achieves reinforcement and reduction through the effect of various manipulations on the points and areas of the body.

Generally speaking, the reinforcement manipulations are effective for raising yang, stimulating and invigorating the physiological functions to nourish the body and strengthen the *zang-fu* organs; the reduction manipulations are good for lowering temperature, inhibiting *zang-fu* functions, eliminating external pathogens and rectifying qi circulation. From ancient times to the present, tui na physicians have accumulated a wealth of experience as the following examples illustrate: pushing and grasping on RN 12 (*zhōng wǎn*), ST 36 (*zú sān lǐ*) and BL 21 (*wèi shù*) can promote intestinal peristalsis to strengthen the spleen, normalize the stomach, promote digestion and resolve food retention; pushing and palm-rubbing on sternocleidomastoid muscle (*Qiáo Gōng Xué*, 桥弓穴) may soothe the liver and pacify yang to treat hypertension, headache and insomnia due to rising hyperactivity of liver yang. Given the external nature of tui na, no substances enter or leave the body, but these manipulations are still essentially referred to as reinforcement and reduction as they achieve these effects. Therefore, reinforcement and reduction in tui na are certain manipulations applied on specific points and areas for an appropriate duration of time to obtain the effects of reinforcing healthy qi and promoting physical functions of the body, or eliminating pathogens and inhibiting hyperactivity of *zang-fu* and the tissues respectively.

1. Main Factors Influencing Reinforcement and Reduction of Tui Na

The reinforcing-reducing effect of tui na is in fact the corresponding functional changes of qi, blood, body fluids and *zang-fu* produced after tui na manipulations have been applied. The therapeutic effect of tui na manipulations depends on two major factors: firstly, the nature and quantity of the manipulation; secondly, the specific areas and points that are stimulated. The reinforcing-reducing effect of tui na manipulations is closely related to the intensity, direction and frequency of manipulations, the nature and duration of the stimulation, and the area(s) of application.

a. Nature and Quantity of Manipulations

As far as the soft tissues are concerned, manipulations which involve prolonged stimulation of shallow parts of the body and are thus able to excite the soft tissues are more effective for reinforcing; conversely, those manipulations which provide brief stimulation, effect deeper parts of the body and are able to inhibit the soft tissues are more effective for reduction. To treat an area with hypertonia, only manipulations which can send strong stimulation deeper into the body are able to inhibit the hyperactive state; for an area with hypotonia, manipulations that produce shallow stimulation are enough to restore physical function. In treating injury of soft tissues, tui na may not only achieve reinforcement by strengthening the local circulation of blood and enhancing the pain threshold of the tissue, but also promote the absorption of local edema and hematoma to relieve sprain and dislocation, thereby eliminating the causes of the soft tissue disorder and achieving reduction. This example demonstrates the coexistence of the reinforcement and reduction effects of tui na on the soft tissues: both aspects promote each other, reduction benefiting reinforcement and reinforcement helping reduction, so as to obtain a satisfactory therapeutic effect.

For certain *zang* or *fu* organs, mild stimulation activates and excites physical function, whereas strong stimulation inhibits physical function. For instance, for weak spleen and stomach, gentle one-finger pushing on BL 20 (*pí shù*), BL 21 (*wèi shù*), RN 12 (*zhōng wǎn*) and RN6 (*qì hǎi*) to create prolonged rhythmic stimulation is appropriate. For gastrointestinal vasospasm, pointing and pressing with strong stimulation on the corresponding back-shu points may produce the desired effect in just a short time. Consequently, for the *zang-fu* organs, strong stimulation over a short time represents reduction and mild stimulation over a long time implies reinforcement.

b. Frequency of Manipulations

For tui na manipulations, a change in the frequency of application within a certain range is just a change of quantity. However, if the frequency varies beyond this range, a manipulation may change in quality from reduction to reinforcement, or vice versa. Clinically, one-finger pushing with a high frequency (220 ~ 250 times/min.) is often used for treating some surgical disorders, such as carbuncles, furuncles and abscesses, since it has the effect of invigorating the blood, eliminating swelling, expelling pus and expressing toxins. As such, it is considered a reducing method. However, one-finger pushing with a lower frequency (120 ~ 160 times/min.) is mainly used to treat internal disorders and gynecological diseases since it has the effect of resuscitating and clearing the mind, strengthening the spleen, harmonizing the stomach, relaxing tendons and removing obstruction from the collaterals, and is thus considered a reinforcing method.

c. Direction of Manipulation

The relationship between the direction of manipulation and the reinforcing-reducing effect is mainly described in the classics about pediatric tui na. These writings state that manipulations along the channels which are slow, gentle and upward are considered reinforcing methods, whereas manipulations against the channels which are rapid, strong and downward are reducing methods.

In the treatment of adult disorders, there is often a relationship between the direction of manipulation and the reinforcing-reducing effect. For example, rubbing the abdomen clockwise has a marked effect in promoting bowel movement and purgation; rubbing the abdomen counterclockwise greatly increases the digestive function of stomach and intestines thus strengthening the spleen and harmonizing the stomach. The former is a reducing method and the latter is a reinforcing method.

d. Area/Points of Application and Reinforcement-Reduction

It should be kept in mind that the specific areas and points of application are a factor which may affect the effect of reinforcing-reducing methods in tui na therapy. During the process of diagnosis by syndrome differentiation and the selection of points, the relation between the diseased area and body surface needs to be identified and then the theory of channels-collaterals and nerve segments is applied in order to select the appropriate point on the body. The same manipulation applied to different points or areas of the body may produce dissimilar effects. The channels and collaterals work to circulate qi and blood, link up the exterior and interior, connect *zang-fu* and the tissues together and a correction application of the theory of channels-collaterals may greatly enhance the therapeutic effect. Points, as reflexes of the body on the surface, are bidirectional as they can reflect internal disorders and pain on the surface but also transmit stimulation signals to the interior from the exterior. Different points work in different ways, and a single point may have different therapeutic effects, depending on the disease that is being treated. For example, when spleen and stomach are hyperactive, ST 36 (*zú sān lǐ*) can inhibit them; otherwise, this point excites them. Therefore, careful attention should be paid to the points in the treatment of *zang-fu* disorders. In tui na clinical practice, some specific points are often selected, such as the five transport points, the *yuan*-source points, the *luo*-connecting points, the *xi*-cleft points, the back-*shu* points, the front-*mu* points, the eight influential points or the confluent points of the eight extraordinary vessels. These points have their own special effect and in combination with tui na manipulations, they serve to supplement deficiency and drain excess for *zang-fu* disorders.

The channels vary in length and physical function. The foot channels are longer than the hand channels, yang channels longer than yin channels. Thus, the foot and yang channels should be manipulated in a strong and heavy way, while for the hand and yin channels, manipulations are usually gentle. Only in this way can reinforcement and reduction be properly achieved. For patients with different body constitutions, tui na therapy should be determined by syndrome differentiation. Patients with a weak constitution should receive slow and gentle manipulations to prevent further exhaustion of qi, consumption of essence and injury to tendons; robust patients should be subject to stronger and more rapid manipulations to obtain fast results. From the point of view of body shape, qi usually circulates smoothly in thin people and with more difficulty in fat people, so reinforcing methods are appropriate for thin people and reducing methods for fat people. As for personal character, reducing methods are suited to people with hyperactivity and a quick temper, reinforcing methods for people with a quiet and easy-going character. The type of disease is also a factor which must be taken into account: acute disease with a short duration should be treated with reducing methods, and long-term chronic disease with reinforcing methods. In addition, sex, age, birthplace and hobbies are also factors to be considered. Tui na therapy should be carried out in a quiet environment with slow and soft background music. The doctor may talk to the patient and use manipulations to put him or her at ease and should also help the patient to understand the sensations that he or she may experience. All these strategies may improve the reinforcement and reduction effect obtained with the treatment.

2. Common Reinforcing-Reducing methods of Tui Na

The common reinforcing-reducing methods of tui na can be divided into five categories: by strength, by direction, by channel direction, by frequency, and by the midnight-noon ebb-flow theory.

a. Reinforcement and Reduction Achieved by Strength

Gentle manipulations are taken to be reinforcing methods, and strong manipulations reducing methods. Waving, rotating, rubbing and scrubbing manipulations are usually gentle and soft, good for regulating the functions of the *zang-fu* organs and tonifying health qi, and therefore considered reinforcing methods. On the other hand, tapping, hitting, pressing, squeezing manipulations as well as the manipulations for moving joints are stronger with heavy stimulation, good at inducing sweating, invigorating blood, stopping vomiting and eliminating pathogens, and therefore considered reducing methods. Therefore, gentle manipulations are suitable for weak patients with lengthy mild diseases; heavy manipulations are more suited to strong patients with severe diseases of a short duration. Experimental evidence shows that gentle manipulations may inhibit central nerves and excite peripheral nerves; heavy manipulations may excite central nerves and inhibit peripheral nerves.

b. Reinforcement and Reduction Achieved by Direction

The ancient physicians, especially pediatric tui na experts, placed great emphasis on the directions of manipulations, and they maintained the following: applying manipulations towards the heart is considered a reinforcing method, away from the heart a reducing method; pushing upward is a reinforcing method, downward a reducing method; pushing inward is a reinforcing method, outward a reducing method; rotating-pushing clockwise is a reinforcing method, counterclockwise a reducing method.

c. Reinforcement and Reduction Achieved by Channel Direction

This method is actually a special case of the direction category; it is given its own category because it is closely related to the flow direction of the channels. The basic principle is that applying manipulations along the channel is a reinforcing method and against the channel is a reducing method. During treatment, rapid and gentle manipulations for a short time on the points along the course of the channel, or pushing and kneading manipulations along the course of the channel, will harmonize circulation of qi and blood and restore normal movement to a weak body, and is thus a reinforcing method achieved by manipulations which can maintain qi along with the flow of qi. Strong pushing, pressing and pinching manipulations against the course of channel, or strong manipulations for long time on the points one by one against the course of channel will weaken the force of pathogens and is thus a reducing method achieved by depriving the force of pathogens against the course of channel. These reinforcing and reducing methods originate from the therapy of acupuncture and moxibustion.

d. Reinforcement and Reduction Achieved by Frequency

Applying manipulations with a fast frequency is a reducing method, and with a slow frequency is a reinforcing method. Clinically, low frequency manipulations are usually gentle and soft, and high frequency manipulations are heavy and strong. Thus, reinforcement and reduction achieved by frequency is often combined with reinforcement and reduction achieved by strength.

e. Reinforcement and Reduction Achieved by Applying the Midnight-Moon Ebb-Low Theory

This method is based on the combination of five transport points, i.e. the *jing*-well point, the *ying*-spring point, the *shu*-stream point, the *jing*-river point point and the *he*-sea point, together with the theory of yin-yang and the five phases. Subsequently, the theory of heavenly stems and earthly branches and the theory of *zang-fu* are applied: points are selected according to time by calculating the circulation, condition, opening and closing of channel qi for a year, a month, a day and an hour with heaven stems and earthly branches. This method is particularly suitable for internal disorders, gynecological diseases and miscellaneous diseases.

Generally, the reinforcement and reduction effects of tui na exist objectively, but they should be understood and applied appropriately. For no reason should any manipulation be thought of as automatically corresponding to reinforcement or to reduction. Reinforcement and reduction are relative, so talking about reinforcement and reduction without taking into account the channels, collaterals, the patient's constitution, the nature of disease and other factors is a one-sided and incomplete view. Therefore, in order to obtain the best therapeutic results, careful and cautious syndrome differentiation is necessary. Reinforcement and reduction in tui na do not simply denote the action of certain manipulations; they form part of systemic treatment under the guidance of the basic theories of TCM, such as yin-yang, *zang-fu*, channels and collaterals.

Chapter 2
Channels, Collaterals & Acupuncture Points

Section 1
Basic Theory of Channels, Collaterals & Acupuncture Points

Channels, collaterals & acupuncture points are the important structures that constitute the human body. The theory of channels, collaterals & acupuncture points is the main component of the theoretical system of traditional Chinese medicine, and it has close relationship with tui na theory. In tui na therapy, for determining the location of disease, the combination of point, line and facet is emphasized. The point implies the corresponding acupuncture point; the line denotes the relative channel; while facet means the corresponding muscular region and cutaneous region.

Jīng Luò is the general term of channels and collaterals. *Jīng* implies "paths and routes" literally, indicating that the channels are the longitudinal courses of the channel system; while *Luò* means "network" literally, indicating that the collaterals are the branches of channels, crisscrossing in the body and running to the various part of the body. Channels and collaterals are the passages for transporting qi and blood, connecting *zang-fu* organs with extremities, linking up the interior to the exterior and the upper part to the lower part, and regulating various vessels of human body. The channels and collaterals, through their regular circulation and complicated communication, form a network linking *zang-fu* organs, sensory organs, orifices, limbs, skin, muscle, tendons and vessels up into an organic whole.

Channel system is constituted by channels and collaterals. Channels include twelve channels and eight extraordinary vessels, and they are the main part of channel system. The collaterals denote the fifteen collateral vessels, superficial collaterals and minute collaterals. The fifteen collateral vessels include the twelve collaterals separating from the twelve channels, the collaterals of the *ren mai and du mai* and the major collateral of the spleen. Since they run to their neighbor channels after separating from the channels they belong to, the collaterals can strengthen and regulate the relationships between yin and yang channels which are externally-internally related. The collaterals distributed in the superficial portion of the body are called "superficial collaterals"; the finest branches of collaterals are named as "minute collaterals". In addition, there are twelve channel divergences, twelve channel sinews and twelve cutaneous regions. The twelve channel divergences are main channels diverged from the twelve channels, they function to strengthen the relationships among the twelve channels in the body cavity, and are distributed to those organs and areas that the main channels never reach, so as to make up the inadequate distribution of the main channels. The twelve sinew channels are the general term of the tendons and muscles system distributed along the courses of the twelve channels, possessing the functions of maintaining the skeleton and dominating the function of joint movement. The twelve cutaneous regions are the reacted regions of the twelve channels on the skin. Since the distribution of twelve sinew channels and cutaneous regions are almost coincident to the distribution of twelve channels on the body surface, they are named in accordance with the twelve channels.

Acupuncture points are the specific sites, through which, qi of *zang-fu* organs and channels is transported to the body surface. Generally, the acupuncture points are called "*shū xué* (腧穴)" in Chinese. These two Chinese characters respectively mean "transportation" and "hole". The names of acupuncture points were different in the past classics, such as "node (*jié* 节)", "meeting (*huì*会)", "qi point (*qì xué*气穴)", "bone hole (*gǔ kǒng*骨孔)" and "point location (*xué wèi*穴位)".

Channels, collaterals and acupuncture points are closely related, and acupuncture points connect with channels, collaterals, *zang-fu* organs, qi and blood. Acupuncture points are attributed to corresponding channels respectively, and the channels pertain to the corresponding *zang-fu* organs. Thus, acupuncture points, channels, collaterals and *zang-fu* organs are formed into an indivisible whole. Once there are any pathogenic changes in the *zang-fu* organs, there must be some reactions in the corresponding acupuncture points. In the same way, stimulation from tui na manipulations on certain acupuncture points would be transmitted to the corresponding *zang-fu* organs through the channels, so as to change the pathological condition of *zang-fu* organs.

Twelve Channels

1. Nomenclature and Classification

Twelve channels are the main part of channel system including three yang channels of the hand, three yang channels of the foot, three yin channels of the hand, and three yin channels of the foot. Twelve channels are named in accordance with yin-yang nature of the internal organs and the distribution of channels on the limbs. The yang channels pertain to *fu* organs, and they run along the lateral aspects of the limbs, while the yin channels pertain to *zang* organs and they run along the medial aspects of the limbs. Hand channels run in the upper limbs, while foot channels run in the lower limbs. Generally speaking, the twelve channels are distributed symmetrically on the head, face, four limbs and trunk, circulating all over the body. On the limbs: the yin channels pertaining to six *zang* organs run along the medial aspects of the limbs. *Taiyin* channels are situated on the anterior side of the medial aspect; *Shaoyin* channels on the posterior side and *jueyin* channels on the middle. The yang channels pertain to six *fu* organs run along the lateral aspects of the limbs. *Yangming* channels are situated on the anterior side of the lateral aspect, *taiyang* channels on the posterior side, and *shaoyang* channels on the middle. On the trunk: the three yang channels of foot are distributed on the lateral side of the trunk; the three yin channels of foot are distributed on the chest and abdomen. Among the six channels of hand, the three yang channels run to the neck by passing the shoulder; hand *taiyin* lung channel and hand *shaoyin* heart channel emerge at the axillary fossa from the chest, while hand *jueyin* pericardium channel only has a short branch on the side of the trunk. On the head and face: the yang channels all reach the head and face to connect with five sensory organs, but their distributions are complicated without obvious rules; the yin channels enter deeply into the head and neck to connect with the throat, tongue and eyes.

- Yin channels ↓ *Zang* organs
  - Three yin channels of the hand (Media aspect of upper limb)
    - *Taiyin* lung channel: anterior
    - *Jueyin* pericardium channel: middle
    - *Shaoyin* heart channel: posterior
  - Three yin channels of the foot (Media aspect of lower limb)
    - *Taiyin* spleen channel: anterior
    - *Jueyin* liver channel: middle
    - *Shaoyin* kidney channel: posterior

* On the lower part of the shank and on the dorsum of foot, the foot *jueyin* liver channel runs along the anterior side and the foot *taiyin* spleen channel runs along the middle line; they cross each other at the level of 8 cun above the medial malleolus, then the foot *taiyin* spleen channel runs along the anterior side and the foot *jueyin* liver channel runs along the middle line.

- Yang channels ↓ *Fu* organs
  - Three yang channels of the hand (Lateral aspect of upper limb)
    - *Yangming* large intestine channel: anterior
    - *Shaoyang sanjiao* channel: middle
    - *Taiyang* small intestine channel: posterior
  - Three yang channels of the foot (Lateral side of lower limb)
    - *Yangming* stomach channel: anterior
    - *Shaoyang* gallbladder channel: middle
    - *Taiyang* bladder channel: posterior

2. Running Direction and Communication

Running direction and communication of the twelve channels are: Three yin channels of the hand run from the chest to hand and communicate with three yang channels of the hand ; three yang channels of the hand run from hand to head and communicate with three yang channels of the foot; three yang channels of the foot run from head to foot and communicate with three yin channels of the foot; three yin channels of the foot run from foot to abdomen and communicate with three yin channels of the hand (Fig. 2-1). Thus, the twelve channels form the circulatory net of qi and blood, since "yin and yang connect like an endless circle".

3. External-Internal Relations and Cyclical Flow of Qi of Twelve channels

The twelve channels pertain to and connect with the corresponding *zang* or *fu* organs respectively, forming the external-internal relations of *zang-fu* and yin-yang, i.e. hand *yangming* large intestine channel is externally and internally related with the hand *taiyin* lung channel; the hand *shaoyang sanjiao* channel with the hand *jueyin* pericardium channel, the hand *taiyang* small intestine channel with the hand *shaoyin* heart channel, the foot *yangming* stomach channel with the foot *taiyin* spleen channel, the foot *shaoyang* gallbladder channel with the foot *jueyin* liver channel, the foot *taiyang* urinary bladder channel with the foot *shaoyin* kidney channel. Thus the twelve channels form six pairs of channels relations. The channels which are externally and internally related run along the symmetrical sides on media and lateral aspects of four limbs (On the shank, at the level of 8 cun above the medial malleolus, the foot *jueyin* liver channel crosses with the foot *taiyin* spleen channel to change their positions), and communicate each other at foot or hand. Because of such external-internal relations, the twelve channels influence each other physiologically and pathologically.

The twelve channels are distributed inside and outside of the human body, while qi and blood circulate in the channels in cycles. That is to say, qi and blood flow from the hand *taiyin* lung channel to the foot *jueyin* liver channel in sequence, and again, flow to the hand *taiyin* lung channel, the beginning and ending are connected like a ring without stop. The rule of cyclical flow of qi and blood in the twelve channels is:

Hand *taiyin* lung channel → Hand *yangming* large intestine channel
↓
Foot *taiyin* spleen channel ← Foot *yangming* stomach channel
↓
Hand *shaoyin* heart channel → Hand *taiyang* small intestine channel
↓
Foot *shaoyin* kidney channel ← Foot *taiyang* urinary bladder channel
↓
Hand *jueyin* pericardium channel → Hand *shaoyang sanjiao* channel
↓
Foot *jueyin* liver channel ← Foot *shaoyang* gallbladder channel

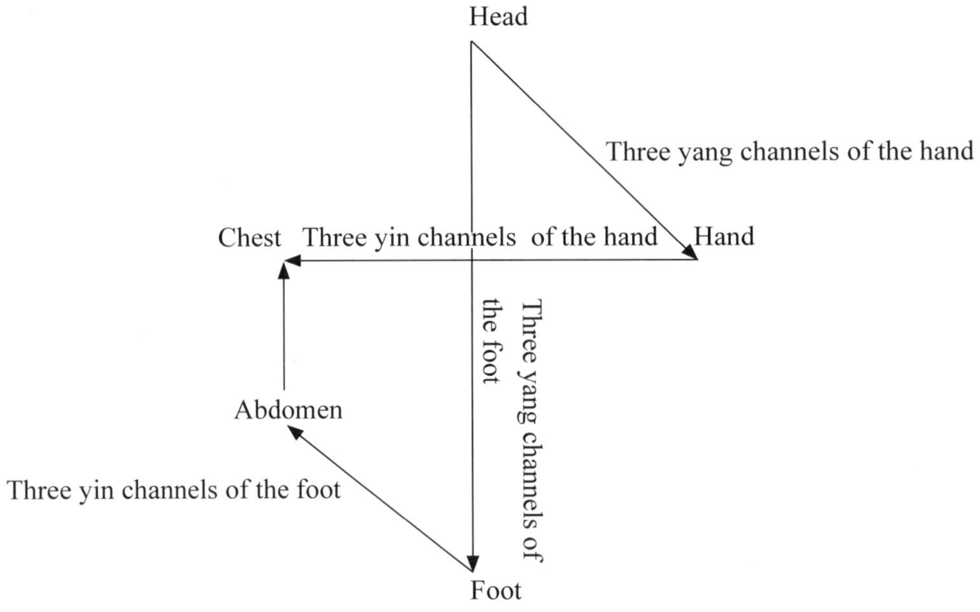

Fig. 2-1 Running Direction and Communication of Twelve channels

Eight Extraordinary Vessels

The eight extraordinary vessels are *du mai, ren mai, chong mai, dai mai, yinqiao mai, yangqiao mai, yinwei mai* and *yangwei mai*. Because they are different from twelve channels, they are named as "extraordinary vessels". They have no direct pertaining and connecting relations with *zang-fu* organs, nor external-internal relations between each other, and they are not distributed as regularly as twelve channels.

The eight extraordinary vessels go across the twelve channels, and function to strengthen the relations among the channels and regulate qi and blood of the twelve channels. When they are overfilled in the twelve channels, qi and blood will be infused into eight extraordinary vessels and be stored there for future use. When the twelve channels are short of qi and blood, the eight extraordinary vessels can make up the insufficiency. The eight extraordinary vessels are closely related with *zang* organs such as liver, kidney, and those extra *fu* organs such as uterus and brain. These relations have great significance to the physiology and pathogenesis of eight extraordinary vessels.

Functions of Eight Extraordinary Vessels

1. *Du mai*

Considered as "sea of yang channels", it functions to govern the general yang qi and maintain qi of whole body. Among the twelve channels, three yang channels of the hand and three yang channels of the foot meet at GV, it is the reason that GV is important in regulating and invigorating general yang qi. Besides, GV ascends and enters into the brain, runs along the spine column and pertains to the kidney, so it influences the functions of brain marrow, spinal cord and kidney.

2. *Ren mai*

Considered as "sea of yin channels", since the six yin channels, Yin LV and TV get together at CV. It functions to regulate qi of yin channels. In addition, there is a saying that "CV dominates conception and fetus", because CV originates in the uterus and is related with the pregnancy of women.

3. *Chong mai*

TV is the communications center of qi and blood of all the channels; it can regulate qi and blood of the twelve channels, so it is called "the sea of the twelve channels". Because TV is closely related with women's menstruation, it is also considered as "the sea of blood".

4. *Dai mai*

BV restricts the channels that run vertically in the trunk and maintains the free circulation of channel qi. All the channels that run in lower limbs are restricted by BV, so it functions to govern these channels. There is a saying that "all the channels are attributed to BV".

5. *Yinqiao mai* and *Yangqiao mai*

Here, "heel" implies moving briskly. Yang HV dominates yang of left and right limbs and Yin HV dominates yin of left and right limbs. Meanwhile, HV can moisten the eyes, control the opening and closing of eyelids and motor functions of lower limbs.

6. *Yinwei mai* and *Yangwei mai*

Here, "link" means maintaining. Yin LV maintains Yin channels of hand and foot, and Yang LV maintains yang channels of hand and foot.

Section 2
Commonly Used Acupuncture Points

Acupuncture point is also named as "point location (*xué wèi*, 穴位)" or "paths (*xué dào*,穴道)". "*shū*" implies transportation and infusion, "*shū xué*" means space and accumulation. The acupuncture points on the courses of fourteen channels with names and locations are called channel points; those experiential points with specific names and definite locations, but not attributed to fourteen channels are called as extra points; those acupuncture points without names and definite locations, selected according to tenderness are called *ashi* points or "heaven reacting point".

The therapeutic properties of acupuncture points are not limited to the local and superficial areas; they would be also used to treat the adjacent, distal or internal disorders.

There are three methods to locate the acupuncture points: proportional measurement, anatomical landmarks, and finger measurement. Locations of acupuncture points, accurate or not, will directly influence the therapeutic results of tui na treatment. In addition to the locating methods mentioned above, sometimes the points can be located according to the landmarks like wrinkles, muscle creases, tendons and joint depressions appeared when the body or limbs are moving or in particular positions. It requires us not only be familiar with the obvious anatomical landmarks, but also to observe landmarks of the bone, muscle and tendon so as to understand the prominence or depression of the tendons and muscles, and characteristics of bones and joints.

In tui na treatment, selection and combination of acupuncture points can be determined by the indications of points and the channels they are attributed to, select adjacent points, distal points, anterior or posterior points, superior or inferior points, left or right points accordingly. The frequently used acupuncture points in clinic are listed in Table 2-1.

Table 2-1 Indications and Manipulations of Frequently Used Acupuncture Points

Channel	Point	Location	Indication	Manipulations
Hand *Taiyin* Lung Channel	LU 1 (*zhōng fǔ*, 中府)	6 cun lateral to the midline of chest, at the same level of the 1st intercostal space	Asthma, fullness in chest, pain of shoulder and back	One-finger Pushing, pressing, kneading, rubbing
	LU 5 (*chǐ zé*, 尺泽)	On the cubital crease, at the lateral side of tendon of m. biceps brachii	Spasmodic pain of elbow and arm, asthma, distending pain in chest and hypochondriac region, infantile convulsion	Pressing, kneading, grasping
	LU 6 (*kǒng zuì*, 孔最)	7 cun above wrist crease, on the line joining LU 9 (*tài yuān*, 太渊) and LU 5 (*chǐ zé*, 尺泽)	Cough, hemoptysis,sore throat, hoarseness of voice, pain of elbow and arm	Pressing, kneading and grasping

Channel	Point	Location	Indication	Manipulations
Hand *Taiyin* Lung Channel	LU 7 (*liè quē*, 列缺)	1.5 cun above the transverse crease of wrist, above styloid process of radius	Cough, shortness of breath, headache, neck rigidity, toothache	One-finger pushing, pressing, kneading
	LU 9 (*tài yuān*, 太渊)	At the radial end of the transverse crease of wrist, in the depression on the radial side of radial artery	Cough, asthmatic breath, mammary swelling, sore throat, pain of wrist and arm	Pressing, kneading, nipping
	LU 10 (*yú jì*, 鱼际)	On the midpoint of the 1st metacarpal bone, at the junction of white and red skin	Chest pain, back pain, headache, dizziness, sore throat, fever, aversion to cold	Pressing, kneading, nipping
	LU 11 (*shào shāng*, 少商)	On the radial side of thumb, 0.1 cun posterior to the corner of the nail	Loss of consciousness due to stroke, spasmodic pain of fingers, infantile convulsion	Nipping
Hand *Yangming* Large Intestine Channel	LI 4 (*hé gǔ*, 合谷)	Between the 1st and 2nd metacarpal bones, on the midpoint of the 2nd metacarpal bone	Headache, toothache, fever, sore throat, contracture of fingers, pain of the arms	Grasping, pressing, kneading
	LI 5 (*yáng xī*, 阳溪)	On the radial side of wrist, between the tendons of m. extensor pollicis brevis and longus	Headache, tinnitus, toothache, sore throat, redness of eyes, pain of the wrist	Nipping, pressing, grasping, kneading
	LI 6 (*piān lì*, 偏历)	3 cun above LI 5 (*yáng xī*, 阳溪), on the line between LI 5 (*yáng xī*, 阳溪) and LI 11 (*qū chí*, 曲池)	Epistaxis, red eyes, tinnitus, deafness, distending sensation in hand and arm	Pressing, kneading, grasping
	LI 7 (*wēn liū*, 温溜)	5 cun above LI 5 (*yáng xī*, 阳溪), on the line between LI 5 (*yáng xī*, 阳溪) and LI 11 (*qū chí*, 曲池)	Abdominal pain, hiccup, pain of tongue & throat, headache	One-finger pushing, pressing, nipping, grasping
	LI 10 (*shǒu sān lǐ*, 手三里)	On the line between LI 5 (*yáng xī*, 阳溪) and LI 11 (*qū chí*, 曲池), 2 cun directly below LI 11 (*qū chí*, 曲池)	distending sensation in arm, elbow pain	Grasping, pressing, kneading, One-finger pushing
	LI 11 (*qū chí*, 曲池)	In the depression at lateral end of transverse cubital crease. Midway between LU 5 (*chǐ zé*, 尺泽) and lateral epicondyle of humerus, when elbow is half flexed	Fever, hypertension, swelling and pain of arm, elbow pain, paralysis of upper limbs	Grasping, pressing, kneading

Channel	Point	Location	Indication	Manipulations
Hand *Yangming* Large Intestine Channel	LI 15 (*jiān yú*, 肩髃)	Anterior and inferior to acromion, in the depression of acromion when arm is in full abduction	Shoulder pain, motor dysfunction of shoulder joint, hemiplegia	One-finger pushing, pressing, kneading
	LI 20 (*yíng xiāng*, 迎香)	In naso-labial groove, at the level of the midpoint of nasal ala	Rhinitis, nasal obstruction, deviation of mouth and eyes	Nipping, pressing, kneading, One-finger pushing
Foot *Yangming* Stomach Channel	ST 2 (*sì bái*, 四白)	Directly below the pupil, in the depression at infra orbital foramen	Deviation of eyes and mouth; redness, pain, itching of eyes	Pressing, kneading, One-finger pushing
	ST 4 (*dì cāng*, 地仓)	0.4 cun lateral to the corner of mouth	Salivation, deviation of mouth and eyes	One-finger pushing, pressing, kneading
	ST 5 (*dà yíng*, 大迎)	In the groove, 1.3 cun anterior to the angle of mandible	Trismus, toothache	Nipping, pressing, kneading
	ST 6 (*jiá chē*, 颊车)	One finger breadth anterior and superior to the lower angle of mandible, at the prominence of m. masseter when the teeth are clenched	Deviation of mouth and eyes, toothache, swelling of cheek and face	One-finger pushing, pressing, kneading
	ST 7 (*xià guān*, 下关)	In the depression between zygomatic arch and mandibular notch, locate the point when the mouth is closed	Facial paralysis, toothache	One-finger pushing, pressing, kneading
	ST 8 (*tóu wéi*, 头维)	0.5 cun within the anterior hairline, at the corner of forehead	Headache	Mopping, pressing, kneading, scattering
	ST 9 (*rén yíng*, 人迎)	1.5 cun lateral to the tip of Adam's apple	Sore throat, asthma, scrofula, goiter, stuffiness	Grasping, lingering
	ST 10 (*shuǐ tū*, 水突)	1 cun below ST 9 (*rén yíng*, 人迎), on the anterior border of m. sternocleidomas toideus	Fullness in the chest, asthma, cough, rigidity of the neck	Grasping , lingering
	ST 12 (*quē pén*, 缺盆)	In the midpoint of the supraclavicular fossa, 4 cun lateral to the anterior midline	Fullness in chest, asthma, cough, rigidity of neck	Pressing, plucking

Channel	Point	Location	Indication	Manipulations
Foot *Yangming* Stomach Channel	ST 25 (*tiān shū*, 天枢)	2 cun lateral to the center of the umbilicus	Diarrhea, constipation, abdominal pain, irregular menstruation	Kneading, rubbing in circles, One-finger pushing
	ST 31 (*bì guān*, 髀关)	On the line connecting anterosuperior ilac spine and superiolateral corner of patella, at the level of gluteal groove	Pain, numbness, atrophy andweakness of leg, cramping, limitation of movement	pressing, grasping, plucking, rolling
	ST 32 (*fú tù*, 伏兔)	on the line connecting anterior superior iliac spine and lateral border of patella, 6 cun above laterosuperior border of patella	Pain, coldness, numbness of knee, paralysis of leg	Rolling, pressing, kneading
	ST 34 (*liáng qiū*, 梁丘)	2 cun above superolateral border of patella	Pain, coldness, numbness of knee	Rolling, pressing, pointing, grasping
	ST 35 (*dú bí*, 犊鼻)	At the lower border of patella, in the depression lateral to patellar ligament	Soreness and pain in knee joint with limitation of movement	Pointing, pressing
	ST 36 (*zú sān lǐ*, 足三里)	3 cun below ST 35 (*dú bí*, 犊鼻), one finger-breadth from the anterior border of tibia	Abdominal pain, diarrhea, constipation, coldness and numbness of leg, hypertension	Pressing, pointing, One-finger pushing
	ST 37 (*shàng jù xū*, 上巨虚)	3 cun below ST 36 (*zú sān lǐ*, 足三里)	Pain around umbilicus, diarrhea, paralysis of leg	Grasping, rolling, pressing, kneading
	ST 39 (*xià jù xū*, 下巨虚)	3 cun below ST 37 (*shàng jù xū*, 上巨虚)	Lower abdominal pain, backache, acute mastitis, paralysis of leg	Grasping, rolling, pressing, kneading
	ST 40 (*fēng lóng*, 丰隆)	Midpoint between lateral EX-LE5 (*xī yǎn*, 膝眼) and the tip of external malleolus	Headache, cough, swelling or paralysis of limbs, constipation, mania, epilepsy	One-finger pushing, pressing, kneading
	ST 41 (*jiě xī*, 解溪)	On the dorsum of foot, at the midpoint of the transverse crease of ankle joint, in the depression between the tendons of m. extensor digitorum longus and hallucis longus	Sprain of ankle joint, numbness of toes	Pressing, grasping, nipping, pointing

Channel	Point	Location	Indication	Manipulations
Foot *Yangming* Stomach Channel	ST 42 (*chōng yáng*, 冲阳)	1.5 cun below ST 41 (*jiě xī*, 解溪), at the highest point of the dorsum of foot where the artery can be felt	Deviation of mouth and eyes, facial swelling, upper teeth pain, stomachache, muscular atrophy and motor impairment of foot, mania, epilepsy	Pressing, kneading, pointing, nipping
Foot *Taiyin* Spleen Channel	SP 3 (*tài bái*, 太白)	Posterior and inferior to the head of the first metatarsal bone, at the junction of red and white skin	Stomachache, abdominal distension, borborygmus, diarrhea, constipation, hemorrhoid	Nipping, pressing, kneading
	SP 4 (*gōng sūn*, 公孙)	Anterior to the base of the 1st metatarsal bone, at the junction of red and white skin	Stomachache, vomiting, indigestion, abdominal pain, diarrhea, dysentery	Nipping, pressing, kneading
	SP 6 (*sān yīn jiāo*, 三阴交)	3 cun above the tip of medial malleolus, on the middle of medial aspect of tibia	Insomnia, abdominal distension with poor appetite, enuresis, dysuria, gynecological disorders	Pressing, pointing, grasping
	SP 8 (*dì jī*, 地机)	3 cun below SP 9 (*yīn líng quán*, 阴陵泉)	Abdominal pain, diarrhea, edema, dysuria, nocturnal emission	Grasping, pressing, kneading
	SP 9 (*yīn líng quán*, 阴陵泉)	In the depression on lower border of medial condyle of tibia	Aching of knee joint, dysuria	Pointing, grasping, pressing, One-finger pushing
	SP 10 (*xuè hǎi*, 血海)	2 cun above medial border of patella	Irregular menstruation, knee pain	Grasping, pressing, pointing
	SP 15 (*dà héng*, 大横)	4 cun lateral to the center of the umbilicus	Diarrhea and dysentery due to deficiency and cold, constipation, lower abdominal pain	One-finger pushing, rubbing in circles, kneading, grasping
Hand *Shaoyin* Heart Channel	HT 1 (*jí quán*, 极泉)	In the center of axilla	Chest distress, hypochondriac pain, cold pain and numbness of elbow and arm	Grasping, plucking
	HT 3 (*shào hǎi*, 少海)	When the elbow is flexed, in the depression at ulnar side of transverse cubital crease	Pain of elbow joint, tremor of hand, spasmodic pain and numbness of hand and arm	Grasping, plucking

Channel	Point	Location	Indication	Manipulations
Hand *Shaoyin* Heart Channel	HT 5 (*tōng lǐ*, 通里)	1 cun above HT 7 (*shén mén*, 神门)	Severe palpitation, dizziness, sore throat, sudden loss of voice, aphasia due to stiffness of tongue, pain of wrist and elbow	Nipping, pressing, kneading, grasping
	HT 6 (*yīn xì*, 阴郄)	0.5 cun above HT 7 (*shén mén*, 神门)	Cardiac pain, hysteria, night sweating, hemoptysis, epistaxis, sudden loss of voice	Nipping, pressing, kneading, grasping
	HT 7 (*shén mén*, 神门)	At ulnar end of transverse crease of wrist, in the depression on radial side of tendon of m. flexor carpi ulnaris	Convulsion, severe palpitation, insomnia, poor memory	Grasping, pressing, kneading
Hand *Taiyang* Small Intestine Channel	SI 1 (*shào zé*, 少泽)	At ulnar side of little finer, about 0.1 cun posterior to the corner of the nail	Febrile disease, coma in stroke, insufficient lactation, sore throat	Nipping
	SI 3 (*hòu xī*, 后溪)	At ulnar side, in the depression proximal to the 5th metacarpo-phalangeal joint, at the end of transverse crease and the junction of the red and white skin	Pain and rigidity of neck and head, deafness, sore throat, toothache, cataract, spasmodic pain and numbness of hand and arm	Nipping
	SI 4 (*wàn gǔ*, 腕骨)	On ulnar side of the dorsum manus, in the depression anterior to pisiform bone	Headache, spasmodic pain of shoulder and arm, pain of wrist, contracture of fingers, febrile disease without sweating	Nipping
	SI 6 (*yǎng lǎo*, 养老)	Dorsal to the head of ulna. When the palm faces chest, the point is in bony cleft on radial side of syloid process of ulna	Blurred vision, shoulder pain, arm pain, lumbago	Nipping, pressing, kneading
	SI 7 (*zhī zhèng*, 支正)	On ulnar side of extended aspect of forearm, 5 cun above wrist	Neck rigidity, contracture of fingers, headache, dizziness	Grasping, pressing, kneading

Channel	Point	Location	Indication	Manipulations
Hand *Taiyang* Small Intestine Channel	SI 8 (*xiǎo hǎi*, 小海)	When elbow is flexed, in the depression between olecronon of ulna and the tip of medial epicondyle of humerus	Toothache, pain in the nape, soreness and pain of arm	Grasping
	SI 9 (*jiān zhēn*, 肩贞)	1 cun above posterior end of axillary fold	Soreness and pain of shoulder joint, motor impairment of shoulder joint, paralysis of arm	Grasping, pressing, kneading, rolling
	SI 11 (*tiān zōng*, 天宗)	In the depression of the center of infrascapular fossa	Soreness and pain of shoulder joint and back, motor impairment of shoulder joint, neck rigidity	One-finger pushing, rolling, pressing, kneading
	SI 12 (*bǐng fēng*, 秉风)	In the centre of suprascapular fossa	Pain in scapular region, failing to raise arm, soreness and numbness of arm	One-finger pushing, pressing, kneading, rolling
	SI 14 (*jiān wài shù*, 肩外俞)	3 cun lateral to lower border of spinous processs of the 1st thoracic vertebra	Soreness and pain of shoulder and back, neck rigidity, cold pain in arm	One-finger pushing, rolling, pressing, kneading
	SI 15 (*jiān zhōng shù*, 肩中俞)	2 cun lateral to DU 14 (*dà zhuī*, 大椎)	Cough, asthmatic breathing, aching of shoulder and back, blurred vision	One-finger pushing, rolling, pressing, kneading
	SI 18 (*quán liáo*, 颧髎)	Directly below the outer canthus, in the depression below the lower border of the zygomatic bone	Deviation of mouth and eyes	One-finger pushing, pressing, kneading
Foot *Taiyang* Bladder Channel	BL 1 (*jīng míng*, 睛明)	0.1 cun lateral to inner canthus	Eye diseases	One-finger pushing, pressing
	BL 2 (*cuán zhú*, 攒竹)	In the depression proximal to medial end of eyebrow	Headache, insomnia, pain in supraorbital region, redness and pain of eyes	One-finger pushing, pressing, kneading
	BL 10 (*tiān zhù*, 天柱)	1.3 cun lateral to DU 15 (*yǎ mén*, 哑门), and in the depression on lateral aspect of m. trapezius	Headache, neck rigidity, nasal obstruction, pain of shoulder and back	One-finger pushing, pressing, grasping

Channel	Point	Location	Indication	Manipulations
Foot *Taiyang* Bladder Channel	BL 11 (*dà zhù*, 大杼)	1.5 cun lateral to lower border of spinous process of the 1st thoracic vertebra	Fever, cough, neck rigidity, soreness and pain in scapular region	One-finger pushing, rolling, pressing, kneading
	BL 12 (*fēng mén*, 风门)	1.5 cun lateral to lower border of spinous process of the 2nd thoracic vertebra	Common cold, cough, neck rigidity, aching of back and lumbar region	One-finger pushing, rolling, pressing, kneading
	BL 13 (*fèi shù*, 肺俞)	1.5 cun lateral to lower border of spinous process of the 3rd thoracic vertebra	Cough, asthmatic breathing, chest distress, muscular injury of back	One-finger pushing, rolling, pressing, kneading, plucking
	BL 15 (*xīn shù*, 心俞)	1.5 cun lateral to lower border of spinous process of the 5th thoracic vertebra	Insomnia, palpitation	One-finger pushing, rolling, pressing, kneading, plucking
	BL 17 (*gé shù*, 膈俞)	1.5 cun lateral to lower border of spinous process of the 7th thoracic vertebra	Vomiting, hiccup, asthmatic breathing, cough, night sweating	One-finger pushing, rolling method, pressing method, kneading method
	BL 18 (*gān shù*, 肝俞)	1.5 cun lateral to lower border of spinous process of the 9th thoracic vertebra	Pain in hypochondriac region, hepatitis, blurred vision	One-finger pushing, rolling, pressing, kneading, plucking
	BL 19 (*dǎn shù*, 胆俞)	1.5 cun lateral to lower border of spinous process of the 10th thoracic vertebra	Pain in hypochondriac region, bitter taste in mouth, jaundice	One-finger pushing, pointing, pressing, kneading
	BL 20 (*pí shù*, 脾俞)	1.5 cun lateral to lower border of spinous process of the 11th thoracic vertebra	Distending pain in epigastric area, indigestion, chronic infantile convulsion due to dysfunction of spleen	One-finger pushing, pointing, pressing, kneading, rolling, plucking
	BL 21 (*wèi shù*, 胃俞)	1.5 cun lateral to lower border of spinous process of the 12th thoracic vertebra	Stomach disorders, infantile vomiting, indigestion	One-finger pushing, pointing, pressing, kneading, rolling, plucking
	BL 22 (*sān jiāo shù*, 三焦俞)	1.5 cun lateral to lower border of spinous process of the 1st lumbar vertebra	Borborygmus, abdominal distension, vomiting, pain and rigidity of lower back	One-finger pushing, pressing, kneading, rolling

Channel	Point	Location	Indication	Manipulations
Foot *Taiyang* Bladder Channel	BL 23 (*shèn shù*, 肾俞)	1.5 cun lateral to lower border of spinous process of the 2nd lumbar vertebra	Kidney deficiency, lumbago, nocturnal emission, irregular menstruation	One-finger pushing, pressing, kneading, rolling
	BL 24 (*qì hǎi shù*, 气海俞)	1.5 cun lateral to lower border of spinous process of the 3rd lumbar vertebra	Lumbago	One-finger pushing, pressing, kneading, rolling
	BL 25 (*dà cháng shù*, 大肠俞)	1.5 cun lateral to lower border of spinous process of the 4th lumbar vertebra	Pain of low back and leg, over-use of lumbar muscle, enteritis	One-finger pushing, pressing, kneading, rolling, plucking
	BL 26(*guān yuán shù*, 关元俞)	1.5 cun lateral to lower border of spinous process of the 5th lumbar vertebra	Lumbago, diarrhea	One-finger pushing, pressing, kneading, rolling
	BL 31, 32, 33, 34 (*bā liáo*, 八髎)	In posterior sacral foramens	Pain of lower back and leg, disorders of urogenital system	Pointing, pressing, kneading, scrubbing
	BL 54 (*zhì biān*, 秩边)	3 cun lateral to posterior midline, on the level of the 4th posterior sacral foramen	Pain in lumbosacral region, muscular atrophy, motor impairment of leg, dysuria, constipation	Rolling, grasping, plucking, pressing
	BL 37 (*yīn mén*, 殷门)	On the line connecting the midpoints of gluteal transverse crease and popliteal transverse crease, 6 cun below BL 36 (*chéng fú*, 承扶)	Sciatica, paralysis of leg, pain of lower back and thigh	Pointing, pressing, patting, rolling, grasping
	BL 60 (*kūn lún*, 昆仑)	In the depression between the tip of external malleolus and tendo calcaneus	Headache, neck rigidity, lumbago, sprain of ankle joint	Pressing, grasping, pointing
	BL 62 (*shēn mài*, 申脉)	In the depression directly below the tip of external malleolus	Depression, mania, epilepsy, soreness and pain of back and leg	Nipping, pointing, pressing
	BL 63 (*jīn mén*, 金门)	Anterior and inferior to BL 62 (*shēn mài*, 申脉), in the depression lateral to cuboid bone	Epilepsy, backache, pain of external malleolus, motor impairment and pain of leg	Nipping, pointing, pressing
	BL 64 (*jīng gǔ*, 京骨)	Below the tuberosity of the fifth metatarsal bone, at the junction of white and red skin	Epilepsy, headache, neck rigidity, pain in lower back and thigh, knee pain, foot pain	Grasping, nipping

Channel	Point	Location	Indication	Manipulations
Foot *Shaoyin* Kidney Channel	KI 1 (*yǒng quán*, 涌泉)	On the sole, in the depression when foot is in plantar flexion	Migraine, hypertension, infantile fever	Scrubbing, pressing, grasping
	KI 3 (*tài xī*, 太溪)	In the depression between the tip of internal malleolus and the tendo calcaneus	Sore throat, toothache, insomnia, nocturnal emission, impotence, irregular menstruation	One-finger pushing, grasping, pressing, kneading
	KI 4 (*dà zhōng*, 大钟)	0.5 cun below KI 3 (*tài xī*, 太溪), on medial side of tendo calcaneus	Stiffness and pain of lower back, heel pain, asthmatic breathing, hemoptysis	One-finger pushing, pressing, kneading
	KI 5 (*shuǐ quán*, 水泉)	1 cun directly below KI 3 (*tài xī*, 太溪)	Irregular menstruation, dysmenorrhea, dysuria, blurred vision	Pressing, kneading, pointing
	KI 6 (*zhào hǎi*, 照海)	In the depression below the tip of medial malleolus	Irregular menstruation	Pressing
	KI 8 (*jiāo xìn*, 交信)	2 cun above KI 3 (*tài xī*, 太溪), posterior to medial border of tibia	Irregular menstruation, diarrhea, constipation, pain and swelling of testis	Pressing, kneading
	KI 9 (*zhù bīn*, 筑宾)	5 cun directly below KI 3 (*tài xī*, 太溪)	Depression, mania, hernia, foot pain and shank pain	Pointing, pressing, kneading , grasping
Hand *Jueyin* Pericardium Channel	PC 3 (*qū zé*, 曲泽)	On transverse cubital crease, at ulnar side of tendon of m. biceps brachii	Soreness, pain and tremor of arm	Grasping, pressing, kneading
	PC 4 (*xì mén*, 郄门)	5 cun above transverse crease of wrist, between tendons of m. palmaris longus and m. flexor carpi radialis	Cardiac pain, palpitation, vomiting	Grasping, pressing, kneading
	PC 6 (*nèi guān*, 内关)	2 cun above transverse crease of wrist, between tendons of m. palmaris longus and m. flexor radialis	Stomachache, vomiting, palpitation, amentia	One-finger pushing, pressing, kneading, grasping
	PC 7 (*dà líng*, 大陵)	In the middle of transverse crease of wrist, between tendons of m. palmaris longus and m. flexor radialis	Cardiac pain, palpitation, stomachache, vomiting, epilepsy, hypochondriac pain	Pressing, kneading, plucking

Channel	Point	Location	Indication	Manipulations
Hand *Jueyin* Pericardium Channel	PC 8 (*láo gōng*, 劳宫)	On the transverse crease of palm, between the 2nd and 3rd metacarpal bones	Palpitation, trembling	Pressing, kneading, grasping
Hand *Shaoyang Sanjiao* Channel	SJ 3 (*zhōng zhǔ*, 中渚)	When the fist is clenched, on dorsum of hand, in the depression posterior to the junction between the head of the 4th and 5th metacarpal bones	Migraine, pain in the fingers and palm, motor impairment of fingers, pain of elbow and arm	Pointing, pressing, kneading, One-finger pushing
	SJ 4 (*yáng chí*, 阳池)	On transverse crease of the dorsum of wrist, in the depression on lateral side of tendon of m. extensor digitorum communis	Pain of shoulder, arm and wrist, malaria, diabetes, deafness	One-finger pushing, pressing, kneading
	SJ 5 (*wài guān*, 外关)	2 cun above dorsal crease of wrist, between radius and ulna	Headache, pain of elbow, arm and fingers, motor impairment of elbow, arm and fingers	One-finger pushing, rolling,pressing, kneading
	SJ 7 (*huì zōng*, 会宗)	3 cun above transverse crease of wrist dorsum, on radial side of ulna	Deafness, epilepsy, arm pain	Rolling, pressing, kneading
	SJ 14 (*jiān liáo*, 肩髎)	Posterior and inferior to acromion, in the depression, about 1 cun posterior to LI 15 (*jiān yú*, 肩髃)	Soreness and pain of shoulder and arm, motor impairment of shoulder joint	One-finger pushing, pressing, kneading, rolling, grasping
Foot *Shaoyang* Gallbladder Channel	GB 20 (*fēng chí*, 风池)	In the depression between upper border of scapula and m. trapezius, on the same level with DU 16 (*fēng fǔ*, 风府)	Migraine, headache, common cold, neck rigidity	Pressing, grasping, One-finger pushing
	GB 21 (*jiān jǐng*, 肩井)	Midway between DU 14 (*dà zhuī*, 大椎) and acromion	Neck rigidity, pain of shoulder and back, difficulty of raising arm	Grasping, rolling, One-finger pushing, pressing, kneading
	GB 29 (*jū liáo*, 居髎)	Midpoint between anterosuperior iliacspine and great trochantar	Pain in thigh and lumbar region, soreness and pain of hip joint, sacroiliitis	Rolling, pointing, compressing, pressing

Channel	Point	Location	Indication	Manipulations
Foot *Shaoyang* Gallbladder Channel	GB 30 (*huán tiào*, 环跳)	At the junction of lateral one third and medial two thirds of the distance between the prominence of great trochanter and hiatus of sacrum	Pain of lower back and leg, hemiplegia	Rolling, pointing, compressing, pressing
	GB 31 (*fēng shì*, 风市)	On the midline of lateral aspect of thigh, 7 cun above transverse popliteal crease	Hemiplegia, soreness and pain of knee joint	Rolling, pointing, compressing, pressing
	GB 34 (*yáng líng quán*, 阳陵泉)	In the depression anterior and inferior to head of fibula	Soreness and pain of knee joint, hypochondriac pain	Grasping, pointing, pressing, kneading
	GB 36 (*wài qiū*, 外丘)	7 cun above the tip of external malleolus, on anterior border of fibula	Fullness in chest and hypochondriac region, muscular atrophy, paralysis and pain of limbs, epilepsy with frothy saliva	Rolling, pressing, kneading
	GB 37 (*guāng míng*, 光明)	5 cun above the tip of the external malleolus, on anterior border of fibula	Headache, muscular atrophy of leg, eye pain, night blindness, distending sensation of breast	Rolling, plucking, kneading
	GB 39 (*xuán zhōng*, 悬钟)	3 cun above the tip of external malleolus, on posterior border of fibula	Headache, neck rigidity, soreness and pain of leg	Grasping, pressing
	GB 40 (*qiū xū*, 丘墟)	Anterior and inferior to external malleolus, in the depression on lateral side of tendon of m. extensor digitorum longus	Ankle pain, pain in hypochondriac region and chest	Pressing, pointing, grasping
	GB 41 (*zú lín qì*, 足临泣)	On foot dorsum, 1.5 cun above the margin of web between the fourth and fifth toe	Scrofula, pain in hypochondriac region, swelling and pain on foot dorsum, spastic pain of foot and toe	Nipping, pointing, pressing
Foot *Jueyin* Liver Channel	LV 3 (*tài chōng*, 太冲)	On foot dorsum, in the depression distal to the junction of the first and second metatarsal bones	Headache, dizziness, hypertension, infantile convulsion	Grasping, pressing, kneading

Channel	Point	Location	Indication	Manipulations
Foot *Jueyin* Liver Channel	LV 5 (*lí gōu*, 蠡沟)	5 cun above the tip of the medial malleolus, on the medial aspect and near the medial border of the tibia	Dysuria, irregular menstruation, weakness and atrophy of the leg	Rolling, grasping, pressing, kneading
	LV 6 (*zhōng dū*, 中都)	7 cun above the tip of the medial malleolus, on the medial aspect and near the medial border of the tibia	Abdominal pain, diarrhea, hernia, uterine bleeding, profuse lochia	Rolling, grasping, pressing, kneading
	LV 13 (*zhāng mén*, 章门)	Below the free end of the 11th rib	Pain in hypochondriac region and chest, chest distress	Rubbing in circles, kneading, pressing
	LV 14 (*qī mén*, 期门)	Directly below nipple, in the 6th intercostals space	Pain in hypochondriac region and chest	Rubbing in circles, kneading, pressing
Ren mai	RN 4 (*guān yuán*, 关元)	3 cun below umbilicus	Abdominal pain, dysmenorrhea, enuresis	One-finger pushing, rubbing in circles, kneading, pressing
	RN 5 (*shí mén*, 石门)	2 cun below umbilicus	Abdominal pain, diarrhea	One-finger pushing, rubbing in circles, kneading, pressing
	RN 6 (*qì hǎi*, 气海)	1.5 cun below umbilicus	Abdominal pain, irregular menstruation, enuresis	One-finger pushing, rubbing in circles, kneading, pressing
	RN 8 (*shén què*, 神阙)	In the centre of umbilicus	Abdominal pain, diarrhea	Rubbing in circles, kneading, pressing
	RN 12 (*zhōng wǎn*, 中脘)	4 cun above umbilicus	Stomachache, abdominal distension, vomiting, indigestion	One-finger pushing, rubbing in circles, kneading, pressing
	RN 15 (*jiū wěi*, 鸠尾)	Below xiphoid process, 7 cun above umbilicus	Pain in cardiac region and chest, nausea, epilepsy	Pressing, kneading
	RN 17 (*dàn zhōng*, 膻中)	On anterior midline, at the level of the 4th intercostal space	Asthma, cough, chest pain, chest distress	One-finger pushing, rubbing in circles, kneading, pressing
	RN 22 (*tiān tū*, 天突)	At the center of suprasternal fossa	Asthma, cough, difficulty of spitting sputum out	Pressing, compressing, One-finger pushing
	RN 24 (*chéng jiāng*, 承浆)	In the center of mentolabial groove	Deviation of mouth and eyes, toothache	Pressing, kneading, nipping
Du mai	DU 1 (*cháng qiáng*, 长强)	0.5 cun below the tip of coccyx	Diarrhea, constipation, prolapse of rectum	Pressing, kneading, pointing

Channel	Point	Location	Indication	Manipulations
Du mai	DU 3 (*yāo yáng guān*, 腰阳关)	Below the spinous process of the 4th lumbar vertebra	Lumbosacral pain	Rolling, One-finger pushing, pressing, kneading, scrubbing, twisting
	DU 4 (*mìng mén*, 命门)	Below the spinous process of the 2nd lumbar vertebra	Lumbosacral pain	Rolling, One-finger pushing, pressing, kneading, scrubbing, twisting
	DU 12 (*shēn zhù*, 身柱)	Below the spinous process of the 3rd lumbar vertebra	Lumbosacral pain	Rolling, One-finger pushing, twisting, pressing
	DU 14 (*dà zhuī*, 大椎)	Below the spinous process of the 7th cervical vertibra	Common cold, fever, stiff neck	One-finger pushing, rolling, pressing, kneading
	DU 16 (*fēng fǔ*, 风府)	1 cun directly above the midpoint of posterior hairline	Headache, rigidity of neck	Pointing, pressing, kneading, One-finger pushing
	DU 20 (*bǎi huì*, 百会)	On the midline of head, 7 cun directly above posterior hairline	Headache, dizziness, syncope, hypertension, prolapse of rectum	Pressing, kneading, One-finger pushing
	DU 26 (*shuǐ gōu*, 水沟)	At the junction of upper third and middle third of philtrum	Infantile convulsion, deviation of mouth and eyes	Nipping
Extra Points	*yìn táng* (EX-HN 3, 印堂)	Midway between medial ends of two eyebrows	Headache, rhinitis, insomnia	Mopping, One-finger pushing, pressing, kneading
	tài yáng (EX-HN 5, 太阳)	In the depression about 1 cun posterior to midpoint between lateral end of eyebrow and outer canthus	Headache, common cold, eye diseases	Pressing, kneading, mopping, One-finger pushing
	yú yāo (EX-HN4, 鱼腰)	At the midpoint of eyebrows	Supraorbital pain, redness, swelling and pain of eyes, trembling of eyelid	Mopping, One-finger pushing, pressing
	yāo yǎn (EX-B 7, 腰眼)	About 3.3 cun lateral to lower border of spinous process of the fourth lumbar vertebra	Lumbar sprain, soreness and pain of back	Rolling, pressing, grasping, scrubbing

Channel	Point	Location	Indication	Manipulations
Extra Points	*jiá jǐ* (EX-B 2, 夹脊)	0.5 cun lateral to lower border of each spinous process from the first thoracic vertebra to the fifth lumbar vertebra	Pain and rigidity of spinal column, disorders of *zang-fu* organs, tonic effect	Rolling, scrubbing, compressing, pushing, One-finger pushing
	shí qī zhuī (EX-B8, 十七椎)	Below the spinous process of the fifth lumber vertebra	Lumbago, thigh pain	Twisting, rolling, pressing
	shí xuān (EX-UE 11, 十宣)	On the tips of ten fingers, about 0.1 cun distal to the nails	Coma	Nipping
	hè dǐng (EX-LE 2, 鹤顶)	In the depression of midpoint of superior patellar border	Swollen and pain of knee joint	Pressing, kneading, pointing
	lán wěi xué (EX-LE 7, 阑尾穴)	About 2 cun below ST 36 (*zú sān lǐ*, 足三里)	Appendicitis, abdominal pain	Pressing, grasping, kneading, pointing method
	jiān nèi líng (肩内陵)	Midway between the end of anterior axillary fold and LI 15 (*jiān yú*, 肩髃)	Soreness and pain of shoulder joint, motor dysfunction	One-finger pushing, rolling, grasping, pressing, kneading
	qiáo gōng (桥弓)	The line between SJ 17 (*yì fēng*, 翳风) and ST 12 (*quē pén*, 缺盆)	Headache, dizziness	Pushing, kneading, grasping
	dǎn náng xué (EX-LE 6, 胆囊穴)	1 cun below GB 34 (*yáng líng quán*, 阳陵泉)	Gallbladder colicky pain	Pressing, kneading, pointing

Chapter 3
Common Diagnostic Methods Used in Tui Na Therapy

Tui na therapy is widely applied, involved in orthopedic diseases, internal diseases, external disorders, gynecological diseases and pediatric disorders. In tui na treatment, the patient's general condition and local symptoms are understood through four diagnostic methods, necessary physical examinations, laboratory checks and image examinations. Next, the disease is analyzed and the primary and secondary factors are distinguished to achieve a correct diagnosis. On this basis, the relative operated area and manipulations are determined under the guidance of combined principles that indicate treatment according to syndrome differentiation and disease differentiation.

Section 1
Examinations with the Four Diagnostic Methods

Inquiry

Inquiry, in any clinical course, is an important part, playing a key role in the four diagnostic methods. Tui na inquiry focuses on the following aspects.

1. General Information

Try to learn more about the patient, such as age, occupation, marriage, nationality, origin, etc.

2. Occurrence of Disease

Ask questions about the chief symptom, when the symptom began, how it occurred, any accompanying symptoms, and any changes, for better or worse. For the patient with traumatic injury, the cause of the injury must be determined in detail, such as falling down from a height, sprain, concussion, tumbling, the type and weight of the striking object, and the direction and intensity of violence. Take falling as an example: falling with the hip striking the ground may cause injury to the lumbar and thoracic vertebrae, and if the patient tries to support his body with his hand, injury of the wrist joint and shoulder joint may occur. As for pain, the starting time, the location, nature, and severity must be asked about in detail. Aching of soft tissues is usually caused by overstrain, and pricking pain by blood stasis, while radiating pain is usually related to nerve injury and oppression. Pain related to weather changes is common in rheumatic and rheumatoid arthritis.

Ask questions about general conditions, such as chills, fever, sweating, urination, defecation, diet, sleep, etc.

3. Other Information

Ask questions about the patient's personal history and family history of disease.

Inspection

In tui na treatment, inspection is an essential step. In addition to observing the patient's general condition, such as complexion, the modality, movement and function of limbs as well as local conditions, should be observed. During inspection, the patient is asked to assume a proper position for full exposure under natural light.

1. Observation of morphological changes

This is done to get a preliminary understanding of the local area and severity of illness. In particular, the patient's walking gait is of great significance in tui na treatment. Normal, straight walking with equal distance between strides keeps both sides of the pelvis horizontal; one side of the pelvis moves forward, leading the body's center of gravity forward, the lumber vertebra and muscles also joining the movement. Any change of this process may cause an abnormal gait. Frequently-seen gait disorders include: (Fig. 3-1).

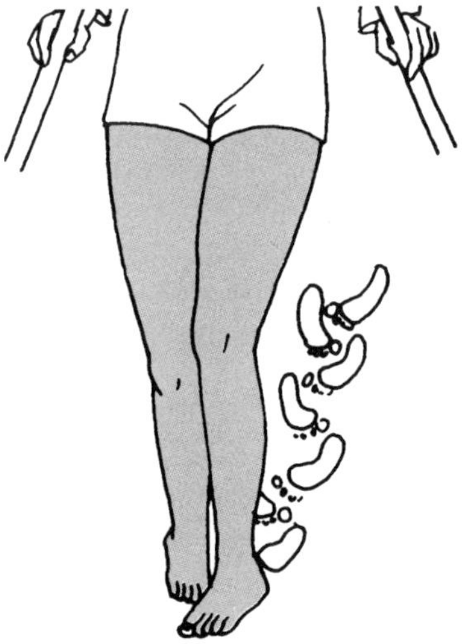

Fig. 3-1 (1) Scissors gait

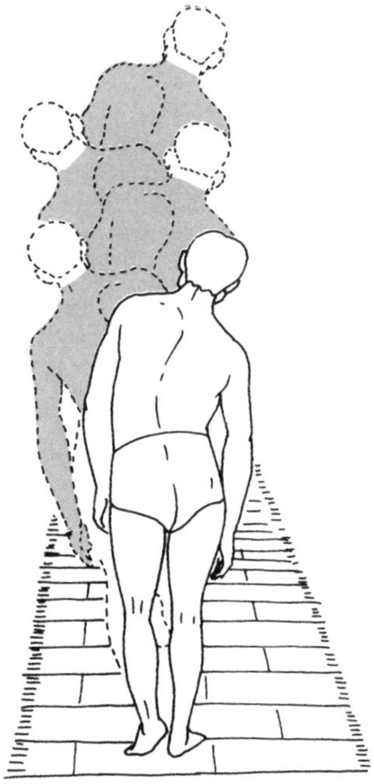

Fig.3-1 (2) Waddling gait (duck step)

Scissors gait: Presented by knees and thighs hitting or crossing in a scissor-like movement, most common in patients with spastic cerebral palsy.

Anti-pain gait: Presented by the normal foot raised quickly to step, with the ailing foot just touching the ground. The gait is hurried, short and unstable, most common in painful disorders due to heavy load on the lower leg.

Short-limb gait. Presented by tiptoeing or the normal knee joint bending due to oblique pelvis and tilted trunk, mostly seen in the patients with one leg at least 3 cm shorter than the other.

Waddling gait (duck step): Presented by the trunk tilted to the affected side when carrying a heavy load, more often seen in congenital dislocation of the hip or paralysis of the gluteus muscle. If the body swings from one side to the other during walking, this is common in paralysis of the bilateral gluteus muscle or dislocation of the hip joint.

2. Observation of Local Area

Observation of local area is particularly important in tui na treatment. By observing abnormal changes of body marker lines or marker points, determine if there are deformities such as depressions or bumps, local swelling, ecchymosis, abnormal functional activities, and so on.

a. Head and Face

Determine whether the skull size and shape are appropriate to age: enlarged head suggests hydrocephalus or cretinism, and small head suggests brain dysplasia. Square head is common in children with rickets, manifesting bilateral frontal and temporal bone protrusion, flat and square vertex, and thin, sparse hair without luster. Normal eyelid fissure of both sides are symmetrical and moderate in size. Blepharophimosis is often seen in oculomotor nerve palsy, cervical sympathetic nerve damage and hemifacial spasm, while wide palpebral fissure is more often seen in facial paralysis. In babies, the head tending to the ailing side with the face towards the healthy side is possibly an infantile muscular torticollis. The situation of one eye failing to close, with the forehead wrinkles flattened out, the mouth angle oblique on the healthy side when teeth are exposed, and the nasolabial groove having disappeared, is usually facial paralysis (Fig. 3-2). Involuntary head tremor is common in the elderly or patients with paralysis agitans.

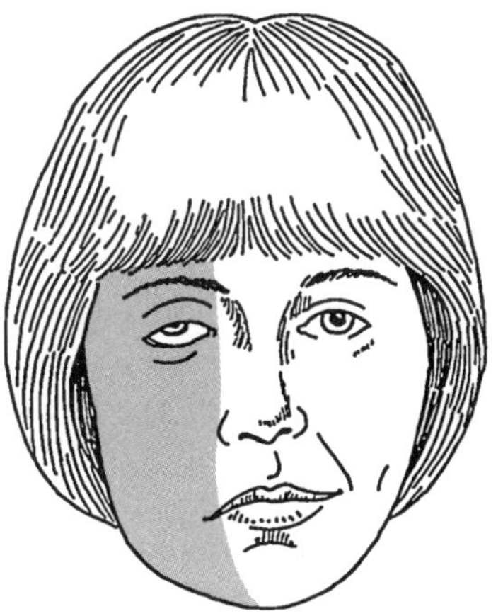

Fig. 3-2 Facial Paralysis

b. Spine

Observation of the spine can be done in standing, sitting and supine positions to expose the spine. First, check to see if there is any change or deformity of the physiological curve of the spine. The normal spine has four physiological flexures: cervical flexure (lordosis), thoracic flexure (kyphosis), lumbar flexure (lordosis), and sacral flexure (kyphosis). Usually, standing and sitting positions are adopted. Examination in a sitting position may exclude the influence of the lower extremity on the spinal flexures. Observation is done to see if there are any changes in posture, such as scoliosis or tilt, kyphosis, lumbar lordosis, increased or decreased, and pelvic skew. Changes of physiological curvatures are common in degenerative diseases of the spine, ankylosing spondylitis and other vertebral disorders. Deformity of lordosis often results from improper posture or polio; kyphosis, manifesting in a hump-shaped angle, is often seen in infantile rickets and spinal tuberculosis. Abnormal lumbar flexure with angular kyphosis is common in disorders of either a single vertebra or 2 ~ 3 vertebrae, such as compression fracture, dislocation, tuberculosis of vertebral body, or tumor, which may damage the bone substance of the vertebrae. Curved kyphosis usually results from a disorder of several vertebrae, such as rheumatoid arthritis and senile osteoporosis. Scoliosis is mostly caused by postural or structural problems. Increased lumbar lordosis can be seen in horizontal sacral vertebrae, lumbar spondylolisthesis, bilateral congenital dislocation of the hip joint, and so on.

Observe the skin color of the spinal area to see if it is normal, with or without mass and ecchymosis. Direct trauma may show local swelling with blue or purple ecchymosis; local redness with swelling usually indicates infection; a hairy spot with dark skin on the lower back indicates the possibility of spina bifida.

c. Chest and Abdomen

Fully expose the chest and abdomen to determine if the shape of the chest is symmetrical. If one side of the chest is bumped and the other side flattened, while the back is also bumped at one side and flattened at the other side, the thoracic vertebrae line is curved into an arc. This is usually a deformity due to thoracic scoliosis. If the sternum, especially the lower part of the sternum, is markedly protruded, the diameter between the anterior and posterior walls of the thoracic cavity extended, and the transverse diameter shortened, forming a shape similar to a chicken breast, it indicates rickets. Marked depression or bulge on the chest and abdomen, for instance, depression in the epigastric region with bulge at the umbilicus and lower abdomen, suggests prolapse of the stomach.

d. Four Limbs

【Shoulder】

Ask the patient expose the shoulder fully while in either a sitting or a standing position, and compare both sides in various areas to see if they are symmetrical at the same level. Any fracture, dislocation or congenital shoulder disorders may cause deformity of the shoulder. When the shoulder joint is dislocated, the acromion is prominent to form subacromial hollowness and a "high shoulder" deformity. The shoulder muscular palsy due to brachial plexus nerve injury often shows "drooping shoulder". "Winged scapula" often appears because of backward protrusion of the scapula, when the joint between the scapular and thorax is loose due to paralysis of the serratus anterior.

Check the shoulder joint for swelling, abrasions, blisters, scars, sinus, skin color changes, and so on. Local swelling with bruising and ecchymosis mostly appears in fractures and dislocations of the shoulder joint. A swollen shoulder joint with red skin more often indicates acute purulent inflammation of the shoulder joint, and dark purple skin with sinus is often a chronic purulent inflammation of the shoulder joint.

Muscular atrophy of the shoulder joint usually occurs at the later stage of shoulder disorders. For example, it may present in peripheral arthritis of the shoulder joint, manifesting long-term pain and limitation of movement. Shoulder fracture, long-term fixed, may cause disuse atrophy. Shoulder nerve injury, muscular paralysis and loss of motor function may cause neuroatrophy of the shoulder muscle.

【Elbow】

In the normal elbow joint, the axis of the upper arm and the axis of the forearm form a valgus carrying angle of 5° ~ 10 ° in the male and 10 ° ~ 15 ° in the female. Congenital abnormalities of the elbow bone, poor reposition of a distal humerus fracture, or an injured distal humeral epiphysis may cause cubitus valgus or cubitus varus, where the valgus carrying angle would be greater than 15 °. Rheumatoid arthritis may form a spindle-shaped deformity on the elbow. When elbow inflammation causes intra-articular effusion, the normal depressions on both sides of the ulnar olecranon disappear, and the joint becomes full. When fluid is present in large quantity, the elbow joint would be in a semi-flexion position with severe swelling. Diffuse swelling of the elbow joint beyond the field of the joint is common in elbow fracture or severe crush injury.

【Wrist and Finger】

The normal wrist joint has a mild ulnar deviation and 10° ~ 15° of dorsiflexion. Deformity of wrist and finger is of great significance in tui na clinic. Dinner-fork deformity of the wrist is usually caused by a distal extension type fracture of the radius, where the distal end of the radius shifts to the dorsum side, and the hand looks like a dinner fork if observed from the side. "Claw hand" is common in injury due to ischemic muscular spasm of the forearm, manifesting in hyperextension of the metacarpophalangeal joints, and flexion of the proximal interphalangeal joint, like a bird claw. Injury to the brachial plexus or ulner nerve may cause hyperextension of the metacarpophalangeal joint, failure of the ring finger and small finger to occlude with the middle finger, and hypothenar muscular atrophy between musculoskeletals. "Ape hand" is common in the combined injury of the ulnar nerve and the median nerve, manifesting in muscular atrophy of the thenar and hypothenar, and the absence of the two transverse arches on the palm: flat palm, also referred to as shovel-shaped hand or flat hand. Radial nerve injury may cause forearm extensor paralysis, with failure of wrist extension, and "drop wrist" appears (Fig. 3-3).

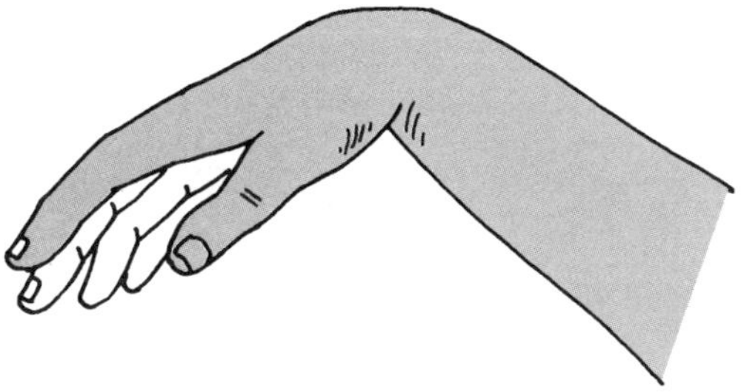

Fig.3-3 Drop wrist

"Mallet fingers" is usually caused by breaking at or nearby the ending point of the extensor tendon of the finger, or by an avulsion fracture at the ending point of the extensor tendon of the finger. Spoon-shaped nails are mostly the results of serious fungal infection, and clubbed nails are common in respiratory diseases or congenital heart diseases.

Wrist swelling is usually found in intra-articular lesions or disorders such as wrist contusions, joint capsule or ligament tears, wrist fractures, or lunate dislocations. Wrist spindle-shaped swelling without redness and warmth is common in wrist joint tuberculosis. Symmetrical swelling of both wrists, sometimes on and sometimes off, is more often seen in rheumatic arthritis, while carpal scaphoid fracture may show full swelling of snuff fossa.

【Pelvis and Hip】

The patient assumes a standing position. Determine whether both sides of the anterior superior iliac spine and posterior superior iliac spine are at the same level. If both sides of the anterior superior iliac spine are not at the same level, it is pelvic tilt due to unequal length of the legs. Asymmetric posterior superior iliac spine, one side shifting upward or protruding backward represents sacroiliac joint dislocation. Above the hip and posterior superior iliac spines, there are two depressions which should be horizontal and at the same level when the pelvis is normal. The depressions would be out of the horizontal line if the pelvis tilts.

On the buttock, there are gluteal lines. Asymmetric gluteal lines in an infant are mostly caused by congenital hip joint dislocation, muscular atrophy, discrepancy of lower limbs and pelvic tilt.

Observe the front of the hips to see if the groin is symmetrical. If one side is fully swollen, it indicates swelling of the hip joint; if one side is depressed, it indicates femoral head dislocation or serious damage. Coxa vara deformity may shorten the affected leg. Valgus deformity of the hip may limit adduction and abduction of the affected leg and the affected leg is usually longer than the healthy leg.

【Knee】

Normally, the knee joint has a 5° ~ 10° physiological valgus angle and a 0° ~ 5°hyperextension when the joint is fully extended. Rickets, polio sequelae, fracture malunion and epiphyseal dysplasia may change the valgus angle of knee joint to form "K" type legs, "X" type legs, "O" type legs and other deformities. Knee joint synovitis, rheumatoid arthritis, knee joint tuberculosis and cancer may cause swelling of the whole knee. Swelling with redness, burning sensation and sharp pain is common in acute purulent inflammation of the knee joint. Limited mass in the capsular part of the patella mostly suggests suprapatellar bursitis. Obvious lumps at the tibial tuberosity suggest inflammation of the tibial tubercle epiphysis. A cystic mass at the back of the knee joint is a popliteal cyst. During examination of the knee joint, special attention should be paid to any quadriceps atrophy, and to any disorders which may disturb the movement of the lower limbs, such as meniscus injury of the knee, long time fixation due to fracture of the lower limb and so on, as all of these may lead to quadriceps atrophy.

【Ankle】

Common deformities of the ankle joint usually include talipes varus, talipes valgus, talipes quinovalgus, talipes calcaneus, talipse cavus, flat foot and other deformities.

Swelling of the ankle joint is usually caused by traumatic injury. Obvious swelling, more on the front of the ankle at the early stage and then progressing to the whole joint, is common in fractures of the external and internal malleolus, or lower tibial fracture. If the swelling progresses slowly, it is most likely ankle joint tuberculosis or osteoarthritis.

Auscultation and Olfaction

These require listening and smelling. It is important to listen to the sound of speaking, moaning, breathing, cough, vomiting and so on. A melodious and mellow voice means sufficient lung qi; a low, feeble and intermittent voice is a sign of primordial qi depletion; a high-pitched voice with rough breathing is common in excess syndrome, while a low-pitched voice with weak breathing is common in deficiency syndrome. The patient with moaning has pain, discomfort, or psychological depression due to liver qi stagnation. It is also necessary to smell vomit, urine, feces, breath and discharges. Foul and sour discharges are common in excess heat syndrome, and stench and fishy discharges common in deficiency cold syndrome.

Palpation

Clinically, palpation indicates feeling the pulse and palpating different parts of the body. Feeling the pulse is required in order to understand the changes of deficiency, excess, cold and heat in *zang-fu*, qi and blood, and palpating the body is required to understand the local changes of the body.

Palpation is of great significance in tui na clinic. It is the main method by which tui na doctors collect clinical information. Through palpation, the doctors can understand the nature of injuries, with or without fracture, dislocation, displacement and so on.

a. Head and Face

Check a baby's fontanelle: which usually close in 12 ~ 18 months after birth. During the examination, place the palms on the baby's temporal regions respectively with the thumbs over the forehead; check the fontanelle with middle and index fingers. Normally, before closed, the fontanelle is flat to the skull. A little tension and pulsing beat can be felt in the anterior fontanelle. The anterior fontanelle is usually bulged when a baby is crying, or when intracranial pressure is increased due to intracranial bleeding.

Mouth-Open Measurement: When the mouth is opened, the distance between the upper and lower teeth equals the width of the distal segments of occluded index, middle and ring fingers. Mandibular joint ankylosis may shorten the distance between the upper and lower teeth, or cause clenched jaw.

Palpation of the head is indicated to locate any tenderness. For instance, tenderness in the frontal, ethmoid or maxillary sinuses are common in sinusitis.

b. Spine

In either a standing or a prone position, do palpation alone to the spinal processes, in the intervertebrae spaces, and at the sides of vertebrae to find tenderness. The interior superior angle of the scapula is at the same level of the 2nd thoracic vertebra plane; the inferior angle of the scapula is at the level of the 7th thoracic vertebra plane; the connecting angle of the 12th rib and thoracic vertebra is at the level of the 12th vertebra; the line between the highest points of the iliac crests is at the level of the 4th lumbar vertebra; and the line connecting the two posterior superior iliac spines is at the level of the 2nd sacral vertebra plane.

Tenderness on the spine should be distinguished as either superficial tenderness, deep tenderness or indirect tenderness. Superficial tenderness indicates shallow disorders, such as supraspinal ligament injury or interspinous ligament injury, and other disorders of superficial tissues. Deep tenderness and indirect tenderness indicate disorders at a deep layer, such as vertebrae, small joints and intervertebral discs. Injuries to the soft tissues of the back mostly manifest in muscular cramping and tenderness at the local area. For examples: interspinous ligament strain often causes tenderness between the spinous processes; supraspinous ligament injury causes tenderness on the spinous process; muscular fasciitis of the lower back often causes tenderness, or muscular cramping, or cord-like nodules on the lumbar region; lumbar muscular strain causes cramping at the local area, and tenderness at the attached area of lumbar muscles. Cervical and lumbar intervertebral disc annulus fibrosus rupture may cause deep tenderness and radiating pain at the area between the spinous processes of the disordered intervertebral disc or at the sides of the disordered spinous processes. If there is only soreness in the lumbar region, no clear tenderness or no tenderness at all, and the pain can be relieved by tapping, it is usually lumbago due to retroversion of the uterus, prolapse of the kidney and neurasthenia. It is also necessary to identify the tenderness on the back and waist to determine whether it is reflexing pain of the internal organs. Heart disease may cause tenderness on the right BL 15 (*xīn shù*), and disorders of liver and gallbladder cause tenderness on the right BL 18 (*gān shù*) and BL19 (*dǎn shù*). Therefore, the clinical examination must be careful and comprehensive. In palpation of the spine, it is also necessary to determine if there is muscular cramping, atrophy, or the existence of tumor.

c. Chest and Abdomen

In initial palpating along the ribs, obvious tenderness suggests rib fracture. Then, in palpating the costal cartilage, bulge and tenderness indicate costal chondritis. Tenderness in the intercostals space is usually caused by intercostals neuralgia.

The Thoracic Compression Test checks whether the rib has a fracture. Ask the patient to assume a sitting or standing position, place the hands respectively over the front and back of thorax of same the side at a symmetrical position, or place the hands symmetrically over the left and right sides of the thorax, then press and squeeze the thorax gently. The tenderness would appear at the local area if there is a fracture of rib. In some cases, bone fricative is often accompanied as a positive sign.

Abdominal Reflex: In a supine position with the legs flexed, ask the patient to relax the abdominal muscle. Gently and rapidly stroke the skin on the hypochondriac regions around the umbilicus and lower abdomen with a blunt object, in an inward direction. Normally, abdominal muscular contraction may appear. The reflex center of the supra abdominal wall is at the segment of T7 –T8 spinal cord; that of the middle abdominal wall is at the segment of T9 – T10 spinal cord; and that of the lower abdominal wall is at the segment of T11– T12 spinal cord. Disappearance of the unilateral abdominal reflex suggests pyramidal tract damage; disappearance of the abdominal reflex at certain level indicates spinal cord damage at the corresponding segment.

d. Limbs

【Shoulder】

Before applying palpation to the shoulder, it is necessary to understand the normal anatomic structure, movement amplitude and bone marks of the shoulder. The acromion is a bony prominence at the highest area on the lateral aspect of the shoulder; below the acromion, another bony prominence is the greater tuberosity of the humerus; in front of the acromion is the lateral end of clavicle; the coracoid is located at one finger’s breadth below the conjunction of the lateral one-third and middle one-third of the clavicle, and superior and medial to the humeral head. The acromion, greater tuberosity and coracoid compose a triangle, referred to as the "shoulder triangle".

During palpation, press the shoulder in detail with the thumb to determine whether the joint structure is normal, and if there is tenderness, abnormal signs, cracking sounds or a rubbing feeling during the movement, and pay attention to rule out the possibility of fracture. As for the tenderness of the shoulder, it should be checked together with shoulder function tests, so as to determine the location of the disorder. Tenderness anterior and inferior to the acromion usually indicates a disorder of the nearby small tuberosity of humerus; tenderness on the lateral aspect of the acromion is common in disorders near the greater tuberosity of humerus. Rotate the patient's shoulder joint outward to check the tubercle sulcus at the proximal end of the humerus and the long head of the biceps tendon which goes through the sulcus. Obvious tenderness suggests tendinitis of the long head of the biceps. Ectopic long head tendon indicates biceps tendon detachment. When the long head tendon is torn, a bulged lump appears at the anterior and middle aspect of the upper arm. The deltoid constitutes a clear appearance of the shoulder shape. Trauma of the shoulder or injury of the axillary nerve may cause deltoid atrophy.

【Elbow】

The humeral medial condyle, the humeral lateral condyle and the olecranon are the important bone marks for palpation of the elbow joint. The changes of "elbow straight line" and "elbow triangle" formed by these three bone marks are of practical significance for distinguishing dislocation of the elbow joint and fracture (Fig. 3-4). The location of the tenderness should be observed during palpation. The humeral lateral epicondyle is attached by the forearm extensors group. Obvious tenderness at this place indicats epicondylitis (Tennis Elbow); the humeral medial epicondyle is attached by the forearm flexors group, and obvious tenderness there also suggests inflammation. The olecranon may manifest tenderness or hypertrophy feeling if there is a fracture, or bursitis. The radial head can be touched at the depression on the radial side above the olecranon, and the rotating feeling of the radial head can be felt when the forearm is rotating. If there is a fracture, the depression would be bulged with tenderness. It is not easy to touch the ulna coracoid below the elbow joint, without pressing forcefully with the thumb, and there would be tenderness at this area in the presence of a fracture. The ulnar nerve passes the ulnar side above the elbow joint, and a disorder of the ulnar nerve may cause a thick feeling with tenderness and radiating numbness

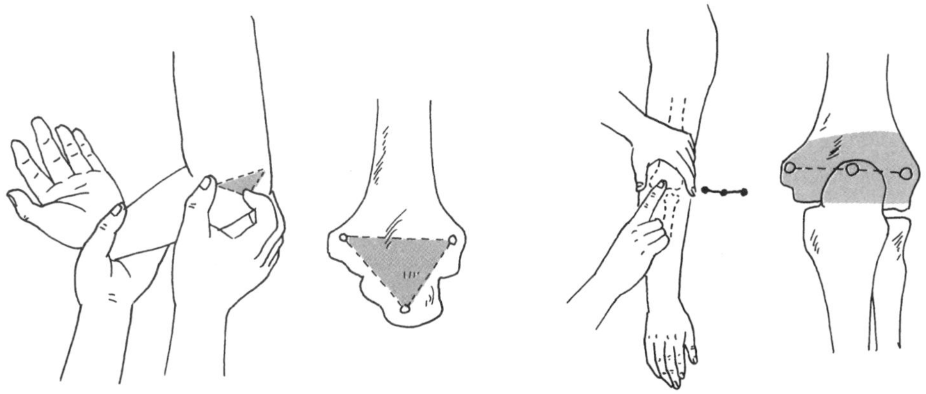

Fig. 3-4 Elbow triangle

at the local area. If the adduction and abduction of the forearm is limited, it indicates injury at the starting points of the forearm extensor and flexor muscles, or injury of the lateral collateral ligament, or the tearing and fracture of the medial and lateral epicondyles. Dislocation or fracture of the elbow joint may cause abnormal adduction and abduction.

【Wrist】

On the wrist, palm and finger, attention should be given to possible tenderness, mass and tapping pain. Tenderness at the radial styloid process is common in tenosynovitis of the musculus extensor pollicis brevis and the musculus abductor policis longus. Tenderness at the palmar side of the metacarpophalangeal joint is common in tenosynovitis of the thumb, index, middle and ring fingers. Tenderness on the middle of the transverse wrist crease accompanied by radiating pain and a numb feeling in the fingers often indicates carpal tunnel syndrome, a compression of the median nerve. Since the ulnar nerve goes through the osseous fiber sheath between the pisiform bone and the hamate bone hook, the patient with ulnar nerve syndrome would manifest hypothenar muscular atrophy and skin bradyesthesia at the ulnar side of the small and ring fingers. Swelling and tenderness of the "snuffbox" indicates scaphoid fracture. Distal radioulnar joint tenderness and a bulged ulnar styloid process with a loose feeling are caused by distal radioulnar joint separation. Lateral pain of the distal and proximal interphalangeal joints, sometimes accompanied by lateral side activities, suggests lateral collateral ligament injury. Wrist and palm usually manifest marked swelling at the fracture line, tenderness, deformity, bone fricative, and axis percussion pain.

Limited mass on the wrist dorsum, which may shift slightly and vertically along the tendon, but not horizontally, is common in thecal cyst.

【Hip】

In a prone position, observe the patient's reaction by pressing the points 2 cm inferior to the middle point of the inguinal ligament using equal force with the thumbs, or hitting the greater trochanter or the heel with the fist. If the test causes hip pain, it indicates hip disorders. Palpate the groin to see if there are swollen lymph nodes or local full swelling and tenderness. Superficial tenderness on the lateral aspect of greater trochanter indicates greater trochanter bursitis. Check the pain due to movement of the hip joint carefully to determine the location of the pain. There are two methods to check rotary pain: I. straight hip rotation test, to check friction pain of the articular surface, and II. Hip flexion-rotation test. Flex the hip joint to relax the iliopsoas, and if pain appears when the hip is rotated slightly, it indicates friction pain of the articular surface, not dragging pain of the iliopsoas; if there is no pain when the hip is rotated slightly, but pain appears when the rotation amplitude is increased, it usually suggests a disorder of the soft tissues of the iliopsoas. In a prone position, palpate the posterior superior iliac spine. An asymmetrical spine accompanied by tenderness at the sacroiliac joints suggests subluxation of the sacroiliac joint. Press the gluteus maximus. Tenderness in this area indicates gluteus maximus fasciitis. Press the greater trochanter and the middle point of the ischial tuberosity forcefully. Deep tenderness or radiating pain along the sciatic nerve usually suggests piriformis syndrome. The patient, in a lateral recumbent position, must try to flex the hip and knee as much as possible, so that the ischial tuberosiry can be touched. If there is obvious tenderness in this area, it indicates ischial bursitis; if there is cystic mass, it would be an ischial tuberosity cyst.

【Knee】

Check the front of the knee joint. When the knee is flexed, the patella is fixed at the anterior aspect of knee joint; when the knee is extended, the patella is moved. Tenderness at the fat pad under the patella suggests hypertrophy of the fat pad or contusion. The medial collateral ligament of the knee joint is part of the knee capsule. It is often torn when the knee is impacted by valgus force. During examination, it is better to palpate the ligament from the starting point to the ending point to see whether there is continuous interruption or tenderness. If the medial collateral ligament is torn at the medial epicondyle, a small piece of torn bone is often attached; if the ligament is torn at the middle area, local defect can be felt.

Check the lateral aspect of the knee joint. The patient must flex the knee while the doctor inserts his thumb into the lateral joint space to touch the lateral meniscus. The iliotibial tract is located slightly anterior to the lateral aspect of the knee joint. Palpate the tract to feel the tension of the tract and determine if there is contracture. Check the posterior aspect of the knee joint. Palpate the deep layer of the popliteal fossa. Cystic mass is common in a popliteal fossa cyst.

Disorders relating to tenderness of the knee joints:

Tenderness on the patella edge - patella chondromalacia

Tenderness in the patella joint space - meniscus injury

Tenderness on the attachment of the lateral collateral ligament - lateral collateral ligament injury

Tenderness on the lower pole of the patella - infrapatellar ligament disease

Tenderness on both sides of the patellar ligament - infrapatellar fat pad lesions

Tenderness on the tibial tubercle - tibial tubercle epiphysitis

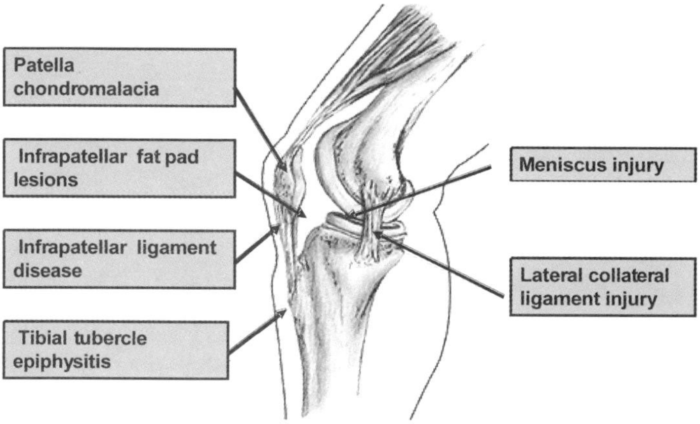

【Ankle Joint】

The soft tissue of the ankle is thin, and the tenderness is often the location of lesion. Tenderness on the ankle and foot usually occur in the joint space, at the bone end and attachment of the tendons, such as the medial lateral malleolus, the ligaments below them, the medial border of the scaphoid, the attachment of the Achilles tendon, the base of the 5th metatarsal bone, the bottom of the heel, and the heads of the 1st, 2nd, and 3rd metatarsal bones. Among these, tenderness in the heel is full of great diagnostic value.

If the tenderness is on the Achilles tendon, a disorder of the tendon or the membrane beside the tendon is possible. If it is on the ending point of the Achilles tendon, bursitis of the posterior Achilles tendon is possible. If tenderness appears inferiorly and posteriorly to the calcaneus in children of 8 ~ 12 years old, an epiphysitis of the calcaneum (Sever's disease) is possible. Tenderness posterior to the middle of the plantar surface of the calcaneum suggests disorders of the calcaneus spine or fat pad. Tenderness anterior to the middle of the plantar surface of the calcaneum indicates a disorder of the plantar aponeurosis. Tenderness on the medial and lateral calcaneum suggests a disorder of the calcaneum itself. Tenderness directly below the medial and lateral malleolus is common in disorders of the subtalar joint.

Section 2
Special Examinations

1. Intervertebral Foramen Compression Test (Knocking Vertex Test)

In a sitting position, bend the head to the affected side. The examiner puts his left hand flatly on the patient's vertex and then knocks the dorsum of his hand with his right fist in a downward direction. If there is radicular damage, the narrow intervertebral foramen may cause neck pain or radiating pain in the limbs, and it is positive. In patients with severe radicular pain, any downward force on the vertex, done by the examiner with one hand over another may induce or exacerbate symptoms (Fig. 3-5).

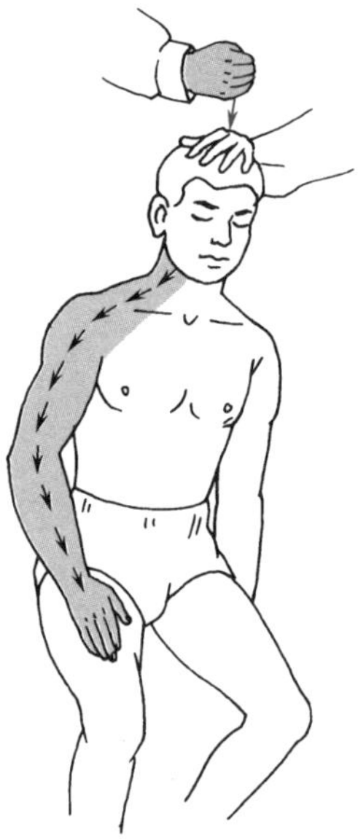

Fig. 3-5 (1) Intervertebral Foramen Compression Test

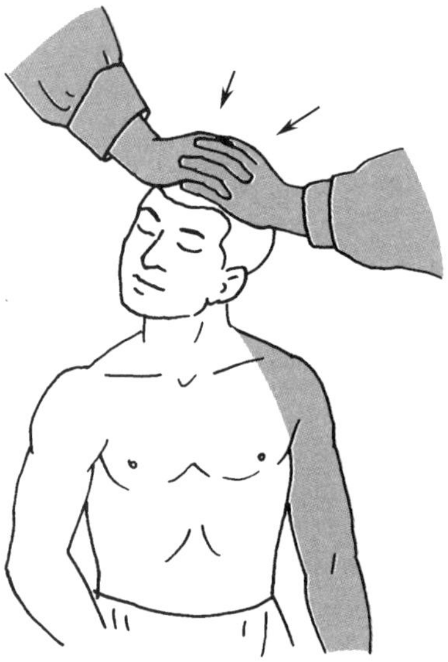

Fig. 3-5 (2) Intervertebral Foramen Compression Test

2. Brachial Plexus Traction Test

Ask the patient to bend the head forward. The examiner should hold the patient's head with one hand at the affected side, and pull the patient's arm in the opposite direction by holding the wrist of the affected side. The test is positive if there is pain or a numb feeling in the ailing limb, suggesting that the brachial plexus is oppressed (Fig. 3-6).

3. Ultra-Abduction Test

This is used to check for thoracic outlet syndrome, where the subclavian artery is compressed by the coracoid process and the pectoralis minor muscle. The patient may stand or sit, then passively raise the ailing arm from the side of body to shoulder lever or head level. It is a positive test if the radial artery pulse weakens or disappears.

4. Neck Rotation Test

Also called vertebral artery distortion test, this is used to determine the status of the vertebral artery. The method is: the patient raises the head backward slightly and rotates the head to the left and right. The signs of vertebral basilar artery insufficiency syndrome such as dizziness and vertigo suggest a positive result. This test may cause vomiting or falling, and so the examiner should take care to observe the patient closely to avoid accident.

5. Neck Flexion Test

The patient assumes a supine position. With one hand below the patient's occiput and the other hand on the patient's chest, the doctor pushes the patients' head forward. Lumbago or sciatica is the positive sign. When the neck flexes forward, the spinal cord is 1 ~ 2 cm up in the spinal canal, and the nerve root is also pulled, resulting in radiating pain. The test is frequently applied to check lumbar disc herniation (Fig.3-7).

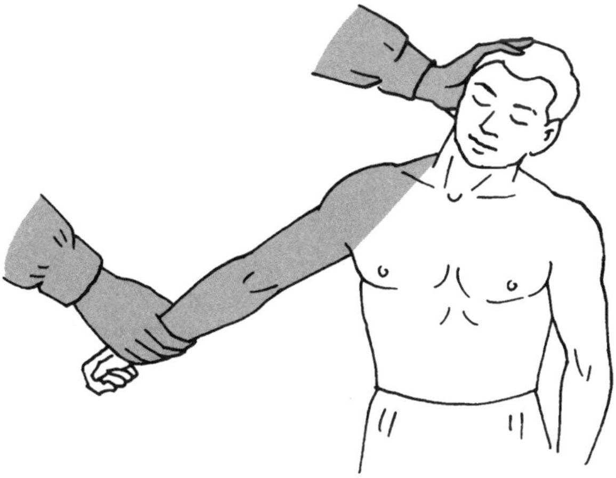

Fig. 3-6 Brachial Plexus Traction Test

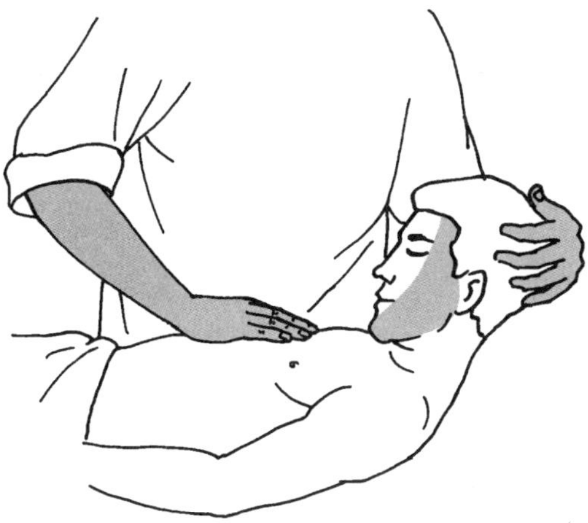

Fig. 3-7 Neck Flexion Test

Abdomen Protruding Test

In a supine position, raise the abdomen so that the waist and pelvis are not touching the bed. Radiating pain in the lumbar region and leg, or pain in the lumbar region and leg during cough is positive, suggesting compression of the lumber nerve root (Fig. 3-8).

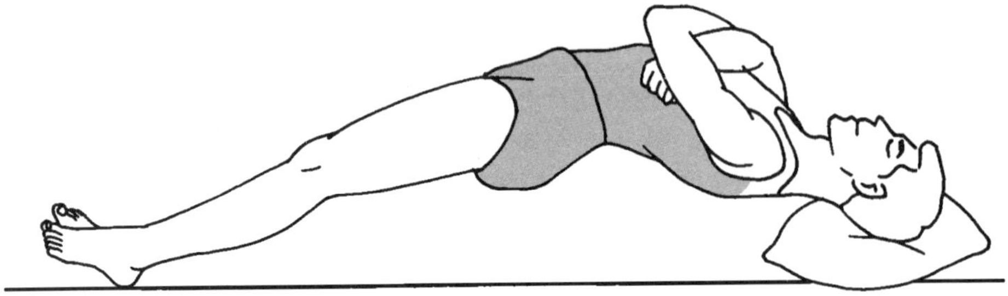

Fig. 3-8 Abdomen Protruding Test

6. Straight Leg Raise Test and Foot Dorsiflexion Test

In a supine position, the patient raises the legs one by one, keeping the knees straight. Measure the pain-free range of the raised leg (the angle between the raised leg and bed surface). If the nerve root is compressed, and limitation of leg movement is very obvious, usually less than 60°, with pain in the distributing area of the compressed nerve when the leg raised, the test is positive. Next, lower the leg 5 ° ~ 10 °, until the pain disappears and perform dorsiflexion suddenly. If sciatic pain appears again, it is positive strengthening test. The latter test has more clinical value in diagnosing ruptures of the fibrosus of the lumbar intervertebral disc, because the tension of the iliotibial tract and hamstring are also positive during the straight leg raise test, while the positive dorsiflexion test is the reaction of sciatic nerve tension when it is pulled (Fig. 3-9).

Fig. 3-9 (1) Straight Leg Raise Test

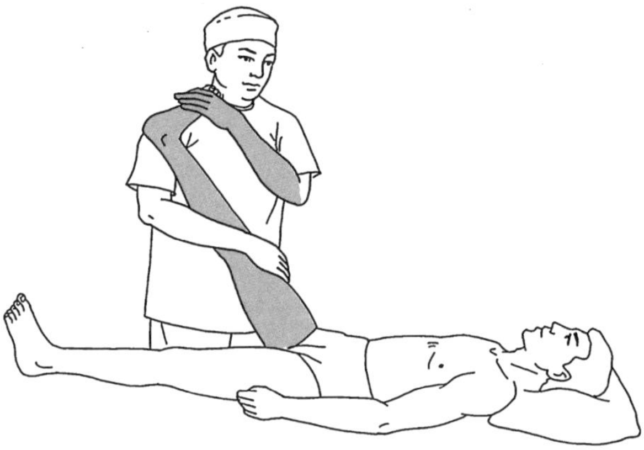

Fig. 3-9 (2) Foot Dorsiflexion Test

7. Femoral Nerve Dragging Test

Ask the patient to assume a prone position. The examiner fixes the patient's pelvis with one hand and holds the calf of the diseased side with the other hand, then extends the thigh extremely, the knee joint extending or flexing. The test would be positive if there is radiating pain along the front of the thigh (Fig. 3-10).

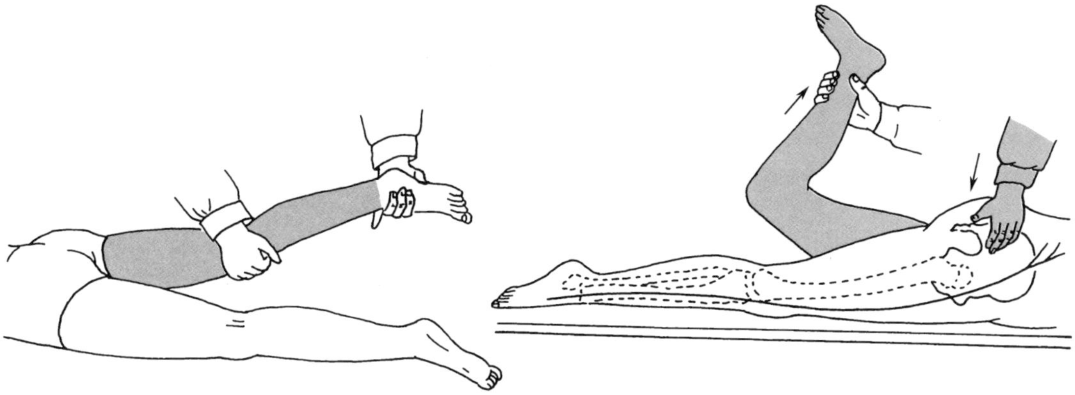

Fig. 3-10 Femoral Nerve Dragging Test

Pelvic Separation, Compression Test

Ask the patient to assume a supine position. Pressing the bilateral iliac crest to the sides with two hands constitutes the pelvic separation test. In the same position, compressing the bilateral iliac crest inward with two hands is the pelvic compression test. Pain is a positive test result, suggesting disorders of the sacroiliac joint or pelvic fracture (Fig. 3-11).

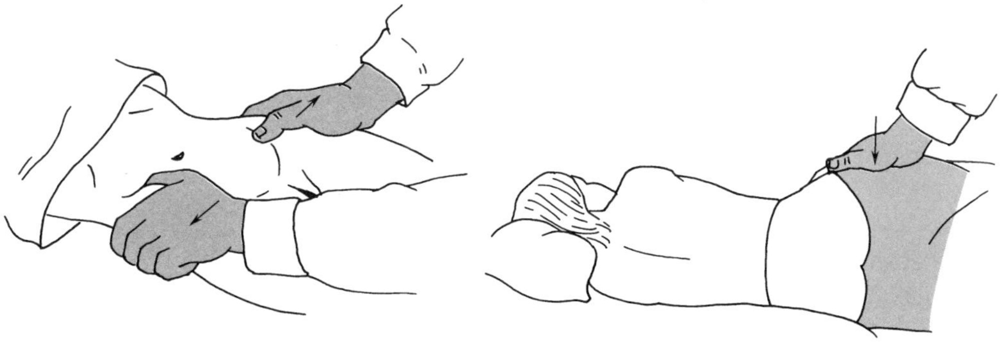

Fig. 3-11 Pelvic Separation, Compression Test

8. Shape of "4" Test

Ask the patient to assume a supine position with the normal leg extended, and the ailing leg bent and outwardly rotated with the foot over the knee of the normal leg. The doctor presses the upper part of the knee of the sick leg with one hand and the anterior-superior iliac spine of the normal side with the other hand to distort the sacroiliac joint. The test is positive if there is pain, suggesting a disorder of the hip joint or lesions of the sacroiliac joint (Fig. 3-12).

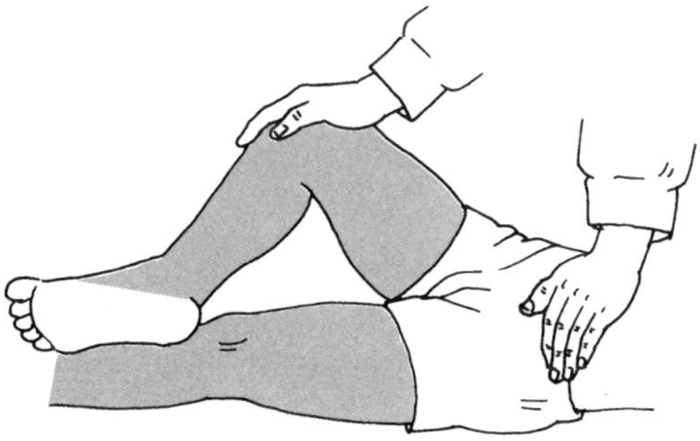

Fig. 3-12 Shape of "4" Test

Bedside Test

Ask the patient to assume a supine position with the buttock of the ailing side over the bedside and the normal leg flexed to fix the pelvis. The doctor should move the ailing leg outside of the bed and try to extend the leg backward as much as possible to stretch and move the sacroiliac joint. Pain in the sacroiliac joint suggests a disorder of the joint (Fig. 3-13).

9. Heel - Buttock Test

Ask the patient to assume a prone position with the legs straightened and relaxed. The doctor holds and moves the patient's heels to touch the buttocks. Disorder of the sacroiliac joint may cause pain in the lumbosacral region, pelvis or waist in tandem with the lift(Fig. 3-14).

Fig. 3-13 Bedside Test

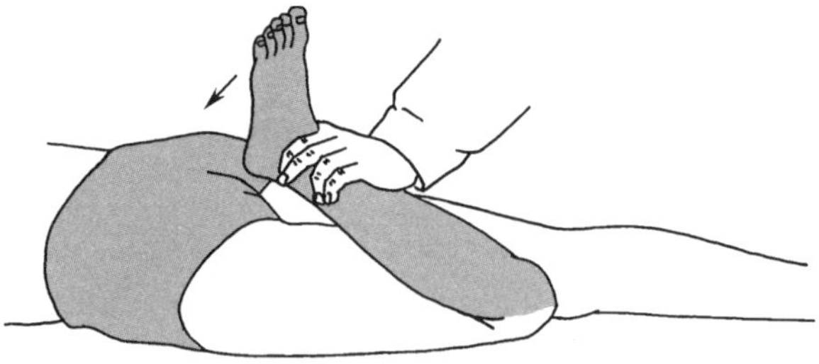

Fig. 3-14 Heel - Buttock Test

10. Putting Hand on Opposite Shoulder (Dugas' Sign) Test

Place the hand of the affected side on the opposite shoulder and bring the elbow to touch the chest. It suggests shoulder dislocation if the patient can not complete the actions or can do only one of two (Fig. 3-15).

11. Ruler Test

Usually, the acromion is located at the medial side of the line between the lateral epicondyle and the greater tuberosity of the humerus. Place a ruler with the edge along the lateral side of the upper arm, and one end on the lateral epicondyle of the humerus. The test is positive if the other end of ruler can touch the acromion, which suggests shoulder dislocation (Fig. 3-16).

12. Dropping Arm Test

Assuming a standing position, first abduct the affected arm 90° passively, and then drop the arm down slowly. If the arm drops quickly to the side of the body, and is unable to fall downward slowly, it suggests a supraspinatus muscle injury.

13. Pain Arc Test

Abduct the shoulder or passively abduct the affected arm. When the arm rises to 60° ~ 90°,

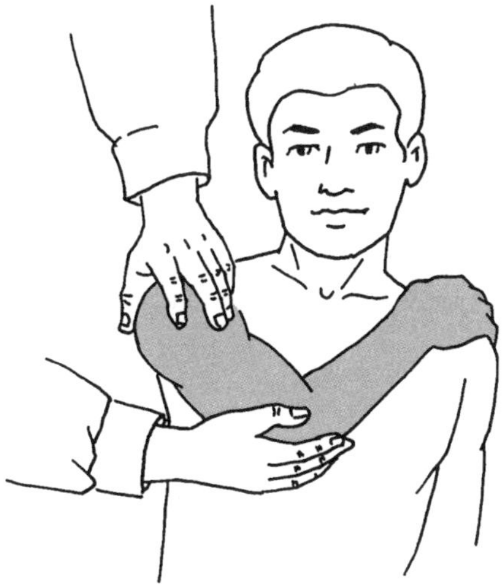

Fig. 3-15 Putting Hand on Opposite Shoulder (Dugas' Sign) Test

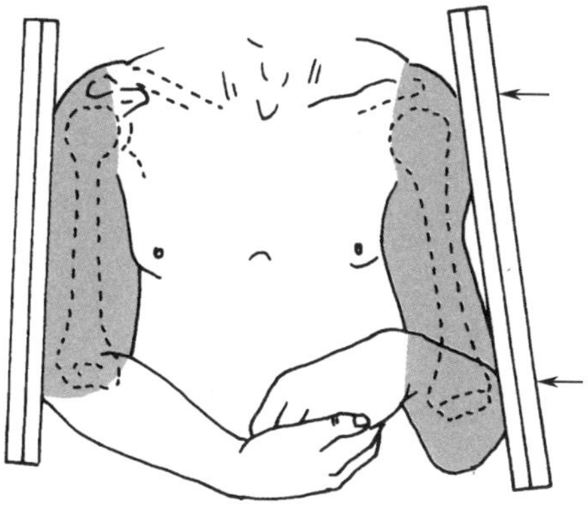

Fig. 3-16 Ruler Test

pain appearing in the shoulder because of friction of the supraspinatus with the acromion, it is a positive sign. The pain in this particular range due to abduction is called the pain arc, suggesting supraspinatus tendinitis (Fig. 3-17).

14. Supraspinatus Tendon Rupture Test

When the shoulder is abducted to 30° ~ 60°, and the deltoid muscle of the affected side contracted forcefully, but the arm fails to abduct and to raise, the harder the patient tries, the more shrugged the shoulder will be. This abduction disturbance in this particular range is a positive sign, suggesting a supraspinatus tendon rupture or tear (Fig. 3-18).

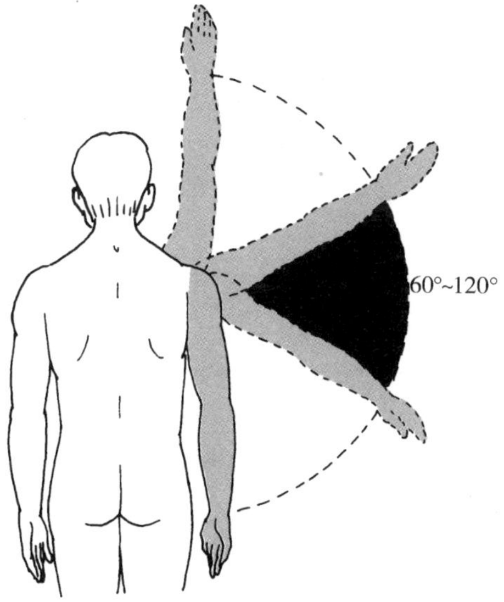

Fig. 3-17 Pain Arc Test

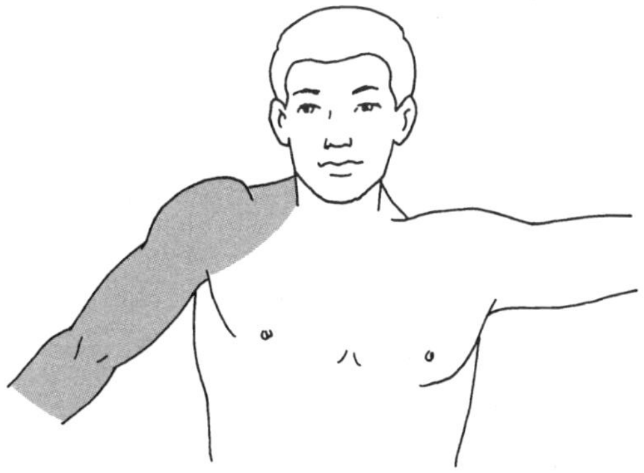

Fig. 3-18 Supraspinatus Tendon Rupture Test

15. Yergason Test

Also known as the biceps resistance test. Ask the patient to flex the arm to a 90° angle. Holding the patient's elbow with one hand and the wrist with the other hand to create resistance, let the patient flex his elbow and rotate the forearm outward forcefully against the resistance. The test is positive if the biceps tendon is slipping out of the groove or if pain occurs in the biceps groove. The former indicates dislocation of the long head of the biceps brachii; the latter is tendonitis of the long head of the biceps brachii (Fig. 3-19).

16. Tennis Elbow Test

Ask the patient to bend the forearm slightly with a half fist and if possible, a flexed wrist. Extend the elbow after the forearm is fully rotated inward. The test is positive if there is pain on the lateral side of the brachioradialis joint (Fig. 3-20).

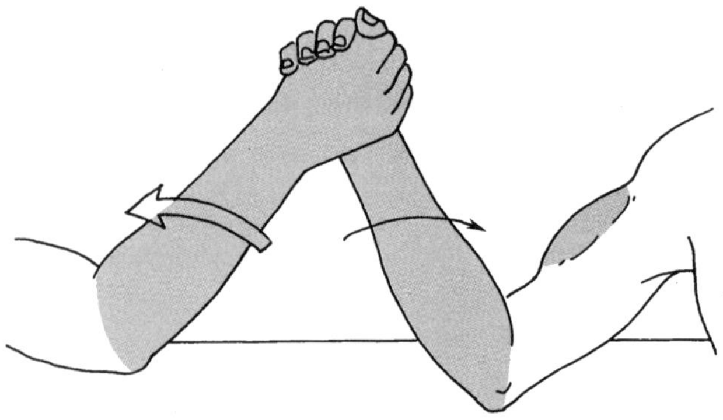

Fig. 3-19 Yergason Test

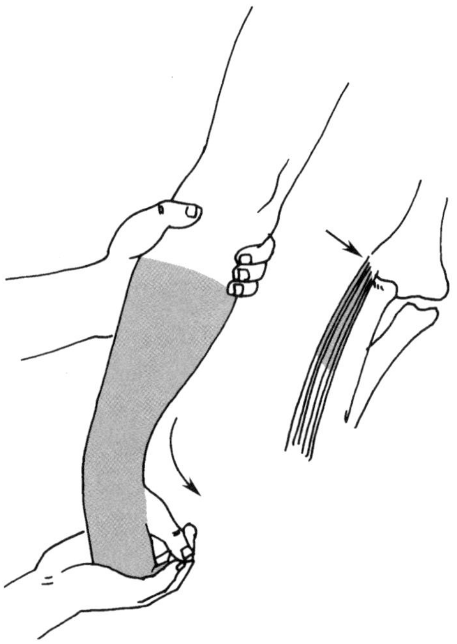

Fig. 3-20 Tennis Elbow Test

17. Forearm Flexor, Extensor Tension (Anti-Resistance) Test

Ask the patient to make a fist with the wrist flexed. The examiner places his hand on the patient's hand dorsum and presses it down. Then, the patient extends the wrist against the resistance. The test is positive if there is pain on the lateral side of the elbow, suggesting inflammatory lesion of the lateral epicondyle of the humerus. Or, the examiner presses the patient's palm down while the patient flexes the wrist against the resistance, and the test is positive if there is pain on the medial aspect of the elbow, suggesting a disorder of the medial epicondyle of the humerus (Fig. 3-21).

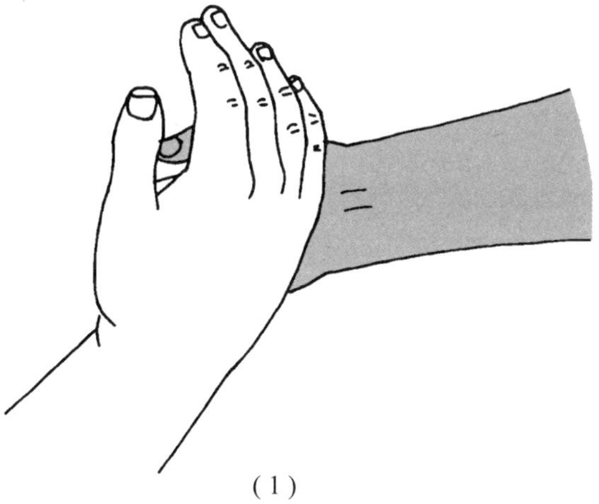
(1)

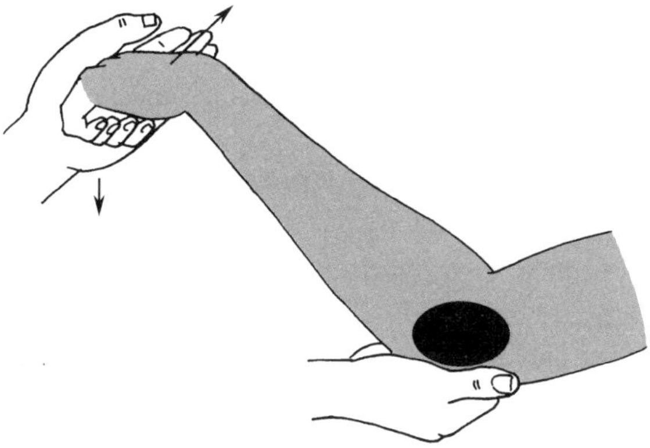
(2)

Fig. 3-21 Forearm Flexor, Extensor Tension (Anti-Resistance) Test

18. Fist Test

Make a fist with the thumb inside of the other four fingers and the wrist deviated toward the ulnar side. The test is positive if there is pain on the radial styloid process, suggesting stenosing tenosynovitis of the radial styloid process (Fig. 3-22).

19. Wrist Flexion Test

Bend the wrist joint as much as possible. Numbness and pain in the fingers indicate carpal tunnel syndrome (Fig. 3-23).

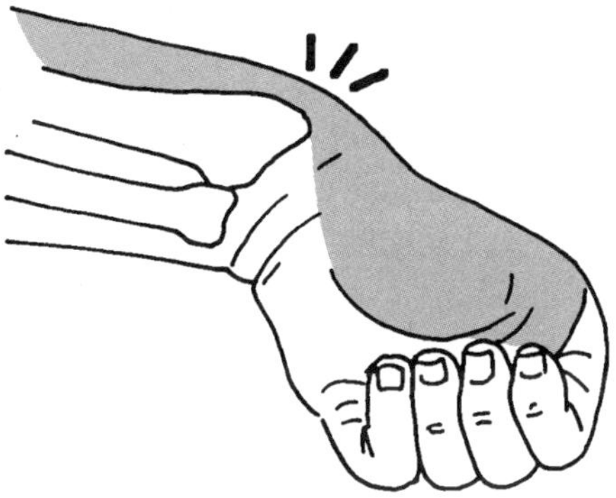

Fig. 3-22 Fist Test

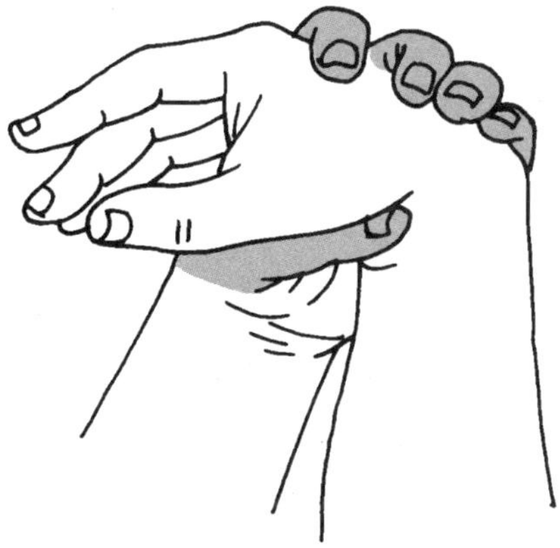

Fig. 3-23 Wrist Flexion Test

20. Wrist Triangular Cartilage Compression Test

This is to determine if there is triangular cartilage damage. Ask the patient to flex the elbow to a 90° angle with the palm downward. Holding the patient's forearm below the wrist with one hand and the patients' hand with the other hand, turn the patient's affected hand toward the ulnar side, then extend and flex the wrist joint to squeeze and ground the ulnocarpal joint. The test is positive if there is obvious pain (Fig. 3-24).

21. Palm - Heel Test

The patient assumes a supine position with straightened legs, and places the heel over the doctor's palm. Under normal conditions, the heel should be erect on the palm. However, in patients with a femoral neck fracture, hip dislocation or paraplegia, the foot falls down to the lateral side (Fig. 3-25).

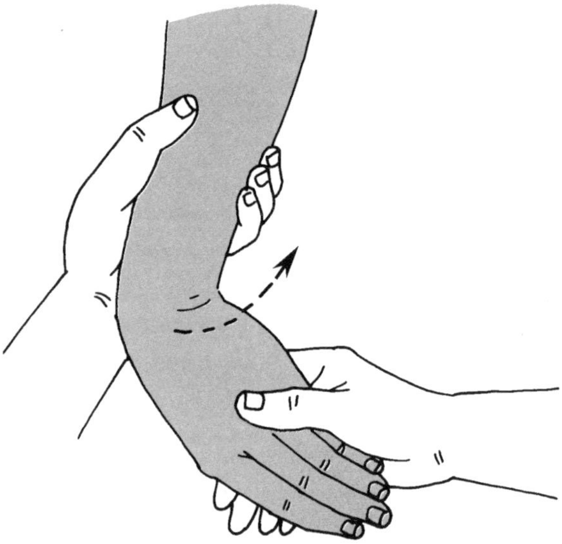

Fig. 3-24 Wrist Triangular Cartilage Compression Test

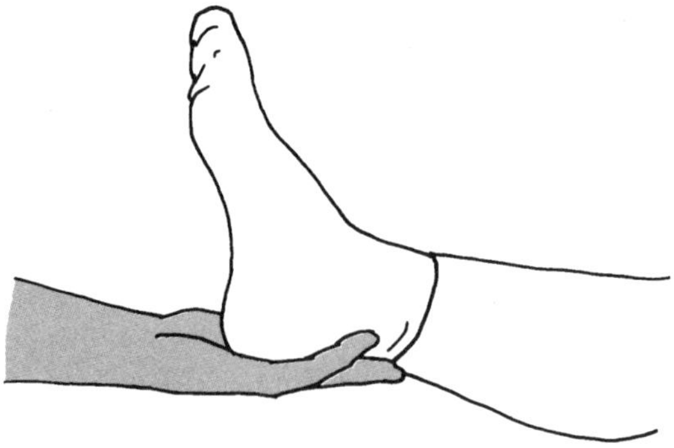

Fig. 3-25 Palm - Heel Test

22. Hip Hyperextension Test

Ask the patient to assume a prone position with the legs extended and straight. The doctor presses the patient's sacral region with one hand to fix the pelvis, and holds the patient's lower leg with the other hand to over-extend the hip joint. If there is a disorder of the hip joint or the sacroiliac joint, the pelvic region will rise in tandem with the over-extension of the hip joint, accompanied by hip pain or pain in the sacroiliac joint (Fig. 3-26).

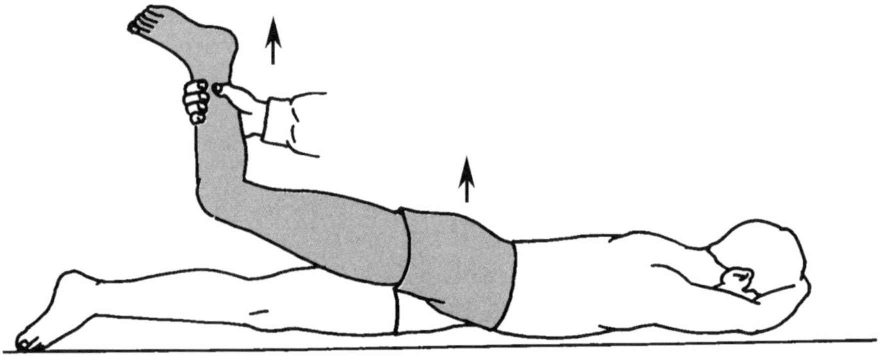

Fig. 3-26 Hip Hyperextension Test

23. Hip Flexion Test (Thomas Sign)

Ask the patient to assume a supine position, flex the normal hip and knee joints as much as possible, and place the pelvis in the forward position. The ailing hip may show flexion deformity, and the angle between the thigh and bed would be a deformed angle (Fig. 3-27).

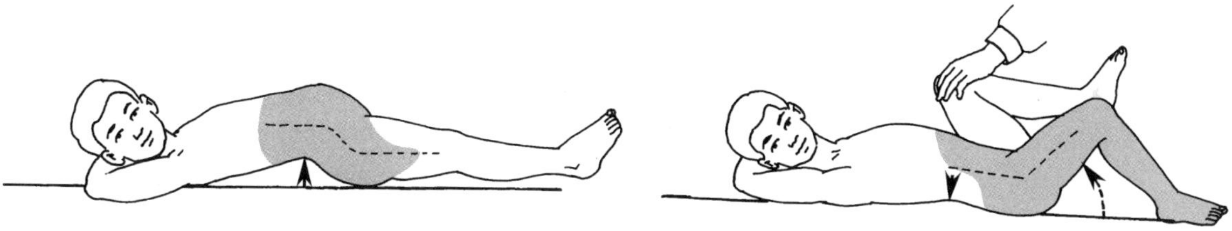

Fig. 3-27 Hip Flexion Test (Thomas Sign)

24. Tapping Heel Test

Ask the patient to assume a supine position with the legs extended and straight. The doctor lifts the sick leg with one hand and taps the heel with the other hand. The test is positive if there is pain at the hip joint, suggesting a disorder of the hip joint (Fig. 3-28).

25. Flexing Knees-Flexing Hip-Separating Legs Test

Ask the patient to assume a supine position with the knees flexed and rotated outward, and the soles of the feet facing each other, the legs continuing to abduct and rotate outward. It is not easy to separate the thighs completely in the patient with femoral adductor syndrome. Pain may appear if the thighs are separated passively (Fig. 3-29).

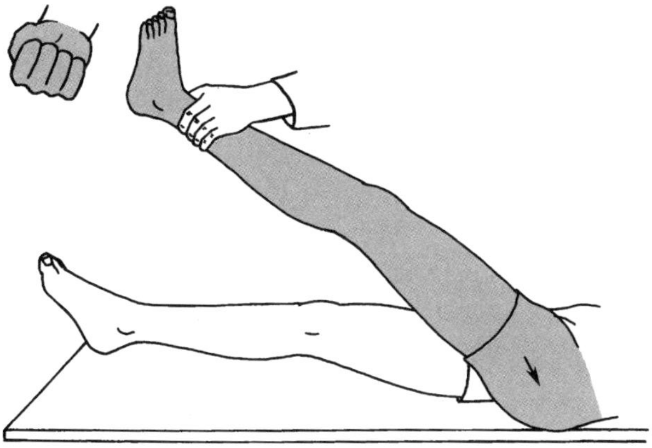

Fig. 3-28 Tapping Heel Test

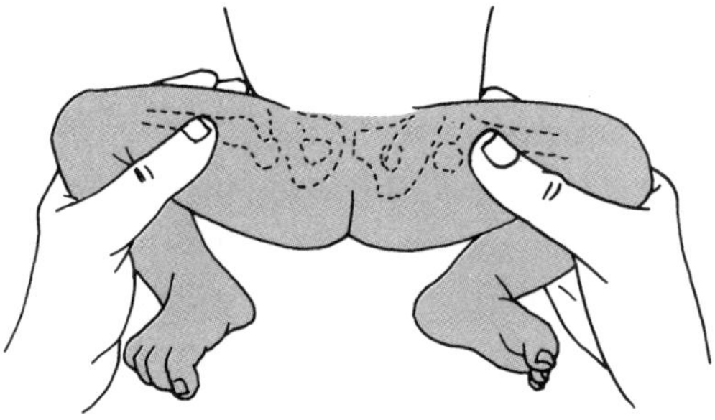

Fig. 3-29 Flexing Knees-Flexing Hip-Separating Legs Test

26. Lower Limb Shortening Test (Allis Sign)

This test is used to check whether the limb is shortened. Ask the patient to assume a supine position with legs bent close to the hips, and feet closed. Observe the height of the knees. The test is positive if the ailing knee is lower, suggesting that the limb is shortened. Clinically, it often occurs in a femoral neck fracture, posterior dislocation of the hip joint, and femoral tibial shortening (Fig. 3–30).

27. Floating Patella Test

Ask the patient to assume a supine position with the legs extended and relaxed. Squeeze the fluid from the patellar articular capsule down into the joint cavity with one hand, press the patella with the index finger of the other hand, and then release. Repeat pressing and releasing a few times. Fluid waving feeling usually suggests effusion in the joint cavity (Fig. 3-31).

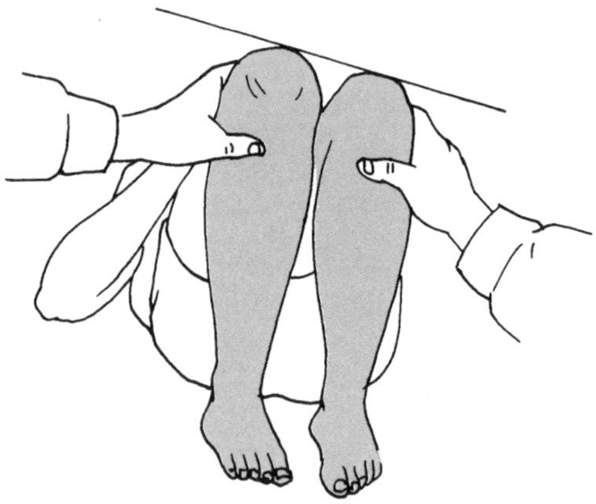

Fig. 3-30 Lower Limb Shortening Test (Allis Sign)

Fig. 3-31 Floating Patella Test

28. Knee Lateral Extrusion Test

Ask the patient to assume a supine position with the ailing knee extended and the quadriceps relaxed. Then, initiate passive varus or valgus movement. There is no lateral movement and no pain under normal conditions. Lateral abnormal movement occurs when the ligament is completely torn, and pain is present when there is ligament injury or a partial ligament tear (Fig. 3-32).

29. Drawer Test

Also known as the push-pull test Ask the patient to assume a supine position with the knee bent to a 90° angle, relaxed, and feet flat on the bed. Push forward and pull backward repeatedly by holding the upper part of the calf. Increased forward activity suggests injury to the anterior cruciate ligament; increased backward activity suggests injury to the posterior cruciate ligament (Fig. 3-33).

30. Knee Rotating-Squeezing Test

Also known as McMurray's test. This is the most common test to diagnose meniscus injury. Ask the patient to assume a supine position with legs straightened. To check for injury to the medial meniscus, the examiner holds the ailing knee with one hand, and the ankle with the other hand. First, bend the knee as much as possible, and then rotate the knee externally, moving the lower leg inward and extending the knee joint slowly. The movement causes squeezing and grounding

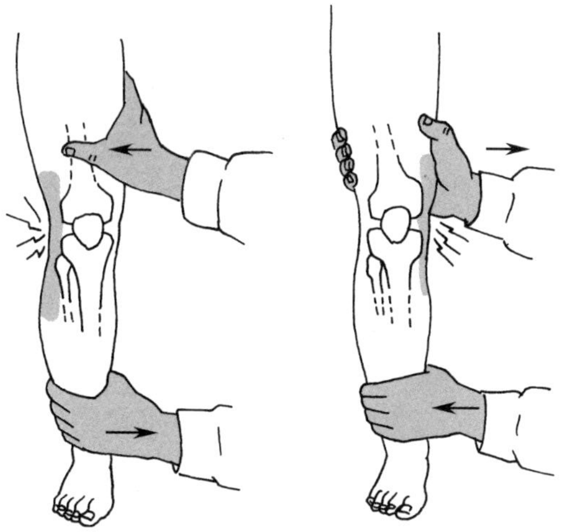

Fig. 3-32 Knee Lateral Extrusion Test

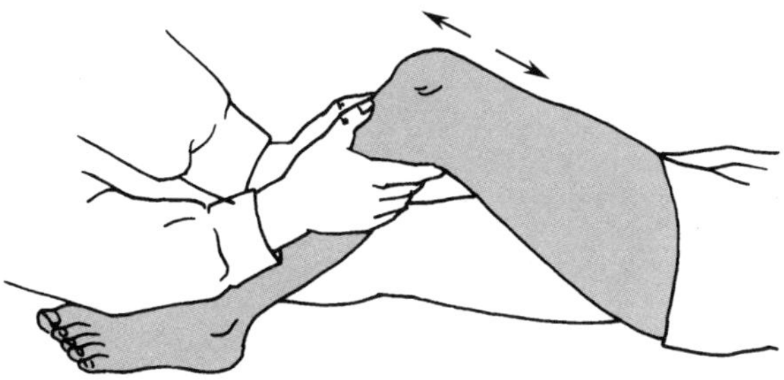

Fig. 3-33 Drawer Test

pressure in the medial knee joint space. If a "click" or pain is felt, this constitutes a positive test. Likewise, the lower leg abducted and the knee internally rotated checks for injury of the lateral meniscus (Fig. 3-34).

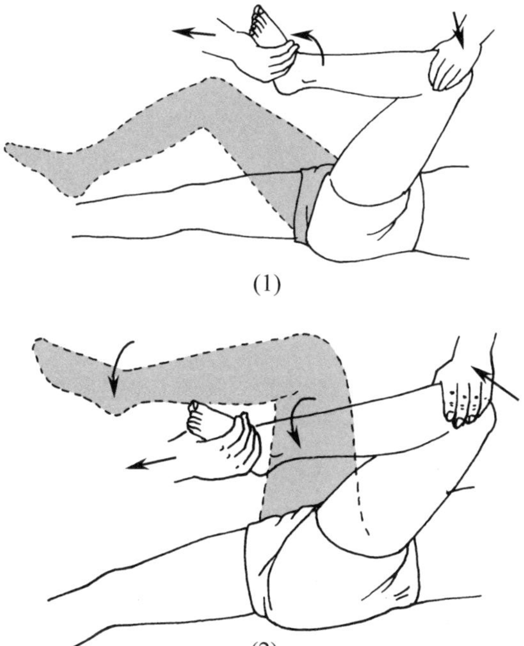

Fig. 3-34 Knee Rotating-Squeezing Test

31. Grinding-Lifting-Pulling Test

This test is used to identify injury of the collateral ligament and rupture of the meniscus. Ask the patient to assume a prone position with the patellofemoral joint straightened and the ailing knee bent to a 90° angle. The examiner fixes the thigh and holds the ailing foot with the hands to squeeze the knee joint and rotate the lower leg. The test is positive if there is pain, suggesting injury of the meniscus. On the contrary, lift the lower leg to broaden the space of the knee joint and rotate the lower leg. If there is pain, it suggests injury of the lateral collateral ligament (Fig. 3-35).

32. Patellar Protrusion Test

Extend the ailing knee and push the patellar forward with the thumb and index finger. The test is positive if there is pain when the quadriceps are contracted, suggesting injury of the patella (chondromalacia patella) (Fig. 3-36).

33. Foot Varus-Valgus Test

The examiner stabilizes the lower leg with one hand and holds the foot with the other hand, rotating the ankle joint externally and internally in an extreme way. Ipsilateral pain indicates the possibility of a medial or lateral malleolus fracture, and contralateral pain suggests collateral ligament injury (Fig. 3-37).

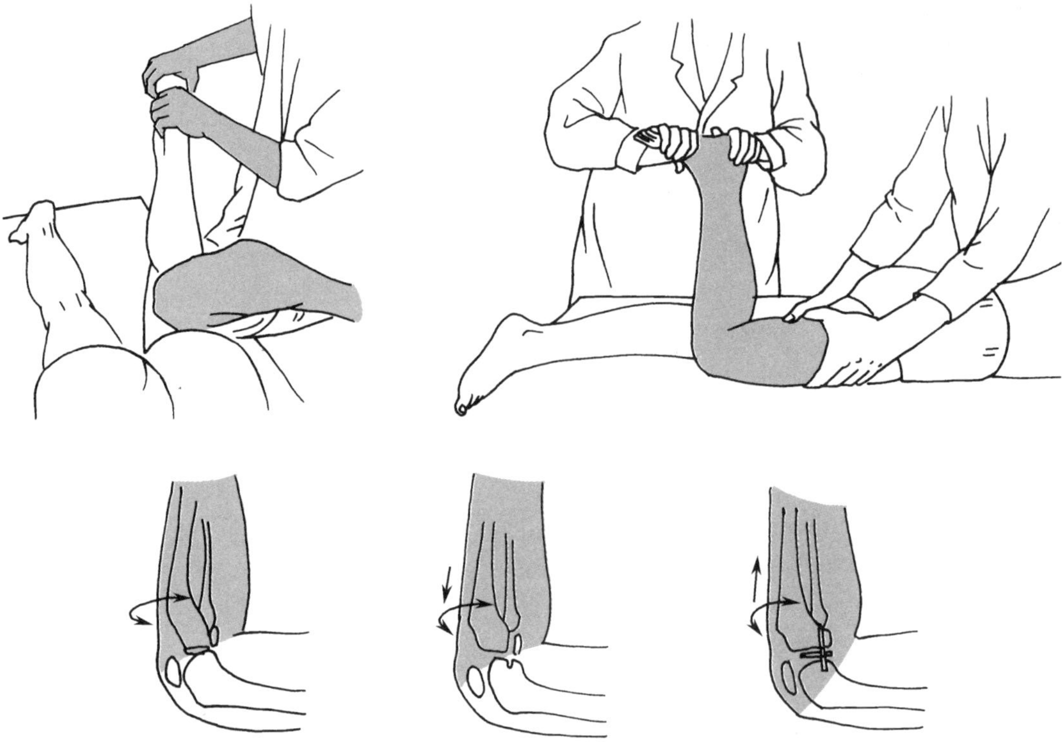

Fig. 3-35 Grinding-Lifting-Pulling Test

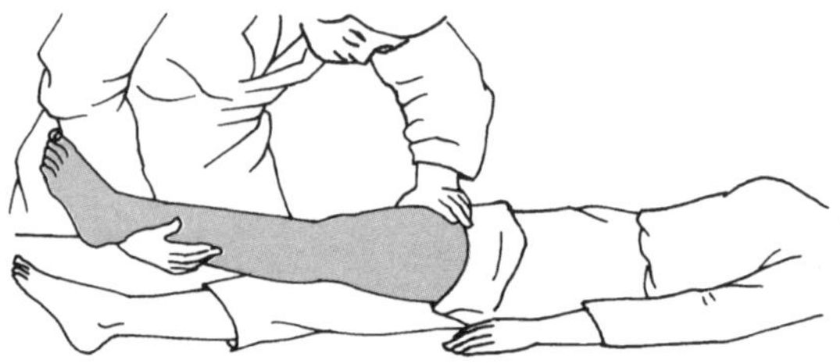

Fig. 3-36 Patellar Protrusion Test

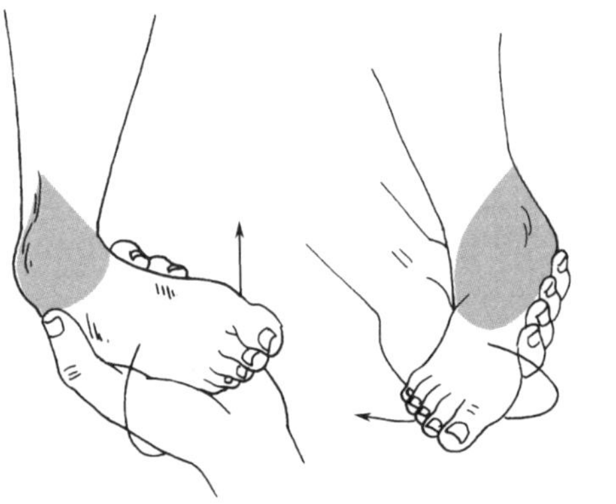

Fig. 3-37 Foot Varus-Valgus Test

Determination of the Foot Index

$$\text{Normal Index} = \frac{\textit{Arch Height} \times 100}{\textit{Foot Length}} \approx 29 \sim 31$$

34. Flatfoot index is 25 ~ 29, or less than 25. High arch foot index is greater than 31

Note: Placing the foot on the table, the arch index is the distance from the arch top to the table surface. Foot length is the length from the heel to the second toe tip.

35. Ankle Reflex (Achilles Tendon Reflex)

The patient assumes a prone position with hip the adducted and the knee bent. The examiner pushes the sole with one hand to make the ankle joint slightly dorsiflexed, and gently taps the Achilles tendon with a percussion hammer. The normal response is sole-toe flexion reflex. If there is no reaction, ask the patient kneel down at the bedside. The examiner pushes the sole to cause dorsiflexion and taps the calf with a percussion hammer. The reflection center is at S1 ~ S2.

36. Ankle Clonus

This sign often appears together with Achilles tendon hyperreflexia. Stabilizing the popliteal fossa with one hand and holding the foot with the other hand, the examiner pushes the ankle to cause a sudden dorsiflexion and then relaxation. This may cause repeated flexion-extension movement of the ankle, suggesting damage of the pyramidal tract.

37. Barbink's Sign

The lateral side of the sole of the foot is rubbed with a blunt instrument from the heel along a curve to the toes. It is positive if the hallux dorsiflex slowly and the other toes fan out, suggesting pyramidal tract damage.

38. Flicking Toes Test

Gently tap the bases of toes or flick the toes upward. If there is plantar flexion, this suggests pyramidal tract damage.

Section 3
Joint Motor Function Examinations

The motor function of joints includes active movements and passive movements. The active movement of joints is closely related to age, sex and exercise, etc. The range of motion in children is wider, and the range of active movement of certain joints in some acrobats and athletes is also obviously wider. The ranges of active movement of adjacent joints are mutually compensated. The passive movement of joints performs in two ways. In passive movement consistent with the active movement, the range is slightly larger than active movement. The other way is a pulling or squeezing movement along the vertical axis of the trunk or limbs, or lateral pulling and squeezing movement. The pulled or squeezed tissues are the muscle, tendon, ligament, joint capsule, bone, joint and nerve roots. The examinations of joint motor function are of great significance for tui na clinical diagnosis. For example, in the case of intra articular disorder due to intra articular adhesion, joint movement in all directions is limited, while in injury of soft tissues, such as muscles, ligaments and so on, movement is limited to a certain direction or within a certain range. The patient with tendonitis of the supraspinatus usually feels pain when the shoulder joint is extended to 60° ~ 120°, but pain disappears when the shoulder joint is out of this range. As it may cause muscular spasm, the pain limits active movement and passive movement of the joint, or the joint may even fail to move.

1. Neck

The movements of the neck include flexion, extension, rotation and lateral bending. The entire cervical spine is involved in neck movement, but 50% of the flexion and extension movement work occurs between the occipital bone and the first cervical vertebra, and 50% relates to the rest of the cervical vertebrae; 50% of rotation movement occurs between the first and second cervical vertebrae (atlas and axial), and 50% relates to the rest of the cervical vertebrae. Lateral bending is often accompanied by rotation of the cervical vertebrae, therefore involving joint activities of all of the cervical vertebrae.

a. Flexion and Extension

Normally, the neck can bend forward 35° ~ 45°. During the examination, ask patient to lower the head as much as possible, attempting to touch the chest with the chin.

b. Rotation

Normally, left rotation and right rotation may reach to 60° ~ 80° with a smooth movement arc. During the examination, ask the patient to rotate the head to the shoulder side as much as possible to force the chin to touch the shoulder.

c. Lateral Bending

Normally, the head can bend to the shoulder 45°. During the examination, ask patient to move the ear close to the shoulder, rather than the shoulder to the ear so as to replace neck movement (Fig. 3-38).

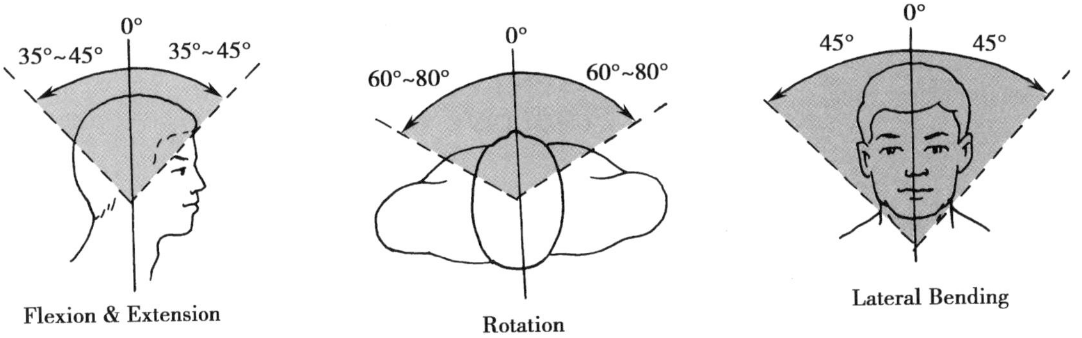

Fig. 3-38 Flexion, extension, rotation and lateral bending of the neck

2. Waist

Because there is no limitation by the ribs, the waist can move in large range. The main movements include flexion, extension, rotation and lateral bending.

a. Flexion and Extension

Normally, the waist can be bent forward 80° ~ 90°, and extended backward 30°. During the examination, the patient assumes a standing position. Standing at the patients' side, the examiner holds the patient's chest with one hand and the upper back with the other hand. Observe the movement of the spine to see if there is an even arc formed gradually in rhythm while the patient is bending forward. Or, ask the patient position to touch the toes with the fingertips while bending forward in a standing position. Normally, the patient can complete this movement with straightened legs. During the backwards extension examination, the patient assumes a standing position while the examiner stands behind the patient, holding his shoulder at the back, and then asks the patient to extend the body backwards.

b. Rotation

Normally, the waist can be rotated to the left and right 30° respectively. The rotation range of both sides should be compared during examination. The patient assumes a standing position, and the examiner stands in front of him. Stabilize the bilateral iliac crests with the hands to maintain pelvic balance, and then ask the patient to rotate the trunk.

c. Lateral Bending

Normally, the waist can be bent to left and right 20° ~ 30°respectively. The bending range of both sides should be compared. The patient assumes a standing position, and the examiner stands behind him. Stabilize the iliac crests with the hands to prevent the pelvis from tilting to one side, and then ask the patient to bend his body from side to side, as much as possible (Fig. 3-39).

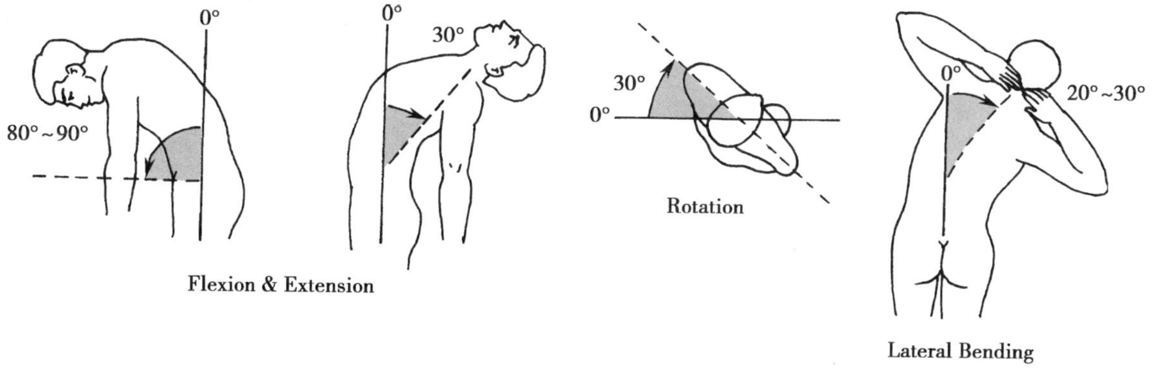

Fig. 3-39 Flexion, extension, rotation and lateral bending of the waist

3. Shoulder

With the arms freely dropping down to the sides in a neutral position, the movements of the shoulder include abduction, adduction, extorsion, intorsion, anteflexion and post-extension, etc.

a. Abduction

Normally, abduction of shoulder can be up to 90°. During the examination, the patient assumes a sitting or standing position, and the doctor stands behind the patient. Ask the patient to flex the arm 90°and abduct the shoulder. The main muscles involved are the deltoid, the supraspinatus and the serratus muscles.

b. Adduction

Normally, adduction of the shoulder can be up to 40°. During the examination, the patient assumes a sitting or standing position while the doctor stands at the tested side. Ask the patient to flex the elbow and move the upper arm inward in front of the chest. The muscles primarily involved are the pectoralis major, the latissimus dorsi, the anterior deltoid, the teres major and so on.

c. Extorsion

Normally, extorsion of the shoulder can be up to 30°. During the examination, the patient assumes a sitting or standing position, and the doctor stands in front of him. Ask the patient to flex the elbow to a 90°with the elbow against the trunk side to stabilize the arm, and then abduct the forearm from the neutral position. The moving range of forearm abduction is the moving amplitude of extorsion of the shoulder. The muscles primarily involved are the infraspinatus, the teres minor and the posterior deltoid.

d. Intorsion

Normally, intorsion of the shoulder can be up to 80°. As in the extorsion examination, ask the patient to adduct the forearm from the neutral position. The moving range of the forearm adduction is the intorsion range of the shoulder joint. The muscles primarily involved are the pectoralis major, the teres minor, the anterior deltoid and so on.

e. Anteflexion

Normally, anteflexion of the shoulder may reach up to 90°. During the examination, the patient assumes a sitting or standing position, and the doctor stands at the tested side and stabilizes the patient's shoulder with the hand. Ask the patient to flex the elbow to a 90°and flex the shoulder joint forward. The muscles primarily involved are the deltoid, the anterior brachial muscle, the pectoralis major and the biceps.

f. Post-Extension

Normally, post-extension of the shoulder may reach up to 45°. During the examination, the patient assumes either a sitting or a standing position, and the doctor stands at the tested side and stabilizes the patient's shoulder with one hand. Ask the patient to flex the elbow and extend the upper arm backward. The muscles primarily involved are the latissimus dorsi, the teres major, the posterior deltoid, the teres minor, etc.

In addition, the shoulder is also capable of shrugging, shoulder contraction and shoulder elevation (Fig. 3-40).

4. Elbow

The main movements of the elbow are elbow flexion, elbow extension, forearm pronation and forearm supination.

a. Elbow Flexion

If full extension is taken as 0°, then flexion can reach up to 140° under normal conditions. During the examination, the patient assumes a sitting or standing position, while the doctor stands in front of the patient. Ask the patient to flex the elbow after fully extending. His fingers should

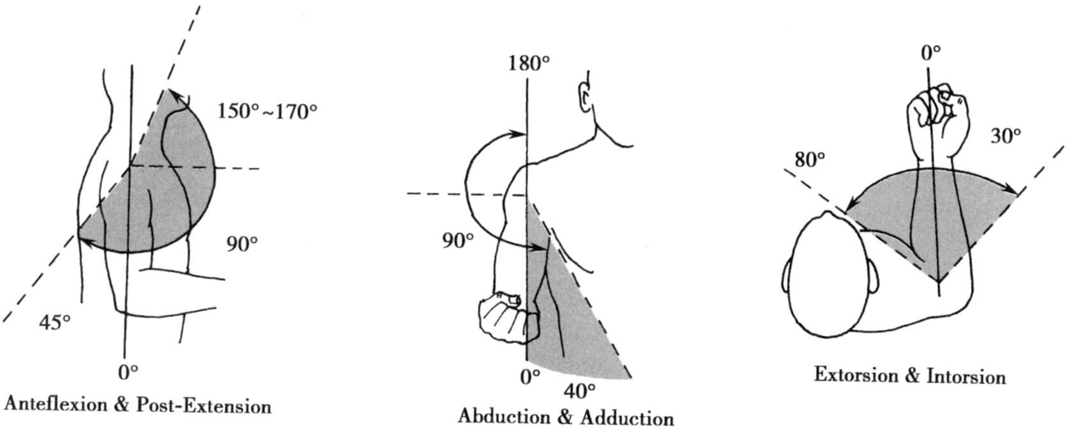

Fig. 3-40 Abduction, adduction, extorsion, intorsion, anteflexion and post-extension of the shoulder

touch the ipsilateral shoulder. The muscles primarily involved are the biceps, the brachialis, the brachioradialis, supinator, etc.

b. Elbow Extension

Normally, the elbow can be extended to 10°. During the examination, the patient assumes a sitting or standing position, and the doctor stands in front of the patient. Ask the patient to flex the elbow as much as possible and then extend the elbow. The muscles primarily involved are the triceps and the anconeus muscle.

c. Pronation

Taking the neutral position of the forearm as 0°, the normal elbow joint has a pronation range of about 80°. Compare the two arms clinically. During the examination, the patient assumes a sitting or standing position, and the doctor stands in front of him. Ask the patient to flex the elbow to a 90° keeping the bilateral forearms against the sides of chest, with empty fists and thumbs upward, and then perform forearm pronation. The muscles primarily involved are the round pronator muscle and the pronator quadratus muscle.

d. Supination

Taking the neutral position of forearm to be 0°, normal elbow supination may reach up to 90°. During the examination, compare the two arms. The patient is asked to perform forearm supination in the same position as that of the pronation test. The primary muscles involved are the supinator and the biceps (Fig. 3-41).

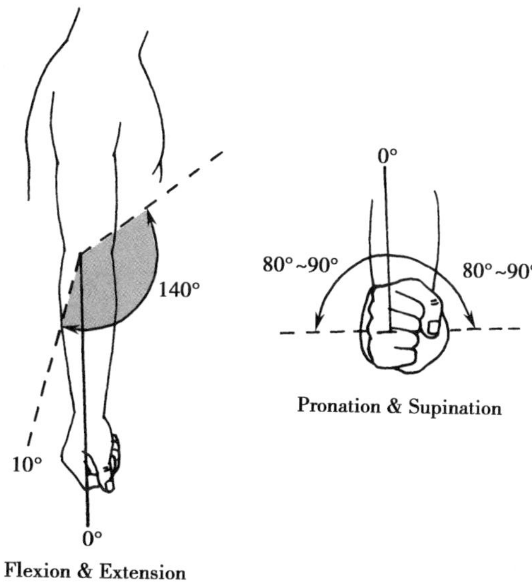

Fig. 3-41 Elbow flexion, elbow extension, forearm pronation and forearm supination

5. Wrist, Palm and Finger

The movement of the wrist joint, taking the straight line formed by the metacarpal bone and the forearm as the neutral position 0°, includes wrist extension, wrist flexion, radial deviation and ulnar deviation. The movement of the metacarpophalangeal joints and the distal proximal interphalangeal joints, by taking the straight line formed by the metacarpal bone and the phalanges as the neutral position 0°, includes finger flexion, extension, abduction and adduction, etc.

a. Wrist Extension

Normally, the wrist joint can extend to 60°. During the examination, the patient is asked to assume a sitting position, and flex the elbow to 90°, keeping the forearm in a position of pronation with the palm facing downward, and then extend the wrist. The primary muscles involved are the extensor carpi radialis long and short, and the extensor carpi ulnaris.

b. Wrist Flexion

Normally, the wrist joint can flex to 60°. During the examination, the patient is asked to assume a sitting position and flex the elbow to 90°, keeping the forearm in a position of pronation with palm facing downward, and then flex the wrist. The primary muscles involved are the flexor carpi radialis and the flexor carpi ulnaris.

c. Radial Deviation

Normally, the movement range of radial deviation is up to 30°. During the examination, the patient is asked to turn the hand to the radial side to achieve radial deviation. The primary muscles involved are the flexor carpi radialis and the extensor carpi radialis.

d. Ulnar Deviation

Normally, the movement range of ulnar deviation is up to 40°. During the examination, the patient is asked to turn the hand to the ulnar side to achieve ulnar deviation. The primary muscles involved are the flexor carpi ulnaris is and the extensor carpi ulnaris.

e. Finger Flexion

Normally, the metacarpophalangeal joint can flex 80° ~ 90°, and the proximal interphalangeal joint 60° ~ 90°. During the examination, the patient is asked to flex the metacarpophalangeal joints, the proximal interphalangeal joints and the distal interphalangeal joints. The primary muscles involved include the lumbrical muscle of the metacarpophalangeal joint, the superficial flexor of the proximal interphalangeal joint and the deep flexor of the distan interphalangeal joint.

f. Finger Extension

Normally, if full extension of the metacarpophalangeal joint is 0°, the metacarpophalangeal joint may hyperextend to 15° ~ 25°. If full extension of the proximal interphalangeal joint and the distal phalangeal joint is 0°, there is no hyperextension. During the examination, the patient is asked to perform hyperextension of the metacarpophalangeal joints. The primary muscles involved include the extensor digitorum, the extensor muscle of the index finger and the extensor muscle of the little finger.

g. Finger Abduction and Adduction

Normally, the little finger, the ring finger and the index finger have 20° of abduction respectively. During the examination, ask the patient to extend the fingers fully, and then perform abduction and adduction (0°) of the little finger, ring finger and index finger one by one, by taking the middle finger as the axis. The primary muscles involved include the dorsal interosseous muscle, the little finger abductor, the volar interosseous muscle and so on.

h. Dorsiextension and Flexion of Thumb

Normally, when the thumb is dorsiextended, the angle between the thumb and index finger is up to 50°. Flexion of the metacarpophalangeal joint of the thumb may reach to 50°, and flexion of the interphalangeal joint is about 90°. During the examination, ask the patient to flex the elbow against the chest with the palm upward to check the dorsiflexion of the thumb, i.e. the thumb is abducted to the radial side. To check the flexion of the thumb, bend the thumb transversely to touch the base of the little finger. Dorsiextension of the thumb is mainly achieved by the extensor pollicis brevis and the extensor pollicis longus. Flexion of the thumb is achieved by the flexor pollicis brevis and the flexor pollicis longus.

i. Abduction and dorsal adduction of the carpo-phalangeal joint

Normal thumb abduction of the carpo-phalangeal joint usually shows an angle of 70° between the thumb and the palmar plane, and dorsal adduction of 0°. During the examination, ask the patient to extend the hand and move the thumb away from the palmar plane to complete a movement of abduction. Move the thumb back to its anatomic position after it is fully abducted, and then do dorsal adduction. Palmar abduction is performed by the abductor pollicis longus and the extensor pollicis brevis, and dorsal adduction by the adductor pollicis.

j. Opposable Thumb

Normally, the thumb tip is capable of touching the tips of the other fingers. During the examination, abduct the thumb and then touch the tips of other fingers with it (Fig. 3-42).

6. Hip

The movements of the hip include anteflexion, post-extension, abduction, adduction, external rotation and internal rotation.

a. Anteflexion

Normal anteflexion of the hip joint is up to 145°. During the examination, ask the patient to assume a supine position with the legs in a neutral position, and the pelvis flattened to keep the line between the bilateral anterior superior iliac crests perpendicular to the long axis of the body. The doctor stands at the side of the patient and places one hand under the patient's back to fix the pelvic region. Ask the patient to perform anteflexion movement of the hip. When the hip is flexed to a certain degree, the patient's lower back is completely placed on the doctor's hand, lumbar lordosis disappears, and the pelvis is fixed, the patient then continues to flex his hip joint as much as possible. The primary muscles **involved** include the iliopsoas muscle and the rectus femoris muscle.

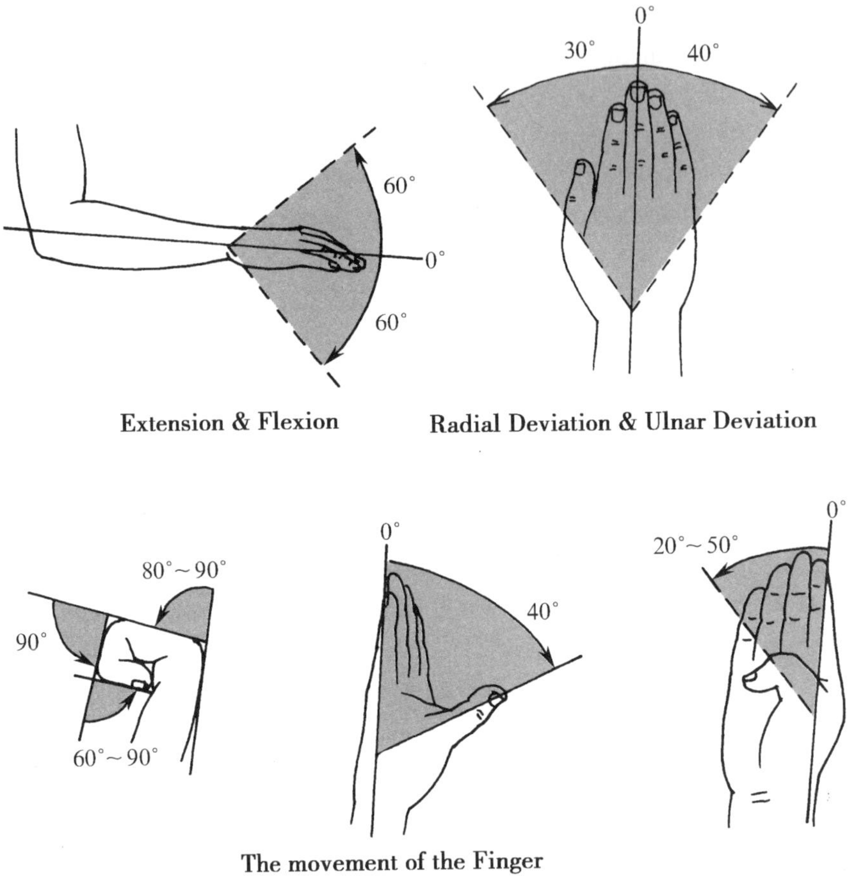

Fig.3-42 The movement of the wrist joint, palm and finger

Anteflexion movement may also determine if the patient has flexion deformity of the hip joint. Ask the patient to flex the unilateral hip joint, i.e. bend one leg to bring the thigh close to the chest and straighten the other leg. Normally, the straightened leg can be placed flat on the bed. If the straightened leg is not capable of lying flat on the bed, or it can be placed flat on the bed but the torso rises up from the bed, it suggests flexion deformity of the hip joint.

b. Post-extension

Normally, post-extension of the hip joint is up to 10° ~ 15°. During the examination, the patient assumes a prone position with the legs fully extended. The doctor stands at the patient's side, placing one hand over the iliac crests and lower lumbar vertebrae to stabilize the pelvis. Ask the patient to raise the thigh backward as much as possible. The gluteus maximus and the hamstrings muscles are involved in this movement. The post-extension movement may also determine whether there is hip flexion contraction. The doctor raises the patient's ailing leg by supporting the upper part of the thigh with one hand. It usually suggests flexion contracture deformity of the hip joint if the patient fails to extend the thigh backward or if the pelvis subsequently lifts from the bed.

c. Abduction

Normally, abduction of the hip joint is up to 45°. During the examination, the patient assumes a supine position with the legs in a neutral position. The doctor stands at the patient's side, pressing the iliac to fix the pelvis with one hand, and holding the knee with the other hand to move the leg slowly outward. The doctor will feel the pelvis begin to move when the leg extends to a certain degree, or to the maximum. The degree of abduction at this time is the movement limitation of hip abduction. The primarily involved muscles are the middle gluteal muscle and the least gluteal muscle.

d. Adduction

Normally, adduction is up to 30°. During the examination, the patient assumes a supine position with the legs in a neutral position. The doctor stands at the patient's side, pressing the iliac to fix the pelvis with one hand. Ask the patient to perform an abduction movement by bending one leg over the middle line of the other leg until the pelvis begins to move. The angle of the bending leg at this time is the angle of hip adduction. The primarily involved muscle is the adductor muscle of the thigh.

e. External Rotation

Normally, external rotation of the hip joint is up to 30°. During the examination, the patient assumes a supine position with the legs in the neutral position, and then performs an external rotation movement. When the external rotation reaches the maximum, the angle perpendicular to the longitudinal axis between the sole and the bed is the angle of external rotation. The primarily involved muscles are the extorter muscles of the hip. This examination can also be done in another way. The patient still assumes the supine position, but with the hip joint and knee flexed to 90° angles respectively, the doctor presses the patient's lower leg toward the thigh by holding the ankle with one hand and the knee with the other hand, and then rotates the thigh externally along the vertical axis. The angle of adduction of lower leg at this time is the angle of external rotation of the hip joint.

f. Internal Rotation

Normally, internal rotation of the hip joint is up to 35°. During the examination, the patient assumes a supine position with legs in the neutral position, and then performs an internal rotation movement. When the leg is rotated to the maximum, the angle between the planter longitudinal axis and the vertical longitudinal axis of the bed is the angle of internal rotation. The primary muscles involved are the gluteus muscle and the minor muscle of the hip. This examination can also be done in another way. The patient still assumes the supine position, but with the hip joint and knee flexed to 90° respectively, the doctor holds the patient's ankle with one hand and the knee with the other hand in order to abduct the lower leg and rotate the thigh internally. The angle of abduction of the lower leg at this time is the angle of internal rotation of the hip joint (Fig. 3-43).

7. Knee

The movements of the knee joint include flexion, extension, external rotation, and internal rotation.

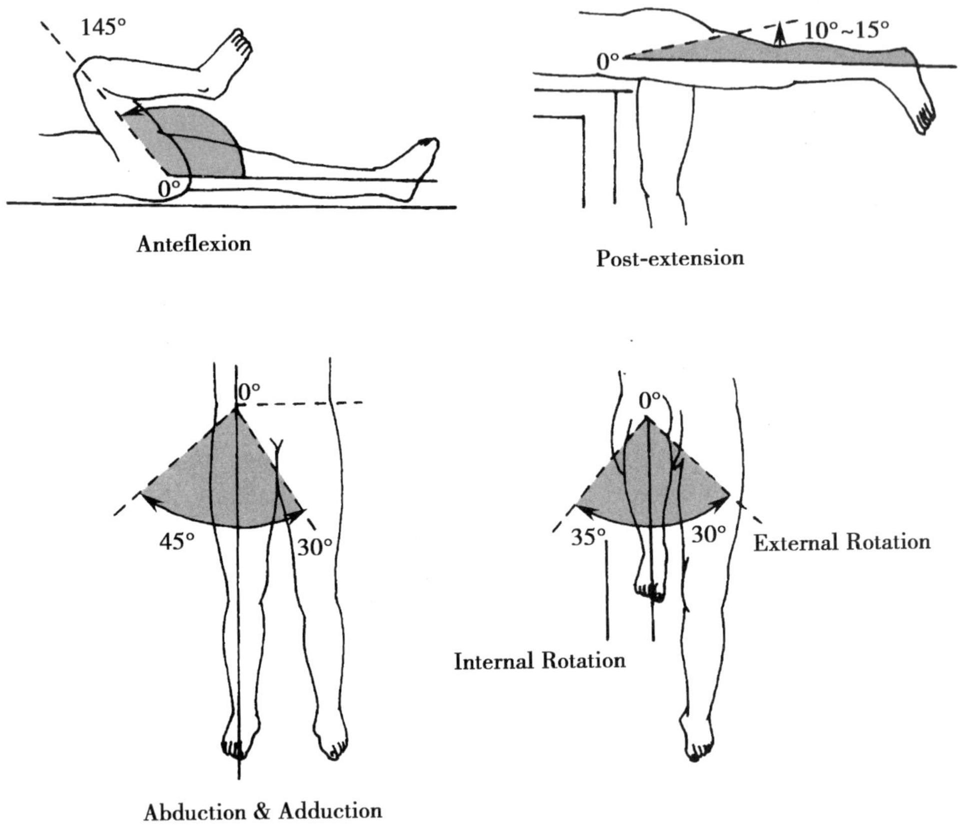

Fig. 3-43 Anteflexion, post-extension, abduction, adduction, external rotation and internal rotation of the hip

a. Flexion

Normally, the knee joint can flex up to 145°. During the examination, the patient assumes a prone position with straightened legs, and the doctor holds the patient's ankle with one hand and presses the lower part of the thigh with the other hand, and then asks the patient to flex the knee. The primary muscle involved is the hamstring muscle.

b. Extension

Normally, the angle of knee extension is 0°. Young people and females have 5° ~ 10° of hyperextension. During the examination, the patient, sitting on the bed side with lower legs dropping down naturally, extends the knee actively. The primary muscles involved are the quadriceps.

c. External Rotation and Internal Rotation

Normally, the knee joint has no external or internal rotation movement when it is extended. However, when the knee joint is flexed to 90°, it has 10° ~ 20° of external or internal rotation. During the examination, the patient is asked to assume a supine position with the knee flexed to 90°. The doctor then holds the patient's ankle with one hand and the knee with the other hand to perform external rotation and internal rotation. The primarily involved muscles include the semitendinosus, the semimembranosus, the biceps femoris, and so on (Fig. 3-44).

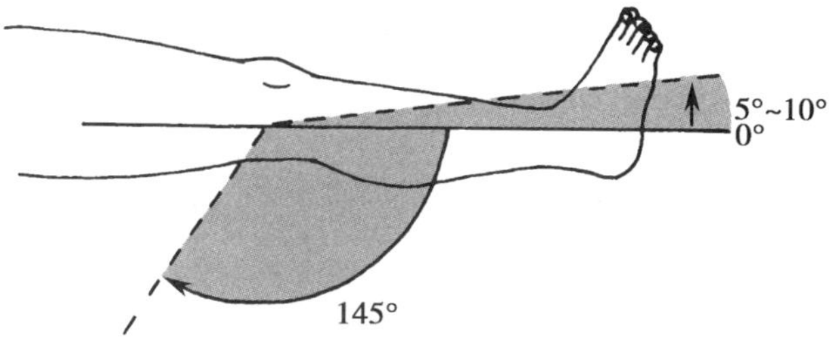

Fig. 3-44 Flexion, extension, external rotation, and internal rotation of the knee joint

8. Ankle and Foot

The main movements of the ankle and foot include ankle dorsiflexion, ankle plantar flexion, ankle varus, ankle valgus, and movement of the toes. During the examination, an angle of 90° between the foot long axis and the vertical axis of the lower leg is taken as the neutral position.

a. Ankle Dorsiflexion

Normally, dorsiflextion of the ankle joint is up to 30°. During the examination, the patient sits on the bed side with legs dropping down naturally. The doctor stands in front of him, holding the patient's heel with the hand to place the ankle joint in a neutral position. Then, the patient is asked to perform an ankle dorsiflexion movement. The priamary muscles involved are the tibialis anterior muscle, the extensor digitorum longus, and so on.

b. Ankle Plantar Flexion

Normally, ankle plantar flexion is up to 45°. During the examination, the position of patient and doctor is the same as in the above examination. Compare the two ankles when the patient is performing an ankle plantar flexion movement. The primary muscle involved is the triceps muscle of the calf.

c. Ankle Varus

Ankle varus movement mainly occurs in talocalcaneal articulation, and it can be up to 30° normally. During the examination, the position of patient and doctor is as same as in the above examination. Compare the ankles when the patient is performing an ankle varus movement. The primary muscle involved is the tibialis posterior muscle.

d. Ankle Valgus

Normally, ankle valgus movement is up to 30°. During the examination, the position of the patient and doctor is the as same as in the above examination. Compare the ankles when the patient is performing an ankle valgus movement. The primary muscles involved are the peroneus longus and the peroneus brevis.

e. Toe Movement

Toe flexion mainly occurs in the distal and proximal interphalangeal articulations of the foot, and dorsiflexion mainly in the metatarsophalangeal joint. For example, flexion of the 1st metatarsophalangeal joint can be up to 30°, and dorsiflexion up to 45° (Fig. 3-45).

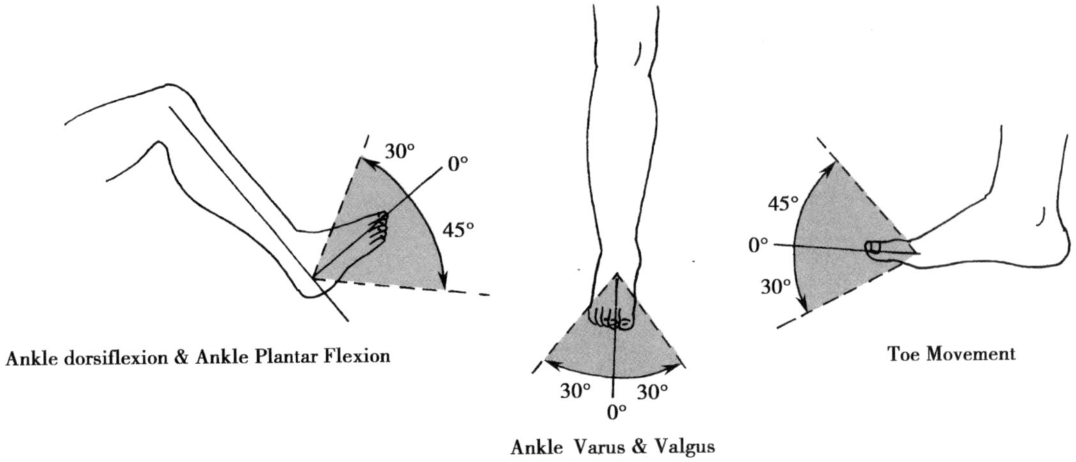

Fig. 3-45 The main movements of the ankle and foot

Chapter 4
Basic Practicing Methods of Tui Na Exercises

(Tui Na practicing methods are shown in the DVD)

Section 1
Characteristics and Actions

The practicing methods of tui na exercises are useful for keeping fit, and for preventing and curing diseases. They can also develop and enhance muscle power, and the functioning of internal organs. They are characterized by the following features:

Clear Movement and Comprehensive Training

The tui na doctor achieves therapeutic purposes by helping the patient to experience passive movement with various manipulations in an active way. Therefore, a tui na doctor must have an excellent body constitution and powerful finger, arm, waist and leg strength, which requires a self-training process. The practicing methods applied in tui na exercises, bare-handed practice, or practice with instruments, are effective in developing body constitution and strength, since they are highly targeted. Taking bare-handed practice as an example, it stresses step forms and stances to train the muscles and ligaments of the legs, as well as the abdominal, lumbar and back muscles, through various movements such as the bending and stretching of the lower limbs. Long-term practice increases the muscular strength of the lower limbs. In bare-handed practice, the movement of the palm is taken as the basis of many other movements. The palms are pushed from the sides of the ribs slowly and forcefully, the hands are moved up and down with spiral turning to twist and screw the forearm muscles, and to produce a kind of spiral energy through contraction, stretching and mutual muscular resistance, so that the muscular strength of the fingers, palms and upper limbs are greatly built up.

Focusing on Mental Qi and Emphasizing Internal Energy

Traditional Chinese medicine teaches that "Qi is the vital foundation of life". Qi and blood, which are circulated in the channels, support and nourish the limbs, the sensory orifices, the five *zang* organs and the six *fu* organs, so as to maintain normal vital activities. Only when qi and blood are abundant in the body does one have a strong body constitution. The special work of tui na therapy requires the tui na doctor have a health status of "equilibrium of yin and yang". So, the practicing methods of tui na exercises emphasize the accumulation of energy to enrich the essence and the blood. Such a good physiological state is achieved by following the principle of martial arts: "train tendons, bones and skin externally, and respiration internally", as well as the principle of qi gong: "breathe in essential qi and hold the mind". In practice, high mental activities are effective in promoting the transformation of "essence, qi and blood", in order to enhance their functions and quality. And then, "to lead qi with the mind transform qi into energy", produces "internal energy". The production of "internal energy" is the best play of the physiological function of the human body. Not only can it benefit vital functions, but it can also work actively to benefit patients during rehabilitation treatments with manipulations.

Combining Medical Treatment with Exercise and Practice to Strengthen Therapeutic Effects

The clinical work of tui na not only focuses on disease treatment, but it also pays more attention to preventing the occurrence and development of diseases, and these purposes are expressed very well in the tui na exercises. Some movements in tui na exercises are suitable for patients to practice, so tui na exercise is also a good approach to reinforce healthy qi and eliminate pathogens, and to inspire the enthusiasm of the patients.

For example, in the movements of bare-handed practice like *Pushing Eight Horses Forward* and *Pulling Nine Oxen Backward,* the hands are pushed forward from the sides of the ribs to make qi circulate in the middle energizer. These movements can invigorate the spleen and harmonize the stomach, promoting the functions of the stomach and intestines, and digestion, while enriching the source of qi and blood, resulting in abundant qi and blood. The movement like Phoenix Spreading Its Wings, performed by abducting the arms horizontally, can open the chest and create qi spreading in the upper energizer, to get the effect of easing the chest, benefiting qi, soothing the liver and strengthening the lung. When qi circulation is regulated, the upward liver qi is pacified, and conditions such as hypertension and dizziness can be prevented and cured. In addition, during practice, the movements of the lower limbs are always emphasized: "tough strength" (a firm stance performed by grasping the ground with all five toes, placing the heels steadily on the ground, with the legs fully straightened, exerting strength from the thighs) can promote qi in the lower energizer to strengthen the spleen and the lumbar regions, so as to prevent diseases of the urinary system and the reproductive system. The training of the neck, shoulders, waist, back, limbs and all of the joints enhances function and muscular strength, but it also prevents and cures the common diseases of these regions.

Section 2
Practicing Method for *The Classic of Sinew Transformation* (*Yì Jīn Jīng*, 易筋经)

The Classic of Sinew Transformation is a type of traditional exercise, known widely throughout Chinese folk culture, and is one of the common exercises that TCM orthopedic doctors and tui na doctors should practice. In Chinese, "*Yi* " means "vary and change", "*Jin*" denotes "tendons and muscles", while "*Jing*" implies "regulations and methods". *The Classic of Sinew Transformation* aims at strengthening and improving the functions of muscles, bones and tendons.

It is reported that *The Classic of Sinew Transformation* was devised by Bodhidharma, a famous monk in both the Southern and Northern Dynasties, because he found that some Buddhist monks were weak and unhealthy. The 12 Postures Moving Exercise, still in use to this day, is an exercise derived from the Songshan Shaolin Temple, and reformed by later generations. The majority of the movements are based on the working postures and movements of ancient peoples laboring in the fields, such as pounding rice, and transporting and storing crops. So *The Classic of Sinew Transformation* can be understood as deriving from the country life-style of the laboring people.

In *The Classic of Sinew Transformation*, most of the movements are coordinated closely with respiration, and are always practiced with static strength. Respiration should be comfortable and easy, it is forbidden to hold the breath. Abdominal breathing can be practiced through reverse breathing and orthodromic breathing. Reverse breathing is performed with abdomen held in and the chest thrust out while inhaling; orthodromic breathing is performed with abdomen thrust out and the chest held in while inhaling, and the abdomen held in while exhaling. Both of them can be used, but it is better to use orthodromic breathing at the beginning, because reverse breathing is comparatively stronger.

Before practicing *The Classic of Sinew Transformation*, some preparations are necessary: changing into loose-fitting clothing, and exercise shoes, or cotton shoes. During practice, keep an easy, static and natural mood, unify vigorousness with gentleness, and concentrate the mind in the pubic region (*dān tián,* 丹田) . This easy, static and natural mood denotes the relaxing of muscle and mind, and keeping quiet; unifying vigorousness with gentleness means to exert strength in the proper way, and not in a rigid way; concentrating the mind in the pubic region (*dān tián,* 丹田) implies meditating on the inside of the lower abdomen, but not too much. The pubic region (*dān tián,* 丹田), in a broad sense, indicates the area one cun below the umbilicus. In order to firm the lower part of the body, concentrating the mind in the pubic region (*dān tián*, 丹田) to assist abdominal breathing an increase the activities of internal organs by relaxing the head and the chest and promoting a downward blood circulation. After practice, or during the interval, don't expose the body to wind. It is better to engage proper movement, such as jogging and stretching the joints. In any case, no strenuous exercise is indicated.

Choose the practice (either doing just a few movements, or completing the whole set of exercises) according to the condition of the individual. However, it must be performed in an orderly, gradual and sustained way. Practice time, along with frequency and intensity of action, should be suited to person, time and place. Usually it is best to end the practice when one is slightly sweating. Don't over-practice. Do practice at least once a day. People with very weak body conditions are not advised to practice *The Classic of Sinew Transformation.*

Wéi Tuó Presenting Pestle (*Wéi Tuó Xiàn Chǔ*, 韦驮献杵)

1. Movement

Move the left foot a half step to the left, so that the feet are parallel and have a shoulder-width distance between them; stand with both knees slightly bent, all five toes firmly grasping the ground, and abduct the arms horizontally with the palms facing downward. Notice: do not extend the elbows or wrists in a rigid manner.

Move the palms forward, slowly close the hands, flex the elbows, and hold the arms and wrists inward to bring the wrists, elbows and shoulders to the same level, with the fingers straight.

Rotate the forearms inward to bring the finger tips facing toward the chest (at the level of

RN 22 (*tiān tū*)).

Slowly stretch the shoulders backward to bring the hands into a shape as if they were holding a ball. Then, the elbows slightly drop down, and the palm centers cave in, the fingertips, bent slightly, are facing each other at a distance of 4-5 inches, and the body leans forward slightly.

Ending: Take a deep breath first, then slowly breathe out and lower the hands.

2. Essential

Stand with the feet a shoulder-width distance apart. Relax the body with the torso erect, leaning forward slightly with the shoulders dropped down. Look forward with half-closed eyes, since this will calm the heart and mind. Staring upward may cause the heart spirit to float upward, and staring downward would cause the heart spirit to descend, resulting in imbalance. The head and neck should be stretched up as if one were holding something on the vertex. Open the mouth slightly with the tongue tip against the palate. Breathe in rapidly and out slowly, contract the buttocks and lower abdomen. Keep the armpits loose, and raise the hands with palms facing each other. Such a standing position puts the lungs into the right position, with freedom of movement, so as to reach an artistic conception with a clarified mind and spirit.

3. Note

Form 1 is used to train the muscles of the arm, such as the deltoid muscle, the brachial triceps, the forearm supinatus muscles and the extensor groups, and also to train the external and internal sphincter of the anus. Long-term practice increases arm strength, energy and stamina, which are the most important links in the training. If the patient practices this form, it can regulate qi circulation, keep the blood vessels free, and enhance therapeutic effect. For example, if the patient with hemorrhoids or hypertension can persist in practicing this form, their disease and health will be much improved. The patient must concentrate the mind during the practice. The beginner practices this form for 3 minutes each time. After one week, add 2 minutes each time every week until reaching 10 minutes. Then, add 1 minute each time every week until 30 minutes is reached. After that, practice for longer or shorter periods, according to the patients' body condition. For those people with weak body conditions, or with chronic disease, only do half of the practice.

Monster Controlling Magic Pestle (*Héng Dǎn Xiáng Mó Chǔ*, 横胆降魔杵)

1. Preparation

The same as the starting position of *Wéi Tuó* Presenting Pestle.

2. Movement

Move the left foot one step away to achieve a shoulder-width distance between the feet, press the hands downward forcefully with the palms facing the ground, and the fingers pointing forward, and look straight ahead.

Turn the palms upward and raise the hands to the chest. Push the hands forward slowly to a level higher than the shoulder. The strength should be concentrated on the lateral side of the thumbs.

Separate the hands to the left and to the right, with strength concentrated on the lateral side of the thumbs. Extend the arms with the palms facing downward to bring the shoulders, elbows and wrists to the same level.

Stretch the knees, and lift the heels with the anterior part of the soles touching the ground. Open the eyes as much as possible and clench the teeth.

Ending: Take a deep breath, and then breathe out slowly; bring down the hands and heels, and close the eyes for a while.

3. Essential

Abduct the arms to shoulder lever. The key point is to stand on tiptoe, so that a sensation similar to carrying a heavy load on the shoulders can occur in this position. Later, when the skill level is greater, it will be possible to stand on only the big toes. In this movement, the mind should be concentrated in the soles of the feet and the tips of the toes. Only in this way can one be calmed down, and the external sign of internal calm is staring eyes and clenched teeth. Looking around, opening and closing the mouth constantly and breathing roughly may run counter to the original goal, or even make standing firmly impossible, so that the practice fails.

4. Note

This form follows Form 1 directly, i.e. when Form 1 ends, raise the elbows slowly to shoulder level, and then turn the palms and extend the arms forward to create the movement of this form. Form 2 focuses on training the deltoid muscle, the triceps muscle of calf, the toe extensor muscular group, the quadriceps muscle of the thigh, the external and internal anal sphincter, the masseter muscle, the orbicular muscle of the eye, and so on. Persisting in the practice increases muscular strength, regulates qi circulation and strengthens the body. Since it is effective in regulating the balance of the body, this form may help patients with cerebellar ataxia to improve symptoms. The beginner does the practice 3 minutes each time, then, one week later, adds 2 minutes each time every week until 20 minutes is reached each time, or usually, up to about 30 minutes each time, or only 15 minutes if the practitioner is sick or weak in body constitution.

Supporting Heaven Gate with Palm (*Zhǎng Tuō Tiān Mén,* 掌托天门)

1. Preparation

The same as the starting position of *Wéi Tuó* Presenting Pestle.

2. Movement

Move the left foot one step away to obtain a shoulder-width distance between the feet. Calm the mind and regulate the breath.

Raise the hands to the chest, and then turn the wrists, and palms with closed fingers, downward. The palm center is slightly hollow, and the distance between the fingertips of the two hands is 1~2 cm, and the hands are not higher than the shoulders.

Raise the hands over the head, and turn the palms upward together with a distance of 1 cm between the fingertips. Close the four fingers with the thumbs abducted to form a quadrangle between LI 4 (*hé gǔ*) of both hands.

Throw the head backward, staring at the dorsum of the hands, lift the heels to shift the body center to the front part of the soles, and clench the teeth.

Ending: The same as *Wéi Tuó* Presenting Pestle.

3. Essential

In this form, stare upward at the hand dorsum but don't throw the head backward too much. It is difficult for the beginner to throw the head backward, because the movement may cause dizziness and an unstable stance. Standing on tiptoe implies that the heels should be lifted as much as possible, but the beginner may do the practice without lifting the heels, if it is difficult for them. The heels should be apart when they are lifted. It is a posture to close yinqiao mai, and open yangqiao mai, so as to make qi and blood of the three yang channels ascend upward to joint du mai. When yang qi flows evenly in du mai, the three passes on the back will be naturally smooth, and the posture of the body will be firm. In addition, relax the body fully to encourage the blood's circulation in following the heart's functions. It is not advisable to hold strength in the arms, because it makes it impossible to maintain a standing posture for long time. Contract the anus and clench the teeth with the tongue tip placed against the palate to link up ren mai and du mai.

4. Note

This form aims to train the strength of various muscle groups of the upper limbs, the triceps muscle of calf, and the levator ani muscul. It improves the overall stability of coordination. The more important thing is that this form allows cerebral blood perfusion, and blood elasticity is significantly increased to maintain an adequate supply of qi and blood, and to refresh the mind. Long-term practice may promote longevity. Patients with hypertension are not advised to practice this form, but it has a marked effect on raising the blood pressure in patients with hypotension, if they persist in practice. The beginner does the practice 3 minutes each time every week. At the second week, add 2 minutes each time every week until 20 minutes is reached each time. Then, add 1 minute each time every week until 30 minutes is reached each time. People with a weak body condition may just do the practice in half the time.

Picking Star and Changing Constellation (*Zhāi Xīng Huàn Dǒu,* 摘星换斗)

1. Preparation

The same as the starting position of *Wéi Tuó* Presenting Pestle.

2. Movement

The right foot steps forward half a step, and the distance between the feet is approximately the width of a fist. Clench the left hand into an empty fist and put it over *yāo yǎn* (腰眼), while the right hand drops down along the medial aspect of the right thigh.

Squat down by bending the left leg. The right foot touches the ground with the toes, the heel lifted. Keep the body straight, without any movement.

Flex the right wrist and bend the fingers slightly to form a hook shape, and then raise the hand along the chest to the right temple. The hand is approximately the width of a fist away from the right temple.

Move the finger tips slightly toward the right side. Raise the head slightly to the right side, staring at the palm center. Inhale quickly and exhale slowly to cause qi sinking. The body center is more on the back leg and less on the front.

Ending: Inhale quickly and exhale slowly, and return to the preparation position. Then, change sides and repeat the same movement.

3. Essential

In this form, only one hand is raised with all five fingers closed slightly, the wrist bent like a hook. The hand is approximately a fist-width away from the right temple, elbow toward the chest, the finger tips outward, the head slightly deviated, and the shoulder relaxed. It is important to stare at the palm center. Open the mouth a bit with the tongue tip placed against the palate to regulate breath. The buttocks should be held in slightly. The front leg steps on tiptoe, carrying 30%-40% of body weight; the back leg stands on the ground to support 60%-70% of body weight. When the posture is changed, the front leg withdraws half of a step backward. The movement is the same on both sides.

4. Note

This form is more difficult than other forms. It plays an important role in tui na exercises. During the practice, concentrate the mind in the palm center, relax the body with the upper part eased and the lower part firmed. Promote qi with the mind and make qi follow the mind. Keep composure to maintain a smooth blood circulation so as to preserve a sufficient potential in the various parts of the body to lay a solid foundation of the clinical application of the manipulations. The practice should follow in order and advance step by step, and hasty action must be avoided. The form may increase the tension of the wrist flexor muscles, the triceps, the lower limb flexion and extension muscles, and the levator ani muscle. Longer-duration practice may cause a warm and numb feeling in the palms. The beginner does the practice 2 minutes each time, and after one week, adds 1 minute each time every week until 7 minutes is reached each time. Then, add 1 minute each time every two weeks until 10 minutes is reached each time. After that, prolong the practice according to concrete conditions. Usually 15 minutes is enough. This form is not suggested for people with weakened body conditions and chronic diseases.

Pulling Nine Oxen by Their Tails (*Dào Zhuài Jiǔ Niú Wěi*, 倒拽九牛尾)

1. Preparation

The same as the starting position of *Wéi Tuó* Presenting Pestle.

2. Movement

Move the left foot one step (wider than shoulder width) away with the tips of the toes inward, bend the knees and squat down to form a horse stance, protect the waist with the fists, and look straight forward.

Raise the fists to the chest, and then open the fists with the palms facing each other, as if holding a ball (the position of the torso is the same as that of Wéi Tuó Presenting Pestle). Relax the shoulders, flex the elbows (which should be lower than the shoulders), keep the head erect and look straight forward.

Rotate the hands and face the palms outward (the four fingers closed and upright, the thumb abducted). Push the palms to the right and left respectively, until the elbows are fully extended. Relax the shoulders, extend the elbows, dorsiflex the wrists, and keep the shoulders, elbows and wrists at the same level.

Turn the body to the right side to form a right bow stance (facing the right). Move the arms simultaneously. Rotate the right arm to the outside, flex the elbow to form a semi-arc shape, the hand clenched into an empty fist, and stare at the fist, keeping the fist and shoulder at the same level. Do not bring the elbow beyond the knee, and do not let the knee protrude beyond the toes. Rotate the left arm inward and extend backward with spiral power, straighten the torso, sink the waist, hold the buttocks in, and regulate the breath.

Ending: Breathe in deeply and breathe out slowly, while returning to the preparation position. Do the same movement on the other side.

3. Essential

Stand in a bow stance with the front leg bent like a bow and the back leg straightened like an arrow, and the front elbow and wrist slightly bent in a semi-arc shape. The hand should be lower than the eyebrow, the elbow is not to exceed the knee, and the knee is not to exceed the foot. Bend the back elbow and wrist slightly and rotate the arm inward. Relax the shoulders and hold strength inward, forcefully, like a spiral turning, or like a rope twisting. Staring at the fist center (PC 8 (*láo gōng*)), lean the torso slightly forward, sink the body center, and open the mouth slightly with the tongue tip placed against the palate. Take an even breath through the nose, receive and send qi to the lower abdomen, and accumulate qi in the pubic region (*dān tián*, 丹田) . Turn to the left and repeat the same movement on the other side.

4. Note

During practice, the mind should concentrate on the movement. Guide the movement with the mind to strengthen the muscles of the arms. Long-term practice can enhance the conditions of the supinator and the pronator muscles, and increase finger strength.

Make empty fists and concentrate the mind on PC 8 (*láo gōng*). Pull the hands backward as if pulling the tail of nine cows. The beginner does the practice 3 minutes each time (1.5 minutes each side). Then, after one week, add 1 minute each time every week until 8 minutes are reached each time. Or, determine the time according to body condition

Displaying Paw and Spreading Wings (*Chū Zhǎo Liàng Chì*, 出爪亮翅)

1. Preparation

The same as the starting position of *Wéi Tuó* Presenting Pestle.

2. Movement

Make the hands into fists and place them at both sides of the waist with the palm centers facing the waist.

Slowly raise the fists to the chest and then open the fists with the thumbs abducted. Then, turn the palms upward and push them forward at shoulder level. The distance between the palms is about

2 inches. Slowly rotate the wrists and turn the palms, the thumbs touching each other, and the four fingers closed and extended, keeping the shoulders, elbows, wrists and palms at the same level. Then, separate and extend all ten fingers as much as possible to release strength into the fingertips. Look straight forward, as if carrying something on the top of the head.

Tilt the fingers upward forcefully with straight elbows and bended wrists, stare at the fingertips, thrust out the chest, and then clench the fists 7 times. Pull the hands backward forcefully.

3. Essential

Hold the fists as if to protect the waist. When breathing out, push the hands forward with the thumbs abducted forcefully at the shoulder level. Thrust out the chest and stretch the back, open the eyes without blinking, and concentrate the mind in the palm centers. Clench the fists 7 times, and then withdraw the hands while breathing in.

4. Note

This form is to train the flexing and extending of the muscle groups of the arm, and the strength of fingers. After much practicing, qi will be free to follow the mind so as to release strength from the shoulders to the finger tips by passing through the elbows and wrists. Therapeutic skill will certainly be enhanced.

The beginner can do the pushing and withdrawing movement of the hands relatively quickly. Later, slow down gradually. Practice meditation on the palm center 1 minute at the beginning. Add 1 minute each time every week until 7 minutes is reached each time, and then do the practice longer, accordingly. Usually 15 minutes is enough.

Nine Ghosts Pulling Sabre (*Jiŭ Guĭ Bá Mă Dāo*, 九鬼拔马刀)

1. Preparation

The same as the starting position of *Wéi Tuó* Presenting Pestle.

2. Movement

Raise the right hand over the head with the palm upward. Extend the elbow fully with the fingertips to the left. Press the left hand down with the fingertips forward.

Rotate the left arm backward with the palms downward and the fingertips to the right.

Flex the right elbow and rotate the wrist to hold the neck, and lean the head slightly forward. Then turn the left palm to face the back.

Raise the head upward and backward as much as possible while the right hand is pressing the neck and the elbow is raised as much as possible, with the movements of pressing and raising forming a resistant strength. Look to the left, with the five fingers behind the back pressing the lower back forcefully.

Ending: Take a deep breath and return to the preparation position while breathing out. Change sides and repeat the movement.

3. Essential

Push upward and press downward with straightened elbows. The fingers of the hand which is pushing up point to the opposite side, and the palm faces the sky. Rotate the wrist and turn the palm to hold the neck and press it down while the head tries to raise and look at the opposite side to form a resistant strength. The fingers of the hand which is pressed down point forward, the palm facing downward. Later, press the back tightly with the finger tips toward the opposite side. Repeat the same movement on the other side.

4. Note

This form is to train the extensor (brachial triceps) muscle, the nuchal muscles, the levator scapulae, and finger strength.

Another method of practicing this form is to lift the heels while doing the above movement. However, it should be done when the skill is perfect, otherwise, it is difficult to stand firmly, and can even cause a disorder of qi, thus failing to achieve training purposes. From the first movement of this form, concentrate the mind in *dān tián* (丹田) with gentle breath (chest resperation) to relax the neck, chest and shoulder and smooth qi circulation; then, gradually shift the mind to upper back (posterior dān tián). This form is not available for the patient with hypertension. Practicing the form 1 minute each time in the first week, add 1 minute each time every week until 5 minutes is reached each time. After that, the practicing time can be prolonged accordingly, usually 10 minutes is long enough.

Three Plates Falling on Ground (*Sān Pán Luò Dì*, 三盘落地)

1. Preparation

The same as the starting position of *Wéi Tuó* Presenting Pestle.

2. Movement

Move the left foot one step away, so that the distance between the feet is wider than shoulder-width. The toes are pointed slightly inward. Bend the knees to squat down with arms akimbo.

Turn both palms upward as if supporting something. Raise the hands along the chest slowly to the shoulder level, and not higher than the eyebrow. The distance between the hands is about 30cm.

Turn both palms downward and press down slowly with all fingers separated in a natural way, LI 4 (*hé gŭ*) of the two hands facing each other as if holding an object with the hands, then press down until the hands are almost toughing the knees (or place the empty fists over the knees). The body leans slightly forward.

Extend the torso fully to achieve a bow-like shape with the back. Relax the shoulders, close the elbows into the trunk, look straight forward, open the mouth, clench the teeth, and contract the anus.

Ending: Take a deep breath and return to the preparation position while breathing out.

3. Essential

Thrust the chest out slightly to shape the back like a bow. Rotate the elbows inward slightly, hold the head erect as if supporting an object with the vertex, look straight forward, place the tongue tip against the palate, with the mouth slightly open, breathe regularly through the nose, contract the anus, maintain the body center between the feet, bend the knees to 90° , but not extending over the tips of the feet, and concentrate the mind in the pubic region (*dān tián*, 丹田).

4. Note

This form, if it is practiced in the correct way, keeps the mind in the vertex and qi in the pubic region(*dān tián*, 丹田) , so as to maintain normal circulation of qi and blood, and make the arms stronger. This form can also train the quadriceps muscle and the muscles of the back, and is one of the exercises that the tui na doctor must practice. The beginner does the practice 2 minutes each time. Then, after one week, add 1 minute each time every week until 5 minutes is reached each time. Then add 1 minute each time every two weeks until 8 minutes is reached.

Blue Dragon Displaying its Claws (*Qīng Lóng Tàn Zhuǎ*, 青龙探爪)

1. Preparation

The left leg takes one step to the left to achieve a shoulder-width distance between the feet. The fists, with the palms facing upward, are placed by the sides of waist, as if protecting the waist. Keep the torso and head erect, and look straight forward.

2. Movement

Stretch the left arm to the right and upward over the head, palm up. Turn the body to the right side at the same time, relax the shoulder, and straighten the elbow and wrist. Place the right fist, palm up, against the waist. Look at the left palm and stand firmly on the ground.

Flex the left thumb to the center of the palm, while staring at the thumb.

Rotate the left arm inward, palm facing down. Bend the body to touch the ground with the hands. The knees should be straight, with the heels fixed on the ground. Raise the head and look forward.

Move the left hand away from the ground and up to the waist by passing around the left knee. Then, turn the left hand palm upward, and withdraw the hand as if to protect the waist. Change sides and repeat the movement.

3. Essential

Place the fists at the sides of waist, the left fist turning into the palm at the right side. Looking forward, keep the palm flat, and no higher than the eyebrow. Bend the thumb inward with the other four fingers closed. Relax the shoulder, and extend the elbow and the palm. Bend the body to press the hands to the ground. Extend the body while the hand passes by the knee and the feet remain firmly on the ground. The movement is done in the same way bilaterally.

4. Note

This form is the movement used to train the lung, liver, gallbladder and *dai mai*. Long-term practice can sooth the liver, and benefit the gallbladder, while ventilating the lungs and contracting *dai mai*. It is a good self-training method for disorders of the lung, liver and gallbladder, as well as gynecological disorders due to looseness of the *dai mai*, and is also a good approach to achieve longevity in healthy people. During the practice, concentrate the mind on the pubic region (*dān tián*, 丹田) , and fill the fingers with power through meditation. The tui na doctor practicing this form can increase the strength of the arms and fingers, and this form is one of the basic movements in practicing one-finger-pushing manipulation. The beginner does the practice 3 minutes each time. Add 2 minutes each time every week until 7 minutes is reached each time. Then, add 1 minute each time every two weeks until 10 minutes is reached each time. After that, add time accordingly.

Hungry Tiger Pouncing on Its Prey (*È Hŭ Pū Shí*, 饿虎扑食)

1. Preparation

The same as the starting position of *Wéi Tuó* Presenting Pestle.

2. Movement

The left foot takes a big step to the left, and the right foot slightly turns toward the left side to form a left bow stance.

Move the hands forward to touch the ground with the fingers, the palms suspended above the ground. Lift the heel of the back leg slightly, and face upward.

Withdraw the front foot and put the dorsum of the foot on the heel of the back foot. Slightly hold the chest and abdomen in, and face upward.

Withdraw the whole body with the buttocks thrusting out, extend the elbows, raise the head; and move the body forward, about 2 inches away from the ground. At this moment, with the elbows bent, the right foot touches the ground with the toes, punching forward with the buttock thrusting out. Repeat the movement to achieve a wave-like movement with the body, or a movement like a hungry tiger pouncing on its prey.

Ending: Slowly stand up with the breath. Change sides and repeat the movement.

3. Essential

Raise the head, neither too high nor too low, look forward, and extend the elbows and knees, but not in a rigid manner. It is forbidden to practice with abrupt force. Hold strength, draw the body backward, with the buttocks thrust out and the chest held in, while breathing in. Punch forward while breathing out with a kind of gentle strength, which may keep the body airborne for a while, maintaining the body's balance. Breathe freely, and do not hold the breath when the movement is repeated; breathe in quickly and breathe out slowly. Change sides and repeat the movement.

4. Note

This form can strengthen the tendons and bones, increase finger skill, enhance the strength of the flexor and extensor muscles of the arm and the toes, and train the muscles of the waist and abdomen. The beginner may touch the ground with the palm and fingers together. After a period of practice, when the arm force is stronger, touch the ground with five fingers and palm suspended above the ground, and later, three fingers (thumb, index and middle fingers), or two fingers, or only one finger. Repeat, with the body waving 4 times on each side at beginning. Later, add 2 times to each practice every week until 10 times is reached at each practice. This form is not recommended for people with a weakened body condition.

Bowing Down to Beat the Drum (*Dǎ Gōng Jī Gǔ*, 打躬击鼓)

1. Preparation

The same as the starting position of Wéi Tuó Presenting Pestle.

2. Movement

The left foot takes a step to the left, the toes turning slightly inward. Slowly raise the hands, palms upward, from the sides of the thighs to shoulder level, the neck erect as if the head were carrying objects. Look straight ahead, relax the shoulders, and extend the elbows and wrists, keeping the body straight, and the wrists, elbows and shoulders at the same level.

Interlace all ten fingers to hold the head by the occiput. Don't protrude the abdomen or buttocks.

Bend the knees and squat down to form a horse stance.

Extend the knees and bend the body. Both hands press the head down to the thighs with the knees straightened and the heels firmly on the ground. Meanwhile, cover the ears with the palms and hit the back of the head with the fingers Hit the Heaven Drum (*Míng Tiān Gǔ*, 鸣天鼓). The left hand and right hand are alternated, 24 times on each side.

Ending: Stretch up, and drop the hands down with the breath.

3. Essential

Hold the head with the palms and fingers, a resistant force between the head and hands, and standing with straight legs. Squat down with an erect torso, leaning the body forward to lower the head. Keep the knees bent, exert strength from the elbows, place the tongue tip against the palate, and keep the breath free, hitting the heaven drum 24 times on each side.

4. Note

There are a few ways to practice this form: with toes-closed stance, with heels-closed stance and with squatting stance. The form is used as a basic exercise to train the waist, legs, nape and buttock. It is useful for the clinical application of pressing manipulation and shaking manipulation. The beginner does the practice 2 minutes each time. One week later, add 1 minute each time every week until 10 minutes is reached each time. The form is not suggested for the people with hypertension.

Shaking the Head and Tail (*Diào Wěi Yáo Tóu*, 掉尾摇头)

1. Preparation

The same as the starting position of *Wéi Tuó* Presenting Pestle.

2. Movement

Raise both hands with palms facing upward in front of the chest until the hands are over the head, with the glance following the hands, while keeping the body straight.

Cross the hands by interlacing the fingers, then push the hands upward, palms facing the sky, extend the elbows, and look straight ahead.

Stretch the body backward, and move the arms backward. Look upward.

Bend the body forward, press the palms down to the ground, raise the head and stare upward. Extend the knees, and do not lift the heels from the ground.

Ending: Slowly finish the movement along with the breath.

3. Essential

Cross the hands by interlacing fingers and extend the arms fully upward. The torso leans forward to push the palms straight down to the ground. The knees and elbows should be straight. Raise the head with eyes wide open.

4. Note

This form is able to relax the channels and collaterals, strengthen the tendons and bones, and enhance the power of the waist, arms and hands. It is the chief exercise to train the tendons and bones. The form is the ending exercise of *The Classic of Sinew Transformation*, and it seems like a simple exercise, but it can achieve the effect of normalizing the twelve channels and the eight extraordinary vessels, so as to promote the circulation of qi and blood, causing a kind of ease and happy feeling after the practice. The beginner repeats the movement 3 times. Then, add 2 times to each practice every week until 15 times is reached at each practice. After that, determine the times accordingly.

The twelve postures of *The Classic of Sinew Transformation* can be practiced one by one for about 30 minutes, or, alternatively, just practice a few forms according to individual conditions, to strengthen the body and dispel diseases.

Section 3
Practicing Method for *Shào Lín* Internal Exercise (*Shào Lín Nèi Gōng*, 少林内功)

Shào Lín Internal Exercise (*Shào Lín Nèi Gōng*, 少林内功) is a component part of internal energy (*Nèi Gōng*, 内功) tui na. It is, according to legend, derived from the movement of *shào lín* martial arts by Bodhidharma. Originally, the exercise was used to strengthen the body by the masters of martial arts. Passed on from generation to generation, this exercise became a training method for associating tui na therapy.

The practicing method of *Shào Lín* Internal Exercise is different from that of other qi gong: it doesn't stress respiration and meditation, but rather emphasizes leading qi with strength. During the practice, one must stand firmly with the toes grasping the ground and the heels firmly planted on the ground, the legs extended fully, and the tips of the feet slightly inward, the thighs closed as much as possible, and the body erect. Thrust out the chest, hold the abdomen in, and keep the chin in. It is necessary to accumulate energy in the shoulders, arms, elbows, wrists and fingers while the upper limbs are trained. Breathe naturally with the movements. During practice, send strength to the four limbs, back and waist. Qi is guided by energy to the meridians to normalize the circulation of qi and blood; to nourish the four limbs, the nine orifices, the five *zang* and the six *fu* organs; to restore the balance of yin and yang; and to tonify qi and blood, so as to strengthen the body constitution and dispel the pathogenic factors. In the practice of *Shào Lín* Internal Exercise, many movements are done with stationary muscle energy, but the breath should be regular and natural, it is not advisable to hold the breath. The movement should be performed firmly and flexibly, tempering toughness with gentleness.

Since the whole body is tensed and energized during the practice, and bit by bit, metabolism is stimulated, digestion is strengthened and the functioning of the nervous system is regulated.

Basic Stances

Standing Stance (*Zhàn Dāng Shì*, 站裆势)

1. Movement

Standing upright, the left foot takes one step to the left to achieve a shoulder-width distance between the feet, and the toes are turned slightly inward to form a pigeon toe pose. Grasping the ground forcefully with the toes, make the power radiate from the torso to the feet.

Slightly protrude the chest, hold the buttocks in, stretch the hands backward, extend the elbows and wrists, close the four fingers with the thumb apart, and look straight ahead (don't move the head). Concentrate the mind and breathe naturally.

2. Essential

The essentials of this stance focuses on three straight lines and four flat surfaces: the buttocks, waist and legs should be kept straight; the head, shoulder, palm and foot should be flat. Stand with the tips of the feet pointed slightly inward to produce a kind of tough force. Hold the shoulders back. Extend the elbows and wrists, and turn the palms with straight fingers. Thrust out the chest and hold in the abdomen, with the tongue tip placed against the palate. Breathe naturally, and look straight ahead.

3. Note

This stance is the basic stance in practicing Shào Lín Internal Exercise. In practice, stand with tough energy by pointing the tips of the feet inward, toes grasping the ground, and holding the thighs tightly closed by contracting the muscle groups in the medial aspect of the thighs such as the phalanx muscle, the gracilis muscle, the long adductor muscle, the short adductor muscle and the large adductor muscle. The strength is released from the upper part to the feet. Extend the arms backward by contracting the latissimus dorsi, the teres major muscle, and the posterior beam of the deltoid muscle. Close the scapulas by contracting the trapezius muscle. Dorsiflex the wrists by contracting the posterior muscle group of the forearm, such as the extensor carpi radialis longus. Extend the fingers fully by contracting the extensor policis longus and the extensor digitorum. In a word, accumulate strength in the four limbs to lead qi to the limbs. The terminal ends of the limbs are the roots of the twelve channels. The free circulation in the channels will nourish the limbs and all the tissues in the superficial portion, but will also support the *zang-fu* organs to regulate yin and yang, promote circulation of qi and blood, and enhance the functions of the *zang-fu* organs, so as to achieve the effect of strengthening healthy qi and eliminating pathogen.

Horse Stance (*Mǎ Dāng Shì*, 马裆势)

1. Movement

Standing upright, the left foot takes a step to the left. Bend the knees to squat down with a distance wider than shoulder-width between the heels, with the knees and toes turning slightly inwards. Focus strength at the posterior and lateral sides of the heel. The shape of the feet is like that of pigeon toe pose.

Stretch the arms backward, extend the elbows and wrists, close four fingers with the thumb apart; or put hands horizontally at the hip sides with LI 4 (*hé gǔ*) towards the hip. Thrust out the chest, hold in the abdomen, set the body center between the legs, the head erect as if supporting an object. Look straight ahead and breathe naturally.

2. Essential

Sink the waist, bend the knees, thrust the chest out and hold the abdomen in, look straight ahead, and keep the breath natural.

3. Note

This stance aims to train the lower part of the body, i.e. to train "stance strength". Based on the semitendinosus, the semimembranosus, the biceps femoris, the sartorius, the gracilis and the gastrocnemius, bend the knees to squat down, with the knees and balls of the feet inward, and contract the antagonist (quadriceps) to maintain horse stance. Additionally, while performing actions of the sacral spine muscle, the rectus abdominis, the external oblique muscle, the internal oblique muscle and the transverse abdominal muscles, thrust the chest out, hold the abdomen in, and keep the body center between the legs, so as to strengthen the lumber region and tonify the kidneys.

Bow Stance (*Gōng Jiàn Dāng Shì*, 弓箭裆势)

1. Movement

Stand upright, turn the body to the right, and then the right foot takes a big step to the right and forward, the distance between the feet determined according to body height. Bend the knee of the front leg (the right leg) to squat down, keep the knee and the toes on a vertical line and turn the balls of the feet slightly inward. Extend the knee of the back leg (the left leg) with the heel touching the ground to form a bow stance.

Slightly lean the torso forward, sink the body center, hold in the buttocks, stretch the arms backward, and extend the elbows and wrists. Focus the strength at the root of the palms (or akimbo pose), set LI 4 (*hé gǔ*) inward, hold the energy inside, concentrate the mind, keep the neck and head erect, and breathe naturally.

2. Essential

The front leg is like a bow and the back leg like an arrow. Sink the body center, thrust the chest out, hold the abdomen in, and breathe naturally.

3. Note

This stance is performed with the front leg like a bow and back leg like an arrow. That is to say, flex the hip and the knee of the front leg mainly with the iliopsoas, the rectus femoris, the tensor fasciae latae, the sartorius, the semitendinosus, the semimembranosus, the biceps femoris and the gastrocnemius muscles. Extend the back leg fully, mainly with the quadriceps muscle. During the practice, focus the energy on the back leg to maintain a state of lunging. After a period of practice, arm movements can be combined with this stance.

Close Stance (*Bìng Dāng Shì,* 并裆势)

1. Movement

Stand upright, kick the heels outward slightly, with the balls of the feet closed, and the toes grasping the ground firmly with equal force.

Extend the wrists and elbows backward, palms downward, the fingers closed and the thumbs apart, and look straight ahead.

2. Essential

The same as that of Standing Stance.

Big Stance (*Dà Dāng Shì,* 大裆势)

1. Movement

The left foot takes a big step to the left. Stand with the knees extended fully and the feet firmly on the ground.

Extend the hands backward with LI 4 (*hé gŭ*) opposite, the fingers closed, the elbows and wrists extended.

2. Essential

The same as that of Standing Stance.

Suspending Stance (*Xuán Dāng Shì,* 悬裆势)

1. Movement

The left foot takes a big step to the left. Bend the knee to achieve a half-squatting position. The distance between the feet is wider than that of horse stance.

Stretch the hands backward with the elbows and wrists extended, fingers closed and the thumbs abducted. This is also called Big Horse Stance (*Dà Mă Dāng,* 大马裆), since the movement of this stance is the same as the movement of horse stance.

2. Essential

The same as that of horse stance.

Basic Movements

Pushing Eight Horses Forward (*Qián Tuī Bā Pǐ Mǎ,* 前推八匹马)

1. Preparation

Stand in standing stance, or appointed stance.

2. Movement

Flex the elbows and place the erect palms at the sides of the costal region.

Keep the palms facing each other, with the thumbs apart, and the four fingers closed and pointing up. Focus the strength in the shoulders, arms and finger tips, and slowly push the arms forward forcefully until the shoulders and palms are on the same level. Slightly straighten the chest and withdraw the arms a little without moving the head. Look straight ahead and breathe naturally.

Move the arms with the thumbs tilted, keep the fingers and arms on the same line, and slowly bend the elbows and draw them back to the sides of the ribs.

Turn the palms from an erect position to a downward position and then press down. Stretch the arms backward and return to the original stance.

3. Essential

Accumulate strength in the arms and fingers, slowly push the hands with erect palms forward, look straight ahead and breathe naturally.

4. Note

This pose is the basic skill of internal energy tui na. It is necessary to accumulate energy in the shoulders, arms and finger tips when the hands are pushed forward. The arms exert strength and push the hands forward, mainly with the brachial triceps.

Pulling Nine Oxen Backward(*Dào Lā Jiǔ Tóu Niú,* 倒拉九头牛)

1. Preparation

Stand in standing stance, or appointed stance.

2. Movement

Flex the elbows and place the upward-facing palms at the sides of the costal region.

Push the palms from the sides of the costal region forward, while gradually rotating the forearms inward. When the arms are fully stretched, LI 4 (*hé gǔ*) of both hands just face downward. The four fingers should be closed with the thumbs apart, and the wrists and elbows are straight at the shoulder level.

Bend the fingers to make fists as if holding something tightly, and focus the strength in the palm centers. Turn the wrists upward to make the index-thumb side of a fist (*Quán Yǎn,* 拳眼), withdraw the arms forcefully, stretch and face the palms up at the sides of the costal region, lean the body forward, and hold in the buttocks slightly.

Rotate the upward-facing palms to face them downward, then press the palms down, extend the arms backward and return to the original stance.

3. Essential

Push the erect palms forward while the arms are rotating, focus the energy in the palm center, stretch the elbows and wrists, keep the shoulders flat, and pull the hands backward forcefully.

4. Note

Rotate the forearms inward while the hands are pushed forward, mainly with the actions of the subscapularis muscle, the pectoralis major, the latissimus dorsi and the teres major muscle; LI 4 (*hé gŭ*) of both hands are facing downward when the arms are fully extended. Then, form the palms into fists with a contraction of the biceps of the humerus, the brachialis, the brachioradialis and the round pronator muscle. Holding the fists tightly with index-thumb side of a fist (*Quán Yăn,* 拳眼) upward, pull the hands backward forcefully, as if pulling nine oxen.

Pulling Golden Ring with One Hand (*Dān Zhăng Lā Jīn Huán,* 单掌拉金环)

1. Preparation

Stand in standing stance, or appointed stance.

2. Movement

Flex the elbows and place the erect palms at the sides of the costal region.

Rotate the forearm inward while pushing the right hand forward to make LI 4 (*hé gŭ*) downward, and face the palm outward when the arm is stretched. Close the four fingers with the thumb apart, focus the strength in the arm and palm, relax the shoulders, and keep the body straight. Look straight ahead and breathe naturally.

Flex the fingers to form a fist, and focus the strength in the palm center. Rotate the wrist to make index-thumb side of a fist (*Quán Yăn,* 拳眼) upward, then pull the hand backward forcefully and place the erect palms at the sides of costal region. After that, do the exercise with left hand. The movement is the same.

Rotate the erect palms downward and then press down. Extend the arms backward, and return to the original stance.

3. Essential

The same as that of Pulling Nine Oxen Backward.

4. Note

The same as that of Pulling Nine Oxen Backward.

Phoenix Spreading Its Wings (*Fèng Huáng Zhăn Chì,* 凤凰展翅)

1. Preparation

Standing in bow stance, or appointed stance.

2. Movement

Flex the elbows and move the hands upward slowly to the chest, and then cross the erect palms in front of the chest.

Rotate the palms from the erect position to the downward position, and then slowly separate the palms and extend the arms forcefully to the left and right like wings. Close the four fingers with the thumbs apart, and keep the head erect. Look straight ahead, slightly lean the body forward, making sure not to shrug the shoulders, and breathe naturally.

Rotate the wrists, flex the elbows inwards, accumulate strength and withdraw the hands slowly to face the palms towards each other, and then cross the erect palms in front of the chest.

Rotate the palms from the erect position to the downward position, press down and stretch the arms backward, and return to the original stance.

3. Essential

Cross the erect palms in front of the chest, abduct the arms forcefully, and keep the shoulders, elbows and wrists horizontal. Accumulate strength to adduct the arms.

4. Note

The abduction of the arms is mainly done by the action of the flexor carpi radialis, the flexor carpi ulnaris, the Palmaris longus, the digitus uperficial flexor and the digitus deep flexor. Rotate the erect palms into a downward position, and then abduct the arms forcefully, like a phoenix extending its wings, by contracting the deltoid muscle, the supraspinatus muscle and the muscle groups of the arm.

Conqueror Supporting Tripot (*Bà Wáng Jǔ Dǐng*, 霸王举鼎)

1. Preparation

Stand in bow stance, or appointed stance.

2. Movement

Flex the elbows and place the upward palms against the waist.

Raise the hands slowly, palms facing upward.

When the hands pass over the shoulders, rotate the palm roots outwards with the fingers turning inwards until LI 4 (*hé gǔ*) are facing each other, as if supporting a heavy object. Stretch the elbows continuously with the fingertips facing each other, and close the fingers with the thumbs apart. Look forward and breathe naturally.

Rotate the wrists until the small thenar are parallel, the fingers upright and the thumbs apart. Accumulate strength and withdraw the hands forcefully to the waist.

When the hands reach the sides of waist, change the palms from the upward position to the downward position, press down and extend the arms backward, and return to the original stance.

3. Essential

Push the hands upward with palms facing upward. Rotate the wrists and turn the palms only when the hands are passing over the shoulders, and then extend the elbows upward. Rotate the wrists and turn the palms while the hands are withdrawing, the fingers upward and the small thenar of both hands facing each other.

4. Note

It is necessary to rotate the wrists and turn the palms only when the hands are raised over the shoulders. Slowly extend the wrists and elbows upward as much as possible by contracting the extensor carpi radialis longus, the extensor carpi radialis brevis, the extensor carpi ulnaris, and all of the digitus extensor muscles.

Pushing the Boat Along the Water Flow (*Shùn Shuǐ Tuī Zhōu*, 顺水推舟)

1. Preparation

Stand in horse stance, or appointed stance.

2. Movement

Flex the elbows and place the erect palms at the sides of the costal region.

While the erect palms are pushing forward slowly, rotate the roots of the palms outward until LI 4 (*hé gǔ*) are facing downward, fingertips facing each other. The four fingers are closed and the thumbs abducted. The elbows are half-extended and the wrists half-flexed to form a ring shape between the arms. Keep the head and body erect. The palms, elbows and shoulders are on the same level.

Slowly rotate the hands outward to erect the palms, the four fingers closed and the thumb abducted forcefully. Bend the elbows, and accumulate energy to withdraw the hands to the sides of the costal region.

Change the palms from the upward position to the downward position, press down and stretch the arms backward to the original stance.

3. Essential

Accumulate energy to push the erect palms slowly, rotate the wrists until the finger tips are pointing to each other, and extend the elbows as if pushing a boat.

4. Note

When the erect palms are pushed forward, contract the subscapularis muscle, the pectoralis major, the latissimus dorsi, the teres major muscle and the muscle groups of the upper arms to rotate the forearms with accumulated strength. At the same time, dorsiflex the wrist joint as much as possible by contracting the extensor carpi radialis longus, the extensor carpi radialis brevis, the extensor carpi ulnaris and the extensor muscles of all the fingers.

Embracing the Moon (*Huái Zhōng Bào Yuè*, 怀中抱月)

1. Preparation

Stand in suspending stance, or appointed stance.

2. Movement

Flex the elbows and the place the upward palms at the sides of the waist.

Raise the palms upward from the waist, and change the palms from the upward position to the erect position and cross them in front of the chest. Then, slowly abduct the arms to the left and right, extend the elbows with the palms facing forward, and keep the palms and the shoulders at the same level.

Turn the hands downward and the palms inward. Slightly lean the torso forward, focus the strength in the palms and arms, and raise them as if embracing something. Finally, cross the hands with erect palms in front of the chest.

Change the palms from the erect position to the downward position, press down and stretch the arms backward, and return to the original stance.

3. Essential

Raise the palms upward, cross the hands with erect palms, and abduct the arms with the palms forward. Keep the wrists, elbows and shoulders at the same level, turn the hands downward with the palms inward, and lean the torso forward slightly. At the same time, move the arms upward slowly as if embracing the moon by contracting the pectoralis major, the latissimus dorsi, the teres major muscle and the biceps.

Immortals Guiding the Way (*Xiān Rén Zhǐ Lù*, 仙人指路)

1. Preparation

Stand in close stance, or appointed stance.

2. Movement

Flex the elbows, and place the palms upward at the sides of the waist.

Lift the right palm to the chest and then change to an erect palm. Push the palm forward with four fingers closed and the thumb apart. The center of the palm is hollow. Focus the strength in the elbow and the arm, and push the erect palm forward with even force.

Flex the wrist and bend the fingers to make a fist when the arm is fully extended. Withdraw the arm backward forcefully while the forearm is rotating outward to form an upward palm at the waist side; the movement of the left palm is the same as that of the right palm.

Change the palms from the upward position to the downward position, press down and stretch the arms backward, and return to the original stance.

3. Essential

Raise the upward palm, change the upward palm to the erect palm in front of the chest, and hollow the palm center. Exert strength with the arm and fingers to push forward forcefully, rotate the wrist and change the palm to a fist, and withdraw the hand to the side of the waist.

4. Note

It is necessary to have an erect palm when the hand is pushed forward. Then, close the four fingers with the thumb abducted, the palm center depressed, and exert strength from the upper arm and elbow to push the hand forward with the action of the volar interosseous muscle, the extensor pollicis longus and the lumbrical muscle.

Holding Tower with Flat Hand (*Píng Shǒu Tuō Tǎ*, 平手托塔)

1. Preparation

Stand in big stance, or appointed stance.

2. Movement

Flex the elbows and place the upward palms at the sides of costal region.

Slowly and forcefully push the upward palms forward, while the thumbs are separated from the other fingers. Keep the palms horizontal. The hands and shoulders should be at the same level when the arms are extremely extended.

Forcefully abduct the thumbs to the left and right, respectively, at a slant, and focus the strength in the fingers. Flex and withdraw the elbows with accumulated strength to the sides of the costal region.

Change the palms from the upward position to the downward position, press down and stretch the arms backward, and return to the original stance.

3. Essential

Push the upward palms forward with accumulated strength, the thumbs abducted at a slant, the elbows straightened and the palms flat as if supporting something in the hands.

4. Note

When the palms are pushed forward, contract the infraspinous muscle and the teres minor to rotate the forearms outward, keeping the palms flat.

Turning Palm to Fold Tile (*Yùn Zhǎng Hé Wǎ*, 运掌合瓦)

1. Preparation

Stand in big stance, or appointed stance.

2. Movement

Flex the elbows and place the upward palms at the sides of the waist.

Change the right palm from the upward position to the downward position, push the hand forward forcefully with strength released from the arm to the fingers, relax the shoulder and extend the elbow, the fingers pointing forward and the palm downward. Hold the strength for the next movement.

Rotate the right wrist to direct the palm upward and slowly withdraw the hand. Then change the left upward palm to the downward position when the right palm is close to the chest. Cross the hands, the left downward palm over the right upward palm, the palms thus facing each other, and then push the left downward palm slowly forward, and withdraw the right upward palm to the side of the waist.

Rotate left wrist to direct the palm upward, and slowly withdraw the hand. Then, turn both palms downward. Stretch the arms backward, and return to the original stance.

3. Essential

Push the upward palms forward with accumulated strength, relax the shoulders, and extend the elbows, finger tips forward.

4. Note

When pushing the palms forward, contract the round pronator muscle, the pronator quadratus muscle and the brachioradialis muscle to change the palms from the upward position to the downward position. Then, continue to push the palms forward.

Wind Blowing Lotus Leaf (*Fēng Bǎi Hé Yè*, 风摆荷叶)

1. Preparation

Stand in bow stance, or appointed stance.

2. Movement

Flex the elbows and place the upward palms at the sides of the waist.

Flex the elbows, palms upward, four fingers closed and thumbs apart. Push the palms upward and forward. At the level of chest, the left palm over the right palm, extend the arms extremely forward. Then, slowly abduct the arms until the shoulders, elbows and palms are at the same level. Focus the strength at the lateral sides of the thumb to bring the hands to a horizontal line. The head should be erect as if supporting an object. Look straight ahead and breathe naturally.

Slowly close the upward palms, the left hand over the right hand, and then withdraw the palms to the sides of the waist.

Change the palms from the upward position to the downward position, stretch the arms backward, and return to the original stance.

3. Essential

Push the hands forward with crossed, upward palms. Rotate the forearms outward, and extend the elbows and abduct the arms, with the shoulders, wrists and palms all at the same level.

4. Note

After placing the upward palms at the sides of the waist, contract the brachial triceps to push the hands forward fully with accumulated strength. Slowly abduct the arms by contracting the deltoid muscle, the supraspinous muscle and the other muscular groups of the upper arm to make bring the hands into a horizontal line.

Supporting the Sky with Two Hands (*Liǎng Shǒu Tuō Tiān*, 两手托天)

1. Preparation

Stand in suspending stance, or appointed stance.

2. Movement

Flex the elbows, and place the upward palms at the sides of the waist.

Slowly raise the palms up, palm centers facing the sky. Accumulate strength in the fingertips, relax the shoulders, and extend the elbows. Look straight ahead, and erect the head, as if supporting an object.

Rotate the palm roots outward with fingers closed, and slowly draw the hands downward with accumulated strength. Then, change the palms into the upward position when the hands are at the level of the chest, and finally, withdraw the upward palms to the sides of the waist, as if to protect the waist.

Change the palms from the upward position to the downward position. Press down and stretch the arms backward, and return to the original stance.

3. Essential

Push the upward palms up, accumulate strength in the finger tips, relax the shoulders, extend the elbows, and look straight ahead.

4. Note

Contract the deltoid muscle, the supraspinatus muscle, the trapezius muscle and the serratus anterior muscle, and push the palms up with accumulated strength, as if supporting the sky.

Single Phoenix Facing the Sun (*Dān Fèng Cháo Yáng*, 单凤朝阳)

1. Preparation

Stand in close stance, or appointed stance.

2. Movement

Flex the elbows and place the upward palms at the sides of the waist.

Change the left palm from the upward position to the downward position. Move the left elbow forcefully upward and to the left, then downward and to the right, and finally, move the hand upward to draw a half-circle back to the sides of the waist.

The movement of the right hand is the same as the movement of the left hand, only in the opposite direction.

Change the palms from the upward position to the downward position, press down and stretch the arms backward, and return to the original stance.

3. Essential

Rotate the wrist to change the position of the palm, move the arm outward with accumulated strength, and drop the hand down slowly, as if drawing a half-circle.

4. Note

Change the palm from the upward position to the downward position, move the hand upward and to the left by contracting the deltoid muscle, the supraspinatus muscle and the muscle groups of the arm. When it is fully abducted, move the arm downward by contracting the pectoralis major, the latissimus dorsi, the deltoid muscle, and the long head of the brachial triceps. Then, flex the elbow and raise the hands up in the shape of semi-circle.

Scooping the Moon from the Sea Bottom (*Hǎi Dǐ Lāo Yuè*, 海底捞月)

1. Preparation

Stand in big stance, or appointed stance.

2. Movement

Flex the elbows and place the upward palms at the sides of the waist.

Raise the arms, with palms facing upward, to the front of chest, then push the hands to the left and right respectively. Rotate the wrists until the palms are facing downward. Bend the body forward with the legs straightened, and the feet planted firmly. Move the arms downward from the sides, the palms turn upward and meeting each other as if engaged in an embrace. Keep the strength in the arms to prepare for the next movement.

Move the arms upward to the chest with the strength in the palm centers and the fingertips, as if holding up heavy objects. While the torso straightens, place the upward palms at the sides of the waist, and look straight ahead. Change the palms from the upward position to the downward position, press down and stretch the arms backward, and return to the original stance.

3. Essential

Raise the upward palms, and separate the hands when the palms are pushed up fully. Rotate the wrists, and turn the palms. Lean the torso with straight legs. The palms are facing upward, as if embracing the moon. Accumulate strength in the upper arms and exert strength in finger tips. Stretch the body slowly.

4. Note

Slowly raise the arms with upward palms to contract the supraspinatus muscle, the deltoid muscle, the serratus anterior muscle and the trapezius muscle; separate the arms to left and right by contracting the deltoid muscle and the supraspinatus muscle. After turning the palms, lean the torso forward slightly with the contraction of the abdominal muscles. Meanwhile, accumulate strength by contracting the pectoralis major, the latissimus dorsi, and the teres major muscle to move the hands from the upper side to the lower side, and then from the lower side to the upper side slowly, as if scooping the moon from the bottom of the sea.

Supporting the Sky and Embracing the Earth (*Dǐng Tiān Bào Dì*, 顶天抱地)

1. Preparation

Standing in big stance, or appointed stance.

2. Movement

Flex the elbows and place the upward palms at the sides of the waist.

Raise the upward palms. When the hands pass by the shoulders, rotate the wrists outward with the fingertips pointing to each other. After that, continue to raise the hands up.

When the arms are fully extended, rotate the wrists and turn the palms, slowly separate the arms, and move the hands downward. At the same time, bend the body forward. Close the palms with the thumbs apart, one over the other (the right palm above the left palm). Try to touch the ground with the dorsum of the hand to prepare for the next movement.

Raise the palms to the chest as if carrying a heavy object; then place the upward palms at the sides of the waist. Straighten up and look straight ahead.

Turn the palms from the upward position to the downward position, stretch the arms backward, and return to the original stance.

3. Essential

Raise the upward palms. When the hands are over the shoulders, rotate the wrists to point the finger tips toward each other. Then, turn the palms over and move the hands downward from the sides to the middle, with the body leaning forward and the hands overlapped, as if rising up an object.

4. Note

It is necessary to rotate the wrists and turn the palms only when the upward palms are raised over the shoulders. Contract the extensor carpi radialis longus, the extensor carpi radialis brevis, the extensor carpi ulnaris and all of the digital extensor muscles to dorsiflex the wrist joints as much as possible, and extend the elbows upward slowly. After that, contract the flexor carpi radialis, the flexor carpi ulnaris, the palmaris longus, the superficial flexor muscle or fingers, the deep flexor muscle of the fingers and the flexor muscle of the thumbs to rotate the wrists, turn the palms, separate the arms to the left and right, lean the torso forward, close and overlap the hands, and raise the hands slowly. Stretch the body along with the hands raised by the action of the sacral spine muscle.

Splitting Hua Mountain with Vigorous Efforts (*Lì Pī Huà Shān*, 力劈华山)

1. Preparation

Stand in bow stance, or appointed stance.

2. Movement

Flex the elbows, and cross the hands with the erect palms in front of the chest.

Slowly separate the arms and push the erect palms to the left and right. Relax the shoulders, and flex the elbows slightly, with the fingers closed, the thumb tilted backward, and the palms forward. Keep the arms at the same level.

Do the chopping movement three times. Don't shake the head during the movement, look straight ahead. Place the upward palms at the sides of the waist after the last chopping movement.

Turn the palms from the upward position to the downward position, press down and stretch the arms backward, and return to the original stance.

3. Essential

Cross the hands with erect palms, and then separate the hands to the left and right. Do the chopping movement forcefully, and look straight forward.

4. Note

When the arms are at a horizontal level, do the chopping movement three times with the accumulated strength from the trapezius muscle, the latissimus dorsi, the pectoralis major, the teres major muscle, the subscapularis muscle and the muscular groups of upper arm.

Chapter 5 Tui Na Manipulations

(Tui Na Manipulations are shown in the DVD)

Tui na manipulations are the methods for diagnosing, treating and preventing diseases by applying various special skilled movements on the body surface with hands or other parts of the body. The manipulations are performed in various ways and forms directly on the patient's body to achieve therapeutic effect by means of exerting strength from the continuous movement of the finger, palm, wrist or elbow, as well as butting or stepping.

Based on different types of stimulation, intensity and duration, miscellaneous basic manipulations such as pushing, pressing, kneading are formed. These basic manipulations are the main components in tui na manipulations. Compound manipulations are formed when two or more basic manipulations are performed in combination like pressing-kneading manipulation (*Àn Róu Fǎ, 按揉法*) and pushing-rubbing manipulation (*Tuī Mó Fǎ*, 推摩法). Compound manipulations are also seen in pediatric tui na. A series of movements are performed in combination and a special name is given like Crossing the heaven river on horseback (*dǎ mǎ guò tiān hé, 打马过天河*) and Wasps Going into Honeycomb (*huáng fēng rù dòng*, 黄蜂入洞). Tui na manipulations stimulate the different parts of the human body with functions of unblocking the channels and collaterals, moving qi and blood, smoothing joints and regulating *zang-fu* functions.

Tui na manipulations are considered as a kind of special skill, main means in tui na therapy. The skill of manipulations directly influences the therapeutic result of the treatment. The essentials of manipulations are sustained movement, forceful manipulation, even speed rhythm, gentle way and deep penetration. "Sustained movement" implies that the manipulations should be maintained strictly by following the skill requirement rules and instructions without any change in a considerable period of time. "Forceful manipulation" implies that the manipulations must possess certain appropriate force and strength. The force and strength should be varied and regulated according to the body constitution of the patient, health conditions and performed area. Unskillful and violent force is forbidden. "Even Speed and Rhythm" implies that the manipulations should be full of rhythm and speed and pressure should be maintained stable within a certain range. "Gentle way" implies that the manipulations should be gentle and careful, not violent. "Deep Penetration" implies that the stimulation must be penetrated deeply into the deep tissues. Only when the manipulations are consistent to sustained, forceful, even and gentle can the purpose of deep penetration be achieved.

Manipulation practice is mainly made to train the skill, arm strength, wrist strength and finger force. Practice can be done firstly on rice sack and on human body later. Prepare a sack with length about 26 cm and width about 20 cm. Fill about 4/5 of the sack with rice and seal the sack. At the beginning, the sack may be tied tight to benefit the training of finger force and the strength of palm, wrist and arm. Later, along with the improvement of skill, loosen the sack gradually. Manipulations including one-finger pushing, rolling, kneading, rubbing and vibrating and so on are practiced when the sack is placed flatly on the table. Rolling is practiced in a standing posture, while one-finger pushing and rubbing are practiced in a sitting posture. But there must be a certain distance between the body and the table, neither too close nor too far, no matter a standing or sitting posture, so as to guarantee the correct operation. At the same time, relax the arm and chest, drop down the shoulder and elbow, hold in the abdomen and buttocks and breathe naturally. Good operating posture should be trained from the beginning.

At the beginning, the main task is to take hold of the Essentials of Movements, not to apply pressure on the performed area, so that the manipulations are correctly performed. If the movements are incorrect and only pressure is heavily given, this will cause the hand muscles stiffness and prevents obtaining the right posture. Furthermore, it might hurt the joints and ligaments. After a period of serious training, one's manipulation would be right and standardized; every time, as long as the practice starts, it will naturally achieve the best mechanical condition, and increase penetration naturally. Meanwhile, it is necessary to enhance the endurance, e.g. maintain a continuous practice without stopping to extend the time of practice gradually. Usually, the single manipulation should last 10~20 minutes. For the convenience of applying manipulation, the hands are often used alternately in clinic to reduce fatigue. In training, the manipulations should be practiced with two hands alternately, not with one hand. After practicing on the sand sack and when the manipulations are skillful, the comprehensive practice can be done on the human body, such as head, face, neck, nape, limbs, back, shoulder, hip, chest, hypochondriac region, abdomen and so on.

Section 1
Basic Tui Na Manipulations for Adults

Basic tui na manipulation refers the manipulation performed with single movement. Basic tui na manipulation has a long history. There are big amounts of manipulations with stable operating movements and strict movement skills. They are the components constituting compound tui na manipulations.

One-finger Pushing (*Yì Zhǐ Chán Tuī Fǎ*, 一指禅推法)

One-finger pushing is a kind of pushing movement done with the tip, fingertips or radial side of the thumb, focusing the force and strength on channels, acupoints or areas. Relax the shoulder, elbow and muscles of the upper limb, effect on the channels, acupoints and areas with constant strength by waving movement of the wrist, flexion and extension of thumb joints.

1. Approaches of Manipulation

The operator makes a hollow fist with the thumb extended naturally and covering the fist hole. The wrist and palm are flexed in a natural way. The fingertip of the thumb is attached to the body surface of the patient.

Drop the shoulder and elbow and suspend the wrist naturally. Wave the forearm actively to lead transverse movement of the wrist and flexion-extension movement of the thumb, so as to effect on the channels and acupoints constantly with alternative change of light and heavy pushing. The frequency is 120 ~ 160 times / min.

2. Essential Movements

a. Shoulder Dropping

Relax the shoulder joint and drop the scapula naturally, keeping the axillary fossa loose with a fist breadth between the body and arm. Don't shrug with unnatural force.

b. Elbow Dropping

Drop down the elbow joint naturally, slightly below the wrist joint. Don't put the elbow too close or too far away from the trunk.

c. Wrist Suspending

Flex and suspend the wrist joint naturally. Try to flex the wrist to 90°, keeping the wrist joint relaxed.

d. Finger Attached

The fingertip or the thumb is placed on the performed area or points with natural strength. Don't press down with rough force.

e. Fist Hollow

Relax the rest of the four fingers and the palm except the thumb to make a hollow fist. Accumulate the strength in the palm and release the strength to the finger.

f. Pushing Quickly While Moving Slowly

This is the essential of one-finger pushing while the hand moving on the body surface. To push quickly implies that the frequency of waving movement is comparatively high, 120 ~ 160times /min. To move slowly implies that the tip of the thumb or fingertip, attached on the body surface, should move slowly along the channels and collaterals or special route without sliding or rubbing.

3. Precautions

Keep the correct body posture and essentials while operating. "Relaxation" is a word that should be kept in mind always when moving the shoulder, elbow and wrist. But "relaxation" doesn't mean slack, natural pressure should be applied in the operation instead of rough strength.

One-finger pushing has two different patterns. It depends on whether the interphalangeal joint of the thumb is flexed or not. If the operator's interphalangeal joint of the thumb is rigid, just able to move in a small range or the stimulation needed in the operation is gentle, the operation with extension and flexion of interphalangeal joint of the thumb may be applied. If the operator's interphalangeal joint of the thumb is tender and soft, it is advisable to do the operation with straight interphalangeal joint of the thumb. The operator should grip and fully understand both of them.

The frequency should be even, not advisable to be sometimes fast and sometimes slow.

4. Appendix: The evolution of one-finger pushing

a. One-finger pushing with radial side of thumb (*Yì Zhǐ Chán Piān Fēng Tuī Fǎ*, 一指禅偏峰推法)

The radial side of thumb at the location of LU11 (*Shào Shāng*) is taken as the working point. Extend and adduct the thumb while the rest the four fingers are extended straightly. Slightly flex the wrist joint, swing the forearm actively to lead a gentle waving movement of the wrist joint. Since the stimulation of this manipulation is swift and gentle, it is often used on the face.

b. One-finger pushing with interphalangeal joint of thumb (*Yì Zhǐ Chán Qū Zhǐ Tuī Fǎ*, 一指禅屈指推法)

Flex the thumb, do one-finger pushing with the radial or dorsal side of interphalangeal joint of the thumb. It is called one-finger pushing with interphalangeal joint of thumb (*Yì Zhǐ Chán Qū Zhǐ Tuī Fǎ*, 一指禅屈指推法) also called *Guì Tuī Fǎ*, 跪推法). This manipulation is done with stable strength, strong and powerful. It is often used on the nape, occipital region and bone aperture of joints.

c. Lingering manipulation (*Chán Fǎ*, 缠法)

Narrow the touching area of tip or radial side of thumb in one-finger pushing; reduce the waving amplitude of the forearm, lower down pressure given to body surface by the thumb and increase the waving frequency to 220 ~ 250 times/ min, it is called lingering manipulation (*Chán Fǎ*, 缠法). This method has a strong dispersing function. It is often used for excessive heat syndrome and external diseases like carbuncles and furuncles.

Rolling (*Gǔn Fǎ*, 㨰法)

With the fifth metacarpophalangeal joint attached on the performed area, roll the hypothenar and a part of the hand back continuously on the local area, which is led by complex movement of extending and flexing of the wrist and rotating of the forearm.

1. Approaches to Manipulation

Flex fingers naturally, place the dorsal part of the fifth metacarpophalangeal joint on the local area or points as the attached point.

Relax the shoulder joint, take the elbow joint as a supporting point. The forearm waves actively to lead flexion and extension of wrist joint and rotation of the forearm.

Taking the third, forth and fifth metacarpophalangeal joint as an axis, the medial side of hypothenar as another axis, the triangular area, formed by crossing of the two axes, is rolled on the performed area continuously, producing force and effect. The frequency of rolling is about 120 times/ min.

2. Essentials of Movements

Relax the shoulder, extend and abduct the upper arm to make the elbow apart from the chest in a distance of 15 cm, too much close to or too much far away may disturb the manipulation.

Flex the elbow into 120°~150°. Too large angle is not conducive to the rotating movement of the forearm; while too small angle is not good for the efficient action of rolling.

Relax the wrist joint, the amplitude of flexing and extending should be large. The rolling amplitude of hand dorsum should be controlled in the range of 120°; flexing amplitude of wrist is 80°~90° and extending amplitude 30°~40°.

The dorsum of the fifth metacarpophalangeal joint should be fixed on the performed area as a supporting point, the dorsum of hypothenar and hand should be attached on the local area to roll without any hauling, sliding and leaping movement.

The pressure, amplitude and speed of rolling should be relatively consistent, not sometimes quick sometimes slower, or sometimes lighter or sometimes stronger. The movement should be coordinated with regular rhythm.

Flex the fingers naturally and relax fingers and palm. It is not advisable to extend the fingers and palm too straight and tightly to make the dorsum of hand into a flat plane, which may affect the manipulation; neither bend the fingers forcefully to produce tension in wrist joint so as to limit the amplitude of rolling.

The operator stands with feet separated, lean upper portion of the body forward about 30°. The frequency of manipulation is 120 ~ 160 times/ min.

3. Precautions

Extend and flex the wrist joint to the maximum to avoid the wrong pattern that the rotation of the forearm is larger than flexing-extending amplitude of wrist joint.

The rolling movement should be fixed on the performed area without any hauling, turning and leaping movement. Avoid hitting activity between dorsum of hand and body surface. While moving the hand, try to avoid the hauling movement on the body surface.

Do not apply the manipulation on spinous process of vertebrae or catapophysis of the joints, since it may cause discomfort feeling.

4. Appendix: The Evolution of Rolling

Metacarpophalangeal-joint-rolling manipulation (*Zhǎng Zhǐ Guān Jié Gǔn Fǎ*, 掌指关节滚法)

Taking Catapophysis of metacarpophalangeal joints as working area, apply simple flexing-extending movement of wrist joint instead of compound movement formed by flexing-extending movement of wrist joint and rotating movement of forearm, it is called metacarpophalangeal-joint-rolling manipulation (*Zhǎng Zhǐ Guān Jié Gǔn Fǎ*, 掌指关节滚法) Compared with rolling, this method is stronger in pressure and stimulation. It is often applied on the regions where the muscles are thick and solid like lower back, buttocks and lower limbs.

Kneading (*Róu Fǎ*, 揉法)

With the fingertip, root of palm or great thenar attached on the performed area or certain point, do a slow and gentle rotating movement to make subcutaneous tissues moving together, it is called kneading. It would be called as finger-kneading manipulation (*Zhǐ Róu Fǎ*, 指揉法) if the manipulation is done with the fingertip; Palm root-kneading manipulation (*Zhǎng Gēn Róu Fǎ*, 掌根揉法) if it is done with palm root and great thenar-kneading manipulation (*Dà Yú Jì Róu Fǎ*, 大鱼际揉法) if it is done with great thenar.

1. Approaches of manipulation

a. Great thenar-kneading manipulation (*Dà Yú Jì Róu Fǎ*, 大鱼际揉法)

The operator exerts the strength to the great thenar, slightly flex the elbow joint to 120° ~ 140°.

Taking the elbow joint as the supporting point, wave the forearm actively to lead the great thenar kneading on the local area with a frequency of 120 ~ 160 times/ min.

b. Palm root-kneading manipulation (*Zhǎng Gēn Róu Fǎ*, 掌根揉法)

Taking the palm root as the working point, flex the fingers naturally and slightly extend the wrist joint. Bend the elbow joint to be the supporting point. Wave the forearm actively to lead palm root kneading on the local area with a frequency of 120 ~ 160 times/ min.

c. Thumn-kneading manipulation (*Mǔ Zhǐ Róu Fǎ*, 拇指揉法)

Taking the belly of thumb as the working point, place the rest fingers on proper area to support the thumb. Slightly flex or extend the wrist joint. Wave the forearm in small amplitude to lead the thumb moving in circles on the performed area with the frequency of 120 ~ 160 times/ min.

d. Middle finger-kneading manipulation (*Zhōng Zhǐ Róu Fǎ*, 中指揉法)

Taking the middle fingertip as the working point, extend the interphalangeal joint of middle finger with the metacarpophalangeal joint slightly bended. Taking the elbow joint as the supporting point, the forearm does an active movement in small amplitude to make the middle finger tip moving in a circle on the local area with the frequency of 120 ~ 160 times/ min.

The manipulation done with index finger, or done with index finger, middle finger and ring finger closed together, is called as index finger-kneading manipulation (*Shí Zhǐ Róu Fǎ*, 食指揉法) and three fingers-kneading manipulation (*Sān Zhǐ Róu Fǎ*, 三指揉法) respectively. The Essentials of Movements are as same as those of middle finger-kneading manipulation (*Zhōng Zhǐ Róu Fǎ*, 中指揉法).

2. Essentials of Movements

Drop down the elbow and relax the shoulder and wrist while doing kneading. Wave the forearm actively in small amplitude to make circling movement on the contacted area.

The subcutaneous tissues are led into movement together by doing kneading. The movement should be flexible, coordinated with regular rhythm.

The pressure applied by kneading should be proper by taking the comfortable feeling of the patient as the standard.

3. Precautions

During operation of kneading, there should not be relative rubbing movement between the working point and body surface.

The strength and effect of kneading is transmitted through the relaxed wrist joint. The wrist joint should maintain the tension at certain degree on the base of being relaxed while applying finger-kneading manipulation (*Zhǐ Róu Fǎ*, 指揉法), avoiding rigidity of the wrist.

Rubbing (*Mó Fǎ*, 摩法)

Rubbing is done by moving the wrist joint in circles with rhythm to lead the palm or the three fingertips including index finger, middle finger and ring finger which are held together rubbing on the performed area and point. If the manipulation is done by fingertips, it is called finger-rubbing manipulation (*Zhǐ Mó Fǎ*, 指摩法). If the manipulation is done by the palm, it is called palm-rubbing manipulation (*Zhǎng Mó Fǎ*, 掌摩法).

1. Approaches of Manipulation

a. Palm-rubbing manipulation (*Zhǎng Mó Fǎ*, 掌摩法)

The operator holds the fingers together and extends the palm naturally. Slightly extend the wrist joint, place the palm on the body surface horizontally. Taking the elbow joint as the supporting point, the forearm moves actively to lead circular rubbing movement of palm on the body surface. The frequency is 100 ~ 120 times/ min. The movement could be either clockwise or counterclockwise.

b. Finger-rubbing manipulation (*Zhǐ Mó Fǎ*, 指摩法)

Hold the four fingers together, and take the fingertip of the index finger, middle finger, ring finger and small finger as contacting area. Extend the palm straight naturally, slightly flex the wrist joint. Taking the elbow joint as the supporting point, the forearm moves actively to lead circular rubbing movement of bellies of four fingers on the performed area with the frequency of 100 ~ 120 times/ min. The movement could be done either clockwise or counterclockwise.

2. Essentials of Movements

The shoulder joint should be relaxed when doing rubbing. The forearm waves actively to lead circular movement of relaxed wrist joint. While applying finger-rubbing manipulation (*Zhǐ Mó Fǎ*, 指摩法), the wrist joint might maintain tension at a certain degree on the base of being relaxed to get the purpose of tension without rigidity.

Rubbing should be done with proper strength and even speed, gentle but not sliding, strong but not sluggish. finger-rubbing manipulation (*Zhǐ Mó Fǎ*, 指摩法) is more swift and springy, while palm-rubbing manipulation (*Zhǎng Mó Fǎ*, 掌摩法) is more slow and stronger.

3. Precautions

Rubbing should be gentle and moderate, not rushing and heavy.

The strength released should be even and stable, it is forbidden to press the local area forcefully.

To distinguish kneading and rubbing: kneading is done with relative strong force, the fingers and palm fixed on the performed area to move subcutaneous tissues, there is no rubbing movement on the body surface, while rubbing manipulation (*Mó Fǎ*, 摩法) is applied gently, the fingers and palm rubbing in circles on the body surface without traction of subcutaneous tissues.

Scrubbing (*Cā Fǎ*, 擦法)

Scrubbing is a kind of straight back and forth rubbing movement with hypothenar, or great thenar, or the palm root. The heat produced by rubbing penetrates downward to deep tissues through body surface. It can be classified to scrubbing manipulation (*Zhǎng Cā Fǎ*, 掌擦法), great thenar-scrubbing manipulation (*Dà Yú Jì Cā Fǎ*, 大鱼际擦法) and hypothenar-scrubbing manipulation (*Xiǎo Yú Jì Cā Fǎ*, 小鱼际擦法).

1. Approaches of Manipulation

a. Scrubbing manipulation (*Zhǎng Cā Fǎ*, 掌擦法)

Place the palm on the skin; straighten the wrist joint, the upper arm moves actively to make the palm rubbing back and forth along a straight line on the body surface by taking the shoulder joint as a supporting point. The frequency is 100 ~ 120 times/ min. This method is often used on chest, hypochondriac region and abdomen.

b. Great thenar-scrubbing manipulation (*Dà Yú Jì Cā Fǎ*, 大鱼际擦法)

The great thenar is taken as the working point. Taking the shoulder joint as the supporting point and keeping the wrist straight, the upper arm moves actively to lead back and forth rubbing movement of great thenar along a straight line on the body surface with a frequency of 100 ~ 120 times/ min. This method is often used on the chest, abdomen, waist, back and four limbs.

c. Hypothenar-scrubbing manipulation (*Xiǎo Yú Jì Cā Fǎ*, 小鱼际擦法)

The hypothenar is taken as the working point. Place the hypothenar on the body surface with the palm erect and wrist straight. Taking the shoulder joint as the supporting point, the upper arm moves actively to lead back and forth rubbing movement of hypothenar along a straight line on the body surface with a frequency of 100 ~ 120 times/ min. This method is often used on the shoulder, back, waist, buttocks and lower limbs.

2. Essentials of Movements

The course that the scrubbing is done along should be straight and long, and the back and forth rubbing movement is repeated along this course, not out of it. The movement should be continuous and smooth without any intermittence.

During the operation, the downward pressure should be even, avoid to making skin wrinkle, and the frequency of the movement should be even as well.

3. Precautions

The operator should breathe naturally during the operation; it is not good to hold the breath.

Scrubbing may produce warm and hot stimulation. *Zhǎng Cā Fǎ* (palm-scrubbing manipulation) is comparatively mild, hypothenar-scrubbing manipulation (*Xiǎo Yú Jì Cā Fǎ*, 小鱼际擦法) is the most warm, and great thenar-scrubbing manipulation (*Dà Yú Jì Cā Fǎ*, 大鱼际擦法) is medium. The standard is the patient's feeling that heat is penetrating downward.

During operation of scrubbing, the lubricants (Ever Green Ointment or Sesame Oil) is often used on the performed area, not only to protect skin but also benefit penetration from heat.

Scrubbing is done directly on body surface, so keep the patient warm.

Generally, it is not advisable to apply other manipulations on the performed area after scrubbing to avoid injury of skin.

Pushing (*Tuī Fǎ*, 推法)

Pushing is a kind of one-way straight pushing movement done on the points or certain area of human body with the thumb or other parts of the operator's body. It can be classified into finger-horizontal pushing manipulation (*Mŭ Zhĭ Píng Tuī Fă*, 拇指平推法), palm-pushing manipulation (*Zhăng Tuī Fă*, 掌推法), elbow-pushing manipulation (*Zhŏu Tuī Fă*, 肘推法), etc.

1. Approaches of manipulation

a. Finger-horizontal pushing manipulation (*Mŭ Zhĭ Píng Tuī Fă*, 拇指平推法)

Place the thumb tip forcefully over the body surface; the other four fingers naturally extend assisting the thumb. Extend and flex the elbow joint to lead the thumb push slowly and firmly to one direction along the course of channels or running direction of muscular fiber. The manipulation is repeated for 5 ~ 15 times continuously.

b. Palm-pushing manipulation (*Zhăng Tuī Fă*, 掌推法)

Place the palm on the body surface; take the root of palm or the whole palm as the working points. Flex and extend the elbow joint to lead the palm pushing forward firmly and slowly to certain direction. Repeat the manipulation for 5 ~ 15 times continuously.

c. Elbow-pushing manipulation (*Zhŏu Tuī Fă*, 肘推法)

Flex the elbow; place the elbow tip (olecranon) on the performed area, do pushing slowly along the running direction of muscular fiber in a straight line.

2. Essentials of Movements

It needs certain pressure while doing pushing; the pushing movement should be done slowly with even and smooth strength along a straight line to one direction.

The amplitude of flexion and extension of elbow joint in finger-horizontal pushing manipulation (*Mŭ Zhĭ Píng Tuī Fă*, 拇指平推法) is comparatively small. The thumb and the wrist arm area exert strength actively, pushing straightly in a short distance to the direction of the thumb.

While doing palm-pushing manipulation (*Zhăng Tuī Fă*, 掌推法), exert the strength in the palm root or whole palm. The wrist joint is extended backward slightly. Taking the shoulder joint as a supporting point, move the upper arm actively to lead the flexion and extension of elbow joint so as to make the palm push to one direction.

Since elbow-pushing manipulation (*Zhŏu Tuī Fă*, 肘推法) is done with the strength almost from the whole body, the stimulation is comparatively strong.

3. Precautions

Pushing is a movement along straight or arc line to one direction, it is forbidden to have back and forth rubbing.

The thumb or other parts of the body should be placed on the body surface tightly, perform manipulation with even and proper strength, and it is not advisable to do pushing in a quick way.

If pushing is done directly on the body surface, the media substances such as Ever Green Ointment, Talcum Powder or ginger juice or scallion juice might are necessary on the performed area.

Mopping (*Mā Fǎ*, 抹法)

Mopping is a back and forth pushing movement done with the tips of two thumbs or two palms to the opposite direction, upward with downward, leftward and rightward, or along arc lines on the bilateral sides. The manipulation is classified into finger-mopping manipulation (*Zhǐ Mā Fǎ*, 指抹法) and palm-mopping manipulation (*Zhǎng Mā Fǎ*, 掌抹法).

1. Approaches of manipulation

a. Inger-mopping manipulation (*Zhǐ Mā Fǎ*, 指抹法)

The thumb tip or both thumbs are taken as the working point; the other four fingers associate the thumbs. Together, they move slowly upward and downward, left and right or in a straight course or in arc repeatedly.

b. Palm-mopping manipulation (*Zhǎng Mā Fǎ*, 掌抹法)

The manipulation is done with the palm of one hand or both palms. Relax the wrist joint. The forearm and upper arm exerts the strength in cooperation to lead the palms, move repeatedly upward and downward, left and right or in a straight course or in arc.

2. Essentials of Movements

During the operation, the thumb tip or palm should be attached to the body surface.

When mopping is applied, the strength should be even, the movement should be soft and gentle but not floating, should be powerful but not hesitant.

3. Precautions

The stimulation produced by mopping is relatively superficial. It is not advisable to drag the deep tissues during the operation.

Mopping is often confused with pushing. Pushing is a movement to single direction along a straight line, while mopping manipulation (*Mā Fǎ*, 抹法) not only a movement to one direction, but also forth and back, or alone a curved line.

When it is applied on face or head, inger-mopping manipulation (*Zhǐ Mā Fǎ*, 指抹法) should follow a fixed procedure.

Scattering Manipulation (*Sǎo Sàn Fǎ*, 扫散法)

Scattering manipulation (*Sǎo Sàn Fǎ*, 扫散法) is a kind of bidirectional pushing and scrubbing movement done by the radial side of thumb and tips of index, middle, ring and little fingers along *shaoyang* channel in temporal region. It is one of the main manipulations in internal energy (*Nèi Gōng*) tui na schools.

1. Approaches to Manipulation

The operator supports the patient's head with one hand, places the radial side of the thumb and the rest of the four finger tips of another hand on the temporal region. Do rapid bidirectional mopping movements forcefully along the course of *shaoyang* channel behind the ear with a frequency about 250 times/ min.

2. Essentials of Movements

The operator should relax the shoulder and drop down the elbow joint naturally. The elbow joint is flexed into an angle 90° ~ 120°. Relax the wrist joint.

Taking the elbow joint as the supporting point, wave the forearm actively to lead the wrist joint waving together, so as to do bidirectional pushing and scrubbing movements with the fingers on temporal region.

3. Precautions

Place the fingers firmly on the scalp during the operation. It should be stronger when pushing and scrubbing forward and be gentle when the fingers moving backward. The manipulation should be gentle but not floating, strong but not hesitant.

The supporting hand should fix the patient's head while doing scattering manipulation, so as to avoid shaking too much the head and discomfort.

Scattering manipulation (*Sǎo Sàn Fǎ*, 扫散法) should be done along the course of the channels from posterior side to the anterior side, each of pushing and scrubbing shouldn't be too long.

Foulage (*Cuō Fǎ*, 搓法)

Foulage is a kind of rapid rubbing movement with strength from two hands which clamp the certain areas of the trunk or limbs.

1. Approaches to Manipulation

Ask patient to relax the limbs. Clamping the performed area of the limb with palms, do foulage with kneading, foulage with rotating or foulage with rubbing forcefully, upward and downward at same time.

a. Foulage on the shoulder joint

The patient takes a sitting position with shoulders and arms relaxed and dropped down naturally. The operator stands by the side of the patient with upper portion of the body lean forward slightly. The palms clamp the patient's shoulder with one on the front of the shoulder and one on the back of it. Do foulage and kneading forcefully and rapidly. This is a kind of foulage with kneading manipulation.

b. Foulage on the upper limb

The patient takes a sitting position with shoulders and arms relaxed and dropped down naturally. The operator stands by the side of the patient with upper portion of the body lean forward slightly. The two palms clamp the upper limb. The foulage is done from upper limb to the wrist repeatedly for 3 ~ 5 times.

c. Foulage on the hypochondriac regions

The patient takes a sitting position with two arms extended slightly. Standing behind the patient and clamping the patient's trunk at the sides of hypochondriac region, the operator does foulage and rubbing from armpits to waist for several times.

2. Essentials of Movements

Relax the shoulder and the upper arm.

Flex the elbow slightly, clamp the performed area tightly, do foulage up and down. The elbow joint is flexed into 150° ~ 160°.

Relax the wrist joint, do movement dexterously in even but quick speed. The two palms should exert the strength in cooperation and be shifted slowly.

The strength should be released and penetrated deeply into the body. The palms are placed tightly on the performed area with continuous movement.

3. Precautions

Foulage shouldn't be too strong with too tight clamping, otherwise, it may cause rigid manipulation.

Foulage is an assistant manipulation. It is usually used on the shoulder or upper limb at the end of tui na treatment.

Vibrating (*Zhèn Fǎ*, 振法)

Vibrating is also called *Zhèn Zhàn Fǎ*. It is a kind of continuous rapid vibration done by fingers or palm on certain points or areas of the human body. It is classified into finger-vibrating manipulation (*Zhǐ Zhèn Fǎ*, 指振法) and palm-vibrating manipulation (*Zhǎng Zhèn Fǎ*, 掌振法).

1. Approaches to Manipulation

The patient takes a sitting or lying position. The operator exerts the strength to the performed area through tips of fingers of one hand or both hands by concentrating the mind on the tips of fingers or centre of the palm.

The muscles of the forearm and hands exert intensive motionless power to make rapid and intensive vibration of the arm. The vibration is transported to the body of the patient through tips of finger or centre of the palm, producing easy and warm feeling in the performed area.

If the power of vibration is released from the fingertips, it is called finger-vibrating manipulation (*Zhǐ Zhèn Fǎ*, 指振法). If it is from the palm, it is called palm-vibrating manipulation (*Zhǎng Zhèn Fǎ*, 掌振法).

2. Essentials of Movements

Relax the shoulder and the upper arm. Slightly flex the elbow joint.

The muscles of the forearm and palm should exert intensive motionless power which is to tighten the muscles of the hand and the forearm without doing active movements. The power is concentrated on the palm or fingers to make vibration of the performed area.

The mind should be concentrated on the fingertips and the centre of the palm with natural and easy breath.

The movements should be continuous and constant with high frequency of 300 ~ 400 times/ min.

3. Precautions

Except the motionless power from the muscles of the forearm and hand, other parts of the body should be relaxed during the operation.

Don't press downward too much during the operation.

Don't hold the breath.

Don't take the working point away from the performed area, and the vibration should be continuous without any intermittence.

Vibrating needs long time practice. The practice of *Shào Lín* internal exercise (*Shào Lín Nèi Gōng*, 少林内功) can improve the quality of the manipulation efficiently.

Shaking (*Dǒu Fǎ*, 抖法)

Shaking is a kind of shaking movement up and down or left and right in small amplitude done by holding the distal part of the affected limb with one hand or both hands.

1. Approaches to Manipulation

The operator holds the distal part of the upper limb or lower limb (wrist or ankle area), raise the sick limb to a certain angle (The upper arm is abducted to the degree around 60° in the sitting position; the lower limb is raised 30° away from the bed in the supine position).

In the state of traction with mild strength, do continuous shaking movements up and down in small amplitude to cause tremor in soft tissues of the limb and let the tremor radiating to the proximal part of the limb.

2. Essentials of Movements

The operated limb should be relaxed and extended in a natural way. The operator should have a natural breath, not to hold the breath.

The shaking amplitude should be small, but in high frequency.

Pull the patient's limb gently to make the limb extended.

Lead the movement of the wrist joint by flexing and extending the forearm slightly.

3. Precautions

When shaking is applied for the lower limb, the shaking amplitude should be larger than that of the upper limb, since the lower limb is heavier.

Shakingis often taken as the ending manipulation and more applied for the upper limb.

Pressing (*Àn Fǎ*, 按法)

It is a pressing movement with gradual increasing force on the local area or point with the belly of thumb or palm. If it is done with the belly of the finger, it is called finger-pressing manipulation (*Zhǐ Àn Fǎ*, 指按法). If it is done with the palm, it is called palm- pressing manipulation (*Zhǎng Àn Fǎ*, 掌按法).

1. Approaches of manipulation

a. Finger-pressing manipulation (*Zhǐ Àn Fǎ*, 指按法)

Extend the thumb straight. Place the tip of the thumb on the body surface to press the points and the course of channel with the rest fingers extended to support and assist the work of the thumb. If the finger force of one hand is not enough, place the thumb of the other hand over it to press together with the tip of the thumb.

b. Palm- pressing manipulation (*Zhǎng Àn Fǎ*, 掌按法)

Press the body surface with the palm root, thenar or the whole palm. If the force of one hand is not enough, the other hand can be placed over it to make the pressure together.

2. Essentials of Movements

The pressing direction should be perpendicular. The strength should be started from gentle to strong, steady but constant, making stimulation penetrate sufficiently downward to deep tissues. Then reduce the pressure gradually, obeying the principle of "gentle-strong-gentle".

If strong stimulation is needed, the operator may lean the body forward slightly to increase the stimulation with the help of body weight.

3. Precautions

It is forbidden to use erupt explosive power to avoid adverse reaction.

The strength of pressing changes in rhythm. It should be distinguished from constant pressing manipulation (*Yā Fǎ*, 压法) which is done with continuous strength of long time. Pressing is often combined with kneading in clinic to form a complex manipulation called pressing-kneading manipualation (*Àn Róu Fǎ*, 按揉法).

Continuous Pressing Manipulation (*Yā Fǎ*, 压法)

Continuous pressing manipulation (*Yā Fǎ*, 压法) is done by pressing those special points or areas with the belly of thumb, palm or olecranon process of the elbow joint continuously and forcefully.

1. Approaches of manipulation

The operator presses the body surface perpendicularly with the tip of thumb, palm or proximal part of forearm when the elbow flexed. It can slide slowly on the body surface while pressing. If it is done by the proximal part of forearm, it is also called elbow-continuous pressing manipulation (*Zhǒu Yā Fǎ*, 肘压法).

2. Essentials of Movements

Pressing and continuous pressing manipulation (*Yā Fǎ*, 压法) are similar to each other, they are often mixed and called "*Àn Yā Fǎ*" . To distinguish them strictly, pressing is more dynamic; Continuous pressing manipulation (*Yā Fǎ*, 压法) is more static. Pressing lasts for shorter time; Continuous pressing manipulation (*Yā Fǎ*, 压法) lasts for longer time. Pressing has gentle pressure and stimulation; Continuous pressing manipulation (*Yā Fǎ*, 压法) has strong pressure and stimulation.

3. Precautions

When continuous pressing manipulation (*Yā Fǎ*, 压法)is applied on the back or lower back, the strength should be carefully controlled to avoid adverse reaction.

Elbow-continuous pressing manipulation (*Zhǒu Yā Fǎ*, 肘压法) is stronger. It is often used on the place where the muscles are rich like lumbar region and buttocks in the patients with strong body build.

Pointing (*Diǎn Fǎ*, 点法)

Pointing manipulation (*Diǎn Fǎ*,点法) is done by pressing and kneading the performed area or point with thumb joint or second interphalangeal joint of index finger or middle finger.

1. Approaches of manipulation

a. Thumb tip-pointing manipulation (*Mǔ Zhǐ Duān Diǎn Fǎ*, 拇指端点法)

Make a loose fist with the thumb tightly against the middle segment of the index finger, press the performed area with the thumb tip perpendicularly downward.

b. Flexed finger-pointing manipulation (*Qū Zhǐ Diǎn Fǎ*, 屈指点法)

Flex the thumb, index finger or middle finger; press the performed area perpendicularly and gradually with the protrusion of thumb and the protrusion of the first interphalangeal joint of index or middle finger.

2. Essentials of Movements

The pointing and pressing direction should be perpendicular to the performed area.

The forearm and wrist exert strength during the manipulation.

The pressure given is increased gradually from gentle to strong, even and continued.

3. Precautions

Pointing manipulation (*Diǎn Fǎ*,点法) contacts the body surface in a small area with intensive stimulation and short duration. It is more often used for arresting pain. It is also called "finger needle". Kneading should be applied, after pointing and pressing, to regulate qi and blood and avoid local soft tissue injury.

Pointing manipulation (*Diǎn Fǎ*,点法) is not available for senior people with weak body constitution and those weak people due to prolonged disease.

When Thumb tip-pointing manipulation (*Mǔ Zhǐ Duān Diǎn Fǎ*, 拇指端点法) is applied, the tip of the thumb must attach lateral border of the index to avoid sprain of interphalangeal joint of thumb due to over exertion of strength.

Pinching (*Niē Fǎ*, 捏法)

Pinching is to squeeze the performed area with symmetric strength from thumb and other fingers. If it is applied on the spine, it is called "pinching along the spine" which is often used in pediatric tui na. See relevant items in pediatric tui na manipulations.

1. Approaches to Manipulation

Hold the performed area with thumb, index and middle fingertips or thumb and the rest of the four fingertips. Squeeze it with opposite strength and relax it right after. Repeat the movements above and move along gradually.

2. Essentials of Movements

The strength from the thumb and the rest of the four fingers should be symmetric, even and gentle, constant with rhythm.

3. Precautions

The bellies of the finger are the working point, not the tip.

Pinching requires a higher finger force, especially the closing force between the thumb and other four fingers, the finger force can be improved by practicing relative exercises.

Grasping (*Ná Fǎ*, 拿法)

Grasping the limbs or muscles to do pinching and kneading movement with closing force between thumb and the other four fingers is called grasping. It can be classified into three-finger grasping manipulation and five-finger grasping manipulation.

1. Approaches to Manipulation

Relax the wrist joint. Hold the performed area tightly with thumb and bellies of index and middle fingers or tips of the rest four fingers. Lift the skin and muscles and make a continuous pinching and relaxing movement or pinching and kneading movement in an forceful and easy, tight and loose way.

2. Essentials of Movements

The shoulder, elbow and wrist should be in a relaxed state, and the movements should be flexible and gentle. Make a loose fist with the fingers extended; hold the performed area with plain bellies of fingers; flex the metacarpophalangeal joint of the fingers which are opposite to the thumb; lift and pinch skin and subcutaneous soft tissues with closing force like a pair of scissors.

Accumulate the energy inside the body to fill it into the fingers, doing continuous movement in pinching and relaxing way alternatively.

Exert strength slowly in a gentle and even way, from mild to strong and then from strong to mild. The kneading and pinching movements should be done continuously.

3. Precautions

When grasping is doing, try to avoid digging and nipping movements of finger tips and nails due to flexion of interphalangeal joints of the fingers.

When is doing, try to pinch and grasp the subcutaneous soft tissues as much as possible in accordance with the clinic requirements, Avoid sliding movement of fingers on the body surface.

After grasping, the gentle kneading and rubbing manipulations are suggested to ease qi and blood.

Twiddling Manipulation (*Niăn Fă*, 捻法)

Twiddling manipulation (*Niăn Fă*, 捻法) is a kind of symmetric twiddling movement on the performed area held with the tips of the thumb and index finger.

1. Approaches to Manipulation

Hold the performed area with the tip of the thumb and radial side of the index finger. The thumb and index finger do rapid comparatively forceful twiddling movement like twiddling thread.

2. Essentials of Movements

The twiddling manipulation should be done with dexterous, continuous, coordinated and powerful movement.

The speed of twiddling should be slightly rapid. The moving speed along the performed area should be slow.

3. Precautions

Twiddling manipulation (*Niăn Fă*, 捻法) is taken as an assistant manipulation. It is often used on joints of fingers and toes.

Plucking (*Bō Fă*, 拨法)

Press the performed area with the tip of the thumb forcefully, then make a transverse plucking movement on the tissues like tendons and muscles running vertically. It is also called *Tán Bō Fă* (弹拨法).

1. Approaches to Manipulation

Extend the thumb straight. The tip of the thumb is taken as the working point; the rest four fingers are placed on the relative areas to assist the thumb. Press the thumb on the side of tendons or muscles until the patient feels soreness and distention. Then make a transverse plucking movement to the vertical tendons or muscular fibers, like plucking the string of a music instrument. If the finger force is not strong enough, the thumbs of both hands can be put together to fulfil the operation.

2. Essentials of Movements

It is not a manipulation of rubbing the skin with the thumb; the plucking movement should make subcutaneous muscular fibers or tendons and ligaments together moving together.

The strength exerted should be increased from gentle to strong gradually. It takes the patient's tolerance as the standard.

3. Precautions

The plucking manipulation is often used on the painful point, because "taking tenderness as an acu-point."

The plucking manipulation works with strong stimulation; it is advisable to apply gentle kneading-rubbing manipulation after to ease qi and blood.

Patting Manipulation (*Pāi Fǎ*, 拍法)

Patting manipulation (*Pāi Fǎ*, 拍法) is to pat the body surface in rhythm with a hollow palm.

1. Approaches to Manipulation

Close the five fingers together and slightly flex the metacarpophalangeal joints. The centre of the palm is depressed forming a hollow palm; pat the performed area in regular rhythm with the frequency of 100 ~ 120 times/ min.

2. Essentials of Movements

Relax the shoulder and wrist joints while doing patting manipulation. The tapping should be gentle, swift and stable; the palm should be raised immediately after touching the skin; the movement should be performed in regular rhythm until the local skin is slightly red.

The manipulation can be performed with one hand or both hands. When it is done with two hands, the hands should do the manipulation alternately.

3. Precautions

The palm should pat the body surface firmly without any dragging and pulling movements.

Make clear about the indications of patting manipulation. It is forbidden to apply this manipulation for patients with tuberculosis, severe osteoporosis, bone tumor and coronary cardiac diseases.

Striking Manipulation (*Jī Fǎ*, 击法)

Striking manipulation (*Jī Fǎ*, 击法) is a kind of rhythmical striking movement on the performed area with palm root, palmar side of hypothenar, dorsal side of the fist, tips of the fingers or a mulberry stick. It can be classified into palm root-striking manipulation (*Zhǎng Gēn Jī Fǎ*, 掌根击法), hypothenar-striking manipulation (*Cè Jī Fǎ*, 侧击法), fist-striking manipulation (*Quán Jī Fǎ*, 拳击法) and finger tip-striking manipulation (*Zhǐ Jiān Jī Fǎ*, 指尖击法).

1. Approaches to Manipulation

a.Palm root-striking manipulation (*Zhǎng Gēn Jī Fǎ*, 掌根击法)

Extend the fingers naturally and wrist joint slightly to the dorsal side. Strike the body surface with palm root.

b. Hypothenar-striking manipulation (*Cè Jī Fǎ*, 侧击法)

Extend the fingers naturally and wrist joint slightly to the dorsal side. Strike the body surface with hypothenars of both hands alternately.

c. Fist-striking manipulation (*Quán Jī Fǎ*, 拳击法)

Make a fist and keep the wrist joint straight. Strike the body surface with dorsal side of the fist flatly. Usually, apply 3 ~ 5 times of striking each time.

d. Finger tip-striking manipulation (*Zhǐ Jiān Jī Fǎ*, 指尖击法)

Close the tips of the five fingers like a plum blossom or scatter the fingers like a claw. Tap and strike the performed area gently and swiftly.

2. Essentials of Movements

The power in striking manipulation should be exerted rapidly in short time; striking the body surface perpendicularly in regular rhythm.

In palm root-striking manipulation (*Zhǎng Gēn Jī Fǎ*, 掌根击法), the palm root is taken as working point, do striking with the strength exerted from the forearm and the arm waving in large amplitude. Usually, apply 3 ~ 5 times of striking each time.

hypothenar-striking manipulation (*Cè Jī Fǎ*, 侧击法)could be performed by one hand or two hands with palm centers face to each other. Taking the elbow joint as the supporting point, the forearms move actively; the hypothenar of palm should be perpendicular to the muscular fibers and do striking swiftly in rhythm.

In fist-striking manipulation (*Quán Jī Fǎ*, 拳击法) the elbow joint is taken as the supporting point. Do striking firmly by flexing and extending the elbow joint with the strength exerted from the forearm.

While doing finger tip-striking manipulation (*Zhǐ Jiān Jī Fǎ*, 指尖击法), relax the wrist joint, and swiftly tap or strike the body surface with finger tips by flexing and extending the wrist joint in small amplitude just like rain drops falling.

3. Precautions

Pay attention to the rebounding feeling of striking manipulation. The hand should be rebounded up immediately after touching the performed area without any stop, dragging or pulling on the body surface.

Have a good understanding on the suitable areas and indications of every striking manipulation, avoiding violent striking.

Fist-striking manipulation (*Quán Jī Fǎ*, 拳击法) is mainly used on Du 14 (*Dà Zhuī*) and lumbosacral region; Palm root-striking manipulation (*Zhǎng Gēn Jī Fǎ*, 掌根击法) could be applied on Du 20 (*Bǎi Huì*) and GB 30 (*Huán Tiào*); and finger tip-striking manipulation (*Zhǐ Jiān Jī Fǎ*, 指尖击法) is usually used on the head.

Flicking (*Tán Fǎ*, 弹法)

Place the belly of middle finger tightly on the dorsum of index finger to flick certain area or point with fingers repeatedly and quickly.

1. Approaches to Manipulation

Flex the index finger; press the belly of middle finger tightly on the dorsal side of the index finger. Then flick the affected area rapidly with the frequency of 120 ~ 160 times/ min.

2. Essentials of Movements

The operation should be even and continuous. The intensity of stimulation is within the limit of causing any pain.

3. Precautions

The manipulation is often used as an assistant manipulation head and face treatment.

Rotation (*Yáo Fǎ*, 摇法)

Rotation is a kind of passive movement of the joint or hemiarticulation within the physiological movement range of these joints and hemiarticulation. It is one of the frequently used manipulation, the approaches are varied according to where the manipulation is applied.

1. Approaches to Manipulation

a. Rotating Neck Manipulation

The patient takes a sitting position with a relaxed neck. The operator stands by the side of the patient, supporting the back of the head vertex with one hand and holding the chin with another hand, two hands exert the strength to opposite directions to slowly rotate the head clockwise and counterclockwise for several times respectively.

b. Rotating Shoulder Manipulation

Ask the patient to take a sitting position. There are three ways to apply the manipulation.

【Rotating shoulder by supporting elbow】

The patient relaxes the shoulder and flexes the elbow. The operator stands by the side of the patient in bow stance with the torso leaning forward slightly. Holding the upper part of the scapula of the patient with one hand to fix it and supporting the elbow of the affected limb with another hand, rotate the shoulder joint clockwise and counterclockwise for several times respectively.

【Rotating shoulder in large amplitude】

The patient drops down the arm naturally. The operator stands by the side of the patient in T-step stance. Holding the wrist of the patient with one hand and putting the dorsum of another hand against the patient's forearm, raise the patient's arm to form 160° between the arm and trunk, then reverse the hand dorsum to hold the wrist. At the same time, the hand, which was holding the patient's wrist, slips downward to hold and press the shoulder, while the other hand, which is hold the wrist, continues to raise the arm. The two hands exert the strength cooperatively (One hand presses the shoulder slightly forward, the other hand holds the wrist to raise the arm) to extend the shoulder joint fully. After that, rotate the arm backward in large amplitude. The movement would be done to the opposite direction if shoulder joint is rotated forward.

c. Rotating elbow

The patient takes a sitting or supine position. Holding the patient's elbow of the affected limb with one hand and the wrist of affected limb with another hand, rotate the elbow clockwise and counterclockwise for several times respectively.

d. Rotating Wrist

Holding the upper portion of the wrist joint of the affected limb with one hand and the palm with another hand, rotate the wrist joint clockwise and counterclockwise for several times respectively while the joint is pulled slightly.

e. Rotating Waist

There are two approaches.

The patient takes a sitting position and relaxes the waist. Standing behind the patient, holding one side of the waist with one hand and the opposite shoulder with another hand, two hands exert the strength cooperatively to make the patient's torso leaning forward, bending to the side and extending backward from left to right or from right to left, so as to rotate the waist. The movement is done clockwise and counterclockwise for several times respectively.

The patient takes a supine position with flexed knees and hips. Pressing two knees with one hand to make the knees closed together and holding the lower parts or ankles of the legs with another hand, rotate two lower legs clockwise and counterclockwise for several times respectively to lead the movement of the waist.

f. Rotating Hip

The patient takes a supine position with knee and hip of the affected limb flexed and healthy leg extended. Standing by the side of the patient, holding the patient's knee with one hand and supporting the heel with another hand, flex the hip joint to 90° and then rotate the hip joint clockwise and counterclockwise for several times respectively with coperformed movement of two hands.

g. Rotating Knee

The patient takes a supine position with knee and hip of the affected limb flexed. Fixing the knee with one hand and holding the ankle with another hand, rotate the knee joint clockwise and counterclockwise for several times respectively. It is advisable to extend the knee joint slowly when it is rotated.

h. Rotating Ankle Manipulation

The patient takes a supine position with the affected limb extended naturally. Holding the lower part of the lower leg with one hand and the anterior part of the foot dorsum with another hand, rotate the ankle joint clockwise and counterclockwise for several times respectively.

2. Essentials of Movements

The movement of rotation should be gentle with stable strength. The speed of rotation should be slow and even.

The amplitude of rotation should be from small to large and be suitable to the pathological condition of the patient, usually it should be within the limitation of normal physical joint movement, but can be slightly over the pathological limit position, anyhow, take the patient's tolerance as the standard.

3. Precautions

It is forbidden to have violent movements or movements against normal physiological activities while making rotating manipulation. For the patients with joint dysfunction, rotating manipulation should be done to suit pathological situation of the patient.

Fully understand the cautions and contraindications of rotating manipulation, it is forbidden to apply this manipulation for the patient with joint bone fracture or joint dislocation, and cervical spondylopathy of vertebral artery type; not advisable for the patient with cervical spondylopathy of spinal marrow type; the manipulation can be done for the patient with muscular tension of nape but in a supine position.

Rotating shoulder Manipulation is often used to improve shoulder joint function. The moving range of rotating shoulder Manipulation by supporting elbow and rotating shoulder by holding wrist is comparatively smaller, they are usually applied for shoulder joint pain and obvious shoulder dysfunction, such as the early stage of peripheral arthritis of shoulder. Rotating shoulder in large amplitude is suitable for the situation that the shoulder function has been improved greatly, such as convalescent stage of periarthritis of shoulder.

Pulling-Stretching Manipulation (*Bá Shēn Fǎ*, 拔伸法)

Fix one end of the limb or joint and keep pulling the other end of the limb or joint forcefully to enlarge the gap of the joint. It is also called pulling-stretching manipulation (*Bá Shēn Fǎ*, 拔伸法) or "traction manipulation", and can be used for different joint disorders.

1. Approaches to Manipulation

a. Pulling-stretching manipulation of neck

It can be classified into pulling-stretching manipulation done by pushing head upward with fingers and palms, pulling-stretching manipulation done by lifting head with elbow and pulling-stretching manipulation in supine position.

【Pulling-stretching neck by pushing head upward with fingers and palms】

Ask the patient to take a sitting position. Standing behind the patient with two thumbs against the area inferior to the occiput of the patient GB 20 (Fēng Chí) and the rest four fingers and palm holding the mandible, place the forearms on the patient's shoulders respectively. The arms exert the strength cooperatively, the hands hold and push the head upward while the forearms press the shoulder forcefully downward so as to pull and stretch the neck slowly upward.

【Pulling-stretching neck by lifting head with elbow】

Ask the patient to take a sitting position with the head lean forward slightly. Standing behind the patient with one hand going round in front of the patient's neck to hold the chin with elbow, stretch the web margin between the thumb and index finger of another hand to hold the occiput of the patient. Then both hands pull and stretch the neck upward slowly along the axis of cervical vertebrae.

【Pulling-stretching neck in supine position】

Ask the patient to take a supine position. Sitting by facing the patient's head, holding and supporting the patient's head at the occiput with one hand and the chin with another hand, two hands exert the strength together to pull and stretch the neck along the axis of cervical vertebrae.

b. Pulling-stretching manipulation of shoulder

The manipulation can be done in two ways:

【Pulling-stretching shoulder by lifting arms】

Ask the patient to sit on a low stool with the affected arm relaxed. Standing behind the patient at the lateral side, holding the patient's wrist with both hands, slowly lift the patient's arms up as much as possible like doing shoulder traction along the vertical axis of arms.

【Pulling-stretching shoulder by abducting arm】

Ask the patient to take a sitting position with the affected arm relaxed and abducted to 45° ~ 60°. Let an assistant stand by the healthy side and hold the trunk of the patient with hands going around through armpit to fix the body. The operator stands by the affected side with two hands holding the patient's wrists to make traction along the vertical axis of the arm with gradually increased strength.

c. Pulling-stretching manipulation of elbow

Ask the patient to take a sitting position. Fixing the proximal end of the elbow joint of the affected limb with one hand (or ask an assistant to fix it), holding the distal end of the forearm with another hand, two hands exert force to opposite directions to pull and stretch the elbow joint.

d. Pulling-stretching manipulation of wrist

Ask the patient to take a sitting position. Holding the proximal end of wrist of the affected limb with one hand and the palm with another hand, two hands exert force to opposite directions to pull and stretch the wrist.

e. Pulling-stretching manipulation of finger

Holding the wrist of the affected finger with one hand, clamping the affected finger with the middle segment of flexed index and middle fingers of another hand, exert resistant force to pull and stretch the affected finger.

f. Pulling-stretching manipulation of waist

Ask the patient to take a prone position. An assistant stands at the bed head side and holds the patient armpits to fix his body (or ask the patient to hold the bed head side with both hands forcefully); the operator stands at the bed foot side to pull the patient's body by holding his ankles with both hands and gradually increased force.

g. Pulling-stretching manipulation of hip

Ask the patient to take a supine position with the knee and hip of the affected limb flexed. Standing by the affected side while the assistant is pressing the anterior superior iliac spines for fixing the hip with both hands, holding the affected knee with one hand and supporting the popliteal fossa with the forearm of another arm, meanwhile, pressing the patient's lower leg with the chest, then, pull and stretch the patient's hip joint along the vertical axis of the thigh with the cooperated force of both arms and trunk.

h. Pulling-stretching manipulation of knee

Ask the patient to take a prone position with the knee of affected limb flexed to 90°. Standing by the affected side with one knee flexed to press the lower part of posterior aspect of the affected thigh and holding the patient's ankles with both hands, pull and stretch the knee joint upward along the vertical axis of lower leg.

i. Pulling-stretching manipulation of ankle

Ask the patient to take a supine position. Supporting the patient's heel of affected foot with one hand and holding the metatarsophalangeal area with another hand, pull the ankle joint along the vertical axis of tibi.

2. Essentials of Movements

The movements of pulling-stretching manipulation should be stable and gentle. The strength released is from mild to strong. When the joint is pulled to a certain extent, keep the traction force stably for a period of time.

The angle of the pulling and stretching should be grasped well; the direction of pulling and stretching should be along the vertical axis of the limb.

3. Precautions

It is forbidden to use abrupt violent strength and do operations against the normal direction of physiological activities of joint.

Pay attention not to squeeze carotid sinuses on both sides of neck when doing pulling-stretching manipulation of neck to avoid adverse reaction.

Back-Carrying (*Bēi Fǎ*, 背法)

Back-carrying is a kind of movement that the operator carries out on the patient with his or her back to pull and vibrate the patient's lumbar vertebrae.

1. Approaches to Manipulation

The operator stands back to back with the patient, holding the patient's elbows of with his own elbows. Bend the waist, flex the knees and erect the buttocks to carry the patient on the back, making the patient's feet away from the ground and the body suspending. With the buttocks against the lumbosacral region of the patient, the operator waves the buttocks left to right a few times, and then extend the knees, flex the hips and erect the buttocks suddenly when the muscles of the patient are relaxed.

2. Essentials of Movements

The patient should be completely relaxed with natural breath. When being carried on the back, the patient should lean the whole body against the back of the operator with the head raised backward. The lumbar vertebrae are pulled and stretched by the weight of lower body.

The waving movement from left to right, the movement extending the knees and erecting buttocks should be continuous in coordination.

3. Precautions

Compare the body weight of the patient with the strength of the operator to avoid the failure of manipulation or even injury to the operator because of overload.

Pulling (*Bān Fǎ*, 扳法)

Pulling is the pulling movement of two hands which exerted strength to same direction or to opposite directions to extend, flex and rotate the diseased joints. It is a manipulation commonly used in orthopedic tui na. The operation methods are different when it is applied on the different areas like neck, lower back and four limbs.

1. Approaches to Manipulation

a. Pulling manipulation of neck

Three ways commonly used:

【Oblique pulling-twisting manipulation of neck】

Ask the patient to take a sitting position with the head bending slightly forward or in neutral position and neck muscles relaxed. Standing by the side of patient with one hand placed on the vertex of patient's head and the other hand holding the chin, rotate the patient's head leftward or rightward. When the head is turned to a flexible limit (when there is a resistance), stop the rotation for a moment, then do a quick, dexterous and controlled twisting movement in small amplitude, cracking sound of reposition is often heard at the moment.

【Pulling manipulation of cervical vertebrae at fixed location】

Ask the patient to take a sitting position with anteflexion of cervical vertebrae in 15°～30°. Take the pulling manipulation with leftward rotation as an example: The operator stands behind the patient at the left side with the tip of right thumb pressing and resisting spinous process or the side of transverse process and left hand holding the chin to make the patient's head turning leftward slowly under the condition of the fixed angle of anteflexion. When there is an elastic resistance, stop the rotation for a moment, then do a quick, dexterous and controlled twisting movement in small amplitude. At the same time, the thumb, which is pressing on the spinous process, pushes the process toward the opposite side forcefully. If the reposition is successful, cracking sound is often heard at the moment. Sometimes there is no cracking sound of reposition, but there will be a "jerking" sensation of spinous process beneath the operator's thumb.

【Pulling manipulation of cervical vertebrae done by rotating atlas-axis joint】

Ask the patient to sit on a low stool. The operator stands by the side of the patient with one thumb pressing the spinous process of second cervical vertebra, holding the patient's chin with another elbow and the occiput with the palm passing by opposite ear. Ask the patient to flex the neck slowly until the operator feels the spinous process of affected vertebra sliding beneath the thumb. Maintaining the neck flexion at this degree, pull and stretch the neck upward along the vertical axis of cervical vertebrae slightly forceful, at the same time, rotate the head toward the direction that the spinous process is deviated until there is an elastic resistance; stop the rotation for a moment, then make a quick, dexterous and controlled twisting movement in small amplitude, and the thumb presses and pushes the spinous process toward the opposite side.

b. Pulling manipulation of thoracic vertebrae

Two ways commonly used:

【Reposition manipulation done by pushing against thoracic vertebrae】

Ask the patient to take a sitting position with two hands holding the occiput and fingers crossed. The operator stands behind the patient, one foot steps on the patient's chair with the knee against the affected spinous process of thoracic vertebra, the arms pass by patient's armpits and go though between forearm and upper arm of the patient to hold patient's lower portion of forearms. The operator presses the patient's forearms downward with both hands and raises his own forearms forcefully to force the cervical vertebrae bending forward and pull the spinal column upward and backward. After a short stop, the operator's both hands and both arms exert strength cooperatively to do a quick, dexterous and controlled twisting movement in small amplitude, at the same time, the knee exerts the strength forward suddenly, cracking sound of reposition is often heard at the moment.

【Reposition manipulation done by pressing thoracic vertebrae】

Ask the patient to take a prone position. The operator crosses two arms and puts the pisiform bones of palms at the sides of transverse processes of the affected vertebra respectively. Ask the patient to breathe deeply to regulate his respiration, at the end of inhalation, the operator exerts the strength with the elbow joints to have a sudden but controlled pressing, cracking sound of reposition is often heard at the moment.

c. Pulling manipulation of waist

Three ways commonly used:

【Oblique pulling-twisting manipulation of lumbar vertebrae】

The patient takes a lateral recumbent position with the healthy leg extended, the affected leg flexed over the healthy leg, the ankle underneath the popliteal fossa of the healthy leg. The operator faces places two elbows (the upper portions of the forearms) on the shoulder front and buttock of the patient respectively. Twist the patient's waist by pushing the shoulder and buttock to the opposite directions until there is an elastic resistance. At this time, do a quick, controlled twisting movement in small amplitude, cracking sound of reposition is often heard at the moment.

【Pulling manipulation done by rotating lumbar vertebrae】

Take pulling manipulation done by rotating lumbar vertebrae rightward as an example. Ask the patient to take a sitting position with lumbar muscles relaxed. An assistant stands in front of the patient to fix the patient's knees with both hands; the operator sits behind the patient at the side with the left thumb pressing the deviated spinous process and the right hand pressing the patient's nape by the arm going through the patient's right armpit. Then press the patient's nape down to force the patient's body bending forward slowly until the operator feels a gap between the spinous processes appearing beneath his left thumb. Maintaining the anteflexion of the body at this degree, the right arm exerts strength slowly by taking the affected spinous process as the supporting point to bend the spinal column rightward and also rotate the patient's waist rightward to an elastic limit position. After a short stop, the operator continues to press the patient's nape downward with right hand and raises his own elbow forcefully. At the same time, he pushes the spinous process toward the opposite side with his thumb to do a quick, controlled twisting movement in small amplitude; cracking sound of reposition is often heard at the moment, and also a "jerking" sensation of spinous process beneath the thumb.

When the manipulation is done by one person, the operator may ask the patient to ride on a narrow bed to fix the pelvis and lower limbs.

【Pulling manipulation of waist done by a backward stretching】

Ask the patient to take a prone position. Standing by the side of the patient, pressing the lumbar area with one hand and raising the affected leg or both legs to a limit position with another hand, the two hands exert strength to opposite directions cooperatively to stretch the lumbar vertebrae backward to fulfil a quick, controlled twisting movement in small amplitude.

d. Pulling manipulation of shoulder

It is classified into four ways in accordance with four directions of shoulder joint movement: raising, adduction, backward extension and abduction.

【Pulling manipulation of shoulder done by raising arm】

Ask the patient to take a sitting position with two arms dropping down naturally. Standing behind the patient to fix the patient's trunk with the body, hold the lower part of the forearm of affected limb to raise it from anteflexion position slowly to 120° ~ 140°. At this moment, hold the same arm at the area close to wrist joint with another hand, two hands exert strength cooperatively to do an upward traction gently. When there is a resistance, make a quick, controlled, upward twisting movement in small amplitude and release the arm right after. The operation can be done repeatedly for 3 ~ 5 times.

【Pulling manipulation of shoulder done by adducting arm】

Ask the patient to take a sitting position and flex the elbow of affected limb in front of the chest. Stand behind the patient abutting against the patient's back to stabilize the patient's body and fix the affected shoulder with the hand which is at the same side of patient's affected shoulder, hold the elbow of affected limb with another hand to help the patient doing adduction until a resistance appearing, make a quick, controlled adducting-twisting movement in small amplitude and release the arm right after. The operation can be done repeatedly for 3 ~ 5 times.

【Pulling-twisitng manipulation of shoulder done by stretching arm backward】

Ask the patient to take a sitting position with the affected arm dropping down naturally. Stand behind the patient at the lateral side with one hand supporting and fixing the affected shoulder, and another hand holding the wrist at the same side to make the arm extended backward and flexed with the hand dorsum touching the back. Pull this hand upward until there is a resistance, then make an sudden, controlled, upward twisting movement in small amplitude, release the arm right after. The operation can be done repeatedly for 3 ~ 5 times.

【Pulling manipulation of shoulder done by abducting arm】

Ask the patient to take a sitting position with the arm extended and abducted. Having a half-squating position by the side of the affected shoulder, the operator, one hand going beneath the patient's armpit to meet his another hand with fingers crossed at the top of patient's shoulder, presses the affected shoulder and stands up slowly by taking the affected shoulder a supporting point, shake the patient's arm slightly at the same time and continue to abduct the patient's arm until a resistance appearing; then, do a quick, controlled abducting-twisting movement in small amplitude and release the arm right after. The operation can be done repeatedly for 3 ~ 5 times.

e. Pulling manipulation of elbow

Ask the patient to take a supine position. Holding the lower part of the upper arm of the patient with one hand and the lower part of the forearm with another hand, extend and flex the elbow joint repeatedly until it reaches to it's limit position of pain, then, do an sudden, controlled, flexing or extending twisting movement in small amplitude.

f. Pulling manipulation of wrist

Holding the lower part of the forearm of the patient with one hand, pull and stretch the patient's wrist joint with another hand. Then, bend and stretch the patient's wrist joint, or bend the wrist joint sideward, to the limit position of pain, make an sudden, controlled extending or flexing or sideward flexing movement in small amplitude.

g. Pulling manipulation of sacroiliac joint

Two ways commonly used:

【Pulling manipulation done by strecthing sacroiliac joint backward】

Ask the patient to take a prone position. Standing by the healthy side with one palm root pressing posterior superior iliac spine and the other hand supporting anterior aspect of lower part of the thigh of affected side, make the knee joint of the affected side flexing, then stretch the affected leg backward to an elastic limit position. At this moment, ask the patient to cough. When the muscles are relaxed after coughing, make an sudden, controlled backward stretching movement to enlarge backward stretching extent of the leg $3° \sim 5°$ more. Meanwhile, the hand, which is pressing the posterior superior iliac spine, does a short downward pressing movement.

【Oblique pulling-twisting manipulation of sacroiliac joint】

The patient takes a lateral recumbent position with the healthy side against the bed and the leg of the healthy side extended and the hip joint slightlyly bended; the hip joint and knee of the affected side flexed. Push the patient's shoulder with one hand to make the torso turned backward; press the lateral aspect of patient's knee with another hand to make the lumbar sacrum rotating forward. When the spine is twisted to an elastic limit position, two hands exert strength cooperatively to do a rapid, controlled pressing movement in small amplitude.

h. Pulling manipulation of knee joint

Two ways commonly applied:

【Pulling manipulation of knee joint done by extending knee】

Ask the patient to take a supine position. Standing by the side of the patient with one hand pressing the area above the affected knee and another hand placed on the posterior aspect of lower part of the lower leg of same side. Two hands exert strength cooperatively to stretch the knee. When a resistance appears, make a rapid, controlled twisting movement in small amplitude.

【Pulling manipulation of knee joint done by flexing knee】

Ask the patient to take a prone position. Standing by the side of the patient with one hand pressing posterior aspect of the thigh to fix it and another hand holding ankle of affected limb, flex the knee joint of affected limb until resistance appearing, and then make a rapid and controlled twisting movement in small amplitude.

i. Pulling manipulation of ankle joint

Ask the patient to take a supine position. Holding the patient's heel with one hand and the plantar digital area with another hand, two hands exert strength cooperatively to make ankle joint flexed and stretched, or turned inward and outward to the limit position of pain, then do an sudden, controlled flexing, or stretching, or turning inward or outward twisting movement in small amplitude.

2. Essentials of Movements

The operation of pulling-twisting manipulation should conform to physiological movement of the joints. Pulling manipulation is a controlled passive movement with certain limitation. It should be done step by step, i.e. stretch or rotate the performed joint to it's extreme limit, then, on the base of it, do an sudden, controlled twisting movement in slightly increased amplitude.

The pulling-twisting movement should be agile and quick at proper time with proper strength.

The patient should be relaxed. Sometimes the patient is required to regulate his breath to cooperate with the operator.

3. Precautions

The strength exerted during the application of pulling-twisting manipulation should be controlled appropriately, it is forbidden to have abrupt violent twisting movement.

The amplitude of pulling-twisting movement should be determined according to the range of physiological activity and pathological condition of the joint. Don't surpass the range of physiological function of the joint movement.

Don't chases bounce sound of the joint deliberately; sometimes, cracking sound can be heard when pulling manipulation is done on cervical and lumbar vertebrae. But the natures of diseases are different, don't try to get it if there is no such bounce sound during clinical treatment, remember the principle that "it would be an effective treatment when the joint is manipulated to its desired position." It is not advisable to trase such bounce sound in joint reposition, so as to avoid unnecessary sprain due to violent manipulation and other bad results.

Have a good understanding on the indications of various pulling-twisting manipulations. It is forbidden to apply pulling-twisting manipulations for the patients with joint fracture, dislocation and tumor.

Section 2
Compound Tui Na Manipulations for Adults

Compound tui na manipulation is constituted by two or more than two basic tui na manipulations which have similar kinematic characteristics or same effected areas, and these two basic manipulations are complementary in the treatment when they are combined into one.

Pressing-Kneading Manipulation (*Àn Róu Fă*, 按揉法)

Pressing-kneading manipulation (*Àn Róu Fă*, 按揉法) is constituted by pressing and kneading. It is classified into two types: pressing-kneading manipulation with finger and pressing-kneading manipulation with palm.

1. Approaches to Operation

a. Pressing-kneading manipulation with finger

Both thumb tips are taken as the working point; the rest of the fingers assist the thumb to exert strength. The wrist joint is flexed slightly, the thumb and forearm move actively to do pressing-kneading movement in rhythm.

b. Pressing-kneading manipulation with palm

The palm root is taken as the working point, the rest fingers are extended naturally. The forearm moves actively to do pressing-kneading movement in rhythm. Pressing-kneading manipulation with two palms overlapped can increase the stimulation; the shoulder joint is taken as the working point, the upper arm exerts strength to lead the hand doing pressing-kneading manipulation in rhythm.

2. Essentials of Movements

Pressing-kneading manipulation (*Àn Róu Fǎ*, 按揉法) is the combination of Pressing manipulation (*Àn Fǎ*, 按法) and kneading, i.e., the gentle movement of kneading manipulation mixed with the strength of pressing manipulation.

The frequency of pressing-kneading manipulation (*Àn Róu Fǎ*, 按揉法) is slower than that of kneading; the operation is rich of rhythm.

Drop down the shoulders and elbows to relax shoulder, elbow and wrist joints, so as to release the strength deeply into internal tissues.

3. Precautions

Pay attention to the intensity of pressing and kneading, the manipulation would be floating if the intensity is too mild and it would be hesitant and unstable if the intensity is too strong.

Pressing-kneading manipulation with finger is similar to grasping; The difference is that the fingers except thumb just function as assistants. While in grasping, the thumb and other four fingers exert strength together from opposite direction.

Grasping-Kneading Manipulation (*Ná Róu Fǎ*, 拿揉法)

It is a compound manipulation that Mixing kneading into grasping.

1. Approaches to Manipulation

The approach of this compound manipulation is similar to that of grasping. Add kneading movement of thumb or other fingers on the base of grasping manipulation.

2. Essentials of Movements

In grasping-kneading manipulation (*Ná Róu Fǎ*, 拿揉法), grasping is the primary and kneading is secondary.

The manipulation can be done along the limb, but the speed of shift should not be too quick.

3. Precautions

In grasping-kneading manipulation (*Ná Róu Fǎ*, 拿揉法), kneading movement of fingers is increased and the closing strength of thumb to other fingers is decreased. It is gentler and more dexterous than the simple grasping manipulation.

Pushing-Rubbing Manipulation (*Tuī Mó Fǎ*, 推摩法)

In pushing-rubbing manipulation (*Tuī Mó Fǎ*, 推摩法), when the thumb does one-finger pushing, the rest of the fingers doing finger-rubbing manipulation (*Zhǐ Mó Fǎ*, 指摩法) at the same time. It is the evolution of one-finger pushing.

1. Approaches to Manipulation

Taking the radial side of thumb as the working point, wave the forearm to do one-finger pushing, at the same time, extend and close the rest of the four fingers together to make a rubbing manipulation with finger tips.

2. Essentials of Movements

It is similar to one-finger pushing: Dropping down the shoulders and elbows, but the suspending amplitude of wrist is smaller. The wrist joint is slightly flexed, the thumb is placed on the body surface firmly, and the rest four fingers exert strength through their bellies to do finger-rubbing manipulation (*Zhǐ Mó Fǎ*, 指摩法).

3. Precautions

The thumb is placed on the chief point and the other four fingers on the secondary points.

One-finger pushing should be done cooperatively with finger-rubbing manipulation (*Zhǐ Mó Fǎ*, 指摩法); neither of them can be neglected.

Chapter 6
Tui Na Treatment for Adult Diseases

Section 1
Orthopedic Diseases

Stiff Neck

1. Overview

Stiff neck is a disease of muscle spasm due to long time pulling of cervical muscles including sternocleidomastoid muscle, trapezius muscle and levator scapulae muscle; it is a common disease of cervical soft tissue injury characterized by aching and distention, pain, rigidity of cervical vertebrae, wry neck and forced posture. The incidence of disease is usually high in winter and spring, in young and middle age people, and often in the male. It refers to impediment (Bi) syndrome in Chinese medicine, and it is considered that the pain is caused by unsmooth flowing of channel qi and malnutrition of channels and collaterals due to deficient body constitution or fatigue with improper sleep posture or an uncomfortable pillow; or caused by obstruction of channels and collaterals due to wind-cold invasion of the neck resulting in blood stasis; or caused by neck sprain resulting in contraction of channels and collaterals. Modern medicine thinks that the occurrence of the disease is related to improper sleep posture and an uncomfortable pillow as well as an external cold invasion of the neck and shoulder and neck sprain.

2. Clinical Manifestations

Most of the patients, when getting up in the morning, may feel pain or rigidity of neck with forced posture of the head often deviated to the sick side. It is usually related to improper sleep posture, uncomfortable pillow, attack of the neck by wind-cold, and improper neck movement. It may show spastic pain and stiffness of the sternocleidoma stoid muscle, trapezius muscle and levator scapulae muscle of one side, obvious limitation of neck movement, failure of turning, raising and lowering the head, and the pain which is always aggravated by moving the head or touching the neck muscle, worse at night and better in daytime. In cases caused by attack of wind and cold, the pain would be more severe if the neck is exposed to these factors.

The patient would have blue and purple tongue or tongue with dark marks, thin or thin white coating, wiry or tense pulse. The patient has to hold their neck to minimize cervical movement in order to relieve pain temporarily.

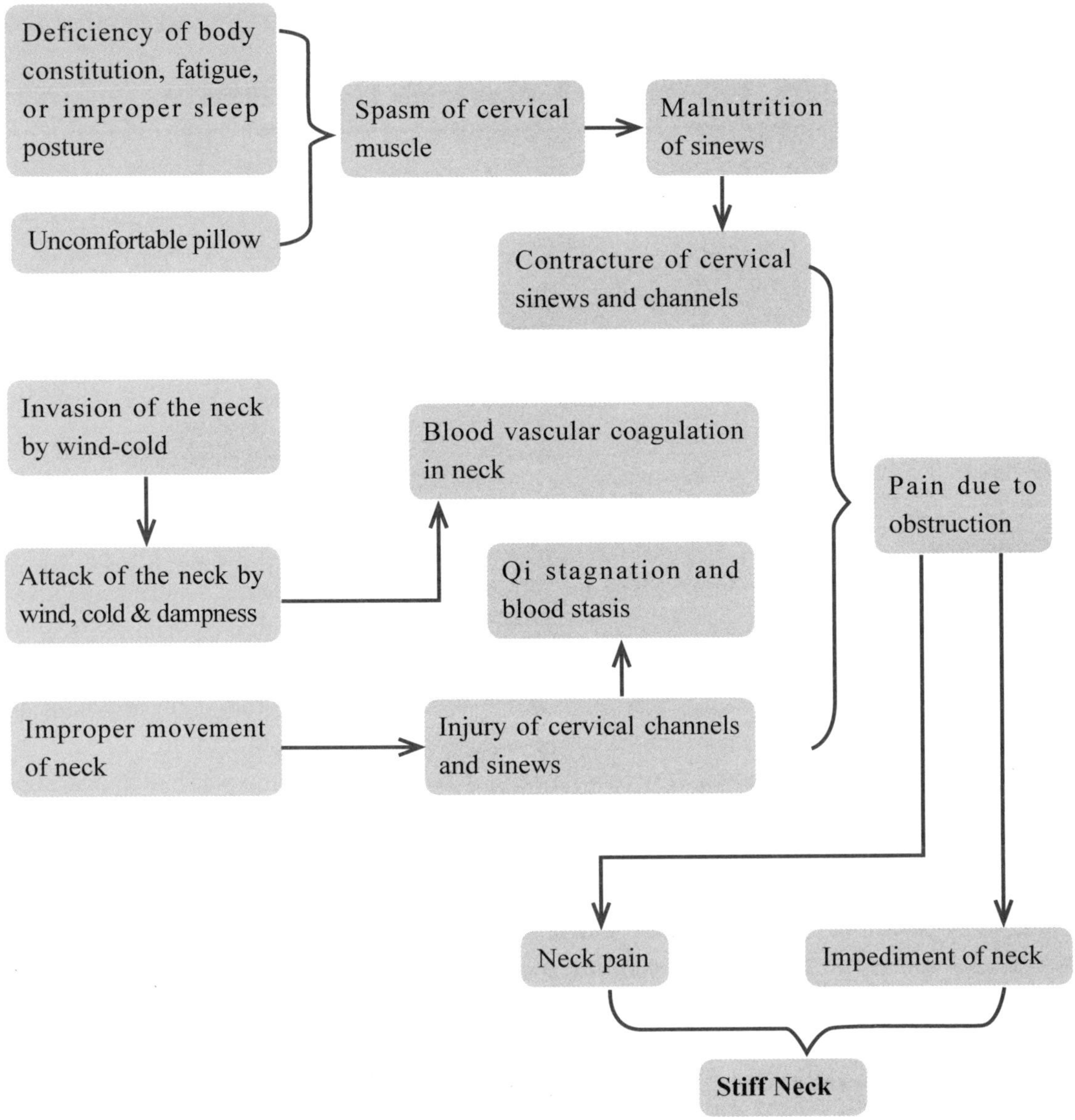

3. Diagnostic Essentials

Cervical muscle tension increases visibly, especially on sternocleidomastoid muscle, trapezius muscle and levator scapulae muscle; cord-like, tense and swollen muscles could be found.

Apparent tender spots often found on the starting and ending points of the muscle and on the belly of the muscles. In the cases with spasm of sternocleidomastoid muscle, tenderness could be found on the belly of the muscle and the mastoid process. In the cases with spasm of trapezius muscle, tenderness could be found on the lateral 1/3 of clavicle or on GB 21 (*jiān jǐng*) or beside the spinal process of cervical and thoracic vertebrae. In the cases with spasm of levator scapulae muscle, tenderness could be found beside spinal process of cervical vertebrae or on the intra-superior angle of scapula.

Limitation of neck movement in turning, raising and lowering the head, forced posture with the head deviated to the sick side, the pain is always worse during movement.

X-ray examination usually shows no special change, only cervical physiological curvature, or scoliosis change. In the middle aged and old patients, degenerative cervical changes could be found by X-ray, but it's not the direct cause of stiff neck, it should be differentiated together with clinical symptoms.

4. Differential Diagnosis

The various tests of the neck show there are no symptoms of nerve root compression. Normally, it is not difficult to distinguish the disease from cervical spondylosis, subluxation of cervical vertebrae, cervical tuberculosis and myofascitis in accordance with the history, body signs and X-ray examination.

5. Tui Na Treatment

【Treatment Principle】

To relax sinew, activate blood, warm channels and dredge collaterals.

【Points and Regions】

EX-UE8 (*wài láo gōng*)	GB 20 (*fēng chí*)	SI 12 (*bǐng fēng*)	GB 21 (*jiān jǐng*)
SI 11 (*tiān zōng*)	SI 14 (*jiān wài shù*)	SI 15 (*jiān zhōng shù*)	LI 11 (*qū chí*)
LI 4 (*hé gǔ*)	GB 34 (*yáng líng quán*)		

Neck and shoulder.

【Method】

Ask the patient to take a sitting position, apply point-kneading manipulation on EX-UE8 (*wài láo gōng*), SI 11 (*tiān zōng*), LI 11 (*qū chí*), LI 4 (*hé gǔ*), GB 34 (*yáng líng quán*), half a minute each point. Ask the patient to move the neck by turning, raising and lowering the head as far as possible when the above points are pointed and kneaded.

Gently apply palm-kneading manipulation and repeatedly on the painful regions for 3~5 times; later, rolling manipulation and one-finger pushing manipulation on both sides of the neck and shoulder, first on the healthy side and then the affected side, but focusing on the affected side. The treatment with these manipulation lasts for 3~5 minutes until the pain is apparently relieved.

Apply pressing-kneading manipulation or one-finger-pushing manipulation on GB 20 (*fēng chí*), SI 12 (*bǐng fēng*), GB 21 (*jiān jǐng*), SI 11 (*tiān zōng*), SI 14 (*jiān wài shù*), SI 15 (*jiān zhōng shù*), 10 seconds each point.

Apply grasping-kneading manipulation on GB 20 (*fēng chí*) for half a minute; grasping-kneading manipulation on the neck for 2~3 times; lifting-grasping manipulation on GB 21 (*jiān jǐng*) for 2~3 times; and flicking manipulation on tense muscle for 2~3 minutes.

Apply pulling-stretching manipulation of neck, rotate the patient's head leftward and rightward slowly, 10 times respectively.

Apply pulling manipulation by rotating the neck.

Apply rotating manipulation of the neck to make the patient's head lower, extend backward and rotate leftward and rightward passively.

Apply scrubbing manipulation on the neck, back and shoulder about 2~3 minutes until it is warm enough at the local area.

6. Precautions

Apply gentle manipulation, increase manipulation force gradually, and avoid the manipulations with strong stimulation and sudden violent force to prevent accidents. Treatment should be started from the distal side of painful region and then gradually close to the affected area, to give the patient's body time for adapting the stimulation. The pulling manipulation of neck should be done stably and quickly, it is not necessary to get cracking sound. The strength of manipulation and rotation degree of manipulation are determined by the patient's tolerance. Forced manipulations are forbidden in order to avoid accident.

For the patient with severe pain, press distal points to relieve pain first.

The pillow should be comfortable, not so high, soft or hard.

For the patients with repeated stiff neck, the neck must be kept warm and away from over-trained.

Functional exercise is necessary after the recovery to improve cervical muscular strength and avoid recurrence.

Medications, acupuncture and physical therapy can be combined with Tui Na Treatment.

Cervical Spondylopathy

1. Overview

Cervical spondylopathy, also called cervical vertebral syndrome, refers to a series of syndromes caused by changes of cervical vertebral function and structure due to degeneration of cervical intervertebral disc, hyperosteogeny of cervical vertebrae and trauma resulting in irritation and compression on cervical nerve root, cervical artery, spinal marrow and sympathetic nerve. The mild cases may manifest pain and numbness of head, neck, shoulder and arm; the severe cases may even have weak limbs, incontinence of urine and stools, and paralysis. If vertebral artery and sympathetic nerve involved, dizziness and palpitation would be found.

There are 7 cervical vertebrae, 6 intervertebral discs; spinal canal and intervertebral foramen are composed of vertebral body and vertebral arch. The structure of C3~C7 are almost same except atlas and axis. The atlas connects with skull to form atlanto-occipital joint. Since it has neither body nor spinous process, the atlas helps to rotate the head. The axis is the second vertebral, it connects with the atlas to form atlanto-odontoid joint for helping head rotation. The spinous process of C2 is long and thick with small and downward transverse process, and no branches, this structure is convenient for the head turning leftward or rightward. From C3 to C7, all the cervical vertebrae have vertebral bodies, vertebral arches and processes. The anterior connection of the vertebrae is Luschka joint, while the posterior connection is zygapophysial joint. Luschka joint takes part in the movement of cervical vertebrae, it can limit the cervical body in the right place so as to improve intervertebral stability and prevent the core of intervertebral disc protruding to the side. When the intervertebral disc degenerates and becomes thinner, the edges of upper and lower cervical bodies may easily collide with each other to wear and cause hyperosteogeny and narrowed intervertebral foramen. The normal intervertebral foramen is in the form of ovate, its vertical diameter is larger than its transverse diameter. Owing to the narrow space between the anterior wall and posterior wall of intervertebral foramen, the diameter would become even smaller, if the posterior articular process and cervical body shift forward or backward or hyperosteogeny forms. Clinically, such changes may compress nerve root and vertebral artery. Zygapophysial joint is almost horizontal, so it has poor stability, and spinal nerve root lies in front of this joint, if the intervetebral disc degenerates, the intervertebral space becomes narrow, the joint capsule of zygapophysial joint is loose, it would cause prolapse of cervical body leading to the symptoms of nerve root irritation resulted from narrowed intervertibral foramen. There is a round hole on the root of transverse process of cervical vertebrae, called transverse foramen or vertebro-arterial foramina. Vertebral artery ascends behind the common carotid artery and enters the transverse foramen of C6, then upward and out from the transverse foramen of the atlas. If the transverse foramen becomes smaller, it would compress the vertebral artery.

The disease is often seen among people over 40 years old as a common disease in the middle aged and old people. Along with the changes of study, profession, and life habits, it has the tendency that incidence is earlier, also fairly common among people at 30 years old. In Chinese medicine, the disease is attributed to cramping of neck tendon, neck and shoulder pain and vertigo, caused by deficiency of liver and kidney, deficiency of qi and blood, together with invasion of exogenous wind, cold and dampness, or trauma and strain. Cervical spondylosis is a degenerative change of cervical vertebrae. The degeneration of cervical intervertebral disc is the internal causative factor; various kinds of acute or chronic traumatic injuries are the external causative factors. Continuous study or work in a lowering head position, incorrect sleep posture, falling down or sprain would cause degeneration of intervertebral disc, looseness of joint capusles and ligaments, the activity degree among vetertebrae is increased to affect the stability of spine and cause ligament calcification and hyperosteogeny. The hyperosteogeny of posterior joints of vertebrae and Luschka joint as well as narrowed intervertebral foramen or narrowed spinal canal are the main pathological factors of compression of spinal marrow, cervical nerve root, vertebral artery and sympathetic nerve. Clinically, cervical spondylopathy is normally divided into five types including nerve root type, spinal marrow type, vertebral artery type, sympathetic nerve type and mixed type according to the affected areas and symptoms.

2. Clinical Manifestations

a. Nerve root type

Symptoms are varied according to the location of compression.

The patient with disorder above the intervertebral space between C3 and C4 may show neck pain radiating to the occipital region, abnormal sensation in the occiput.

The patient with disorder in the intervertebral space between C4 and C5 may show nape pain and numbness radiating to the wrist along shoulder, anterior side of lateral aspect of upper arm and anterior side of radial aspect of forearm, but not to the hand.

The patient with the disorder in the intervertebral space between C5 and C6 may show pain of nape and back and abnormal sensation radiating to the thumb along hand *taiyin* lung channel.

The patient with disorder in the intervertebral space between C6 and C7 may show pain of nape and back and abnormal sensation radiating to the index finger and middle finger along the middle line of posterior aspect of the upper arm and forearm.

The patient with disorder in the intervertebral space between C7 and T1 may show pain and abnormal sensation radiating along the interior aspect of the upper arm and the ulnar aspect of forearm to the ring finger and small finger.

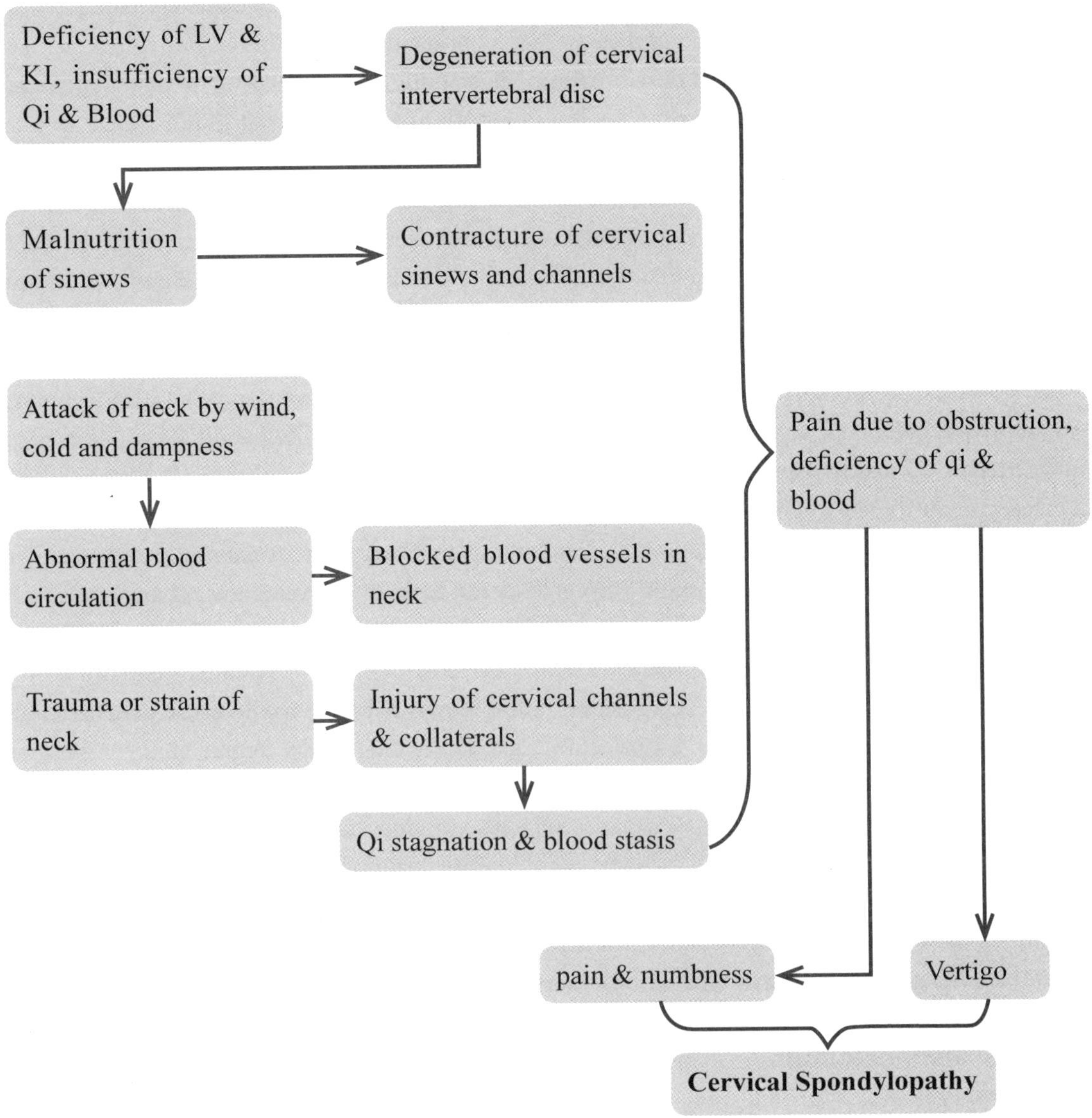

The above are the symptoms showing compression of single nerve. But in clinic, several nerve roots could be compressed simultaneously due to pathogenic changes of several vertebral bodies, it make the symptoms much more complicated.

Physical examination may reflect muscular tension of the neck, tenderness or radiating pain at the side of disordered vertebral spinous process and on distribution area of the nerve, limited cervical movement, tenderness on the upper part (C5 and C6), the middle part (C6 and C7) and the lower part (C7 and T1) of medial border of the scapula. Intervertebral foramen pressure test (+). Brachial plexus stretching test (+). Abnormal sensation: Hyperesthesia may appear in the case with mild compression of nerve root and short duration; on contrary, it is hypoesthesia. The patient with long duration may manifest muscular atrophy on the areas controlled by corresponding nerves. X-ray examination may show shallow cervical physiological curve with hyperosteogeny of different degrees.

b. Vertebral artery type

Neck and shoulder pain or neck and occiput pain, but not always obvious.

Vertigo

It usually happens suddenly when the head turns to a certain angle, which could be relieved if the head changes its position.

Falling down suddenly and disturbance of consciousness.

There would be no signs before the onset. The patient may fall down due to muscular tension of lower limbs, when turning the head or when rotating the neck in the posture of walking or standing.

Tinnitus and deafness

Headache

It is a kind of pumping or distending pain, appearing alternatively with vertigo, on one side of the head, in the neck or in top of the occiput. It is the sign of cerebrovascular spasm.

Dysfunction of vegetative nerve and internal organs

The symptoms include nausea, vomiting, uncomfortable sensation in epigastric region, profuse sweating or absence of sweating, flowing of saliva, arrhythmia, burning sensation in the nape, back and chest, formication, chest stuffiness, irregular breathing. Physical examination: neck rotation test (+), X-ray examination: Hyperplasia on the lateral side of Luschka joint. Oblique film shows narrowed intervertebral foramen. Vertebral arteriography, rheoencephalogram and magnetic resonance angiography (MRA): compression of vertebral artery.

c. Spinal marrow type

At the early stage of spinal marrow type, only mild abnormal sensation in the neck like that of the nerve root type, even no symptoms and no local signs to differentiate the symptoms of the limbs, so it is often misdiagnosed as neurosis to delay the treatment. At the late stage, the symptoms related to sensory system, motor system, sympathetic nerve and vessels may manifest:

Compression of pyramidal tract or spastic ischemia symptoms of anterior spinal artery

They may manifest weakness and heaviness of lower limbs, staggering, trembling, falling down, muscular spasm; and spastic paralysis at the late stage.

Spinothalamic tract symptom

It refers to numbness of limbs first appearing in the lower limbs and then gradually developing upward.

Ataxia

Unstably standing, staggering gait, vibratory sensation, disorders of position sense, swing gait when walking with closed eyes.

Dysfunction of vegetative nerve and sphincter

They may manifest cold, aching and distending feeling in the paralyzed or numb limbs, accompanied by poor blood circulation and edema. At the early stage, there are urgent micturition and vesical tenesmus; while at the later stage, urinary retention, constipation and incontinence of stools may occur. Physical examination shows incomplete paralysis of limbs with significant sensory disturbance plane. Lin Mite's sign (+). In standing position with the head lowered or erected, if the patient feels electric-shock like numbness in the upper limbs, which radiating downward along the trunk to the shank and the foot, it is an important sign of compression of cervical spinal marrow. Increased muscular tension and decreased muscular force. Abnormal reflex: Disappearance of superficial reflex, abdominal reflex, cremasteric reflex and levator ani reflex. Hyperactivity of deep reflex: biceps jerk, triceps jerk, knee jerk and Achilles tendon reflex. Appearance of pathological reflex: Hoffmann's sign (+), Babinski sign (+).

CT and MRI can help to make diagnosis.

d. Sympathetic nerve type

【Symptoms of the head】

Neck and occipital pain, migraine, dizziness without obvious relations to the movement of head.

【Symptoms of the heart】

Tachycardia or bradycardia, precordial pain, unstable blood pressure.

【Peripheral vascular symptoms】

Positive Raynaud's sign, dull sensation of limbs, head, neck and face.

【Abnormal sweating】

Profuse sweating or scanty sweating on the affected limb or unilateral limbs.

【Symptoms of the eye】

Weakness of eyelid, blurred vision, distending pain in behind the eyeball, lachrymation.

【Dysfunction of stomach and intestine】

Diarrhea or constipation.

【Other symptoms】

Tinnitus, deafness, numbness of tongue, uncomfortable sensation or foreign sensation in the throat, ataxia. Physical examination shows no typical symptoms; a part of the patients may show Horner's sign, i.e. myosis, ptosis, enophthalmos.

e. Mixed type

Though the cervical spondylopthy of simple type could be seen in clinic, the most are mixed type with two types and three types as well. Their clinical manifestations are varied and complicated too.

3. Diagnostic Essentials

a. Nerve root type

Typical compression symptoms of nerve root and tenderness beside corresponding spinous process.

Intervertebral foramen pressure test (+).

X-ray examination shows: Shallow physiological curve of cervical vertebrae, hyperosteogeny, narrowed intervertebral space, narrowed intervertebral foramen.

Rule out the possibility of cervical vertebral tuberculosis, tumor, thoracic outlet syndrome, scapulohumeral periarthritis, tennis elbow, bicipital tenosynovitis.

b. Vertebral artery type

Cervical vertigo, suddenly falling down.

Neck rotation test (+).

X-ray examination shows: unstable intervertebral joints or hyperosteogeny of Luschka joint.

Rule out the possibility of aural vertigo and ocular vertigo.

Rule out the possibility of intracranial tumor and neurosis.

The disease can be diagnosed with the results of vertebral arteriography, CT and MRI. The results of cerebral aorticrheogram and EEG are taken as reference.

c. Spinal marrow type

Compression Symptoms of spinal marrow. The case with symptoms spreading from upper limbs to the whole body is considered as central type; the case with symptoms spreading from lower limbs to the whole body is considered as peripheral type.

X-ray examination shows: Hyperplasia of posterior border of vertebral body, narrowed sagittal diameter of spinal canal.

Rule out the possibility of amyotrophiclateralsclerosis (ALS), spinal marrow tumor, adhesive arachnoiditis secondary to spinal injury, multiple peripheral neuritis.

For the difficult cases, myelography or CT and MRI can be taken to help diagnosis.

d. Sympathetic nerve type

A series of sympathetic nerve symptoms, such as dizziness, blurred vision, tinnitus, hand numbness, tachycardia and precordial pain.

X-ray results agree with clinical symptoms.

Normal ECG.

4. Differential Diagnosis

The cervical spondylopthy of nerve root type should be distinguished from vertebral tuberculosis, tumor and thoracic outlet syndrome according to history of disease, body signs and imaging examinations. The cervical spondylopthy of vertebral artery type should be distinguished from subclavian steal syndrome, meniere's syndrome, disorders of vegetative nerve and acoustic neuroma. The cervical spondylopthy of spinal marrow type should be distinguished from syringomyelia, vertebral tuberculosis and vertebral tumor. The cervical spondylopthy of sympathetic nerve type should be mainly distinguished from angina pectoris due to coronary insufficiency; both of them manifest the symptoms of vegetative nerve, but the symptoms of vegetative nerve are obvious in the cervical spondylopthy of sympathetic nerve type, while cardiac symptoms are obvious in coronary insufficiency; in addition, ECG is normal in cervical spondylopathy, but ST segment downshift and T wave is low and flat in angina pectoris.

5. Tui Na Treatment

【Treatment Principle】

To dredge channels and collaterals, activate blood, eliminate blood stasis, and reposite sinews.

【Points and Locations】

GB 20 (*fēng chí*)	DU 16 (*fēng fǔ*)	GB 21 (*jiān jǐng*)	SI 11 (*tiān zōng*)
LI 11 (*qū chí*)	LI 4 (*hé gǔ*)	LI 10 (*shǒu sān lǐ*)	SJ 5 (*wài guān*)

The neck and upper arms of the sick side.

【Method】

Basic manipulations:

Ask the patient to take a sitting position. Apply rolling manipulation or four-finger-pushing manipulation on the shoulder and neck for relaxation.

Apply pressing-kneading manipulation on GB 20 (*fēng chí*), DU 16 (*fēng fǔ*), SI 11 (*tiān zōng*), and grasping manipulation on GB 20 (*fēng chí*).

Apply pressing-kneading manipulation on LI 11 (*qū chí*), LI 4 (*hé gǔ*), LI 10 (*shǒu sān lǐ*), rubbing manipulation on the shoulder, shaking manipulation on the upper arm and pulling-extending manipulation on the finger joints.

Apply rotating manipulation on the neck.

Take the pillow away, apply pulling-extending manipulation of the neck.

The manipulations determined according to the types.

⋆.Nerve root type

Apply pressing-kneading and flicking manipulation on the tender spots of the neck, the manipulations for reposting the neck such as pulling manipulation by rotating the neck, pulling manipulation of cervical vertebrae at fixed location or oblique-pulling manipulation; cervical traction is suggested with low weight and longer time.

⋆. Spinal marrow type

Give cervical traction with low weight and longer time (40~60 min, 3~5 kg)

⋆. Vertebral artery type

Apply common manipulations on the face and head and give cervical traction with low weight and longer time.

⋆. Sympathetic nerve type

Apply pressing-kneading manipulation on bilateral PC 6 (*nèi guān*), BL 15 (*xīn shù*), BL 22 (*sān jiāo shù*), and RN 17 (*dàn zhōng*).

6. Precautions

Before Tui Na Treatment for cervical spondylopathy, it should be made clear if the disease is at an acute stage or at recovery stage. In acute stage, gentle manipulations are suggested, neither oblique-pulling manipulation nor pulling manipulation of cervical vertebrae at fixed area by rotating the neck. In recovery stage, stronger manipulation can be given but within the patient's endurance.

The principle of increasing manipulation strength bit by bit must be followed during treatment; when passive movement is done, the manipulations should be slow and gentle, violent and rough manipulations in large amplitude are forbidden to avoid accident.

Advice the patient not to work with bowing the head for long time, avoid carrying heavy object by the head and hand, or work with improper posture.

The pillow for sleep should be comfortable and suitable, better a small cushion under the neck.

During the treatment period and the period 1~2 weeks after the treatment, it's better to take a neckband to fix cervical vertebrae.

Keep the neck and shoulder warm.

Have functional neck exercise of neck during and after treatment period, especially the exercise for strengthening anterior and posterior muscle groups of neck.

The therapeutic effect of Tui Na Treatment of cervical spondylopthy of spinal marrow type is not good, sometimes, even shows a tendency of progressive aggravation. For spinal marrow type, combined treatment or surgical operation should be considered.

Acute Lumbar Sprain

1. Overview

Acute lumbar sprain refers to acute injury of muscles, fascia and ligaments of lumber region as well as the injury of small intervertebral joints and lumbosacral joints during working or sports. The most are caused by indirect force due to sudden excessive pulling or pressing. Clinically, acute lumbar sprain is a common disease with high incidence among young and middle aged people, the laborers and the people who are lack of exercises and exertion. It seems the male is more than the female.

The causative factors of acute lumbar sprain are various, including intensity of labor, movement skills, health condition of the waist and back, strain and even the changes of weather and season. Most of the patients are able to illustrate the posture when they were injured and point out the painful areas.

The following are the factors which may causes lumbar injury:

a. Improper posture of exertion

For example, bow to pick up a heavy object with the legs straighten, the center of gravity is far from the body axis, the movement increases load to lumbar muscle because of leverage and easily cause acute sprain of lumbar muscle.

b. Slipping and falling

When slipping during walking on uneven road or going down stairs, the torso falls to the front while the legs are still straight; it is a posture easily causes sprain and tear of lumbar muscular fascia.

c. Disharmonious movement

For example, two persons are carrying an object, they can not coordinate each other and lose imbalance; since the center of gravity deviates suddenly, the lumbar muscle contracts abruptly and forcefully under the condition with no preparedness, the consequence is the onset of acute lumbar muscular sprain.

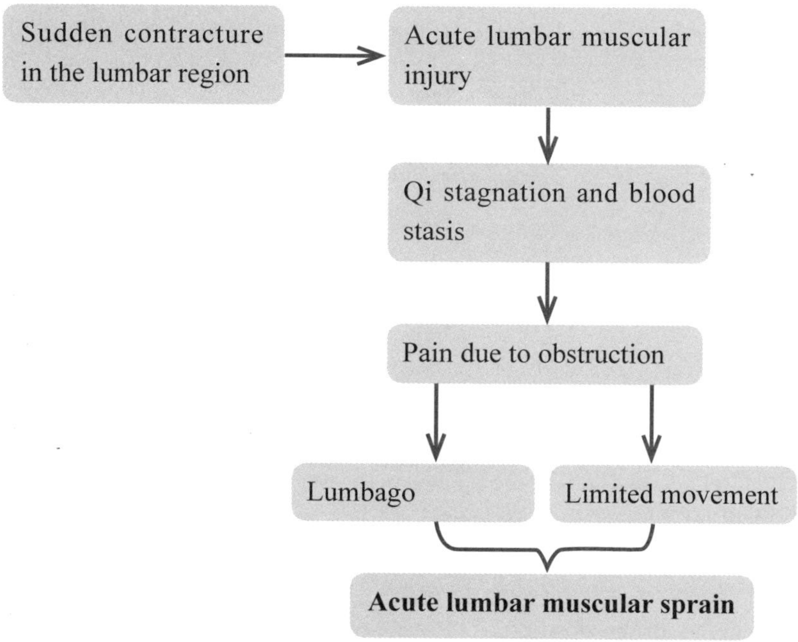

2. Clinical Manifestations

The patient usually manifests unilateral or bilateral sharp pain in the lumbar region, stiffness of the back, failure of stretching the body. The pain would be aggravated by bowing, stretching, turning, standing up and sitting down. In severe cases, even getting up from the bed, exerting, coughing and sneezing may worsen the pain; in mild cases, the pain is mild and the patient can still work, but the symptoms would become worse in a few hours or next day. In order to diminish the pain, the patient has to hold his back with his hands. The pain is mostly in lumbosacral region, sometimes in the hip, one side or both sides, or in the posterior aspect of the thigh; the exact location and nature of the pain are usually not clear, but the most complaints are distending pain and aching. In acute lumbar muscular pain, the tongue is purple, or purple with dark marks, tongue coating is thin, and the pulse is wiry or slow.

Physical examination

At the early stage of sprain, protective spasm of the muscle caused by pain due to tear of muscle, fascia and ligament is often seen; physiological lordosis of the lumbar vertebrae decreases; asymmetrical muscular spasm may cause lateral curvature of spine column. Many patients have obvious limited tenderness, which are the injured areas and also the essentials for making diagnosis. X-ray examination shows no change of bone substance.

3. Diagnostic Essentials

A traumatic history of sudden lumbar injury.

Severe lumbago aggravated by cough and sneeze, limitation of movement.

Obvious tenderness on the lumbar region aggravated by tapping, lumbar muscular spasm, possible deviated spinous process, enlarged space between the spinous processes and scolosis of the spinal column.

Usually no lower limb pain. Sometimes, there is reflecting pain in posterior aspect of the thigh or in medial side of anterior aspect of the thigh nearby the groin.

X-ray examination usually shows no particular changes.

4. Differential Diagnosis

X-ray examination is suggested to rule out fracture, tumor and tuberculosis.

5. Tui Na Treatment

【Principle】

To relax sinew and activate blood.

【Points and Regions】

BL 23 (*shèn shù*)	BL 25 (*dà cháng shù*)	GB 30 (*huán tiào*)
BL 37 (*yīn mén*)	BL 40 (*wěi zhōng*)	BL 57 (*chéng shān*)
GB 34 (*yáng líng quán*)	BL 60 (*kūn lún*)	*ashi* point

The back and lumbar region.

【Method】

Ask the patient to take a prone position. Apply rolling manipulation around the tender spot and gradually shift the hand to the tenderness; meanwhile, the passive movement by stretching the patient's lower back backward is done from small range to large range with manipulation strength enhanced gradually. The treatment with these manipulations last about 5 minutes.

Ask the patient to take a prone position. Apply rolling manipulation and kneading manipulation on BL 23 (*shèn shù*), BL 25 (*dà cháng shù*), GB 30 (*huán tiào*), BL 37 (*yīn mén*), BL 57 (*chéng shān*), GB 34 (*yáng líng quán*), BL 60 (*kūn lún*) and *ashi* points. Then, apply grasping manipulation on BL 40 (*wěi zhōng*) till the patient feels soreness and distention, plucking manipulation above and below the tender spot with gentle but strong force. The treatment lasts about 5 minutes.

Apply scrubbing manipulation on the lumbar region till it is hot enough at the local area.

Apply oblique-pulling manipulation or rotating-pulling manipulation on the lumbar region.

For severe lumbar pain, apply pressing manipulation on BL 57 (*chéng shān*), meanwhile, ask the patient to move his lower back actively.

6. Precautions

After the treatment, ask the patient to have a bed rest, don't do any movement with the lower back in a short period.

Acute symptoms could be relieved instantly after the treatment, but the pain and stiff feeling in the lumbar region doesn't disappear, the physical therapy at the local area could be applied to relieve the symptoms gradually.

The exercises which can train m. extensor of the back may consolidate the therapeutic effect and prevent reoccurrence of the disease.

Keep the lumbar region warm.

Chronic Lumbar Strain

1. Overview

Chronic lumbar strain refers to chronic accumulated injury of muscle, fascia, ligament, bone, joint and other tissues in lumbar region. It is called functional lumbago in western medicine. The disease is usually caused by long time working in bowing and squatting position, overloading and straining of the back, improper posture during work, or lumbar anatomic specialty and defect. In addition, improper treatment or delayed treatment of acute lumbar injury or repeated traumatic injuries of the back. Chronic lumbar strain is the most common causative factor of lumbago. It appears gradually and slowly without obvious trauma and influences the people's work and life significantly, so it should be treated and prevented actively.

2. Clinical Manifestations

The main symptom is chronic lumbago manifesting dull pain, better after rest or proper exercise or by changing position, worse after exertion or when weather changes. It is difficult to work in bowing position; the pain would be exacerbated if the patient forces himself to work in this position. The patient likes to tap the lumbar region with his hands for relieving pain; a few patients complain distending pain in the area of hip joint. The tongue is light red, the coating is thin white, and the pulse is superficial and tight.

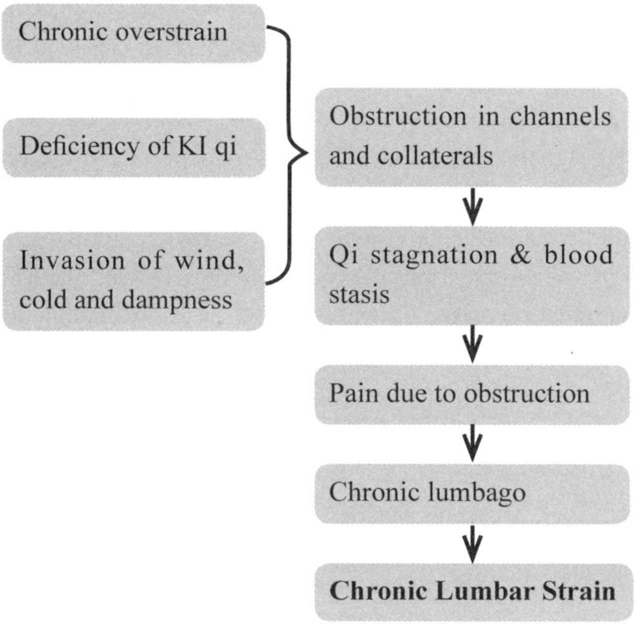

Physical examination: The appearance of spine is normal, no problem in movement; tenderness can be found in one or both sacrospinalis muscle, in posterior side of iliac crests or at the ends of back muscle. In severe cases, the pain is worse with mild limitation of movement.

Neurologic examination: Usually no changes.

X-ray examination: It is possible to find the changes of spinal physiological bow, such as scoliosis, weakening or disappearance of lumbar lordosis, or congenital variations like sacralization of L 5, lumbarization of S 1 and occult cleft spine, or hyperosteogeny.

3. Diagnostic Essentials

A long medical history of lumbago with repeated attacks.

Uncomfortable feeling or pain aggravated after exertion or during cloudy and rainy days.

Straight leg raising test is generally normal, unobvious limitation of movement.

Block therapy with 1% procaine 2~3 ml on the tender spot may relieve or eliminate the symptoms.

X-ray examination only shows congenital variation of lumbosacral vertebrae or hyperosteogeny.

4. Differential Diagnosis

It should be distinguished from strain of supraspinal ligament.

5. Tui Na Treatment

【Principle】

To relax sinew, activate blood, warm channels and dredge collaterals.

【Points and Regions】

BL 23 (*shèn shù*)	BL 25 (*dà cháng shù*)	BL 26 (*guān yuán shù*)
BL 54 (*zhì biān*)	GB 30 (*huán tiào*)	BL 40 (*wěi zhōng*)

The back and lumbosacral region.

【Method】

Ask the patient to take a prone position, apply palm-pushing manipulation, pressing manipulation and kneading manipulation on erector muscles on both sides of the spine. The treatment with these manipulations lasts 5 minutes.

Apply finger-pressing manipulation and plucking manipulation on sacrospinalis muscle for several times, and then, apply pushing manipulation, pressing manipulation and plucking manipulation with the thumb on the tender spots. The treatment with these manipulations lasts 5 minutes.

Apply pressing manipulation, kneading manipulation and trembling manipulations with finger tips and finger bellies on BL 23 (*shèn shù*), BL 25 (*dà cháng shù*), BL 26 (*guān yuán shù*), BL 54 (*zhì biān*), GB 30 (*huán tiào*), BL 40 (*wěi zhōng*), half a minute each point.

Apply scrubbing manipulation transversely on the lumbosacral region till it is warm enough at the local area.

6. Precautions

Take care of posture and note to correct habitual poor posture to maintain the normal physiological curves of the spine.

Get more sports exercise to strengthen lumbar muscles.

Regulate and improve the environment and condition of the work and study. For the people who have to work in single position, exercise is necessary; avoid long time of working in poor posture.

Keep a proper balance between work and rest. For the patient with relative diseases or other chronic diseases, have proper rest and exercise to prevent overstrain.

Degenerative Spondylitis

1. Overview

Degenerative spondylitis, also called hypertrophic spondylitis, refers to osteoarthropathy characterized by degenerative changes of lumbar cartilage and hyperosteogeny. The disease is common in middle age and old age, more frequently seen in the male. It is a kind of chronic osteoarthritis of lumbar vertebrae showing chronic pain of lower back and leg; the occurrence of disease is usually earlier in the over-weight people, manual workers and athletes.

The disease is classified into two types: primary type and secondary type. The primary type indicates physiological retrogression in the old people, including hyperosteogeny of various degrees on the body margin of lumbar vertebrae, degeneration of intervertebral disc, narrowed intervertebral space and foramen; these changes compress and stimulate nerve root to cause pain of lower back and leg. The secondary type usually follows variety of injuries, chronic inflammation, anemia, metabolic disorders or endocrine disorders; these disorders may affect blood circulation and nutrition supply of the osteoarticular cartilage, resulting in inflammatory changes of the cartilage and reactive hyperosteogeny of the subchondral bone, leading to lumbago and leg pain.

Modern medicine thinks that the pathological change of degenerative spondylitis is based on degeneration of intervertebral disc. The spine has three physiological curves; hyperosteogeny relatively more happens on the concave side of the spine due to stress concentration.

It should be made clear that hyperosteogeny is a kind of normal compensative reaction of vertebrae to the pressure over its own load for increasing stability and ability of load bearing due. Due to natural limited space in the body, the hyperosteogeny is possible to affect the function of adjacent tissues and cause those symptoms. To the pain, the local (including articular surface and tissues like paravertebral ligaments) inflammations (including congestion and edema) are the significant factors. The pain appears only when the tissues react to the stimulus like drag and compression due to inflammation. Along with the gaining of age, hyperosteogeny stops to develop because it has grew big enough to counteract abnormal increase of load, and then the inflammation decrease (the occurrence of inflammation is greatly related with abnormal increase of pressure) and the pain would be obviously eased. At this moment, the patient may have no marked subjective symptoms, though X-ray examination possibly shows severe hyperosteogeny. It is not advisable to make diagnosis as degenerative spondylitis for this situation.

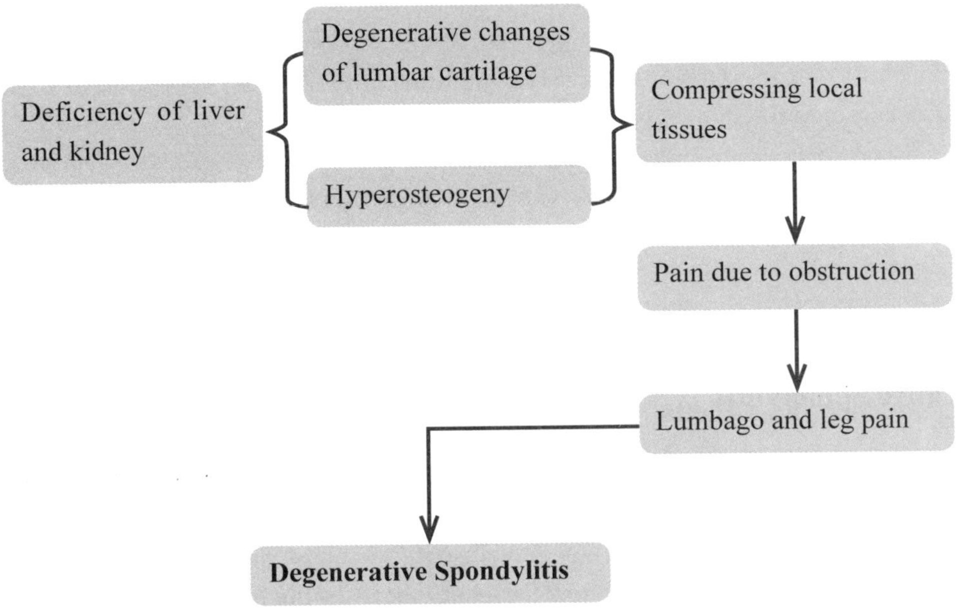

2. Clinical Manifestations

Lower back pain gradually appears after middle and old age without systemic symptoms. It is the fastigium of lower back pain due to degenerative spondylitis during 45~55 years old. Usually, the lumbago is not severe; or just uncomfortable feeling or rigid feeling in the lumbar region with less flexible movement. The lumbago would be worse in the morning when the patient gets up from the bed or at daytime after long time sitting; the pain could be better or disappear after moving around and be worse after overstrain. Sometimes, the pain may radiate to the hip or thigh, and get worse during rainy, cloudy, windy and cold days. The patient usually manifests a tongue with thin white coating or white greasy coating, deep and tense or soft and slow pulse.

Physical examination: Deformation of spinal column, physiological lordosis of lumbar vertebrae decreases or even disappears, limitation of spinal movement, occasional percussion pain of lumbar vertebral process, tension or tenderness of bilateral psoas. Tenderness or even sciatic irritation symptoms may occur on the courses of superior gluteal nerve and sciatic nerve. Straight leg raising test is positive, tendon reflex is weak, neck flexed and abdomen pressed test is positive. X-ray examination may show the degree of hyperosteogeny.

3. Diagnostic Essentials

Chronic lower back pain and leg pain.

No significant deformity of the spinal column. If there is olisthy, lordosis of lumbar vertebrae increases. There is no evident limitation or just mild limitation of lumbar movement. Straight leg raising test is false positive.

Usually, there is no fixed tender spot on the lumbar region; if there are any, they usually appear on bilateral psoas muscles and the lumbar vertebrae of L 3 ~ L 4, L 4 ~L 5.

X-ray examination may show: Hyperosteogeny on the body margin of lumbar vertebrae, lipping or bony spur on the anterior border of lumbar vertebrae, narrowed or irregular intervertebral space, blurred articular process, and possible senile bone atrophy.

4. Differential Diagnosis

The disease is mainly distinguished from other lumbar diseases such as the third lumbar transverse process syndrome and prolapse of lumbar intervertebral disc. X-ray examination may help to rule out other lumbar vertebral diseases, such as tuberculosis, tumor, fracture, congenital deformity of lumbar and sacrum vertebrae.

5. Tui Na Treatment

【Principle】

To promote qi, activate blood, relax sinew and dredge collaterals.

【Points and Regions】

DU 4 (*mìng mén*)	DU 3 (*yāo yáng guān*)	BL 24 (*qì hǎi shù*)
BL 25 (*dà cháng shù*)	BL 26 (*guān yuán shù*)	EX-B2 (*jiā jǐ*)
BL 40 (*wěi zhōng*)	GB 34 (*yáng líng quán*)	BL 57 (*chéng shān*)

The lower back.

【Method】

Ask the patient to take a prone position. Apply rolling manipulation on the lumbar region and both sides of lumbar vertebrae. Increase the force gradually. The treatment lasts 3~5 minutes.

Apply finger-pressing manipulation on DU 4 (*mìng mén*), DU 3 (*yāo yáng guān*), BL 24 (*qì hǎi shù*), BL 25 (*dà cháng shù*), BL 26 (*guān yuán shù*), or press EX-B2 (*jiā jǐ*) on bilateral sides of lumbar vertebrae with palm root, then apply rolling manipulation from the lumbar region to the buttocks. For dragging pain in the leg, apply pinching manipulation, grasping manipulation and pressing-kneading manipulation along the posterior aspect of the thigh to the calf; pointing, pressing and kneading manipulations on BL 40 (*wěi zhōng*), GB 34 (*yáng líng quán*) and BL 57 (*chéng shān*); at the same time, ask the patient to raise leg backward to associate the treatment. The treatment lasts about 10 minutes.

At last, apply scrubbing manipulation on the back and relative areas. Warm compression therapy is suggested.

6. Precautions

Rest on hard bed, and keep the lower back warm.

Have necessary exercises such as bowing, stretching the body backward and turning the loin leftward and rightward.

Oral intake of herbal medicine is recommended to strengthen sinew and bone, activate blood and eliminate stasis, if the stomach and intestine functions are allowed.

Third Lumbar Transverse Process Syndrome

1. Overview

The third lumbar transverse process syndrome refers to chronic lumbago marked by the evident tenderness on the third lumbar transverse process. It is also known as peripheral inflammation or bursitis of the third lumbar transverse process. It belongs to the category of lumbar myofascial strain. The third lumbar vertebra, with longer transverse process, is located at the center of the whole lumbar vertebrae. It has wider range of movement with stronger anti-stress ability. Therefore, it has a higher incidence of strain which always leads to lumbago and buttock pain. The disease is mainly seen among young and middle-aged people, especially among those who are engaged in physical work.

The internal causative factor of the disease is that lumbar muscles are not well-developed, so it usually occurs to thin and tall people. Its external factors are chronic strain and acute sprain. The lumbar transverse processes are located at both sides of the lumbar vertebrae without any protection from bones. The third lumbar transverse process is the longest one and attached by psoas major muscle, quadratus lumborum muscle, transverse abdominis muscle and the deep fascia of latissimus dorsi muscle. When the lumbar and abdominal muscles contract forcefully, the third lumbar transverse process is exposed to the strongest stress. As a result, the muscles attached to the third lumbar transverse process are apt to be pulled and damaged, resulting in pathological changes as inflammatory swelling, hyperemia and exudation of the local tissues, and followed by secondary changes as hyperplasia of synovium, fibrous tissues and fibrocartilage, etc. In addition, the prolonged irritation to the external branch of the lumbar posterior ramus will lead to degenerative changes of nerve fibers, consequently causing lumbago, hip pain and lumbosacral muscular spasm. Besides, exogenous pathogenic factors and trauma can also cause the laceration of the muscles and fasciae surrounding the third lumbar vertebra, consequently leading to injurious inflammation. Improper treatment may cause pathological changes as scar adhesion, thickened fascia, tendon contracture around the transverse process and other corresponding symptoms.

2. Clinical Manifestations

The disease is often characterized by lumbar fatigue feeling and diffused pain that spreads to the posterior part of the thigh and even to the popliteal fossa. The pain, which tends to be persistent, may be aggravated by exertion, weather changes, or worse in the morning or when the body is bent. However, it may be alleviated by moving around. In some cases, the disease may be marked by intermittent ache, distension and lassitude with the pain radiating to the buttock or the lateral side of the thigh. Numbness or hypersensation is often shown at the side of the intervertebral space between the second and third lumbar vertebrae. Other manifestations include pale tender tongue with white coating, and deep thready pulse.

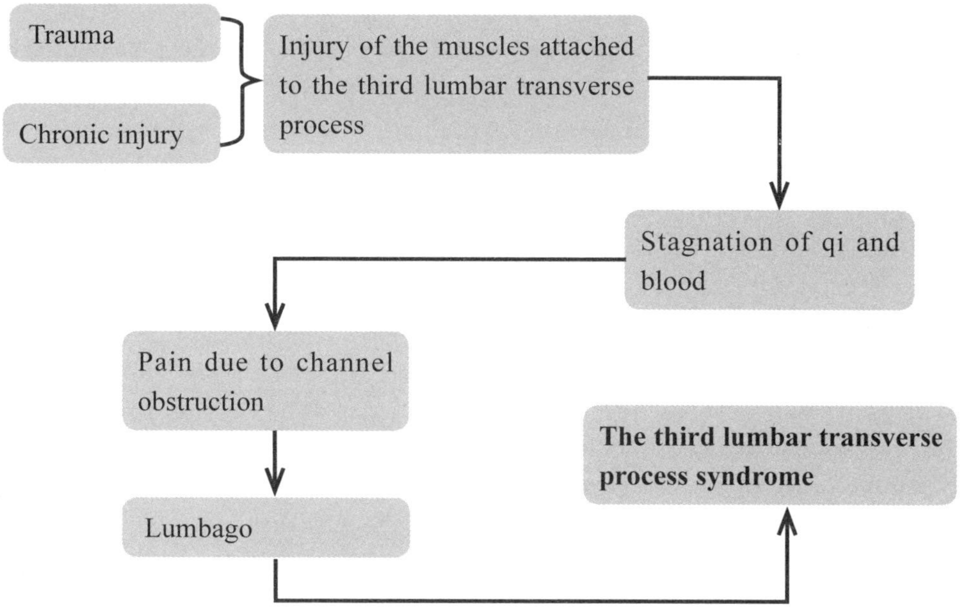

The examination may show local tenderness at the tip of the third lumbar transverse process lateral to the margin of sacrospinalis. Sometimes fibrous nodules of soft tissue can be touched, which often cause reflecting pain in the affected leg, and weakened lumbar muscular tension, but lumbar movement is basically normal. Straight leg raising test may be positive. X-ray examination shows that the third lumbar transverse process is evidently longer, which may present asymmetry between bilateral transverse processes or backward tilt.

3. Diagnostic Essentials

Often accompanied by history of lumbar injury, mild or severe.

Unilateral or bilateral lumbago pain, worse in the morning, after exertion or during bending movement. In severe cases, the pain may radiate to the lower leg along the thigh.

Evident pain and nodular fibrous indurations at the tip of the third lumbar vertebra transverse process.

X-ray film shows that the third lumbar transverse process is longer than usual with calcification shadow at the distal edge of the transverse process asymmetrical processes.

4. Differential Diagnosis

This disease should be differentiated from acute lumbar sprain, chronic lumbar muscle injury, herniated lumbar disk and so on. X-ray exam can exclude other lumbar diseases like tuberculosis and tumor.

5. Tui Na Treatment

【Principle】

To move qi and invigorate blood, relax the sinews and unblock the collaterals.

【Points and Regions】

GB 30 (*huán tiào*)	BL 36 (*chéng fú*)	BL 40 (*wěi zhōng*)	BL 57 (*chéng shān*)

Lower back.

【Method】

Ask patient to take a prone position. Apply rolling or four-finger-pushing manipulations on both sides of lumbar region to relax the muscles.

Apply plucking manipulation on the third lumbar vertebra transverse process.

Apply pointing and kneading manipulations or one-finger pushing manipulation on BL 23 (*shèn shù*), BL 24 (*qì hǎi shù*), BL 25 (*dà cháng shù*), BL 54 (*zhì biān*), GB 30 (*huán tiào*), BL 36 (*chéng fú*), BL 40 (*wěi zhōng*), BL 57 (*chéng shān*), BL 60 (*kūn lún*) and GB 34 (*yáng líng quán*), 1 minute each point.

Ask patient to take a lateral recumbent position, apply oblique-pulling manipulation of the lumbar vertebrae.

Apply palm-vibrating manipulation on the third lumbar vertebra transverse process.

Apply vertical scrubbing manipulation along bilateral courses of the foot taiyang bladder channel, transverse scrubbing manipulation and patting manipulation on lumbosacral region.

6. Precautions

It is better to sleep or rest on a hard bed during the attack and treatment period.

Keep warm, avoid invasion of exogenous pathogenic factors which may influence the therapeutic effect. Apply hot compress to enhance the therapeutic effect during treatment period.

Avoid any hard work that may cause the exertion of the lumbar region.

Rectify bad postures.

Lumbar Disc Herniation

1. Overview

Lumbar disc herniation, also known as herniated lumbar discus intervertebralis nucleus pulposus due to ruptured annular fibrosus, refers to a series of symptoms including pain in lower back and leg. These symptoms are caused by the bulged or herniated nucleus pulpsus pressing nerve root, followed by degenerative lumbar intervertebral disc and partially or completely ruptured annular fibrosus due to external forces. The disease is one of the common diseases marked by lower back and leg pain. It is often seen among young and middle-aged manual workers. The incidence is high among the workers from 20 to 40 years of age. Lumbar disc herniation between L4 and L5 is the most common; and that between L5 and S1 is less; herniation between L3 and L4 happens occasionally and that between L2 and L3 or L1 and L2 rarely seen. In TCM, the disease pertains to the category of *bi* syndrome since there is no name of lumbar disc herniation. TCM holds that the disease is caused by the obstruction of channels and collaterals due to wind-cold-dampness attack with the deficiency of liver and kidney as the root cause. Western medicine thinks that it results from a series of pathological changes due to degenerative intervertebral discs.

Lumbar intervertebral discs lie between adjacent vertebrae. They serve as the weight-bearing parts and the movement pivot of the spinal column. Intervertebral disc consists of annulus fibrosus, nucleus pulposus and cartilaginous end plate. Annulus fibrosus is composed of elastic and tenacious fibers embedded in cartilaginous matrix and connected tightly with adjacent vertebrae. Nucleus pulposus is a hydrous gel-like center, which is encased in the global cavity by annulus fibrosus and cartilaginous plates of adjacent vertebrae. Along with the increase of age and the influence of the external forces as pressing, pulling and twisting, the discs degenerate gradually marked by dehydrated nucleus pulposus and decreased elasticity, which are followed by narrowed intervertebral spaces, loosened and ruptured ligaments. The series of pathological changes are the internal causes of lumbar disc herniation. Under the external force, the annulus fibrosus may rupture and nucleus pulposus may extrude posterolaterally when posterior pressure in disc increased. Therefore, obvious nerve pain would be caused by irritation and compression of the spinal nerve (or spinal cord). In the cases without any evident traumatic injury, cold invasion is the main cause. In these cases, lumbar muscle spasm may lead to herniation of degenerative lumbar disc and resultant compression of nerve root after cold invasion resulting in hyperemia, edema and degeneration or hyperplasia and hypertrophy or even adhesion to herniated disc in chronic cases. Mostly, the disc is herniated towards one side through longitudinal ligament to compress spinal cord or nerve root, so the symptoms are ipsilateral. However, herniated disc may irritate and compress bilateral nerve roots causing symptoms in both legs or alternating symptoms.

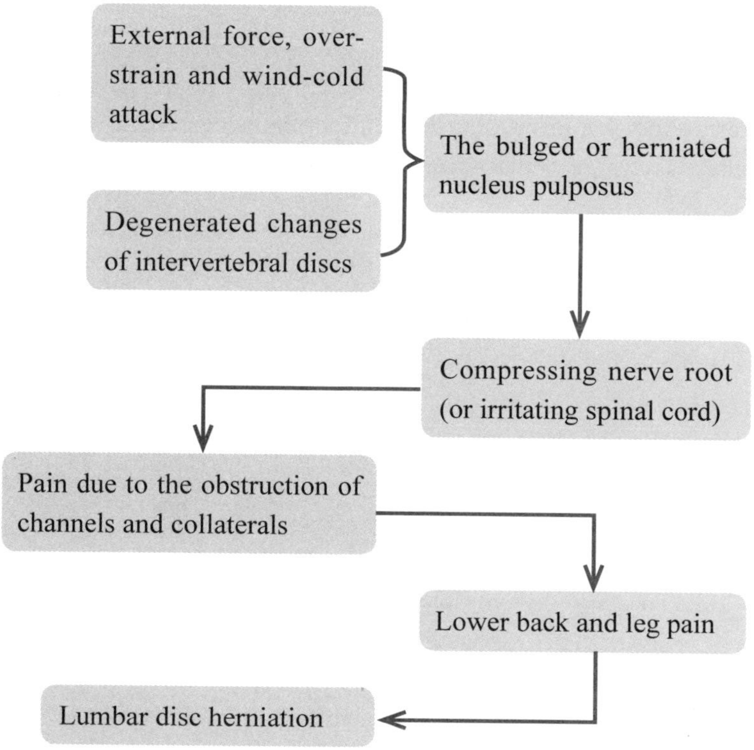

2. Clinical Manifestations

The main symptoms are lower back pain (or lumbago) and radioactive leg pain (sciatica). Lower back pain is limited in lumbosacral region. Usually, there is local deep tenderness in the spaces between spinous processes of L4-L5, L5-S1, or L3-L4, which may radiate to the affected leg. Sciatica often occurs unilaterally and the pain radiates down along the posterior aspect of the thigh and the lateral side of the shank to the heel or to the lateral side of the dorsum of foot. If the herniation of intervertebral disc is severe or exists in the center of vertebral canal, bilateral pain may occur. Coughing, sneezing and straining with bowel movements may tense the nerves and worsen the symptoms. Walking, bending and standing up from a sitting position may stretch the nerve root and then worsen the pain. The pain may be relieved when hip and knee are flexed or during bed rest. The pain is usually paroxymal and seldom persistent. The pain may be evidently reduced after a good rest, especially a bed rest. But it may recur because of mild injury. For cases with a long duration, there may be numbness in the affected area, accompanied by dark purple tongue, or a tongue with purple spots and marks, deep and unsmooth pulse.

3. Clinical Examination

a. Lumbar deformity

The patient may show functional scoliosis, reduction or disappearance of lumbar lordosis, evident limitation of bending forward and less limitation of bending backward. Pain or movement limitation appearing in scoliosis is based on the deformity direction; bending toward the concave side of the scoliosis may relieve pain while bending toward the convex side may worsen pain.

b. Tender points

The location of tenderness is contributive to the position of herniated lumbar disc.

c. Paresthesia

The paresthesia of the affected limb is significant in the diagnosis.

d.Neck bending test, abdomen protruding test and straight leg raising test (Laseque's Test) are positive; tendon reflex is reduced or disappears.

4. Diagnostic Essentials

There is history of lumbar trauma, chronic lumbar strain or cold-dampness attack. Most of the patients had chronic lumbago before the onset of lumbar disc herniation.

It is often seen in young and middle-aged people.

Lower back pain radiates down to the buttock and lower limb. Increase of abdominal pressure induced by coughing or sneezing can worsen the pain.

Scoliosis, disappearance of lumbar lordosis, tenderness on the side of affected vertebrae which radiating down to the leg and limited lumbar movement.

Hyperesthesia and hypoesthesia may appear in the corresponding area of the leg which is controlled by the affected nerve; myoatrophy in the cases with long duration; straight leg raising test (Laseque's Test) positive; reflex of patellar tendon or achilles tendon decreased or disappeared; muscular strength of hallux dorsiflexion weakened.

X-ray film shows scoliosis, reduced or disappeared lumbar lordosis and osteophytes around the edges of adjacent vertebrae. CT and MRI may show the location and severity of herniated lumbar disc.

5. Differential Diagnosis

This disease should be differentiated mainly from chronic lumbar muscle strain, third lumbar transverse process syndrome and so on. X-ray exam can exclude other lumbar diseases like tuberculosis, tumor, fracture and congenital lumbosacral deformity, etc.

6. Tui Na Treatment

【Principle】

To relax the sinews, unblock the collaterals and relieve the adhesion.

【Points and Regions】

DU 3 (*yāo yáng guān*)	BL 25 (*dà cháng shù*)	GB 30 (*huán tiào*)	GB 29 (*jū liáo*)
BL 36 (*chéng fú*)	BL 37 (*yīn mén*)	BL 40 (*wěi zhōng*)	BL 57 (*chéng shān*)
GB 34 (*yáng líng quán*)	GB 39 (*xuán zhōng*)	GB 40 (*qiū xū*)	

Lower back and lower limb.

【Method】

Ask patient to take a prone position. Apply rolling, pressing and kneading manipulations along bilateral courses of urinary bladder channel on the lumbar region, buttock and the posterolateral aspect of the leg for 3~5 minutes, especially on the lumbar region.

Apply pressing manipulation with overlapped palms on the lumbosacral region up and down for 5 minutes.

Apply pointing, pressing and kneading manipulations on DU 3 (*yāo yáng guān*), BL 25 (*dà cháng shù*), GB 30 (*huán tiào*), GB 29 (*jū liáo*), BL 36 (*chéng fú*), BL 37 (*yīn mén*), BL 40 (*wěi zhōng*), BL 57 (*chéng shān*), GB 34 (*yáng líng quán*), GB 39 (*xuán zhōng*), GB 40 (*qiū xū*) and *ashi* point for 5~10 minutes to relieve spasm and pain.

Apply plucking manipulation on the tender points located on the side of the affected spinous process for 3~5 minutes.

Apply pointing, pressing, kneading and plucking manipulations on the sciatic distributing area of the affected side for 1-3 minutes.

Methods of reposition:

Oblique pulling manipulation.

Apply pulling manipulation of waist done by a backward stretching if oblique pulling manipulation fails.

Reposition manipulation of waist done by rotating lumbar vertebrae is suggested if there is evident deviation of spinous process.

Apply treading manipulation if it is possible.

Apply springy continuous palm-pressing manipulation when the waist is in a state of continuous confrontation traction.

Apply pulling-stretching manipulations of leg in the state of leg raised straightly or hip flexed and knee extended in supine position.

Apply scrubbing manipulation along bilateral courses of the foot *taiyang* bladder channel and Du vessel; transverse scrubbing manipulation on lumbosacral region.

7. Precautions

Sleep on a hard bed.

Keep the back warm, avoid catching cold.

Avoid any bending movement with exertion like mopping. Pay attention to the working posture and avoid bending too long or bearing heavy load, which may speed up the degeneration of intervertebral discs.

Have a bed rest and avoid vigorous movements at the acute stage. Proper rest is necessary even if lumbago is improved, avoid over-strained at remission stage to prevent aggravation of disease.

Take food rich in calcium, such as milk, dairy product and sea food. Pay attention to dietary nutrition.

The patients with improved or stable condition can gradually increase functional exercise of the back muscles. (It is forbidden to have intense activities during acute stage, when a bed rest is suggested).

Usually, it is not advisable to apply Tui Na Treatment for patient with large central herniation, especially pulling manipulation, to avoid nerve root injury; but, it is not absolute.

For those patients with poor surgical effect or repeated attacks, the treatment should be given accordingly; it should be very careful if reposition manipulations are used.

Closed Injury of Chest and Hypochondrium

1. Overview

Closed injury of chest and hypochondrium is characterized by rigidity, dragging pain and oppression in the chest due to the obstruction of qi activity in the chest and hypochondrium, mostly caused by violent impact or compression which is not severe enough to cause rib fracture, or caused by poor posture and improper exertion. There are three types of closed injury of chest and hypochondrium, i.e. injury of qi, injury of blood and injury of both qi and blood. Injury of qi, also known as chà qì (岔气) or hypochondriac pain, is caused by indirect violent twisting or pulling which damages the joints and soft tissues of thorax without obvious local tenderness. Blood injury is caused by direct violent impact resulting in thoracic tissue bleeding which disturb circulation of qi manifesting obvious and fixed tenderness. Injury of both qi and blood is caused by direct or indirect violence, such as compression or impact together with pulling or stretching, resulting in thoracic tissue bleeding and extensive injury of the thorax, manifesting clinical features of injury of both qi and blood.

The costovertebral joints consist of two articulations: the joint of capitulum costae and costotransverse joint. They are independent joints, but functionally, are associated. Normally, the two joints are harmonious in movement, however, when there is a violent twisting due to external force, subluxation of joints may compress intercostal nerves causing pain; meanwhile, when the body is twisting, the joint space at a particular area may open to offer the chance for joint synovium inserted. Since there are sensory nerve ends in the synovium, pain and acute injurious pathological changes would occur when the synovium is compressed. In addition, improper bending, weightlifting or pulling may pull and squeeze thoracic proper muscles (intercostales externi, intercostales interni, endothoracic fascia and transversus thoracis) to cause tear or spasm of muscles which may irritate intercostal nerves and cause pain.

2. Clinical Manifestations

The patients usually have evident history of injury. Injury usually causes pain on one side of the chest and hypochondrium spreading to the shoulder and upper back. The pain is worse during coughing or breathing. Superficial short breath and chest oppression often occurs due to reduced respiratory range. The manifestations also include blue-purple tongue or a tongue with dark purple marks or spots with slightly thick coating, and slow choppy pulse. In the cases with severe injury of both qi and blood, pale tongue with purple marks and thin coating, thready choppy pulse may be found. Clinical manifestations are varied in different types.

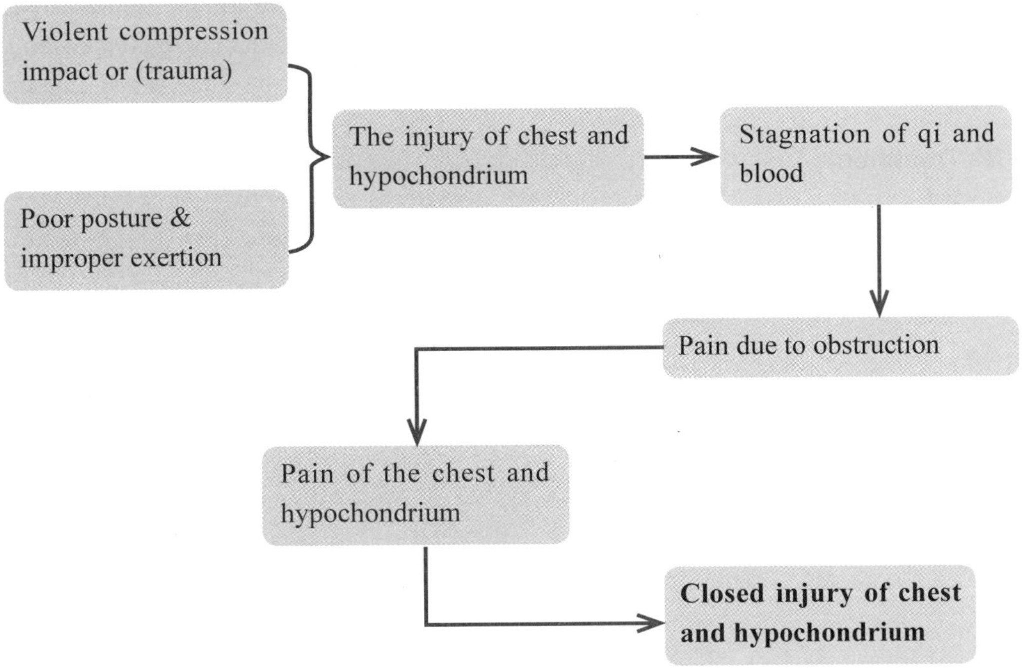

Injury of qi: It is characterized by wandering pain, no obvious local tenderness, dragging pain during breathing or speaking, even inability to lie down or difficulty to turn around in severe cases. In the cases with costovertebral subluxation, there may be tenderness in the affected joints.

Injury of blood: It is characterized by fixed pain with obvious local swelling. If the muscles attached to the chest wall are injured, evident swelling and tenderness can be found in the affected region. If there is tear or spasm in thoracic proper muscles, swelling and tenderness in the corresponding intercostal space and narrowed intercostal space can be found.

Injury of both qi and blood: It is characterized by symptoms of both above two kinds of syndromes.

3. Diagnostic Essentials

The patients usually have evident history of injury.

Palpation can help to find if there is marked tenderness or costovertebral subluxation, help to determine the location, severity and the affected range. The patients with injury of qi often have difficulties to point out the location of the pain; or show local tenderness in a small area. The patients with injury of blood and injury of both qi and blood may show bruise, swelling and obvious local tenderness which is usually aggravated by pressing.

Breathing and speaking induce dragging pain. In severe cases, inability to lie down and difficulty to turn around are seen.

Thoracic squeezing test is negative.

X-ray examination can help to exclude fracture.

4. Differential Diagnosis

X-ray exam is the main method to determine if there is costovertebral subluxation, and to exclude costal fracture. This disease should be also distinguished from intercostal neuralgia, the early stage of chest herpes zoster, tuberculosis or tumor of thoracic vertebrae, pleurisy and costal chondritis, etc.

5. Tui Na Treatment

【Principle】

To invigorate blood, dissolve stasis, move qi, relieve pain, relax the sinews to reposition.

【Points and Regions】

GB 34 (*yáng líng quán*)	RN 17 (*dàn zhōng*)	LU 1 (*zhōng fǔ*)	LU 2 (*yún mén*)
LV 13 (*zhāng mén*)	LV 14 (*qī mén*)	SP 21 (*dà bāo*)	GB 24 (*rì yuè*)

The points of the foot *taiyang* bladder channel on the back, the affected side of the chest, hypochondrium, shoulder and upper back are taken as the main points.

【Method】

Ask patient to take a sitting or supine position. To relieve pain, apply pointing-pressing manipulation on GB 34 (*yáng líng quán*) when the patient is having deep breathing and chest expanding movement.

Ask patient to take a supine position. Apply pointing-pressing manipulation with thumb belly on RN 17 (*dàn zhōng*), LU 1 (*zhōng fǔ*), LU 2 (*yún mén*), LV 13 (*zhāng mén*), LV 14 (*qī mén*), SP 21 (*dà bāo*) and GB 24 (*rì yuè*), 10 seconds each point to relieve local pain. Then apply kneading and rubbing manipulations with palm on the affect part for 3~5 minutes.

Apply pulling manipulation on costovertebral joint. Ask patient to take a sitting position. The operator stands at the affected side of the patient, facing the patient. Inserting one hand under the patient's armpit and holding the patient's affected upper arm with the other hand, pulling the affected side shoulder with the joint efforts of both hands; now, ask the patient breath naturally, do a controlled pulling up movement in small amplitude at the end of breathing in, a cracking sound is often heard if it is costovertebral subluxation or synovial incarceration.

If it fails, pulling manipulation with traction by expanding thorax or back-carrying manipulation can be used.

Ask patient to take a deep breath, apply palm-root-striking manipulation on the corresponding area of the affected rib nearby the spine while the patient is breathing in.

Apply scrubbing manipulation on the back and the local areas.

6. Precautions

Before Tui Na Treatment, it is important to define the diagnosis to exclude the chest and hypochondriac pain caused by fracture and tumor.

At an acute stage, it is not advisable to apply strong manipulations and thermotherapy, so as to prevent bleeding or exudation. Painkillers can be suggested to relieve pain temporarily.

For the patient with facet joint disorder of thoracic vertebrae, pulling manipulation with traction by expanding thorax or reposition manipulation done by pushing against thoracic vertebrae are recommended.

Sleep on a hard bed and avoid heavy physical work during the treatment period.

Keep warm and avoid wind-cold-dampness attack, especially during outdoor work.

After recovered, functional exercises of back muscles and deep breathing exercise should be practiced.

Subluxation of the Sacroiliac Joint

1. Overview

Sacroiliac joint is the weight-bearing pivot of the human body through which the weight that the spine bears is conducted down to the leg and the feet; the external force to the ischial tuberosity is sent up to the trunk. Since sacroiliac joint is stable and movable in small range, only the strong external force can cause sacroiliac subluxation. Subluxation of sacroiliac joint may be caused by violent injury, such as sudden falling down with unilateral buttock knocking on the land; the ground force is conducted upwards from ischial tuberosity, while the impact force due to the body falling down is conducted downward through the sacroiliac joint. Therefore, the two forces converge at the sacroiliac joint pushing the iliac bone upwards and inwards, resulting in subluxation of sacroiliac joint. Similarly, sudden weight bearing of one leg, such as hopping and kneeling, can also cause subluxation of sacroiliac joint. Besides, sprain due to standing up with weightbearing from a squatting position, or over-rotation of sacroiliac joint during falling down with body bending forward or backward may push the lilac bone inwards and upwards to cause subluxation of sacroiliac joint. During pregnancy and after childbirth, the change of endocrine may relax the sacroiliac joint, any of twist, pulling, impacting or slip may cause subluxation of sacroiliac joint.

Subluxation of sacroiliac joint is one of the common diseases marked by lumbago and leg pain. Its incidence is high in young people, especially in females. Improper treatment may lead to persistent pain in the lower back.

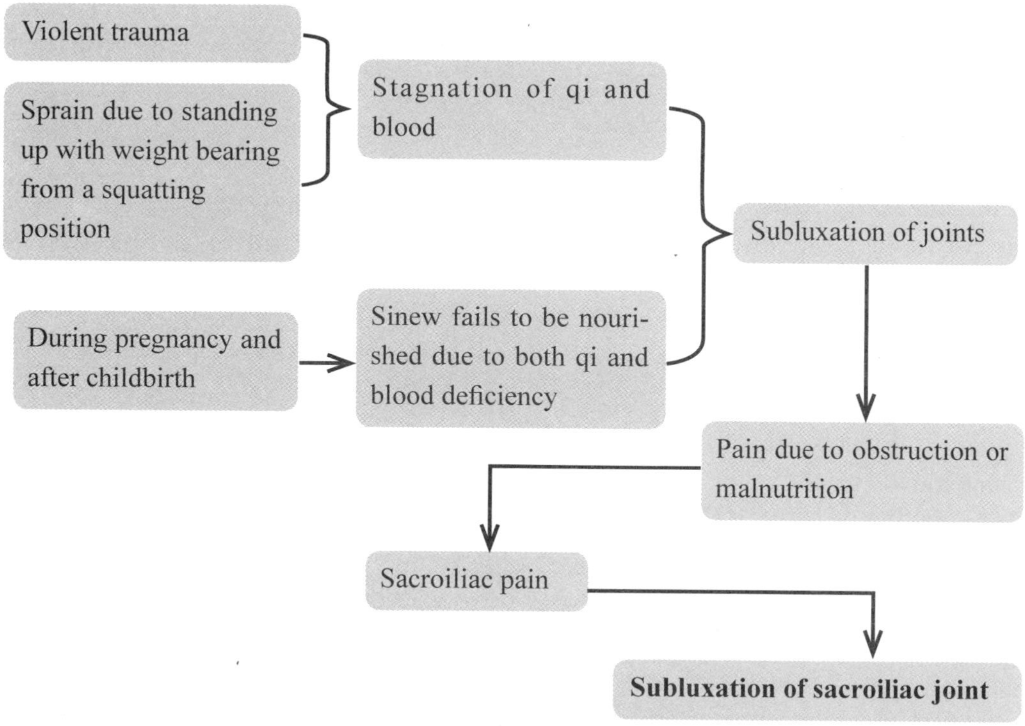

2. Clinical Manifestations

Most of the patients have history of injury and manifest lower back pain and unilateral or bilateral sacroiliac pain. Some patients have unilateral or bilateral alternate sciatica-like pain. On the affected side, there is muscle spasm around the sacroiliac joint, limited movement of lower limb, incapability of bearing weight, walking with a stick or hobbling. The movement like bending, turning, or lying on the back may make pain worse. The patients can neither wear shoes or socks nor laugh or cough because these activities can increase the abdominal pressure to worsen the pain in the affected sacroiliac joint. There is pain with weakness and sometimes radioactive pain or seldom numbness in the lower limbs. The patients often feel that their legs become longer or shorter, and have to walk by holding the affected legs to diminish vibration from walking, have to step with the affected legs first when walking upstairs or downstairs, and need someone to help them when lying down or getting up due to the painful legs. They usually have pale tongue white thin coating, and wiry tense pulse.

Physical examination may find swelling of the affected sacroiliac joint which is more prominent than the healthy side, tenderness and percussion pain at the interior inferior angle of the posterior inferior lilac spine; painful nodules may be touched sometimes. Palpation of the bilateral posterior superior iliac spine may show convex or concave at the posterior superior iliac spine. X-ray examination shows no obvious abnormality. In the patients with old injury, osteophyte can be found on the edges of the sacroiliac joint.

3. Diagnostic Essentials

History of injury.

Lower back pain accompanied by unilateral or bilateral sacroiliac pain.

Limited movement of lower limbs, incapability to tolerate weight.

Leg length discrepancy examination, pelvic separation test, shape of 4 test (Patrick sign) and bedside test (Gaenslen sign) are all positive.

No obvious abnormality in X-ray exam.

4. Differential Diagnosis

This disease should be distinguished from sprain and contusion of the sacroiliac joint, lumbar disk herniation and sacroiliac tuberculosis.

5. Tui Na Treatment

【Principle】

To unblock channels and collaterals, and relieve adhesion.

【Points and Regions】

BL 23 (*shèn shù*)	BL 25 (*dà cháng shù*)	BL 57 (*chéng shān*)	BL 31-34 (*bā liáo*)
BL 54 (*zhì biān*)	GB 30 (*huán tiào*)	BL 40 (*wěi zhōng*)	

Lower back and sacroiliac joint.

【Method】

Ask patient to take a prone position. Apply rolling, pressing and kneading manipulations on sacrospinalis, sacroiliac joint and buttock for 5 minutes, and then apply pressing, kneading, pointing and plucking manipulations with thumb on BL 31-34 (*bā liáo*), BL 54 (*zhì biān*) and GB 30 (*huán tiào*) till it has sour and distending feeling in the local area to relieve spasm and stop pain.

For patient with leg pain, apply pinching, grasping, pressing and kneading manipulations on the thigh and shank. Apply scrubbing manipulation on the affected area till it is warm enough in the local area, or offer hot- wet compression on the sick area.

Approach of reposting subluxation

Ask patient to have a lateral recumbent position on the healthy side over the bedside with the healthy leg straightened. Standing behind the patient, hold the posterior part of iliac wing of the patient with the left hand and the ankle of the affected side with the right hand, flex the patient's knee to 90 degree. Pull the leg backwards to a maximum by holding the ankle together by pushing the ilium forward with the left hand, and then, drag the leg backward further more with a sudden force, sometimes, a cracking sound can be heard. This manipulation is applicable to the backward subluxation of sacroiliac joint.

Ask patient to take a supine position with the left leg flexed to the chest and abdomen (take left leg as an example) and the right leg straightened. Standing firmly at the left side of the patient with the feet naturally apart, the operator holds the ankle of the affected side with one hand and flexes the other elbow, pressing the patient's knee forcefully 2-3 times, which makes the patient's hip and knee over-flexion with the knee touching the chest or abdomen. It may achieve better effect if a cracking sound can be heard or if the patient feels reduction in pain. The method is applicable to forward subluxation of sacroiliac joint.

6. Precautions

Although the symptoms can be relieved a lot after Tui Na Treatment, it is not advisable to do any movement in large amplitude with the waist and legs within two weeks after the treatment, because the recovery of sacroiliac ligaments injury takes time.

It is better to have a bed rest and keep warm during the treatment period.

Piriformis Syndrome

1. Overview

Piriformis syndrome refers to a series of symptoms marked by sciatica, caused by direct or indirect injury of piriformis resulting in tear, bleeding, exudation, adhesion and protective spasm of piriformis; or caused by invasion of wind, cold and dampness resulting in spasm, thickening, local inflammatory exudation, edema, and increased tension of piriformis; and all these factors irritate and compress sciatic nerve which runs through piriformis. It is also called piriformis injury syndrome or piriformis spasm syndrome. Clinically, buttock pain, usually complained as the chief symptom, radiates down along the posterior aspect of the thigh, anterolateral aspect of the shank, lateral malleolus, foot dorsum and toes. The syndrome may occur at any ages, but mostly in young and middle-aged people; it is related closely with anatomical variation of piriformis.

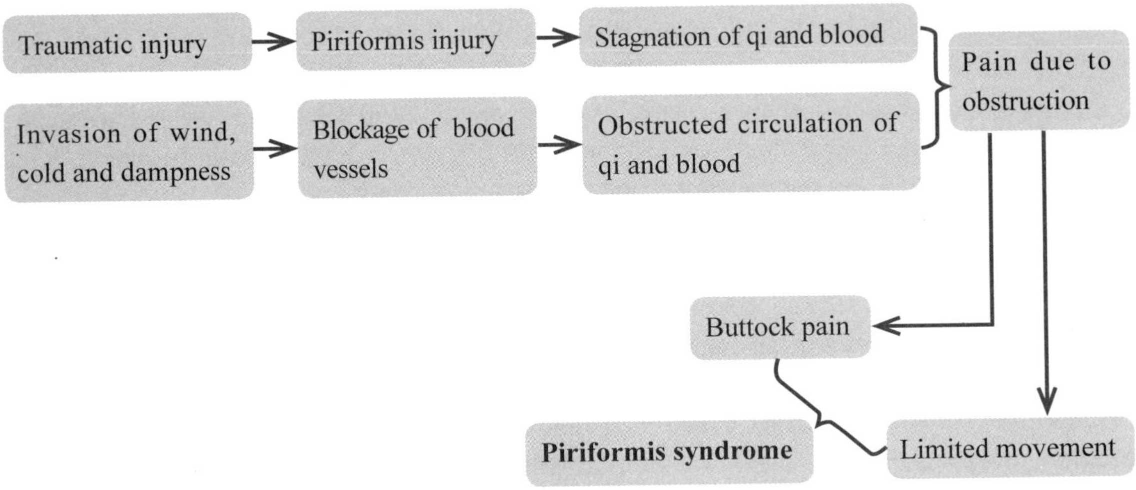

2. Clinical Manifestations

The main clinical manifestations include pricking or knife-cutting pain on one side or both of buttocks; which may radiate along the posterior aspect of the thigh, anterior border of lateral aspect of the shank, lateral malleolus, foot dorsum and toes; the pain may make the patient hobble with hip stick out and aggravated after long walk and exertion or in wet weather. When abdominal pressure is increased by cough, defecation or sneezing, the pain becomes worse. The accompanied manifestations are light red tongue with white coating, wiry and tense pulse.

Physical examination may show evident tenderness on the location of piriformis of the affected buttock. Nodule-like spasm of piriformis can be touched; radioactive pain along the affected leg may appear if the local area is pressed. In chronic cases, mild muscular atrophy in buttock is possibly found. Straight leg raising test (Laseque's Test) shows that the pain is worse when the leg is raised less than 60 degree; and better when the leg raised more than 60 degree. Piriformis tension test is usually positive and flat film of pelvis X-ray reveals no changes.

3. Diagnostic Essentials

A history of injury and cold invasion of the buttock.

Buttock pain, hobbling with hip stick out.

Tenderness of piriformis, nodule-like spasm can be touched on the hip, radioactive pain along ipsilateral leg.

X-ray examination shows no abnormality.

4. Differential Diagnosis

X-ray examination shows no abnormality. X-ray examination of hip joint should be done to exclude any pathological changes of hip joint for the patients suspected to have fracture, tuberculosis or tumor. It is not difficult to make diagnosis according to the history of disease, body signs and results of X-ray examination, but this disease should be distinguished from lumbar disk herniation.

5. Tui Na Treatment

【Principle】

To relax the sinews, unblock the collaterals, activate blood and stop pain.

【Points and Regions】

BL 23 (*shèn shù*)	BL 25 (*dà cháng shù*)	GB 30 (*huán tiào*)	BL 54 (*zhì biān*)
GB 29 (*jū liáo*)	BL 36 (*chéng fú*)	BL 40 (*wěi zhōng*)	GB 34 (*yáng líng quán*)
ST 36 (*zú sān lǐ*)	BL 57 (*chéng shān*)		

Lower back and buttock.

【Method】

Ask patient to take a prone position. Standing at the affected side of the patient, apply rolling, pressing and kneading manipulations on the affected buttock, focusing on the projected area of the piriformis. The manipulations should be performed slowly and firmly about 5 minutes.

Apply pointing and pressing manipulations on BL 40 (*wěi zhōng*), BL 57 (*chéng shān*), GB 34 (*yáng líng quán*), BL 59 (*fū yáng*), GB 39 (*xuán zhōng*), GB 40 (*qiū xū*), GB 41 (*zú lín qì*), GB 30 (*huán tiào*), BL 54 (*zhì biān*).

Ask patient to take a supine position with flexed hips and knees. Gently wave and shake the patient's hip and knee, and also pull and shake the leg a few times, after that, raise the affected leg to 80 degrees and make the affected foot have a dorsiflexion.

Apply scrubbing manipulation transversely on lumbosacral region till it is warm enough in the local area.

6. Precautions

Avoid excessive flexion, extension and rotation of the waist and leg during treatment period.

Keep warm and away from over-strained.

Myofascitis of the Back

1. Overview

Myofascitis of the back, also known as functional lumbago, is marked by diffused pain on one side or both sides of the back due to chronic injury of soft tissues such as back muscles, fasciae and ligaments resulting in local aseptic inflammation. The spinal column is an independent back bone, it relies on the surrounding soft tissues like muscles, fasciae and ligaments to maintain its normal structure and functions, and these soft tissues are the important factors to sustain the stability of the spine. The muscles on the back are classified into superficial and deep muscles. The superficial muscles are constituted of trapezius muscle and latissimus dorsi muscle; deep muscles are of erector spinae distributed from superficial layer to deep layer, transversospinales and deep short muscles. Fascia of the back is classified into superficial and deep layers to wrap erector spinae. The superficial layer covers the surface of erector spinae with its medial side attaching spinous process and suprsaspinal ligament and its lateral side closely connected with aponeurosis of latissimus dorsi; the deep layer, located between the 12th rib and iliac crest, is attached to lumbar transverse process with its medial side and separates erector spinae and quadratus lumborum with its lateral side. The deep and the superficial layers join each other at the lateral side of erector spinae to become the starting part of obliquus internus abdominis and transverses abdominis. The muscles and fasciae of back are connected closely, the later plays a solid part to protect and support the former. Based on the anatomical features above, the injury of back myofascitis can be divided into three parts, i.e. muscles, fasciae and ligaments. Clinically, the injury of muscles and fasciae are inseparable, and usually worse than ligament injury. Therefore, the disease is called myofascitis of the back. TCM thinks that kidney qi deficiency is the root cause of myofascitis of back; together with wind-cold-dampness invasion resulting in obstruction of channels and collaterals, stagnation of qi and blood, malnutrition of sinews, lower back pain is thus induced. Therefore, it is also called lumbago due to kidney deficiency. This disease is common in young and middle-age people, possibly related to their professions and working environment, because there is no evident injury history sometimes.

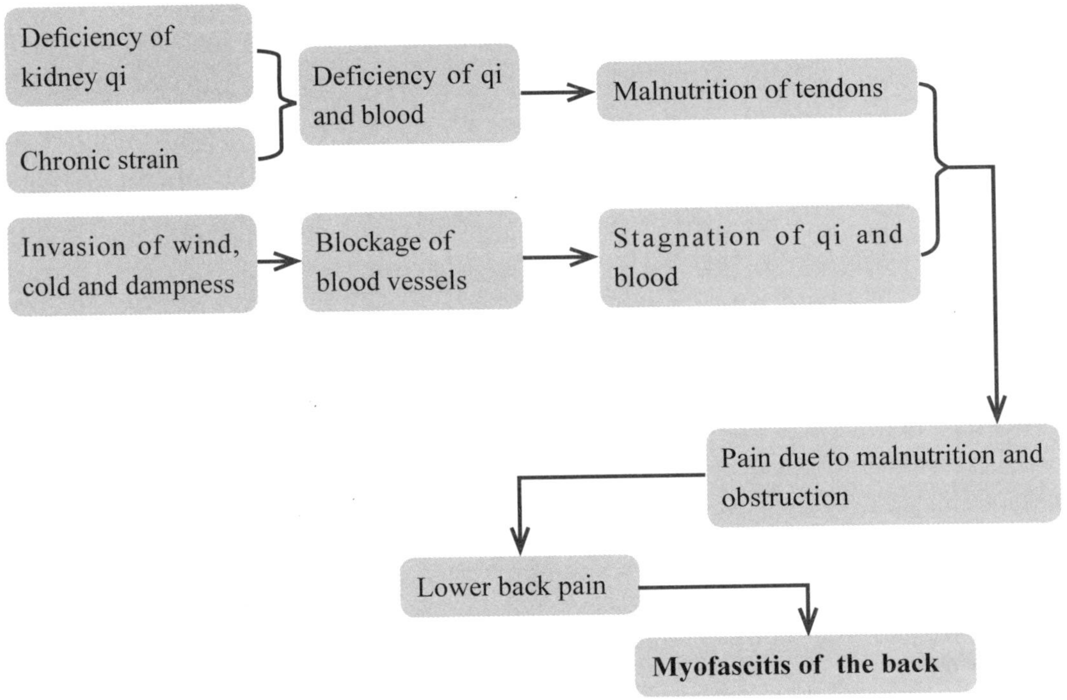

2. Clinical Manifestations

Clinically, it is marked by recurrent distending or aching pain on one side or both sides of lower back, sometimes mild and sometimes severe. Rest, proper exercises or frequent changes of posture may relieve the symptoms, while over-worked, humid weather or attack of wind, cold and dampness may aggravate the symptoms. The patient may have hypoesthesia of lower back, preference for warmth, aversion to cold, rigidity of the back; and often pounds his back with hands to relieve lumbar discomfort. Lumbar movement is generally normal without obvious functional disorder, but sometimes with dragging feeling. The patient is not able to stand or sit for long time, or work in bending position for long time since it would be difficult to stretch the body. The accompanied manifestations are red tongue, sometimes with purple marks, little tongue coating and a thready rapid pulse.

Examination shows nodulars or cord-like mass on the back; evident muscular spasm, or even lumbar scoliosis and leg pain may be seen during acute attack. X-ray exam is usually normal.

3. Diagnostic Essentials

It is possible to have history of acute traumatic injury, history of catching cold or over-strained.

Aching or distending pain in the lower back marked by recurrent attacks, sometimes better and sometimes worse, inconspicuous limitation of lumbar movement.

It is possible to manifest extensive inconspicuous tenderness according to the injured area, without radiating pain. The tenderness usually appears on the back of sacroiliac joint and sacrum, or on the lumbar transverse process. In mild case, the pain is not evident; but in severe case, the tenderness could be accompanied by spasm and stiffness of unilateral or bilateral erector spinae.

The physiologic arc of the lumber vertebrae may diminish or disappear. In the case with long duration, evident myatrophy on one side or both sides of lower back may appear; nodules or cord-like mass can be touched on the sacroiliac region.

The patients with acute attacks often show increased muscular tension on one side or both sides of the lower back, or apparent scoliosis with functional disorders at different degrees.

Straight leg raising test (Laseque's Test) and Bragard's test are usually negative.

X-ray examinations may help to find congenital deformity of lumbosacral vertebrae in a few cases; degenerative bone changes of vertebrae in aged patients; or no obvious changes in most of the patients with lumbosacral disorders.

4. Differential Diagnosis

This disease should be distinguished from hypertrophic spondylitis, old lumbar fracture, lumbar tuberculosis and lumbar disk herniation.

5. Tui Na Treatment

【Principle】

To relax the sinews, unblock the collaterals, warm the channels, activate blood, relieve spasm and stop pain.

【Points and Regions】

BL 23 (*shèn shù*)	DU 3 (*yāo yáng guān*)	BL 60 (*kūn lún*)	BL 31-34 (*bā liáo*)
BL 54 (*zhì biān*)	GB 34 (*yáng líng quán*)	KI 3 (*tài xī*)	BL 57 (*chéng shān*)
BL 40 (*wěi zhōng*)	BL 25 (*dà cháng shù*)		

Lower back and buttock.

【Method】

Ask patient to take a prone position. After rolling manipulation, apply kneading manipulation with palm or palm root along bilateral courses of the foot *taiyang* bladder channel, repeat the manipulations up and down for 3~5 times respectively.

Apply pressing-kneading manipulation with both thumbs or tips of elbows on BL 23 (*shèn shù*), DU 3 (*yāo yáng guān*), BL 25 (*dà cháng shù*), BL 31-34 (*bā liáo*), BL 54 (*zhì biān*), BL 40 (*wěi zhōng*), GB 34 (*yáng líng quán*), BL 57 (*chéng shān*), BL 60 (*kūn lún*), KI 3 (*tài xī*), about 10 seconds each point until there is sour and distending feeling in the local areas.

Apply plucking manipulation with the thumb on the tenderness, spasm areas or nodules. Repeat the manipulation 3-5 times.

Apply grasping manipulation with the bellies of the thumb and index and middle finger of both hands on bilateral EX-B7 (*yāo yǎn*), repeat the manipulation 2-3 times.

Standing beside the patient's head, the operator apply pushing manipulation with one hand or both hands along bilateral courses of the foot *taiyang* bladder channel from the upper back to the lower back, repeat the manipulation 2~3 times.

Apply oblique pulling manipulation on the lumbar region.

Apply scrubbing manipulation on the back along bilateral courses of the foot *taiyang* bladder channel; scrubbing manipulation transversely on lumbosacral region till it is warm enough at the local area.

At last, apply alternate tapping manipulation with hollow fists from the upper back to the lumbosacral region, repeat the manipulation 2~3 times.

6. Precautions

In daily life and work, keep proper posture and change posture every now and then to avoid fatigue and prevent recurrence.

Wear a wide leather belt or waist belt to protect the lumbar region during treatment period.

It is better to combine tui na treatment with traction, hot compress, fumigating therapy with Chinese medications, physical therapy and other methods to improve therapeutic effect.

Sleep or rest on a hard bed to prevent distortion of the spinal column.

Have proper rest, keep warm and control sexual activities.

Persist in functional exercises of the lower back muscles during treatment period and after recovery, since the exercises can help to reduce the possibility of recurrence.

External Humeral Epicondylitis

1. Overview

External epicondylitis refers to a series of symptoms caused by the irritation of nerve ending or periosteum, resulted from non specific inflammation due to pulling injury of the attachment of extensor carpi radialis caused by excessive rotation of forearm, forceful extension of wrist or chronic strain of elbow. It is also known as tennis elbow, humeral epicondyle syndrome, radiohumeral bursitis or radiohumeral arthritis. It is marked, clinically, by swelling and pain of humeral epicondyle and limited elbow movement. Known as tennis elbow, it is a condition commonly associated with playing tennis. It occurs more on the right side and is often seen in the workers who often rotate the forearm for work. This disease is attributed to category of sinew injury in TCM.

When the forearm is in the pronation position, the sudden and forceful active dorsiflexion of the wrist may make extensor carpi radialis contract intensively to cause the injury of its attachment. Long-term of the work involving repeated forearm pronation may keep extensor carpi radialis in a tense state resulting in chronic strain. The pathological changes are usually induced by the following: firstly, tear of the attachment of extensor carpi radialis; secondly, subperiosteal bleeding, swelling and hematoma organization at the attachment of extensor carpi radialis leading to periostitis and increase of subperiosteal tension; thirdly, traumatic inflammation or fibrositis of annular ligament; lastly, radiohumeral bursitis or inflammation due to incarceration of radiohumeral synovium.

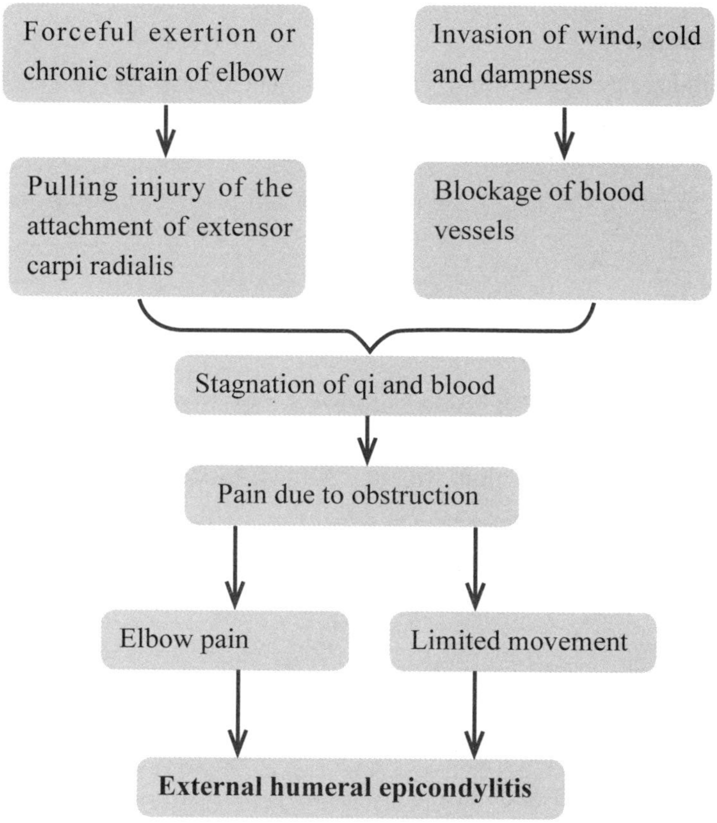

2. Clinical Manifestations

The patients with acute attack usually have a history of evident sprain or strain; while the patients with chronic condition have no evident trauma history, the disease usually develops slowly. The main manifestations include aching pain on the posterolateral part of the affected elbow, radiating pain down along extensor carpi radialis, weakness of the forearm rotation and holding movement. The pain becomes worse when the arm is over used, or during rainy and cloudy days, or when the affected forearm rotates with wrist stretching backwards, or when the patient performs lifting, pulling, holding, pushing movements, especially twisting a towel. Sometimes, mild swelling can be found on the affected area. Other manifestations are light red tongue with thin white coating, wiry or wiry choppy pulse.

The examinations may show mild swelling and tenderness in the external humeral epicondyle; a small synovial bursa could be touched at the local area in a few cases. The locations of tender points indicate the injured tissues. The tenderness on external humeral epicondyle indicates injury of the insertion of extensor carpi radialis brevis; tenderness at the upper part of external humeral epicondyle indicates the injury at the insertion of extensor carpi radialis longus; tenderness nearby the capitulum radii indicates annular ligament injury combined with radial collateral ligament injury. Extensor carpi tension test and Mill test are positive. X-ray examination of the elbow usually shows no abnormality. But in some patients, the external humeral epicondyle is rough or density increased.

3. Diagnostic Essentials

History of acute injury or chronic strain.

Tenderness, aching or distending pain of the external humeral epicondyle, which may radiate down along the radial side of forearm.

Weakness of the forearm during lifting movement and pain becomes worse when twisting a towel.

Mill test is positive.

4. Differential Diagnosis

X-ray examination shows no abnormality in most cases, roughness or increase of density on external humeral epicondyle in part of the cases. In accordance with the history of the disease, body sign and the result of X-ray examination, it is not difficult to distinguish the disease from medial humeral epicondylitis.

5. Tui Na Treatment

【Principle】

To activate blood, dissolve stasis, relax sinews and unblock collaterals.

【Points and Regions】

LI 11 (*qū chí*)	PC 3 (*qū zé*)	LI 10 (*shǒu sān lǐ*)	LI 4 (*hé gǔ*)

Lateral epicondyle of humerus and muscle groups on the radial side of the forearm.

【Method】

Ask patient to take a supine or sitting position. Apply rolling manipulation from the radial side of elbow to radial side of forearm for several times. Apply pressing, kneading, point-pressing and plucking manipulations on LI 11 (*qū chí*), PC 3 (*qū zé*), LI 10 (*shǒu sān lǐ*), LI 4 (*hé gǔ*), 1 minute each point.

Apply one-finger pushing, pressing, kneading, point-pressing manipulations as the main, and alternate with plucking manipulation on the external humeral epicondyle for about 5 minutes.

Press the tenderness at the external humeral epicondyle by holding the medial humeral epicondyle with the other four fingers, pull and stretch the wrist with the other hand to the opposite direction for a while; then bend the elbow slowly and make the forearm pronate to a maximum; at this moment, extend and pull the forearm quickly 3 times consecutively to break the bursa, so as to benefit the absorption of exudate.

Apply pushing and kneading manipulations on the external humeral epicondyle and extensor carpi radialis; then apply scrubbing manipulation along radial aspect of the forearm to external humeral epicondyle until the warmth penetrates into the inside of arm.

6. Precautions

During treatment period, avoid excessive rotation of the forearm and forceful dorsiflexion of the wrist.

Keep the local area warm.

Cold compress is suggested in the affected area at acute stage and wet-warm compress in chronic stage.

Wrist Sprain

1. Overview

Sprain of wrist joint indicates peripheral ligaments injury, tendons and capsule of wrist joint caused by direct or indirect external force or over-twisting of the wrist surpassing the normal limitation of wrist ligaments. The injury may disturb the wrist functional activity, also known as traumatic carpal arthritis or soft tissues injury of wrist joint. Sprain of wrist joint should be distinguished from wrist fracture due to direct or indirect violent injury. Clinically, sprain of wrist joint is characterized by pain and swelling around the wrist joint and limited wrist movement. It may occur in people of all ages, especially in young and middle-aged people who are active in sports. TCM thinks that it is caused by "qi stagnation and blood stasis due to the injury of muscles and tendons", included in "dislocation of bone and sinew".

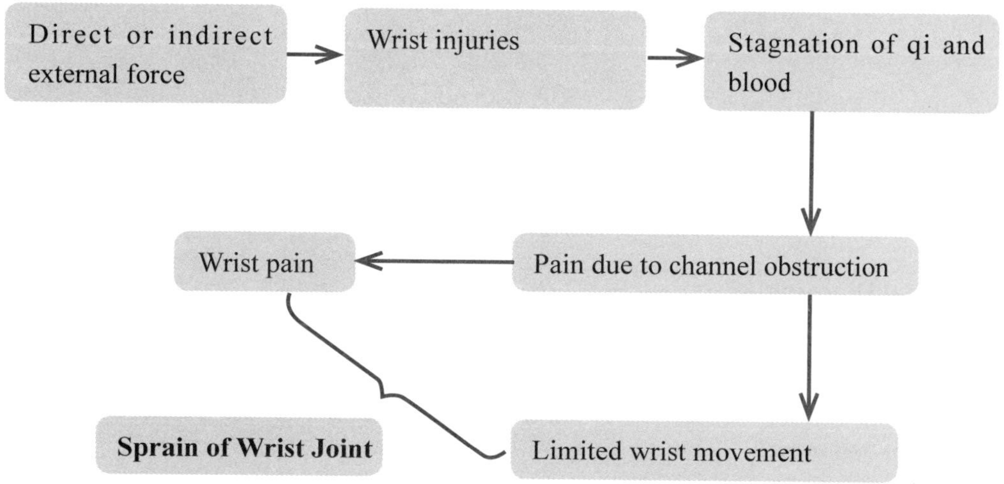

2. Clinical Manifestations

An evident injury history, such as falling down on your hands supporting the body, twisting wrist during work or sport, holding heavy object or long-term of work with wrist, can be traced back. The patient with mild sprain may just have inflexible wrist and mild pain in the wrist, which could be worse when the wrist is moving in large amplitude. The patient with severe condition may complain pain immediately after an injury, fail in moving the wrist. Swelling in different degrees may appear. In severe cases, there may be subcutaneous ecchymosis in the wrist, bluish purple at early stage and purple-yellow or soil-yellow at later stage. As for limitation of movement, evident limited wrist movement or even failure of moving the wrist may occur in acute cases; while in chronic cases, it is not clear or only limited when the wrist is moving to a particular direction, the symptoms are usually worse after exertion or during cloudy or rainy days.

Pain and tenderness at the affected area and the direction of limited movement are contributed to have definite diagnosis.

a. Tenderness

The tenderness is usually found at dorsal radiocarpal ligament in injury of dorsal carpal ligament;

at volar radiocarpal ligament in injury of volar carpal ligament; at radial aspect of the anatomical snuffbox (or radial fossa) in injury of radial carpal collateral ligament; at ulnar head in injury of ulnar carpal collateral ligament; at the space of distal radioulnar joint and ulnar aspect of the wrist in injury at the triangular cartilages.

b. Limitation of movement

Injury of dorsal carpal ligament may cause limited wrist movement with pain due to palmar flexion; injury of volar carpal ligament cause limited wrist movement with pain due to wrist dorsiflexion; injury of radial collateral ligament cause limited wrist movement with pain due to ulnar flexion; injury of the ulnar collateral ligament cause limited wrist movement with pain due to radial flexion; injury of the triangular cartilages cause limited wrist movement with pain during joint rotation. The other manifestations are light red tongue with thin white coating, wiry choppy or wiry tense pulse.

3. Diagnostic Essentials

History of acute or chronic injury of the wrist.

Wrist pain at the injured area.

Wrist swelling, which is not obvious in chronic cases, but evident and accompanied by subcutaneous ecchymosis in acute cases.

Limited wrist movement. The limited direction is opposite to the injured area.

X-ray examination shows no obvious abnormality in wrist bones.

4. Differential Diagnosis

X-ray examination can help to exclude wrist facture and dislocation.

5. Tui Na Treatment

【Principle of treatment】

To relax sinews, activate blood, dispel stasis and unblock collaterals.

【Points and Regions】

SJ 5 (*wài guān*)	LI 5 (*yáng xī*)	SI 5 (*yáng gǔ*)	SJ 4 (*yáng chí*)
LI 4 (*hé gǔ*)	LU 9 (*tài yuān*)	HT 3 (*shào hǎi*)	LU 5 (*chǐ zé*)
LI 11 (*qū chí*)	HT 7 (*shén mén*)	LU 7 (*liè quē*)	PC 7 (*dà líng*)
SI 4 (*wàn gǔ*)	HT 5 (*tōng lǐ*)		

And injured area. Select the points according to the area of injury.

【Method】

Only when fracture and dislocation are ruled out by X-ray, can tui na treatment be applied. For acute injury, tui na treatment should be applied 24 to 48 hours after the injury, if swelling and subcutaneous ecchymosis are evident.

Apply rolling, thenar-pressing, pressing-kneading manipulations on the attachments of injured ligament or tendon and injured area, together with rotation of wrist. Then, apply plucking manipulation gently and vertically along the injured tissues.

Apply pulling-extending manipulation on the affected wrist. If injured area is on the dorsum of wrist, have palmar flexion when the affected wrist is pulling and extending. If injured area is on the palmar side of the wrist, have dorsal flexion when the wrist is pulling and extending. If injured area is on the radial side of the wrist, have ulnar flexion when the wrist is pulling and extending. If injured area is on the ulnar side of the wrist, have radial flexion when the wrist is pulling and extending.

Apply foulage, shaking and rotating manipulations on the affected wrist.

Apply scrubbing manipulation on the local area.

6. Precautions

For acute injury with subcutaneous hemorrhage, ice compress should be used before the treatment to prevent continuous bleeding.

For severe injury, X-ray exam should be taken to rule out fracture and dislocation.

Tui na manipulations should be applied gently and slowly to avoid further injury.

Keep the local area warm and take wristband during treatment period.

If the case is complicated with dislocation or avulsion fracture, the treatment is as same as that of dislocation or fracture. The affected wrist should be immobilized for 6-8 weeks or till clinical union of fracture, only at that time, can tui na treatment be applied to restore wrist functions.

Strain of the Iliotibial Tract

1. Overview

Strain of the iliotibial tract is caused by long-term friction between the posterior margin of the iliotibial tract and greater trochanter of femur, or between the anterior margin of gluteus maximus and greater trochanter of femur. The friction leads to strain of iliotibial tract or thickening of the anterior margin of gluteus maximus, which may cause snapping sound because the iliotibial tract slides on the great trachanter of femur when the hip joint is doing active flexion and extension or when the patient is walking. Therefore, it is also called "snapping hip" syndrome, clinically characterized by snapping sound in hip during walking without any obvious discomfort. It occurs frequently in women and mostly attacks one side, sometimes both sides are involved. Strain of iliotibial tract is resulted from chronic inflammation or hyperplasia of posterior margin of iliotibial tract or the attachment of gluteus maximus; from chondroma, hypertrophy or bursitis of greater trochanter; from thickening and fibrous adhesion of cyst wall due to inflammatory exudates of greater trochanter synoviae. Strain of iliotibial tract is attributed to the category of sinew injury in traumatology of TCM.

2. Clinical Manifestations

Usually there is no obvious history of injury. The patient just feels uncomfortable in the hip. Snapping sound in the hip is heard when the hip joint is flexed, extended, adducted or internally rotated; but snapping sound may not occur during passive flexion and extension of the hip. In the cases with increased exudate due to greater trochanter bursitis, pain often appears at the posterior side of the greater trochanter, which may further radiate to the posterolateral side of the thigh, accompanied by aching, distending, intense and weak feeling. The manifestations also include light red tongue with thin white coating, normal or wiry tense pulse.

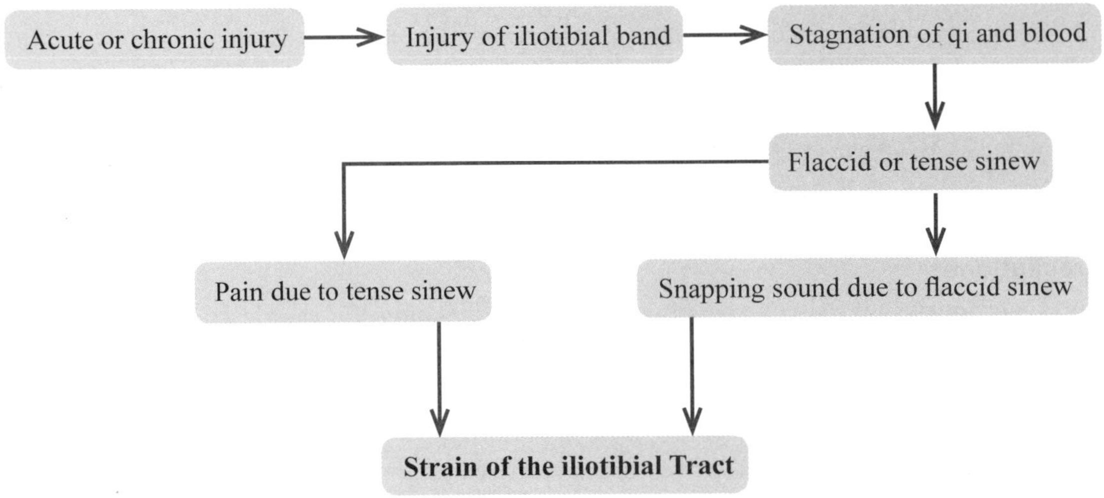

Physical examination may show hard mass or cord-like tissue at the area of snapping sound. When the hip joint flexes and extends actively, snapping sound can be heard and sliding iliotibial tract over the greater trochanter can be touched. X-ray examination usually shows no evident abnormality. The most discomforting symptom of the disease is the movement always followed by snapping sound, it makes the patient nervous psychologically.

3. Diagnostic Essentials

Absence of any acute or chronic injury history.

Snapping sound of the hip.

No pain, no motor impairment.

X-ray examination shows no evident abnormality.

4. Differential Diagnosis

X-ray examination shows no evident abnormality. It is not difficult to make diagnosis in accordance with the history of the disease, typical snapping sound and the result of X-ray examination, and is easy to be distinguished from other diseases.

5. Tui Na Treatment

【Principle】

To relax sinews, activate blood, unblock channels and dredge collaterals.

【Points and Regions】

GB 29 (*jū liáo*)	GB 30 (*huán tiào*)	BL 36 (*chéng fú*)	GB 31 (*fēng shì*)	ST 31 (*bì guān*)

And the area of greater trochanter.

【Method】

Apply pressing-kneading manipulation with thumb on GB 29 (*jū liáo*), GB 30 (*huán tiào*), BL 36 (*chéng fú*) , GB 31 (*fēng shì*) and ST 31 (*bì guān*), 1 minute each point. Then apply palm-kneading manipulation on the area of greater trochanter for 3 minutes.

Ask patient to take a prone position. Standing by the affected side, apply rolling manipulation along the running direction of gluteus maximus and iliotibial tract 3 minutes, together with passive movement by backward extending and abducting hip joint to relax the local muscles.

Apply pressing, kneading, point and plucking manipulations on the tensor fasciae latae and lateral side of thigh for 5 minutes. Then apply plucking manipulation on the greater trochanter vertically along the nodules for 3 minutes.

Ask patient to take a supine position, holding the affected side knee with one hand, and the lower part of the calf with the other hand to move the affected leg by flexing knee and hip for 10 to 15 times; then apply foulage manipulation from upper end of the thigh to the knee for 3 minutes.

Apply scrubbing manipulation on the local area from the area of nodules on the hip to lateral side of the thigh until it is warm enough at the local area.

6. Precautions

Explain the disease to the patient to calm the patient down.

Keep the local area warm to avoid cold irritation.

Less movement of hip, such as long walking.

Osteoarthritis of the Knee Joint

1. Overview

Osteoarthritis of the knee joint indicates a group of clinical symptoms caused by intra-articular imbalance and dysfunction due to non-inflammatory degenerative disorders like hyperplasia of tibiofemoral joint and patellofemoral joint as well as mechanical abrasion, excluding arthritis due to soft tissue problems. It is also called degenerative arthritis, hypertrophic arthritis, or senile arthritis of knee joint. Clinically, it is characterized by joint pain, limitation of movement and deformity of knee joint. The disease is more frequently seen in aged people, especially women and fat persons. In TCM, osteoarthritis of knee joint is attributed to the category of bone Bi syndrome caused by invasion of wind, cold and dampness based on the root cause of deficiency of liver and kidney.

Western medicine thinks the chronic accumulated injury, mechanical pulling and irritation are the main causative factors of osteoarthritis of knee joint. Since it is common in aged people, some experts think the disease is related to metabolism. The disease can be divided into primary and secondary types according to causative factors. Primary type is often related with the age. Along with gaining of age, connective tissues degenerate gradually and cartilages are worn, and osteophytes is formed. And secondary type is usually caused by chronic cartilage injuries due to trauma or deformity.

When the knee joint is moving, osteophytes may irritate soft tissues of the joint or the articular surface causing pain. Since osteophytes gradually make the joint space narrow, nonspecific exudate of synovium and increased pressure in the joint cavity, swollen joint, fibrotic thickening and thickened synovium of joint capsule may happen. At later stage, the intra-articular synovia decreases resulting in dryness in the joint, friction increases, and cracks or exfoliation appear on the surface of patella cartilage. All these factors may irritate local blood vessels and nerves to make the symptoms worse, manifesting muscular adhesion and atrophy around the joint and limited movement.

This disease is referred to the category of bone *bì* syndrome in TCM. The knee joint is one of the eight cavities (*bā xū*), the place where tendons meet and is abundant with qi and blood. Weakness of body due to the age, deficiency of liver and kidney and malnutrition of qi and blood may deprive nourishment from the joint; or invasion of the joint by wind, cold and dampness may cause Bi syndrome, in which the accumulation of those exogenous pathogenic factors may accumulate in the joints to cause pain and swelling. Looseness of bone may lead to osteophytes and spasm of tendons turn into contraction, resulting in rigidity of joint.

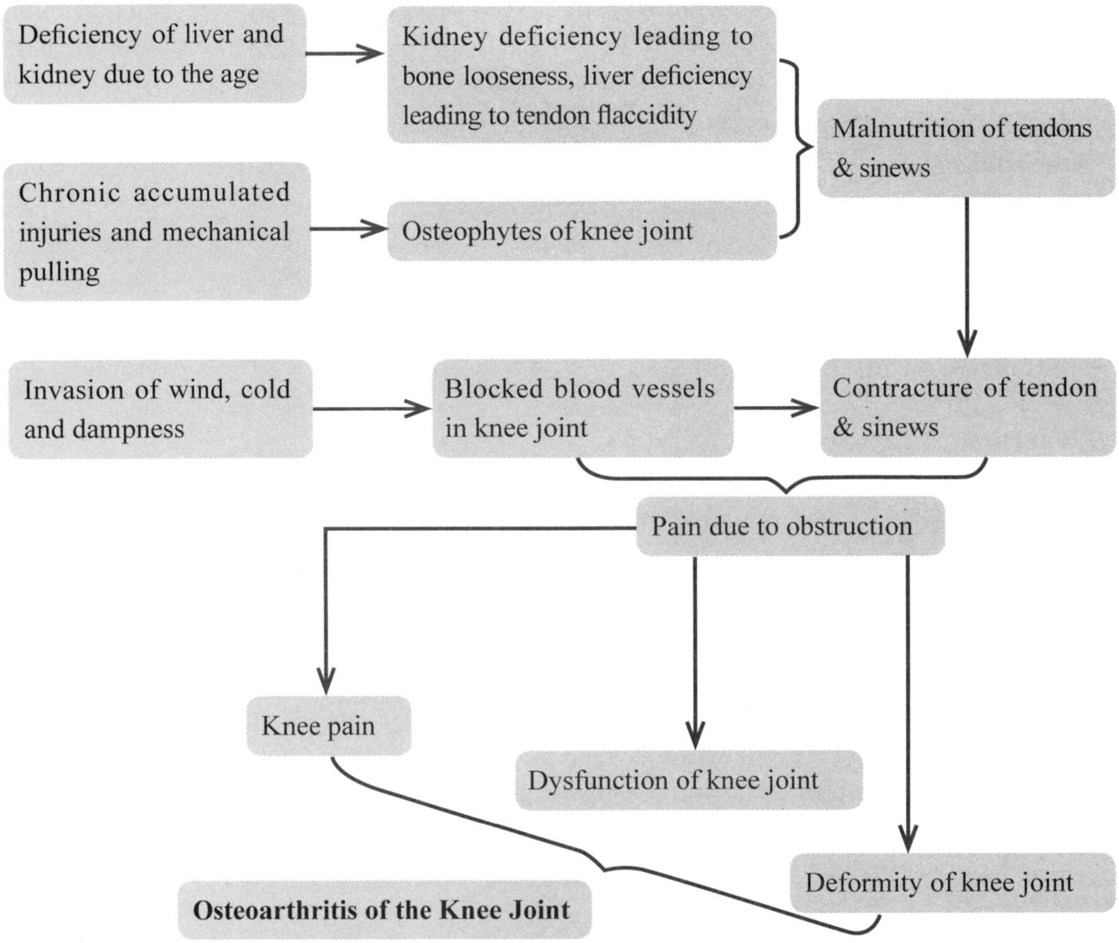

2. Clinical Manifestations

It is frequently seen in middle-aged and old people. It develops slowly, mostly with the history of chronic knee strain. At beginning, the patient only manifests weakness of the knee, gradually pain appears during walking, first in one side and then in both knees, but mostly in one side. The pain may appear alternately in both knees, sometimes better and sometimes worse, with a nature of wandering. The pain is usually sharp when the patient is gets up in the morning, when standing up from a sitting position or when going up or down stairs. The pain would be better after moving around but worse again after exertion. Later, the walking distance would be shorter and shorter, the duration of pain is longer and longer; and at last, the pain can not be relieved anymore by rest. As for the nature of the pain, at the beginning, it is a kind of aching, and then it develops to a distending, stabbing and tingling pain. The patient becomes nervous when walking or going on stairs because every step causes stabbing pain in the joint. The movement of knee is limited gradually; the range of flexion and extension is getting smaller. The patient dares not to stretch or bend their knees fully. Crackling sound or friction in the joint can be heard and felt when the knee is moving. In the cases with obvious inflammatory exudation, the knee would be swollen due to hydrops of the suprapatellar bursa, resulting in stiffness of knee joint in severe cases. In part of the patients, because of dysfunction of knee joint, the hip joint and ankle joint have to work more as compensation; and the consequence is the hip and ankle are also affected. The patients with this disease usually manifest pale or light red tongue with thin white coating, wiry tense or tense choppy pulse.

Physical examination shows tenderness in bilateral depressions on the sides of patellar ligaments and in popliteal fossa in the cases with tibiofemoral arthritis; tenderness around the margin of patella, friction sound between patella and femur, positive ballottable patella sign, and atrophic quadriceps femoris of different degree in the cases with patellofemoral arthritis. Lab tests shows normal blood sedimentation, negative antistreptolysin O test and negative rheumatoid factor. X-ray examination shows evident sharp bony spurs on the facet of tibial condyle or hyperosteogeny on the margin of patellar, narrowed joint space and calcified ligaments. X-ray can help to exclude other osteogenic pathological changes.

3. Diagnostic Essentials

Frequently seen in middle-aged and old people with the history of chronic knee strain.

Progressive knee pain, especially worse when going upstairs or downstairs.

Dysfunction of knee joint, friction sound in the knee and myatrophy around the knee.

X-ray examination shows severe osteophytes and narrowed joint space.

Rheumatoid arthritis is ruled out by lab test.

4. Differential Diagnosis

X-ray examination shows apparent osteophytes and narrowed joint space. The diagnosis can be confirmed in accordance with the history of disease, body signs and the report of X-ray examination. It should be distinguished from rheumatic arthritis, rheumatoid arthritis and injury of soft tissue around the knee.

5. Tui Na Treatment

【Principle】

To relax sinews, activate blood, relieve spasm, stop pain, and benefit the joint.

【Points and Regions】

ST 35 (*dú bí*)	EX-LE5 (*xī yǎn*)	EX-LE2 (*hè dǐng*)	SP 10 (*xuè hǎi*)
ST 34 (*liáng qiū*)	GB 31 (*fēng shì*)	BL 40 (*wěi zhōng*)	GB 34 (*yáng líng quán*)
SP 9 (*yīn líng quán*)	BL 57 (*chéng shān*)		

And the area around knee joint.

【Method】

Ask patient to take a supine position. Standing by the affected side, apply pinching, grasping, pressing and kneading manipulations along the quadriceps femoris down to the patella and the areas beside patellar. The areas beside patellar are the important places to be manipulated. Then apply pressing and kneading manipulations on the anterolateral part of the affected shank. The treatment with these manipulations lasts about 5 minutes.

Apply pressing-kneading manipulation on ST 35 (*dú bí*), EX-LE5 (*xī yǎn*), EX-LE2 (*hè dǐng*), SP 10 (*xuè hǎi*), ST 34 (*liáng qiū*), BL 40 (*wěi zhōng*), GB 34 (*yáng líng quán*), SP 9 (*yīn líng quán*) and BL 57 (*chéng shān*) selectively according to painful areas, 1 minute each point.

Ask patient to take a prone position. Standing by the affected side, apply rolling, pressing and kneading manipulations on the popliteal fossa, lower part of the thigh and upper part of the calf, focusing on the popliteal fossa or BL 40 (*wěi zhōng*), together with passive movement by flexing and extending the patient's knee. Then apply point-pressing manipulation on BL 40 (*wěi zhōng*) and BL 57 (*chéng shān*). The treatment with these manipulations lasts about 5 minutes.

Ask patient to take a supine position with the affected knee flexed to 45 degree. Apply one-finger pushing, pressing and kneading manipulations repeatedly on bilateral EX-LE5 (*xī yǎn*).

Apply scrubbing manipulation on bilateral sides of the knee and the area around patellar till it is warm at the local area. Then apply foulage, kneading and rotating manipulations on the knee to finish the treatment.

6. Precautions

Keep the knee warm. Hot-wet compress with water temperature at 45~50°C can be done at home.

Have a rest and less knee movements when there are severe pain and swelling.

Avoid heavy load on the affected knee. Knee band can be taken to protect knee.

Persist in functional exercises of the knee to prevent myatrophy and adhesion of joint.

It is advisable to do self-massage on the knee, twice a day.

Ankle Sprain

1. Overview

Ankle sprain indicates the medial and lateral collateral ligaments injuries caused by a sudden twisting of the ankle leading to inversion or eversion. The injuries include partial tear, complete rupture of ligament, or avulsion fracture in severe cases. Clinically, sprain of ankle is characterized by local pain, bruise and limited ankle movement. The sprain due to inversion is mostly common because of the following causes: ①lateral malleolus is thin and long, posterior to medial malleolus and lower than medial malleolus; ②lateral ligaments are thinner and weaker than medial ligaments; ③the fibers of tibiofibular transverse ligaments run downward to lateral side, and the medial facet of lateral malleolus is incline to make lateral aspect of the ankle move inward more freely.

Awkwardly planting the foot when running, jumping on uneven ground or ankle sudden inversion with plantar flexion when stepping down may cause lateral collateral ligaments exposed to strong stretching force. After the onset of injury, the mild cases may show periosteal laceration at the attachment of ligament and subperiosteal hemorrhage; the severe cases show partial tear of ligaments, or even complete rupture along with avulsion fracture or subluxation of talus. In injuries due to inversion, the injury of anterior talofibular ligament is mostly common, and the injury of calcaneofibular ligament is possible in severe cases. But it is seldom to see the injury of posterior talofibular ligament. Eversion of ankle usually causes the fracture of lateral malleolus.

Sprain of ankle is attributed to the category of sinew injury in TCM traumatology.

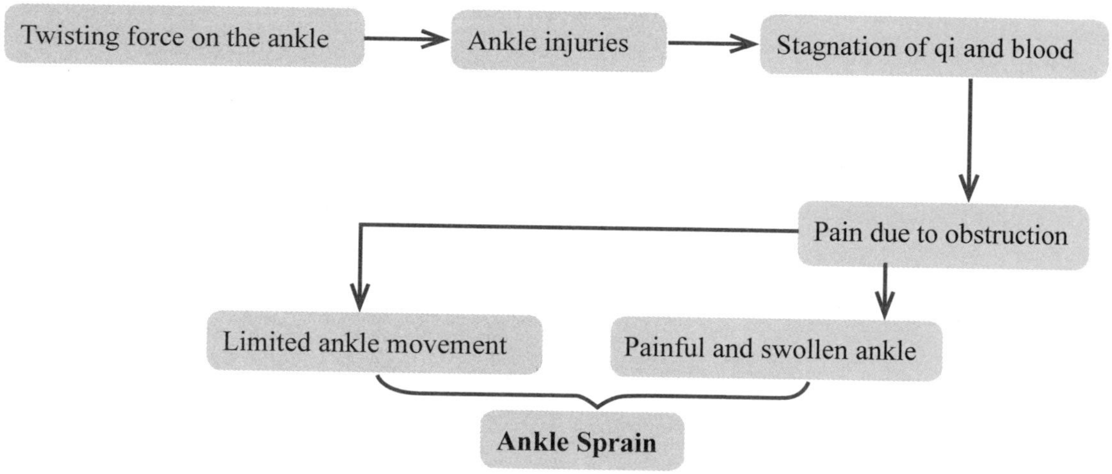

2. Clinical Manifestations

There is an evident history of injury. Local pain in the affected side may occur immediately after injury. The patient with mild injury has to walk on tiptoe, mild swelling could be found at the local area; the patient with severe injury would fail to walk, obvious swelling could be found at the local area, accompanied by limited ankle movement. In 2~3 days, subcutaneous ecchymosis may appear; which may spread to the opposite side in severe condition. The size of ecchymosis is, more or less, related with the severity of injury and hemorrhage. It is blue and purple at beginning; it becomes purple and yellow in 5~7 days and then gradually turns into brown yellow; meanwhile, the swelling begins to abate and blood stasis be absorbed. The color of ecchymosis is important for judging the duration of injury. This disease is differentiated as the syndrome due to stagnation of qi and blood, the patient may have light red tongue with thin white coating, wiry or wiry tense pulse.

The body signs vary according to the areas of injury.

Injury of lateral collateral ligaments: Obvious tenderness on the area anterior and inferior to lateral malleolus on anterior talofibular ligament (also called injury of anterior talofibular ligament). The pain is sharp with ankle inversion. In cases with the rupture of both anterior and posterior talofibular ligaments, there is a separation sensation on the lateral side of ankle during lateral ankle movement test. Fracture fragment may be felt if there is avulsion fracture of lateral malleolus. X-ray examination can help to decide whether there is a fracture or dislocation. In cases with ruptured ligament, X-ray shows an angle formed by the lower joint surface of tibia and upper joint surface is over 15 degree with forceful ankle inversion.

Injury of medial collateral ligaments: There is obvious tenderness on the medial side of the ankle which is just located under medial malleolus. There is also tenderness under medial malleolus in the cases with the injury of inferior tibiofibular ligaments. The pain may get worse with ankle eversion. Fracture fragment can be felt when avulsion fracture of medial malleolus occurs. X-ray examination can help to decide whether there is a fracture or dislocation. In cases with rupture of inferior tibiofibular ligaments, X-ray shows widened space between lateral and medial malleolus.

3. Diagnostic Essentials

The evident history of ankle twisting.

Pain and swelling on the medial or lateral side of ankle and tenderness on the injured place.

Limited ankle movement. Pain may get worse when repeating the injury movement.

Fracture and dislocation are ruled out by X-ray examination.

4. Differential Diagnosis

X-ray examination can help to exclude ankle facture and dislocation.

5. Tui Na Treatment

【Principle】

To relieve swelling and pain, activate blood, dispel stasis, adjust sinew and dredge the collaterals.

【Points and Regions】

Injury of lateral collateral ligaments:

ST 36 (*zú sān lǐ*)	GB 34 (*yáng líng quán*)	ST 41 (*jiě xī*)
GB 40 (*qiū xū*)	BL 62 (*shēn mài*)	BL 63 (*jīn mén*)

And the area anterior and inferior to lateral the malleolus.

Injury of medial collateral ligaments:

SP 6 (*sān yīn jiāo*)	SP 5 (*shāng qiū*)	KI 6 (*zhào hǎi*)	KI 3 (*tài xī*)

And the area inferior to the medial malleolus.

【Method】

【Injury of lateral collateral ligaments】

Ask patient to take a supine position. Apply one-finger pushing, rolling, pressing and kneading manipulations along the lateral side of anterior aspect of the lower leg to lateral aspect of the ankle for 5 minutes.

Apply pressing-kneading manipulation with thumb or thenar on the area anterior and inferior to lateral malleolus. Apply pressing-kneading manipulation on the area around injured place and then focus on the injured place after pain is relieved a little. The manipulations should be applied gently for 5 minutes.

Apply pressing, kneading, point-pressing, plucking manipulations or one-finger pushing manipulation on ST 36 (*zú sān lǐ*), GB 34 (*yáng líng quán*), ST 41 (*jiě xī*), GB 40 (*qiū xū*), BL 62 (*shēn mài*), BL 63 (*jīn mén*), 1 minute each point.

Apply pulling-extending manipulation on the affected ankle with one hand holding the heel of the affected side and the other hand holding the toes on the affected side. Then apply rotating manipulation on the affected ankle, together with pulling-extending the ankle, and turning the ankle inward and outward.

【Injury of medial collateral ligaments】

Ask patient to have a lateral recumbent position on the healthy side with the affected limb straightened and the healthy limb bent. Apply pushing or pressing and kneading manipulations along the medial aspect of the lower leg and the medial malleolus down to the medial side of foot repeatedly about 5 minutes.

Apply pressing and kneading manipulations on the area under the medial malleolus to relieve pain. Then apply pressing, kneading, point-pressing and plucking manipulations on the injured area gently. The treatment with these manipulations lasts about 3 minutes.

Apply pressing, kneading or one-finger pushing manipulation on SP 6 (*sān yīn jiāo*), SP 5 (*shāng qiū*), KI 6 (*zhào hǎi*) and KI 3 (*tài xī*), 1 minute each point.

Apply pulling and rotating manipulations on the affected ankle.

6. Precautions

For acute cases with bleeding and swelling, an ice compress should be applied immediately after injury. Tui na treatment should be applied 24~48 hours after the injury according to severity of bleeding.

For severe cases, X-ray examination should be taken. Only when fracture and complete rupture of ligament are excluded can Tui Na therapy be applied.

At acute stage, the affected foot should be immobilized and the affected limb should be raised to abate swelling. Immobilization in varus position for injury of medial collateral ligaments and immobilization in valgus position for injury of lateral collateral ligaments should be applied for 1~2 weeks to benefit the recovery ligament.

During the convalescence stage, do functional exercises by flexing and stretching the knee joint and ankle joint, rotating the ankle clockwise and counter-clockwise respectively, twice a day, 3 minutes each movement.

At the early stage of acute cases, manipulations should be gently applied not for a long time on the injured part; otherwise, local bleeding and edema would be worsened. At convalescence stage, plucking manipulation is taken as the main manipulation to loosen adhesion, cooperated with pulling-extending and rotating manipulations.

Temporomandibular Joint Dysfunction

1. Overview

Temporomandibular joint dysfunction (TMJD), also known as snapping jaw, refers to a series of manifestations such as pain and clicking in temporomandibular joints, popping motions and deviation in the movement of the joint, caused by the pathological changes of temporomandibular capsule, cartilage disc, surrounding ligaments and muscles. It's etiology is not clear, may be a violent punch to the jaw, preference for hard food, asymmetry of temporomandibular joints, invasion of cold, peripheral inflammation of the joint, habitual unilateral chewing movement, overstress clenching teeth habit or mouth opening for long time. It is a common disease in stomatology department, usually seen in young people at the age of 20~40 years. It often occurs in one joint, occasionally in both joints.

2. Clinical Manifestations

The main clinical manifestations include snapping sound and pain in temporomandibular joints and abnormality of opening mouth.

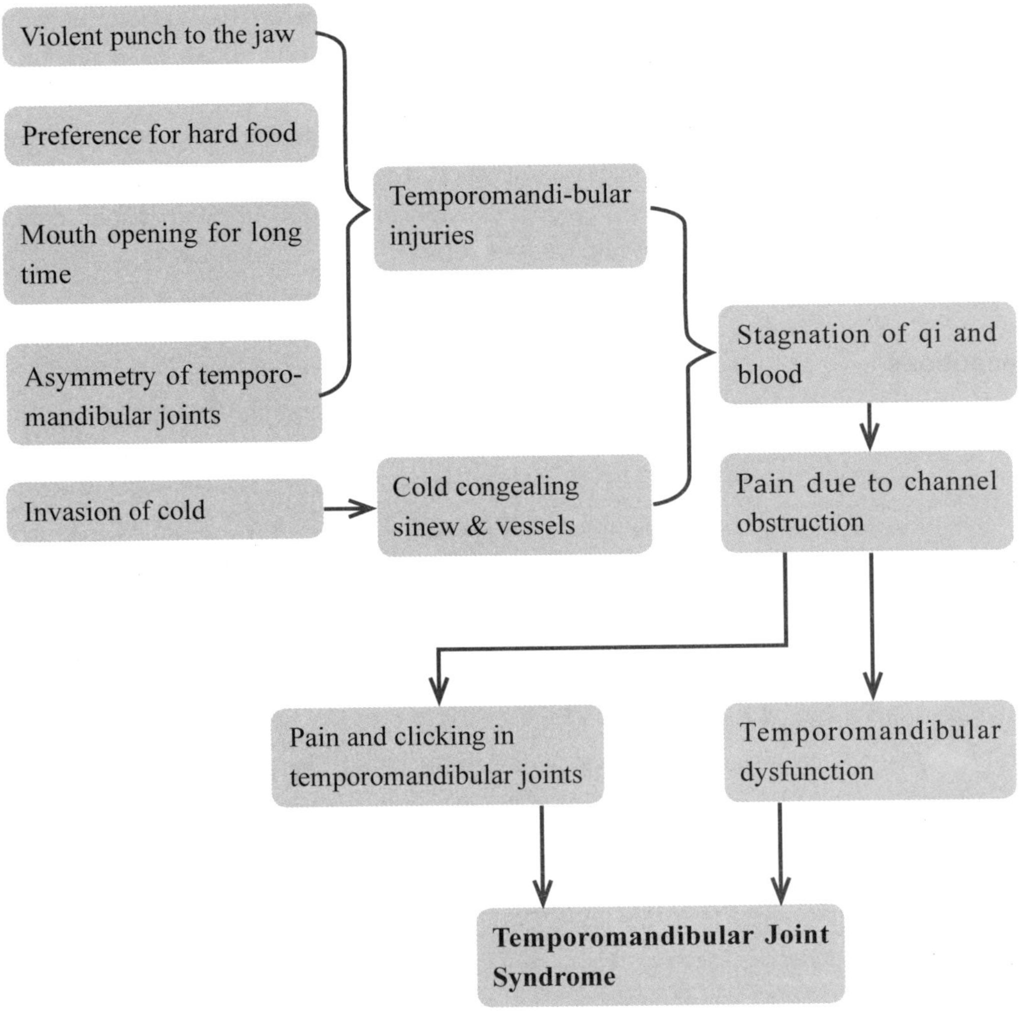

a. Clicking

Some patients have clicking while opening the mouth and when closing the mouth, while some patients have the sound at the end of opening the mouth and the beginning of closing then mouth. There may be temporomandibular discomfort and pain when clicking occurs. Grinding sound may appear in those patients with injured articular cartilage and bone substance when opening and closing the mouth.

b. Pain

Pain of temporomandibular joints may be mild or just a kind of aching in some patients, while the pain appears when the mouth is opening, during chewing movement, or when the mandible is protruding or moving to one side. The location of pain may vary in the individuals; some patients may have pain at the area posterior to sigmoid notch and articular tubercle, and some patients have pain in the posterior region of temporomandibular joint, or in the area of articular tubercle, or on the anterior oblique surface of condyle. A part of patients could be accompanied by spasm of jaw-closing muscles.

c. Abnormality of mouth opening

It indicates limited mouth opening due to pain, over mouth-opening or temporomandibular subluxation due to looseness of ligaments and capsules and hyperactivity of lateral pterygoid muscle. It also means locked jaw due to spasm of masseter muscles. Some patients may manifest deviated lower jaw when opening the mouth.

3. Diagnostic Essentials

A history of temporomandibular injury or congenital dysplasia.

There may be facial asymmetry and improper meeting of the upper and lower teeth due to long-term of unilateral temporomandibular disorder or the habit of masticating food with teeth of one side.

Tenderness may be found on one side or both sides of temporomandibular joints, sigmoid notch, the area posterior to articular tubercle, or on the posterior area of temporomandibular joints, articular tubercle or the anterior oblique surface of condyle. Muscular spasm may be touched in the cases with spasm of jaw-closing muscles.

Clicking is possible in the movement of temporomandibular joints.

Mouth motion abnormalities or limited mouth opening function. If only one side is sick, the mandible may deviate to the affected side; if both sides are affected, the mandible would be still in the right place or deviated to the side more limited.

X-ray examination shows congenital deformity, degeneration or subluxation of temporomandibular joints.

4. Differential Diagnosis

X-ray examination can help to distinguish the disease from facture, subluxation or osteopathy of temporomandibular joints.

5. Tui Na Treatment

【Principle of treatment】

To relax sinew, activate blood and reposit sinew and joints.

【Points and Regions】

GB 3 (*shàng guān*)	ST 7 (*xià guān*)	SJ 17 (*yì fēng*)	ST 6 (*jiá chē*)	LI 4 (*hé gǔ*)

Also the area of the unilateral or bilateral temporomandibular joint.

【Method】

Ask patient to take a sitting or supine position. Apply kneading manipulation with middle finger gently to relax the muscles around the affected temporomandibular joint.

Apply one-finger pushing manipulation swiftly and gently on ST 6 (*jiá chē*), ST 7 (*xià guān*), SJ 17 (*yì fēng*) and GB 3 (*shàng guān*). Then apply point-pressing manipulation on LI 4 (*hé gǔ*).

Press bilateral ST 6 (*jiá chē*) with both thumbs and support the lower edge of the mandible with the other fingers of both hands. Then move the mandible slightly when the thumbs are pressing and kneading bilateral ST 6 (*jiá chē*). The patient with subluxation of temporomandibular joint may have a light popping feeling in the joint. For the patient with mandible deviation to the healthy side and abnormal occlusion, it is necessary to have reposition treatment. Standing behind the patient who is in a sitting position, press temporal area and condyle of the affected side with one palm and healthy side of the mandible with the other palm, then squeeze and compress the joint forcefully with opposing force to adjust the occlusion when the patient is doing opening and closing movement of the mouth.

Apply scrubbing manipulation with the great thenar on the affected temporomandibular joint.

6. Precautions

Select proper reposition manipulation with appropriate strength when it is necessary during Tui Na Treatment. Immobilization of temporomandibular joint is needed for certain time except during food intake and treatment after reposition, since it can prevent subluxation and help to restore soft tissues. However, immobilization is not suggested for long time.

It is not allowed to take raw, cold and hard food during the period of Tui Na treatment, since they may irritate temporomandibular joints.

Keep face warm and avoid cold stimulation.

Rectify bad chewing habit and avoid overstrain of the muscle on the affected side.

After recovery, to consolidate the therapeutic effect, functional exercises should be done aimed to make muscular strength of the affected side consistent with the muscular strength of the healthy side.

The patient with osteogenic changes should be transferred to stomatology department, if Tui Na treatment fails.

Hot compress, acupuncture, moxibustion, physiotherapy can be used together with Tui Na treatment.

Section 2
Treatment for Disorders of Internal Medicine, Gynecology and the Five Sense Organs

Epigastric Pain

1. Overview

Epigastric pain indicates frequently occurred pain near the cardiac area; it is similar to certain digestive diseases in western medicine, such as stomach cramps, acute and chronic gastritis, gastric and duodenal ulcers, and gastrointestinal neurosis. But the condition discussed here excludes serious organic disorders like severe upper digestive tract bleeding, intestinal obstruction, perforation, gastric torsion and cancer, as well as upper abdominal pain due to angina pectoris, myocardial infarction, liver disorders and gallbladder disorders. Epigastric pain which could be helped by tui na therapy includes 4 syndromes of 2 major categories, e.g. obstruction of pathogenic factors and dysfunction of *zang-fu* organs.

2. Clinical Manifestations

Clinically, epigastric pain is classified into two major categories as obstruction of pathogens and dysfunction of *zang-fu* organs. But, if there is no thorough treatment, both of them may turn into internal retention of blood stasis after a period.

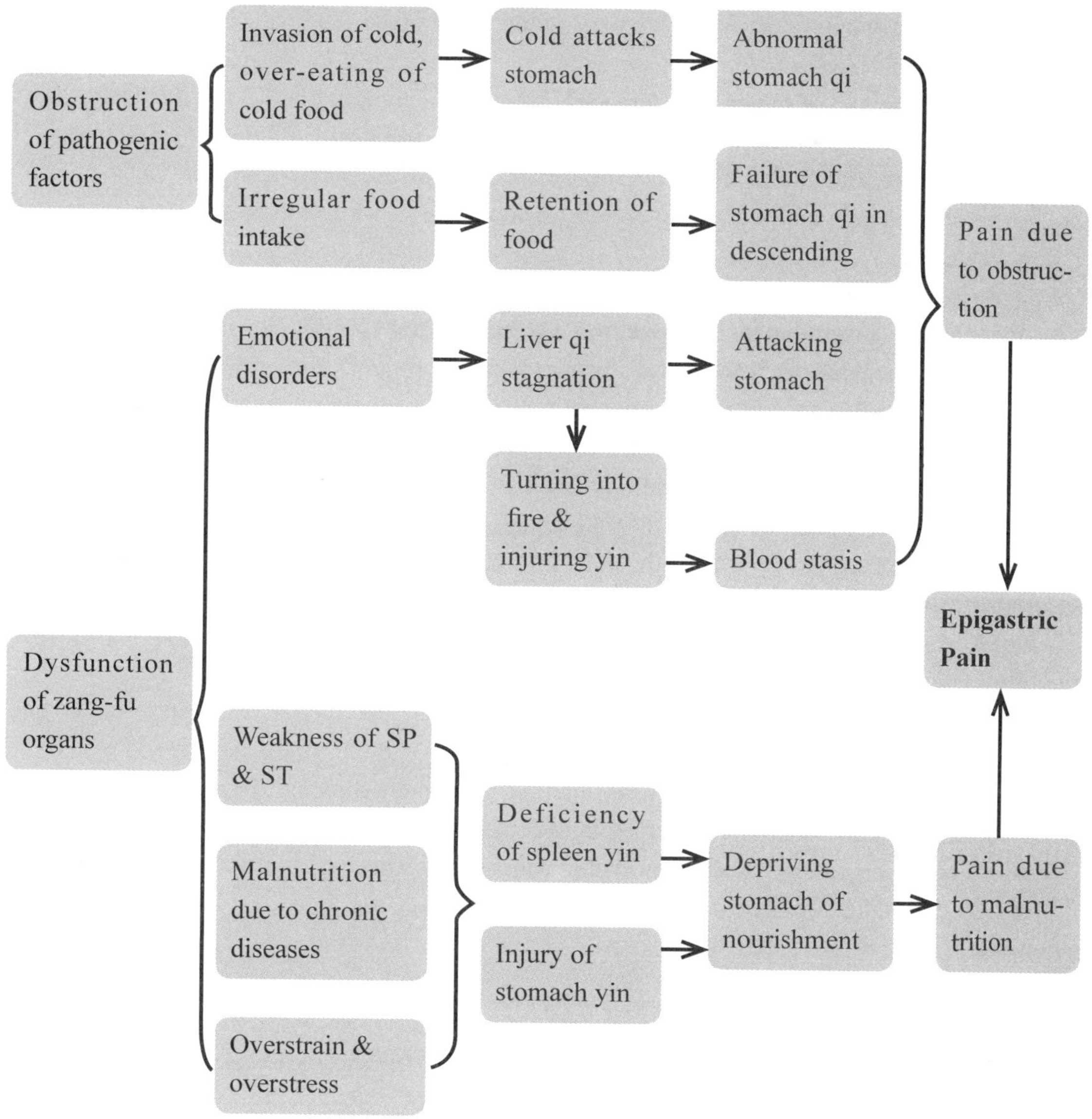

a. Obstruction of pathogens

【Attack of stomach by cold】

Sudden onset of epigastric dull or colic pain which could be alleviated by warmth and aggravated by cold, absence of thirst or thirst with desire of hot drinking, thin white tongue coating, wiry tense pulse.

【Retention of food】

Epigastric distention or pain, sour regurgitation, or vomiting undigested food, anorexia, hesitant bowel movement, white greasy tongue coating, and slippery pulse. The pain is better after vomiting or breaking wind.

b. Dysfunction of *zang-fu* organs

【Attack of stomach by liver qi】

Epigastric fullness and pain which may radiate to hypochondriac regions, frequent belching, hesitant bowel movement, thin white tongue coating, wiry pulse. The pain is usually induced by drastic emotional changes.

【Deficiency and cold of spleen and stomach】

Dull stomach ache which could be alleviated by warmth and pressing; worse when the stomach is empty and better by food intake, regurgitation of clear water, poor appetite, listlessness, cold hands and feet in severe cases, loose stool, white tongue coating, weak pulse or slow pulse.

Epigastric pain due to obstruction of pathogens usually manifests acute pain, while the pain due to dysfunction of zang-fu organs shows chronic pain. It is not so difficult to cure the case due to obstruction of pathogens, but if the disease is not treated thoroughly, the acute case may turn into a chronic case. Clinically, the above syndromes do not appear simply or invariably, they may show complicated conditions with simultaneous occurrence of deficiency and excess, alternation of cold and heat. In clinic, the treatment should be determined flexibly by tracing back the causative factors according to differentiation.

3. Diagnostic Essentials

Epigastric pain is often accompanied by fullness or distention, belching, sour regurgitation, uncomfortable feeling in the stomach, nausea and vomiting.

The pain is often induced by emotional changes, irregular food intake, overstrain, catching cold and other factors.

Upper digestive tract barium meal examination, fiber endoscopy and tissue biopsy may show stomach and duodenum mucosal inflammation, ulcers and other diseases.

Positive occult blood tests of stool and vomit suggest digestive tract bleeding.

Ultrasonic examination, liver function test and bile duct X-ray image are helpful to distinguish the diseases.

4. Differential Diagnosis

Epigastric pain should be distinguished from cardiac vascular diseases, liver and gallbladder diseases, stomach obstruction, perforation, tumor and ulcer bleeding.

The patient with heart disease is usually accompanied by palpitation, abnormal ECG; the patient with liver and gallbladder disease accompanied by Murphy's sign (+), percussive pain in liver area, increased proportion of total WBC and neutral, jaundice, etc; the patient with pancreatitis accompanied by pain in zones on the back, increased pancreatic amylase and trypsin. The tumor of the stomach, pancreas, liver and gallbladder may manifest various symptoms according to the location and severity of tumor. Clinically, physical examination must be carefully done or make necessary lab tests for an accurate diagnosis; even if there are difficulties to determine the diagnosis, at least, rule out the above diseases which are not indications of tui na therapy, so as to avoid the delay of treatment and medical accidents.

5. Tui Na Treatment

【Principle】

To regulate qi and stop pain.

【Points and regions】

RN 12 (*zhōng wǎn*)	ST 25 (*tiān shū*)	ST 36 (*zú sān lǐ*)	RN 6 (*qì hǎi*)
BL 17 (*gé shù*)	BL 18 (*gān shù*)	BL 20 (*pí shù*)	BL 21 (*wèi shù*)
BL 22 (*sān jiāo shù*)	GB 21 (*jiān jǐng*)	LI 10 (*shǒu sān lǐ*)	LI 4 (*hé gǔ*)
PC 6 (*nèi guān*)			

【Method】

Ask the patient to take a supine position, apply one-finger pushing on RN 17 (*dàn zhōng*), RN 12 (*zhōng wǎn*), RN 6 (*qì hǎi*), and RN 4 (*guān yuán*) about 5~10 minutes.

Rub the abdomen, focusing on the epigastric region about 10~20 minutes.

Apply rolling manipulation along the courses of urinary bladder channel on the back, focusing on BL 20 (*pí shù*), BL 21 (*wèi shù*), BL 22 (*sān jiāo shù*), about 5~10 minutes.

Manipulations determined according to syndromes.

* Attack of stomach by cold

Apply kneading manipulation specially on BL 20 (*pí shù*), BL 21 (*wèi shù*) and ST 36 (*zú sān lǐ*).

Apply palm-vibrating manipulation on epigastric region.

Apply vertical scrubbing manipulation along the courses of urinary bladder channel on the back.

* Retention of food

Manipulations are focused on RN 12 (*zhōng wǎn*), PC 6 (*nèi guān*) and ST 25 (*tiān shū*).

Rub the abdomen clockwise for longer time.

* Attack of stomach by liver qi

Apply one-finger pushing on RN 17 (*dàn zhōng*), LV 13 (*zhāng mén*) and LV 14 (*qī mén*) about 5~10 minutes.

Apply pressing manipulation on BL 18 (*gān shù*) and BL19 (*dǎn shù*) forcefully.

* Deficiency and cold of spleen and stomach

Apply one-finger pushing on RN 6 (*qì hǎi*), and RN 4 (*guān yuán*) about 5~10 minutes.

Apply pressing and kneading manipulations specially on ST 36 (*zú sān lǐ*).

Apply palm-vibrating manipulation on RN 12 (*zhōng wǎn*) and RN 6 (*qì hǎi*).

Apply vertical scrubbing manipulation along governor vessel (GV) and the courses of urinary bladder channel on the back until it is warm enough at the local area.

6. Precautions

It is not advisable to give treatment with manipulations to the patients with bleeding due to stomach, duodenum ulcer.

Have a regular life style; keep an easy mood and proper diet.

It is forbidden to have voracious eating of spicy food and drinking alcoholics. It is better to have more meals with less light food.

For the patient with continuous stomach ache, it is better to take liquid food or half liquid food during certain period.

Diarrhea

1. Overview

Diarrhea indicates increased defecation with loose or watery stool due to pathological changes of lower digestive tract. It may occur at any age. The disease could be seen in various intestinal inflammatory syndromes such as acute or chronic enteritis, ulcerative colitis, dumping syndrome after major gastrointestinal surgery, intestinal neurosis, tumor or uremia. Here, emphasis is put on diarrhea due to acute or chronic enteritis and intestinal neurosis. In TCM, the location of disease is in the spleen, the large and small intestines are also involved; pathologically, the disease is characterized by spleen deficiency and excessive dampness.

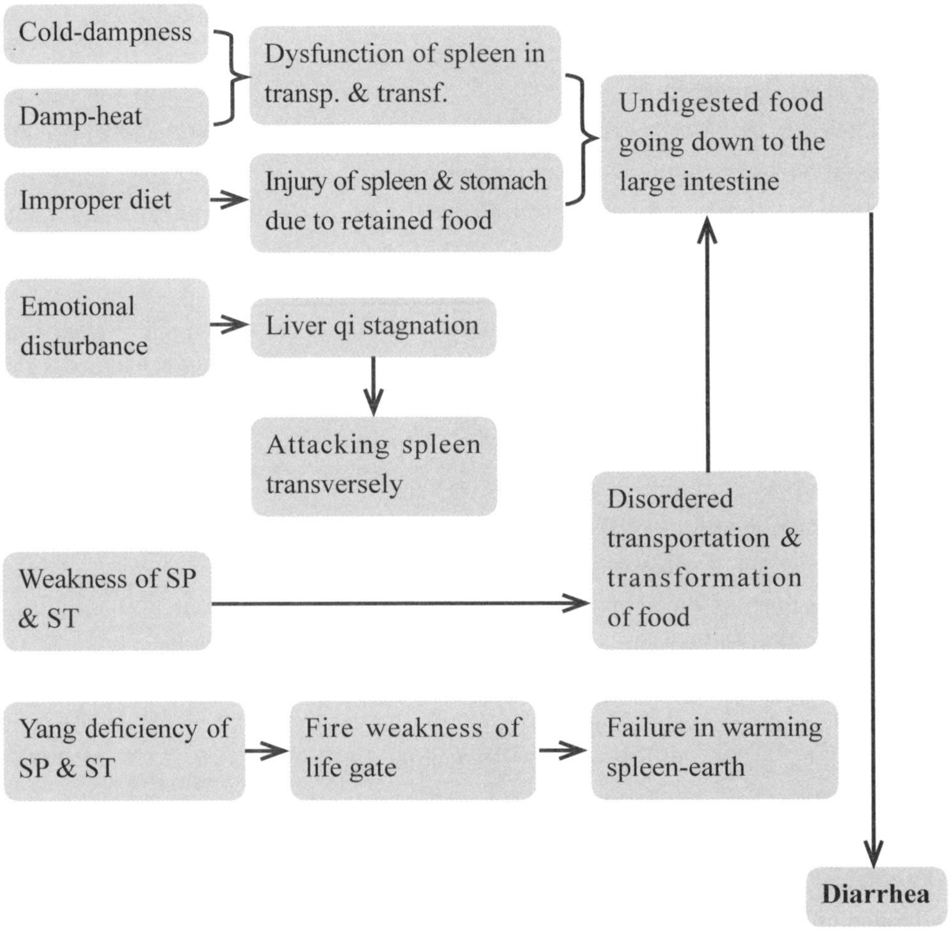

2. Clinical Manifestations

a. Acute diarrhea

【Attack of dampness】

Sudden onset, loose or watery stool or stool mixed with mucus, frequent bowel movements several or more than ten times a day, abdominal pain, borborygmus, aching pain and heaviness of the limbs, sometimes complicated by exterior syndrome manifesting chills and fever, white greasy or yellow greasy tongue coating, soft or slippery rapid pulse.

【Improper food intake】

A history of gluttony or unsanitary food intake, abdominal distending pain alleviated after defecating, diarrhea with offensive smell like rotten egg and a sensation of incompletely defecating, belching with fetid odor, acid regurgitation, thick greasy tongue coating, a slippery rapid pulse.

b. Chronic diarrhea

【Spleen and stomach weakness】

It usually manifests intermittent diarrhea with loose or watery stool, often induced or aggravated by intake of greasy or heavy food, poor appetite, pale tongue with white coating, weak pulse.

【Yang deficiency of spleen and stomach】

It indicates diarrhea before dawn with pain around the umbilicus, immediately appeared after borborygmus, pain relieved after diarrhea, cold feeling in abdomen, soreness and weakness in lumbar region and knees, pale tongue with white coating, a deep and thready pulse.

【Attack of spleen by liver qi】

It is often induced by emotional disturbance, manifesting abdominal pain, borborygums, stuffiness and fullness in the chest and hypochondriac regions, belching, thin tongue coating and wiry pulse.

Tenderness in left lower abdomen or around the umbilicus may be found in some cases, but usually, there is no positive sign during physical examination. Do palpation carefully to see if there is any mass. A routine stool test is always asked to the patients with diarrhea. For the patients with mucopurulent diarrhea, stool test for Amoeba should be done. For the patients with chronic diarrhea, stool culture should be taken to exclude mycotic enteritis, even if routine stool test is negative. For those patients with abdominal mass, ultrasonic examination, barium enema, fibro-colonoscopy and even biopsy should be done to make an accurate diagnosis; for the patients with severe chronic diarrhea, small intestine absorption test should be taken; for patients with fever, a routine blood test should be asked.

3. Diagnostic Essentials

Frequent bowel movements.

Loose stool or even watery stool.

Exclude dysentery and other intestinal organic diseases.

4. Differential Diagnosis

It should be distinguished from dysentery.

Dysentery is marked by abdominal pain, tenesmus and loose stool with red and white mucus. Red blood cells are found in routine stool test. Dysentery bacillus can be found in stool culture; while in the cases with common diarrhea, only increased pus cells, undigested food or fat globules can be seen with routine stool test; in the cases with ulcerative colitis, mucopurulent stool can be seen, no dysentery bacillus shows in stool culture and it can be confirmed by colonoscopy. As for amebic dysentery, it usually manifests caramel loose stools and amebic trophozoites in the colonoscopy.

Besides, it should be distinguished from diarrhea due to tumor characterized by alternation of diarrhea and constipation, abdominal pain, complete or incomplete intestinal obstruction and positive fecal occult blood test. Diarrhea due to tumor can be confirmed by colonoscopy and barium enema.

In addition, there is drug-induced diarrhea which may disappear after stopping the drug.

5. Tui Na Treatment

【Principle】

To invigorate spleen and resolve dampness as a general rule.

Pathogenic dampness can be divided into cold-dampness and dampness-heat; for cold-dampness, warm middle energizer and dissipate cold; and for dampness-heat, clear heat and resolve dampness. For injury due to improper food intake, promote digestion and remove obstruction; for weakness of spleen and stomach, invigorate spleen and harmonize stomach; for yang deficiency of spleen and stomach, warm kidney and spleen; for attack of spleen by liver qi, sooth liver and regulate qi.

【Points and Regions】

RN 12 (*zhōng wǎn*)	RN 17 (*dàn zhōng*)	RN 6 (*qì hǎi*)	RN 4 (*guān yuán*)
BL 21 (*wèi shù*)	BL 23 (*shèn shù*)	ST 36 (*zú sān lǐ*)	LI 4 (*hé gǔ*)
LI 11 (*qū chí*)	SJ 5 (*wài guān*)	LV 13 (*zhāng mén*)	LV 3 (*tài chōng*)
BL19 (*dǎn shù*)	BL 20 (*pí shù*)	BL 18 (*gān shù*)	

【Method】

Ask patient to take a supine position. Apply one-finger pushing on RN 12 (*zhōng wǎn*), RN 6 (*qì hǎi*), RN 4 (*guān yuán*) and RN 8 (*shén què*).

Apply pressing-kneading manipulation on RN 12 (*zhōng wǎn*), ST 25 (*tiān shū*), BL 20 (*pí shù*), BL 21 (*wèi shù*) and BL 25 (*dà cháng shù*).

Apply rubbing manipulation counterclockwise on the abdomen.

Apply rolling manipulation along bilateral courses of foot taiyang urinary bladder channel.

Manipulations determined according to syndrome differentiation.

⋆ Inhibition of spleen by cold-dampness

Add grasping manipulation on GB 20 (*fēng chí*), GB 21 (*jiān jǐng*) and LI 4 (*hé gǔ*), scrubbing manipulation on DU 14 (*dà zhuī*), BL 20 (*pí shù*) and BL 21 (*wèi shù*); also apply rubbing manipulation on abdomen for longer time till it is warm enough in abdomen.

⋆ Retention of dampness-heat

Add kneading manipulation on LI 11 (*qū chí*), SJ 5 (*wài guān*), ST 36 (*zú sān lǐ*) and ST 37 (*shàng jù xū*).

⋆ Injury due to retained food

Add scrubbing manipulation clockwise on abdomen for longer time, and pressing-kneading manipulation on ST 36 (*zú sān lǐ*).

⋆ Weakness of spleen and stomach

Add pressing-kneading manipulation on ST 36 (*zú sān lǐ*).

⋆ Yang deficiency of spleen and kidney

Add pressing-kneading manipulation on RN 6 (*qì hǎi*), RN 4 (*guān yuán*), ST 36 (*zú sān lǐ*) and DU 4 (*mìng mén*), transverse scrubbing manipulation along Du vessel and on BL 23 (*shèn shù*) and DU 4 (*mìng mén*), pinching the spine or patting manipulation on the back.

⋆ Attack of spleen by liver qi

Add pressing-kneading manipulation on RN 17 (*dàn zhōng*), LV 13 (*zhāng mén*), BL 18 (*gān shù*), BL 19 (*dǎn shù*) and LV3 (*tài chōng*); heavyage manipulation on hypochondrium, separating-pushing manipulation and combing manipulation on abdomen.

6. Precautions

Care should be taken to observe whether there is dehydration or acidosis in the cases with severe acute diarrhea. If there is, fluid infusion should be administered to correct water and electrolyte disturbance. It is advised to take high-carbohydrate, high-protein, low-fat and light diet. Avoid uncooked, cold, greasy food or food that may produce gas, or roughage which may increase intestinal peristalsis.

Chronic diarrhea is most encountered in tui na clinic since the drugs of western medicine and TCM can not achieve good effect on chronic diarrhea. While acute diarrhea is rarely seen in tui na clinic since it can be controlled by drugs at first. Actually, tui na is also effective to acute diarrhea.

For patient with chronic diarrhea, it is advised to adhere to proper diet, balanced lifestyle, regular exercises. Avoid overstrain and keep abdomen warm.

Acute diarrhea has good prognosis and shorter period of treatment, sometimes two or three treatments are enough. As for chronic diarrhea, the period of treatment varies according to individuals and condition of disease; the most of cases can achieve satisfactory result excluding the cases with organic pathological change.

Constipation

1. Overview

Constipation is a condition due to various causes manifesting dry and hard stool, prolonged defecation or difficult defecation. It could be a symptom or a disease. Constipation can occur at any age, but less in children. As for its incidence, there is no significant difference between male and female. The constipation applicable to tui na is functional constipation (or called simple constipation).

2. Clinical Manifestations

Dryness-heat in the stomach and intestines.

Dry and hard stool, abdominal distension and fullness, flushed face, feverish sensation in the body, scanty and dark urine, dry mouth, vexation, or fetid breath, lip sores, red tongue with yellow or dry yellow coating, a slippery rapid pulse.

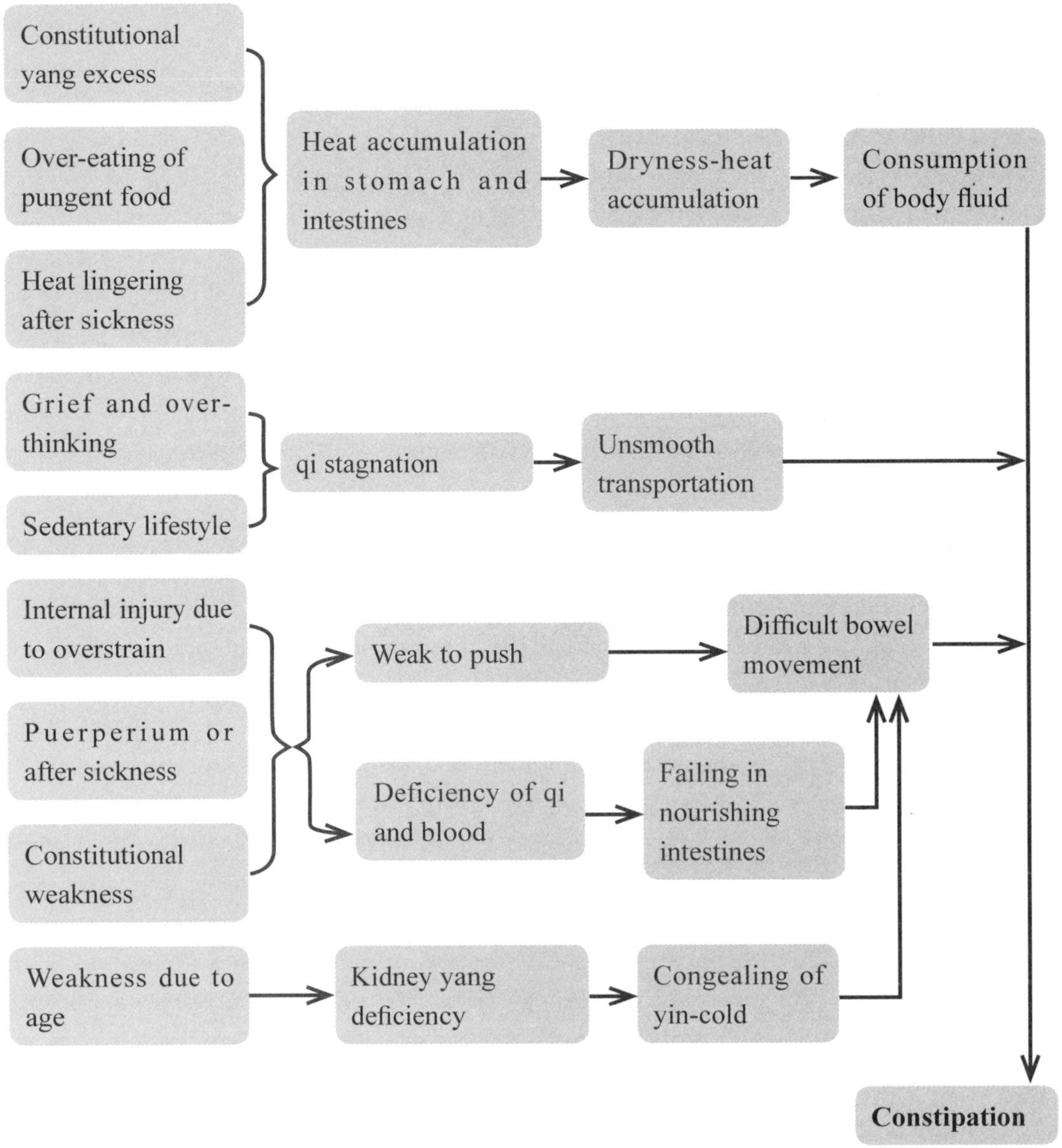

a. Qi stagnation

Inability of defecation, stuffiness and fullness in abdomen and hypochondrium, even abdominal distending pain, frequent belching, poor appetite, mental depression or irritability, thin white tongue coating and a wiry pulse.

b. Deficiency of qi and blood

【Qi deficiency】

Weakness of defecation though patient has a desire, or sweating and shortness of breath if patient exerts defecation, tiredness after defecation with soft stool, no abdominal distending pain, pale complexion, listlessness, lassitude, pale tongue with thin white coating, a weak and soft pulse.

【Blood deficiency】

Dry and hard stool, sallow complexion without luster, vertigo, palpitation, pale tongue and thready pulse.

c. Congealing of yin-cold

Difficult defecation, cold pain in abdomen, profuse and clear urine, cold limbs, pale complexion, soreness and cold feeling in the back, pale tongue with moist white coating, a deep and slow pulse.

Usually, there is no obvious positive physical sign; maybe mild abdominal tenderness in excess syndrome, while no obvious discomfort in deficiency syndrome. For middle-aged patients who have frequent constipation with bloody stool or mucous stool, or accompanied by abdominal dull pain, poor appetite and emaciation, digital rectal examination, sigmoidoscopy, colonoscopy or air-barium double contrast radiography should be administered to exclude tumor in lower digestive tract. For female patients, gynecological examination should be taken together to exclude gynecological tumor.

3. Diagnostic Essentials

Absence of bowel movement for 48 hours.

Dry and hard stool or difficult defecation.

Exclude hemorrhage or tumor of lower digestive tract.

4. Differential Diagnosis

It is not difficult to make diagnosis, just need to distinguish the disease from gynecological tumor and tumor of lower digestive tract.

5. Tui Na Treatment

【Principle of treatment】

Take harmonizing intestines to relieve constipation as a general rule.

For constipation due to dryness-heat in the stomach and intestines: clear heat and descend the turbid.

For constipation due to qi stagnation: sooth liver and regulate qi.

For constipation due to deficiency of qi and blood: tonify qi and blood.

For constipation due to congealing of yin-cold: reinforce yang and dissipate cold.

【Points and Regions】

RN 12 (*zhōng wǎn*)	ST 25 (*tiān shū*)	RN 6 (*qì hǎi*)	RN 4 (*guān yuán*)
BL 25 (*dà cháng shù*)	BL 18 (*gān shù*)	BL19 (*dǎn shù*)	BL 20 (*pí shù*)
BL 23 (*shèn shù*)	ST 36 (*zú sān lǐ*)	DU 4 (*mìng mén*)	BL 31-34 (*bā liáo*)

【Method】

Ask patient to take a prone position. Apply rolling manipulation along bilateral courses of foot *taiyang* bladder channel, focusing on BL 20 (*pí shù*), BL 21 (*wèi shù*), BL 25 (*dà cháng shù*) and BL 31-34 (*bā liáo*).

Ask patient to take a supine position. Apply one-finger pushing on RN 12 (*zhōng wǎn*), ST 25 (*tiān shū*), RN 6 (*qì hǎi*) and RN 4 (*guān yuán*).

Apply rubbing manipulation clockwise on abdomen.

The manipulations determined according to syndrome differentiation

⋆ Dryness-heat in the stomach and intestines

Apply strong manipulations to stimulate ST 36 (*zú sān lǐ*) and BL 25 (*dà cháng shù*), apply pressing-kneading manipulations on SJ 5 (*wài guān*), LI 4 (*hé gǔ*) and LI 11 (*qū chí*) to purge heat.

⋆ Qi stagnation

Add one-finger pushing on RN 17 (*dàn zhōng*), LV 14 (*qī mén*), LV 13 (*zhāng mén*), LU 1 (*zhōng fǔ*) and LU 2 (*yún mén*); pressing-kneading manipulation on BL 13 (*fèi shù*), BL 18 (*gān shù*), BL19 (*dǎn shù*) and BL 17 (*gé shù*); heavyage manipulation on hypochondriac regions and combing manipulation on the chest and abdomen.

⋆ Deficiency of qi and blood

Add pressing-kneading manipulation on ST 36 (*zú sān lǐ*), SP 6 (*sān yīn jiāo*) and SP 10 (*xuè hǎi*); one-finger pushing on RN 6 (*qì hǎi*), RN 4 (*guān yuán*) and RN 8 (*shén què*) for longer time; scrubbing manipulation along bilateral courses of foot taiyang urinary bladder channel and transverse scrubbing manipulation on BL 31-34 (*bā liáo*) and pinching along the spine manipulation.

⋆ Congealing of yin-cold: Add pressing-kneading manipulation on DU 4 (*mìng mén*) and BL 23 (*shèn shù*); one-finger pushing on RN 6 (*qì hǎi*) and RN 4 (*guān yuán*) for longer time; scrubbing manipulation on the back along bilateral courses of foot taiyang urinary bladder channel and Du vessel and transverse scrubbing manipulation on BL 31-34 (*bā liáo*); patting-striking manipulation on both sides of back.

6. Precautions

Drink cold water or salty water in the morning to promote intestinal peristalsis.

Cultivate a habit to have a regular bowel movement.

Intake of more roughage to promote intestinal peristalsis.

Proper exercise to promote intestinal peristalsis.

Adhere to self massage on the abdomen clockwise.

For the patient with constipation due to little food intake at convalescence stage after an acute febrile disease or during attack of other diseases, it is not necessary to worry about it because it can be relieved when stomach qi recovers and eating returns to normal.

Avoid taking *Má Zǐ Rén Wán* (Cannabis Fruit Pill, 麻子仁丸) without differentiation.

Hypertension

1. Overview

Hypertension is a commonly encountered chronic disease marked clinically by a persistent elevated arterial blood pressure, also named primary hypertension. At its later stage, pathological changes of heart, kidney and brain may occur. It has high incidence associated with age, occupation and family history. In TCM, it pertains to the category of vertigo or headache. The causative factors are generally related to wind, fire, phlegm and blood stasis due to emotional disturbance resulting in hyperactivity of liver yang, yin depletion of liver and kidney failing in controlling yang and liver fire, over-eating of fat, sweet or greasy food leading to injury of spleen and stomach resulting in production of phlegm and dampness. Visceral qi and blood is consequently damaged, manifesting vertigo, headache and pathological changes of heart, kidney and brain.

Hypertension is characterized by constant elevated blood pressure. Clinically, 80%~90% of hypertension is referred to primary hypertension. Secondary hypertension is only a symptom of certain diseases, which may be temporary or persistent and occupies 10%~20% of hypertension. In general, it can be diagnosed as hypertension if blood pressure often exceeds 140/90 mmHg during rest. Elevated diastolic pressure is taken as major criteria for diagnosing hypertension, and diagnostic criteria for hypertension can be taken as reference.

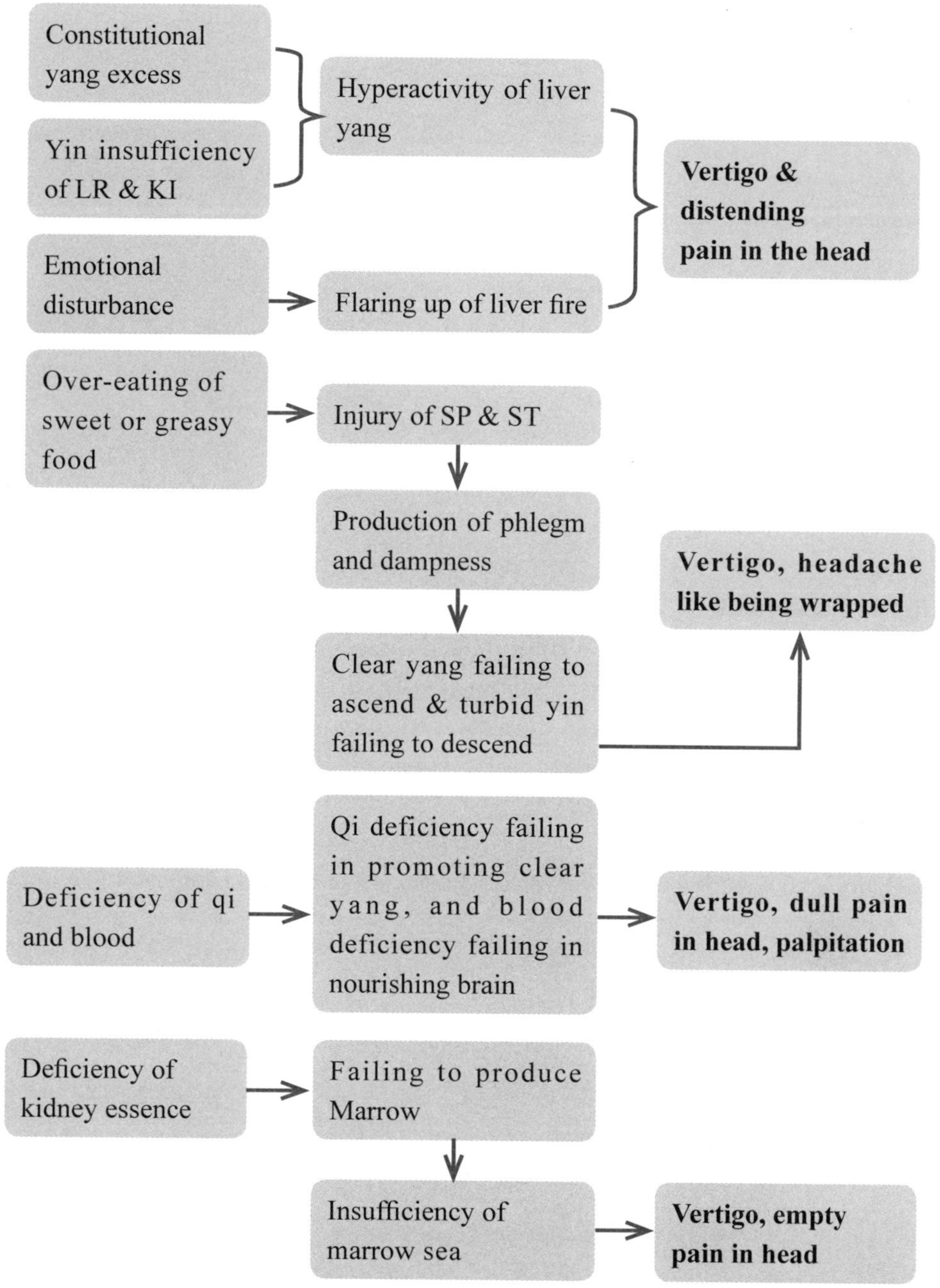

2. Clinical Manifestations

The clinical manifestations of hypertension vary in severity. Some patients is absent of subjective symptoms and is often detected during physical examination. The common manifestations are vertigo, headache, flushed face, bloodshot eyes, bitter taste in mouth, palpitation, constipation, red tongue and wiry a pulse.

a. Fire due to liver qi stagnation

Vertigo, headache, eye distension, photophobia, irritability, flushed face, bloodshot eyes, bitter taste in mouth, dry throat, constipation, scanty dark urine, red tongue, big wiry or wiry rapid pulse. The symptoms could be worse after vexation and exertion or by drastic emotional changes.

b. Retention of phlegm-dampness

Vertigo, headache like being wrapped by cloth, stuffy sensation in chest, nausea, poor appetite, obesity, profuse sputum, numbness and edema of the limbs, thick greasy or yellow greasy tongue coating, a soft and slippery pulse.

c. Yang hyperactivity due to yin deficiency

Dizziness and distending pain in the head, tinnitus, amnesia, soreness and weakness in lumbar region and knees, flushed face, blurred vision, dry mouth and throat, red tongue, a wiry thready pulse.

d. Insufficiency of kidney essence

Dizziness and empty pain in the head, mental fatigue, lassitude, insomnia, dreamful sleep, aching pain in lumbar region, frequent urination at night, pale or red tongue, a thready and weak pulse.

3. Diagnostic Essentials

According to the criteria made by WHO/ISH and Guidelines for Prevention and Treatment of Hypertension in China (October 1999), hypertension is defined as a condition of systolic blood pressure 140 mmHg or more or/and diastolic blood pressure 90 mmHg or more without taking any antihypertensive for adults over 18.

The patient with a past history of hypertension, whose blood pressure can be controlled under 140/90 mmHg by taking antihypertensive, is also diagnosed as hypertension.

4. Tui Na Treatment

【Principle of treatment】

To pacify liver, subdue yang, nourish yin, reduce fire, resolve phlegm, invigorate spleen, harmonize and reinforce yin and yang.

【Points and Regions】

GB 20 (*fēng chí*)	EX-HN3 (*yìn táng*)	EX-HN5 (*tài yáng*)	LV 14 (*qī mén*)
LV 13 (*zhāng mén*)	RN 12 (*zhōng wǎn*)	GB 34 (*yáng líng quán*)	SJ 20 (*jiǎo sūn*)

qiáo gōng (桥弓)	LI 11 (*qū chí*)	ST 36 (*zú sān lǐ*)	KI 1 (*yǒng quán*)
GB 21 (*jiān jǐng*)	LV 3 (*tài chōng*)	KI 3 (*tài xī*)	ST 40 (*fēng lóng*)
BL 18 (*gān shù*)	BL 23 (*shèn shù*)	BL 20 (*pí shù*)	

Back and abdomen.

【Method】

⋆ Fire due to liver qi stagnation

To clear liver, resolve stagnation, pacify liver and subdue yang.

Ask patient to take a supine position. The practitioner sits at the side of patient's head facing to the patient. Apply pushing manipulation with two hands along the course from EX-HN3 (*yìn táng*) to the midpoint of anterior hairline, which is called opening *tiān mén* (*kāi tiān mén*, 开天门) for 1 minute; apply separating-pushing manipulation along the eyebrows, which is called pushing *kǎn gōng* (*tuī kǎn gōng*, 推坎宫) for 20 times.

Apply thenar-kneading manipulation on the forehead for 1 minute; separate-pushing manipulation and meeting-pushing manipulation with both thumb bellies for 10 times respectively.

Prop patient's head with the bellies of the middle fingers and apply pressing-kneading manipulation on both GB 20 (*fēng chí*) for 1~2 minutes and on both EX-HN5 (*tài yáng*) for 1 minute.

Sitting at right side of patient and facing to patient, apply one-finger pushing on bilateral LV 14 (*qī mén*) 1 minute, and along the course of conception vessel from RN 22 (*tiān tū*) to RN 15 (*jiū wěi*) 5~10 times.

Apply pointing-kneading manipulation on bilateral LV 3 (*tài chōng*), GB 34 (*yáng líng quán*) and BL 18 (*gān shù*), 1 minute each point.

Ask patient to take a sitting position. Standing and facing to the patient, apply scattering manipulation on both sides of head.

Standing behind patient, apply grasping-five-channels manipulation on the head for 20 times.

⋆ Retention of phlegm-dampness in middle energizer

To resolve phlegm, eliminate dampness, invigorate spleen and normalize middle energizer.

Ask patient to take a supine position. Sitting at right side of patient and facing to patient, apply one-finger pushing on RN 12 (*zhōng wǎn*) and bilateral LV 13 (*zhāng mén*), 1 minute each point.

Apply rubbing-kneading manipulation clockwise on abdomen in circular way by taking umbilicus as the center, gradually enlarging the circles and then shorten the circles back to umbilicus, 5 minutes all together or until warm feeling appearing in abdomen.

Apply pointing-kneading manipulation on bilateral ST 40 (*fēng lóng*), ST 36 (*zú sān lǐ*) and SP 6 (*sān yīn jiāo*), 1 minute each point.

Apply grasping manipulation on the lateral side of legs repeatedly for 20 times; rolling manipulation on lateral side of legs 2 minutes each side.

Ask patient to take a prone position. Apply rolling manipulation on the back 3~5 minutes, focusing on BL 20 (*pí shù*) and BL 21 (*wèi shù*).

Apply pinching-spine manipulation from upper back to lower back repeatedly for 5~10 times.

⋆ Hyperactivity of yang due to yin deficiency
To tonify liver and kidney, nourish yin and subdue yang.

Ask patient to take a supine position. Sitting at right side of patient and facing to patient, apply one-finger pushing along conception vessel from upper back to lower back repeatedly for 20 times.

Apply one-finger pushing on LV 14 (*qī mén*), RN 6 (*qì hǎi*) and RN 4 (*guān yuán*), 1 minute each point.

Apply pointing-kneading manipulation on bilateral KI 3 (*tài xī*), SP 6 (*sān yīn jiāo*) and KI 1 (*yǒng quán*), 1 minute each point.

Apply four-finger-pushing manipulation on the medial aspects of legs for 20 times.

Ask patient to take a prone position. Apply rolling manipulation on the back 3~5 minutes, focusing on BL 18 (*gān shù*) and BL 23 (*shèn shù*).

Ask patient to take a sitting position. Apply grasping manipulation on GB 21 (*jiān jǐng*) 1 minute, on the lateral sides of arms up and down repeatedly 10 times.

⋆ Insufficiency of kidney essence
To tonify and nourish kidney essence.

Ask patient to take a supine position. Sitting at right side of patient and facing to patient, apply one-finger pushing along conception vessel from upper back to lower back repeatedly for 20 times.

Apply one-finger pushing on RN 12 (*zhōng wǎn*) and RN 4 (*guān yuán*), 1 minute each point.

Apply palm-vibrating manipulation on RN 6 (*qì hǎi*) 2 minutes till a warm feeling appear in the abdomen.

Apply pointing-kneading manipulation on bilateral KI 3 (*tài xī*), SP 6 (*sān yīn jiāo*) and ST 36 (*zú sān lǐ*), 1 minute each point.

Apply scrubbing manipulation on bilateral KI 1 (*yǒng quán*) till it is warm at the local area.

Ask patient to take a prone position. Apply rolling manipulation on the back 3~5 minutes, focusing on BL 20 (*pí shù*), BL 18 (*gān shù*) and BL 23 (*shèn shù*).

Apply scrubbing manipulation on the back along the courses of foot *taiyang* bladder channel and governor vessel until it is warm at local area.

5. Precautions

Tui Na treatment above is done mainly for primary hypertension; while for secondary hypertension, the primary disease should be treated as the basis, some manipulations can be added to control blood pressure.

Avoid over-stress, keep an optimistic mood and maintain enough sleeping time.

To have regular and proper exercise for preventing over-weighted or obesity. Stop smoking and take low-fat, low-salt and light food.

For the patient with hypertensive crisis or presymptoms of stroke, combined treatments should be administered immediately and try to calm the patient down.

Tui na manipulations are suggested to correct the disorders of small joints.

Add manipulation of pushing *qiáo gōng*(桥弓) 10~20 times for the cases with severely elevated blood pressure.

Coronary Heart Disease

1. Overview

Coronary heart disease is referred to myocardiac damage caused by imbalance of blood supply and demand between coronary artery blood flow and heart muscle. Coronary heart disease is divided into functional and organic types. Tui Na treatment is effective for functional coronary heart disease, and only an accessory treatment for organic coronary heart disease. It pertains to the category of chest impediment or palpitation in TCM. Coronary heart disease usually manifests stuffy sensation and pain in the chest, shortness of breath, dyspnea and inability to lie down flatly, or even heart pain radiating to the back or back pain radiating to heart. It occurs more in middle-aged people over 40, more in male and mental workers.

Western medicine thinks the disease is turned from coronary atherosclerosis, but its etiology is not very clear. So far, it is believed that the disease is caused by variety of factors acting on the different segments including age, sex, occupation, diet, blood fat, blood pressure, smoking, obesity, heredity, diabetes, etc.. Among these factors, hyperlipemia, hypertension, smoking and diabetes are the most important risk factors. The pathogenesis of the disease is closely related to anatomy and location of coronary artery as well as the condition of platelet function. TCM holds that the occurrence of disease is associated with invasion of exogenous pathogenic cold, improper diet, emotional disturbance and weak body constitution. The disease may show excess and deficiency syndromes. Excess syndrome indicates chest pain caused by congealing of cold, qi stagnation, blood stasis or turbid phlegm; while deficiency syndrome means precordial pain caused by emotional disturbance or weakness due to age.

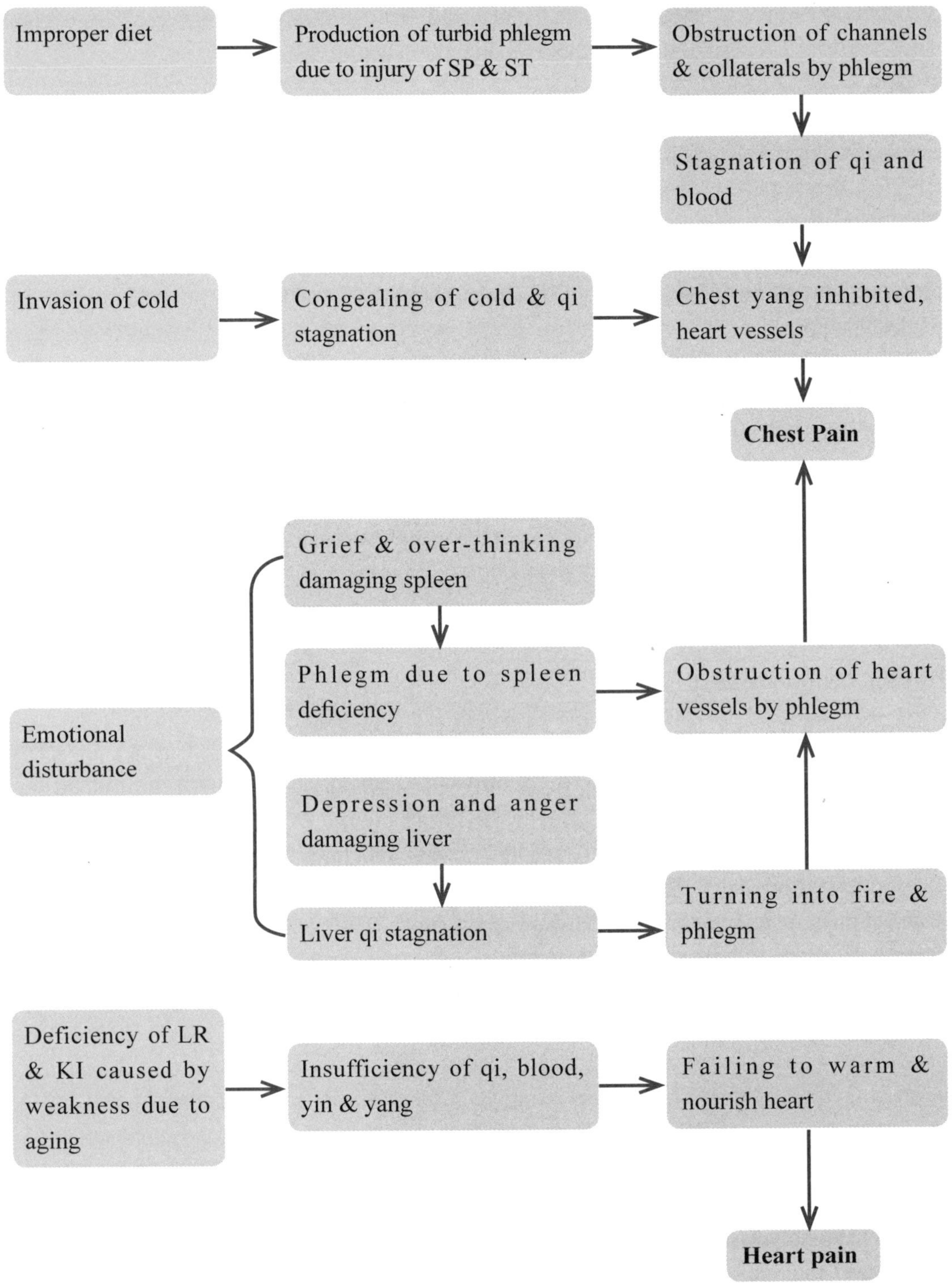

2. Clinical Manifestations

Typical angina pectoris is marked by sudden onset of squeezing, distending or suffocating pain behind upper or middle segment of sternum, which may spread over the most part of precordial region or may radiate to left shoulder, anteromedial aspect of left arm and even to ring and little fingers. Occasionally, the patient may have near-death experiences and has to stop doing any things, the severe case is also accompanied by sweating. Such pain usually lasts 1~5 minutes, rarely more than 15 minutes. It may disappear within 1~2 minutes (rarely more than 5 minutes) after rest or taking Nitroglycerin.

In TCM, the disease is classified into the following syndromes according to different causes.

a. Disturbance of heart by turbid phlegm

Angina pectoris, alternation of pain and suffocation, radiating pain to left shoulder and arm, shortness of breath, dyspnea, heavy limbs, profuse sputum, tongue with dark marks and turbid greasy coating, and slippery pulse.

b. Deficiency of yang qi

Dull pain or suffocating sensation in chest, shortness of breath, dizziness, mental fatigue, dislike of speaking, aversion to cold, cold limbs, pale complexion, sweating after exertion, blue-purple lips and nails, pale flabby tongue with teeth-marks, deep thready pulse.

c. Obstruction of heart by blood stasis

Fixed stabbing pain in the chest which is usually worse at night, palpitation, restlessness, purple and dark tongue with dark marks on the margin, and deep hesitant pulse.

d. Yin deficiency of heart and kidney

Suffocating feeling and pain in chest, dysphoria, poor sleep, palpitation, night sweating, warm feeling in chest, palms and soles, dry throat and mouth, poor memory, dizziness, soreness and weakness in lumbar region and knees, red tongue with dark marks, thready and rapid pulse.

e. Deficiency of qi and yin

Intermittent suffocating feeling and dull pain in chest, palpitation, shortness of breath, dizziness, lassitude, dislike of speaking, red tongue or tongue with teeth-marks, thready rapid forceless or intermittent knotted pulse.

f. Congealing of yin-cold

Chest pain radiating to the back which is often aggravated by cold, suffocating feeling in chest, shortness of breath, palpitation, pale complexion, cold limbs, even dyspnea and inability to lie down flatly, white tongue coating, and deep thready pulse.

3. Diagnostic Essentials

It is not difficult to make the diagnosis according to the medical history, main clinical manifestations such as suffocating chest pains, palpitation, shortness of breath, and results of physical examination. The disease should be distinguished from cardiovascular neurosis and pericarditis.

4. Tui Na Treatment

【Principle】

To nourish heart, warm yang, eliminate obstruction and stop pain.

For obstruction of heart by turbid phlegm, it is to invigorate yang, drain the turbid, eliminate phlegm and remove obstruction.

For deficiency of yang qi, it is to replenish qi, warm yang, activate blood and dredge collaterals.

For obstruction of heart by blood stasis, it is to activate blood, eliminate stasis, dredge collaterals and stop pain.

For yin deficiency of heart and kidney, it is to nourish kidney yin, tonify heart and calm the mind.

For deficiency of both qi and yin, it is to replenish qi, nourish yin, activate blood and dredge collaterals.

For congealing of yin-cold, it is to invigorate yang with warming method, remove obstruction and disperse cold.

【Points and Regions】

RN 1 (*huì yīn*)	RN 17 (*dàn zhōng*)	PC 6 (*nèi guān*)	BL 15 (*xīn shù*)	BL 14 (*jué yīn shù*)

Chest and back.

【Method】

Ask patient to take a sitting or supine position.

Apply one-finger pushing manipulation, finger-pressing and finger-kneading manipulations on RN 1 (*jù queē*) and RN 17 (*dàn zhōng*), 3 minutes each point.

Apply pressing-kneading manipulation on PC 6 (*nèi guān*) 5 minutes when the patient is having deep breath.

Apply rolling, finger-pressing, finger-kneading manipulations on BL 15 (*xīn shù*) and BL 14 (*jué yīn shù*), 3 minutes each point.

Apply transverse scrubbing manipulation on the chest till warm sensation appears at the local area.

Ask patient to take a prone position. Apply hypothenar-scrubbing manipulation on the back along the courses of foot *taiyang* bladder channel and governor vessel till warm sensation appears at the local area.

Manipulations determined according to syndrome differentiation.

*. Obstruction of heart by turbid phlegm in the heart

Add pointing-pressing manipulation on ST 40 (*fēng lóng*), BL 20 (*pí shù*), BL 21 (*wèi shù*), BL 13 (*fèi shù*), SP 9 (*yīn líng quán*) and ST 36 (*zú sān lǐ*) to invigorate yang, drain the turbid, resolve phlegm and remove obstruction. It is better to have strong manipulations as reducing method, not less than 1 minute each point.

*. Deficiency of yang qi

Add rubbing manipulation on lower abdomen; pressing manipulation on RN 3 (*zhōng jí*); pushing manipulation on RN 4 (*guān yuán*), RN 6 (*qì hǎi*) and RN 3 (*zhōng jí*); transverse scrubbing manipulation on BL 31-34 (*bā liáo*), BL 23 (*shèn shù*) and DU 4 (*mìng mén*) to replenish qi, warm yang, activate blood and dredge collaterals. It is better to have gentle manipulations as reinforcing method.

* Obstruction of heart by blood stasis

Add pressing-kneading manipulation on SP 21 (*dà bāo*), GB 25 (*jīng mén*), BL 17 (*gé shù*) and

SP 6 (*sān yīn jiāo*) to activate blood, resolve stasis, dredge collaterals and stop pain.

⋆ Yin deficiency of heart and kidney

Add one-finger pushing or rolling manipulation on BL 15 (*xīn shù*) and BL 23 (*shèn shù*); pressing-kneading manipulation on RN 6 (*qì hǎi*), RN 4 (*guān yuán*) and SP 6 (*sān yīn jiāo*); scrubbing manipulation on bilateral KI 1 (*yǒng quán*) to nourish yin, benefit kidney, tonify heart, and calm the mind.

⋆ Deficiency of qi and yin

Add pressing-kneading manipulation on RN 12 (*zhōng wǎn*), SP 10 (*xuè hǎi*) and ST 36 (*zú sān lǐ*); one-finger pushing or rolling manipulation on BL 20 (*pí shù*) and BL 21 (*wèi shù*) to replenish qi, nourish yin, activate blood and dredge collaterals.

⋆ Congealing of yin-cold

Add transverse scrubbing manipulation on the shoulder and upper back, BL 23 (*shèn shù*), DU 4 (*mìng mén*) and BL 31-34 (*bā liáo*); vertical scrubbing manipulation on the back along the courses of governor vessel until warm sensation appearing to invigorate yang, eliminate obstruction and disperse cold with warming method.

5. Precautions

Regulate and calm the mood, avoid over-stressed, keep warm and prevent catching cold.

Adhere to regular lifestyle and diet with low-salt, low-fat and low-cholesterol food, more meals less food, and avoid intense sports.

Have proper exercise to strengthen body constitution, improve heart function, help to generate collateral circulation, regulate lipid metabolism and prevent obesity.

Have regular checkup to protect heart.

Tui Na Treatment is significant to non-attack stage of angina pectoris with stable condition and ischemic change of ECG.

Headache

1. Overview

Headache is the pain of the upper half of skull caused by intracranial or extracranial diseases stimulating sensitive tissues of pain. It is a subjective symptom commonly seen in the clinic in various acute and chronic diseases. There are four types of diseases that can cause a headache: intracranial disorders, extracranial disorders, systemic diseases and neurosis. The headache discussed here is in the scope of internal diseases with headache as the main symptom. If it is just the accompanied symptom occurring in traumatic disorders or some other diseases, it will disappear when the primary disease goes away. The etiology of headache can be generalized into two types, exogenous and endogenous pathogenic factors. Wind-cold headache, wind-heat headache, summer-dampness headache are caused by exogenous pathogenic factors. Liver yang headache, turbid phlegm headache, blood deficiency headache, kidney deficiency headache and blood stasis headache are caused by endogenous pathogenic factors.

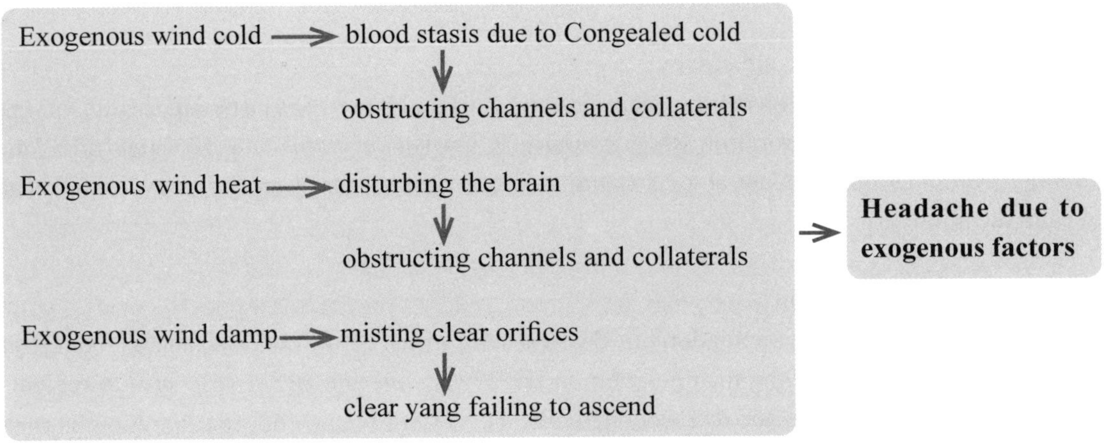
Exogenous wind cold
blood stasis due to Congealed cold
obstructing channels and collaterals
Exogenous wind heat
disturbing the brain
obstructing channels and collaterals
Exogenous wind damp
misting clear orifices
clear yang failing to ascend
Headache due to exogenous factors

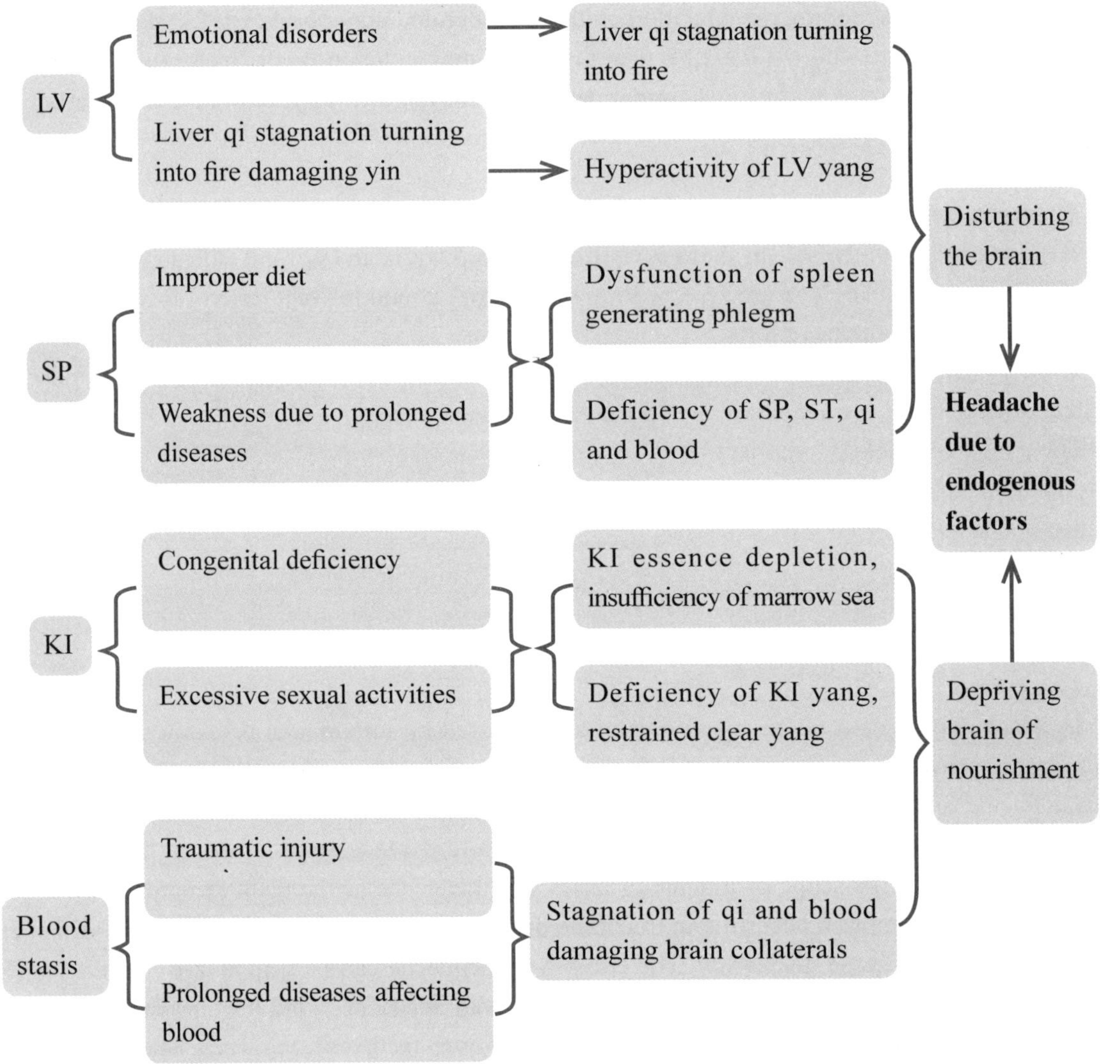
LV
Emotional disorders
Liver qi stagnation turning into fire damaging yin
Liver qi stagnation turning into fire
Hyperactivity of LV yang
SP
Improper diet
Weakness due to prolonged diseases
Dysfunction of spleen generating phlegm
Deficiency of SP, ST, qi and blood
KI
Congenital deficiency
Excessive sexual activities
KI essence depletion, insufficiency of marrow sea
Deficiency of KI yang, restrained clear yang
Blood stasis
Traumatic injury
Prolonged diseases affecting blood
Stagnation of qi and blood damaging brain collaterals
Disturbing the brain
Headache due to endogenous factors
Depriving brain of nourishment

2. Clinical Manifestations

a. Wind-cold headache

It is often induced by exposing to wind or cold, accompanied by repeated attacks, pain extending to nape and upper back, aversion to wind and cold, soreness of joints, preference for having headband, no thirst, thin and white tongue coating, a floating or tight pulse.

b. Wind-heat headache

Distending pain of head, or even like splitting, aversion to wind, fever, red face and eyes, thirst with desire of drinking, red, swollen and sore throat, yellow urine or constipation, thin and yellow tongue coating or red tongue tip, a floating rapid pulse.

c. Summer-dampness headache

Headache like the head being wrapped, fullness in epigastrium and poor appetite, weakness and heaviness of limbs, fever with sweating, vexation, thirst, greasy tongue coating, a soggy and rapid pulse.

d. Liver yang headache

Headache with dizziness and giddiness, worse in temple regions, irritation, irritability, restless sleep, red face, dryness and bitterness in mouth, distending pain in hypochondriac regions, thin and yellow tongue coating or red tongue body with scanty coating, a wiry forceful pulse or wiry thready pulse.

e. Turbid phlegm headache

Distending pain of head, fullness in epigastric region and discomfort in chest, poor appetite, fatigue, salivation, nausea, white greasy tongue coating, a slippery pulse.

f. Blood deficiency headache

Headache, dizziness, worse after exertion, listlessness, lassitude, lusterless complexion, poor appetite, palpitation, shortness of breath, pale tongue.

g. Kidney deficiency headache

It manifests empty pain, listlessness, lassitude, tinnitus, blurred vision, poor memory, insomnia, soreness in lumbar region, weakness of legs, nocturnal emission, leucorrhea, cold limbs. Yang deficiency syndrome may show pale puffy tongue and deep thready forceless pulse, and yin deficiency syndrome show dry mouth with scanty fluid, red tongue body, and a thready rapid pulse.

h. Blood stasis headache

It manifests repeated attacks with fixed stabbing pain and long duration, or with the history of head trauma, dusky purple tongue, or with stasis maculae, a choppy pulse.

3. Diagnosis

Headache is the main symptom in the diseases, appearing in the forehead, tempora, vertex, occipital region or the whole head with different nature such as pounding pain, stabbing pain, distending pain, dizzy pain and dull pain. It might be intense with an abrupt onset without a break, or have repeated attacks with long duration. Each attack can last for several minutes, hours, days or even weeks.

Headache might have an abrupt onset caused by exogenous or endogenous pathogenic factors, or have the history of repeated attacks.

Blood test, blood pressure measurement should be done. To exclude organic diseases and make correct diagnosis, cerebrospinal fluid examination, electroencephalogram (EEG) should be done if necessary, Doppler, cranial CT and MRI should be done if possible.

4. Tui Na Treatment

【Principle of treatment】

To dredge channels and collaterals, move qi and activate blood.

【Points and regions】

yìn táng (EX-HN3)	ST 8 (*tóu wéi*)	*tài yáng* (EX-HN5)	*yú yāo* (EX-HN4)
BL 2 (*cuán zhú*)	GB 14 (*yáng bái*)	DU 20 (*bǎi huì*)	*sì shén cōng* (EX-HN1)
GB 21 (*jiān jǐng*)	GB 20 (*fēng chí*)		

Head, face, neck and nape.

【Method】

The patient in sitting position, apply one-finger pushing on the neck along bilateral courses of urinary bladder channel upward and downward about 3 minutes. Then, apply pressing manipulation on GB 20 (*fēng chí*), DU 16 (*fēng fǔ*) and BL 10 (*tiān zhù*); grasping manipulation on bilateral GB 20 (*fēng chí*), GB 21 (*jiān jǐng*) about 1 minute each point, do it 4~5 times along bilateral courses of urinary bladder channel from upper part to lower part.

The patient in sitting position, apply one-finger pushing from *yìn tang* (EX-HN3), along hairline to ST 8 (*tóu wéi*), and to *tài yáng* (EX-HN5), repeat the manipulation 3~4 times; pressing manipulation on *yìn táng* (EX-HN3), *yú yāo* (EX-HN4), *tài yáng* (EX-HN5), DU 20 (*bǎi huì*); five-finger grasping manipulation from vertex to GB 20 (*fēng chí*), where change to three-finger grasping manipulation along urinary bladder channel till sides of DU 14 (*dà zhuī*), repeat the manipulation 3~4 times.

Points and regions selected according to syndrome:

* Wind-cold headache

Apply rolling manipulation on the nape and upper back 2~3 minutes; pressing and kneading manipulations on BL 13 (*fèi shù*) and BL 12 (*fēng mén*); grasping manipulation on GB 21 (*jiān jǐng*) on both sides and scrubbing manipulation along bilateral courses of urinary bladder channel until it is warm in the local area.

* Wind-heat headache

Apply pressing and kneading manipulations on DU 14 (*dà zhuī*), BL 13 (*fèi shù*) and BL 12 (*fēng mén*), 1 minute each point; grasping manipulation on GB 21 (*jiān jǐng*) of both sides; pressing and grasping manipulations on bilateral LI 11 (*qū chí*), LI 10 (*shǒu sān lǐ*) and LI 4 (*hé gǔ*) until there are soreness and distension in the local area; patting and striking manipulations along bilateral courses of urinary bladder channel on the back until local skin is slightly red.

* Summer-dampness headache

Apply pressing and kneading manipulations on DU 14 (*dà zhuī*) and LI 11 (*qū chí*); grasping manipulation on GB 21 (*jiān jǐng*) and LI 4 (*hé gǔ*); patting and striking manipulations along bilateral courses of urinary bladder channel on the back until local skin is slightly red; lifting and pinching the skin at the areas of *yìn táng* (EX-HN3) and nape till local skin is red.

* Liver yang headache

Apply pushing manipulation along *qiáo gōng* (Extra Point) from upper side to lower side, more than 20 times each side; scattering manipulation on lateral aspect of head along the course of gallbladder channel from anterior superior side to posterior inferior side about ten times each side; pressing manipulation on SJ 20 (*jiǎo sūn*); pressing and kneading manipulation on LV 3 (*tài chōng*) and LV 2 (*xíng jiān*) until there is local soreness and distension; scrubbing manipulation on bilateral KI 1 (*yǒng quán*) until it is warm enough in the local area.

* Turbid phlegm headache

Apply one-finger pushing and rubbing manipulation on abdomen, focusing on RN 12 (*zhōng wǎn*) and ST 25 (*tiān shū*) for 6~8 minutes; pressing and kneading manipulations on BL 20 (*pí shù*), BL 21 (*wèi shù*) and BL 25 (*dà cháng shù*). Then, do transverse scrubbing manipulation on left side of the back until it is warm enough in the local area; pressing and kneading manipulations on bilateral ST 36 (*zú sān lǐ*), ST 40 (*fēng lóng*) and PC 6 (*nèi guān*).

* Blood deficiency headache

Apply rubbing manipulation on abdomen for 6~8 minutes, focusing on RN 6 (*qì hǎi*), RN 12 (*zhōng wǎn*) and RN 4 (*guān yuán*); transverse scrubbing manipulation on left side of the back and along governor vessel until it is warm enough in the local area; pressing and kneading manipulations on bilateral BL 15 (*xīn shù*), BL 17 (*gé shù*), ST 36 (*zú sān lǐ*) and SP 6 (*sān yīn jiāo*) till there is mild soreness and distention.

* Kidney deficiency headache (insufficiency of kidney yang)

Apply rubbing manipulation on abdomen for 6~8 minutes, focusing on RN 6 (*qì hǎi*) and RN 4 (*guān yuán*); scrubbing manipulation on the back, governor vessel and transverse scrubbing manipulation on lumbar area including BL 23 (*shèn shù*),DU 4 (*mìng mén*) and lumbosacral area until it is warm enough in the local area.

* Blood stasis headache

Apply pressing, kneading and mopping manipulations on *tài yáng* (EX-HN5), BL 2 (*cuán zhú*) and forehead, course of gallbladder channel on the sides of head; scrubbing manipulation on the forehead and bilateral *tài yáng* (EX-HN5) until it is warm enough in the local area.

5. Precautions

It is not advisable to apply tui na manipulations for the patient at acute stage of cerebrovascular disease, or with encephalopyosis, intracranial space occupying lesion, contusion and laceration of brain and traumatic intracranial hematoma.

For headache caused by exogenous pathogenic factors, keep warm, avoid wind-cold attack and have proper rests.

For liver yang headache, measure blood pressure frequently and be cautious the change of blood pressure affecting the heart.

For blood deficiency headache or kidney deficiency headache, have less sexual activities.

For all kinds of headache, smoking and alcoholics are not allowed.

Insomnia

1. Overview

Insomnia refers to a syndrome characterized by inability to have normal sleep including inadequate quantity and quality of sleep, and functional impairment while awake. The people with mild insomnia may have difficulty in falling asleep, or no sound sleep, intermittent sleep, difficulty in falling asleep again after waking. The people with severe insomnia would be asleep for whole night. The syndrome might to occur alone, or together with other symptoms like headache, dizziness, palpitation and poor memory. Insomnia is often seen in neurosis, menopausal syndrome, etc. It can be caused by over-thinking, over-worry or overstrain, which may lead to heart-spleen depletion, or heart and gallbladder deficiency, or disharmony of stomach due to retention of food and water or turbid phlegm in middle-energizer. Generally, the occurrence of insomnia relates to dysfunctions of qi, blood, spirit and zang-fu or disturbance of pathogenic qi. Though the heart is a chief organ involved, the liver, spleen and kidney are also related.

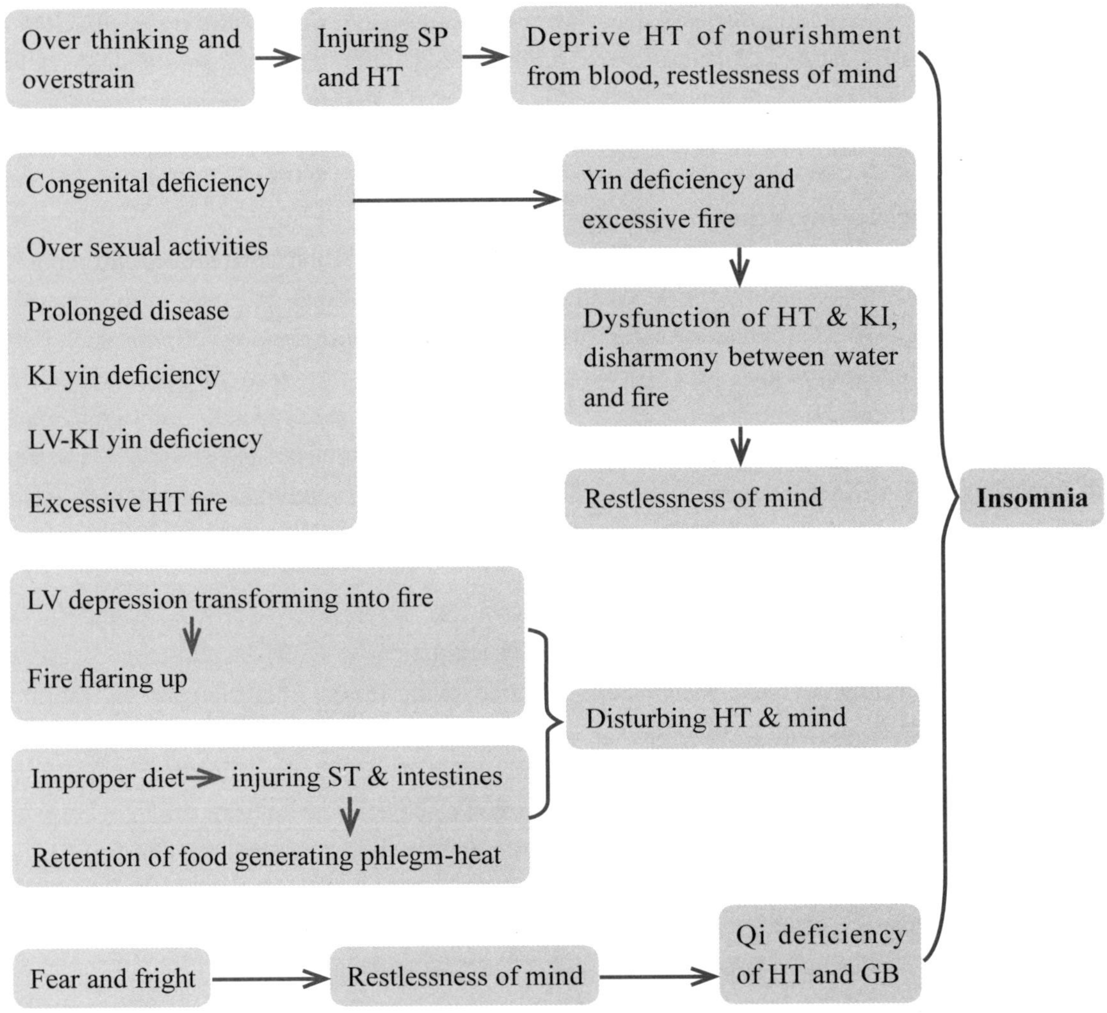

2. Clinical Manifestations

Clinically, the syndrome should be differentiated if it is deficiency or excess syndrome. Deficiency syndrome is often caused by insufficiency of yin blood; excess syndrome often caused by liver depression transforming into fire, phlegm-heat harassing internally, or phlegm-heat in stomach.

a. Deficiency of both heart and spleen

Dreamful sleep, nocturnal awakenings, difficulty maintain sleep, or even inability to fall asleep all the night, palpitation, amnesia, listlessness, lassitude, poor appetite, lusterless complexion, pale tongue with thin coating, thready weak pulse.

b. Yin deficiency and effulgent fire

Dysphoria, insomnia, dizziness, tinnitus, dry mouth with scanty fluid, vexing heat in chest, palms and soles, or nocturnal emission, amnesia, palpitation, lumbar soreness, red tongue with a thready raid pulse.

c. Phlegm-heat harassing internally

Insomnia, dreamful sleep, dysphoria, irritability, chest distress, heaviness of head, blurred vision, distending pain in hypochondriac regions, anorexia, thirst with desire for water, red eyes, bitter taste in mouth, dark urine, constipation, red tongue with a yellow greasy coating, wiry and a slippery pulse.

d. Liver depression transforming into fire

Insomnia, fussy temper, irritability, anorexia, thirst with desire for water, red eyes, bitterness in mouth, dark urine, constipation, red tongue with yellow coating, a wiry rapid pulse.

3. Diagnostic Essentials

Sleep disorder is the primary symptom, followed by the other symptoms including difficulty in falling asleep, light sleep, nocturnal awakening, dreamful sleep, waking too early in the morning, difficulty returning to sleep after awakening, discomfort after awakening, fatigue or sleepiness in daytime.

The sleep disorder described above occurs at least three times a week and lasts for more than one month.

Insomnia is not one part of symptoms in any physical diseases or mental disorders.

4. Tui Na Treatment

【Principle】

To regulate *zang-fu* organs, calm and tranquilize the mind.

【Points and regions】

EX-HN3 (*yìn táng*)	DU 24 (*shén tíng*)	*tài yáng* (EX-HN5)	BL 1 (*jīng míng*)
BL 2 (*cuán zhú*)	*yú yāo* (EX-HN4)	SJ 20 (*jiǎo sūn*)	DU 20 (*bǎi huì*)
GB 20 (*fēng chí*)	GB 21 (*jiān jǐng*)	RN 12 (*zhōng wǎn*)	RN 6 (*qì hǎi*)
RN 4 (*guān yuán*)	BL 15 (*xīn shù*)	BL 18 (*gān shù*)	BL 20 (*pí shù*)
BL 21 (*wèi shù*)	BL 23 (*shèn shù*)	DU 4 (*mìng mén*)	

Head, face, neck, shoulder and abdominal areas.

【Method】

Ask the patient to take a sitting position or supine position, apply one-finger pushing or kneading manipulation, starting from *yìn táng* (EX-HN3) upward to DU 24 (*shén tíng*); then from *yìn táng* (EX-HN3), along bilateral superciliary arches, to *tài yáng* (EX-HN5), and apply one-finger pushing around orbital areas. The whole treatment is about 5 minutes.

Then, starts from *yìn táng* (EX-HN3), along sides of nose, passing by LI 20 (*yíng xiāng*), SI 18 (*quán liáo*), to the front of ears. Apply pressing manipulation and kneading manipulation *yìn táng* (EX-HN3), DU 24 (*shén ting*), *tài yáng* (EX-HN5), BL 1 (*jīng míng*) and BL 2 (*cuán zhú*). The treatment lasts about 5 minutes.

Press and knead BL 1 (*jīng míng*) and *yú yāo* (EX-HN4) along the areas described above with two hands about 3 minutes.

Apply scattering manipulation on lateral aspect of head along the course of gallbladder channel, coordinated by pressing manipulation on SJ 20 (*jiǎo sūn*). Apply five-finger manipulation from vertex downward and change into three-finger grasping manipulation at the lower part of occiput, pressing and grasping bilateral GB 21 (*jiān jǐng*). The treatment lasts about 3 minutes.

Apply palm-rubbing manipulation on abdomen clockwise, pressing and kneading RN 12 (*zhōng wǎn*), RN 6 (*qì hǎi*), RN 4 (*guān yuán*) at the same time about 5 minutes.

Points and regions selected according to syndrome:

⋆ Deficiency of both heart and spleen

Apply pressing manipulation and kneading manipulation on BL 15 (*xīn shù*), BL 18 (*gān shù*), BL 21 (*wèi shù*), BL 27 (*xiǎo cháng shù*) and ST 36 (*zú sān lǐ*), about 1 minute each point. Then apply scrubbing manipulation transversely on the left side of back and along governor vessel until it is warm enough in the local area.

⋆ Yin deficiency and effulgent fire

Apply pushing manipulation on *qiáo gōng* (桥弓) side by side; transverse scrubbing manipulation on BL 23 (*shèn shù*) and DU 4 (*mìng mén*) until it is warm enough in the local area; then scrubbing manipulation on bilateral KI 1 (*yǒng quán*) to lead fire back to its origin.

⋆ Phlegm-heat harassing internally

Apply gentle rolling manipulation on bilateral sides of the spine, focusing on BL 20 (*pí shù*), BL 21 (*wèi shù*) and BL 15 (*xīn shù*) about 5 minutes; pressing manipulation and kneading manipulation on the same points and RN 12 (*zhōng wǎn*), RN 6 (*qì hǎi*), ST 25 (*tiān shū*), RN 8 (*shén què*), ST 36 (*zú sān lǐ*), ST 40 (*fēng lóng*) while rubbing abdomen; transverse scrubbing manipulation on the left side of back, BL 31 (*shàng liáo*), BL 32 (*cì liáo*), BL 33 (*zhōng liáo*), and BL 34 (*xià liáo*) in sacral region until it is warm enough in the local area.

⋆ Liver depression transforming into fire

Apply pressing and kneading manipulations with fingers on BL 18 (*gān shù*), BL 19 (*dǎn shù*), LV 14 (*qī mén*), LV 13 (*zhāng mén*), LV 3 (*zhāng mén*) 1~2 minutes each point. Apply foulage manipulation on two hypochondriac regions about 1 minute.

5. Precautions

Insomnia is often seen in neurasthenia, but also seen in some organic diseases. It is important to distinguish one from another, because the cause should be treated if it is insomnia caused by organic disease.

Before go to bed, don't smoke and drink alcohol, tea and coffee, and don't read and watch sensational and excitant books and movies, take footbath with warm water everyday.

Have proper exercises and physical labor to strengthen body constitution.

Strike a proper balance between work and rest and have proper sexual activities, regular living habit, getting up and going to bed early.

Help the patient to be eased away from worry, avoid emotional changes, and keep an open and optimistic mood.

Sequelae of Wind Stroke

1. Overview

Sequelae of wind stroke, also called "unilateral withering" or "hemiplegia", refers to the syndrome characterized by muscular weakness and atrophy of unilateral limbs failing to have voluntary movement, it is often accompanied by deviated eyes and mouth, slurred speech and so on. It usually follows cerebral vascular accidents or other cerebral diseases. Wind stroke includes various symptoms occurring in cerebral hemorrhage, cerebral thrombosis and subarachnoid hemorrhage. Tui na therapy is mainly used during restoration and sequela stages of wind stroke, for symptoms like hemiplegic, paralysis, deviation of mouth and eyes, speech disorder, etc. The pathological location of this disease is in the brain and closely related to the heart, kidney, liver and spleen. The pathogenesis of wind stroke are deficiency (yin deficiency and qi deficiency), fire (liver fire and heart fire), wind (liver wind and external wind), phlegm (wind phlegm and dampness phlegm), qi (adverse flowing of qi) and blood (blood stasis). They affect and work on each other under certain conditions. The nature of the disease is, generally speaking, root deficiency with branch excess, upper excess and lower deficiency. Clinically, hemiplegic, paraplegia or limb paralysis due to other cerebral or spinal diseases like tumor, encephalitis, traumatic injury can be treated by same method.

2. Clinical manifestations

a. Hemiplegia

It takes paralysis and weakness of unilateral limbs, deviation of eyes and mouth, tongue stiffness and slurred speech as the main signs. In initial stage, the patient usually manifests weakness, perceptual retardation or rigidity, limited movements of limbs. Gradually, the limbs become rigid and spastic, which change the posture of limbs resulting in deformity of the limbs.

b. Deviation of eyes and mouth

The mouth and nasolabial grooves are deviated to the healthy side, air leeking when cheeks are bulged. But the patient can still do frowning and close the eyes.

3. Examinations

a. Hemiplegic

It shows increased muscular tension of the limbs, contracture and deformity of joints, slight perceptual retardation and loss of motor functions, hyperreflexia of biceps brachii muscle, brachial triceps muscle, patella and Achilles tendon of the affected side.

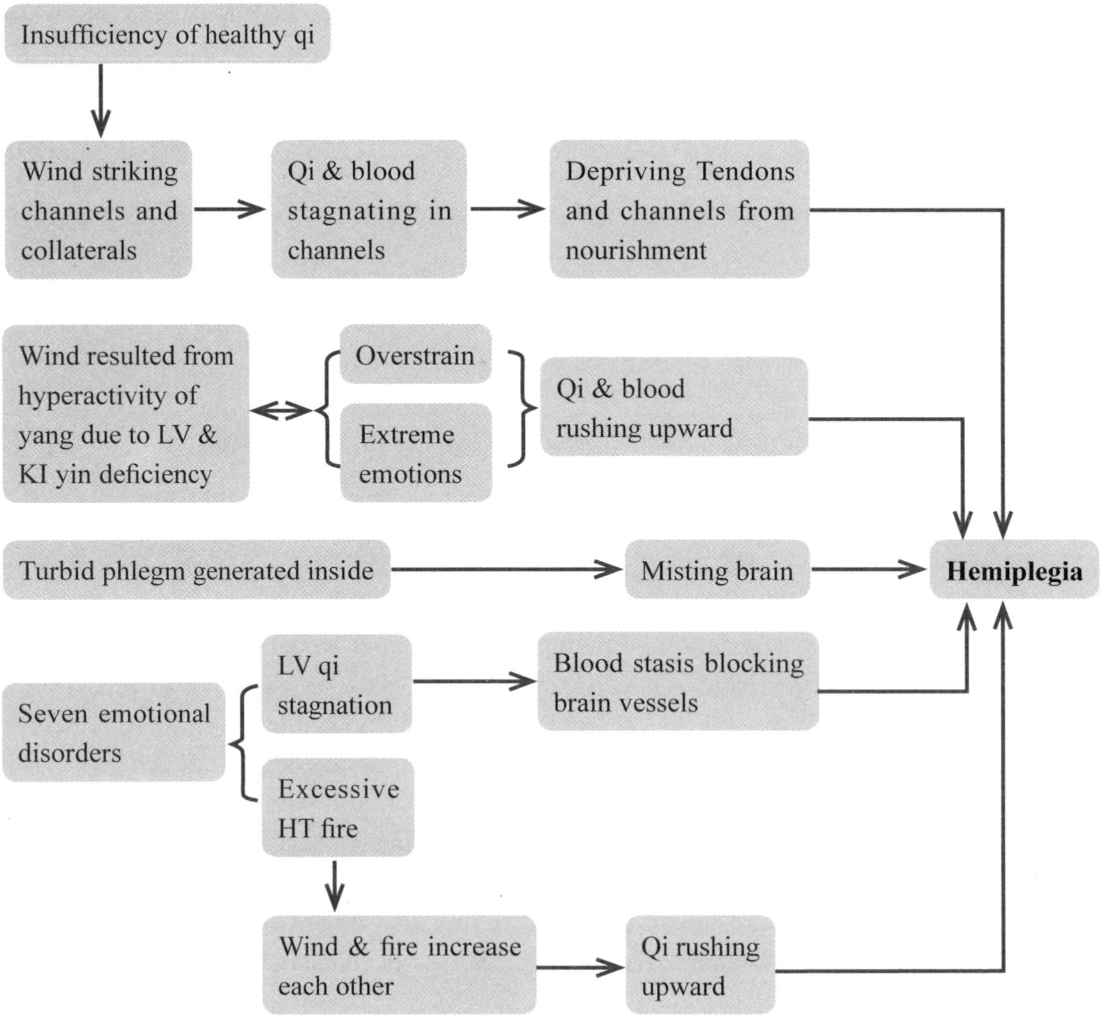

b. Blood pressure

The blood pressure is usually higher in the patients with cerebral hemorrhage and cerebral thrombosis; positive meningeal irritation signs are often seen in the patients with subarachnoid hemorrhage; and neurologic signs are common in the patients with cerebral embolism.

c. Cerebrospinal fluid examination

The cerebrospinal fluid of the patients with cerebral hemorrhage and subarachnoid hemorrhage is bloody, while that of the patients with cerebral thrombosis and cerebral embolism is normal.

4. Diagnostic Essentials

The patient has past history of hypertension, cardiac diseases, headache and vertigo.

The patient had sudden falling and loss of consciousness, or gradual development of hemiplegia, deviation of eyes and mouth, tongue stiffness and slurred speech in static condition.

5. Tui Na Treatment

The treatment is suggested to be given at early stage, usually two weeks after the onset of disease.

【Principle of treatment】

To relax sinew and dredge collaterals, move qi and activate blood.

【Points and regions】

SI 11 (*tiān zōng*)	BL 18 (*gān shù*)	BL 19 (*dǎn shù*)	BL 17 (*gé shù*)
BL 23 (*shèn shù*)	GB 30 (*huán tiào*)	GB 34 (*yáng líng quán*)	BL 40 (*wěi zhōng*)
BL 57 (*chéng shān*)	GB 31 (*fēng shì*)	ST 32 (*fú tù*)	*xī yǎn* (EX-LE5)
ST 41 (*jiě xī*)	LU 5 (*chǐ zé*)	LI 11 (*qū chí*)	LI 10 (*shǒu sān lǐ*)
LI 4 (*hé gǔ*)	*yìn táng* (EX-HN3)	BL 1 (*jīng míng*)	*tài yáng* (EX-HN5)
SJ 20 (*jiǎo sūn*)	GB 20 (*fēng chí*)	DU 16 (*fēng fǔ*)	GB 21 (*jiān jǐng*)

The back, four limbs, head and face areas.

【Methods】

Ask patient to take a prone position, apply pressing manipulation on both sides of spinal column from upper part to lower part; pointing, pressing, kneading manipulations on SI 11 (*tiān zōng*), BL 18 (*gān shù*), BL 19 (*dǎn shù*), BL 17 (*gé shù*) and BL 23 (*shèn shù*). Then apply rolling manipulation on both sides of spinal column downward to hip, posterior aspect of thigh and lower leg, focusing on the sides of lumbar vertebrae, GB 30 (*huán tiào*), BL 40 (*wěi zhōng*), BL 57 (*chéng shān*) and Achilles tendon; at the same time, make passive movements by stretching the patient's back and hip joint of affected side backward. The process is about 5 minutes.

Ask patient to take a lateral recumbent position with healthy side against bed. Apply rolling manipulation along lateral aspect of the thigh, knee and lower leg, focusing on hip joint and knee joint, about 3 minutes.

Ask patient to take a supine position. Apply rolling manipulation on the affected lower limb from anterior superior iliac spine downward to the dorsum of foot along the anterior aspect of thigh, lower leg, ankle joints; pointing, pressing, kneading manipulations on ST 32 (*fú tù*), *xī yǎn* (EX-LE5), ST 41 (*jiě xī*). At the same time, make the passive movement by extending and flexing the patient's hip joint, knee joint and ankle joint, and rotating the patient's lower limb inward. Then apply grasping manipulation on the affected leg, on BL 40 (*wěi zhōng*), BL 57 (*chéng shān*), the middle of medial aspect of thigh and knee area. The process is about 5~10 minutes.

Ask patient to be in a supine position. Apply rolling manipulation along the medial aspect of affected arm downward to the forearm, focusing on elbow joint and areas around. At the same time, make passive movement by abducting the patient' s affected arm as well as extending and flexing the patient' s elbow joint. Do pressing and kneading manipulations on LU 5 (*chǐ zé*), LI 11 (*qū chí*), LI 10 (*shǒu sān lǐ*), LI 4 (*hé gǔ*); then rolling manipulation on the wrist, palm and fingers of affected side, together with passive movement of extending and flexing the wrist joint and interphalangeal joints. Twiddling manipulation is also suggested for the joints of fingers. The process is about 5 minutes.

Ask patient to take a sitting position. Apply rolling manipulation around scapula of affected side and sides of nape, combined with passive movements of rotating the affected arm backward, adducting the shoulder joint upward and adducting the arm. Then apply grasping manipulation from the shoulder to the wrist together with the movement of the shoulder, elbow and wrist joints. Finally, apply foulage manipulation from the shoulder to the wrist up and down repeatedly. The process is about 3 minutes.

Apply to-and-fro mopping manipulation from *yìn táng* (EX-HN3) to *tài yáng* (EX-HN5), pressing and kneading BL 1 (*jīng míng*) and *tài yáng* (EX-HN5) at the same time. Then apply scattering manipulation on the lateral aspect of head along course of gallbladder channel from anterior superior area to posterior inferior area and press and knead SJ 20 (*jiǎo sūn*). The process is about 2 minutes.

Deviation of eyes and mouth

Apply one-finger pushing repeatedly along EX-HN3 (*yìn táng*), GB 14 (*yáng bái*), BL 1 (*jīng míng*), ST 2 (*sì bái*), LI 20 (*yíng xiāng*), ST 7 (*xià guān*), ST 6 (*jiá chē*) and ST 4 (*dì cāng*) and then gentle scrubbing manipulation on these points; again one-finger pushing on GB 20 (*fēng chí*) and the nape. Finally, apply grasping manipulation on GB 20 (*fēng chí*) and LI 4 (*hé gǔ*) to finish the treatment.

6. Precautions

Since the duration of disease is directly related with recovery, it is very important to give the treatment as early as possible. Generally, tui na therapy is recommended when the condition is stable.

Activating blood and resolving stasis is taken as the first treatment for the patient with the disease within half a year; tonifying qi and blood to strengthen healthy qi, stabilize the body condition and strengthen the tendons and bones is considered as the important principle for the patient with disease over half a year. The manipulations are almost same for both conditions, except the passive movements of limbs and joints of the latter are more. The effect of tui na Treatment for the patients with the disease more than one year is comparatively poorer. Usually, it takes long time to treat sequlae of wind stroke, so the stimulation of manipulation, the duration of the operation and focused areas or points should be varied according to the changes of pathological conditions.

Keep stable emotions and regular life style, keep away from smoking, alcohol drinking, pungent and fatty food. Keep personal hygiene and pay attention to nursing, preventing bedsores. Rehabilitant therapies like herbal medicine, acupuncture, physiotherapy and medicated diet are suggested.

During the recovery, do systemic and gentle exercises to strengthen motor function of the affected limbs such as rolling gymnastic ball, holding exercise hoop, pulling pulley, stretching the shoulder backward, moving the hands in front of the chest, the movements which can contract quadriceps of thigh, kicking the air and tapping the limbs. But, it is not advisable to do these exercise too much or forcefully.

Dysmenorrhea

1. Overview

Dysmenorrhea is characterized by periodic lower abdominal pain or lumbar pain during, before or after menstruation, or even intense pain beyond endurance, often accompanied with pale complexion, nausea and vomiting, cold sweating, cold hands and feet, cyclical occurrence with the period. So it is also called "menstrual abdominal pain", often seen in unmarried young women. The occurrence of the disease is usually related to underlying physiological environment of the body, periodic physiological change of *chong mai, ren mai* and the uterus, emotional injuries, irregular life style or invasion of six exogenous pathogenic factors. In western medicine, primary dysmenorrhea is often seen in young women since menarche, related to dysfunction of vegetative nerve, uterine spasm, or uterine hypoplasia, cervical stenosis, uterine over-flexion which affects smooth menstrual flow. Secondary dysmenorrhea is usually resulted from organic changes of reproductive organs such as inflammation, hysteromyoma or endometriosis.

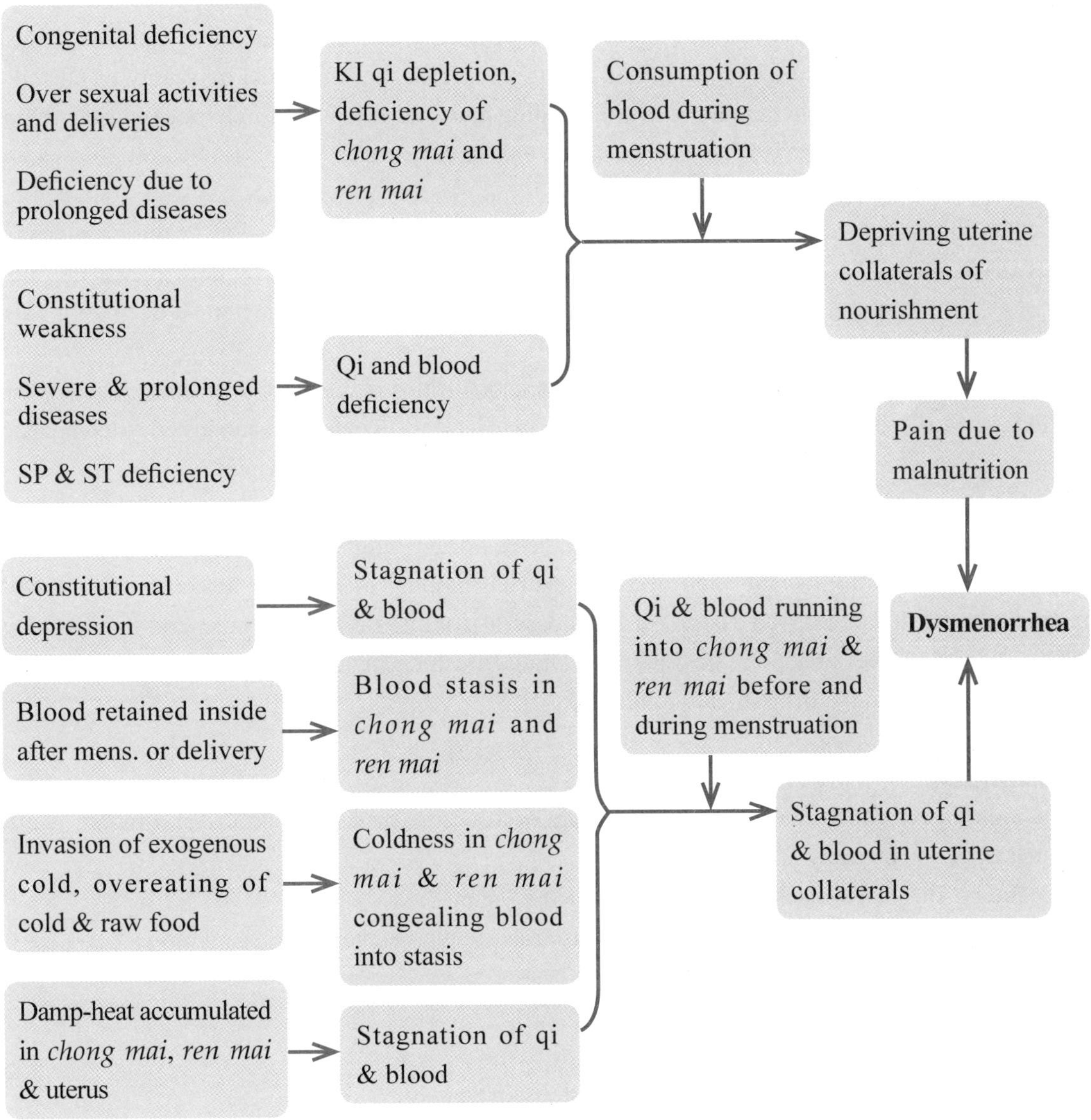

2. Clinical Manifestations

The main clinical manifestation is lower abdominal pain during menstruation, which may attack whole abdomen or lumbosacral region, or accompanied by bearing down pain of external genitalia and anus. If pain is intense, the patient may have pale complexion, profuse cold sweating, cold hands and feet, or even syncope and collapse. The symptoms are periodic with cycles of period. Distinguish cold, heat, deficiency and excess conditions according to the time and nature of pain. It is an excess syndrome if the pain occurs before or during menstruation and deficiency syndrome if the pain occurs after menstruation; excess syndrome if pain is aggravated by pressing and deficiency syndrome if pain is alleviated by pressing; cold syndrome if pain is better with warm compression and heat syndrome if pain is worse with warm compression; blood stasis syndrome if pain is worse than distending feeling and pain relieved when clots expelled, and qi stagnation syndrome if distention is worse than pain.

a. Qi stagnation and blood stasis

Lower abdominal distending pain, aggravated by pressing and alleviated when clots out, appears one or two days before menstrual period or during the period; accompanied by scanty or unsmooth menstrual flow, dark purple in color, clots, distending pain and discomfort in hypochondriac regions and breasts, dark tongue or tongue with petechia, a deep wiry pulse.

b. Cold-dampness coagulation

Lower abdominal cold pain appearing a few days before menstrual period or during menstrual period, alleviated by warming and alleviated by pressing; accompanied by dark menstrual blood with clots, or aversion to cold and general ache, white greasy tongue coating, and a deep tight pulse.

c. Qi and blood deficiency

Dull pain in lower abdomen after or during menstruation which is alleviated by pressing; accompanied by dilute menstrual blood light in color, or mental fatigue, lack of strength, pale and lusterless complexion, or anorexia, loose stools, pale tongue with thin tongue coating, a feeble thready pulse.

d. Liver-kidney depletion

Dull pain in lower abdomen, soreness and distension in lumbar region, appearing one or two days after menstruation, scanty and dilute menstrual blood dark or light in color; accompanied by tinnitus, dizziness, blurred vision, or lumbosacral soreness and pain, cold and bearing down sensation in the lower abdomen, or tidal fever, malar flushing, pale tongue with thin white or thin yellow tongue coating, a deep thready pulse.

3. Diagnosis

Periodic lower abdominal pain during, before or after menstruation, lumbosacral region is often affected, syncope possibly appears.

Dysmenorrhea is common in young unmarried women.

Abdominal pain caused by pelvic organic diseases should be excluded.

4. Tui Na Treatment

【Principle】

To regulate qi and blood, warm channels and dissipate cold.

【Points and regions】

RN 6 (*qì hǎi*)	RN 4 (*guān yuán*)	BL 23 (*shèn shù*)	BL 31 (*shàng liáo*)
BL 32 (*cì liáo*)	BL 33 (*zhōng liáo*)	BL 34 (*xià liáo*)	

Abdomen, lower abdomen, lumbar and back areas.

【Methods】

Ask patient to take a supine position, apply rubbing manipulation clockwise on lower abdomen; one-finger pushing or pressing, kneading manipulation on RN 6 (*qì hǎi*), RN 4 (*guān yuán*), about 5 minutes each point.

Ask patient to take a prone position, apply rolling manipulation on bilateral lumbar areas along the spine and lumbosacral area. Then apply one-finger pushing or pressing, kneading manipulations on BL 23 (*shèn shù*), BL 31 (*shàng liáo*), BL 32 (*cì liáo*), BL 33 (*zhōng liáo*), BL 34 (*xià liáo*) until there is local distending feeling. Apply scrubbing manipulation on lumbosacral area and BL 31 (*shàng liáo*), BL 32 (*cì liáo*), BL 33 (*zhōng liáo*), BL 34 (*xià liáo*) until it is warm enough in the local area. The process takes 5 minutes.

Points and regions selected according to syndrome.

☆ Qi stagnation and blood stasis

Apply pressing and kneading manipulations on LV 13 (*zhāng mén*), LV 14 (*qī mén*), BL 18 (*gān shù*), BL 17 (*gé shù*) and grasp SP 10 (*xuè hǎi*) and SP 6 (*sān yīn jiāo*) until there is local distending feeling.

☆ Cold-dampness coagulation

Apply scrubbing manipulation first along governor vessel, and then, transversely over lumbosacral region including BL 23 (*shèn shù*) and DU 4 (*mìng mén*) until it is warm enough in the local area. Then, apply pressing and kneading manipulation on SP 10 (*xuè hǎi*) and SP 6 (*sān yīn jiāo*).

☆ Qi and blood deficiency

Apply scrubbing manipulation along governor vessel, and then, transversely over both sides of the back until it is warm enough in the local area. Next, do rubbing manipulation on the abdomen; pressing and kneading manipulations on RN 12 (*zhōng wǎn*); Finally, pressing and kneading manipulations on BL 20 (*pí shù*), BL 21 (*wèi shù*) and ST 36 (*zú sān lǐ*).

☆ Liver-kidney depletion

Apply scrubbing manipulation first along governor vessel, and then, transversely over lumbar area including BL 23 (*shèn shù*) and DU 4 (*mìng mén*) until it is warm enough in the local area; pressing and kneading manipulations on KI 6 (*zhào hǎi*), KI 3 (*tài xī*), BL 18 (*gān shù*), BL 23 (*shèn shù*) and KI 1 (*yǒng quán*).

☆ Special therapy for dysmenorrhea excess syndrome

For dysmenorrhea of excess syndrome with deviation of spinal process of lumbar vertebrae (mostly L4) and mild tenderness, apply reposition manipulation with rotating or oblique pulling manipulation to rectify deviated spinal process. Do scrubbing manipulation along governor vessel and transversely over lumbosacral area, BL 31 (*shàng liáo*), BL 32 (*cì liáo*), BL 33 (*zhōng liáo*) and BL 34 (*xià liáo*) until it is warm enough in the local area.

Treatment is made twice a week before menstruation every month for three months in sequence. Six times are taken as one course.

5. Precautions

Keep warm during menstruation. Pay attention to menstrual hygiene.

Have a proper rest and avoid overstrain.

Keep ease mood and avoid irritability and depression.

Tiuna does not have a satisfactory long-term effect for dysmenorrhea caused by organic changes.

Climacteric Syndrome

1. Overview

Climacteric syndrome or menopausal syndrome, now named premenopausal syndrome, refers to a series of syndrome characterized by dysfunction of vegetative nerve and metabolic disorders due to dysfunction of ovary and declining of estrogen level during transition of a woman from child-bearing age to agedness.

The occurrence of the disease is closely related to the physiological features at premenopausal period. When a woman is around age of 49, the kidney qi begins to decline and reproduction-stimulating essence is gradually decreased or even exhausted, *chong mai* and *ren mai* start to decline as well. During the physiological transition, influenced by internal or external environment, such as constitutional preponderance or weakness of yin or yang, underlying depression, prolonged disease, or environmental changes of family or society may easily cause disorder of kidney yin and yang, and later lead to the disease. "Kidney being innate foundation", so the root of the disease is kidney, and involvement of other zang organs like heart, liver, spleen and numerous channels make the disease complicated.

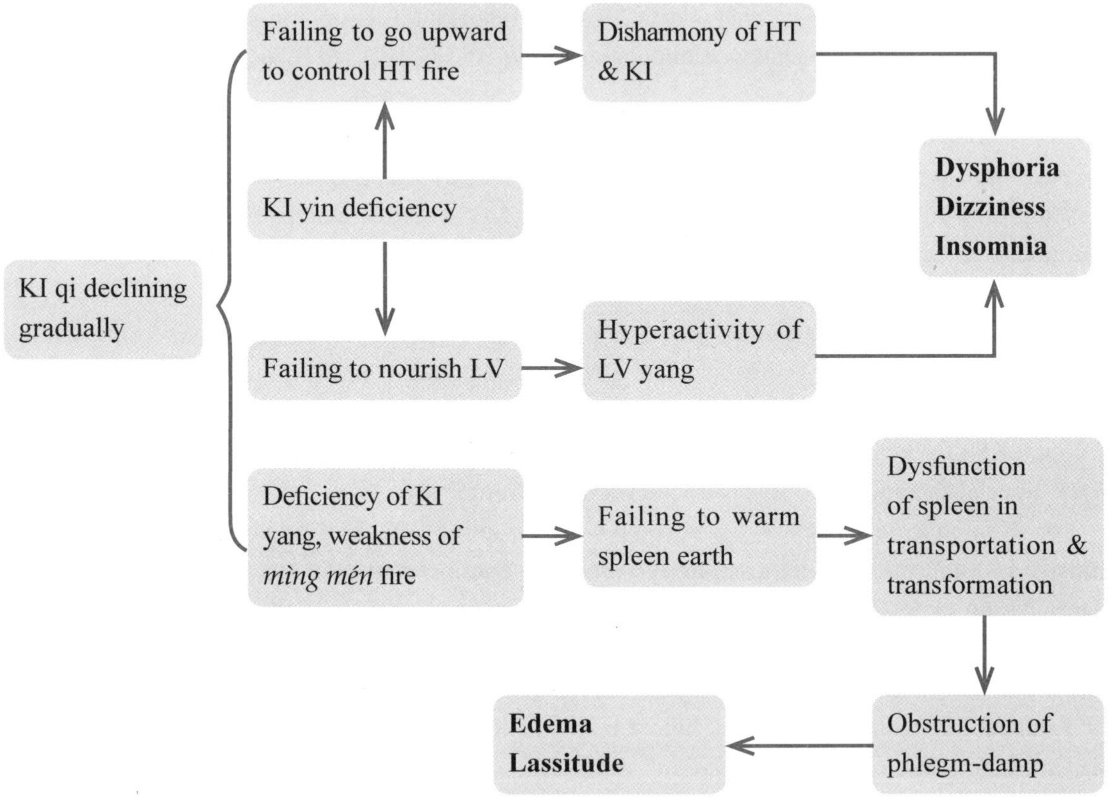

2. Clinical manifestations

The disease usually happens on the patients with age from 45 to 55 years old. Clinically, it needs to make clear if the patient had any special changes in her work or life before onset of the disease, any history of psychic trauma and bilateral ovarian resection or history of radiotherapy. The early symptoms include tidal fever, sweating and emotional change. Tidal fever starts from the chest, surging to the head, neck, face, and sweating comes after. After sweating, tidal fever goes away. The whole process lasts for seconds or minutes. The frequency of attack everyday is irregular. Emotional changes like agitation, dysphoria, irritability and unreasonable sweeping beyond control are often accompanied by dizziness, headache, insomnia, palpitation, lumbar soreness and back pain, irregular menstruation, etc. The later symptoms include dry and burning heat in the vagina, pruritus vulvae, frequent and urgent urination or incontinence of urine, skin itching, etc.

3. Examination

a. Gynecological examination

There might have vaginal or uterine atrophy in different degrees and decreased cervical and vaginal secretion in the late phase.

b. laboratory examination

Exfoliative cytoscopy of vaginal smear shows decreased estrogen level in different degrees, increased level of ESH while E2 decreased. The report is significant for making a diagnosis of menopausal syndrome.

4. Diagnostic Essentials

Menopausal syndrome, with various complicated clinical symptoms and messy complains and few physical signs, is easy to be confused with other diseases. Determine the diagnosis only when other organic diseases are excluded.

Menopausal syndrome often happens in patients more than 40 years old with irregular menstruation or amenorrhea, tidal fever, sweating, palpitation, excitability, insomnia or depression, etc.

There is atrophy of reproductive organs and secondary sex characteristics in different degrees.

Level of urine and blood estrogen is decreased and FSH, LH is obviously increased.

Cervix and uterine body become smaller and vaginal fornix becomes shallower.

There is internal contraction of cervical canal and atrophy of endometrium.

Vaginal mucosa becomes thinner and superficial cells are absent.

PH of vagina is increased.

Vagina is dry and lack of elasticity.

5. Tui Na Treatment

【Principle】

To harmonize yin and yang, regulate *chong mai* and *ren mai*.

【Points and regions】

RN 17 (*dàn zhōng*)	RN 12 (*zhōng wǎn*)	RN 6 (*qì hǎi*)
RN 4 (*guān yuán*)	RN 3 (*zhōng jí*)	

Lumbar area and upper back:

BL 14 (*jué yīn shù*)	BL 17 (*gé shù*)	BL 18 (*gān shù*)
BL 20 (*pí shù*)	BL 23 (*shèn shù*)	DU 4 (*mìng mén*)

Governor vessel on the back, the first lateral line of urinary bladder channel on the back.

Head, face, neck and shoulder areas:

EX-HN5 (*tài yáng*)	BL 2 (*cuán zhú*)	ST 2 (*sì bái*)	LI 20 (*yíng xiāng*)
DU 20 (*bǎi huì*)	GB 20 (*fēng chí*)	GB 21 (*jiān jǐng*)	

The abdomen, neck, nape and back.

【Method】

Ask patient to take a supine position, apply one-finger pushing on RN 17 (*dàn zhōng*), RN 12 (*zhōng wǎn*), RN 6 (*qì hǎi*), RN 4 (*guān yuán*), RN 3 (*zhōng jí*), 2~3 minutes each point. Then apply kneading and rubbing manipulations clockwise on epigastric and lower abdominal areas, 5 minutes each area.

Ask patient to take a prone position, apply one-finger pushing or thumb-pressing, kneading manipulations on BL 14 (*jué yīn shù*), BL 17 (*gé shù*), BL 18 (*gān shù*), BL 20 (*pí shù*), BL 23 (*shèn shù*), DU 4 (*mìng mén*), 2 minutes each point. Then apply hypothenar-scrubbing manipulation along governor vessel on the back, the first lateral line of urinary bladder channel on the back and BL 23 (*shèn shù*), DU 4 (*mìng mén*) until it is warm enough in the local area.

Ask patient to take a sitting position, apply pinching and grasping manipulations on GB 20 (*fēng chí*) and neck-nape area 2 minutes; repeat pinching and grasping manipulations on the head (from anterior hairline to posterior hairline) 5~10 times; one-finger pushing or thenar-kneading manipulation on forehead 5 minutes; bidirectional mopping manipulation on the forehead, orbits and sides of ala nasi 5~10 times; pressing and kneading manipulations with both thumbs on *tài yáng* (EX-HN5), BL 2 (*cuán zhú*), ST 2 (*sì bái*), LI 20 (*yíng xiāng*) 0.5 minute each point; thumb-pressing and kneading manipulations on DU 20 (*bǎi huì*) 0.5 minute and grasping manipulation on GB 21 (*jiān jǐng*) 5~10 times.

Points and regions are selected according to syndrome.

* Yin deficiency of liver and kidney

Apply pressing and kneading manipulations on BL 52 (*zhì shì*), SP 10 (*xuè hǎi*), SP 9 (*yīn líng quán*), SP 6 (*sān yīn jiāo*), KI 3 (*tài xī*), LV 3 (*tài chōng*), half a minute each point. Then push Extra Point (*qiáo gōng* 桥弓) on both sides alternately.

*. Non-interaction between heart and kidney

Apply kneading and pressing manipulations on HT 5 (*tōng lǐ*), PC 6 (*nèi guān*), LI 4 (*hé gǔ*), BL 13 (*fèi shù*), BL 15 (*xīn shù*), SP 10 (*xuè hǎi*), SP 6 (*sān yīn jiāo*) and KI 3 (*tài xī*), half a minute each point; then twisting and scrubbing manipulations on KI 1 (*yǒng quán*) until it is warm enough in the local area.

* Yang deficiency of spleen and kidney

Apply kneading and pressing manipulations on ST 25 (*tiān shū*), LI 11 (*qū chí*), LI 4 (*hé gǔ*), ST 36 (*zú sān lǐ*), GB 34 (*yáng líng quán*), ST 40 (*fēng lóng*), GB 39 (*xuán zhōng*), BL 40 (*wěi zhōng*), BL 57 (*chéng shān*), BL 60 (*kūn lún*), half a minute each point. Then apply palm-vibrating manipulation on RN 4 (*guān yuán*) and scrubbing manipulation over BL 31 (*shàng liáo*), BL 32 (*cì liáo*), BL 33 (*zhōng liáo*), BL 34 (*xià liáo*) transversely until it is warm enough in the local area.

* Deficiency of heart and spleen

Apply kneading and pressing manipulations on PC 8 (*láo gōng*), HT 5 (*tōng lǐ*), PC 6 (*nèi guān*), LI 4 (*hé gǔ*), BL 15 (*xīn shù*), SP 10 (*xuè hǎi*), ST 36 (*zú sān lǐ*), SP 9 (*yīn líng quán*), GB 39 (*xuán zhōng*) and SP 6 (*sān yīn jiāo*), half a minute each point. Then do twisting and scrubbing manipulations on KI 1 (*yǒng quán*) until it is warm enough in the local area.

⋆ Deficiency of yin and yang

Apply kneading and pressing manipulations on LI 4 (*hé gǔ*), ST 36 (*zú sān lǐ*), GB 34 (*yáng líng quán*), SP 10 (*xuè hǎi*), SP 9 (*yīn líng quán*), SP 6 (*sān yīn jiāo*), KI 3 (*tài xī*), LV 3 (*tài chōng*), GB 39 (*xuán zhōng*), half a minute each point. Then do scrubbing manipulation transversely on BL 31 (*shàng liáo*), BL 32 (*cì liáo*), BL 33 (*zhōng liáo*) and BL 34 (*xià liáo*); twisting and scrubbing manipulations on KI 1 (*yǒng quán*) until it is warm enough in the local area.

⋆ Insufficiency of yin blood

Apply pressing and kneading manipulations on PC 8 (*láo gōng*), HT 5 (*tōng lǐ*), PC 6 (*nèi guān*), LI 4 (*hé gǔ*), BL 15 (*xīn shù*), SP 10 (*xuè hǎi*), ST 36 (*zú sān lǐ*), GB 39 (*xuán zhōng*), SP 6 (*sān yīn jiāo*), LV 3 (*tài chōng*), half a minute each point. Then do twisting and scrubbing manipulations on KI 1 (*yǒng quán*) until it is warm enough in the local area.

⋆ Liver depression and spleen deficiency

Apply kneading and pressing manipulations on PC 6 (*nèi guān*), ST 36 (*zú sān lǐ*), GB 34 (*yáng líng quán*), ST 40 (*fēng lóng*), GB 39 (*xuán zhōng*), SP 6 (*sān yīn jiāo*), LV 3 (*tài chōng*), half a minute each point. Then do scrubbing and twisting manipulations on KI 1 (*yǒng quán*) and scrubbing manipulation transversely on BL 31 (*shàng liáo*), BL 32 (*cì liáo*), BL 33 (*zhōng liáo*) and BL 34 (*xià liáo*) until it is warm enough in the local area.

⋆ Insecurity of *chong mai* and *ren mai*

Apply kneading and pressing manipulations on LI 4 (*hé gǔ*), ST 36 (*zú sān lǐ*), GB 34 (*yáng líng quán*), SP 9 (*yīn líng quán*), SP 6 (*sān yīn jiāo*), KI 3 (*tài xī*), LV 3 (*tài chōng*), half a minute each point. Then apply palm-vibrating manipulation on RN 4 (*guān yuán*) and scrubbing manipulation on BL 31 (*shàng liáo*), BL 32 (*cì liáo*), BL 33 (*zhōng liáo*) and BL 34 (*xià liáo*) transversely, twisting and scrubbing manipulations on KI 1 (*yǒng quán*) until it is warm enough in the local area.

⋆ Qi depression and phlegm stagnation

Apply kneading and pressing manipulations on SJ 6 (*zhī gōu*), LI 4 (*hé gǔ*), ST 36 (*zú sān lǐ*), RN 22 (*tiān tū*), ST 40 (*fēng lóng*), SP 6 (*sān yīn jiāo*), KI 3 (*tài xī*), LV 3 (*tài chōng*), half a minute each point. Then do scrubbing manipulation transversely on BL 31 (*shàng liáo*), BL 32 (*cì liáo*), BL 33 (*zhōng liáo*) and BL 34 (*xià liáo*); scrubbing and twisting manipulations on KI 1 (*yǒng quán*) until it is warm enough in the local area.

6. Precautions

Every woman would have her menopause since it is a normal physiological process. Enlighten the patient to be objective and positive to the symptoms of autonomic dysfunction, so as to eliminate worries.

Tui na therapy has an affirmative effect for the disease. It is effective for various symptoms in the disease.

Impotence

1. Overview

Impotence is referred to malnutrition and weakness of penis due to deficiency, fear and damp heat, characterized by the inability to develop or maintain an erection of the penis. In western medicine, impotence is a kind of astysia often accompanied by premature ejaculation, nocturnal emission, reduced libido or no sexual desire, caused by cerebral cortex dysfunction, spinal dysfunction of central nerve system and genital organic diseases. The occurrence of the disease is usually related to the dysfunction of the liver and kidney. Insufficiency of heart and spleen, weakness of *mìng mén* (*gate of vitality*, 命门) fire, deficiency of kidney yang, coldness and deficiency of essence qi may disturb the function of the penis to cause the disease.

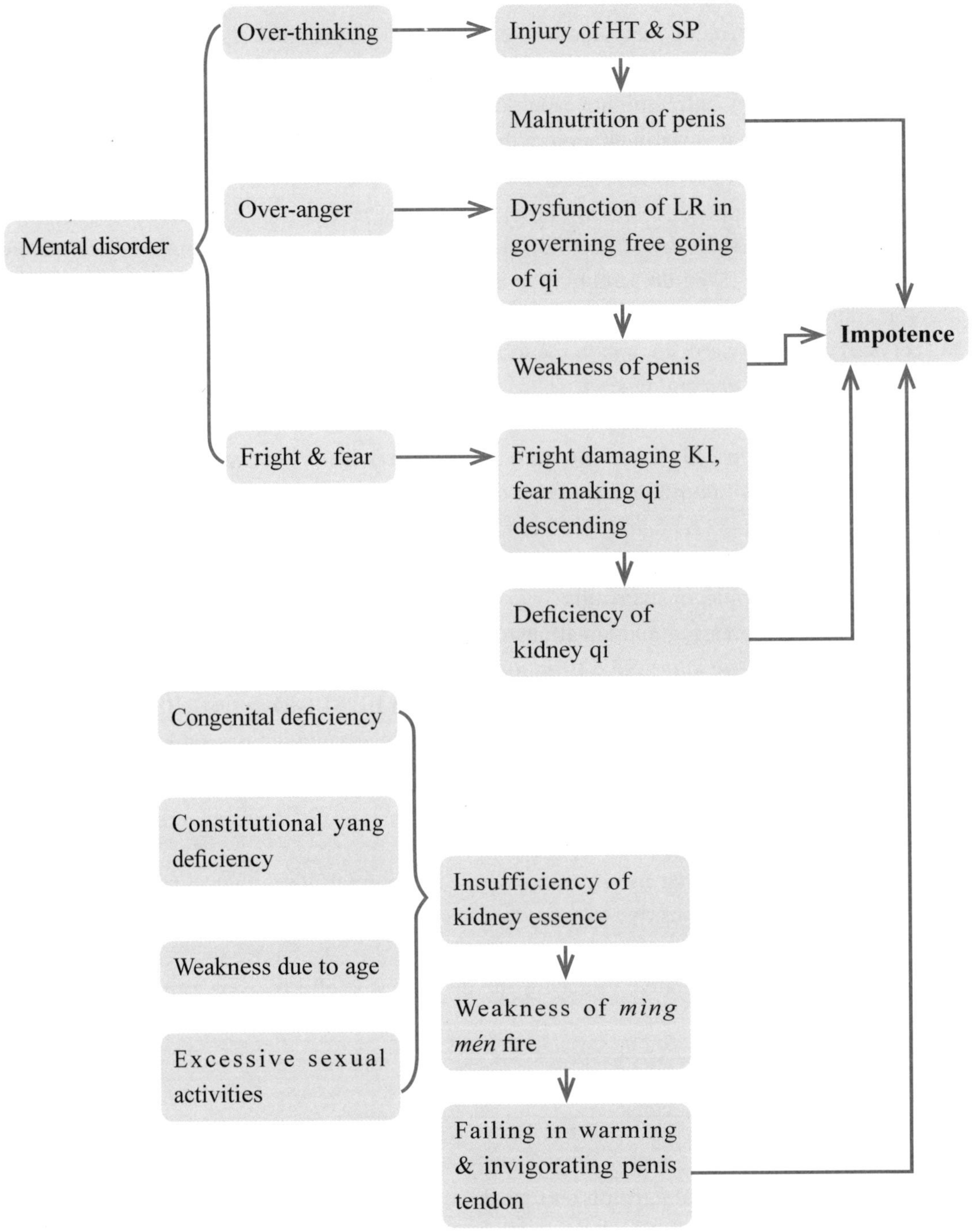

2. Clinical Manifestations

a. Weakness of *mìng mén* fire

Failure of erection, dilute cold semen, dizziness, tinnitus, blurred vision, listlessness, pale complexion, soreness and weakness in the lumbar region and knees, aversion to cold, cold limbs, pale tongue with white coating, a deep thready pulse.

b. Deficiency of heart and spleen

Failure of erection, listlessness, poor sleep, sallow complexion, poor appetite, pale tongue with thin greasy coating, and a thready pulse.

c. Dampness-heat pouring down

Thin, soft and weak penis with foul scrotum, aching and heavy limbs, dark yellow urine, dribbling of urine, red tongue with yellow greasy coating, a soggy pulse.

d. Injury of kidney by fear

Failure of erection or difficulty of maintaining erection, timid, suspicion, palpitation, insomnia, a tongue with thin coating, a wiry and thready pulse.

3. Diagnostic Essentials

Impotence is characterized by the inability to develop or maintain an erection of the penis sufficient for satisfactory sexual performance.

Impotence is classified into primary and secondary types and also classified as organic and functional types. The patient with primary impotence is never successful to insert the penis into the virginal; the patient with secondary impotence had sexual activities before, but had sexual disorder later. The patient with organic impotence is impossible to have erection at any time, neither when there is sexual arousal (during sleep and when the bladder is full), nor spontaneous erection; the patient with functional impotence may have spontaneous erection, but is not capable to maintain erection before ejaculation.

Impotence is mostly caused by psychological factors, the patients with impotence are more or less in the state of tension, fear, depression, worry and vaxation.

Exclude functional impotence by analyzing the other body signs and tracing primary disorders. For example, for impotence due to diabetes, blood and urine tests are necessary.

4. Tui Na Treatment

【Principle】

To tonify kidney and strengthen yang.

【Points and Regions】

RN 8 (*shén què*)	RN 6 (*qì hǎi*)	RN 4 (*guān yuán*)	RN 4 (*guān yuán*)
BL 15 (*xīn shù*)	BL 20 (*pí shù*)	BL 23 (*shèn shù*)	DU 4 (*mìng mén*)
DU 3 (*yāo yáng guān*)	SP 6 (*sān yīn jiāo*)		

Abdominal region, lumbar region and lower limbs.

【Method】

Ask patient to have a supine position, apply kneading manipulation with palm root on RN 8 (*shén què*) for 5 minutes, then one-finger pushing on RN 6 (*qì hǎi*), RN 4 (*guān yuán*) and RN 4 (*guān yuán*), 2 minutes on each point; after that, apply rubbing manipulation with palm on the lower abdomen until it is warm at the local area; Finally, vibrating manipulation with palm on the lower abdomen.

Ask patient to have a prone position, apply pressing and kneading manipulations with fingers on BL 15 (*xīn shù*), BL 20 (*pí shù*), BL 23 (*shèn shù*), DU 4 (*mìng mén*), 2 minutes on each point. Then apply scrubbing manipulation on DU 3 (*yāo yáng guān*) until it is warm enough deeply in the local area.

Apply pressing and kneading manipulations together on SP 6 (*sān yīn jiāo*) about 2 minutes. Finally, apply pinching and grasping manipulations alternately on bilateral legs 3~5 minutes.

Points and Regions Selected According to Syndrome

⋆ Weakness of *Mìng Mén*

Apply pressing and kneading manipulations with fingers on BL 23 (*shèn shù*), DU 4 (*mìng mén*), 5 minutes on each point; scrubbing manipulation along du mai, spinal column and bilateral course of foot taiyang bladder channel, apply scrubbing manipulation transversely over BL 23 (*shèn shù*), DU 4 (*mìng mén*) and BL 31-34 (*bá liǎo*) until it is warm enough in the local area.

⋆ Deficiency of heart and spleen

Apply pressing and kneading manipulations with finger on PC 6 (*nèi guān*), ST 36 (*zú sān lǐ*) and SP 10 (*xuè hǎi*), 1~2 minutes each point; same manipulations on BL 15 (*xīn shù*) and BL 20 (*pí shù*), 3~5 minutes each point.

⋆ Dampness-heat pouring down

Apply pressing and kneading manipulations with finger on ST 25 (*tiān shū*), ST 40 (*fēng lóng*), ST 36 (*zú sān lǐ*), BL 25 (*dà cháng shù*), SP 9 (*yīn líng quán*) and BL 28 (*páng guāng shù*), 2 minutes each point; apply palm-rubbing manipulation on the lower abdomen about 5 minutes.

⋆ Injury of kidney by fear

Apply sideward-mopping manipulation on the forehead about 10 times; finger-pressing and kneading manipulations on EX-HN5 (*tài yáng*), HT 7 (*shén mén*), PC 7 (*dà líng*) and EX-LE6 (*dǎn náng*), 1~2 minutes each point; alternate pinching and grasping manipulations on the arm about 2 minutes.

5. Precautions

Correctly guide the patient to relieve tension and fear and maintain a good mood.

Encourage the patient to set up the confidence of overcoming the disease, sexual partners should be considerate and gentle to each other.

Strike a proper balance between work and rest and have proper exercises and physical labor.

Have less worldly desire, abstain from masturbation, and moderate sexual activities.

Toothache

1. Overview

Toothache refers to pain caused by various reasons, which is one of the common symptoms in oral diseases. It will be aroused and aggravated by the cold, hot, sour and sweat irritations. It can be seen in the caries, pulpitis, peri-apical and dentin hypersensitivity. In TCM, it is related to wind fire, stomach fire, kidney deficiency and caries.

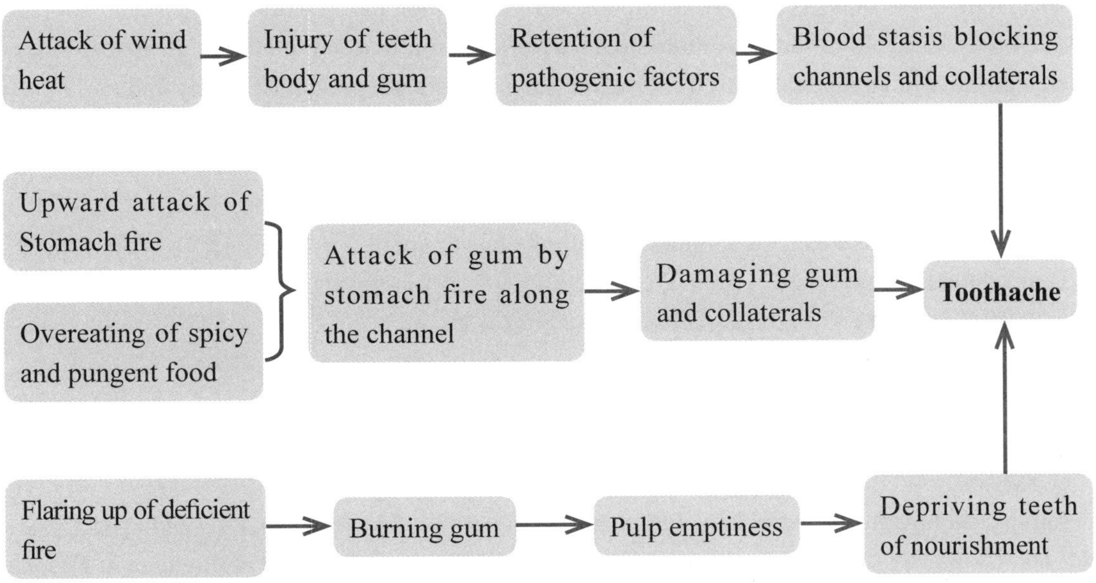

2. Clinical Manifestations

Clinically, the disease can be seen at any ages and seasons.

a. Toothache due to wind heat

Toothache with paroxysmal attack induce by wind, aggravated by warmth and alleviated by cold, red and swollen gum; accompanied by fever, chills, thirsty, red tongue with white and dry coating, superficial and a rapid pulse.

b. Toothache due to stomach fire

Severe pain, dark red and severe swollen gum, or even bleeding and pus, swollen cheek, headache, thirsty with desire of drinking, heavy breath, constipation, yellow greasy tongue coating, a surging and rapid pulse.

c. Toothache due to deficient fire

Dull or mild toothache, light red gum, mild swollen gum, or gum atrophy due to chronic disease, weak biting due to loose teeth; toothache is usually worse in the afternoon. It is also accompanied by lumbago, back pain, dizziness, dry mouth without desire of drinking, red and tender tongue without coating, a thready and rapid pulse.

3. Diagnostic Essentials

a. Toothache due to wind heat

Toothache is the main symptom; the pain which is alleviated by cold and aggravated by warmth, red and swollen gum, fever, chills and thirsty are taken as the essentials of differentiation; accompanied by red tongue with white and dry coating, superficial and a rapid pulse.

b. Toothache due to stomach fire

Toothache is the main symptom; red and severe swollen gums, swollen cheeks, headache, thirst with desire of drinking, heavy breath and constipation are taken as the essentials of differentiation; accompanied by yellow greasy tongue coating, and a surging and rapid pulse.

c. Toothache due to deficient fire

Toothache is the main symptom; dull pain, light red gums, mild swollen gums, gum atrophy in chronic case, weak biting loose teeth and pain worse in the afternoon are taken as the essentials of differentiation; accompanied by a red and tender tongue without coating, a thready and rapid pulse.

4. Tui Na Treatment

【Principle of treatment】

To dispelling wind, clear fire, eliminate swelling and stop pain.

【Points and Regions】

LI 4 (*hé gǔ*)	ST 7 (*xià guān*)	ST 6(*jiá chē*)	ST 44 (*nèi tíng*)
KI 3 (*tài xī*)	LV 2 (*xíng jiān*)	LV 3 (*tài chōng*)	

And the face.

【Method】

Apply pointing, pressing and kneading manipulation on ST 44 (*nèi tíng*), KI 3 (*tài xī*), LV 2 (*xíng jiān*) and LV 3 (*tài chōng*). Give the treatment with strong stimulation, and the treatment lasts about 3 minutes.

Apply one-finger pushing or pressing and kneading manipulations on ST 7 (*xià guān*) and ST 6 (*jiá chē*). The strength of manipulations should be increased gradually to strong, and the treatment lasts about 3 minutes.

Apply pressing, kneading, pinching and grasping manipulations on LI 4 (*hé gǔ*). The treatment lasts about 1 minute.

Finally, apply pinching, grasping, pressing and kneading manipulations on the corresponding area of sick gum to end the treatment.

Points and Regions Selected According to Syndrome:

⋆ Toothache due to wind fire

Add one-finger pushing on EX-HN5(*tài yáng*) and grasping on GB 20 (*fēng chí*), LI 11 (*qū chí*) and TE 5 (*wài guān*).

⋆ Toothache due to stomach fire

Add pressing and kneading manipulations on LI 2 (*èr jiān*), LI 3 (*sān jiān*) and ST 44 (*nèi tíng*).

⋆ Toothache due to deficient fire

Add one-finger pushing on BL 23 (*shèn shù*) and pressing and kneading manipulations on KI 3 (*tài xī*) and LV 2 (*xíng jiān*).

5. Precautions

No matter what kind of toothache, it is important to have a good health habit, persist in gargling and brushing teeth after eating.

During the face treatment, the manipulation should be fixed without any pulling and dragging movements to prevent aggravation of gum swelling.

Anti-inflammatory drugs can be prescribed together with Tui Na Treatment to enhance therapeutic effect, since caries, pulpitis and apical inflammation are referred to acute inflammatory changes.

Tinnitus and Deafness

1. Overview

Tinnitus and deafness refer to an abnormal acoustic symptom. Tinnitus indicates high or low conscious ringing inside the ear, like cicada tweeting or tidal sound, accompanied by hypoacusis or hearing disability. And deafness is often developed from tinnitus. Modern medicine thinks they are attributed as inner ear diseases, or ear disease caused by certain drugs.

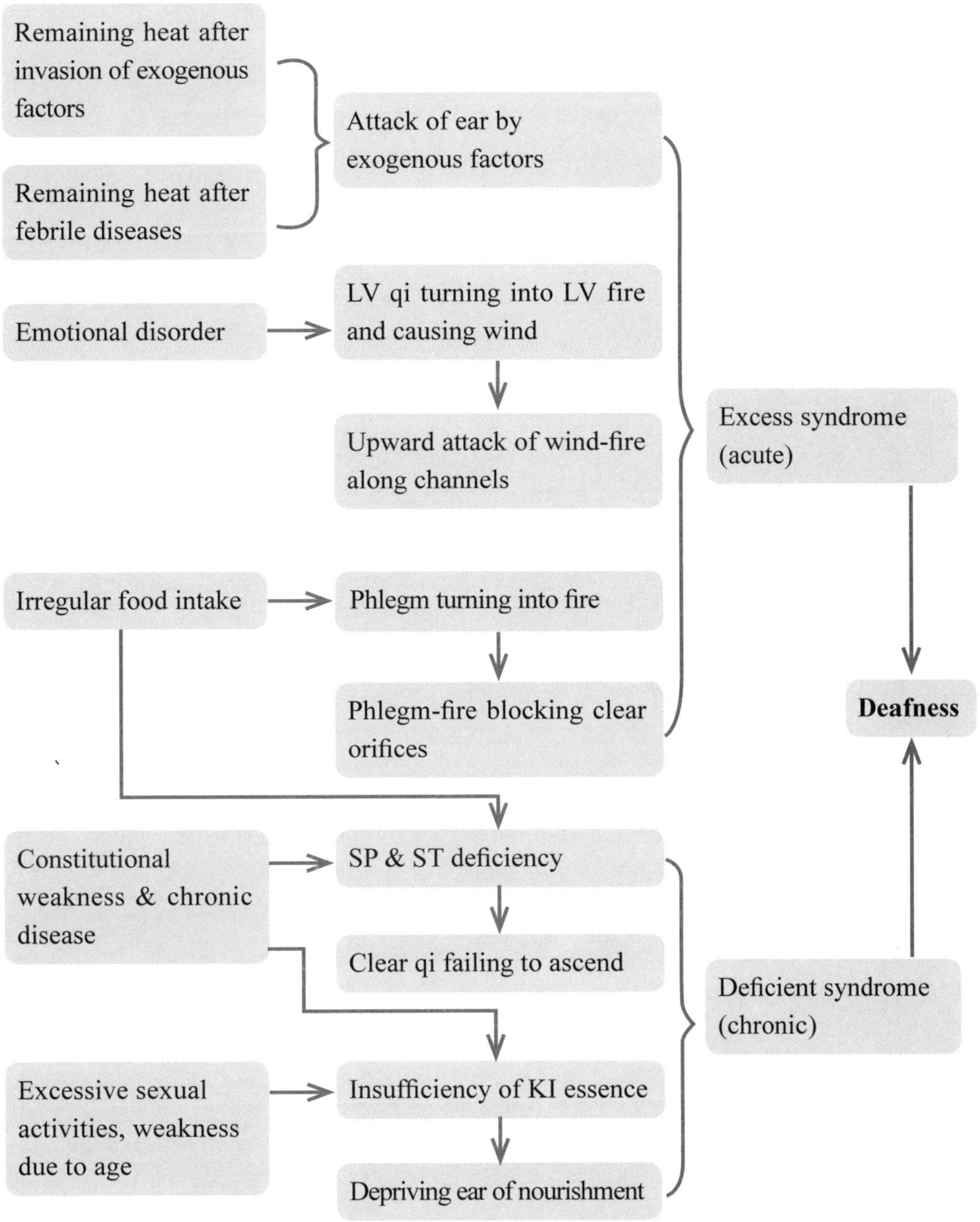

2. Clinical Manifestations

a. Excess syndrome

The main symptoms: Sudden onset of deafness, or distending feeling in the ear with continuous rumble which can't be helped by pressing the ear.

The accompanied symptoms: Tinnitus like cicada tweeting, sometimes blocking feeling in the ear, chest stuffiness, profuse sputum, bitter taste in the mouth, thin yellow greasy tongue coating, wiry and slippery pulse. In the cases due to upward attack of wind-heat, distending feeling in the head, red face, dry throat, irritability and wiry pulse can be seen; in the cases due to invasion of exogenous wind, chills, fever and superficial pulse can be found.

b. Deficiency syndrome

The main symptoms: Deafness due to long time illness, tinnitus like cicada tweeting, sometimes on and sometimes off, aggravated after exertion and alleviated by pressing the ear.

Accompanying symptoms: In the cases due to deficiency of kidney essence, dizziness, soreness and weakness in lumber region and knees, lassitude, spermatorrhea, leukorrhea, weak thready pulse can be found; in the cases due to deficiency of spleen and stomach, poor appetite, listlessness, short breath, thin white tongue coating and a thready pulse can be found.

3. Diagnostic Essentials

The main symptoms are tinnitus and descending of hearing, accompanied by with mild dizziness.

The disease is often induced by anger, overstrain and invasion of exogenous pathogenic factors, caused by ototoxicity drugs, constitutional weakness due to age and malnutrition.

Ear examination shows no obvious tympanic changes, but shows turbid drum membrane, otopiesis, thickened drum membrane, adhesion or calsinosis of drum membrane.

The acoustic examination shows sensorineural hearing loss or conductive hearing loss in the patient with deafness.

Tinnitus and deafness should be distinguished from distending feeling in the ear, blocked feeling in the ear, Menlere's syndrome and acoustic neuromas.

4. Tui Na Treatment

【Principle of treatment】

To remove obstruction from the orifice, sharpen the ear and clear liver fire.

【Points and Regions】

SJ 21 (*ěr mén*)	SI 19 (*tīng gōng*)	GB 2 (*tīng huì*)	SJ 17 (*yì fēng*)
DU 20 (*bǎi huì*)	DU 15 (*yǎ mén*)	GB 20 (*fēng chí*)	DU 16 (*fēng fǔ*)

The head and the area around ear

【Method】

Apply pinching and grasping manipulations on five courses of channels of the head; one-finger-pushing, grasping, pressing and kneading manipulations on the neck and nape; pressing and kneading manipulations on DU 20 (*bǎi huì*), DU 15 (*yǎ mén*), GB 20 (*fēng chí*), DU 16 (*fēng fǔ*), about 5 minutes.

One-finger pushing on SJ 21 (*ěr mén*), SI 19 (*tīng gōng*), GB 2 (*tīng huì*); pressing and kneading manipulation on SJ 17 (*yì fēng*) for about 5 minutes.

Holding the patient's ears with index and middle fingers, rub the ear up and down until it is warm enough in the auricle for about 5 minutes.

Apply vibrating manipulation with fingers or palm on the ear to end the treatment.

Points and Regions Selected According to Syndrome:

⋆ Upward attack of wind-fire

Apply pointing and pressing manipulations on LV 3 (*tài chōng*), LV 2 (*xíng jiān*), BL 19 (*dǎn shù*), BL 22 (*sān jiāo shù*) until the patient starts to have soreness and distending feeling in the local area; heavyage manipulation on hypochondriac region 1 minute; kneading manipulation on medial aspect of the thigh 2 minutes.

⋆ Attack of exogenous wind

Apply rolling manipulation on the neck and back for 2~3 minutes, pressing and kneading manipulations on EX-HN5 (*tài yáng*), DU 14 (*dà zhuī*), BL 13 (*fèi shù*), BL 12 (*fēng mén*); vertical scrubbing manipulation on bilateral courses of bladder channel until it is warm enough at the local area. Apply grasping manipulation on bilateral GB 21 (*jiān jǐng*); tap bilateral courses of bladder channel on the back until it is slightly red on the local area.

⋆ Deficiency of kidney essence

Apply gentle pressing and kneading manipulations on RN 6 (*qì hǎi*), RN 4 (*guān yuán*), 1 minute each point; scrubbing manipulation along governor vessel; scrubbing manipulation along transverse line on BL 23 (*shèn shù*), DU 4 (*mìng mén*) and BL 31-34 (*bá liǎo*) on the lumbosacral region until it is warm enough at the local area.

⋆ Deficiency of spleen and stomach

Apply pressing and kneading manipulations on BL 20 (*pí shù*), ST 36 (*zú sān lǐ*), SP 9 (*yīn líng quán*), RN 12 (*zhōng wǎn*) 2 minutes each point. Rub the abdomen and apply scrubbing manipulation on the back and lumbar region until it is warm enough on the local area.

5. Precautions

Tui na therapy can increase cerebral blood flow and improve the oxygen supply of the damaged auditory nerve to benefit blood vessel elasticity and decrease vascular resistance, so it has certain effect to restore auditory nerve function. But the treatment is not effective for complete loss of hearing due to tympanic membrane injury.

Since the causative factors of tinnitus and deafness are complicated, it is necessary to have definite diagnosis. It is also important to treat primary disease which causes tinnitus and deafness. As for tinnitus and deafness caused by neck disorders, the treatment of cervical spondylosis can be taken as reference.

Regular life style and harmony mood are of great significance to the health of the patient with tinnitus and deafness. Overstrain and drastic emotional changes should be avoided.

Depression Syndrome

1. Overview

Depression syndrome is a general term for disorders resulted from emotional depression and stagnation of qi. The chief symptoms are depression, restlessness, chest fullness, hypochondriac distending pain, irritability, and foreign body sensation in the throat.

Depression syndrome covers a wide range including disorders of *zang-fu* organs due to six excesses and emotional depression, as well as food accumulation and phlegm stagnation, which may cause many syndromes, such as blood stasis, phlegm retention, food accumulation and fire.

Some diseases in the scope of western medicine, like neurosis, neurasthenia, hysteria, reactive psychosis, and menopausal syndrome, are included in depression syndrome. Tui na is mainly used to treat depression syndrome due to emotional constraining and qi stagnation.

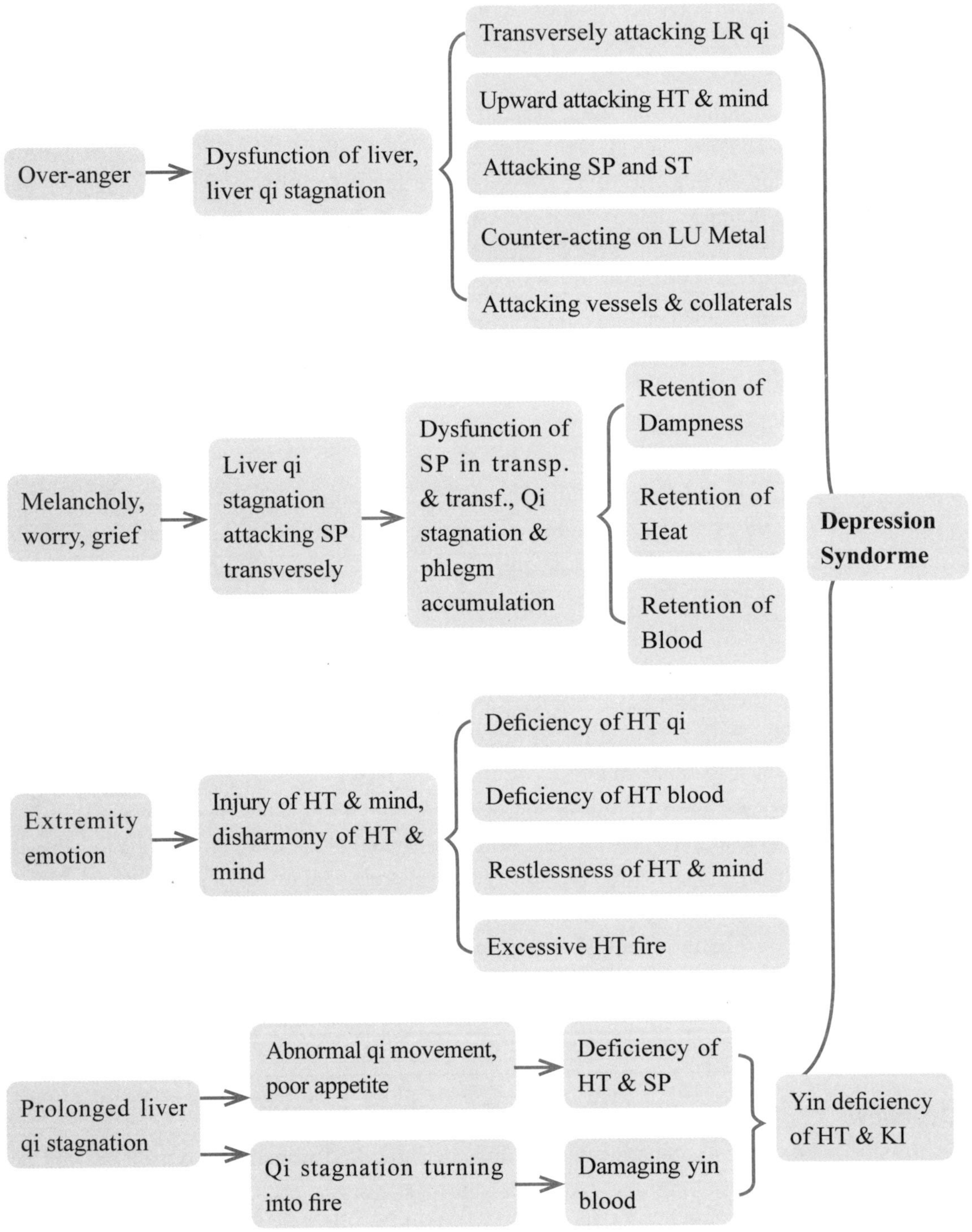

2. Clinical Manifestations

a. Liver qi depression

Emotional depression, chest fullness, distending and wandering pain in the chest and hypochondriac region, poor appetite, or abdominal pain, vomiting, or frequent belching, irregular bowel movement, a tongue with thin white or slightly greasy coating, a wiry and tense pulse.

b. Fire due to Qi depression

Irritability, chest and hypochondriac distension, dry mouth and bitter taste in the mouth, or headache, red eyes, tinnitus, or sour regurgitation, constipation, red tongue with yellow coating, wiry and rapid pulse.

c. Phlegm due to qi stagnation

Depression, foreign body sensation in the throat hard to spit it out or to swallow it, chest and hypochondriac distention, a tongue with thin white coating, a wiry and slippery pulse.

d. Malnutrition of heart and mind

Depression, restlessness, blurred mind, unreasonable crying and laughing, preference of yawn, a tongue with thin white coating, a wiry and thready pulse.

e. Deficiency of heart and spleen

Over-thinking, dizziness, listlessness, palpitation, timid, insomnia, poor memory, poor appetite, pale complexion, pale tongue with thin white coating, a thready pulse.

f. Yin deficiency of heart and kidney

Dizziness, tinnitus, palpitation, insomnia, restlessness, irritability, soreness and weakness in the lumbar region and knees, nocturnal emission, irregular menstruation, red tongue with little coating, a wiry, thready and rapid pulse.

3. Diagnosis

Mental symptoms include hyperthermia or hypothermia with flight of ideas or thought retardation.

The disease is characterized by paroxysmal attack and normal psychological state in intermission.

Commonly, no positive signs founded in the body, nerve system and laboratory examination.

4. Tui Na Treatment

【Principle of treatment】

Soothing liver, regulating qi, resolving phlegm and easing depression.

【Points and Regions】

BL 18 (*gān shù*)	BL 20 (*pí shù*)	BL 21 (*wèi shù*)
LV 13 (*zhāng mén*)	LV 14 (*qī mén*)	

Back, hypochondriac region, abdominal region.

【Method】

Ask the patient to have a prone position; apply rolling manipulation on the back and lumbar region along bilateral courses of bladder meridian at the side of spine for 5 minutes. Apply one-finger pushing or finger-pressing and finger-kneading manipulation on BL 18 (*gān shù*), BL 20 (*pí shù*), BL 21(*wèi shù*), 2 minutes on each point.

Ask the patient to have a supine position; apply finger-pressing and finger-kneading manipulations on LV 13 (*zhāng mén*), LV 14 (*qī mén*), 1 minute on each point. Apply finger or palm-rubbing manipulation on the hypochondriac region and abdomen for 3 minutes respectively.

Treatment according to differentiation syndrome.

* Liver qi depression

Apply pointing or pressing manipulation on LV 3 (*tài chōng*), LV 2 (*xíng jiān*), 2 minutes for each point. Rub the hypochondriac region for 1 minute.

* Fire due to qi stagnation

Apply pointing or pressing manipulation on BL 19 (*dǎn shù*), BL 22 (*sān jiāo shù*), 2 minutes for each point. Apply grasping manipulation on muscles on the medial aspect of the thigh for 5 minutes.

* Stagnation of qi and phlegm

Apply acupoint-pressing or pressing manipulation with figers on BL 13 (*fèi shù*), BL 19(*dǎn shù*), RN 22 (*tiān tū*), 2 minutes for each point. Apply the palm-kneading manipulation on RN 12 (*zhōng wǎn*) for 3 minutes.

* Malnutrition of heart spirit

Apply pressing or kneading manipulation on BL 15 (*xīn shù*) and ST 36 (*zú sān lǐ*), 2 minutes for each point. Apply grasping manipulation to grasp the muscles on the medial and anterior aspects of legs.

* Deficiency of heart and spleen

Apply finger-pressing or finger-kneading manipulation on BL 15 (*xīn shù*), PC 6 (*nèi guān*), SJ 5 (*wài guān*), ST 36 (*zú sān lǐ*), 1 minute for each point. Apply palm-kneading manipulation on RN 12 (*zhōng wǎn*) for 3 minutes.

* Yin deficiency of heart and kidney

Apply finger-pressing or finger-kneading manipulation on BL 23 (*shèn shù*), RN 6 (*qì hǎi*), RN 4 (*guān yuán*), SP 6 (*sān yīn jiāo*), 2 minutes for each point. Apply scrubbing manipulation on KI 1 (*yǒng quán*) till it is warm in the local area.

5. Precautions

Depression syndrome is mostly caused by drastic emotional changes. In addition to medicinal drugs and tui na therapy, the psychological treatment should be also suggested, so as to guide the patient getting rid of worries and depression, strike a proper balance between work and rest and ensure enough sleep.

Try to stay in quiet environment and keep away from noise; it is better to have dim light in the room, avoid irritation of intense light.

It is advisable to have food containing rich nutrient, such as vegetables, fishes, lean meat, dairy products and soy products; forbidden to have spicy food, smoking and alcohol, and have less greasy, fatty and sweet food.

Irregular Menstruation

1. Overview

Irregular menstruation, a kind of common gynecological disease, is a general term of menstrual cycle disorders. Including advanced menstruation, delayed menstruation or irregular menstrual

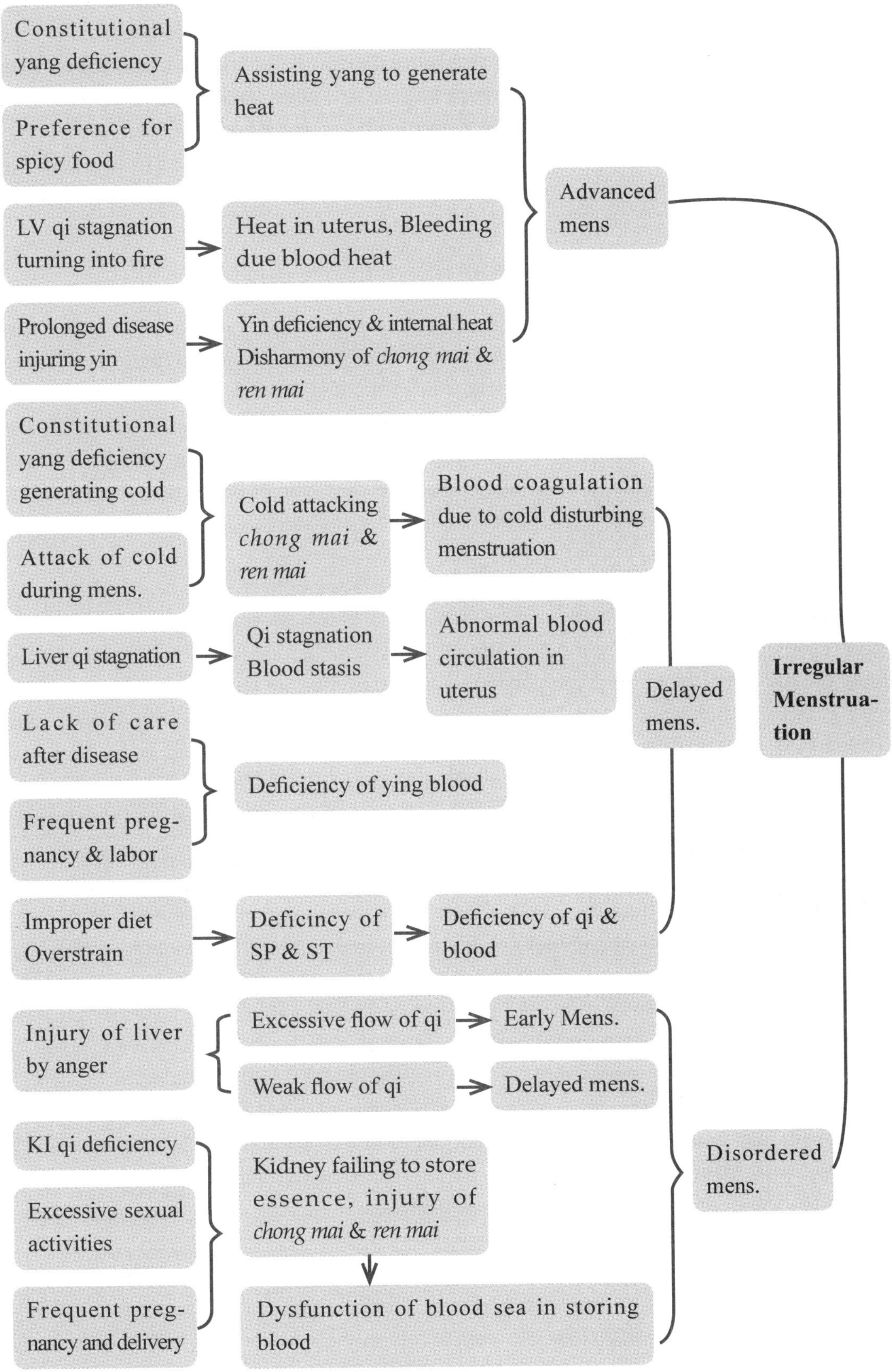
Constitutional yang deficiency
Preference for spicy food
Assisting yang to generate heat
LV qi stagnation turning into fire
Heat in uterus, Bleeding due blood heat
Prolonged disease injuring yin
Yin deficiency & internal heat Disharmony of *chong mai* & *ren mai*
Advanced mens
Constitutional yang deficiency generating cold
Attack of cold during mens.
Cold attacking *chong mai* & *ren mai*
Blood coagulation due to cold disturbing menstruation
Liver qi stagnation
Qi stagnation Blood stasis
Abnormal blood circulation in uterus
Lack of care after disease
Frequent pregnancy & labor
Deficiency of ying blood
Improper diet Overstrain
Deficincy of SP & ST
Deficiency of qi & blood
Delayed mens.
Irregular Menstruation
Injury of liver by anger
Excessive flow of qi
Early Mens.
Weak flow of qi
Delayed mens.
KI qi deficiency
Excessive sexual activities
Frequent pregnancy and delivery
Kidney failing to store essence, injury of *chong mai* & *ren mai*
Dysfunction of blood sea in storing blood
Disordered mens.

cycle, it's mainly characterized by disorders of menstrual cycle, menstrual period, menstrual volume, menstrual color and menstrual property. Clinically, menstruation earlier than due time by 7 days, or even twice a month, is regarded as advanced menstruation, while menstruation later than due time by 7 days, or even once every forty to fifty days, is considered as "delayed menstruation". Irregular menstruation, manifesting irregular menstrual cycle, earlier or later than due time by more than 7 days, is called "disordered menstruation". Modern medicine considers that it could be caused by disorders of estrogen secretion, dysfunction of vegetative nerve, mental disorders, cold, fatigue or some general diseases.

2. Clinical Manifestations

Irregular menstruation usually shows disorders of menstrual cycle, menstrual volume, menstrual color, and menstrual property. Menstrual cycle disorders include advanced menstruation, delayed menstruation, irregular menstrual cycle, short or prolonged menstrual period. The disorders of menstrual volume are manifested by hypermenorrhea or hypomenorrhea. The disorders of menstrual color implies sticky or thin menses, with blood clots or odor smelling. Or accompanied by discomfort and distending pain in lower abdomen, distending pain of breast or in the hypochondriac region, headache, nausea, vomiting, disorders of urination and stools.

a. Advanced menstruation

Menstruation is earlier than due time, even twice every month. Excess heat syndrome usually manifests profuse purple and sticky menstrual blood, restlessness, chest fullness, red tongue with yellow coating, floating and rapid pulse. Blood heat syndrome due to yin deficiency often shows scanty red menstrual blood, red complexion, hot sensation in the palms, red tongue with yellow coating, thready and rapid pulse. The fire syndrome due to liver qi depression may manifest blood clots in menses, distending pain in chest, hypochondriac region, breast and lower abdomen, irritability and wiry pulse. Qi deficiency syndrome often reflect scanty, light and thin menstrual blood, fatigue, lassitude, short breath, palpitation, dropping sensation in the lower abdomen, pale tongue with thin coating, and feeble pulse.

b. Delayed menstruation

Menstruation is later than due time. Excess cold symptom usually manifests scanty dark red menstrual blood, lower abdominal colicky pain which could be alleviated by warmth, blue complexion, cold limbs, a tongue with white thin coating, a deep and tight pulse. Deficiency cold syndrome shows scanty menstrual blood light in color, abdominal pain alleviated by pressing and warmth, pale complexion, pale tongue with white coating, a deep, slow and weak pulse. In the syndrome of qi depression, scanty menstrual blood, lower abdominal distending pain, depression, stuffiness and fullness in chest and hypochondriac region, preference for sigh, a tongue with yellow coating, wiry and an unsmooth pulse could be found; In the syndrome of blood deficiency, lower abdominal empty pain, yellow complexion, dry skin, palpitation, blurred vision, pale tongue with thin coating, feeble, thready and weak pulse could be seen.

c. Disordered Menstruation

Menstruation is earlier or later than due time. In the syndrome of liver qi stagnation, unsmooth menstruation, distending pain in chest, breast and lower abdomen, depression, chest fullness, preference for sigh, wiry pulse could be seen. While in the syndrome of kidney deficiency, the symptoms including scanty dilute menstrual blood light in color, dark complexion, dizziness and tinnitus, soreness and weakness in lumbar region and knees, frequent urination at night, pale tongue with thin coating, a deep and weak pulse could be found.

3. Diagnosis

a. Advanced menstruation

Menstruation is about 7 days earlier than due time, even once every two weeks, the situation has happened more than 2 times.

If menstruation is half a month earlier than due time, it should be distinguished from intermenstrual bleeding, advanced menstruation in the periods of adolescence and menopause.

b. Delayed menstruation

Take manifestation of 7 days later than normal menstrual period as the main symptom.

Menstrual cycle exceeds 35 days for more than 2 continuous cycles.

If the women of child-bearing age has delayed menstruation, it should be distinguished from delayed menstruation in the periods of pregnancy, adolescence and menopause.

Gynecological examination, type-B ultrasonic examination or pneumoperitoneography are necessary to exclude organic diseases of the uterus and ovary.

c. Disordered menstruation

Take irregular menstrual cycles as the main symptom.

Menstruation is 7 days earlier or later than normal menstrual cycle, and such situation has lasted more than 2 continuous menstrual cycles.

Disordered menstruation must be distinguished from disordered menstruation in the periods of adolescence and menopause.

Gynecological examination and type-B ultrasonic are necessary to exclude organic diseases. Basal body temperature (BBT), stain smear and cervical mucus crystallization (CMC) are necessary to understand the function of the ovary.

4. Tui Na Treatment

【Principle】

Harmonizing qi and blood, soothing liver and regulating qi.

【Points and Regions】

RN 4 (*guān yuán*)	RN 6 (*qì hǎi*)	RN 3 (*zhōng jí*)
BL 20 (*pí shù*)	BL 18 (*gān shù*)	BL 23 (*shèn shù*)
SP 6 (*sān yīn jiāo*)	LV 3 (*tài chōng*)	KI 3 (*tài xī*)

Abdominal region, back, lumbar region and lower limbs.

【Method】

Ask the patient to have a supine position; Apply one-finger pushing or kneading manipulation on RN 4 (*guān yuán*), RN 6 (*qì hǎi*), RN 3 (*zhōng jí*), about 1 minute for each point till obtaining qi. Then apply rubbing manipulation clockwise on the lower abdomen for about 10 minutes.

Ask the patient to have a prone position; apply one-finger pushing manipulation on the bilateral courses of Bladder meridian, especially on BL 20 (*pí shù*), BL 18 (*gān shù*), BL 23 (*shèn shù*), for 3~5 minutes. And then, apply pressing and kneading manipulation on BL 20 (*pí shù*), BL 18 (*gān shù*), BL 23 (*shèn shù*), about 1 minute for each point till obtaning qi.

Ask patient to have a supine position; Apply pressing and kneading manipulation with both thumbs on SP 6 (*sān yīn jiāo*), LV 3 (*tài chōng*), KI 3 (*tài xī*), about 1 minute for each point till the patient feels soreness and distention.

Treatment according to syndrome differentiation.

⋆ Blood Heat

Apply pressing and kneading manipulation with thumb on LV 1 (*dà dūn*), LV 2 (*xíng jiān*), SP 1 (*yǐn bái*), SP 6 (*sān yīn jiāo*), ST 41 (*jiě xī*), SP 10 (*xuè hǎi*), about 1 minute each point till obtaining qi. Or apply pressing and kneading manipulation with thumb, or index finger, or middle finger on BL 18 (*gān shù*), BL 21 (*wèi shù*), BL 25 (*dà cháng shù*) for 3~5 minutes.

⋆ Blood Cold

Apply palm-pressing manipulation on RN 8 (*shén què*) continuously for 3~5 minutes and make patient feel a hot sensation on lower abdomen. Then, apply palm-rubbing manipulation on governor vessel (GV) and BL 23 (*shèn shù*), DU 4 (*mìng mén*), frequently rub for 1~2 minutes till the skin is hot.

⋆ Qi and blood deficiency

Apply palm-pressing manipulation on patient's abdominal points like RN 12 (*zhōng wǎn*), RN 6 (*qì hǎi*), continuously press each point for 3 minutes and make the patient feel a hot sensation on the abdomen. Then, press and knead ST 36 (*zú sān lǐ*), SP 6 (*sān yīn jiāo*) with thumb, about 3 minutes each point until obtaining qi. After that, apply pressing and kneading manipulation with thumb on BL 20 (*pí shù*), BL 21 (*wèi shù*), 1 minute each point. Finally, apply palm-rubbing manipulation on BL 20 (*pí shù*), BL 21 (*wèi shù*) until the local area is warm.

⋆ Liver qi stagnation

Apply pressing and kneading manipulation with thumb on LV 13 (*zhāng mén*), LV 14 (*qī mén*) about 2 minutes, and then, press and knead BL 17 (*gé shù*), BL 18 (*gān shù*) with the thumb for 3~5 minutes.

⋆ Kidney deficiency

Apply finger-pressing manipulation on RN 4 (*guān yuán*) for 3~5 minutes till the ward sensation goes deeply into the lower abdomen; press and knead both KI 1 (*yǒng quán*) with the thumb continuously for 1 minute; palm-rubbing manipulation along the vertical axis on foot bottom repeatedly till it is warm at the local area. Finally, apply rubbing manipulation on governor vessel (GV) and bladder channel repeatedly for 5~7 times, and BL 23 (*shèn shù*), DU 4 (*mìng mén*), BL 30 (*bái huán shù*) until it is warm at the local area.

5. Precautions

The manipulations should be gentle and moderate, step by step, avoid violent manipulations for quick result.

It's better to give tai na treatment before or after menstrual period. Take care of diet, avoiding veracious eating or over-eating of fatty, sweet, greasy, spicy, cold and raw food.

Pay attention on the weather changes; be careful not to catch cold and not over-warmed.

Keep ease mood, avoid drastic emotional changes which may disturb *chong mai* and *ren mai* to cause the disease.

Have proper rest, avoid over-work or severe exercise. It is not advisable to have excessive sexual activities, practice contraception to avoid abortion which may damage *chong mai*, *ren mai* and kidney qi.

For the patient with irregular menstruation due to organic disorders, it is better to offer medicine and acupuncture at the same time to enhance therapeutic effect.

Chapter 7
Tui Na Treatment for Common Pediatric Diseases

Section 1
Basic Tui Na Manipulations for Children

Pushing

Pushing manipulation is one of the frequently used manipulations in pediatric tui na. It is a kind of straight, circular or arc pushing movement done on the operated area or points with thumb or fingertips of index and middle fingers. It can be classified as straight-pushing manipulation (*zhí tuī fǎ*, 直推法), circular-pushing manipulation (*xuán tuī fǎ*, 旋推法), separating-pushing manipulation (*fēn tuī fǎ*, 分推法) and inward-pushing manipulation (*hé tuī fǎ*, 合推法) according to different directions of pushing movement.

Straight-pushing Manipulation (*zhí tuī fǎ*, 直推法):

It is a kind of one-way straight pushing movement done on the points with the radial side or thumb ball or fingertips of the index and middle finger.

1. Manipulation

Do straight pushing movement on the point with radial side or thumb ball or thumb ball or fingertip of the index and middle finger (Fig. 7-1).

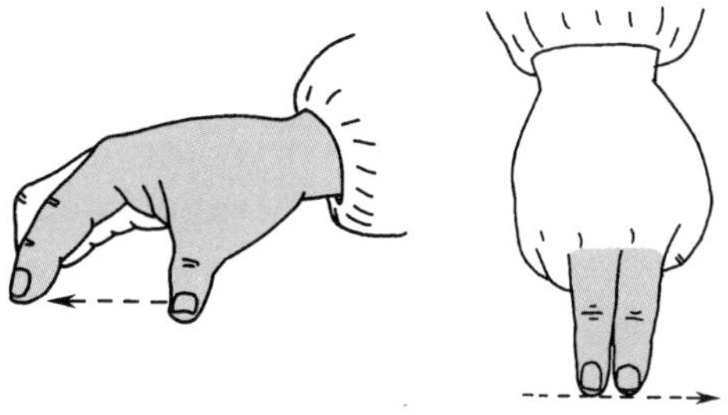

Fig. 7-1 Straight-pushing manipulation (*zhí tuī fǎ*, 直推法)

2. Essential Movements

Relax the shoulder, elbow and wrist joints. Do pushing movement straight by a fist with extended thumb or extended index and middle fingers.

Straight-pushing manipulation done with radial side of thumb mainly relies on active adduction and abduction of the thumb; straight-pushing manipulation done with fingertips of index and middle fingers mainly relies on flexion and extension of elbow joint.

The movement should be swift and continuous, done along a straight line with a frequency of 250~300 times /min.

3. Precautions

During the application of straight pushing manipulation, pay attention to strength and speed of the manipulation as well as stability and harmony of the movement to achieve the reinforcing or reducing effect.

The media substances like ginger juice, scallion juice, or sesame oil should be used as medium to prevent skin injury on children and enhance the therapeutic effect.

Circular-pushing Manipulation (*xuán tuī fǎ*, 旋推法)

It is a kind of clockwise circular-pushing and rubbing movement on the point with the right thumb ball.

1. Manipulation

Do clockwise circular-pushing and rubbing movement on the points with the thumb ball (Fig. 7-2).

Fig. 7-2 Circular-pushing manipulation (*xuán tuī fǎ*, 旋推法)

2. Essentials of Movements

Relax the shoulder, elbow and wrist joint, do circular-pushing movement with the thumb in small amplitude.

Circular-pushing manipulation is similar to one-finger-rubbing manipulation, just rubbing skin surface with no pulling of subcutaneous tissues.

The speed of circular-pushing manipulation is slower than that of straight-pushing manipulation, with even and gentle strength, harmonious movement and frequency about 160~200 times /min.

3. Precautions

During the application of circular- pushing manipulation, the contacted area of the thumb should be flat and stable, together with media substances like scallion juice and herbal juice.

Circular-pushing manipulation is often used as a tonifying method, selected according to the pathological conditions of children.

Separating-pushing Manipulation (*fēn tuī fǎ*, 分推法)

It is a kind of pushing movement from the point center to bilateral sides with radial sides or both thumb balls, or fingertips of both index fingers and middle fingers.

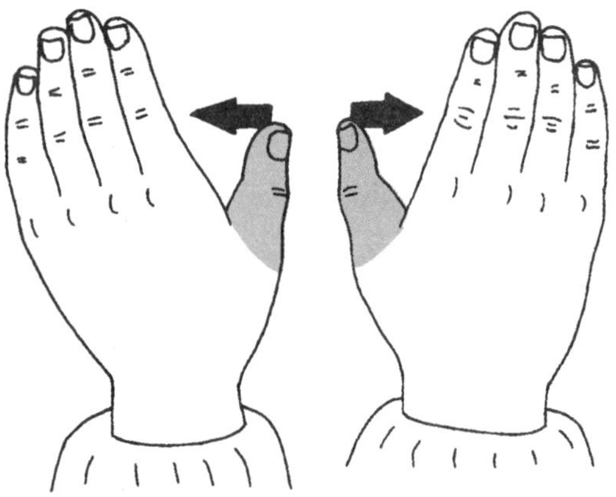

Fig. 7-3 Separating-pushing manipulation (*fēn tuī fǎ*, 分推法)

1. Manipulation

Do pushing movement from the middle to opposite directions with radial sides or both thumb balls, or fingertips of both index fingers and middle fingers, or do pushing movement in shape of Chinese character "八" (Fig. 7-3).

2. Essential Movements

The strength of pushing movement to the sides should be even, gentle, swift and harmonious.

Do manipulation in a straight line or an arc line along the body surface, 30~50 times continuously in all.

3. Precautions

Separating-pushing manipulation in a straight line should be even and steady; it is forbidden to push and press heavily.

Mediums like talcum powder, sachet, or shallot, ginger juice are suggested to prevent skin injury on children.

Inward-pushing Manipulation (*hé tuī fǎ*, 合推法)

It is a kind of pushing movement starting from sides of the point to the middle with the thumbs or the palms of both hands.

1. Manipulation

Stretching the thumbs of both hands from the other fingers, effect pushing movement from the sides of the point to the middle with the of thumb balls or palms (Fig. 7-4).

2. Essentials of Movements

The movement of inward-pushing manipulation is similar to that of separating-pushing manipulation, but different in direction (opposite) and amplitude (smaller).

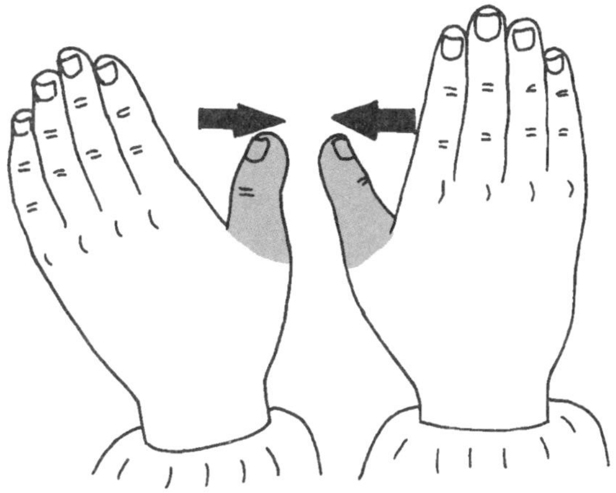

Fig. 7-4 Inward-pushing manipulation (*hé tuī fǎ*, 合推法)

3. Precautions

During the application of inward-pushing manipulation, the exerted strength should be even and steady.

Mediums like talcum powder, sachet, or shallot, ginger juice is suggested to prevent skin injury on children.

Kneading

It is one of the frequently used manipulations in pediatric tui na, a kind of clockwise or counterclockwise rotating movement with the thumb ball, middle finger or thenar area fixed on the operated area or certain points. The manipulation can be classified into middle finger-kneading manipulation (*zhǐ róu fǎ*, 指揉法), palm root-kneading manipulation (*zhǎng gēn róu fǎ*, 掌根揉法) and thenar-kneading manipulation (*yú jì róu fǎ*, 鱼际揉法) according to different operating areas.

1. Manipulation

a. Middle finger-kneading manipulation (*zhǐ róu fǎ*, 指揉法)

Fix the fingertips of index finger, middle finger and ring finger, or thumb tip and middle finger tip on the area or the point; do gentle rotating movements in a small amplitude to make subcutaneous tissues move together. It can be further classified into thumb-kneading manipulation (*mǔ zhǐ róu fǎ*, 拇指揉法), middle finger-kneading manipulation (*zhōng zhǐ róu fǎ*, 中指揉法), index and middle fingers-kneading manipulation (*shí zhǐ zhōng zhǐ róu fǎ*, 食指中指揉法) and three fingers-kneading manipulation (*sān zhǐ róu fǎ*, 三指揉法).

b. Palm root-kneading manipulation (*zhǎng gēn róu fǎ*, 掌根揉法)

Put the palm root on the area with the wrist relaxed and slightly pressed downward. Taking the elbow joint as the supporting point, the forearm does an active movement to lead the palm root kneading in small circles gently.

c. Thenar-kneading manipulation (*yú jì róu fǎ*, 鱼际揉法)

Put the great thenar on the operated area with the relaxed wrist; the forearm does active movement swiftly and gently to lead the local skin moving in circles through wrist joint.

2. Essential Movement

Relax the shoulder, elbow and wrist joints and naturally extend the fingers.

The strength of the kneading movement should be constant, even, coordinated with regular rhythm to achieve the purpose of rotating smoothly and moving orderly.

The amplitude of the kneading movement should be from small to large; the force is from gentle to strong; the direction can be clockwise or counterclockwise, and slow shifting, 200~300 times /min.

3. Precautions

The manipulation should be light and soft on fixed point without any pulling or scrubbing movement on the local area.

It is forbidden to have any forceful pressing movement in kneading manipulation.

Pressing

It is a downward pressing movement with gradually increased force on the local area or point with the finger or palm, classified into finger-pressing manipulation (*zhǐ àn fǎ*, 指按法) and palm-pressing manipulation (*zhǎng àn fǎ*, 掌按法) according to operating areas.

1. Manipulation

a. Palm-pressing manipulation (*zhǎng àn fǎ*, 掌按法)

Stretch the wrist joint dorsally with five fingers naturally extended. Press the local area with palm or palm root for a few minutes, the strength should be exerted downward perpendicularly; after that, release the hands and do downward pressing movement with gradually increased strength again. Repeat the manipulation a few times.

b. Finger-pressing manipulation (*zhǐ àn fǎ*, 指按法)

Press downward perpendicularly by taking the thumb ball and middle fingertips as operating unit. The movement is similar to that of palm- pressing manipulation.

2. Essential Movement

Sink qi in *Dantian* and breathe naturally, avoid holding the breath.

Do pressing stably without any pulling; increase the strength gradually.

3. Precautions

Keep the pressing on the local area for a few minutes; it is not advisable to release the hands suddenly, forbidden are rough and violent movements.

Press a larger area when palm- pressing manipulation is applied, the pressure should be slightly stronger with mild and slow stimulation.

Press a smaller area when finger-pressing manipulation is applied, the stimulation should be gentle and soft.

Rubbing

Move the wrist joint and forearm in circles clockwise or counterclockwise to lead the rubbing movement of palm or the index fingertip, middle finger and ring finger tips on the local area and point.

1. Manipulation

a. Palm-rubbing manipulation (*zhǎng mó fǎ*, 掌摩法)

Extend palm and fingers naturally and make wrist joint stretched slightly toward dorsal side. Put the palm on the operated area to exert strength. Relax the wrist joint and move the forearm actively to lead the wrist joint and hand moving in circles clockwise or counterclockwise.

b. Finger-rubbing manipulation (*zhǐ mó fǎ*, 指摩法)

Extend and close the index, middle, ring and little fingers together; flex and suspend the wrist joint slightly; move the forearm actively to lead the fingers rubbing in circles by the fingertips fingers exerting strength on the local area or point.

2. Essentials of Movements

Relax the shoulder, elbow and wrist joints with the elbow joint slightly flexed.

Relax wrist joint and extend the palm naturally; slightly flex and suspend the wrist joint with metacarpophalangeal joints slightly bended.

Release the strength naturally with slow and harmonious movements. The frequency of rubbing is 120~160 times/ min.

3. Precautions

During the operation, avoid pulling subcutaneous tissues.

The fingers should perform a rubbing movement in circles as the manipulation requires, not a tapping or knocking movement.

Nipping

It is a kind of strong clutching movement on the point or certain areas with the nail.

1. Manipulation

Make a hollow fist with the thumb extended, put thumb nail on the operated point or area to press and irritate the point with gradually increased strength (Fig. 7-5).

2. Essential Movements

Exert the strength perpendicularly and increase the intensity gradually, or intermittently to increase the stimulation. The location of the point should be accurate.

The operation is usually given 4~5 times or stopped immediately as soon as the disease improves. It is not advisable to offer this manipulation repeatedly for long time. If the manipulation performs for emergency cases, the strength should exert suddenly; repeat the manipulation until the child awakes.

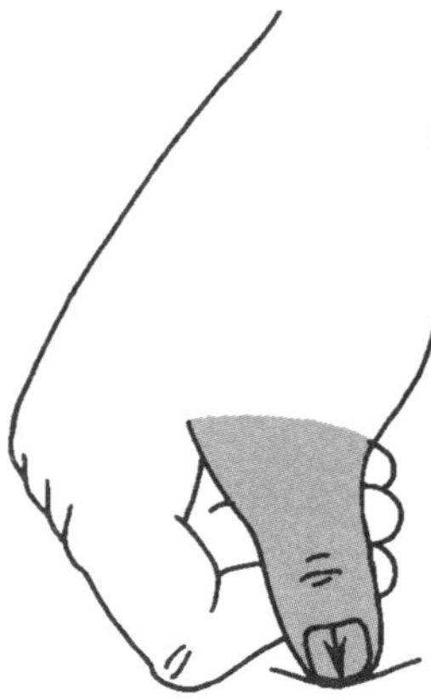

Fig. 7-5 Nipping manipulation (*qiā fǎ*, 掐法)

3. Precautions

Nipping manipulation is one of the manipulations with strong stimulation; not available for long time of repeated application. It is better to place a piece of cloth over the operated area to avoid injury of the skin. Kneading manipulation is often done after nipping manipulation to diminish stimulation and reduce local pain or discomfort.

Pinching

Compress the skin or limb of the child with thumb and index, middle and ring fingers with symmetric strength like alternation of lifting and grasping movements.

1. Manipulation

For children, pinching along the spine is taken as the main manipulation.

a. Three fingers-pinching manipulation (*sān zhǐ niē*, 三指捏)

Push the skin with the thumb ball, the index and middle fingers press the skin in front of the thumb, the three fingers perform a lifting and grasping movement together with symmetric strength. Two hands squeeze the skin alternately, grasping and releasing to move forward (Fig. 7-6).

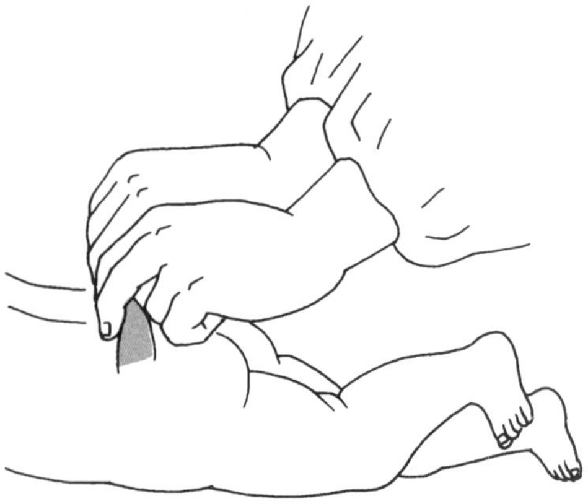

Fig. 7-6 Three fingers-pinching manipulation (*sān zhǐ niē*, 三指捏)

b. Two fingers-pinching manipulation (*liǎng zhǐ niē*, 两指捏)

Flex the index finger with radial side of middle segment against skin. The thumb presses the skin in the front of thumb. Two fingers perfom a lifting and grasping movements with symmetric strength and two hands shift forward alternately (Fig. 7-7).

2. Essential Movements

The forearm releases static strength, the wrist joint moves to lead the metacarpophalangeal joints twisting continuously, swiftly and lightly.

Do manipulations in the order of pinching, lifting, twisting and pushing the skin. Repeat the movements along this order continuously.

Shift the hand slowly with gentle force, agility movement and even rhythm.

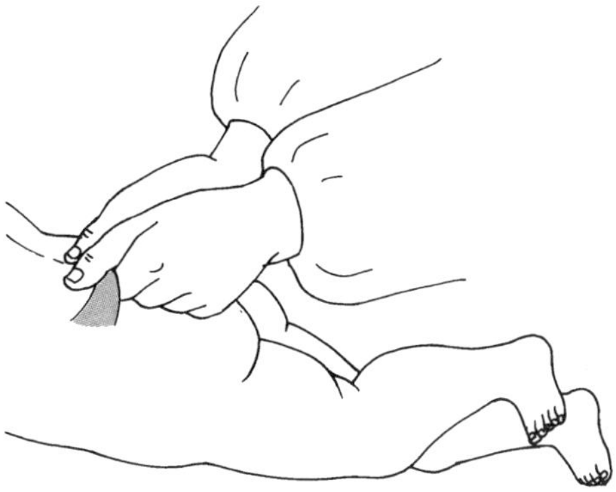

Fig. 7-7 Two fingers-pinching manipulation (*liǎng zhǐ niē*, 两指捏)

3. Precautions

Do the movements continuously without intermittance but with appropriate force when pinch and grasp the skin.

Don't screw, nip and press the skin by nails while pinching. The hands shift forward along a straight line.

Transporting Manipulation (*yùn fǎ*, 运法)

Transporting manipulation is a kind of pushing movement along an arc or in circles from one point to another with thumb ball or middle finger.

1. Manipulation

Put the thumb ball or middle finger gently on the operated area to do pushing movement along an arc from one point to another or in circles around a point continuously (Fig. 7-8).

2. Essential Movements

Stretch the wrist naturally with the thumb straightened, the other fingers flexed and the web margin between the thumb and index finger flat. Exert the strength with the radial side of thumb tip, or with middle finger tip when thumb, index, ring and little fingers flexed.

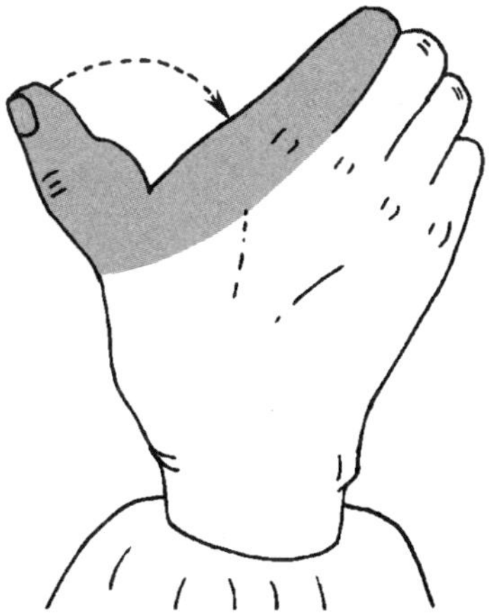

Fig. 7-8 Transporting manipulation (*yùn fǎ*, 运法)

The movement of metacarpophalangeal joint or wrist joint leads the thumb and middle finger tip shifting along an arc or in circles.

The manipulation should be gentle like soft rubbing on the skin surface during the operation. The frequency is 80~120 times /min generally.

3. Precautions

Don't influence deep muscular tissues. Transporting manipulation is lighter than pushing manipulation and rubbing manipulation.

Use lubricants as medium during the operation to protect the skin of children.

Pounding Manipulation (*dǎo fǎ*, 捣法)

Pounding manipulation is to strike the point in rhythm with tip of the middle finger or interphalangeal joints of the flexed index and middle fingers.

1. Manipulation

The striking of fingertip should be elastic, 5~20 times generally. Raise the fingertip right after striking (Fig. 7-9).

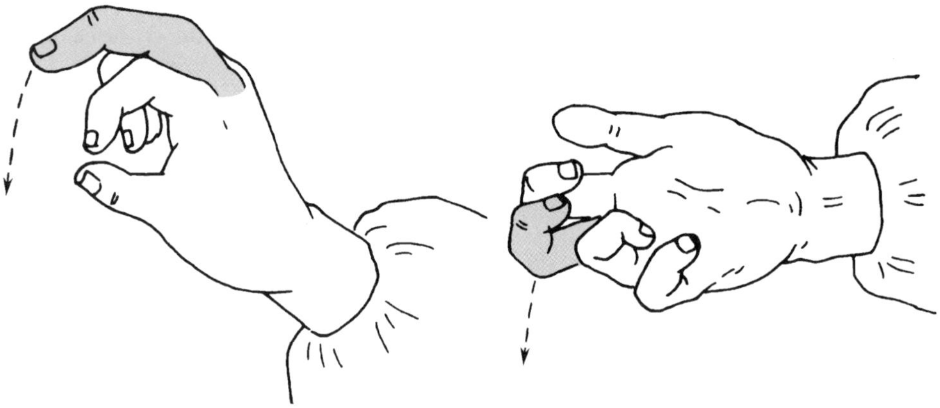

Fig. 7-9 Pounding manipulation (*dǎo fǎ*, 捣法)

2. Precautions

Relax interphalangeal joints, the flexion and extension of wrist joint is active movement.

The area for pounding should be accurate. The movement should be elastic.

Don't do pounding violently. Cut the fingernails before the treatment to prevent skin injury to the children.

Section 2
Compound Manipulations of Pediatric Tui Na Therapy

Wasps Going into the Honeycomb (*Huáng Fēng Rù Dòng*, 黄蜂入洞)

1. Manipulation

Support the head of child with one hand to fix the head, and put the tips of index and middle fingers on the lower border of the nostrils. The wrist joint moves actively to lead the fingertip, knead the points 50~100 times (Fig. 7-10).

2. Action

To induce sweating, release the exterior, ventilate lung and remove obstruction from the nose.

To treat fever due to invasion of exogenous wind-cold with absence of sweating, nasal congestion and unsmooth breathing in both acute and chronic rhinitis.

Scrubbing and Rubbing like Pressing String (*Àn Xián Zǒu Cuō Mó*, 按弦走搓摩)

1. Manipulation

Keep the child in sitting position or ask the parent to embrace the child sitting in his or her arms. Put the palms on bilateral hypochondriac regions of the child to apply symmetric scrubbing movement downward to the angle of belly 100~200 times (Fig. 7-11).

Fig. 7-10 Wasps going into honeycomb (*huáng fēng rù dòng*, 黄蜂入洞)

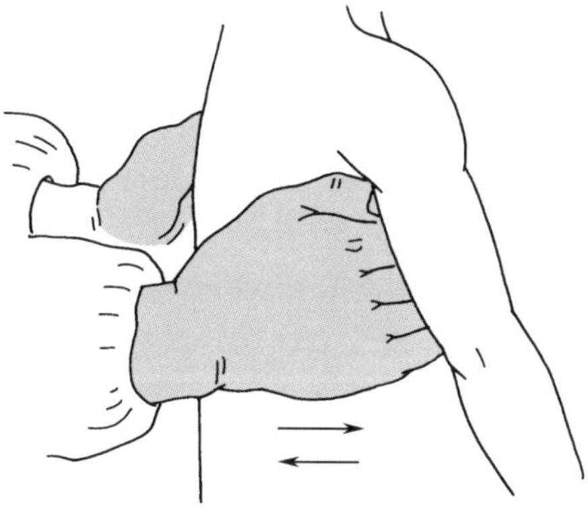

Fig. 7-11 Scrubbing and rubbing like pressing string (*àn xián zǒu cuō mó*, 按弦走搓摩)

2. Action

To regulate qi, resolve phlegm, strengthen the spleen and promote digestion.

To treat phlegm accumulation, discomfort in the chest and hypochondrium, cough, dyspnea, abdominal pain and distention, food retention.

Scooping the Moon up from The Water (*Shuǐ Dǐ Lāo Yuè*, 水底捞月)

1. Manipulation

Keep the child in sitting position or supine position. Hold four fingers of the child with left hand, drip cold water on *nèi láo gōng* (内劳宫) with the right hand. Do pushing and transporting manipulation with the tip of the middle finger which was dipped in water from the root of little finger to *nèi láo gōng* (内劳宫), via *zhǎng xiǎo héng wén* (掌小横纹) and *kǎn gōng* (坎宫); blow on the child's palm to cool it while doing manipulation (Fig. 7-12).

2. Action

This manipulation, cold in nature, acts to clear heat, cool blood, calm the mind and eliminate restlessness, usually used to treat excess syndromes manifesting unconsciousness due to high fever, disturbance of nutrient blood by heat, restlessness and constipation.

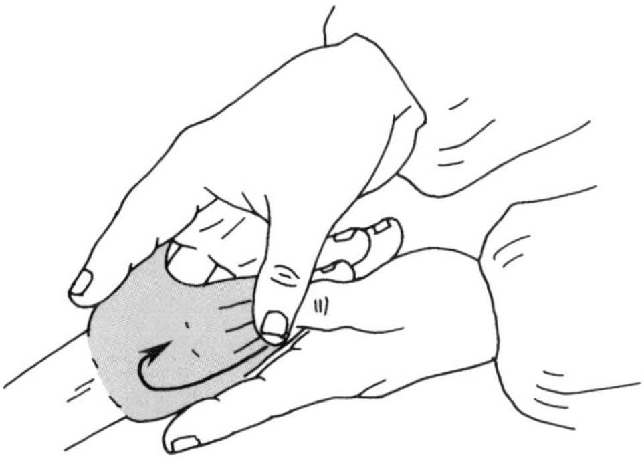

Fig. 7-12 Scooping the moon up from the water (*shuǐ dǐ lāo yuè*, 水底捞月)

Crossing the Heaven River On Horseback (*Dǎ Mǎ Guò Tiān Hé*, 打马过天河)

1. Manipulation

Keep the child in sitting position or supine position. Hold four fingers of the child to make the palm upward with one hand. After doing transporting manipulation on *nèi láo gōng* (内劳宫) with the tip of middle finger of another hand, tap and flick the child's forearm from *zǒng jīn* (总筋) to *hóng chí xuè* (洪池穴) along *tiān hé shuǐ* (天河水) with the fingertips of index and middle fingers dipped in water, 20~30 times all together. Blow on the arm to cool it while tapping and flicking the arm (Fig. 7-13).

2. Action

To clear heat, cool blood and dredge collaterals, usually used to treat excessive heat syndromes manifesting high fever, dysphoria, unconsciousness, delirium, numbness and convulsion of upper limbs.

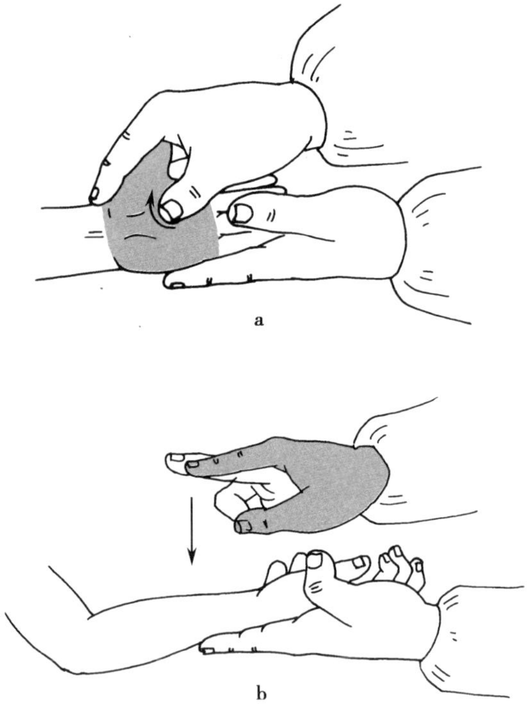

Fig. 7-13 Crossing the heaven river on horseback (*dá mǎ guò tiān hé*, 打马过天河)

Transporting Earth into Water (*Yùn Tǔ Rù Shuǐ*, 运土入水)

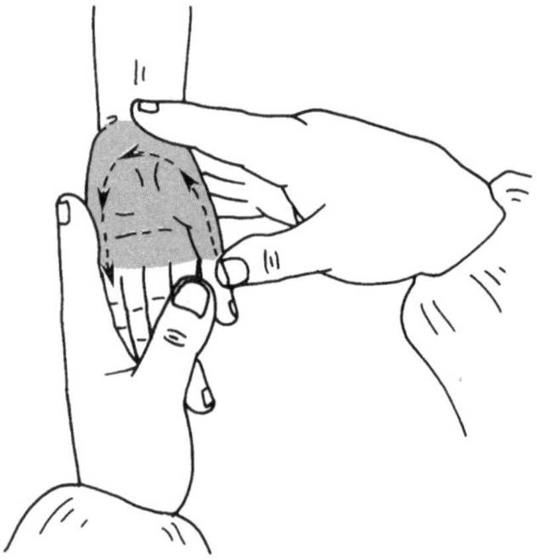

Fig. 7-14 Transporting earth into water (*yùn tǔ rù shuǐ*, 运土入水)

1. Manipulation

Hold the child's four fingers to make the palm upward with the left hand. Perform pushing and transporting manipulation from the root of the thumb to the root of the little finger, via *xiǎo tiān xīn* (小天心) and *zhǎng xiǎo héng wén* (掌小横纹), with the tip of the right thumb along in a one-way direction repeatedly for 100~300 times (Fig. 7-14).

2. Action

To clear damp-heat from the spleen and stomach, benefit urination, check diarrhea and tonify kidney water, usually used to treat frequent and hesitant urination with dark yellow urine, lower abdominal distention and diarrhea.

Transporting Water into Earth (*Yùn Shuǐ Rù Tǔ*, 运水入土)

1. Manipulation

Keep the child in sitting or supine position. Hold the child's four fingers to make the palm upward with left hand. Perform pushing and transporting manipulation from the root of the little finger to the root of the thumb, via *zhǎng xiǎo héng wén* (掌小横纹) and *xiǎo tiān xīn* (小天心), with the tip of the right thumb along in a one-way direction repeatedly for 100~300 times (Fig. 7-15).

2. Action

To strengthen the spleen, benefit transportation and transformation of food, moisten dryness and promote bowel movement, usually used to treat indigestion, anorexia, constipation, abdominal distension and diarrhea due to weakness of spleen and stomach.

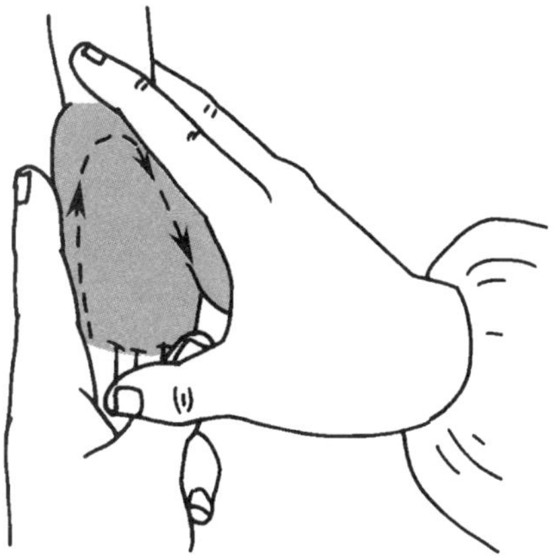

Fig. 7-15 Transporting water into earth (*yùn shuǐ rù tǔ*, 运水入土)

Section 3
Specific Points for Infants

Specific points of infants imply points used only for infants. They have locations like "point", but also like "route" and "facet". Mostly, these specific points are located on the hands and area below the elbow. Unlike the points of fourteen channels, these specific points are plain without theoretic system. To facilitate the study and application, the times of operation recommended in the book are for infants between 6 months to one year old, as reference in clinical application. There should be determined according to the age and body constitution of infants and severity of disease in clinic. As a habit, the left hand of the child is taken as an operated hand when the specific points on the upper limb are manipulated, no matter whether a boy or girl. Usually, the operation for infant starts from the head and face, then upper limbs, chest and abdomen, lumbar area and back to lower limbs at last. This order can be also determined flexibly according to the condition of disease and the posture of the infant during the treatment.

Kǎn gōng (坎宫)

1. Location

The transverse line from the medial end to the lateral end of the eyebrow.

2. Manipulation

Apply separating-pushing manipulation from the medial ends of the eyebrows to the lateral ends with both thumbs; it is called pushing *kǎn gōng* (坎宫) (Fig. 7-16). Do the manipulation 50~100 times.

3. Action

To disperse wind, release the exterior, resuscitate the consciousness, sharpen the vision and relieve headache.

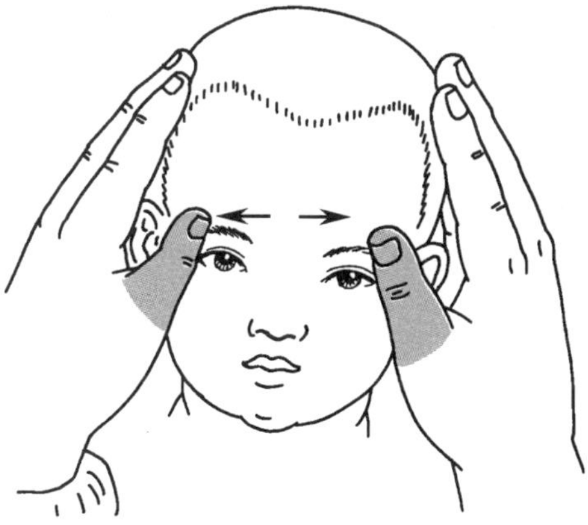

Fig. 7-16 Pushing *kǎn gōng* (坎宫)

4. Indication

Headache due to external pathogens, fever, redness and pain of eyes, infantile convulsion, myopia.

5. Application

It is often applied together with manipulations of pushing BL 2 (*cuán zhú*), kneading *tài yáng* (太阳) for fever and headache due to external pathogens; together with the manipulations of clearing *gān jīng* (肝经), nipping and kneading *xiǎo tiān xīn* (小天心) and clearing *tiān hé shuǐ* (天河水) for redness and pain of eyes.

Tiān mén (天门)

1. Location

The vertical line from the midpoint between the eyebrows to the anterior hairline.

2. Manipulation

Apply pushing manipulation from the midpoint between the eyebrows to the midpoint of anterior hairline with the thumb balls alternately, it is also called pushing BL 2 (*cuán zhú*) (Fig. 7-17). Repeat the manipulation 50~100 times.

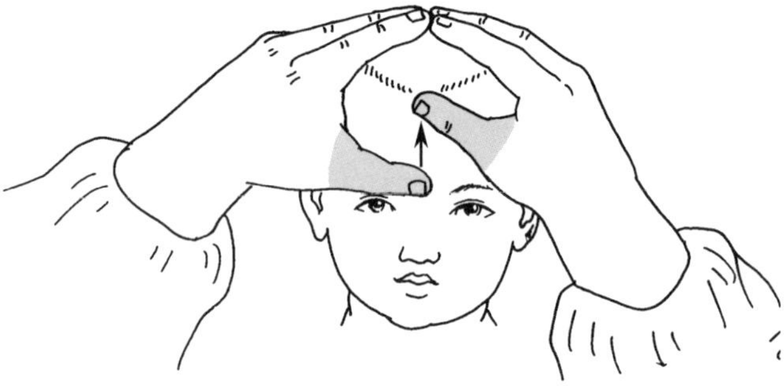

Fig. 7-17 Pushing *tiān mén* (天门)

3. Action

To induce sweating, release the exterior, sedate and calm the mind and open the orifices.

4. Indication

Headache, common cold, vertigo, night crying and insomnia.

5. Application

Together with the manipulation of pushing *kǎn gōng* (坎宫) and kneading *tài yáng* (太阳), it is often used for common cold due to wind-cold, headache, absence of sweating and fever; together with the manipulation of clearing *gān jīng* (肝经), pounding *xiǎo tiān xīn* (小天心), nipping and kneading *wǔ zhǐ jié* (五指节) and kneading DU 20 (*bǎi huì*) for fright and restlessness.

Tài yáng (太阳)

1. Location

In the depression posterior to the eyebrow.

2. Manipulation

Kneading the point with tip of middle finger or thumb is called kneading *tài yáng* (太阳) or transporting *tài yáng* (太阳). Do kneading manipulation toward the eye is considered as reinforcing method and kneading toward the ear is considered as reducing method. Do pushing manipulation backward straight with radial side of the thumb is called pushing *tài yáng* (太阳). The manipulation is done repeatedly 50~100 times each (Fig. 7-18).

3. Action

To release the exterior, sharpen the vision and relieve headache.

4. Indication

Headache, vertigo, common cold, fever, redness and pain of eyes.

5. Application

Reducing method is applied for headache appearing in exterior syndrome of excess type; reinforcing method for headache in exterior syndrome of deficiency type and headache due to internal injury. The manipulation of pushing *tài yáng* (太阳) is mainly used for fever in exterior syndrome.

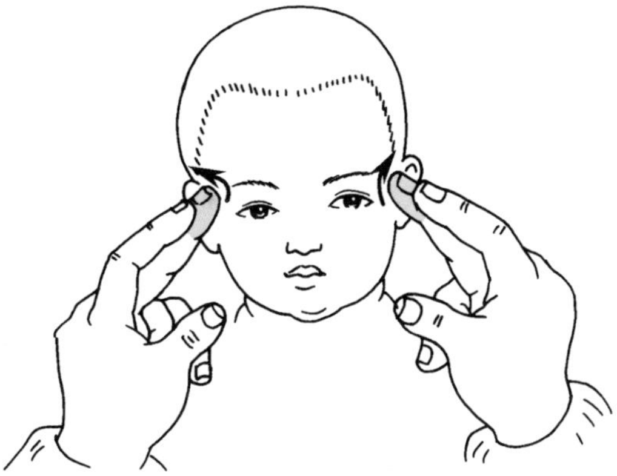

Fig. 7-18 Kneading *tài yáng* (太阳)

Ěr hòu gāo gǔ (耳后高骨)

1. Location

In the depression inferior to the mastoid process behind the ear, and superior to the posterior hairline.

2. Manipulation

Kneading the point with the tips of the thumbs or middle fingers is called kneading *ěr hòu gāo gǔ* (耳后高骨) (Fig. 7-19). Repeat the manipulation 50~100 times.

3. Action

To disperse wind, release the exterior, calm the mind and relieve restlessness.

4. Indication

Headache, dysphoria, common cold, etc.

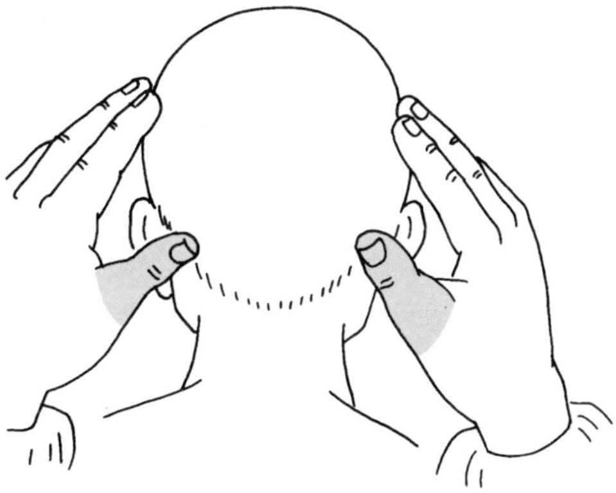

Fig. 7-19 Kneading *ěr hòu gāo gǔ* (耳后高骨)

5. Application

Together with the manipulation of pushing *tiān mén* (天门), *kǎn gōng* (坎宫) and kneading *tài yáng* (太阳), it is often used to treat headache due to common cold (wind-cold type in exterior excess syndrome). These four manipulations are taken as four major pediatric tui na manipulations.

Tiān zhù gǔ (天柱骨)

1. Location

The vertical line from the midpoint of the posterior hairline to Du 14 (*dà zhuī*).

2. Manipulation

Pushing the point straight downward with thumb ball or the surface of last segments of index and middle fingers is called pushing *tiān zhù gǔ* (天柱骨) (Fig. 7-20). Repeat the manipulation 100~500 times.

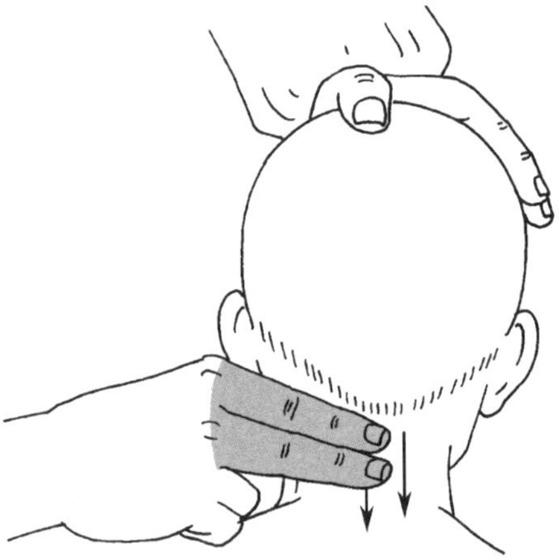

Fig. 7-20 Pushing *tiān zhù gǔ* (天柱骨)

3. Action

To pacify adverse qi, stop vomiting, dispel wind and disperse cold.

4. Indication

Nausea, vomiting, common cold, fever, sore throat and rigidity of neck.

5. Application

For vomiting and nausea, the manipulation is often coordinated with the manipulations of pushing manipulation from *héng wén* (横纹) to *bǎn mén* (板门) and kneading RN 12 (*zhōng wǎn*). For fever due to invasion of exogenous pathogens, rigidity and pain of the nape, it is commonly used together with the manipulation of grasping GB 20 (*fēng chí*), nipping and kneading *èr shàn mén* (二扇门).

Rǔ páng (乳旁)

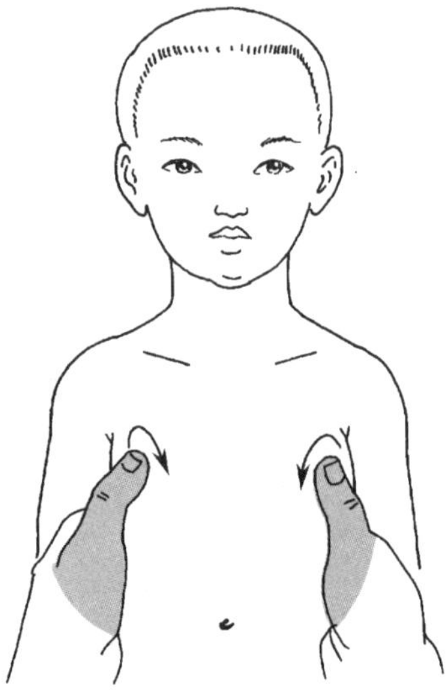

Fig. 7-21 Kneading *rǔ páng* (乳旁)

1. Location

0.2 cun lateral to the breast.

2. Manipulation

Kneading the point with the tip of middle finger is called kneading *rǔ páng* (乳旁) (Fig. 7-21). Repeat the manipulation 100~200 times.

3. Action

Ease the chest, regulate qi, stop cough and resolve phlegm.

4. Indication

Stuffiness in the chest, gurgling with sputum, cough and vomiting.

5. Application

Clinically, the manipulations of ST 18 (*rǔ gēn*)and *rǔ páng* (乳旁) are often used in combination with the tips of index and middle fingers.

Rǔ gēn (乳根)

1. Location

0.2 cun below the breast.

2. Manipulation

Kneading the point with the tip of middle finger is called kneading ST 18 (*rǔ gēn*) (Fig. 7-22). Repeat the manipulation 100~200 times.

3. Action

To ease the chest, regulate qi, stop cough and resolve phlegm.

4. Indication

Stuffiness in the chest, cough, wheezing and chest pain.

5. Application

As same as that of *rǔ páng* (乳旁).

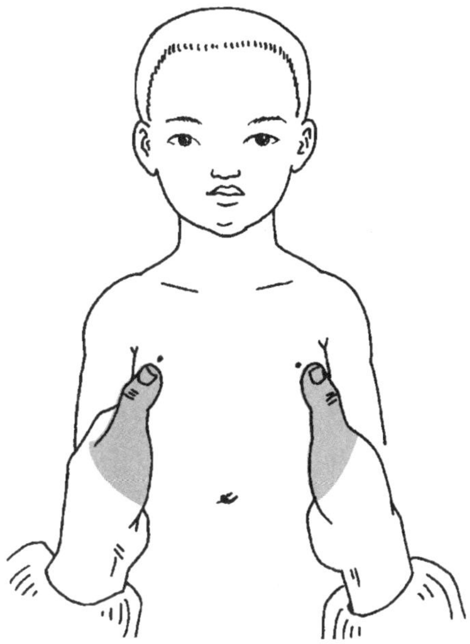

Fig. 7-22 Kneading ST 18 (*rǔ gēn*, 乳根)

Xié lèi (胁肋)

1. Location

Hypochondriac regions from axillary line to ST 25 (*tiān shū*).

2. Manipulation

Rubbing the hypochondriac regions with both palms from axillary line to ST 25 (*tiān shū*) is called scrubbing and rubbing *xié lèi* (胁肋), also named scrubbing and rubbing like pressing string (*àn xián zǒu cuō mó*, 按弦走搓摩) (Fig. 7-11). Repeat the manipulation100~200 times.

3. Action

To normalize qi, resolve phlegm and eliminate chest stuffiness.

4. Indication

Stuffiness in chest, wheezing with sputum, shortness of breath, hypochondriac pain, etc.

5. Application

The point is characterized by opening and descending. It is often used for infantile food retention and phlegm accumulation, chest stuffiness and abdominal distention due to adverse qi.

Fù (腹)

1. Location

Abdomen

2. Manipulation

Pushing along the border of costal arch, or separating-pushing from RN 12 (*zhōng wǎn*) and the umbilicus to the sides of the abdomen is called separating-pushing abdomen (*fēn tuī fù yin yang*, 分推腹阴阳). Rubbing the abdomen with the palm or four fingers is called rubbing abdomen (*mó fù*, 摩腹). Repeat separating-pushing abdomen for 100~200 times, rubbing abdomen for 5 minutes (Fig. 7-23).

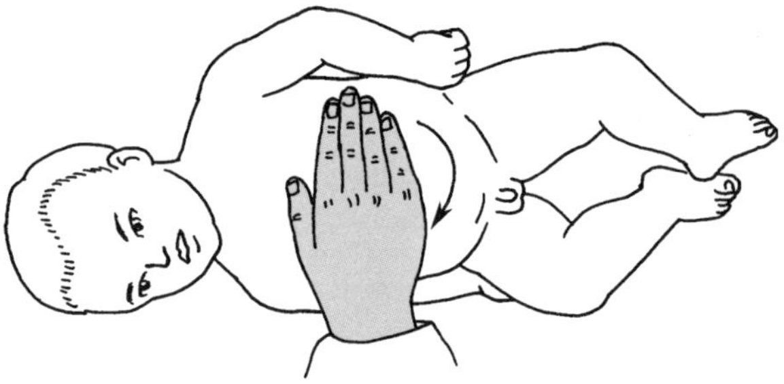

Fig. 7-23 Rubbing abdomen (*mó fù*, 摩腹)

3. Action

To strengthen the spleen, normalize the stomach, regulate qi and promote digestion.

4. Indication

Diarrhea, abdominal distension and pain, constipation, nausea and vomiting.

5. Application

For excessive syndromes like infantile diarrhea, constipation, abdominal distension and anorexia, rub and knead abdomen clockwise (reducing method); for deficient syndromes like diarrhea due to spleen deficiency, rub and knead abdomen counterclockwise (reinforcing method). The manipulation of rubbing abdomen is often combined with the manipulation of pinching spine and kneading ST 36 (*zú sān lǐ*). For vomiting due to indigestion, the manipulation of separating-pushing abdomen is taken as the main together with pushing manipulation from *héng wén* (横纹) to *bǎn mén* (板门) and pushing *tiān zhù gǔ* (天柱骨). In addition, the point is often used for general healthcare of the infant.

Qí (脐)

1. Location

Umbilicus

2. Manipulation

Apply rubbing manipulation on the umbilicus with finger or palm is called rubbing umbilicus (*mó qí*, 摩脐); apply kneading manipulation on the umbilicus with tip of thumb or middle finger is called kneading umbilicus (*róu qí*, 揉脐) (Fig. 7-24). Repeat the kneading manipulation 100~300 times and rubbing manipulation 5 minutes.

3. Action

Counterclockwise rubbing and kneading can warm yang, disperse cold, tonify qi and blood; clockwise operation can benefit digestion, eliminate food retention and promote bowel movement.

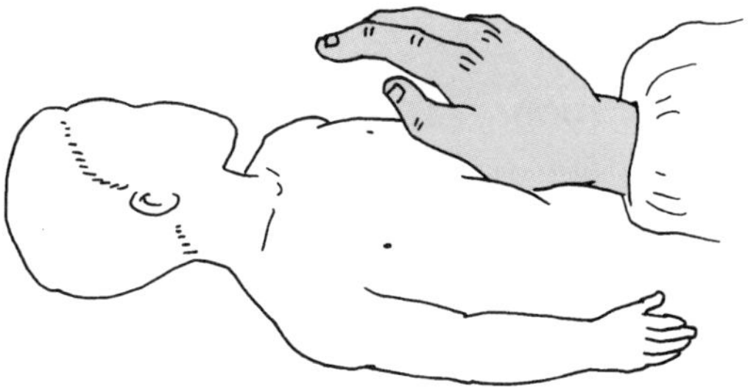

Fig. 7-24 Kneading umbilicus (*róu qí*, 揉脐)

4. Indication

Abdominal pain, constipation, abdominal distension, food retention and diarrhea, etc.

5. Application

Clinically, the manipulation of kneading umbilicus is often used together with manipulations of rubbing abdomen, pushing *qī jié gǔ* (七节骨) and kneading *guī wěi* (龟尾) to treat diarrhea. Counterclockwise rubbing and kneading umbilicus is effective for deficiency and cold syndromes such as pediatric diarrhea, borborygmus and abdominal pain; clockwise rubbing and kneading umbilicus is good for excess syndromes such as pediatric constipation and abdominal distention.

Dān tián (丹田)

1. Location

On the lower abdomen (2 or 3 cun below the umbilicus).

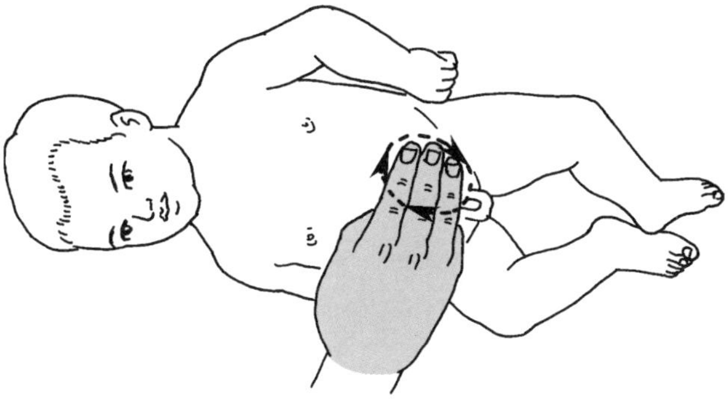

Fig. 7-25 Rubbing *dān tián* (丹田)

2. Manipulation

Kneading or rubbing the point is respectively called kneading *dān tián* (丹田)or rubbing *dān tián* (丹田) (Fig. 7-25). Repeat kneading *dān tián* (丹田)50~100 times or rubbing *dān tián* (丹田) 5 minutes.

3. Action

To strengthen the kidney to stabilize the root, warm and tonify kidney qi, separate the clear from the tubid.

4. Indication

Enuresis, abdominal pain, etc.

5. Application

It is often used to treat congenital deficiency, cold accumulation in the lower abdomen, abdominal pain and enuresis, together with the manipulations of reinforcing *shèn jīng* (肾经), pushing *sān guān* (三关) and kneading SJ 5 (*wài guān*).

Dù jiǎo (肚角)

1. Location

The large tendons 2 cun lateral to the umbilicus.

2. Manipulation

Grasping the large tendon 2 cun lateral to the umbilicus with the thumb, index and middle fingers is called grasping *dù jiǎo* (肚角) (Fig. 7-26). Pressing the tendon with the tip of the middle finger is called pressing *dù jiǎo* (肚角). Repeat the manipulation 3~5 times.

3. Action

To relieve abdominal pain.

4. Indication

Abdominal pain and diarrhea.

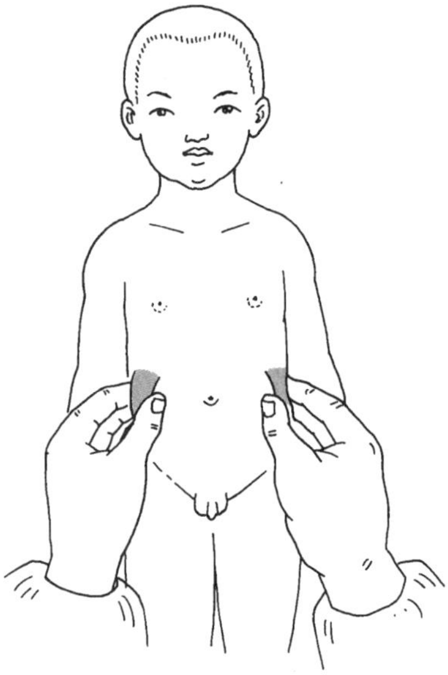

Fig. 7-26 Grasping *dù jiǎo* (肚角)

5. Application

It is effective for abdominal pain due to various factors, especially good for cold pain and abdominal pain due to improper food intake. To avoid crying which often influences treatment the manipulation of grasping *dù jiǎo* (肚角) can be done at the end of treatment after the other manipulations.

Fèi shù (肺俞)

1. Location

1.5 cun lateral to lower border of the spinous process of the third thoracic vertebra.

2. Manipulation

Kneading the point with tips of index and middle fingers of one hand or two thumbs is called kneading BL 13 (*fèi shù*); pushing downward along medial borders of the scapulas with tips of two thumbs is called pushing BL 13 (*fèi shù*) or separating-pushing scapulars (*fēn tuī jiān jiǎ gǔ*, 分推肩胛骨). Repeat kneading manipulation 50~100times; sideward–pushing manipulation 100~300 times (Fig. 7-27).

3. Action

The manipulation of separating-pushing scapulas can descend lung qi, stop cough and shortness of breath; kneading BL 13 (*fèi shù*) can regulate lung qi and tonify deficiency.

4. Indication

Cough, asthma, chest stuffiness, chest pain, gurgling with sputum, sore throat, common cold, fever and back pain, etc.

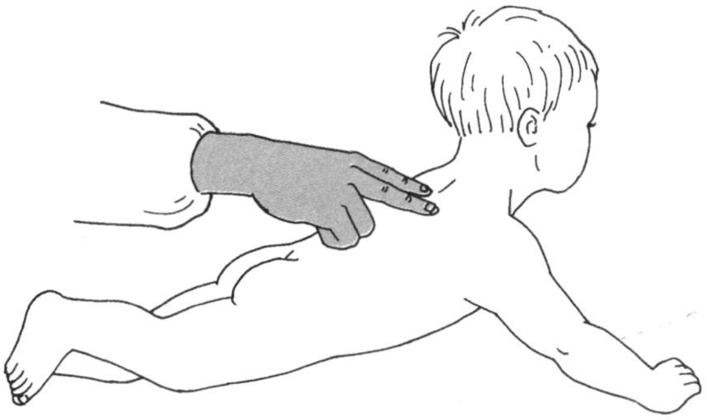

Fig. 7-27 (1) Kneading BL 13 (*fèi shù*)

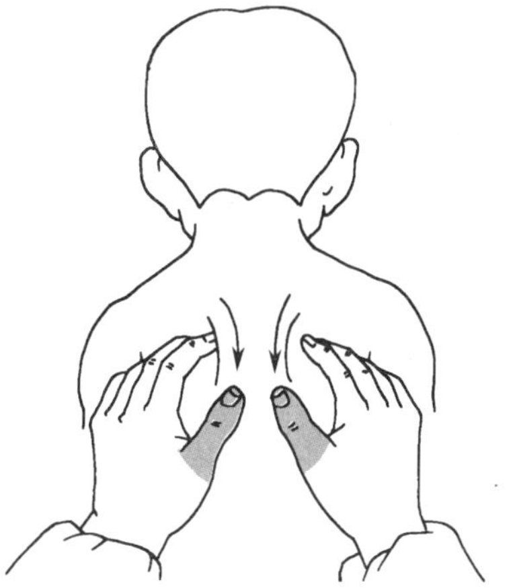

Fig. 7-27 (2) Pushing BL 13 (*fèi shù*)

5. Application

This point is often used for pediatric respiratory diseases, together with the manipulations of pushing and kneading RN 17 (*dàn zhōng*), kneading ST 18 (*rǔ gēn*) and *rǔ páng* (乳旁), pushing *fèi jīng* (肺经), moving *nèi bā guà* (内八卦), kneading RN 22 (*tiān tū*), kneading *zhǎng xiǎo héng wén* (掌小横纹) and pushing *xiǎo héng wén* (小横纹).

Jǐ zhù (脊柱)

1. Location

The straight line between DU 14 (*dà zhuī*) and DU 1 (*cháng qiáng*).

2. Manipulation

Pinching along the spine from the lower side to upper side is called pinching along the spine (*niē jǐ*, 捏脊) (Fig. 7-28); lifting the skin on the spine once after every 3 times of pinching is called the method of one lifting after three pinching (*niē sān tí yī fǎ*, 捏三提一法). Pushing the spine straight from upper side to lower side with the fingertips of index and middle fingers is called pushing the spine (*tuī jǐ*, 推脊) (Fig. 7-29). Repeat the manipulation of pushing the spine 100~300 times, the manipulation of pinching the spine 3~5 times along the spine.

3. Action

The manipulation of pinching along the spine can harmonize yin and yang, regulate qi and blood, normalize *zang-fu* organs, dredge channels and collaterals, strengthen original qi; the manipulation of pushing the spine can clear heat.

4. Indication

Diarrhea, abdominal pain, vomiting, constipation, fever and night crying, etc.

5. Application

The manipulation of pinching along the spine is one of the commonly used manipulations for

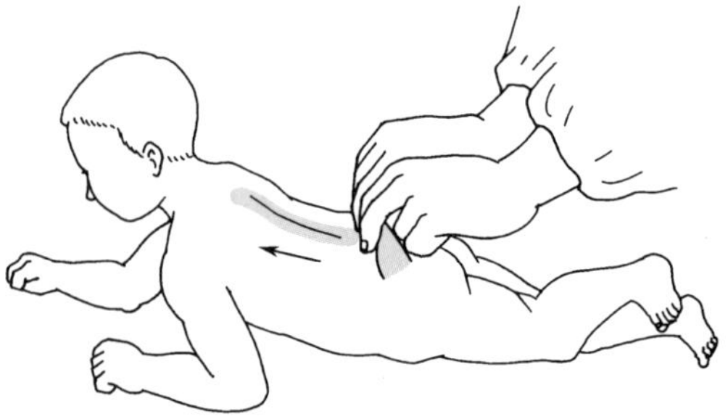

Fig. 7-28 Pinching along the spine (*niē jǐ*, 捏脊)

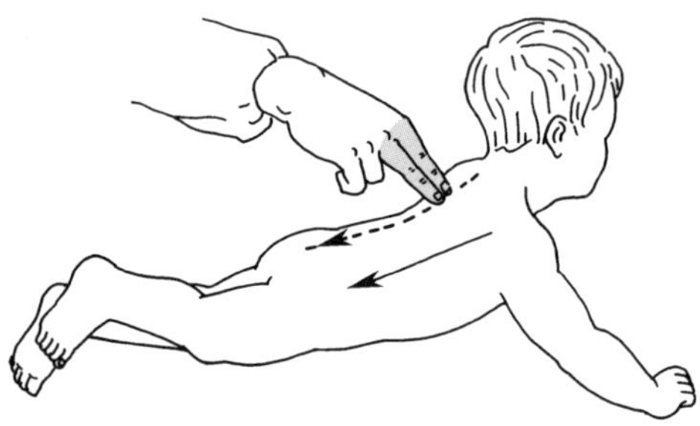

Fig. 7-29 Pushing the spine (*tuī jǐ*, 推脊)

child healthcare. Clinically, it is often used together with the manipulations of reinforcing *pí jīng* (脾经), reinforcing *shèn jīng* (肾经), pushing *sān guān* (三关), rubbing abdomen (*mó fù*, 摩腹), pressing and kneading ST 36 (*zú sān lǐ*) to treat all kinds of deficiency syndromes due to congenital deficiency and acquired insufficiency. If the treatment is given only with this manipulation, it would be called pinching-spine-therapy (*niē jǐ liáo fǎ*, 捏脊疗法).

The manipulation of pushing along the spine is often used for infantile fever, together with the manipulations of clearing *tiān hé shuǐ* (天河水), pushing *liù fǔ* (六腑) and KI 1 (*yǒng quán*).

Qī jié gǔ (七节骨)

1. Location

The straight line from the 4th lumbar vertebra to DU 1 (*cháng qiáng*).

2. Manipulation

Pushing along the spine upward or along the spine downward with the radial side of the thumb or the fingertips of the index and middle fingers is respectively called pushing *qī jié gǔ* upward (*tuī shàng qī jié gǔ*, 推上七节骨) and pushing *qī jié gǔ* downward (*tuī xià qī jié gǔ*, 推下七节骨) (Fig. 7-30). Repeat the manipulation 100~300 times.

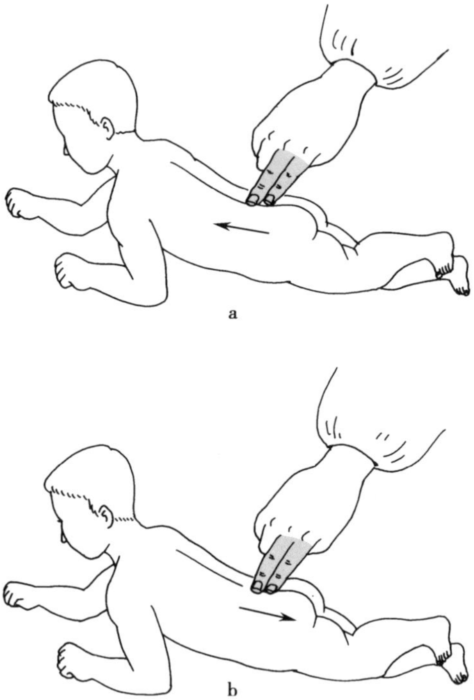

Fig. 7-30 Pushing *qī jié gǔ* (七节骨)

3. Action

To warm yang, check diarrhea, purge heat and promote bowel movement.

4. Indication

Diarrhea, constipation, fever, etc.

5. Application

The manipulation of pushing *qī jiē gǔ* (七节骨) upward is effective for warming yang to check diarrhea, commonly used for diarrhea and abdominal pain due to deficiency and cold. Clinically, it is often applied together with reinforcing *dà cháng* (大肠), pushing *sān guān* (三关), pressing and kneading DU 20 (*bǎi huì*) and kneading *dān tián* (丹田). It is not advisable to use this manipulation for diarrhea due to damp-heat, because it may cause abdominal distension or other problems in infants.

The manipulation of pushing *qī jié gǔ* (七节骨) downward acts to purge heat and induce defecation. It is often used for constipation due to retention of heat in the intestines and fever.

Guī wěi (龟尾)

1. Location

The end of the coccyx.

2. Manipulation

Kneading the point with the tip of thumb or middle finger is called kneading *guī wěi* (龟尾) (Fig. 7-31). Repeat the manipulation 100~300 times.

3. Action

To regulate large intestine.

4. Indication

Constipation, diarrhea, enuresis, etc.

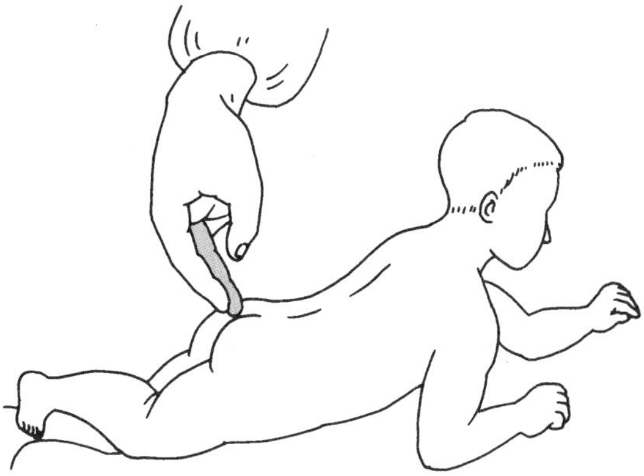

Fig. 7-31 Kneading *guī wěi* (龟尾)

5. Application

Guī wěi (龟尾) is just at the location of DU 1 (*cháng qiáng*). Kneading the point can regulate and dredge qi of governor vessel. The point, even in nature, can either check diarrhea or promote bowel movement. It is often used together with the manipulations of kneading umbilicus and pushing *qī jié gǔ* (七节骨) for diarrhea and constipation.

Pí jīng (脾经)

1. Location

The thumb ball, or the line from the tip to root on the radial border of thumb.

2. Manipulation

Bend child's thumb, pushing along the radial border of thumb to finger root is considered as reinforcing method, named reinforcing *pí jīng* (脾经) (Fig. 7-32), while pushing from the root of thumb to the tip is considered as clearing method, called clearing *pí jīng* (脾经). Repeat the manipulation 100~500 times respectively.

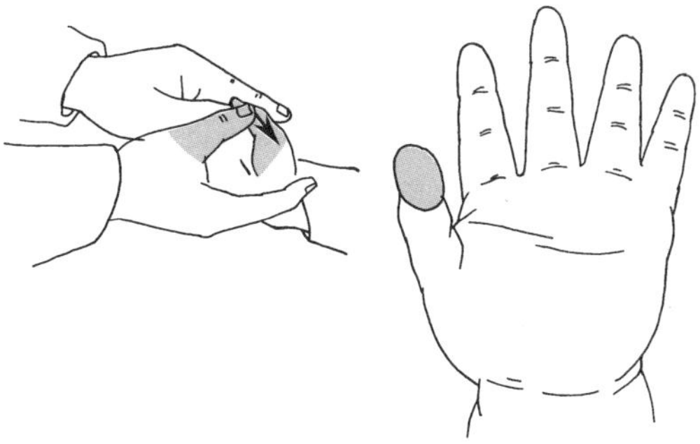

Fig. 7-32 Reinforcing *pí jīng* (脾经)

3. Action

The manipulation of reinforcing *pí jīng* (脾经) can invigorate spleen and stomach, tonify qi and blood; clearing *pí jīng* (脾经) can clear heat and drain dampness, resolve phlegm and arrest vomiting.

4. Indication

Diarrhea, constipation, abdominal distention, dysentery, anorexia, jaundice due to dampness-heat, etc.

5. Application

The manipulation of reinforcing *pí jīng* (脾经) is used to treat poor appetite, emaciation and indigestion caused by weakness of spleen-stomach and deficiency of qi and blood. The spleen and stomach of children are tender, reinforcing method is usually used on the point *pí jīng* (脾经).

Gān jīng (肝经)

1. Location

The index fingertip.

2. Manipulation

Pushing the point in circles or straight is called pushing *gān jīng* (肝经). Usually, pushing in circles is considered as reinforcing method and pushing straight is reducing method. Pushing from the distal interphalangeal joint crease of the index finger towards the finger tip is considered as clearing method, called clearing *gān jīng* (肝经) (Fig. 7-33). Repeat the manipulation 100~500 times.

3. Action

The manipulation of clearing *gān jīng* (肝经) can clear the liver, drain fire, extinguish wind, sedate fright, relieve depression and dysphoria.

4. Indication

Red eyes, bitter mouth, dry throat, infantile convulsion, dysphoria, warm feeling in chest, palms and soles.

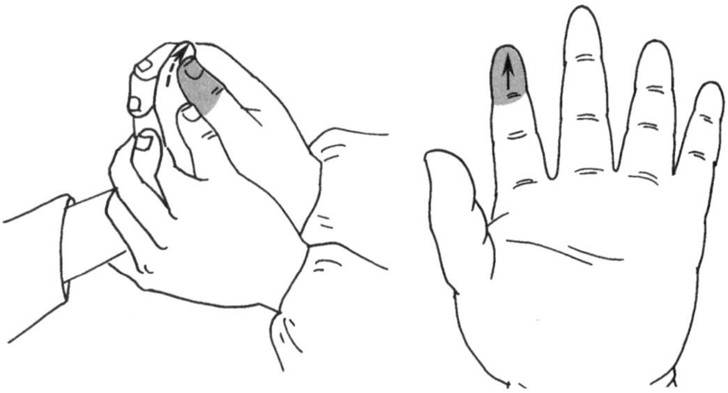

Fig. 7-33 Clearing *gān jīng* (肝经)

5. Application

The manipulation of clearing *gān jīng* (肝经) is effective for redness, swelling and pain of eyes, infantile convulsion and dysphoria caused by up-flaming liver fire, together with the manipulations of clearing *xīn jīng* (心经) and *tiān hé shuǐ* (天河水). *gān jīng* (肝经) should be cleared rather than reinforced, it is used to reinforce *shèn jīng* (肾经) instead of reinforcing *gān jīng* (肝经) when the liver is deficient and needs to be reinforced; this is called the method of tonifying liver by nourishing kidney.

Xīn jīng (心经)

1. Location

The fingertip of the middle finger.

2. Manipulation

Pushing the fingertip of the middle finger in circles or straight is called pushing *xīn jīng* (心经). Pushing in circles on the belly is considered as reinforcing method, and pushing straight from the distal interphalangeal joint crease towards finger tip is clearing method, called clearing *xīn jīng* (心经) (Fig. 7-34). Repeat the manipulation 100~ 500 times.

3. Action

The manipulation of clearing *xīn jīng* (心经) is effective to clear heart and purge fire; the manipulation of reinforcing *xīn jīng* (心经) is good to nourish the heart and tranquilize the mind.

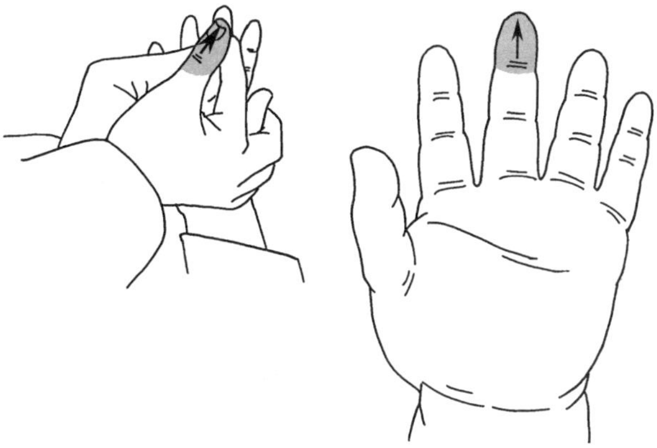

Fig. 7-34 Clearing *xīn jīng* (心经)

4. Indication

Sores in mouth or on tongue, scanty dark urine, unconsciousness due to high fever, warm feeling in palms and soles, etc.

5. Application

The manipulation of clearing *xīn jīng* (心经) is used to treat unconsciousness due to high fever, red face, sores in the mouth, scanty dark urine caused by excessive heart fire. The manipulation is usually applied together with the manipulations of clearing *tiān hé shuǐ* (天河水) and clearing *xiǎo cháng* (小肠). It is advisable to apply the clearing method on *xīn jīng* (心经) because reinforcing can stir up heart fire.

Fèi jīng (肺经)

1. Location

The fingertip of the ring finger.

2. Manipulation

Push the fingertip of the ring finger in circles or straight is called pushing *fèi jīng* (肺经). Pushing in circles is considered as reinforcing method, called reinforcing *fèi jīng* (肺经) (Fig. 7-35), and pushing straight from the distal interphalangeal joint crease towards the finger tip is clearing method, called clearing *fèi jīng* (肺经) (Fig. 7-35). Repeat the manipulation 100~500 times.

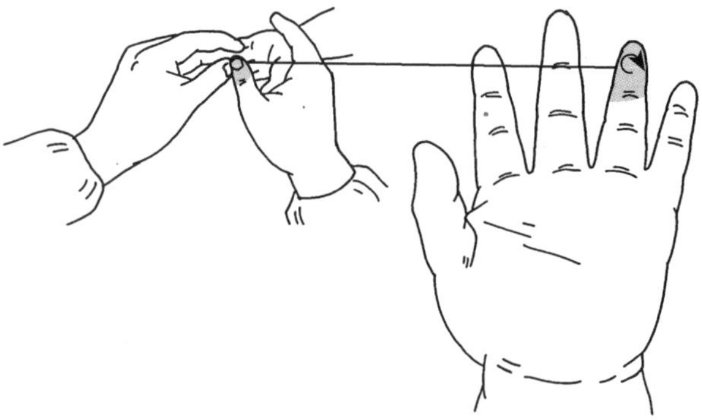

Fig. 7-35 (1) Reinforcing *fèi jīng* (肺经)

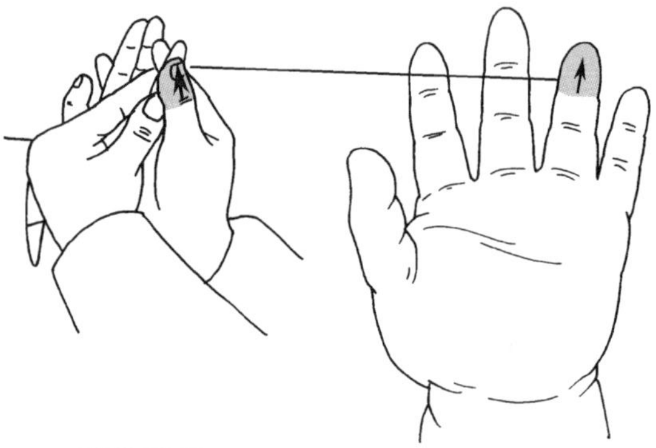

Fig. 7-35 (2) Clearing *fèi jīng* (肺经)

3. Action

The manipulation of reinforcing *fèi jīng* (肺经) is effective to tonify lung and replenish qi; the manipulation of clearing *fèi jīng* (肺经) is good to ventilate the lung, clear heat, disperse wind, release the exterior, resolve phlegm and stop cough.

4. Indication

Common cold, cough, dyspnea, gurgling with sputum, spontaneous sweating, night sweating, pale complexion, prolapse of rectum, enuresis, constipation, etc.

5. Application

The manipulation of reinforcing *fèi jīng* (肺经) is used for deficiency and cold syndrome of the lung channel manifesting deficiency of lung qi, cough, asthmatic breathing, spontaneous sweating and aversion to cold. The manipulation of clearing *fèi jīng* (肺经) is used for excess heat syndrome of the lung channel manifesting fever due to common cold, cough, asthmatic breathing and gurgling with sputum.

Shèn jīng (肾经)

1. Location

The fingertip of the little finger.

2. Manipulation

Pushing the fingertip of little finger in circles or straight is called pushing *shèn jīng* (肾经). Pushing in circles is considered as reinforcing method, called reinforcing *shèn jīng* (肾经) (Fig. 7-36); and pushing straight from the distal interphalangeal joint crease towards finger tip is clearing method, called clearing *shèn jīng* (肾经). Repeat the manipulation 100~500 times.

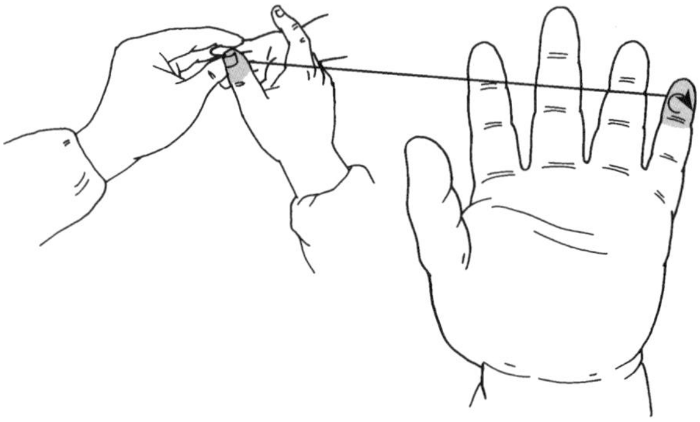

Fig. 7-36 Reinforcing *shèn jīng* (肾经)

3. Action

The manipulation of reinforcing *shèn jīng* (肾经) is effective to nourish kidney, tonify brain, warm and strengthen kidney qi; the manipulation of clearing *shèn jīng* (肾经) is good to clear heat and drain dampness from the lower energizer.

4. Indication

Congenital deficiency, constitutional weakness due to prolonged diseases, diarrhea in early morning, enuresis, cough, shortness of breath, red eyes, painful urination with dribbling and turbid urine.

5. Application

The manipulation of reinforcing *shèn jīng* (肾经) is used to treat congenital deficiency, constitutional weakness due to lingering illness, chronic diarrhea resulted from kidney deficiency, profuse urine, enuresis, spontaneous sweating, and shortness of breath. The manipulation of clearing *shèn jīng* (肾经) is applied for retention of damp-heat in urinary bladder, and difficult urination with dark urine. Clinically, *shèn jīng* (肾经) is usually stimulated with the reinforcing method. Even if the clearing method is needed, clear *xiǎo cháng* (小肠) instead.

Xiǎo cháng (小肠)

1. Location

On the ulnar side of little finger, the line from finger tip to its root.

2. Manipulation

Pushing from the finger tip to its root is considered as a reinforcing method, called reinforcing *xiǎo cháng* (小肠). Pushing to the opposite direction is considered as a clearing method, called clearing *xiǎo cháng* (小肠). Repeat the manipulation 100~300 times (Fig. 7-37).

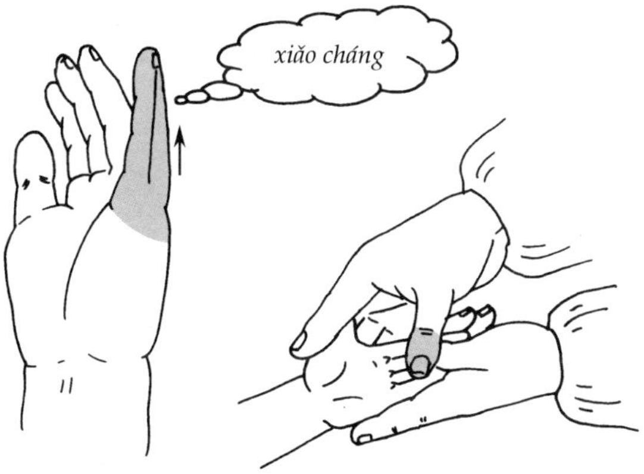

Fig. 7-37 (1) Reinforcing *xiǎo cháng* (小肠)

Fig. 7-37 (2) Clearing *xiǎo cháng* (小肠)

3. Action

To clear heat, benefit urination, separate the clear from the turbid, nourish yin and tonify deficiency.

4. Indication

Difficult urination with dark urine, watery stool, sores in mouth or on tongue, afternoon fever, etc.

5. Application

The manipulation of clearing *xiǎo cháng* (小肠) is effective to separate the clear from the turbid. It is often used to treat difficult urination with scanty and dark urine, etc. Together with the manipulation of clearing *tiān hé shuǐ* (天河水), it can strengthen the effect of clearing heat and benefiting urination, when heat of heart channel transmitting into small intestine. It is better to reinforce *xiǎo cháng* (小肠) for frequent urination and enuresis due to deficiency and cold of the lower energizer.

Dà cháng (大肠)

1. Location

On the radial border of the index finger, a line from fingertip to finger root.

2. Manipulation

Pushing from the fingertip to finger root is considered as a reinforcing method, called reinforcing *dà cháng* (大肠). Pushing to the opposite direction is considered as a clearing method, called clearing *dà cháng* (大肠). Repeat the manipulation 100~300 times (Fig. 7-38).

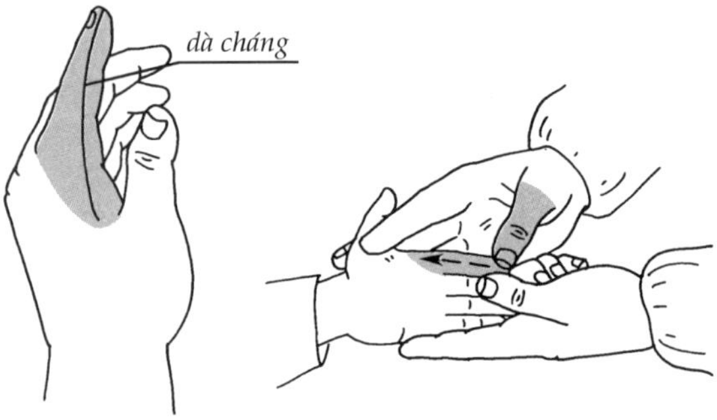

Fig. 7-38 (1) Reinforcing *dà cháng* (大肠)

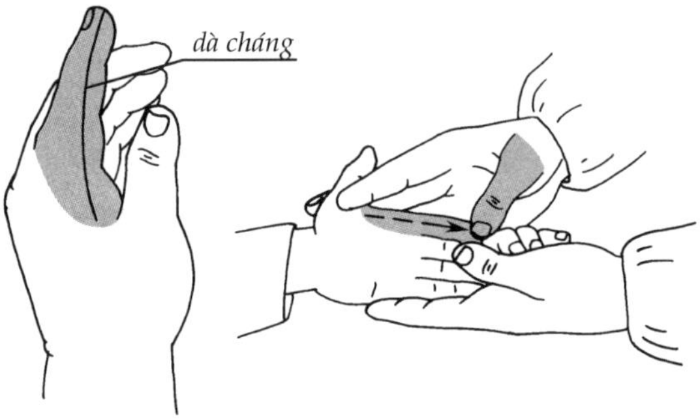

Fig. 7-38 (2) Clearing *dà cháng* (大肠)

3. Action

The manipulation of reinforcing *dà cháng* (大肠) is effective to warm the middle energizer, astringe intestines and check diarrhea; the manipulation of clearing *dà cháng* (大肠) is good to clear heat, drain dampness and eliminate constipation.

4. Indication

Diarrhea, dysentery, constipation, abdominal pain, etc.

5. Application

The manipulation of reinforcing *dà cháng* (大肠) is often applied for deficiency-cold diarrhea. The manipulation of clearing *dà cháng* (大肠) is used for retention of damp-heat or retention of food in the intestines, feverish sensation of the body, abdominal pain, dysentery with mucous and bloody stools, damp-heat diarrhea and constipation.

Shèn dǐng (肾顶)

1. Location

On the fingertip of little finger.

2. Manipulation

Pressing and kneading the point with the tip of thumb or middle finger is called kneading *shèn dǐng* (肾顶). Repeat the manipulation 100~500 times (Fig. 7-39).

3. Action

To astringe original qi, consolidate superficial portion of the body and check sweating.

4. Indication

Night sweating, spontaneous sweating, and profuse sweating.

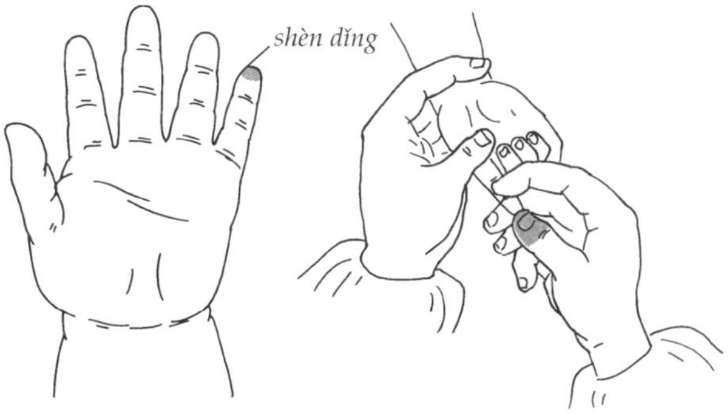

Fig. 7-39 Kneading *shèn dǐng* (肾顶)

5. Application

The manipulation of kneading *shèn dǐng* (肾顶) is effective for spontaneous sweating, night sweating or lingering massive sweating.

Sì héng wén (四横纹)

1. Location

On the palmar surface, the transverse creases of the 1st interphalangeal joints of the index, middle, ring and little fingers.

2. Manipulation

Pressing and kneading the point with the nail of thumb is called nipping *sì héng wén* (四横纹); pushing the creases from index finger to little finger is known as pushing *sì héng wén* (四横纹). Repeat the manipulation of nipping *sì héng wén* (四横纹) on each finger 3~5 times or do manipulation of pushing *sì héng wén* (四横纹) 100~300 times (Fig. 7-40).

3. Action

The manipulation of nipping *sì héng wén* (四横纹) is effective to eliminate fever, relieve dysphoria and dissipate blood-stasis and mass; the manipulation of pushing *sì héng wén* (四横纹) is good to regulate the middle energize, promote qi, harmonize qi and blood, resolve fullness and distention.

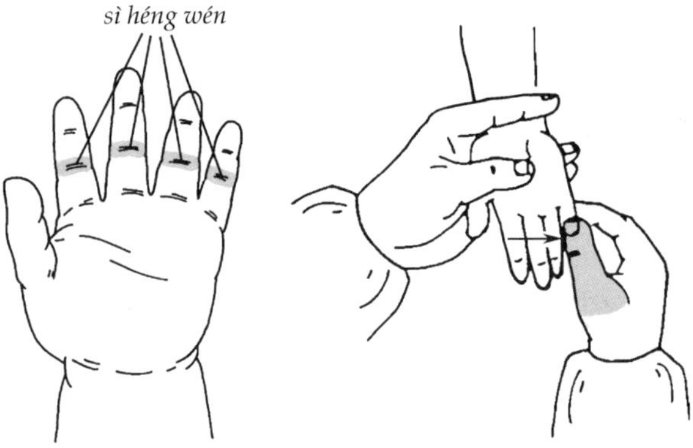

Fig. 7-40 Pushing *sì héng wén* (四横纹)

4. Indication

Indigestion, abdominal distension, abdominal pain, disharmony of qi and blood, dyspnea, chapped lips.

5. Application

Clinically, it is often used to treat abdominal distension, disharmony between qi and blood and indigestion. It is often used together with the manipulation of reinforcing *pí jīng* (脾经) and kneading RN 12 (*zhōng wǎn*). It is suggested to prick *sì héng wén* (四横纹) with a filiform needle or a three-edged needle to cause bleeding for infantile malnutrition.

Xiǎo héng wén (小横纹)

1. Location

On the palmar surface, at the transverse creases of metacarpophalangeal joints of the index, middle, ring and little fingers.

2. Manipulation

Nipping the creases with thumb nails is called nipping *xiǎo héng wén* (小横纹); pushing the creases with thumb sides is called pushing *xiǎo héng wén* (小横纹) (Fig. 7-41). Repeat nipping manipulation 3~ 5 times each finger, or do pushing manipulation 100 ~ 300 times.

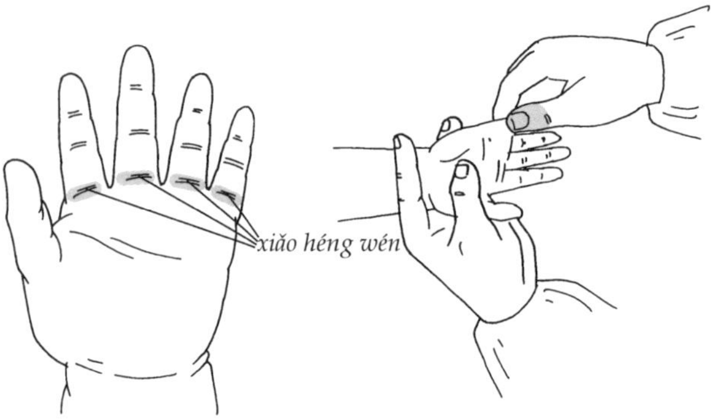

Fig. 7-41 Pushing *xiǎo héng wén* (小横纹)

3. Action

To clear fever, resolve distention, dissipate mass.

4. Indication

Chapped lips, sores in mouth, abdominal distension, fever, dysphoria, etc.

5. Application

Pushing and nipping the point is often applied for retention of heat in spleen and stomach, chapped lips, and abdominal distention. Clinically, pushing *xiǎo héng wén* (小横纹) is effective in treating pulmonary dry rales.

Zhǎng xiǎo héng wén (掌小横纹)

1. Location

On the palmar surface, at the root of little finger, on the ulnar end of the transverse crease.

2. Manipulation

Pressing and kneading the point with the tips of thumb or middle finger is called kneading *zhǎng xiǎo héng wén* (掌小横纹) (Fig. 7-42).
Repeat the manipulation 100~500 times.

3. Action

To clear heat, dissipate mass, open the chest, disperse lung qi, resolve phlegm and relieve cough.

4. Indication

Sores and ulcers in mouth and on the tongue, salivation, pneumonia, cough and asthma due to phlegm retention.

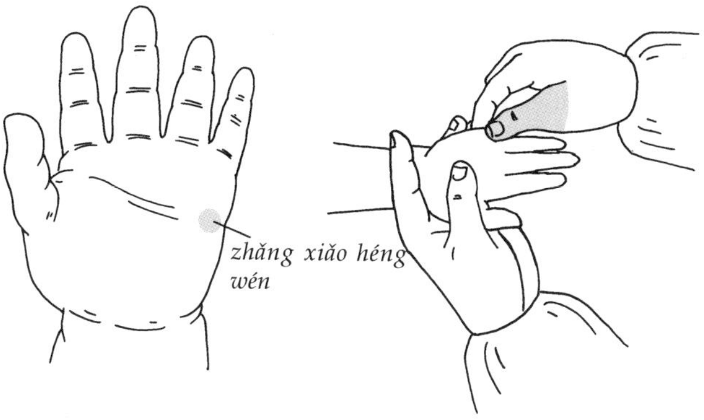

Fig. 7-42 Kneading *zhǎng xiǎo héng wén* (掌小横纹)

5. Application

The point is mainly used in treating cough, asthma and sores on the tongue; it is an important point for treating pneumonia. Clinically, kneading *zhǎng xiǎo héng wén* (掌小横纹) has a certain effect in treating pulmonary wet rales.

Wèi jīng (胃经)

1. Location

On the radial side of the greater thenar, at the junction of red and white skin.

2. Manipulation

Pushing the point in circles is considered as reinforcing method, called reinforcing *wèi jīng* (胃经). Pushing from the palmar root to the thumb root straightly is considered as clearing method, called clearing *wèi jīng* (胃经). Repeat the manipulation 100~500 times (Fig. 7-43).

3. Action

Clearing *wèi jīng* (胃经) can clear heat and drain dampness from middle energizer, normalize

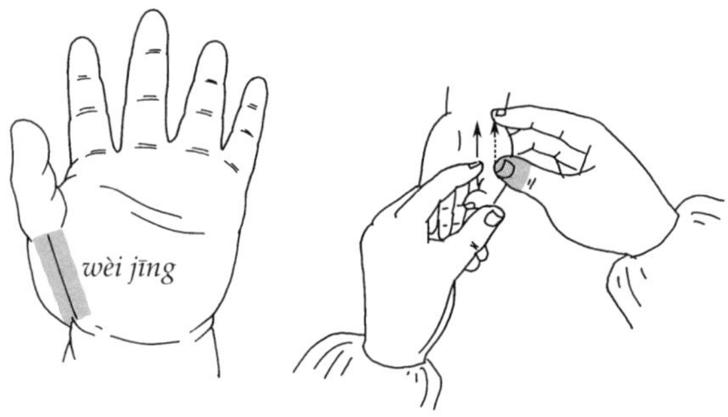

Fig. 7-43 (1) Reinforcing *wèi jīng* (胃经)

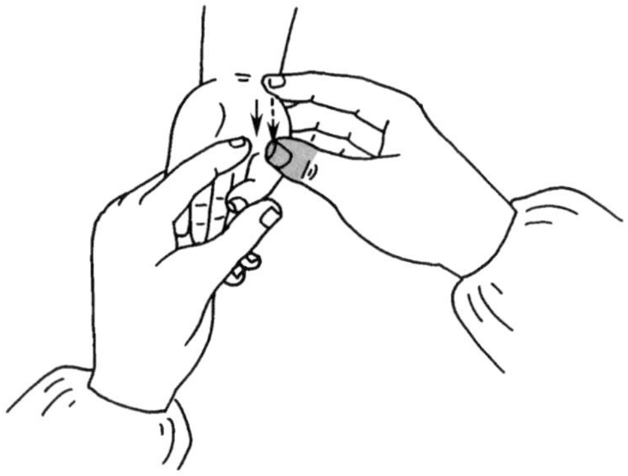

Fig. 7-43 (2) Clearing *wèi jīng* (胃经)

stomach, pacify adverse qi, quench stomach fire, relieve dysphoria and thirst; reinforcing *wèi jīng* (胃经) can invigorate spleen and stomach and promote digestion.

4. Indication

Nausea, vomiting, hiccup, belching, anorexia, abdominal distension, fetid breath, constipation, etc.

5. Application

Together with clearing *pí jīng* (脾经), pushing *tiān zhù gǔ* (天柱骨) and pushing from *héng wén* (横纹)to *bǎn mén* (板门), clearing *wèi jīng* (胃经) is often used to treat nausea, vomiting and abdominal distension due to dampness-heat of spleen and stomach or disharmony of stomach qi. Together with clearing *dà cháng* (大肠), pushing *liù fǔ* (六腑), kneading ST 25 (*tiān shū*) and pushing *qī jié gǔ* downward (*tuī xià qī jié gǔ*, 推下七节骨), the method can be also used to treat excess syndromes such as fever, dysphoria, thirst, and constipation. Together with reinforcing *pí jīng* (脾经), kneading RN 12 (*zhōng wǎn*), rubbing abdomen (*mó fù*, 摩腹), pressing and kneading ST 36 (*zú sān lǐ*), reinforcing *wèi jīng* (胃经) is often applied to treat deficiency-cold syndromes such as spleen-stomach weakness, indigestion, anorexia, etc.

Bǎn mén (板门)

1. Location

The flat surface of the greater thenar.

2. Manipulation

Kneading the point with finger tip is called kneading *bǎn mén* (板门) (Fig. 7-44). Pushing from thumb root to the transverse crease of wrist is called pushing from *bǎn mén* (板门) to *héng wén* (横纹). Pushing to opposite direction is called pushing from *héng wén* (横纹) to *bǎn mén* (板门). Repeat the manipulation 100~300 times.

3. Action

To promote digestion, resolve food retention, check diarrhea, and arrest vomiting.

4. Indication

Anorexia, internal injury due to indigestion of milk and irregular food intake, vomiting, diarrhea, abdominal distention, dyspnea and belching.

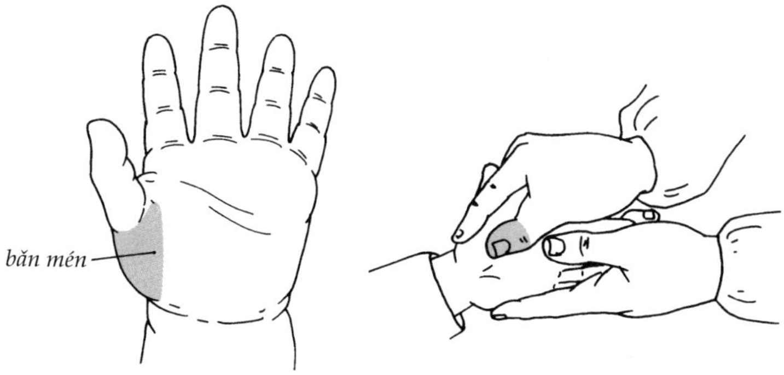

Fig. 7-44 Kneading *bǎn mén* (板门)

5. Application

Kneading *bǎn mén* (板门) can promote digestion and resolve food retention. It is mostly used for retention of milk and food, anorexia, or belching, abdominal distention, diarrhea, vomiting, together with moving *nèi bā guà* (内八卦) clockwise and rubbing RN 12 (*zhōng wǎn*). Pushing from *bǎn mén* (板门) to *héng wén* (横纹) is effective for checking diarrhea, while pushing from *héng wén* (横纹) to *bǎn mén* (板门) is able to arrest vomiting.

Nèi láo gōng (内劳宫)

1. Location

On the centre of the palm, the midpoint between the middle and ring fingers when these two fingers flexed.

2. Manipulation

Kneading the point with middle finger tip is called kneading *nèi láo gōng* (内劳宫). Apply Transporting manipulation (*yùn fǎ*, 运法) around *nèi láo gōng* (内劳宫) is called moving *nèi láo gōng* (内劳宫). Repeat kneading manipulation 100~300 times and transporting manipulation 10~30 times (Fig. 7-45).

3. Action

To clear heat, relieve dysphoria, clear deficiency-heat.

4. Indication

Fever, dysphoria, thirst, sores in mouth, bloody stool, erosion of gum, dysphoria due to internal deficiency-heat.

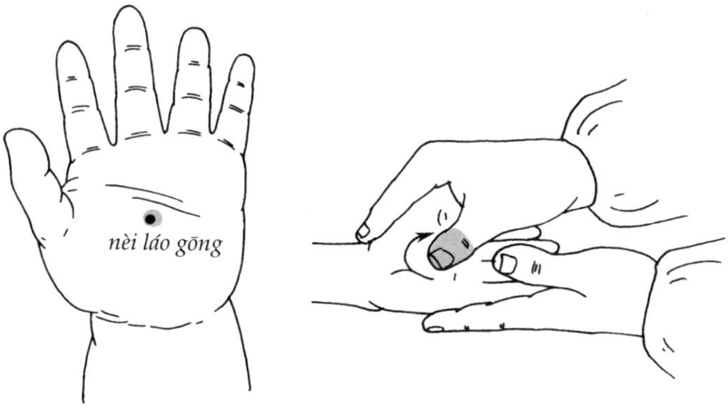

Fig. 7-45 Transporting *nèi láo gōng* (内劳宫)

5. Application

Kneading *nèi láo gōng* (内劳宫) is used for the disorders due to heat in heart channel, such as boils on the tongue, fever, dysphoria and thirst. Transporting *nèi láo gōng* (内劳宫) is a compound manipulation of transporting *zhǎng xiǎo héng wén* (掌小横纹), kneading *xiǎo tiān xīn* (小天心) and transporting *nèi láo gōng* (内劳宫), and it is mostly suitable for deficiency- heat of the heart channel and kidney channel.

Xiǎo tiān xīn (小天心)

1. Location

In the depression of the junction between greater and hypothenar eminences.

2. Manipulation

Kneading the point with middle finger tip is called kneading *xiǎo tiān xīn* (小天心). Nipping with the thumb nail is called nipping *xiǎo tiān xīn* (小天心). Pounding the point with middle finger tip or flexed interphalanngeal joint is called pounding *xiǎo tiān xīn* (小天心). Repeat kneading manipulation 100~ 300 times; nipping and pounding manipulations 5~20 times respectively (Fig. 7-46).

3. Action

To clear heat, sedate convulsion, diuresis and improve vision.

4. Indication

Convulsion, night crying, dysuria with dark urine, red, swollen and painful eyes, boils on the tongue and in mouth, and strabismus, etc.

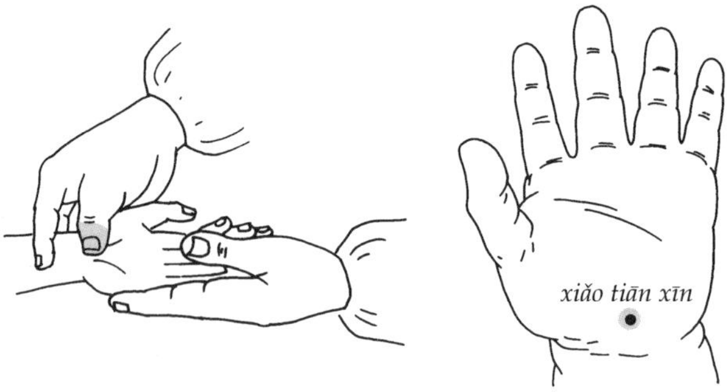

Fig. 7-46 Kneading *xiǎo tiān xīn* (小天心)

5. Application

Kneading *xiǎo tiān xīn* (小天心) is mainly used for symptoms caused by heat of heart channel, such as redness, swelling and pain of eyes, tongue ulcer, fear, restlessness; Or scanty dark urine caused by transmission of heat from heart channel into small intestine. Additionally, the manipulation is also effective for infantile retention of urine. Nipping and pounding *xiǎo tiān xīn* (小天心) is mainly used for night crying, etc.

Nèi bā guà (内八卦)

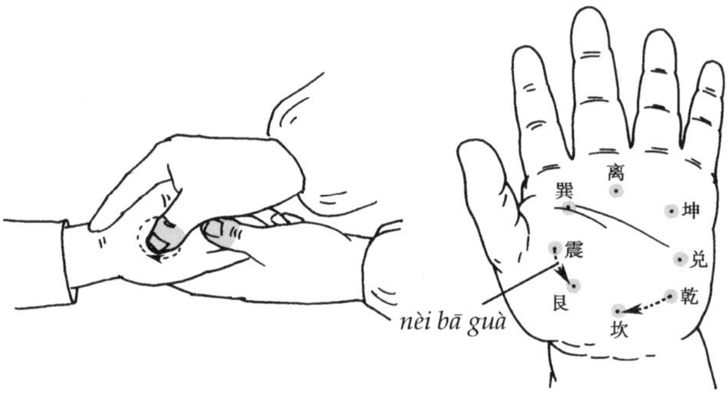

Fig. 7-47 Transporting *nèi bā guà* (内八卦)

1. Location

Taking palm center as the center, draw a circle with the radius from the center to the point at inner 2/3 of distance between palm center and transverse crease of middle finger root. *Nèi bā guà* (内八卦) indicates the area within the circle.

2. Manipulation

Apply transporting manipulation on the area with thumb belly is called moving *nèi bā guà* (内八卦) (Fig. 7-47). Repeat the manipulation 100~300 times.

3. Action

To open the chest, benefit diaphragm, regulate qi, resolve phlegm, remove food retention and promote digestion.

4. Indication

Chest stuffiness, counter-flow of qi, diarrhea, and vomiting.

5. Application

Together with transporting *bǎn mén* (板门), moving *nèi bā guà* (内八卦) is used to treat chest stuffiness, cough, abdominal distension, anorexia. Counter-moving *nèi bā guà* (内八卦) can descend qi and relieve dyspnea. Together with pushing RN 17 (*dàn zhōng*) and pushing *tiān zhù gǔ* (天柱骨), the manipulation is used for severe dyspnea with phlegm and vomiting.

Zǒng jīn (总筋)

1. Location

At the midpoint of the palmar transverse crease of the wrist.

2. Manipulation

Pressing and kneading the point is called kneading *zǒng jīn* (总筋) (Fig. 7-48). Nipping the point with the thumb nail is called nipping *zǒng jīn* (总筋). Repeat kneading manipulation 100~300 times, and nipping manipulation 3~5 times.

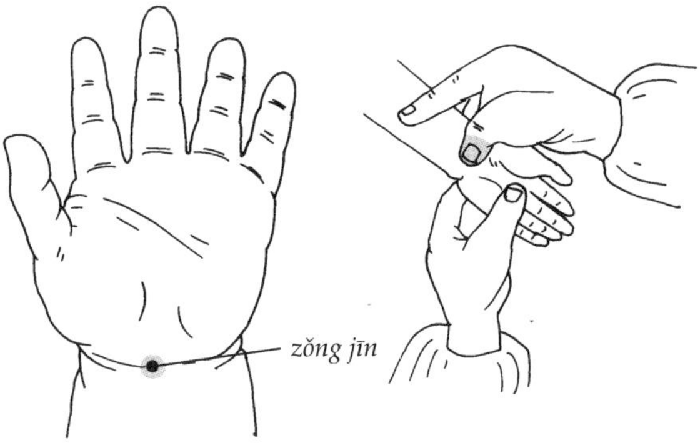

Fig. 7-48 Kneading *zǒng jīn* (总筋)

3. Action

To clear heat in the heart channel, dissipate mass, sedate convulsions and regulate qi circulation all over the body.

4. Indication

Sores and ulcers on tongue and in mouth, tidal fever, night crying, toothache, etc.

5. Application

Kneading *zǒng jīn* (总筋) is often associated by clearing *tiān hé shuǐ* (天河水) and *xīn jīng* (心经) to treat excess heat syndromes such as sores and ulcers on the tongue and in mouth, tidal fever and night crying. The manipulation should be applied quickly with stronger force.

Dà héng wén (大横纹)

1. Location

On the palmar transverse crease of the wrist, the radial end close to the thumb is known as SJ 4 (*yáng chí*), and the ulnar end close to the little finger is called *yīn chí* (阴池).

2. Manipulation

Pushing from the midpoint of the palmar transverse crease of wrist (where *zǒng jīn* (总筋) is located) towards the sides of wrist with the two thumbs respectively is called separating-pushing *dà héng wén* (*fēn tuī dà héng wén*, 分推大横纹), also known as separating yin and yang (*fēn yīn yáng*, 分阴阳). Pushing from sides, i.e. SJ 4 (*yáng chí*) and *yīn chí* (阴池), towards *zǒng jīn* (总筋) is called closing yin and yang (*hé yīn yáng* , 合阴阳). Repeat the manipulation 30~50 times (Fig. 7-49).

3. Action

To balance yin and yang, harmonize qi and blood, resolve food retention, promote digestion, resolve phlegm and eliminate masses.

4. Indication

Alternation of chills and fever, diarrhea, vomiting, food retention, lingering fever, restlessness, chest stuffiness, cough and asthma, etc.

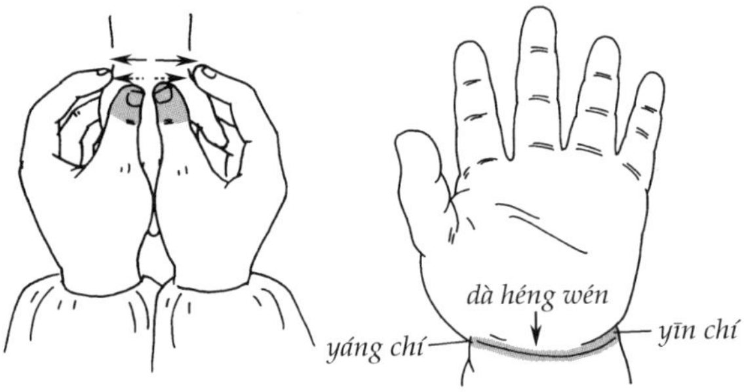

Fig. 7-49 Separating-pushing *dà héng wén* (大横纹)

5. Application

Separating yin and yang (*fēn yīn yáng*, 分阴阳) is commonly used for alternation of chills and fever, restlessness due to imbalance of yin and yang and disharmony of qi and blood; or retention of milk and food, abdominal distention, diarrhea and vomiting. Pushing toward *yīn chí* (阴池) should be applied with stronger force for excess heat syndrome; Pushing toward SJ 4 (*yáng chí*)should be applied with stronger force for deficiency cold syndrome. Closing yin and yang (*hé yīn yáng*, 合阴阳) is often used to treat cough, asthma and chest stuffiness.

Duān zhèng (端正)

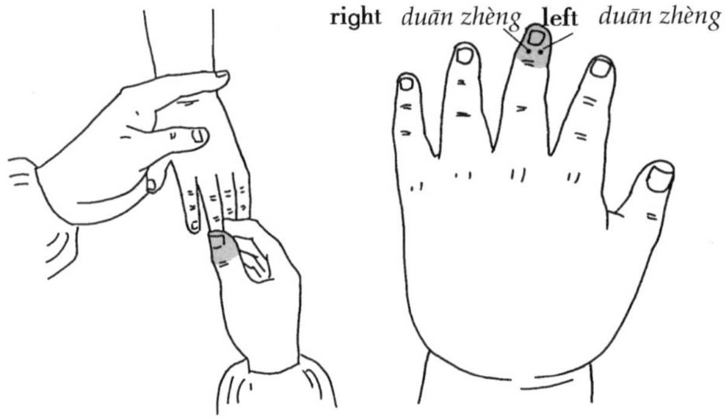

Fig. 7-50 Kneading *duān zhèng* (端正)

1. Location

On both sides of nail root of middle finger, at junction of red and white skin, close to the 2nd interphalangeal joint. The one at radial side of nail root of middle finger is called left *duān zhèng* (左端正), the one at ulnar side is called right *duān zhèng* (右端正) (Fig. 7-50).

2. Manipulation

Nipping the points with symmetric strength by the nails of thumb and index fingers is called nipping *duān zhèng* (端正);

kneading the points with symmetric strength by the thumb ball and index finger is called kneading *duān zhèng* (端正). Repeat nipping manipulation 5 times, or kneading manipulation 50 times.

3. Action

Kneading right *duān zhèng* (右端正) can pacify adverse qi and arrest vomiting; kneading left *duān zhèng* (左端正) can raise yang and check diarrhea.

4. Indication

Vomiting, counter-flow of qi, hemorrhage, diarrhea with watery stool, dysentery, etc.

5. Application

Kneading right *duān zhèng* (右端正) is mainly used for nausea, vomiting and other symptoms caused by upward attack of stomach qi. Kneading left *duān zhèng* (左端正) is mainly used for diarrhea with watery stool and dysentery. Nipping *duān zhèng* (端正) is commonly used to treat infantile convulsion together with nipping PC 8 (*láo gōng*) and clearing *gān jīng* (肝经). The point is also effective for epistaxis with the method as: wind a thin string (not very tight) round the transverse crease of the 2nd interphalangeal joint of the middle finger, and then ask child to have a bed rest.

Wǔ zhǐ jié (五指节)

1. Location

On the dorsal sides of the 1st interphalangeal joints of five fingers.

2. Manipulation

Nipping the points with thumb nail is called nipping *wǔ zhǐ jié* (五指节). Kneading the points with the thumb and index finger is called kneading *wǔ zhǐ jié* (五指节). Repeat nipping manipulation on each point 3~5 times, or kneading the points 30~50 times (Fig. 7-51).

3. Action

To calm the mind, sedate convulsion, dispel wind and phlegm, remove obstruction from the orifices.

4. Indication

Cough due to wind and phlegm, salivation, fear and restlessness, etc.

5. Application

Nipping *wǔ zhǐ jié* (五指节) is mainly used for fear and restlessness together with clearing *gān jīng* (肝经); kneading *wǔ zhǐ jié* (五指节) is chiefly used for chest fullness, asthmatic breathing due to phlegm and cough, together with moving *nèi bā guà* (内八卦), pushing and kneading RN 17 (*dàn zhōng*).

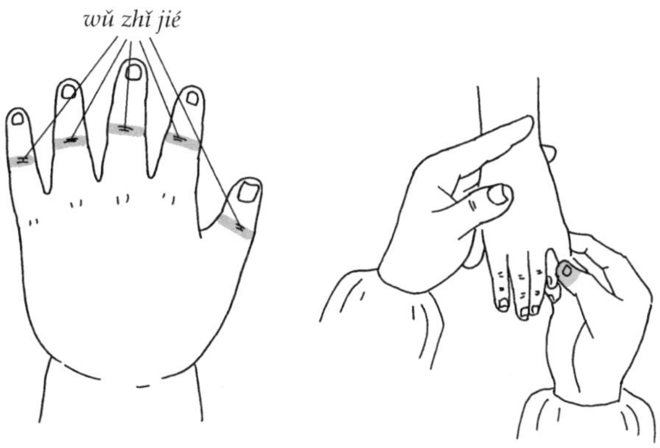

Fig. 7-51 Kneading *wǔ zhǐ jié* (五指节)

Èr shàn mén (二扇门)

1. Location

On the dorsum of the hand, in the depressions on both sides of the middle finger root.

2. Manipulation

Nipping the point with the thumb nail is called nipping *èr shàn mén* (二扇门). Pressing and kneading the point with radial border of thumb is called kneading *èr shàn mén* (二扇门). Repeat the nipping manipulation 5 times, or kneading manipulation 100~300 times (Fig. 7-52).

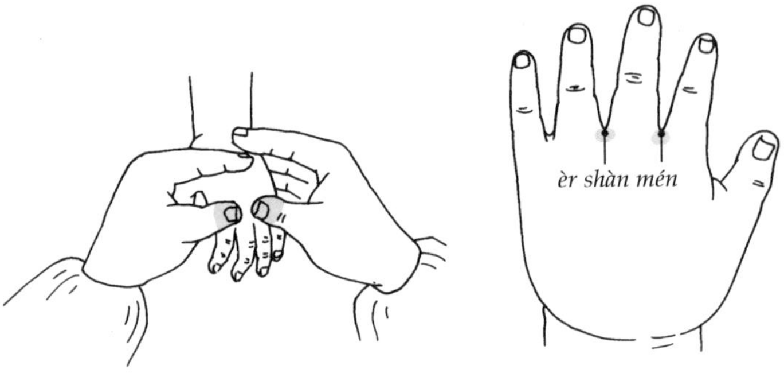

Fig. 7-52 Kneading *èr shàn mén* (二扇门)

3. Action

To induce sweating to let pathogens out from the exterior, eliminate fever and relieve asthmatic breathing.

4. Indication

Common cold, fever without sweating, asthmatic breathing and coarse breath with expectoration of sputum, etc.

5. Application

Nipping or kneading *èr shàn mén* (二扇门) is an effective manipulation for inducing sweating. Do manipulations quickly with stronger force to treat the common cold due to wind-cold. Together with kneading *shèn dǐng* (肾顶), reinforcing *pí jīng* (脾经) and *shèn jīng* (肾经), the point is good for common cold due to constitutional weakness.

Èr rén shàng mǎ (二人上马)

1. Location

On the dorsum of the hand, in the depressions proximal to the metacarpophalangeal joints of the ring and little fingers.

2. Manipulation

Kneading the point with thumb tip is called kneading *èr rén shàng mǎ* (二人上马), and nipping the point with thumb nail is called nipping *èr rén shàng mǎ* (二人上马). Repeat nipping manipulation 3~5 times, or kneading manipulation 100~300 times (Fig. 7-53).

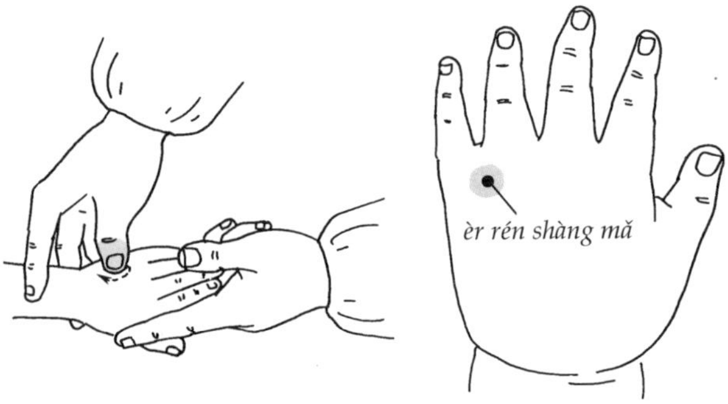

Fig. 7-53 Kneading *èr rén shàng mǎ* (二人上马)

3. Action

To nourish yin, tonify kidney, normalize qi circulation, eliminate masses, benefit water metabolism and relieve stranguria.

4. Indication

Dysuria with dark urine, abdominal pain, enuresis, indigestion, shortness of breath, toothache, etc.

5. Application

Clinically, kneading *èr rén shàng mǎ* (二人上马) is more frequently used for yin deficiency and yang hyperactivity, tidal fever, restlessness, toothache, and dysuria with dark urine. Together with kneading *xiǎo héng wén* (小横纹), the point is effective to treat pulmonary infection with dry rales lasting for long time because of weak body constitution. For wet rales, the point can be used together with kneading *zhǎng xiǎo héng wén* (掌小横纹).

Wēi líng (威灵)

1. Location

On the dorsum of hand, in the depression between the 2nd and 3rd metacarpal bones.

2. Manipulation

Nipping the point is called nipping *wēi ling* (威灵). Repeat the manipulation 3~5 times, or until child wakes (Fig. 7-54).

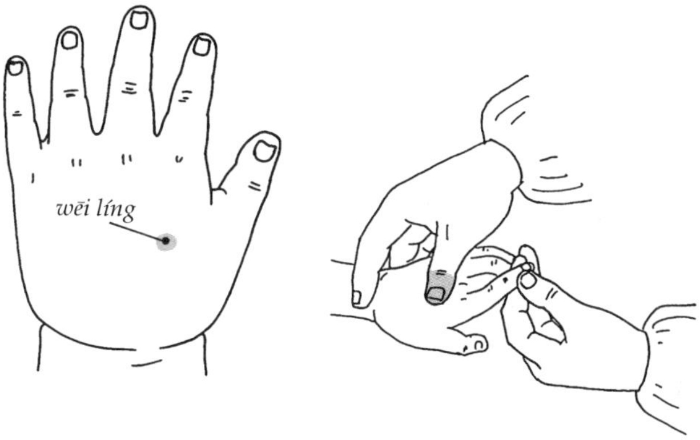

Fig. 7-54 Nipping *wēi ling* (威灵)

3. Action

To resuscitate conciousness.

4. Indication

Syncope, loss of consciousness, headache, etc.

5. Application

Mainly use the point in emergency treatment for syncope and loss of consciousness, together with nipping DU 26 (*shuǐ gōu*) and *shí xuān* (十宣)

Jīng nìng (精宁)

1. Location

On the dorsum of hand, in the depression between the 4th and 5th metacarpal bones.

2. Manipulation

Nipping the point is called nipping *jīng nìng* (精宁). Repeat the manipulation 3~5 times, or until child wakes (Fig. 7-55).

3. Action

To promote qi, break masses and resolve phlegm.

4. Indication

Retention of food and phlegm, asthmatic breathing, dry vomiting, infantile malnutrition, syncope, etc.

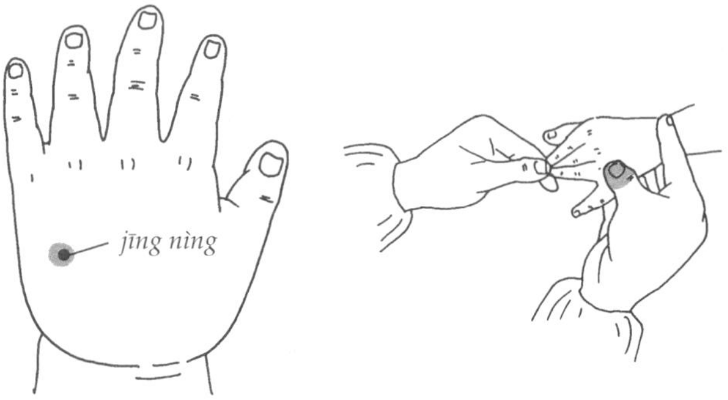

Fig. 7-55 Nipping *jīng nìng* (精宁)

5. Application

Jīng nìng (精宁) is often used to treat retention of food and phlegm, wheezing, asthmatic breathing and dry vomiting. It is not advisable to use the point for children with constitutional weakness. If it must be used, it is better to add the manipulations of reinforcing *pí jīng* (脾经), pushing *sān guān* (三关), pinching along the spine (*niē jǐ*, 捏脊) to avoid damage of original qi.

The point is often used together with nipping *wēi ling* (威灵) for syncope, so as to strengthen the function of resuscitating consciousness.

Bó yáng chí (膊阳池)

1. Location

On the dorsum of the hand, 3 cun above *yī wō fēng* (一窝蜂).

2. Manipulation

Nipping the point with the thumb nail is called nipping *bó yáng chí* (膊阳池), and kneading the point with the finger tip is called kneading *bó yáng chí* (膊阳池). Repeat nipping manipulation 3~ 5 times, or kneading manipulation 100~300 times (Fig. 7-56).

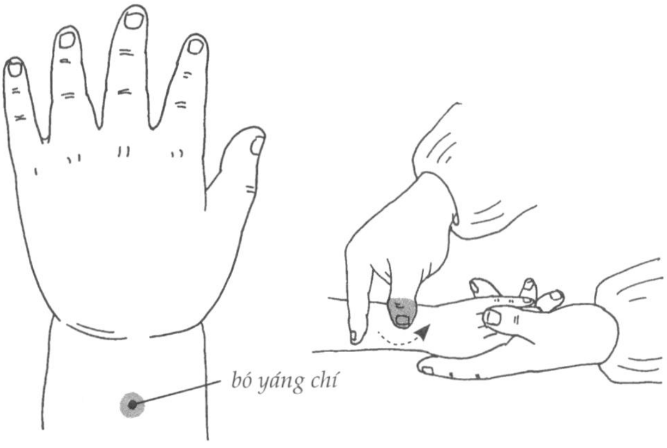

Fig. 7-56 Kneading *bó yáng chí* (膊阳池)

3. Action

To relieve headache, normalize bowel movement and benefit urination.

4. Indication

Constipation, dysuria with dark urine, headache due to common cold.

5. Application

Long time kneading on the point has marked effect for constipation, but forbid to use the point for diarrhea with efflux stool. Usually, use the point together with other points good for relieving the exterior and benefiting urination to treat headache due to common cold, or dysuria with scanty dark urine.

Yī wō fēng (一窝蜂)

1. Location

On the midpoint of dorsal transverse crease of the wrist.

2. Manipulation

Kneading the point with the finger tip is called kneading *yī wō fēng* (一窝蜂). Repeat the manipulation 100~300 times (Fig. 7-57).

3. Action

To warm middle energizer, promote qi circulation, relieve joint pain, promote functions of joints, disperse and eliminate pathogens of the exterior and interior.

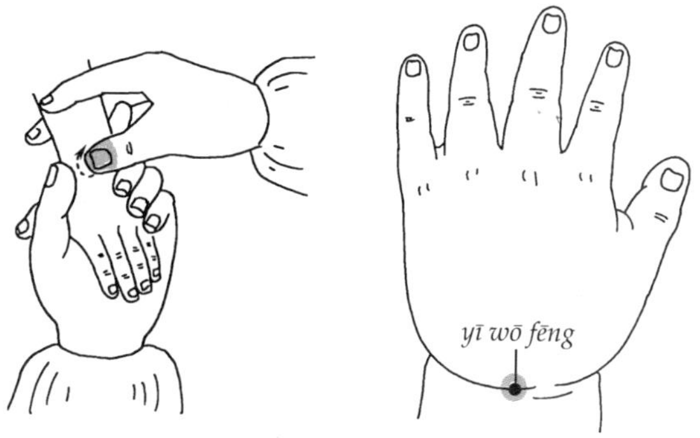

Fig. 7-57 Kneading *yī wō fēng* (一窝蜂)

4. Indication

Abdominal pain, borborygmus, common cold due to wind cold, acute or chronic infantile convulsion, poor movement of joints, etc.

5. Application

Kneading *yī wō fēng* (一窝蜂) is often applied for abdominal pain caused by cold or food retention, together with grasping *dù jiăo* (肚角), pushing *sān guān* (三关) and kneading RN 12 (*zhōng wăn*). The point is also effective for arthralgia due to cold in channels and collaterals or common cold due to wind-cold.

Sān guān (三关)

1. Location

On the radial aspect of the forearm, the straight line between SJ 4 (*yáng chí*) and LI 11 (*qū chí*).

2. Manipulation

Pushing from transverse crease of wrist to transverse crease of elbow with fingertips of index and middle fingers is called pushing *sān guān* (三关) (Fig. 7-58). Repeat the manipulation 100~300 times.

3. Action

To warm yang, disperse cold, replenish qi, activate blood, induce sweating to relieve the exterior.

4. Indication

Abdominal pain, diarrhea, aversion to cold, lassitude, constitutional weakness after diseases, and all deficiency and cold syndromes like common cold due to wind-cold.

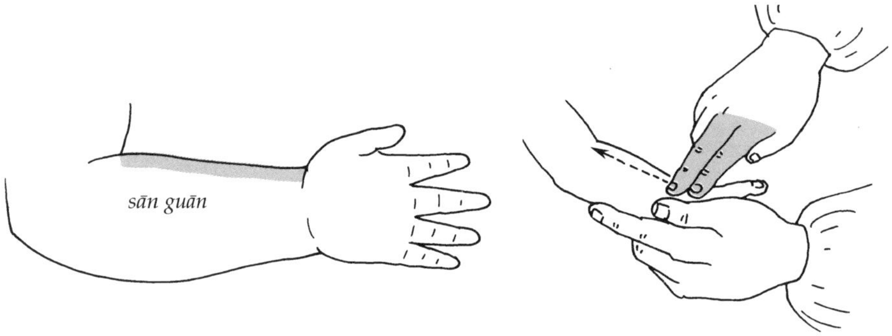

Fig. 7-58 Pushing *sān guān* (三关)

5. Application

Sān guān (三关) is warm in nature. The indication of *sān guān* (三关) includes all kinds of deficiency and cold syndromes. Use the point carefully for the patients with non deficiency-cold syndromes. Clinically, together with the manipulations of reinforcing *pí jīng* (脾经) and *shèn jīng* (肾经), kneading *dān tián* (丹田), pinching along the spine (*niē jǐ*, 捏脊) and rubbing abdomen (*mó fù*, 摩腹), pushing *sān guān* (三关) is used to treat the syndromes due to deficiency of qi and blood, weakness of *mìng mén* fire, deficiency and cold of lower energizer and deficiency of yang qi, manifesting with a cold feeling in four limbs, pale complexion, poor appetite, vomiting and diarrhea.

Liù fǔ (六腑)

1. Location

On the ulnar aspect of forearm, the straight line between *yīn chí* (阴池) and the elbow.

2. Manipulation

Pushing from transverse crease of elbow to transverse crease of wrist with the thumb ball or fingertips of index and middle fingers is called pushing *liù fǔ* (六腑) (Fig. 7-59). Repeat the manipulation 100~300 times.

3. Action

To clear heat and cool blood.

4. Indication

All kinds of excess-heat syndromes such as high fever, restlessness, thirst, infantile convulsion, sore throat and constipation.

5. Application

Liù fǔ (六腑) is cool and cold in nature and functions to treat excess-heat syndromes including febrile diseases showing the signs of heat entering nutrient-blood and retention of heat in *zang-fu* organs, such as high fever, restlessness, thirst and constipation. Together with reinforcing *pí jīng* (脾经), the point has the effect of stopping sweating. For chronic loose stool and diarrhea due to spleen deficiency; use the point carefully.

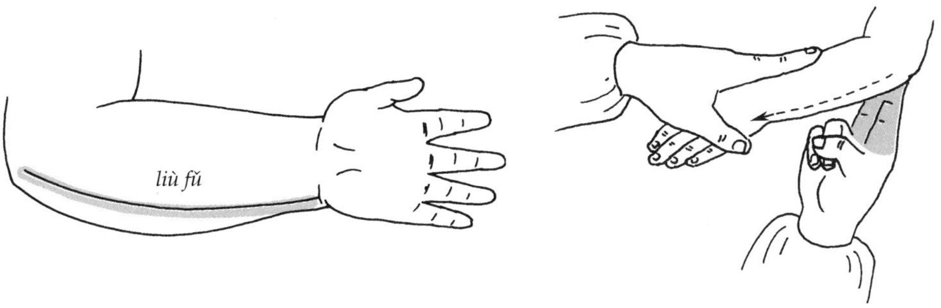

Fig. 7-59 Pushing *liù fǔ* (六腑)

Pushing *liù fǔ* (六腑) and pushing *sān guān* (三关), the former is cool in nature and the latter is warm in nature. They can be used together or singly. For kids with constitutional qi deficiency manifesting aversion to cold, pushing *sān guān* (三关) is used alone; for high fever, restlessness, thirst and eruption, pushing *liù fǔ* (六腑) alone. When used together, the two points can balance yin and yang, prevent massive cold and massive heat damaging healthy qi. For a mixture of cold and heat, if heat is predominant, pushing *liù fǔ* (六腑) three times and *sān guān* (三关) one time; if cold is predominant, pushing *sān guān* (三关) three times and *liù fǔ* (六腑) one time.

Tiān hé shuǐ (天河水)

1. Location

Along the midline of medial aspect of forearm, the straight line from *zǒng jīn* (总筋) to *hóng chí* (洪池) or PC 3 (*qū zé*).

2. Manipulation

Pushing from transverse crease of wrist to transverse crease of elbow with the fingertips of index and middle fingers is called clearing (pushing) *tiān hé shuǐ* (天河水). Repeat the manipulation 100~300 times (Fig. 7-60).

3. Action

To clear heat, relieve the exterior, purge heart fire, resolve restlessness and moisten dryness.

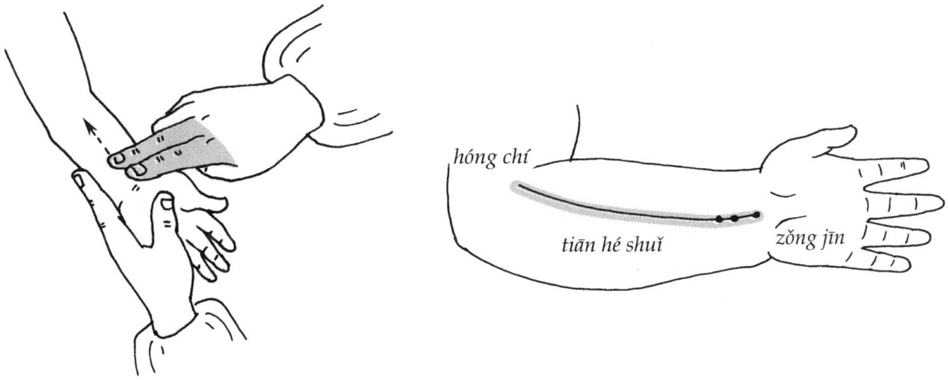

Fig. 7-60 Clearing *tiān hé shuǐ* (天河水)

4. Indication

All kinds of heat syndromes showing ever due to invasion of exogenous pathogenic factors, warm feeling, tidal fever, restlessness, thirst, sores and ulcers in mouth and on the tongue, cough, asthmatic breathing with sputum, and sore throat.

5. Application

Tiān hé shuǐ (天河水) is slightly cool and even in nature, mainly used for heat syndromes. It can clear heat without damaging yin, often applied for warm feeling in chest, palms and soles, dry mouth and throat, herpes on the lip, sores on the tongue, and night crying. The method is also used together with the manipulations of pushing BL 2 (*cuán zhú*), pushing *kǎn gōng* (坎宫) and kneading *tài yáng* (太阳) to treat external contraction of wind-heat with symptoms of fever in the common cold, headache, aversion to wind, slightly sweating, and sore throat. This point is good for clearing heat from the defense aspect and qi aspect.

RN 22 (*tiān tū*, 天突)

1. Location

In the depression, 0.6 cun superior to the midpoint on upper border of sternal notch, on conception vessel.

2. Manipulation

Press and knead the point with middle finger tip about 30 times (Fig. 7-61); or press the point in and out with finger by following inhalation and exhalation, about 3~5 times.

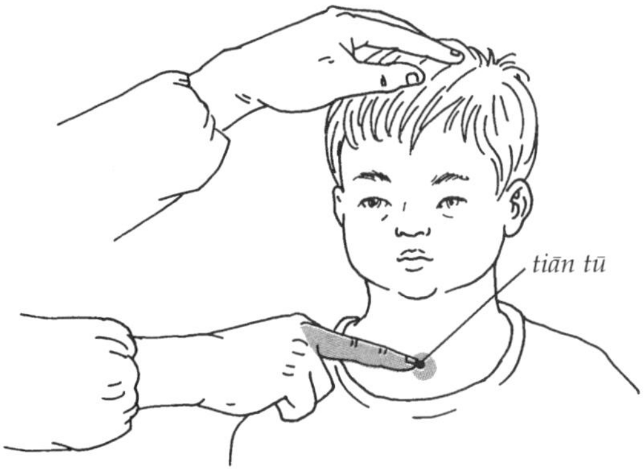

Fig. 7-61 Kneading RN 22 (*tiān tū*, 天突)

3. Action

To regulate qi, resolve phlegm, pacify upward attack of qi, sooth asthma and stop vomiting.

4. Indication

Phlegmatic asthma and difficult expectoration of sputum.

5. Application

Together with manipulations of pushing and kneading RN 17 (*dàn zhōng*), kneading RN 12 (*zhōng wǎn*) and moving *nèi bā guà* (内八卦), the point is used for phlegmatic asthma and vomiting due to upward attack of stomach qi, accumulation of phlegm and fluid. Pressing the point inward and downward quickly with slightly a bent finger may induce vomiting.

RN 17 (*dàn zhōng*, 膻中)

1. Location

On the sternum, at the midpoint between two breasts.

2. Manipulation

Kneading the point with the middle finger tip is called kneading RN 17 (*dàn zhōng*). Pushing from the point straightly to bilateral nipples with the thumbs is called separating-pushing RN 17 (*dàn zhōng*). Pushing from the sternal notch downward to xiphoid is called pushing RN 17 (*dàn zhōng*). Repeat pushing or kneading manipulation 50~100 times (Fig. 7-62).

Fig. 7-62 (1) Kneading RN 17 (*dàn zhōng*, 膻中)

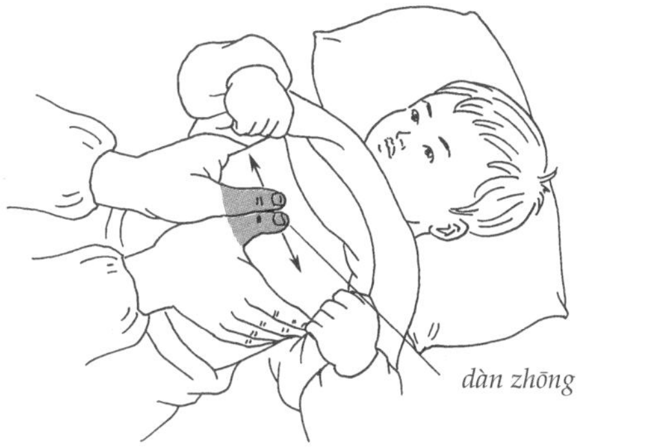

Fig. 7-62 (2) Separating-pushing RN 17 (*dàn zhōng*, 膻中)

3. Action

To ease the chest, regulate qi, relieve cough and resolve phlegm.

4. Indication

Chest fullness, vomiting, belching, cough, shortness of breath and gurgling sound in the throat due to sputum, etc.

Fig. 7-62 (3) Pushing RN 17 (*dàn zhōng*, 膻中)

5. Application

RN 17 (*dàn zhōng*) is the influential point of qi, located in the chest. Chest and upper back are referred to the lung. Pushing and kneading the point can ease the chest, regulate qi, check cough and resolve phlegm; it is also effective for chest fullness, vomiting, belching, cough, asthma and wheezing caused by various kinds of reasons. It is used together with manipulations of moving *nèi bā guà* (内八卦), pushing from *héng wén* (横纹) to *bǎn mén* (板门), separating-pushing abdominal *yīn yáng* (*fēn tuī fù yīn yáng*, 分推腹阴阳) to treat vomiting and belching. Together with manipulations of pushing *fèi jīng* (肺经), kneading BL 13 (*fèi shù*), it is often used to treat cough and asthma. Together with manipulations of kneading RN 22 (*tiān tū*), pressing and kneading ST 40 (*fēng lóng*), it is used to treat difficult expectoration of sputum.

Section 4
Common Pediatric Diseases

Pediatric tui na is an important branch of tui na therapy, a kind of external therapy for children to prevent and treat diseases or promote development and intelligence with manipulations applied on special points or areas on body surface, under the guidance of basic Chinese medical theories and in accordance with physiological and pathological characteristics of children.

Physiologically, children have characteristics of delicate *zang-fu* organs, insufficiently developed body, fullness of vitality and rapid development. After a baby was born, his or her five zang-organs and six fu-organs are tender and weak; his or her configuration, four limbs, tendons, muscles, bones, qi, blood, body fluid and function of qi are immature and insufficient. Traditional Chinese medicine generalizes such phenomena as "childish yin and yang" and "Childish yang is yang insufficient and childish yin is yin incompletely developed." Both material basis and physiological functions of children are immature and incomplete, still on the way of growing and developing. On the other hand, their growth and development are rapid, the younger the quicker. In this way, they urgently need abundant essence of water and food as well as other kinds of nutrition.

Pathologically, children have characteristics of poor body resistance, easily getting disease, quick transmission and change of disease if they are sick, easily getting well since they have clear and pure zang qi. Because of the frail body constitution and physiological functions, environmental changes are liable to affect children resulting in lower body resistance. Since children are not able to dress and diet accordingly, the exogenous pathogenic factors may attack them easily and irregular food intake would influence their body condition possibly. Clinically, lung and spleen are mostly involved in pediatric disorders. In a word, the changes of cold, heat, deficiency and excess in children are more rapid and complicated than that in adults. Therefore, it is much more important to have correct diagnosis, pattern differentiation and treatment in time for children's diseases. The inappropriate treatment will aggravate the diseases and lead a severe condition into a crisis. Clear and pure zang qi, easily getting well indicates that children would recover quickly when they are sick, since they have vibrant and energetic body with responsive reaction of qi and blood.

Pattern differentiation of pediatric tui na is also based on four diagnostic methods and eight principles. Among the four diagnostic methods, inquiry is often indirect, because infants cannot speak and elder children are not able to express themselves appropriately although they can speak. Since qi and blood of infants have not matured, and vessels and channels have not fully filled, it is difficult to make diagnosis by feeling their pulse. Though listening and smelling can present some information, it is still not complete, only inspection and observation can reflect reliable pathological conditions, especially the inspection of infants' finger stria.

Since pediatric diseases often show as diseases due to invasion of exogenous pathogens and disease due to irregular food intake, yang syndrome, excess syndrome and heat syndrome are frequently seen in pediatric department. Therefore, the commonly used methods of tui na treatment include relieving the exterior with the manipulations of pushing BL 2 (*cuán zhú*), pushing *kǎn gōng* (坎宫), pushing *tài yáng* (太阳), grasping GB 20 (*fēng chí*), etc., clearing heat with manipulations of clearing *tiān hé shuǐ* (天河水), pushing *liù fǔ* (六腑), pushing along the spine (*tuī jǐ*, 推脊), etc., promoting digestion and eliminating food retention with manipulations of pushing *pí jīng* (脾经), clearing *dà cháng* (大肠), kneading *bǎn mén* (板门), kneading RN 12 (*zhōng wǎn*), kneading ST 25 (*tiān shū*), etc. The most of points used in pediatric tui na are specific points for infants besides a few channel points and extra points. They have locations not only in the form of "point", but also in the forms of "course" and "area". The points like *jīng nìng* (精宁), *wēi líng* (威灵), *yī wō fēng* (一窝蜂) and *xiǎo tiān xīn* (小天心) are the points in the form of "point"; *tiān hé shuǐ* (天河水), *sān guān* (三关) and *liù fǔ* (六腑) are points in the form of "course"; *fù* (腹), *qí* (脐) and *bā guà* (八卦) are the points in the form of "area". These points are seldom, even not used in adult tui na. The most of them are located below two elbows, different from the points in adult tui na. The location of these specific points makes the clinical treatment very convenient.

The infants have delicate *zang-fu* organs, insufficiently developed body and tender skins and muscles. The manipulations are required to be gentle and soft with proper strength. So it is very important to practice the manipulations. There are many ways to practice the manipulations, but practicing on human body is the main; the most of manipulation can be practiced as same as practicing manipulations of adults' tui na. Pushing and kneading manipulations have higher frequency while rubbing manipulation has lower frequency. Nipping manipulation is heavier, quicker and less. Kneading manipulation is usually applied after nipping manipulation, and pressing manipulation is often combined with kneading manipulation. Nipping, grasping and pinching manipulations which have stronger stimulation are usually applied at the end of treatment, in case too much stimulation makes infants crying, affecting the operation.

There are some precautions in pediatric tui na treatment.

The nails of the doctor should be carefully cut and polished.

The hands should warm.

The treatment can be given in three orders which can be determined flexibly according to clinical situation.

I The points on head and face are operated first, and then the points on upper limbs, chest, abdomen, waist, upper back and lower limbs.

II The chief points are operated first and then secondary points.

III The secondary points are operated first and chief points such as pinching along the spine (*niē jǐ*, 捏脊) later.

But no matter which way is adopted and no matter chief points or combined points, nipping, grasping, pinching manipulations and manipulations with strong stimulation are operated at last, because they may irritate infant to cry, affecting the operation and therapeutic effect.

The duration of operation is determined according to the age of child, the pathological condition, the body constitution and nature of manipulation; usually finish the treatment within 15minutes. It could be also determined according to the condition of disease, giving treatment once every day or twice a day for acute diseases like high fever.

Habitually, the points of upper limb are operated only on the left, no matter boys or girls; the points on other parts of the body can be operated bilaterally.

The media substances such as Talcum powder should be used during the operation to lubricate the skin, prevent injury and enhance the therapeutic effect.

It is not good to give tui na treatment when kids are hungry or full in stomach. The best time to give tui na treatment is one hour after meal.

Cough

Cough is one of the main symptoms in lung diseases. It may happen in any season, especially in winter and spring. The incidence of disease is higher on infants. The cough discussed in this section refers to the diseases taking cough as the main symptom such as acute and chronic bronchitis.

The causative factors include invasion of exogenous pathogens and internal injury. The location of disease is in lung and spleen. Lung is a delicate organ, opening into nose, manifesting its condition on skin hair externally and dominating the exterior of whole body. The cough due to invasion of exogenous pathogens is caused by exogenous pathogenic qi or pathogenic dryness, resulting in lung qi ascending. Cough due to internal injury is often caused by constitutional weakness, lung yin depletion or deficiency-cold of spleen and stomach. In western medicine, physicochemical irritation, infection and allergens are considered as external causes of the disease; while weak body resistance, allergic constitution and low respiratory tract immune function are thought as internal causes. The cough reflex, contractile function of smooth muscles of airway and ciliary motility of children are comparatively weak, it is difficult to clean inhaled dusts and foreign granules out efficiently, it is the reason that children are more liable to catch respiratory tract infection.

1. Clinical Manifestations

a. Cough due to exogenous pathogens

Cough with expectoration of sputum, nasal obstruction, running nose, aversion to cold, headache, thin tongue coating and floating pulse. Cough due to wind-cold may manifest clear sputum and nasal discharge, severe chills without sweating, thin white tongue coating; cough due to wind-heat may show yellow and thick sputum and nasal discharge, mild cold feeling with slightly sweating, thirst, sore throat, fever, thin yellow tongue coating, a floating rapid pulse.

b. Cough due to internal injury

Prolonged cough, lower fever or dry cough with scanty sputum, or cough with profuse sputum, poor appetite, listlessness, lassitude and emaciation.

2. Tui Na Treatment

【Principle of treatment】

To disperse lung qi and check cough.

【Commonly used methods】

Clearing *fèi jīng* (肺经), pressing RN 22 (*tiān tū*), kneading *rǔ páng* (乳旁), kneading ST 18 (*rǔ gēn*), scrubbing RN 17 (*dàn zhōng*), scrubbing BL 13 (*fèi shù*).

⋆ Cough due to exogenous pathogens

Add manipulations of pushing *tiān mén* (天门), pushing *kǎn gōng* (坎宫), pushing *tài yáng* (太阳), wasps going into honeycomb (*huáng fēng rù dòng* 黄蜂入洞), grasping GB 20 (*fēng chí*), pushing *sān guān* (三关) upward, pushing *liù fǔ* (六腑) downward. Push *sān guān* (三关) more times if cold is predominant.

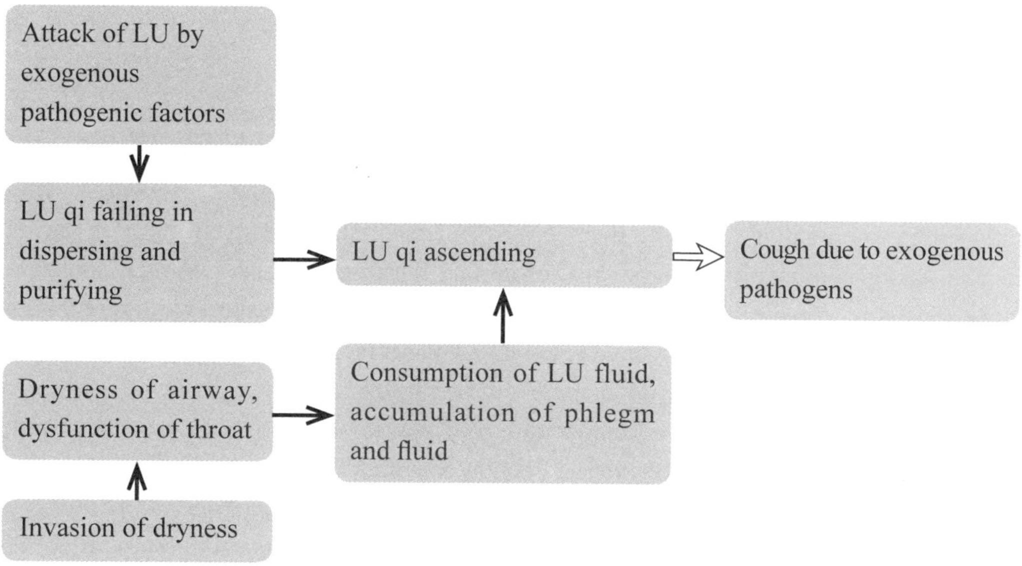

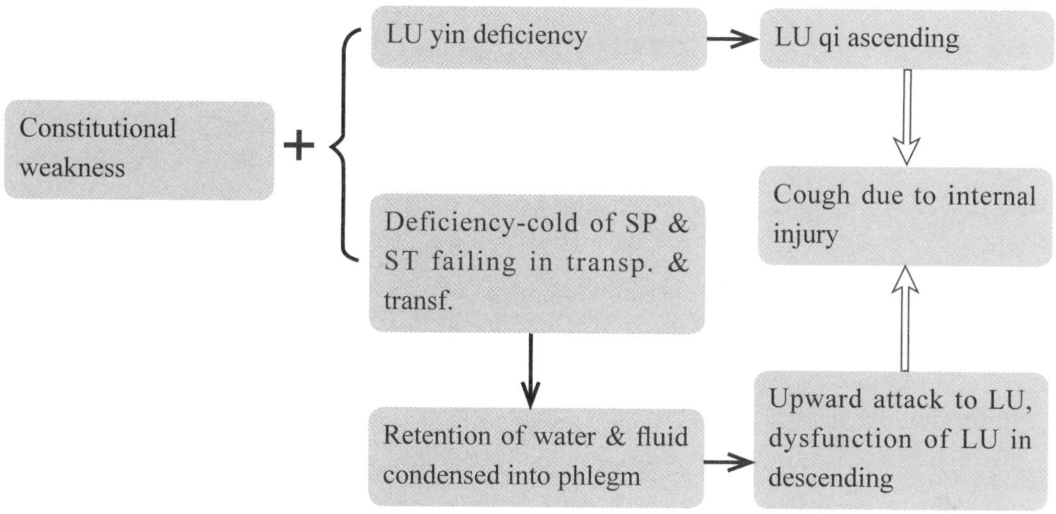

⋆ Cough due to internal injury

Add manipulations of reinforcing *pí jīng* (脾经), reinforcing *shèn jīng* (肾经), kneading RN 12 (*zhōng wǎn*), pressing and kneading ST 36 (*zú sān lǐ*), kneading BL 13 (*fèi shù*), kneading BL 23 (*shèn shù*).

3. Nursing Care

Have light food during treatment; raw, cold, sour, sweetish, pungent, spicy food and fishes are forbidden to prevent aggravation of cough.

Have proper rest, drink more water, pay attention to weather change, avoid exposure to wind and cold.

Improve living environment, keep ventilation in room and away from smog and oil gas.

Fever

Fever is a disease often seen in children characterized by abnormal elevation of body temperature. Clinically, syndrome of excess-heat of lung and stomach, syndrome of yin deficiency and internal heat, and syndrome of fever due to qi deficiency are often seen. Fever due to exogenous pathogens generally refers to common cold. The disease may occur in any season, but more in spring and winter. The younger infants have higher risk of getting the disease. Sick kids with constitutional weakness are liable to have complications, they need more cares. Western medicine thinks that children have lower immunity, easily have respiratory tract infection resulting fever. Children have vigorous metabolism and incomplete development of thermoregulation center, any of sports, crying, eating and heavy dressing, high room temperature may elevate their body temperature. Clinically, pathological fever is related to bacteria, virus infection or central thermoregulation disorder. Chinese medicine thinks either exogenous pathogens or internal injury can induce fever. In children, yang is always excessive and yin is always deficient, the pathogens are liable to turn into heat after they are attacked by those pathogens.

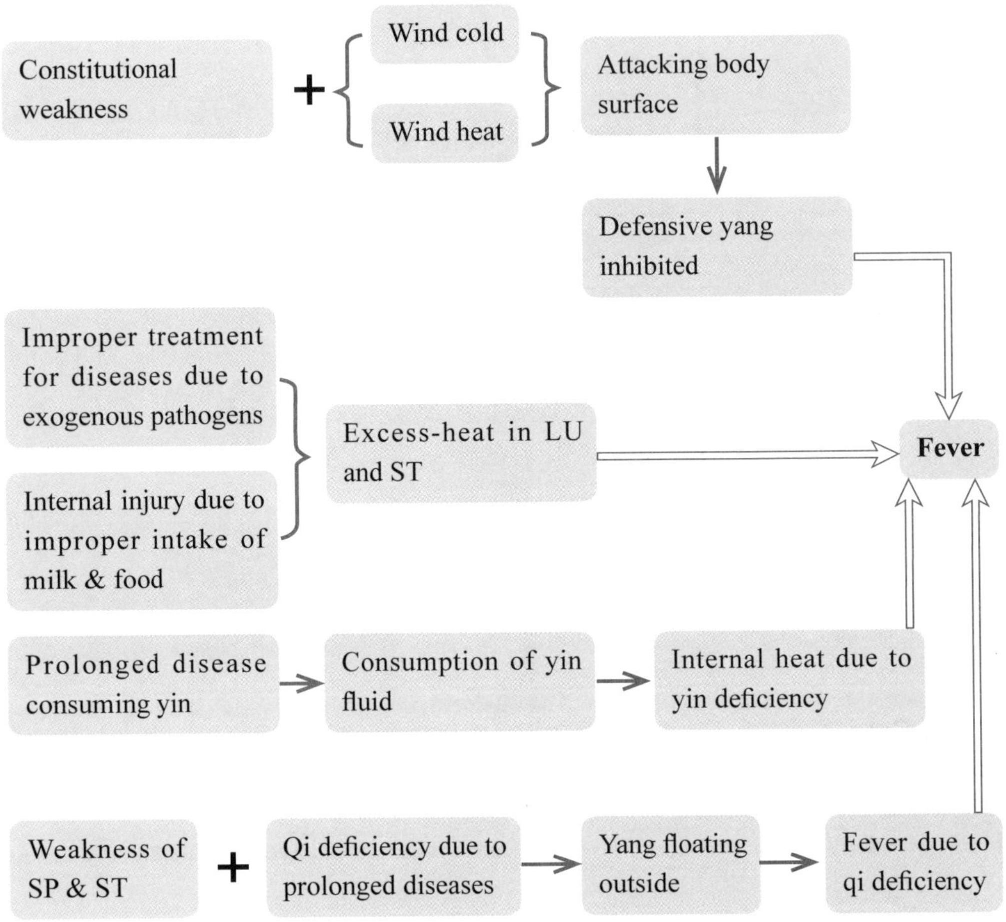

1. Clinical Manifestations

a. Fever due to exogenous pathogens

Fever, absence of sweating, aversion to cold, headache, general aching, nasal obstruction, clear nasal discharge, cold hands and feet, thin white tongue coating, fresh red finger stria indicating wind cold; fever, slightly sweating, yellow or turbid nasal discharge, swelling and pain of throat, dry mouth, red tongue tip, thin yellow tongue coating, red purple finger stria indicating wind heat.

b. Fever due to excess-heat in lung and stomach

High fever, profuse sweating, thirst with desire of drinking, reduced appetite, red face, shortness of breath, constipation, restlessness, red tongue, yellow dry tongue coating, dark purple finger stria.

c. Fever due to yin deficiency

Afternoon fever, lower grade fever, accompanied by warm sensation in chest, palms and soles, night sweating, red cheek, reduced appetite, emaciation, thready rapid pulse, red tongue with little coating or without coating, purplish finger stria.

d. Fever due to qi deficiency

Fever after exertion, lower grade fever, feeble voice, dislike of speaking, lassitude, spontaneous sweating after movements, anorexia, emaciation or diarrhea right after meals, pale tongue with thin white coating, a weak pulse or a deep thready forceless pulse, pale finger stria.

2. Tui Na Treatment

【Principles of treatment】

To clear heat.

【Commonly used manipulations】

Pushing *tiān mén* (天门), pushing *kǎn gōng* (坎宫), transporting *tài yáng* (太阳), clearing *tiān hé shuǐ* (天河水), pushing *liù fǔ* (六腑), scooping the moon up from the water (*shuǐ dǐ lāo yuè*, 水底捞月), crossing the heaven river on horseback (*dá mǎ guò tiān hé*, 打马过天河).

⋆ Fever due to exogenous pathogens

To clear heat, relieve the exterior and disperse pathogens.

For wind-cold, add clearing *fèi jīng* (肺经), pushing *sān guān* (三关), kneading *èr shàn mén* (二扇门), grasping GB 20 (*fēng chí*), pushing *tiān zhù gǔ* (天柱骨); For wind-heat, add clearing *fèi jīng* (肺经), pushing along the spine (*niē jǐ*, 捏脊), kneading DU 14 (*dà zhuī*).

⋆ Fever due to excess-heat in lung and stomach

To clear and purge heat, regulate qi and promote digestion.

Add manipulations of clearing *fèi jīng* (肺经), clearing *wèi jīng* (胃经), clearing *dà cháng* (大肠), kneading *bǎn mén* (板门), transporting *nèi bā guà* (内八卦), kneading ST 25 (*tiān shū*). For difficult defecation due to dry stools, add pushing *qī jié gǔ* (七节骨) downward, rubbing abdomen (*mó fù*, 摩腹) clockwise, kneading *bó yáng chí* (膊阳池), scrubbing and rubbing hypochondriac regions.

⋆ Fever due to yin deficiency and internal heat

To nourish yin and clear heat

Add manipulations of kneading *èr rén shàng mǎ* (二人上马), reinforcing *pí jīng* (脾经), reinforcing *fèi jīng* (肺经), kneading ST 36 (*zú sān lǐ*), pushing and scrubbing KI 1 (*yǒng quán*). For night sweating or spontaneous sweating, add kneading *shèn dǐng* (肾顶), pinching the spine (*niē jǐ*, 捏脊) and reinforcing *shèn jīng* (肾经); for restlessness and insomnia, add clearing *gān jīng* (肝经), kneading DU 20 (*bǎi huì*), pushing *tiān mén* (天门), nipping and kneading *wǔ zhǐ jié* (五指节), pounding *xiǎo tiān xīn* (小天心).

⋆ Fever due to qi deficiency

To invigorate spleen and replenish qi, with assistance of clearing heat.

Add manipulations of reinforcing *pí jīng* (脾经), reinforcing *fèi jīng* (肺经), transporting *nèi bā guà* (内八卦), rubbing abdomen (*mó fù*, 摩腹), kneading ST 36 (*zú sān lǐ*), kneading BL 20 (*pí shù*), kneading BL 13 (*fèi shù*), pinching along the spine (*niē jǐ*, 捏脊). For abdominal distension and anorexia, add kneading *bǎn mén* (板门), rubbing RN 12 (*zhōng wǎn*), separateing-pushing abdomen (*fēn tuī fù yīn yáng*, 分推腹阴阳); For loose stools with undigested food, add rubbing abdomen (*mó fù*, 摩腹) counterclockwise, reinforcing *dà cháng* (大肠), pushing *qī jié gǔ* upward (*tuī shàng qī jié gǔ*, 推上七节骨), pushing from *bǎn mén* (板门) to *héng wén* (横纹); For nausea and vomiting, add pushing *tiān zhù gǔ* (天柱骨), pushing from *héng wén* (横纹) to *bǎn mén* (板门), pushing RN 12 (*zhōng wǎn*), and kneading right *duān zhèng* (端正).

3. Nursing Care

Keep room ventilated and the environment clean.

Have light diet but nutritious.

Take care of body temperature, have bath with warm water to induce sweating so as to lower down body temperature.

Drink warm water to supplement the source of sweat.

Asthma

Asthma is a kind of respiratory disease often seen in pediatrics. It is characterized by paroxysmal dyspnea, prolonged expiration, wheezing sound in throat, or even inability to lie down flatly in a horizontal position with mouth opened and shoulders raised. The disease often occurs in spring and winter induced by abrupt weather change, abnormal changes of cold or heat, improper diet, overstrained, drastic emotional changes. The occurrence of the disease is caused by allergy status of the body resulting from contacting allergens such as pollen, paint, fish and crayfish, etc., which may lead to spasm of small bronchial smooth muscles, causing a series of symptoms. Chinese medicine thinks that infantile asthma is usually caused by endogenous and exogenous pathogenic factors. Endogenous pathogenic factors are related to the function of lung, spleen and kidney. Exogenous pathogenic factors include catching wind cold, irregular food intake or contacting foreign body. Recurrent asthma may consume lung qi and long time of illness may disturb kidney leading to kidney-yang deficiency and dysfunction of kidney in receiving qi.

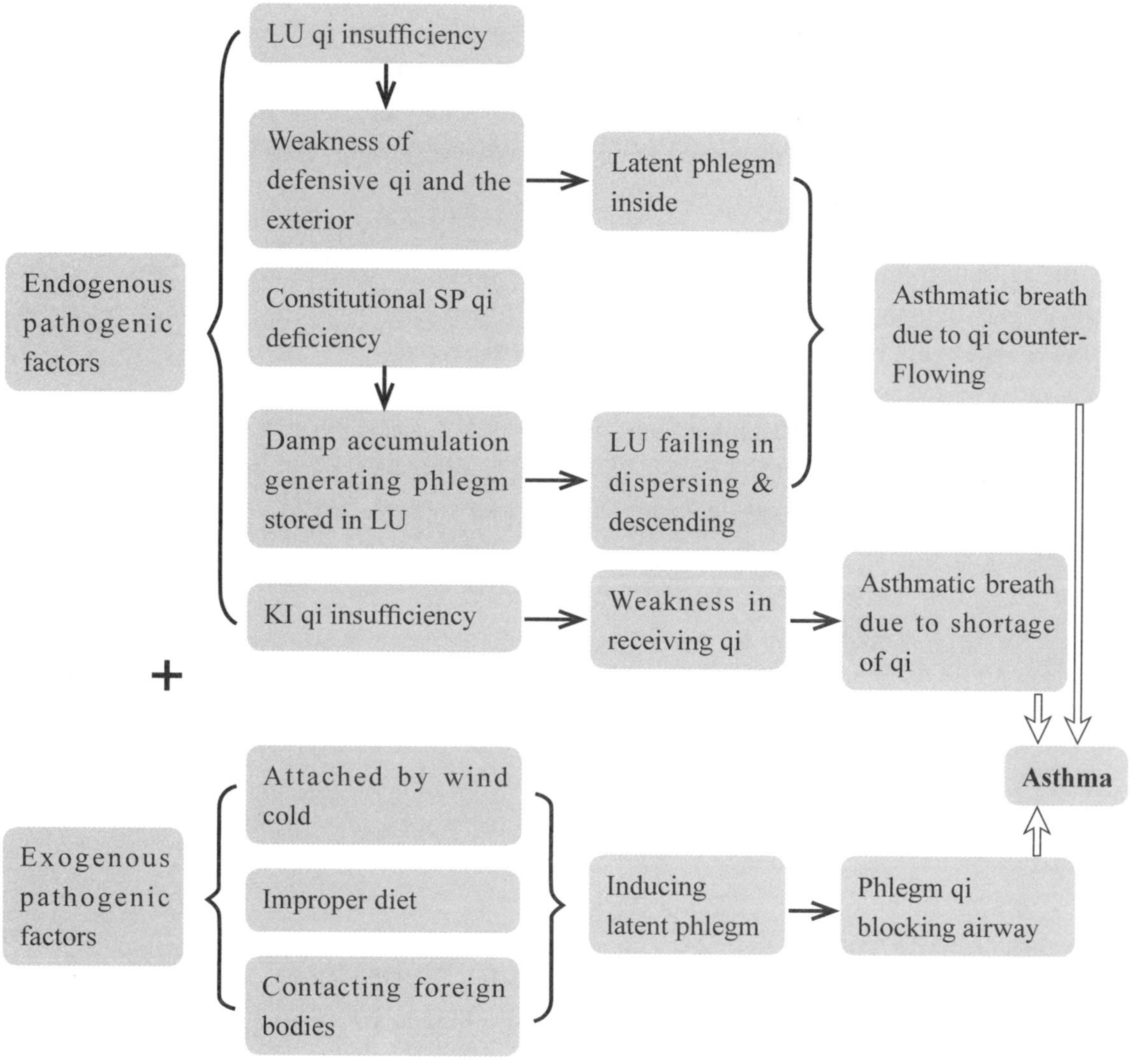

1. Clinical Manifestations

a. Asthma due to cold

Cough, difficult respiration with wheezing, or even with mouth opened and shoulders raised, inability to lie down flatly, expectoration of clear and dilute sputum white in color with foam, aversion to cold, absence of sweating, pale or bluish complexion, cold limbs, no thirst or thirst with desire of warm drinking, clear and profuse urine, light red tongue with thin white coating, a soggy rapid or floating slippery pulse, light red finger stria.

b. Asthma due to heat

Cough, shortness of breath, suffocating breath, wheezing during breathing, expectoration of thick yellow sputum, red face, fever, chest stuffiness, epigastric fullness, restlessness, thirst with desire of cold drinking, dark urine, dry stool, red tongue with thin yellow coating, a floating rapid pulse, deep red finger stria.

c. Dysfunction of kidney in receiving qi accompanied by kidney-yang deficiency

Shortness and difficult breath, wheezing during breath, bluish and grayish complexion, no thirst, fatigue, lassitude, poor appetite, orthopnea with mouth opened and shoulders raised, cold limbs, aversion cold, soreness and weakness in lower back and knees, frequent urination with clear and profuse urine, pale tongue with thin white coating, a deep thready and forceless pulse, light finger stria.

2. Tui Na Treatment

【Principles of treatment】

To open the chest, regulate qi, resolve phlegm and ease asthma.

【Commonly used manipulations】

Pushing *fèi jīng* (肺经), pushing *sì héng wén* (四横纹), kneading *bǎn mén* (板门), pressing RN 22 (*tiān tū*), kneading RN 17 (*dàn zhōng*), kneading ST 18 (*rǔ gēn*), *rǔ páng* (乳旁), scrubbing and rubbing like pressing string (*àn xián zǒu cuō mó*, 按弦走搓摩), kneading BL 13 (*fèi shù*).

* Asthma due to cold

Add manipulations of wasps going into honeycomb (*huáng fēng rù dòng*, 黄蜂入洞), pressing GB 20 (*fēng chí*), reinforcing *fèi jīng* (肺经), grasping LI 4 (*hé gǔ*), pushing *sān guān* (三关) upward, scrubbing RN 17 (*dàn zhōng*), scrubbing BL 13 (*fèi shù*). If cold asthma is together with yang deficiency, add reinforcing *pí jīng* (脾经), *fèi jīng* (肺经) and *shèn jīng* (肾经), kneading *dān tián* (丹田), BL 20 (*pí shù*), BL 23 (*shèn shù*), pressing and kneading SP 6 (*sān yīn jiāo*).

* Asthma due to heat

Add manipulations of clearing *fèi jīng* (肺经), clearing *dà cháng* (大肠), pushing *liù fǔ* (六腑), change kneading RN 17 (*dàn zhōng*) into separating-pushing RN 17 (*dàn zhōng*) and pushing the spine (*tuī jǐ*, 推脊).

* Dysfunction of kidney in receiving qi accompanied by kidney-yang deficiency

Add manipulations of reinforcing *fèi jīng* (肺经), pushing *xiǎo cháng* (小肠), *sān guān* (三关), rubbing RN 12 (*zhōng wǎn*), kneading *dān tián* (丹田), BL 23 (*shèn shù*), reinforcing *shèn jīng* (肾经), *pí jīng* (脾经), moving *nèi bā guà* (内八卦), kneading RN 12 (*zhōng wǎn*), pressing and kneading ST 36 (*zú sān lǐ*).

3. Nursing Care

Patients with constitutional weakness or rickets should be supplemented with nutrition.

Keep warm to prevent attack of exogenous pathogenic factors.

The mother should have less pungent, spicy, fragrant, roasted and baked food, or greasy and sweetish food to prevent milk being influenced.

Have proper rest during asthma attack. Do outdoor exercises to strengthen body constitution during remission stage. Change dressing in time to avoid common cold.

Vomiting

Vomiting is a disease caused by dysfunction of stomach qi in descending, upward running of stomach qi forcing stomach contents rushing out from mouth and nose. Literally, vomiting with content and sound is called "*ǒu*"; vomiting with content but without sound is called "*tù*". Since "*ǒu*" and "*tù*" often occur together so vomiting in Chinese is called with a joint name "*ǒu tù*". Vomiting is often seen in infants as a chief symptom in various diseases such as acute gastritis, cardiospasm, pylorospasm and pyloric obstruction. Western medicine thinks vomiting is a kind of instinctive reflex of body to expel harmful substances out to protect stomach. However, frequent intense vomiting will disturb normal food intake and lead to dehydration, imbalance of electrolyte and acid-base and dystrophy if vomiting lasts for long time. In addition, infantile vomiting could be also seen in diseases of other systems, it is necessary to make history of disease clear and analyze the disease carefully.

Milk flowing out from mouth corner is a common phenomenon in the neonatal period. This is caused by too much milk in the stomach or air in the stomach which was taken in during breast feeding. It is also related to the infantile anatomical features such as horizontal position of stomach, incomplete development of stomach muscles, weak cardiac muscle and high tension of pyloric muscle. Therefore, this phenomenon is not taken as disease.

In Chinese medicine, stomach is considered as sea of water and food, it works well only when its function in descending is normal. The spleen and stomach of infants are weak and tender, any of six exogenous pathogenic factors, irregular eating habit, voracious eating of raw and cold fruits, greasy food; or fear and fright, may induce vomiting.

1. Clinical Manifestations

a. Vomiting due to cold

Intermittent vomiting after over-eating with vomitus not very foul, pale complexion, cold limbs,

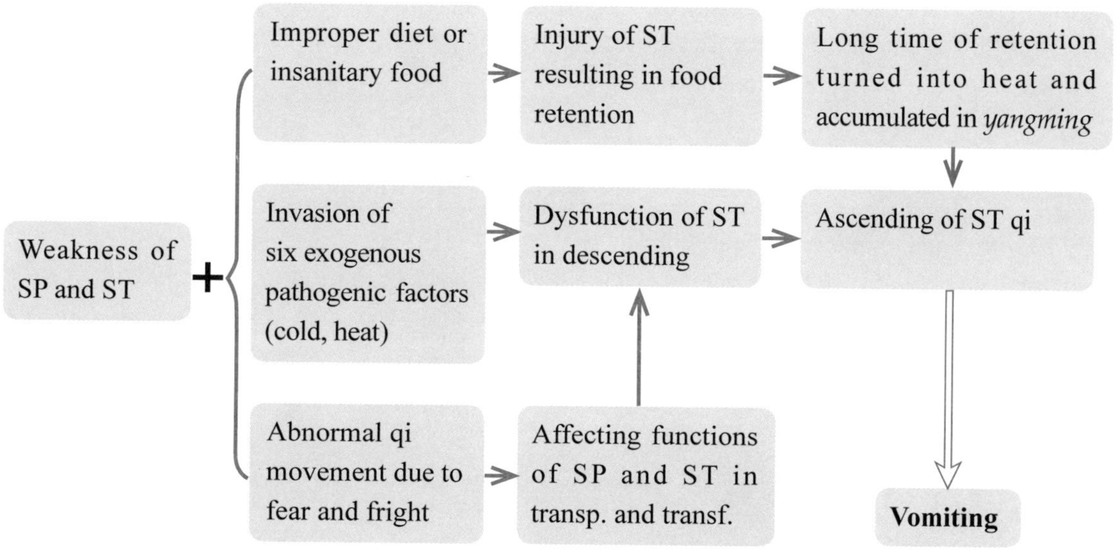

abdominal pain alleviated by warmth and pressing, loose stools, pale tongue with thin white coating, red finger stria.

b. Vomiting due to heat

Vomiting right after eating with foul vomitus, restlessness, thirst, fever, constipation or defecation with foul stools, dark yellow urine, dry lips, red tongue with yellow greasy coating, purple finger stria.

c. Vomiting due to improper feeding

Frequent vomiting with foul vomitus, bad breath, anorexia, abdominal distending pain, sour loose stool, red tongue with thick greasy coating, a slippery full pulse, purple or red finger stria.

d. Vomiting due to fear and fright

Sudden onset of vomiting after being frightened, or frequent vomiting with clear fluid, nervous expression, restlessness and fear at daytime and disturbed sleep at night, easily crying, bluish nose bridge, bluish finger stria, and a rapid pulse.

2. Tui Na Treatment

【Principles of treatment】

To normalize stomach and pacify adverse qi.

【Commonly used manipulations】

Reinforcing *pí jīng* (脾经), *wèi jīng* (胃经), pushing from *héng wén* (横纹) to *bǎn mén* (板门), pushing *tiān zhù gǔ* (天柱骨), kneading RN 12 (*zhōng wǎn*), rubbing abdomen (*mó fù*, 摩腹), pressing and kneading ST 36 (*zú sān lǐ*).

* Vomiting due to cold

Add manipulations of kneading EX-UE8 (*wài láo gōng*), pushing *sān guān* (三关).

* Vomiting due to heat

Add manipulations of pushing *liù fǔ* (六腑), clearing *dà cháng* (大肠), pushing along the spine (*niē jǐ*, 捏脊), pushing *qī jié gǔ* downward (*tuī xià qī jié gǔ*, 推下七节骨).

* Vomiting due to improper feeding

Kneading *bǎn mén* (板门), moving *nèi bā guà* (内八卦), separateing-pushing abdomen (*fēn tuī fù yīn yáng*, 分推腹阴阳), scrubbing and rubbing like pressing string (*àn xián zǒu cuō mó*, 按弦走搓摩), pressing and kneading RN 17 (*dàn zhōng*), kneading BL 20 (*pí shù*).

* Vomiting due to fear and fright

Pressing and kneading RN 22 (*tiān tū*), clearing *gān jīng* (肝经), kneading *xiǎo tiān xīn* (小天心), nipping and kneading *wǔ zhǐ jié* (五指节), separateing-pushing abdomen (*fēn tuī fù yīn yáng*, 分推腹阴阳), kneading right *duān zhèng* (端正).

3. Nursing Care

Feed the baby regularly, don't leave the baby too hungry or too full, or don't give food too cold or too hot.

Severe vomiting may cause apnea and asphyxiation, babies with such vomiting should be under close observation to prevent gastric content inhaled, resulting in aspiration pneumonia and other diseases of respiratory tract.

Recurrent vomiting may lead to dehydration, acidosis and so on. Integrated treatment with western and Chinese medicine should be recommended at this moment.

Diarrhea

Diarrhea is characterized by loose stools, or even watery stools, and increased bowel movements every day. The disease is more often seen in infants younger than one and half years old, often happens in summer and autumn. Diarrhea can be classified into two categories: acute diarrhea and chronic diarrhea. The disease is mainly related to spleen, large intestine and small intestine. Spleen governs transportation and transformation, small intestine sends the clear upward and the tubid downward, and large intestine is the organ in charge of transportation. Therefore, disorders of spleen, large and small intestines may lead to diarrhea. Western medicine thinks, in infants, immature development and incomplete functions of digestive system, weak neuroregulation, less secretion of gastric acid and digestive enzymes, low enzyme activity are endogenous pathogenic factors of the disease. Improper diet, exposure to cold, or invasion of pathogenic escherichia coli and enterovirus are exogenous pathogenic factors. In severe cases, water and electrolyte would be disturbed resulting in crisis like dehydration and acidosis.

Diarrhea is liable to consume qi and blood. Persisting diarrhea, if it is not treated in time, may affect nutrition, growth and development of infants, resulting in crisis of liquid depletion due to qi deficiency or even death.

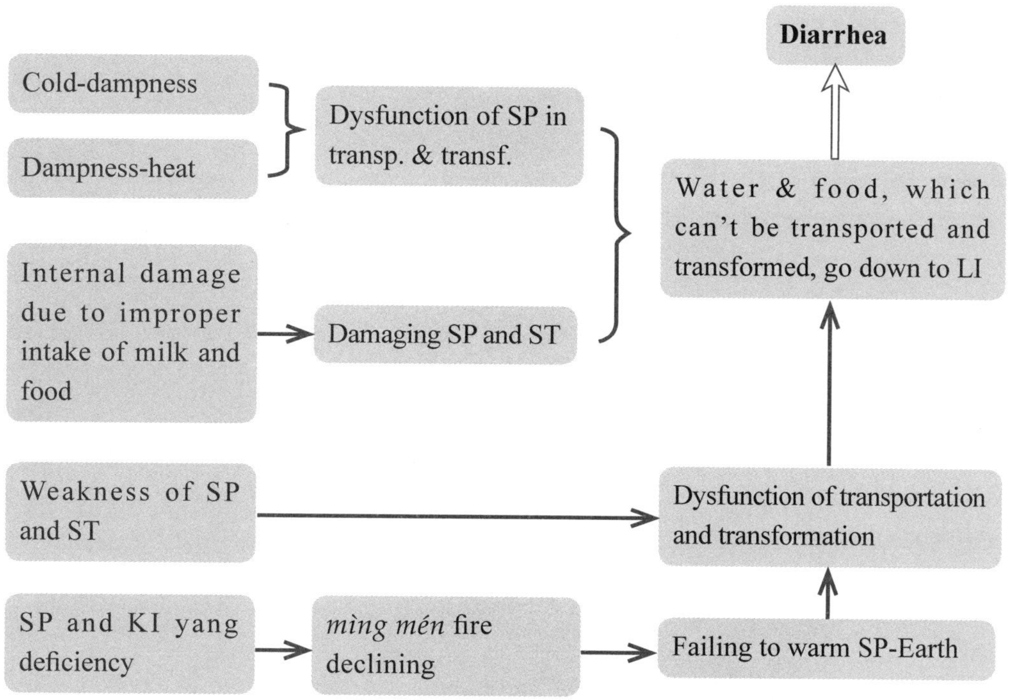

1. Clinical Manifestations

a. Diarrhea due to cold-dampness

Loose stools with foam, light in color, no foul smell, profuse clear urine, nausea, vomiting, chest stuffiness, poor appetite, borborygmus, abdominal pain, mild fever, chills, cold hands and feet, no thirst, white greasy tongue coating, a soft pulse.

b. Diarrhea due to dampness-heat

Loose yellow stools with foul smell, dark scanty urine, restlessness, thirst, high fever, yellow greasy tongue coating and a rapid pulse.

c. Diarrhea due to improper intake of milk and food

Abdominal distention and pain, crying before bowel movement, pain relieving after defecation, big amount of foul stools, poor appetite, belching, restless sleep at night, feverish palms, sallow complexion, thirst, thick tongue coating and a slippery pulse.

d. Diarrhea due to spleen-deficiency

Recurrent diarrhea right after meals or intake of greasy food, loose stools with undigested food, light in color and no foul smell, sallow complexion, listlessness, lassitude, cold limbs, pale tongue with white coating, soft pulse.

e. Yang deficiency of spleen and kidney

Immoderate defecation with watery stools, undigested food in stools, sallow complexion, listlessness, weak limbs, cold limbs, white tongue coating, and thready pulse. Any kind of severe diarrhea might cause crisis of collapse resulted from yang floating outside due to yin exhausted inside.

2. Tui Na Treatment

【Principles of treatment】

To invigorate spleen and drain dampness.

【Commonly used manipulations】

Reinforcing *pí jīng* (脾经), pushing *dà cháng* (大肠), clearing *xiǎo cháng* (小肠), rubbing abdomen (*mó fù*, 摩腹), kneading umbilicus (*róu qí*, 揉脐), kneading *guī wěi* (龟尾), pushing *qī jié gǔ* upward (*tuī shàng qī jié gǔ*, 推上七节骨).

⋆ Diarrhea due to cold-dampness

Add manipulations of kneading EX-UE8 (*wài láo gōng*), kneading ST 25 (*tiān shū*), pressing BL 20 (*pí shù*) and BL 21 (*wèi shù*).

⋆ Diarrhea due to dampness-heat

Add manipulations of clearing *dà cháng* (大肠), pushing *sān guān* (三关) upward, pushing *liù fǔ* (六腑) downward.

⋆ Diarrhea due to improper intake of milk and food

Add manipulations of clearing *pí jīng* (脾经) and *wèi jīng* (胃经), kneading RN 12 (*zhōng wǎn*), scrubbing umbilicus (*cuō qí*, 搓脐), grasping *dù jiǎo* (肚角).

⋆ Diarrhea due to spleen-deficiency

Add manipulations of pushing *bǎn mén* (板门), moving *nèi bā guà* (内八卦), kneading BL 20 (*pí shù*) and BL 21 (*wèi shù*), pinching along the spine (*niē jǐ*, 捏脊), kneading ST 36 (*zú sān lǐ*); For yang deficiency of spleen and kidney, additionally add manipulations of kneading BL 23 (*shèn shù*), pushing and scrubbing lumbosacral region.

3. Nursing Care

Take care of dietary hygiene to prevent the disease caused by eating.

Feed the baby at fixed time with limited milk and food; it is not advisable to leave the baby sometimes full or too hungry, or sometimes too cold and sometimes too warm.

Take light food easy for digesting and keep away from greasy food during the attack of diarrhea.

Anorexia

Anorexia refers to long time inappetence of children, disinterest in eating. It is often seen in children among 1~6 years old. The incidence of the disease is obviously lower in school children, higher in city children. The disease has no obvious seasonality. In western medicine, it is thought the disease is caused by insufficiency of calories and protein, lack of vitamin B family or certain microelements, or excessive intake of protein, sugar, fat and Vitamin D or vitamin A. Besides, bad mood because the child is forced to eat by parents, or disrupted eating habits because of frequent feeding, may also cause anorexia. Tension, worry, fear, excitement of the child can influence the appetite as well. In Chinese medicine, it is thought that the disease is mainly related to functions of spleen and stomach, eating habit and emotional factors. Tension, anxiety, fear, excitement of the child can influence the appetite as well. In Chinese medicine, it is thought that the disease is mainly related to functions of spleen and stomach, eating habit and emotional factors.

1. Clinical Manifestations

a. Dysfunction of spleen in transportation and transformation

Refusing to take milk or food, or no desire of taking food, tasteless, lusterless complexion, emaciation, pale tongue with thin white or greasy coating, a soft moderate pulse.

b. Stomach yin deficiency

No desire of eating, poor appetite, preference for drinking water, dry mouth and tongue, lusterless complexion, dry skin, dry stools, yellow urine, dry red tongue with little coating or peeled coating, a thready rapid pulse.

c. Weakness of spleen and stomach

No desire for eating, sallow complexion, thin body, listlessness, lassitude, dislike of speaking, frequent sweating, stool with undigested food, pale tongue with thin white coating, a feeble weak pulse.

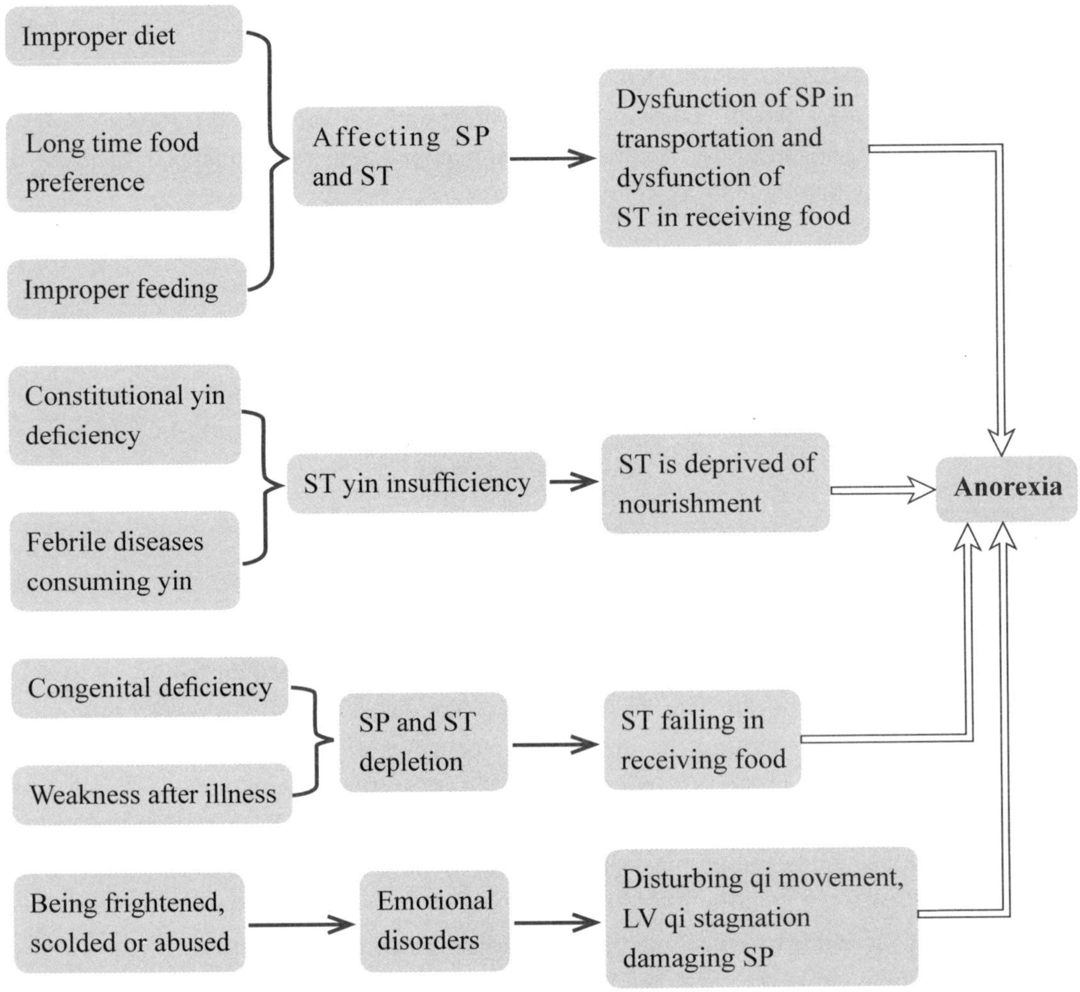

d. Liver qi stagnation

Poor appetite, no desire for eating, depressed mood, epigastric fullness, belching, hypochondriac distention, sighing, pale tongue with peeled coating, a wiry moderate pulse.

2. Tui Na Treatment

【Principles of treatment】

To invigorate spleen and promote digestion.

【Commonly used manipulations】

Reinforcing *pí jīng* (脾经), moving *nèi bā guà* (内八卦), kneading *bǎn mén* (板门), pushing *sì héng wén* (四横纹), kneading RN 12 (*zhōng wǎn*), rubbing abdomen (*mó fù*, 摩腹), pinching along the spine (*niē jǐ*, 捏脊).

⋆ Dysfunction of spleen in transportation and transformation

Add manipulations of reinforcing *wèi jīng* (胃经), kneading BL 20 (*pí shù*) and BL 21 (*wèi shù*), pressing and kneading ST 36 (*zú sān lǐ*).

⋆ Stomach yin deficiency

Add manipulations of kneading *èr rén shàng mǎ* (二人上马), clearing *dà cháng* (大肠), clearing *tiān hé shuǐ* (天河水), scooping the moon up from the water (*shuǐ dǐ lāo yuè*, 水底捞月), transporting earth into water (*yùn tǔ rù shuǐ*, 运土入水).

⋆ Weakness of spleen and stomach

Add manipulations of reinforcing *wèi jīng* (胃经), transporting water into earth (*yùn shuǐ rù tǔ*, 运水入土), pushing *sān guān* (三关), rubbing RN 12 (*zhōng wǎn*), rubbing *dān tián* (丹田), kneading BL 20 (*pí shù*), BL 21 (*wèi shù*) and ST 36 (*zú sān lǐ*).

⋆ Liver qi stagnation

Add manipulations of clearing *gān jīng* (肝经), kneading RN 17 (*dàn zhōng*), scrubbing and rubbing like pressing string (*àn xián zǒu cuō mó*, 按弦走搓摩), kneading BL 18 (*gān shù*), BL 20 (*pí shù*) and BL 21 (*wèi shù*).

3. Nursing Care

Feed the child in a correct way at fixed time, rectify bad eating habits.

Don't force the child to eat; it may make the child disgust with eating.

Offer varied food good for digestion according to the age to increase eating desire and benefit stomach and intestines.

Constipation

Constipation indicates prolonged bowel movement, or difficult and hesitant defecation. The incidence of infantile constipation is 3%-8%, among which functional constipation occupies 90%-95%. Infantile constipation can be classified into excess and deficiency types. The pathological change is mainly related to the conditions of stomach, intestines, qi, blood and body fluid. In western medicine, infantile constipation is classified into functional constipation and constipation due to intestinal tract malformation. Functional constipation is more often seen in clinic, its etiology includes: I. Irregular defecation habit results in feeble defecation reflex and weak intestinal muscles. II. Used to take liquid and soft food which are lack of dietary fibers, or food lack of carbohydrate. III. Perianal disorders like hemorrhoid and anal fissure, which may cause pain during defecation resulting retention of feces. IV. Malnutrition like rickets may cause dysfunction of intestinal tract, weakness or paralysis of abdominal muscles.

1. Clinical Manifestations

a. Excess constipation

Dry stools, difficult defecation, scanty dark urine, red face, warm body, hypochondriac and abdominal distension, abdominal distending pain, reduced appetite, dry mouth, restlessness, red tongue with yellow coating, rapid pulse, purple finger stria.

b. Deficiency constipation

Hesitant bowel movement, hard and difficult defecation, sweating and shortness of breath after defecation, no dry stools, lusterless complexion, listlessness, timidity, fatigue, lassitude, pale tongue with thin coating, feeble thready pulse, pale finger stria.

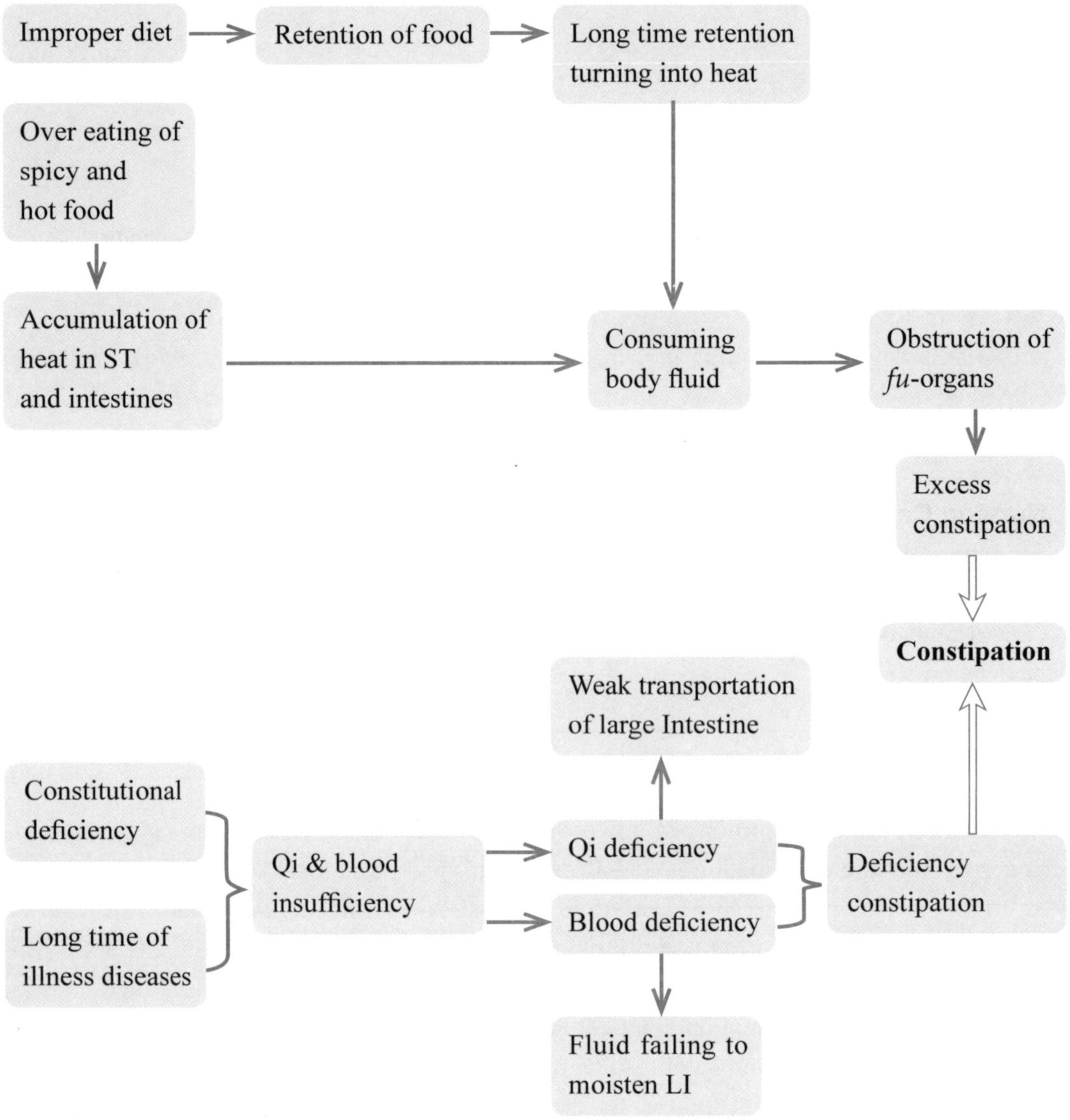

2. Tui Na Treatment

【Principle of treatment】

To remove obstruction and promote bowel movement.

【Commonly used manipulations】

Reinforcing *pí jīng* (脾经), clearing *dà cháng* (大肠), kneading ST 25 (*tiān shū*), rubbing abdomen (*mó fù*, 摩腹) clockwise, kneading *guī wěi* (龟尾), pushing *qī jié gǔ* downward (*tuī xià qī jié gǔ*, 推下七节骨), pressing and kneading *bó yáng chí* (膊阳池).

⋆ Excess constipation

Add manipulations of pushing *liù fǔ* (六腑), scrubbing and rubbing like pressing string (*àn xián zǒu cuō mó*, 按弦走搓摩), kneading ST 25 (*tiān shū*).

* Deficiency constipation

Add manipulations of pushing *sān guān* (三关), kneading ST 25 (*tiān shū*), pinching along the spine (*niē jǐ*, 捏脊), pressing and kneading ST 36 (*zú sān lǐ*).

3. Nursing Care

Build up habit of defecation at fixed time.

Take more fruits, vegetables and grain, keep away from spicy, pungent and high flavored food.

Have proper outdoor exercise.

Night Crying

Night crying refers to infant crying at night, or crying at certain time every night, but normal in daytime. In mild cases, the infant can still fall asleep after crying; in severe cases, the infant may cry all night. The problem can last several days or even over one month. It is often seen in infants younger than one year old and can happen in any season. Prolonged night crying is often caused by disorders of digestive system and nutritional deficiencies. In Chinese medicine, it is thought that night crying is mainly related to the functions of spleen, stomach and heart. The main causative factors include spleen cold, heart heat, fear and fright, and food retention.

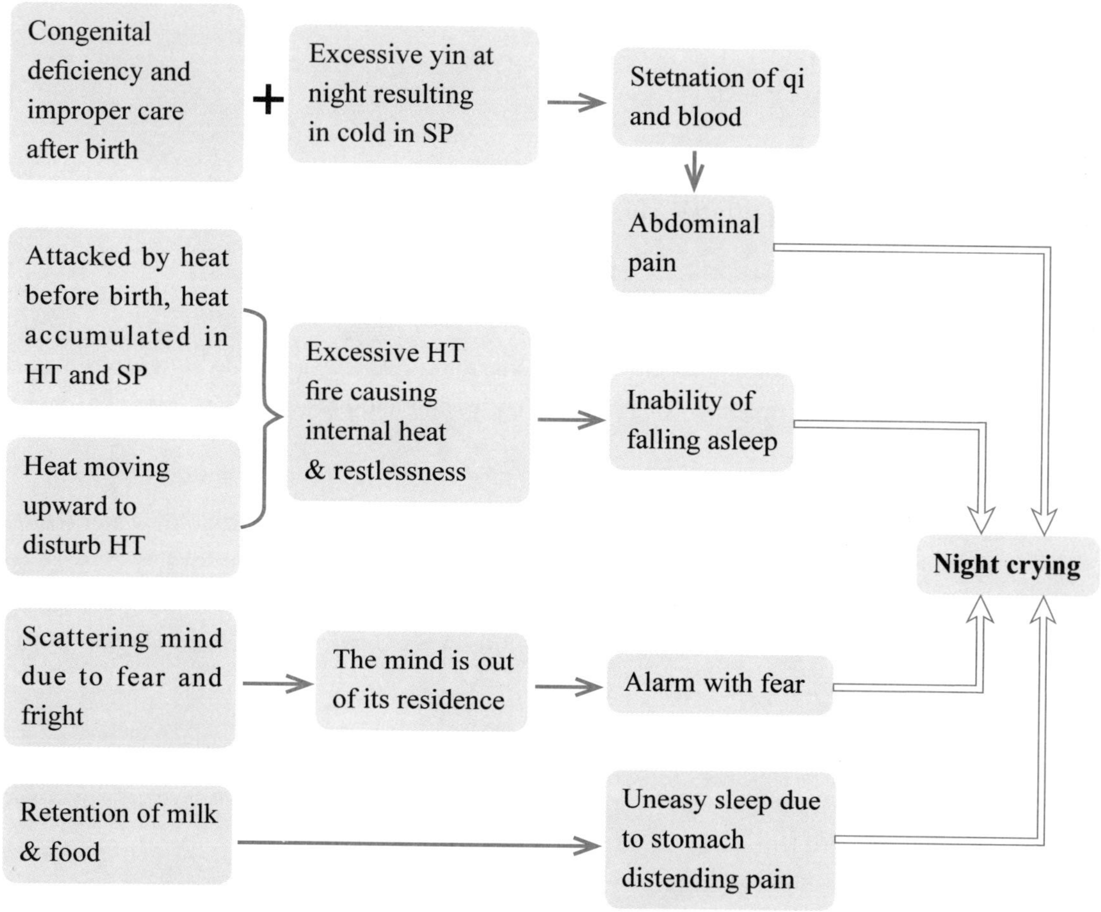

1. Clinical Manifestations

a. Spleen cold

Pale or bluish complexion, timidity, sleepiness, cold limbs, or accompanied by diarrhea, curled up during abdominal pain, feeble crying, preference for pressing his or her belly by hands, pain alleviated by warmth.

b. Heart heat

Red face and eyes, restlessness, preference for lying on the back, photophobia, loud crying, warm hands and abdomen, constipation, scanty and dark urine.

c. Fear and fright

Alternation of pale and bluish complexion, fear, alarm, miserable and urgent cry during dreams, frightened appearance, like to sleep by cuddled up.

d. Food retention

Dislike eating, vomiting milk, belching, acid regurgitation, abdominal pain and distension, uneasy sleep.

2. Tui Na Treatment

【Principles of treatment】

To calm the mind and ease mood.

【Commonly used manipulations】

Pressing and kneading DU 20 (*bǎi huì*), clearing *xīn jīng* (心经), clearing *gān jīng* (肝经), kneading *xiǎo tiān xīn* (小天心).

* Spleen cold

Add manipulations of reinforcing *pí jīng* (脾经), kneading EX-UE8 (*wài láo gōng*), pushing *sān guān* (三关) upward, rubbing abdomen (*mó fù*, 摩腹), pressing and kneading BL 20 (*pí shù*) and ST 36 (*zú sān lǐ*).

* Heart heat

Add manipulations of clearing *xiǎo cháng* (小肠), scooping the moon up from the water (*shuǐ dǐ lāo yuè*, 水底捞月), clearing *tiān hé shuǐ* (天河水), pushing *liù fǔ* (六腑) downward.

* Fear and fright

Add manipulations of nipping and kneading *gān jīng* (肝经), *xīn jīng* (心经), *xiǎo tiān xīn* (小天心) and *jīng níng* (精宁).

* Food retention

Add manipulations of clearing *pí jīng* (脾经) and *wèi jīng* (胃经), clearing *dà cháng* (大肠), kneading *bǎn mén* (板门), moving *nèi bā guà* (内八卦), pushing RN 12 (*zhōng wǎn*) downward, pushing *qī jié gǔ* downward (*tuī xià qī jié gǔ*, 推下七节骨).

3. Nursing Care

Have proper clothing; keep warm to prevent cold for the baby with spleen cold; don't put on too much clothes for the baby with heart heat.

Feed baby at fixed time with limited milk and food; it is not advisable to let the baby be sometimes too full, sometimes too hungry, sometimes too cold and sometimes too warm.

Pregnant women and mothers in breast feeding should avoid eating too much cold, pungent, spicy and hot food.

Keep the room quiet and avoid scaring the infant.

Enuresis

Enuresis refers to involuntary bed-wetting while asleep in children over three years of age. Bed-wetting of infants younger than three years of age is not considered as a disease because their cerebral marrow is not fully filled and intelligence not well developed, the ability of controlling urination is not formed yet. In modern medicine, it is thought that infantile urination is regulated by sympathetic and parasympathetic nerve of autonomic nervous system, but the efficient control from cerebral cortex to the urination has not established in infants. After three years old, the function of bladder in urination starts to be controlled efficiently by cerebral cortex. If cerebral cortex decontrol spinal micturition center, detrusor may contract to have urination. In Chinese medicine, it is thought that infantile enuresis is related to dysfunctions of lung, spleen and kidney, often caused by congenital insufficiency of kidney qi and deficiency-cold of lower energizer, or by spleen-lung depletion or heat of the liver channel resulting from various diseases.

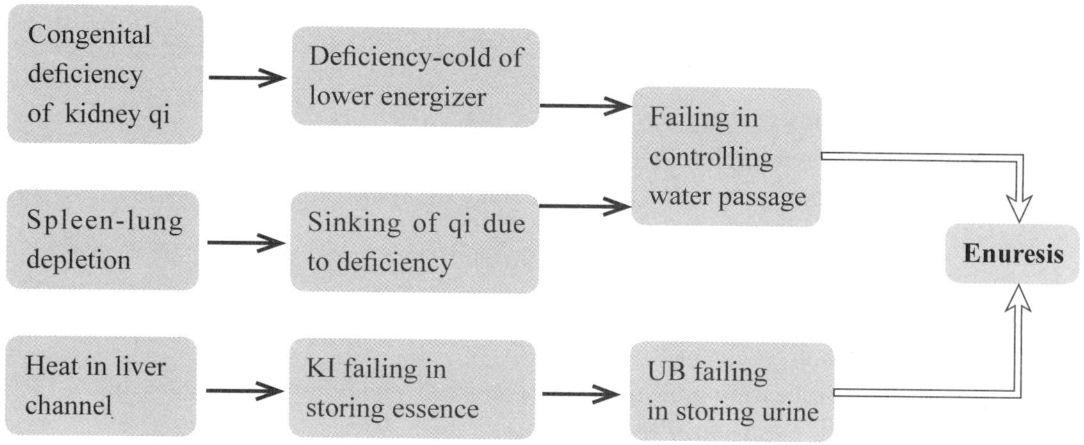

1. Clinical Manifestations

Involuntary urination while asleep, especially worse after fatigue or in cloudy and rainy days; the child with mild condition may have bed-wetting once a few nights, while the child with severe condition may have bed-wetting once, twice or more every night, some children even have enuresis at daytime. The child with enuresis for a long time usually manifest sallow complexion, lower intelligence, lassitude, dizziness, lumbar soreness and cold limbs. The child of older age may show coyness or nervousness.

a. Insufficiency of kidney qi

Bed-wetting while asleep, once or twice or even more times every night; the child at elder age is able to complain tiredness, lassitude, soreness and weakness in lumbar region and knees, cold limbs, clear profuse urine, or accompanied by dizziness, or even cold limbs, aversion to cold, sleep with the body curling up, pale tongue with thin white coating, a deep thready and forceless pulse.

b. Qi deficiency of lung and spleen

Bed-wetting while asleep, frequent urination with scanty urine, lusterless complexion, shortness of breath, spontaneous sweating, poor appetite, loose stools, emaciation, lassitude, pale tongue with thin white coating, a moderate forceless pulse.

c. Retention of heat in liver channel

Bed-wetting, scanty dark yellow urine, frequent incontinent urination, quick temper, feverish feeing in palms and soles, red face and lips, thirst with desire of drinking, or even dark red eyes, red tongue with yellow greasy coating, a wiry rapid pulse.

2. Tui Na Treatment

【Principles of treatment】

To warm kidney and astringe urine.

【Commonly used manipulations】

Kneading DU 20 (*bǎi huì*), *dān tián* (丹田) and BL 23 (*shèn shù*), rolling BL 31-34 (*Bá liǎo*), kneading *guī wěi* (龟尾), pressing and kneading SP 6 (*sān yīn jiāo*).

* Deficiency-cold of lower energizor

Add manipulations of reinforcing *shèn jīng* (肾经), pushing *sān guān* (三关), kneading BL 23 (*shèn shù*), scrubbing lumbosacral region, pinching along the spine (*niē jǐ*, 捏脊).

* Qi deficiency of lung and spleen

Add manipulations of reinforcing *pí jīng* (脾经), *fèi jīng* (肺经), kneading EX-UE8 (*wài láo gōng*), kneading RN 12 (*zhōng wǎn*), pressing and kneading ST 36 (*zú sān lǐ*).

* Retention of heat in liver channel

Add manipulations of clearing *gān jīng* (肝经) and *xiǎo cháng* (小肠), pushing *liù fǔ* (六腑), kneading *xiǎo tiān xīn* (小天心) and *èr rén shàng mǎ* (二人上马).

3. Nursing Care

Train the child to have urination at fixed time and build up a methodical life for child to prevent from tiredness.

In addition to active treatment, necessary nutrition should be supplemented and proper rest should be arranged. Don't offer drinks to the child two hours before sleep and give less liquid food.

While asleep, wake the child at a fixed time for urination to build up an orderly life habit.

Parents should consider the child's emotional welfare; try to diminish their nervousness.

Infantile Myogenic Torticollis

Infantile myogenic torticollis is characterized by the head tilted toward the affected side and bent forward with the face toward healthy side. Clinically, it generally refers to myogenic torticollis caused by spasm of unilateral sternocleidomastoid muscle. If the disease has lasted more than one year with obvious malformation, surgical operation should be considered.

The pathology of myogenic torticollis is fibrotic contraction of affected sternocleidomastoid muscle, manifesting hyperplasia of fiber cells and degeneration of muscle fibers, which would be replaced by connective tissues at last. The etiology of the disease is not sure until now, but there are several sayings as follows.

Mostly, it is thought the disease is related to trauma. Sternocleidomastoid muscle of one side is damaged by compression of birth canal or obstetric forceps during delivery, bleeding causes hemotoma which is organized later to form contraction.

Secondly, it is thought malposition of baby's head during delivery affects the blood supply of the sternocleidomastoid muscle of one side, causing ischemia of the muscle, edema of muscular fibers, or even necrosis and secondary fiber hyperplasia, at last resulting in muscular contraction to form myogenic torticollis.

And also, it is thought intrauterine deflexion of fetus' head to one side affects blood supply of sternocleidomastoid muscle of one side, causing ischemia of the muscle. This condition has no relation with delivery process.

1. Clinical Manifestation

After birth, a spindle-shaped mass could be found on one side of the neck, the sternocleidomastoid muscle of affected side gradually gets contracted and tensed, and the prominence is cord-like.

The infant's head bends toward affected side and the face toward healthy side.

A few infants only show hard mass like warts around attachment point of sternocleidomastoid muscle at the clavicle of affected side.

Prolonged condition may influence the development of face at affected side; the healthy side of the face will have adaptive change, making the face asymmetric. At later stage, the disease would be accompanied by compensatory thoracic scoliosis.

2. Tui Na Treatment

【Principles of treatment】

To relax sinew, dredge collaterals, soften hard mass and eliminate hemotoma. The treatment is mainly done on a local area.

【Commonly used manipulations】

Keep the infant in a supine position. Apply three-finger kneading manipulation on the affected sternocleidomastoid muscle (on hard nodule).

Apply grasping manipulation on affected sternocleidomastoid muscle (on hard nodule).

Apply three-finger kneading manipulation on affected sternocleidomastoid muscle (on hard nodule).

Bend infant's neck towards healthy side to rotate affected side.

At last, do gentle grasping manipulation on GB 21 (*jiān jǐng*) 5~6 times.

3. Nursing Care

Parents may often pull affected sternocleidomastoid muscle to extend the muscle.

To correct the pathological posture by adopting certain movements to opposite direction, such as feeding, sleeping on particular pillow, or attracting the infant's attention with toys.

Parents may have home-massage for the infant by taking kneading manipulation with fingertips of index, middle and ring fingers on infant's neck of the affected side, and kneading local nodules.

Infantile Subluxation of Radius Head

Infantile subluxation of radius head is caused by abnormal locations of radius head and annular ligament. As a common elbow injury in clinic, it often occurs in children under five years of age.

When infant's wrist is pulled suddenly under the condition of elbow joint stretched, for example, the wrist held by adult during dressing or falling down, the joint space of humeroradial articulation is enlarged, intra-articular vacuum is increased suddenly, joint capsule and annular ligament could be sucked into the joint space, annular ligament may stick radius head to affect it's returning, resulting in subluxation of the radius head.

1. Clinical Manifestations

The disease often occurs in infants with affected limb once injured by pulling, manifesting elbow pain with semiflexion of elbow joint and pronation of forearm, tenderness on the area of capitulum radii and absence of obvious swelling or malformation on local area. The child stops using the arm to take things and other elbow movements, and dislikes being touched. The locations of lateral epicondyle, medial epicondyle of humerus and olecranon are normal. X-ray examination can't show the lesion.

2. Tui Na Treatment

【Principles of treatment】

To relax sinew for reposition and stop pain.

【Method】

It is not necessary to have any anaesthesia. Face the child when the parent holds the infant. The condition that the right side is affected is taken as an example.

Place left thumb on lateral side of radius head and hold the upper part of wrist with right hand, stretch and rotate forearm backward.

Then, flex affected elbow joint, the radius head would be returned to its normal position.

3. Nursing Care

After reposition, elbow pain may disappear immediately, the infant stops crying and can flex the elbow and raise the arm to take things normally.

Generally, it is not necessary to have external treatment if there is no obvious swelling. Neck wrist sling can be used to append the elbow in flexed position 2~3 days.

Don't pull the affected limb during dressing or undressing in case of second injury or habitual dislocation.

Don't walk hand in hand with the child, because the adult is much taller than the child, it is liable to cause subluxation of the radius head when the forearm of the child is pulled in a raising up position.

Chapter 8 Self-Healthcare Tui Na Therapy

Section 1
Functions of Self-Healthcare Tui Na therapy

Self-healthcare tui na therapy implies some basic tui na manipulations that everybody can do on themselves together with some exercises to move their limbs so as to treat the diseases at early stage or keep fit.

Self-healthcare tui na therapy takes the person himself as the operated object. Active tui na manipulations are taken as the major treatment. Through active manipulations, it can not only stimulate all parts of the body and relative channels, collaterals and points, regulate the functions of important tissues and organs to enhance body's ability in preventing diseases; but also can excite right qi of the body and promote the circulation and metabolism of qi and blood, therefore the body can be kept in the harmonious healthy condition that "only when yin is in peace and yang is compact can the essence-spirit be normal" and "only when right qi is abundant inside the body can it keep away from the attack of pathogenic qi."

Self-healthcare tui na therapy consists of various exercises with rich contents. It is easy to be learned and available for the people at different ages to prevent and to treat diseases. In practical application, the people are required to concentrate the mind and keep an easy mood. The manipulations should be gentle, flexible and efficient.

Section 2
Approaches to the Manipulations

Soothing Liver Regulating Qi

The liver stores the soul, is attributed to "wood" in the five elements, and characterized by "moving" and "ascending". The main physiological function of the liver is to govern the free flow of qi and to store blood. Thus, the liver can regulate the movement of qi, harmonize channels, promote and ensure normal physiological functions of various *zang-fu* organs. Furthermore, it can promote the circulation of qi, blood and body fluid and strengthen transporting and transforming functions of spleen and stomach. The liver opens into the eyes, dominates the tendons and manifests its condition on the nails. Its will is anger and its fluid is the tear. A sufficient liver qi gives strong tendons, powerful strength, hard nails and bright eyes. On the contrary, the deficiency of liver qi results in soft and weak tendons and blurred vision. On the other hand, liver and gallbladder are related not only because of their pertaining and connecting relations between the foot *jueyin* liver channel and the foot *shaoyang* gallbladder channel, but also because of their external-internal relations. Therefore, applying the method of soothing the liver and regulating qi can prevent and cure illness of liver and gallbladder system in TCM effectively.

1. Rubbing intercostal spaces

In sitting position, put the right hand under the left armpits with fingers parted and the left hand under the right armpit. The distance between the fingers is equal to the distance between the ribs. Push rightward to the sternum with left hand, and then push leftward to the sternum with right hand. Do pushing movement with left and right hand alternately and shift bit by bit to the navel level, repeat the whole process 9 times. Attention: the fingers should touch the spaces and the movement should be stable and even until there is warm feeling in the intercostal spaces (Fig. 8-1).

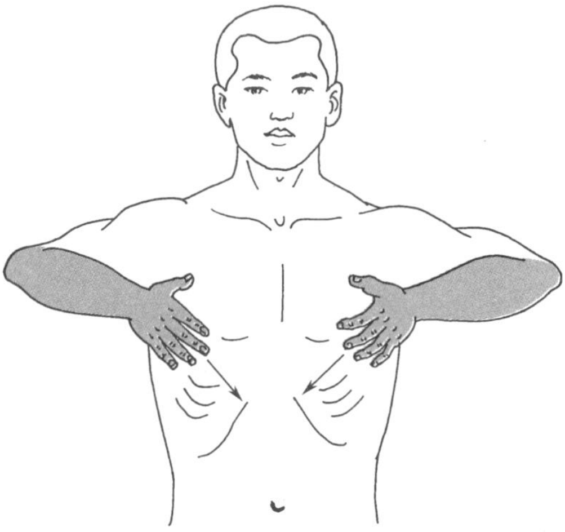

Fig. 8-1 Rubbing intercostal spaces

2. Kneading RN 17 (*dàn zhōng*, 膻中)

In sitting position, close four fingers of both hand and put them on RN 17 (*dàn zhōng*). Do kneading movement clockwise and counterclockwise 36 times in each direction with slight forceful strength.

3. Scrubing hypochondriac regions

In sitting position, close five fingers of both hands and put them over the chest at the nipple sides. The hands are overlapped, the left over the right. Scrubbing the chest and hypochondriac regions horizontally along the ribs and gradually shift downward to the floating ribs. And then put right hand over the left to do same movement again. Repeat the operation until there is warm feeling in the hypochondriac regions.

4. Plucking GB 34 (*yáng líng quán*, 阳陵泉)

In sitting position, put the thumbs on bilateral GB 34 (*yáng líng quán*). Press and knead the point for one minute, and then pluck the tendons transversely at the local area 3-5 times until there is sour and numb feeling radiating like electric shock.

5. Pressing LV 3 (*tài chōng*, 太冲)

In sitting position, press bilateral LV 3 (*tài chōng*) with the thumb tips forcefully about one minute till there is sour and numb feeling. Then knead the point gently with the thumb bellies.

6. Scrubbing lower abdomen

In sitting position or supine position, put the hands below hypochondriac regions, scrubbing forcefully along an oblique line to the lower abdomen to pubis, repeat the scrubbing 36 times (Fig. 8-2).

7. Pointing LV13 (*zhāng mén*, 章门)

Put tips of middle fingers on LV 13 (*zhāng mén*), press the point for about one minute with slightly strong force until there is sour and numb feeling.

8. Kneading LV 14 (*qī mén*, 期门)

In sitting position or supine position, put palm root of left hand on right LV 14 (*qī mén*) to knead the point forcefully clockwise and counterclockwise 36 times respectively. And then change hands and repeat the same process on left LV 14 (*qī mén*).

9. Grasping lumbar muscles

In sitting position, put the webs between the thumbs and index fingers over the lumbar muscles bilaterally to grasp the muscles from lumbar region to sacral region for 36 times.

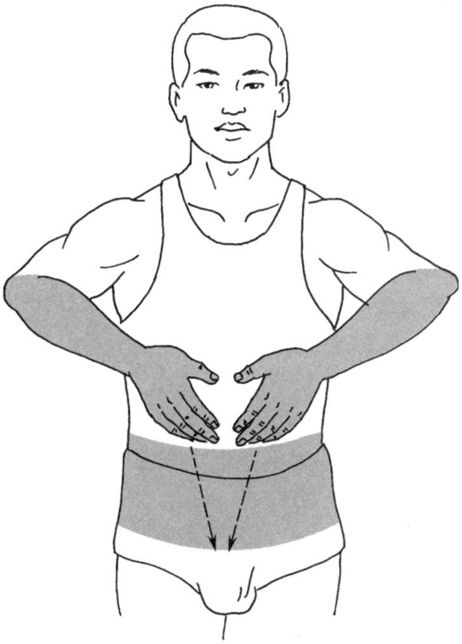

Fig. 8-2 Scrubbing lower abdomen

10. Moving both eyes

In sitting position, keeping the torso erect, gazing forward straightly, rotate two eyeballs clockwise slowly 9 times, then open the eyes widely and stare forward for a while. Repeat the counterclockwise rotation also 9 times.

Soothing Heart and Tranquilizing Mind Method

The main physiological function of the heart is to dominate blood vessels, which is considered as the key of vital activities. Only when the function of dominating blood vessels works normally, the blood can circulate normally in the vessels to nourish the body and to maintain the normal physiological activities. The heart is connected with the small intestine. The condition of the heart is shown through spirit, consciousness, mental activities, motor movement, pulse and tongue. Sufficient heart qi and abundant blood in vessels may manifest vigorous spirit, good mental activities, agile movement, mild and forceful pulse, and light red and moist tongue. On the contrary, insufficient heart qi may cause low spirit, slow reaction, and choppy or irregular pulse, and dusky purple or pale tongue. Therefore, the disorders of the heart system in TCM can be prevented and cured effectively by applying the method of soothing the heart and tranquilizing mind.

1. Invigorating heart channel

In a standing position with feet in a distance of the width of the shoulder, relax the body and stretch the hands naturally. Turn the waist left and right quickly to make the arms swinging around the body. Pat the chest with the palm; and the middle of the back with the hand dorsum when the arms are in the front and at the back respectively. At beginning, pat the body gently, the strength can be increased properly if there is no uncomfortable feeling. Repeat the same process about 36 times (Fig. 8-3).

2. Rubbing the chest

Put the right palm on the area between the breasts with fingers pointing obliquely downward to the side of the abdomen. Start rubbing around the left breast from the area below the left breast, then withdraw the hand to the area below the right breast to repeat the rubbing in the same way to form a figure of "∞" (horizontal 8) 36 times (Fig. 8-4).

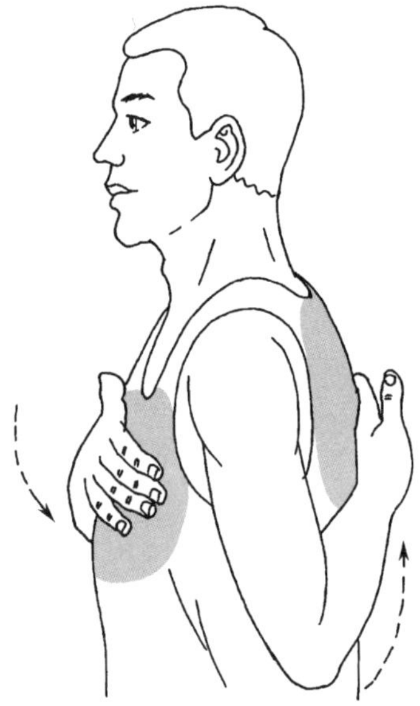

Fig. 8-3 Invigorating heart channel

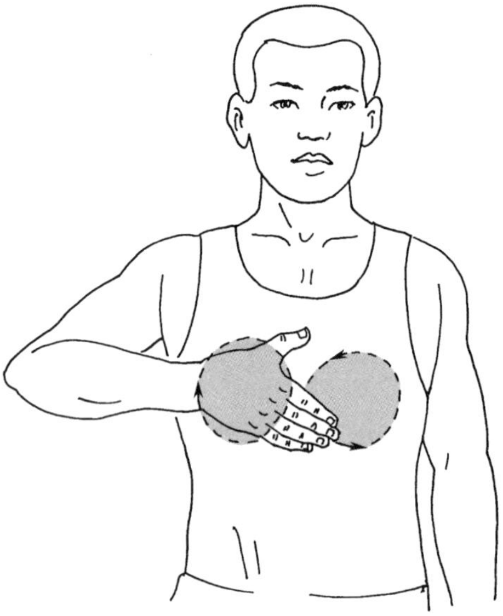

Fig. 8-4 Rubbing the chest

3. Hooking HT 1 (*jí quán*, 极泉)

Putting four fingers of right hand on the left greater pectoral muscle, press and knead the muscle with the palm root for a few minutes. Then, hold the anterior wall of armpit with the web between index and thumb and put middle finger on HT 1 (*jí quán*), hook and pluck the tendon there 9 times to cause sour and numb feeling which may radiate like electric shock. Then do the same process on the right side with left the hand.

4. Pinching PC 9 (*zhōng chōng*, 中冲)

Clip the tip of middle finger PC 9 (*zhōng chōng*) of left hand with thumb and index finger of right hand, do pressing and pinching forcefully 9 times. After that, change the side and do same process.

5. Kneading SP 10 (*xuè hǎi*, 血海)

In sitting position, put hands above the knee joints respectively, press and point SP 10 (*xuè hǎi*) with tips of thumbs about 1 minute, then knead the point gently and slowly 36 times.

6. Grasping heart channel

Put right thumb under the left armpit and the rest four fingers on the medial aspect of the upper arm; do grasping, pinching, pressing and kneading movements simultaneously, and shift the hands bit by bit down to HT 7 (*shén mén*). Repeat the same process up and down 9 times. After that, change the side to do the same operation on the right arm.

7. Kneading HT 7 (*shén mén*, 神门)

In sitting position, middle finger and index finger of right hand are overlapped to knead HT 7 (*shén mén*) of left hand about 1 minute. After that, change the side and repeat the same process.

8. Pressing PC 6 (*nèi guān*, 内关)

In sitting position, press PC 6 (*nèi guān*) on the left side with thumb of right hand, the other four fingers assist to squeeze the point from the back of wrist. Press and squeeze the point 9 times. After that, change the side and do the same process.

9. Hitting heaven drum

Put both the hand's palms on the ears with the root of the palms forward and five fingers backward. Hit the occiput region with index, middle and ring fingers 3 times, and then move the hands away suddenly. Repeat the same process 9 times (Fig. 8-5).

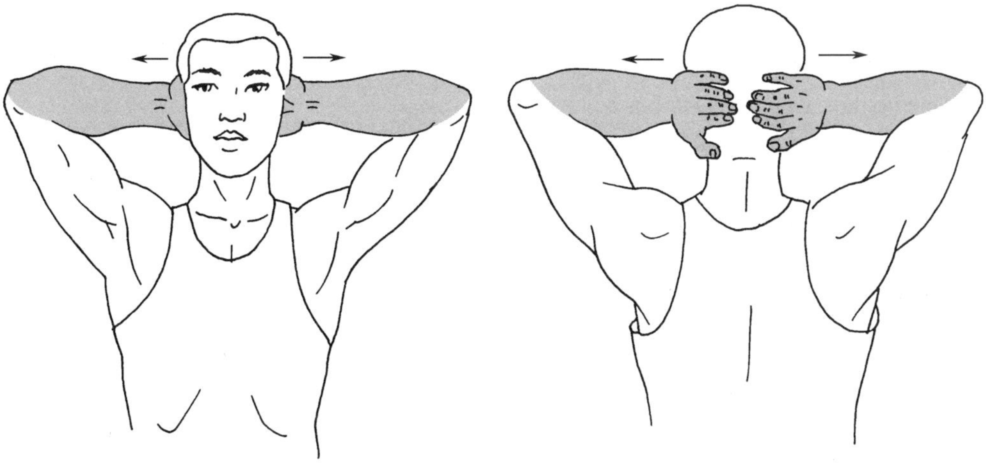

Fig. 8-5 Hitting heaven drum

10. Stirring the sea

Rotate the tongue inside the mouth to rub the outside and inside of the gum, from right to left and left to right, 9 times respectively. Swallow the saliva excreted by the movement three times.

Strengthening Spleen and Harmonizing Stomach Method

The main physiological function of the spleen is the transportation and transformation of food and water. The spleen plays an important role in digesting, absorbing, transporting and transforming nutrient substances and promoting the metabolism of water. Many functions of internal organs and an healthy condition of the body depend on the function of the spleen. As a result, in TCM, the spleen is called “acquired foundation”. Spleen has the function of controlling and keeping blood in the vessels. The spleen is related to the stomach via their exteriorly-interiorly related channels. On the body surface, the spleen manifests its condition through limb muscle, lips and taste in the mouth. When the spleen functions is well in transportation and transformation, the food essence is absorbed continuously, qi and blood are produced and turn into enough nutrition and lips are red and lustrous. On the contrary, the body would manifest emaciation, muscular atrophy, weakness, tastelessness or abnormal taste in the mouth and pale lips without luster. The method of strengthening spleen and benefiting stomach can prevent and cure illness of spleen- stomach system in TCM.

1. Rubbing the epigastric region

Putting left or right hand on RN 12 (*zhōng wǎn*), rubbing the epigastric region in circles 36 times counterclockwise from small circle to big circle. Then do the same rubbing movement 36 times but clockwise, from a big circle to a small circle (Fig. 8-6).

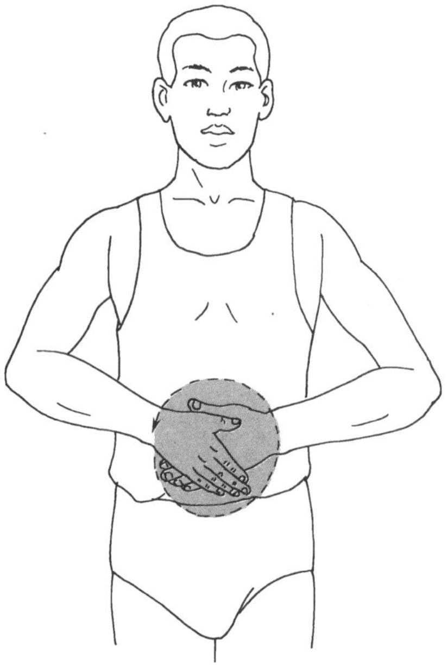

Fig. 8-6 Rubbing the epigastric region

2. Swaying the stomach

In supine position with two limbs flexed, put the hands overlapped on RN 12 (*zhōng wǎn*). With abdominal respiration, push upward and sway the abdomen with the root of overlapped palms when breathe out and release the hands when breathing in. Repeat the whole process 36 times.

3. Separating yin and yang

In sitting position or supine position, putting the hands with fingers toward fingers below the xiphoid process, pull from the front midline to the hypochondriac regions along the rib arcs and shift down to the lower abdomen bit by bit. Repeat the whole process 9 times.

4. Pressing ST 36 (*zú sān lǐ*, 足三里)

Putting the thumbs or index fingers or middle fingers on ST 36 (*zú sān lǐ*), press and knead the point forcefully about 3 minutes until there is a sour and distending feeling in the local area.

5. Kneading ST 25 (*tiān shū*, 天枢)

In sitting position or supine position, press and knead ST 25 (*tiān shū*) with the index fingers and middle fingers simultaneously clockwise and counterclockwise 36 times respectively.

6. Pressing the epigastric region

Close four fingers and put them on RN 12 (*zhōng wǎn*). With abdominal respiration, do a pressing movement downward when breathing in and gentle kneading movement in circles when breathing out. Repeat the whole process 36 times.

7. Kneading SP 10 (*xuè hǎi*, 血海)

In sitting position, knead SP 10 (*xuè hǎi*) with the thumbs clockwise and counterclockwise 36 times respectively.

Ventilating Lung and Releasing Exterior Method

The main physiological function of the lung is "governing qi and controlling breathing". It is the chief organ for exchanging air between the interior and exterior of the body. The body inhales fresh air and exhales waste air to stimulate the creation of qi and adjust the ascending, descending, exiting and entering movement of qi, so as to ensure the normal metabolism of the human body. The lung also has the function of "ventilating, purifying, descending, dredging and regulating water passage". The normal function of the lung may maintain respiration, nutrition and water metabolism in good condition so that the body can stay healthy. On the contrary, the abnormal function of the lung may manifest difficulty in breathing, stuffiness in the chest, cough and asthmatic breathing, and even edema. The lung is connected with the large intestine via channels and collaterals. The condition of the lung can be shown through luster of the skin, the nature of disease, or changes of the nose. Therefore, the method of dispersing the lung and benefiting qi may prevent and cure illness of the lung system in TCM.

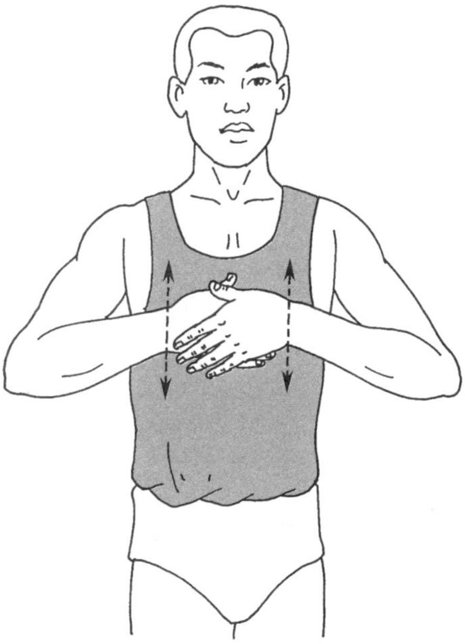

Fig. 8-7 Easing the influential point of qi

1. Easing the influential point of qi

Overlap the hands on RN 17 (*dàn zhōng*) between nipples; rub the area up and down 36 times (Fig. 8-7).

2. Freeing the movement of qi

In sitting position, put right hollow palm above the right breast, pat with proper force and move leftward horizontally, back and forth 9 times; then, cross the hands with fingers and put them above or below the breasts, do transverse rubbing back and forth forcefully 36 times. Finally, hold the side of body with the webs between thumbs and index fingers. Do rubbing up and down from the hypochondriac regions to ilium 36 times until there is a warm feeling at the local area.

3. Invigorating the chest

In sitting position, hold and grasp greater pectoral muscle of the left side with the right hand 9 times and repeat the same method on the right side with the left hand. Then, cross the fingers, hold the nape with the elbows flexed in a horizontal way. Try to extend the elbows backward as much as possible when breathing in and move the elbows inward and forward when breathing out. Repeat the same process 9 times (Fig. 8-8).

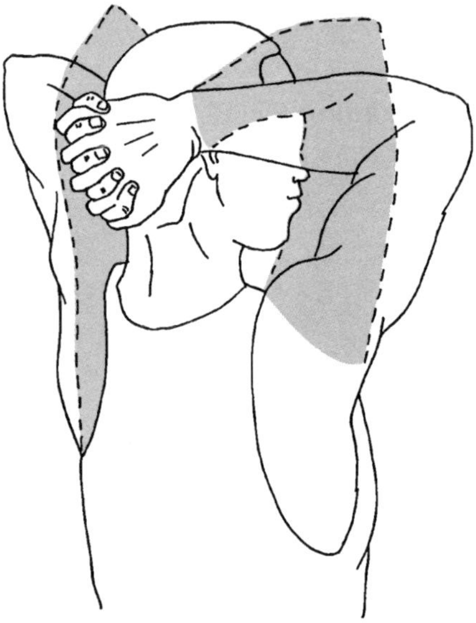

Fig. 8-8 Invigorating the chest

4. Kneading LU 1 (*zhōng fǔ*, 中府)

In sitting position, cross the hands in front of the chest with the tips of middle fingers on bilateral LU 1 (*zhōng fǔ*). Knead the point with slightly forceful strength clockwise and counterclockwise 36 times respectively.

5. Hooking RN 22 (*tiān tū*, 天突)

Hook RN 22 (*tiān tū*) with the tip of index finger and knead for 1 minute.

Regulating Triple Energizers

In sitting position or supine position, cross the fingers and put the hands horizontally on RN 17 (*dàn zhōng*) with the palm roots on the medial borders of the breasts. Do pushing movement from RN 17 (*dàn zhōng*) to RN 4 (*guān yuán*) forcefully. Repeat the same process 36 times (Fig. 8-9).

6. Removing obstruction from the lung channel

In sitting position or standing position, put right hand above the left breast and do rubbing in circles till it is warm at the local area. Then, do scrubbing and pushing along the frontal part of the shoulder, anterior border of medial aspect of the arm, radial side of the wrist and dorsum of the index finger (the course of the lung channel) up and down 36 times. After that, repeat the same process with the left hand on the right side (Fig. 8-10).

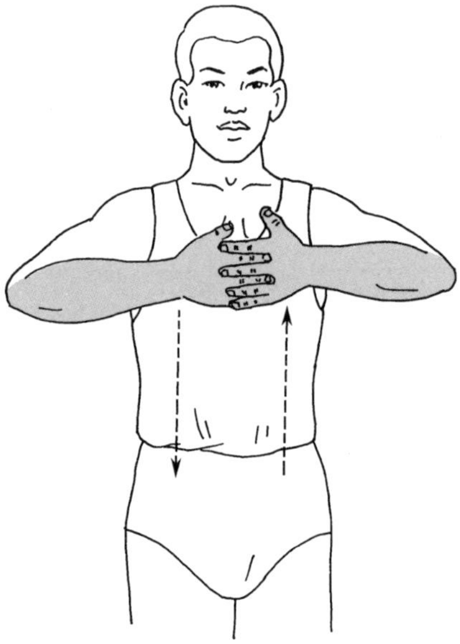

Fig. 8-9 Regulating Triple Energizers

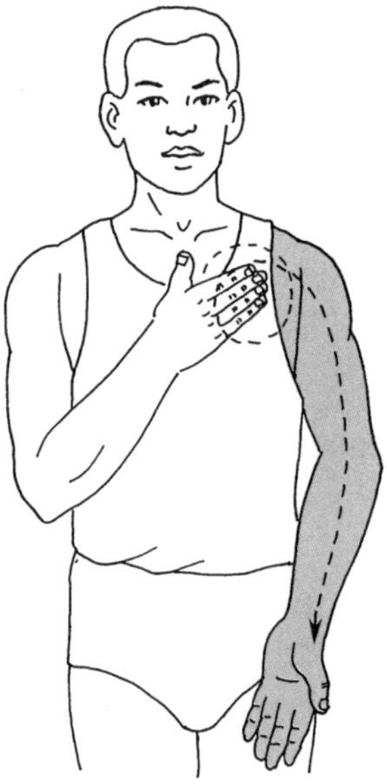

Fig. 8-10 Removing obstruction from the lung channel

7. Nipping LI 4 (*hé gŭ*, 合谷)

In sitting position, nip left LI 4 (*hé gŭ*) with the thumb and index finger of the right hand applying a closing force about 1 minute. After that, do the same process with the left hand on the right side.

8. Scrubbing LI 20 (*yíng xiāng*, 迎香)

In sitting position, put greater thenar of two hands or radial sides of index fingers on LI 20 (*yíng xiāng*) to rub the local area up and down with fast breath until there is a warm feeling at the local area.

Stabilizing Kidney Increasing Essence

The kidney is an important organ of the human body. In TCM, it is considered as the "congenital foundation" and it is the dynamic source of life. The major functions of the kidney are to store essence, to govern reproduction and development, and to regulate the metabolism of body fluid letting the clear part of the body fluid ascending to the lung for further distribution to the various parts of the body and the turbid part descending to the urinary bladder for discharging out of the body. In addition, the function of kidney in receiving qi is important for the respiration. The condition of the kidney is often shown from firmness of bones, luster or dryness of hair, outer spiritual status and hearing of the ears. The method of stabilizing kidney and increasing essence can strengthen and consolidate the kidney's function, but also has a certain effect in preventing and curing disorders of the kidney system in TCM.

1. Rubbing KI 1 (*yǒng quán*, 涌泉)

In a sitting position with tailor-fashion, rub two hands till they are warm, then do scrubbing back and forth from SP 6 (*sān yīn jiāo*) to the toe by passing ankle joint until the skin is very warm, and then rub KI 1 (*yǒng quán*) with two hands respectively until it is warm inside. The rubbing movement should be even in proper rhythm.

2. Rubbing kidney area

Put hands tightly over BL 23 (*shèn shù*), do rubbing in circles from lateral side to the spinal side with two hands simultaneously 36 times. [Rubbing clockwise is reinforcing method, and vice versa. It is not advisable to apply reducing method on BL 23 (*shèn shù*), so take care of rubbing direction during the operation]. For the people with kidney deficiency or lumbago, it is necessary to increase the rubbing times.

3. Kneading DU 4 (*mìng mén*, 命门)

Put index finger and middle finger on DU 4 (*mìng mén*) and knead the point in circles clockwise and counterclockwise 36 times respectively.

4. Scrubbing the lumbosacral region

Lean the body forward slightly with the elbow flexed and the palms placed on the lower back. Then, scrub the sacral region up and down with the whole palm or small thenar until it is warm at the local area (Fig. 8-11).

5. Rubbing RN 4 (*guān yuán*, 关元)

By taking RN 4 (*guān yuán*) as the centre of a circle, rub RN 4 (*guān yuán*) in circles clockwise or counterclockwise with left or right hand 36 times respectively. After that, press RN 4 (*guān yuán*) three minutes with the rhythm of the respiration.

6. Scrubbing the lower abdomen

With both hands push and rub repeatedly along an oblique course from the area below hypochondriac regions to the pubis until it is warm at the local area.

7. Vibrating the ears

First, put two hands over the ears, do rubbing and pushing movements back and forth 36 times. Then, hold the earlobes with thumbs and index fingers and do shaking movement 36 times. After that, insert the index finger into the ear tracts, do vibrating manipulation quickly several times, and pull out the fingers suddenly. Repeat the whole process 9 times (Fig. 8-12).

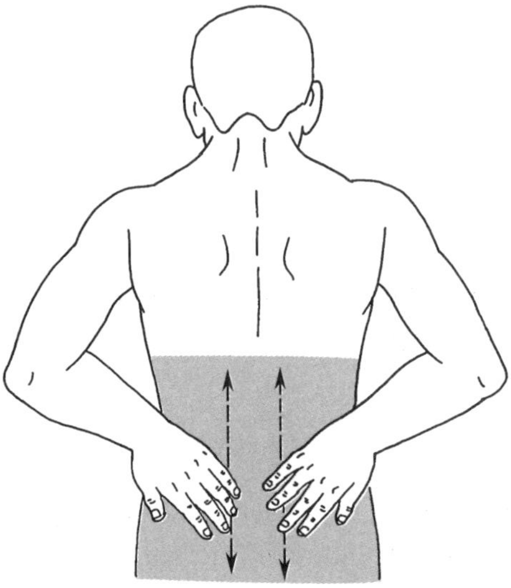

Fig. 8-11 Scrubbing the lumbosacral region

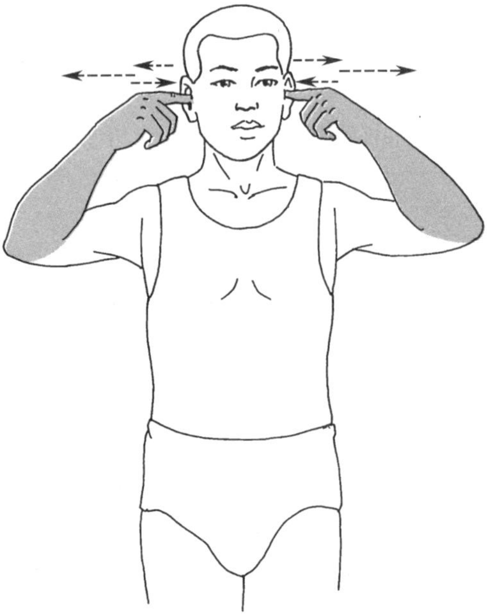

Fig. 8-12 Vibrating the ears

8. Contracting the anus and external genitalia

Keep the body relaxed with abdominal respiration. Contract the anus and external genitalia during expiration; relax the abdomen during inspiration. Repeat the whole process 36 times.

Appendix 1
Glossary of Tui Na Manipulations for Adults

One-finger Pushing	*Yī Zhǐ Chán Tuī Fǎ*	一指禅推法
Rolling	*Gǔn Fǎ*	滚法
Kneading	*Róu Fǎ*	揉法
Rubbing	*Mó Fǎ*	摩法
Scrubbing	*Cā Fǎ*	擦法
Pushing	*Tuī Fǎ*	推法
Mopping	*Mā Fǎ*	抹法
Scattering Manipulation	*Sǎo Sǎn Fǎ*	扫散法
Foulage	*Cuō Fǎ*	搓法
Vibration	*Zhèn Fǎ*	振法
Shaking	*Dǒu Fǎ*	抖法
Pressing	*Àn Fǎ*	按法
Continuous Pressing Manipulation	*Yā Fǎ*	压法
Pointing	*Diǎn Fǎ*	点法
Pinching	*Niē Fǎ*	捏法
Grasping	*Ná Fǎ*	拿法
Twiddling Manipulation	*Niǎn Fǎ*	捻法
Plucking	*Bō Fǎ*	拨法
Patting Manipulation	*Pāi Fǎ*	拍法
Striking Manipulation	*Jī Fǎ*	击法
Flicking	*Tán Fǎ*	弹法
Rotatingon	*Yáo Fǎ*	摇法
Pulling-stretching Manipulation	*Bá Shēn Fǎ*	拔伸法
Back-carrying	*Bēi Fǎ*	背法
Pulling	*Bān Fǎ*	扳法
Pressing-kneading Manipulation	*Àn Róu Fǎ*	按揉法
Grasping-kneading Manipulation	*Ná Róu Fǎ*	拿揉法
Pushing-rubbing Manipulation	*Tuī Mó Fǎ*	推摩法

Appendix 2
Glossary of *Shào Lín* Internal Practicing Methods

Standing stance	*Zhàn Dāng Shì*	站裆势
Horse Stance	*Mǎ Dāng Shì*	马裆势
Bow Stance	*Gōng Jiàn Dāng Shì*	弓箭裆势
Close Stance	*Bìng Dāng Shì*	并裆势
Big Stance	*Dà Dāng Shì*	大裆势
Suspending Stance	*Xuán Dāng Shì*	悬裆势
Pushing Eight Horses Forward	*Qián Tuī Bā Pǐ Mǎ*	前推八匹马
Pulling Nine Oxen Backward	*Dào Lā Jiǔ Tóu Niú*	倒拉九头牛
Pulling Golden Ring with One Hand	*Dān Zhǎng Lā Jīn Huán*	单掌拉金环
Phoenix Spreading Its Wings	*Fèng Huáng Zhǎn Chì*	凤凰展翅
Conqueror Supporting Tripot	*Bà Wáng Jǔ Dǐng*	霸王举鼎
Pushing Boat along Water-Flowing	*Shùn Shuǐ Tuī Zhōu*	顺水推舟
Embracing the Moon	*Huái Zhōng Bào Yuè*	怀中抱月
Immortals Guiding Way	*Xiān Rén Zhǐ Lù*	仙人指路
Holding Tower with Flat Hand	*Píng Shǒu Tuō Tǎ*	平手托塔
Turning Palm to Fold Tile	*Yùn Zhǎng Hé Wǎ*	运掌合瓦
Wind Blowing Lotus Leaf	*Fēng Bǎi Hé Yè*	风摆荷叶
Supporting the Sky with Two Hands	*Liǎng Shǒu Tuō Tiān*	两手托天
Single Phoenix Facing the Sun	*Dān Fèng Cháo Yáng*	单凤朝阳
Scooping the Moon from Sea Bottom	*Hǎi Dǐ Lāo Yuè*	海底捞月
Supporting the Sky and Embracing the Earth	*Dǐng Tiān Bào Dì*	顶天抱地
Splitting Hua Mountain with Vigorous Efforts	*Lì Pǐ Huá Shān*	力劈华山

Index of Point Names—Numerical Codes

B

BL 1 (*jīng míng*, 睛明) 38
BL 2 (*cuán zhú*) 258, 288
BL 2 (*cuán zhú*, 攒竹) 38
BL 10 (*tiān zhù*, 天柱) 38
BL 11 (*dà zhù*, 大抒) 39
BL 12 (*fēng mén*, 风门) 19, 39
BL 13 (*fèi shù*) 19, 22
BL 13 (*fèi shù*, 肺俞) 39
BL 15 (*xīn shù*) 10
BL 15 (*xīn shù*, 心俞) 39
BL 17 (*gé shù*, 膈俞) 39
BL 18 (*gān shù*) 20, 21
BL 18 (*gān shù*, 肝俞) 39
BL 19 (*dǎn shù*, 胆俞) 39
BL 19 (*dǎn shù*) 21
BL 20 (*pí shù*) 7, 8, 18, 20, 23
BL 20 (*pí shù*, 脾俞) 39
BL 21 (*wèi shù*) 7, 8, 18, 20, 22, 23
BL 21 (*wèi shù*, 胃俞) 39
BL 22(*sān jiāo shù*, 三焦俞) 39
BL 23 (*shèn shù*) 17, 18
BL 23 (*shèn shù*, 肾俞) 40
BL 24 (*qì hǎi shù*, 气海俞) 40
BL 25 (*dà cháng shù*, 大肠俞) 40
BL 26(*guān yuán shù*, 关元俞) 40
BL 31 (*shàng liáo*) 22
BL 31, 32, 33, 34 (*ba liao*, 八髎) 40
BL 32 (*cì liáo*) 22
BL 33 (*zhōng liáo*) 22
BL 34 (*xià liáo*) 22
BL 37 (*yīn mén*, 殷门) 40
BL 52 (*zhì shì*) 18
BL 54 (*zhì biān*, 秩边) 40
BL 60 (*kūn lún*, 昆仑) 40
BL 62 (*shēn mài*, 申脉) 40
BL 63 (*jīn mén*, 金门) 40
BL 64 (*jīng gǔ*, 京骨) 40

D

dǎn náng xué (EX-LE 6, 胆囊穴) 46
DU 1 (*cháng qiáng*) 19, 265, 267
DU 1 (*cháng qiáng*, 长强) 44
DU 3 (*yāo yáng guān*, 腰阳关) 45
DU 4 (*mìng mén*) 17, 18
DU 4 (*mìng mén*, 命门) 45, 323
DU 12 (*shēn zhù*, 身柱) 45
DU 14 (*dà zhuī*) 19, 21, 265
DU 14 (*dà zhuī*, 大椎) 45
DU 16 (*fēng fǔ*) 19
DU 16 (*fēng fǔ* , 风府) 45
DU 20 (*bǎi huì*, 百会) 45
DU 26 (*shuǐ gōu*) 283
DU 26 (*shuǐ gōu*, 水沟) 45

G

GB 20 (*fēng chí*) 19, 260
GB 20 (*fēng chí*, 风池) 42
GB 21 (*jiān jǐng*, 肩井) 42
GB 29 (*jū liáo*, 居髎) 42
GB 30 (*huán tiào*, 环跳) 43
GB 31 (*fēng shì*, 风市) 43
GB 34 (*yáng líng quán*, 阳陵泉) 43, 316
GB 36 (*wài qiū*, 外丘) 43
GB 37 (*guāng míng*, 光明) 43
GB 39 (*xuán zhōng*, 悬钟) 43
GB 40 (*qiū xū*, 丘墟) 43
GB 41 (*zú lín qì*, 足临泣) 43

H

hè dǐng (EX-LE 2, 鹤顶) 46
HT 1 (*jí quá*, 极泉) 36

HT 1 (*jí quán*, 极泉) 318
HT 3 (*shào hǎi* , 少海) 36
HT 5 (*tōng lǐ*, 通里) 37
HT 6 (*yīn xì*, 阴郄) 37
HT 7 (*shén mén*, 神门) 37, 319

J

jiá jǐ (EX-B 2, 夹脊) 46
jiān nèi líng, 肩内陵 46

K

KI 1 (*yǒng quán*, 涌泉) 41, 323
KI 3 (*tài xī*, 太溪) 41
KI 4 (*dà zhōng*, 大钟) 41
KI 5 (*shuǐ quán*, 水泉) 41
KI 6 (*zhào hǎi*, 照海) 41
KI 8 (*jiāo xìn*, 交信) 41
KI 9 (*zhù bīn*, 筑宾) 41

L

lán wěi (EX-LE 7, 阑尾穴) 46
LI 4 (*hé gǔ*, 合谷) 33, 323
LI 4 (*hé gǔ*) 19, 87, 92, 98, 99, 100, 101, 102, 103
LI 5 (*yáng xī*, 阳溪) 33
LI 6 (*piān lì*, 偏历) 33
LI 7 (*wēn liū*, 温溜) 33
LI 10 (*shǒu sān lǐ*, 手三里) 33
LI 11 (*qū chí*, 曲池) 33
LI 15 (*jiān yú*, 肩髃) 34
LI 20 (*yíng xiāng*, 迎香) 34, 323
LU 5 (*chǐ zé*, 尺泽) 32
LU 6 (*kǒng zuì*, 孔最) 32
LU 7 (*liè quē*, 列缺) 33
LU 9 (*tài yuān*,太渊) 33
LU 10 (*yú jì*, 鱼际) 33
LU 11 (*shào shāng*, 少商) 33
LU 11 (*Shào Shāng*) 114
LV 3 (*tài chōng*, 太冲) 43, 316
LV 5 (*lí gōu*, 蠡沟) 44
LV 6 (*zhōng dū*, 中都) 44
LV 13 (*zhāng mén*) 20
LV 13 (*zhāng mén*, 章门) 44, 317
LV 14 (*qī mén*) 20
LV 14 (*qī mén*, 期门) 44, 317

N

nèi láo gōng (内劳宫) 255, 277

P

PC 3 (*qū zé*, 曲泽) 41
PC 4 (*xì mén*, 郄门) 41
PC 6 (*nèi guān*) 10, 22
PC 6 (*nèi guān*, 内关) 41, 319
PC 7 (*dà líng*, 大陵) 41
PC 8 (*láo gōng*) 90, 281
PC 8 (*láo gōng*, 劳宫) 42
PC 9 (*zhōng chōng*, 中冲) 318

Q

qiáo gōng, 桥弓 46

R

RN 4 (*guān yuán*) 17, 18
RN 4 (*guān yuán*, 关元) 324
RN 5 (*shí mén*, 石门) 44
RN 6 (*qì hǎi*, 气海) 44
RN 6 (*qì hǎi*) 8, 17, 18, 21, 23
RN 8 (*shén què*) 19
RN 8 (*shén què*, 神厥) 44
RN 10 (*xià wǎn*) 21
RN 12 (*zhōng wǎn*, 中脘) 8, 17, 18, 20, 22, 23, 44, 260, 262, 274, 285, 288
RN 13 (*shàng wǎn*) 20
RN 15 (*jiū wěi*, 鸠尾) 44
RN 17 (*dàn zhōng*) 22, 288
RN 17 (*dàn zhōng*, 膻中) 44, 316
RN 22 (*tiān tū*) 21, 22, 86
RN 22 (*tiān tū*, 天突) 44, 322
RN 24 (*chéng jiāng*, 承浆) 44

S

shí qī zhuī (EX-B8, 十七椎) 46
shí xuān (EX-UE 11, 十宣) 46
shí xuān (十宣) 283
SI 1 (*shào zé*, 少泽) 37
SI 3 (*hòu xī*, 后溪) 37
SI 4 (*wàn gǔ*, 腕骨) 37
SI 6 (*yǎng lǎo*, 养老) 37
SI 7 (*zhī zhèng*, 支正) 37
SI 8 (*xiǎo hǎi*, 小海) 38

SI 9 (*jiān zhēn*, 肩贞) 38
SI 11 (*tiān zōng*, 天宗) 38
SI 12 (*bǐng fēng*, 秉风) 38
SI 14 (*jiān wài shù*, 肩外俞) 38
SI 15 (*jiān zhōng shù*, 肩中俞) 38
SI 18 (*quán liáo*, 颧髎) 38
SJ 3 (*zhōng zhǔ*, 中渚) 42
SJ 4 (*yáng chí*) 279
SJ 4 (*yáng chí*, 阳池) 42
SJ 5 (*wài guān*) 19, 263
SJ 5 (*wài guān*, 外关) 42
SJ 7 (*huì zōng*, 会宗) 42
SJ 14 (*jiān liáo*, 肩髎) 42
SP 3 (*tài bái*, 太白) 36
SP 4 (*gōng sūn*, 公孙) 36
SP 6 (*sān yīn jiāo*, 三阴交) 36
SP 8 (*dì jī*, 地机) 36
SP 9 (*yīn líng quán*, 阴陵泉) 36
ST 10 (*shuǐ tū*,水突) 34
SP 10 (*xuè hǎi*) 21
SP 10 (*xuè hǎi*, 血海) 36, 318, 321
SP 15 (*dà héng*,大横) 36
ST 2 (*sì bái*, 四白) 34
ST 4 (*dì cāng*, 地仓) 34
ST 6 (*jiá chē*, 颊车) 34
ST 7 (*xià guān*, 下关) 34
ST 8 (*tóu wéi*, 头维) 34
ST 9 (*rén yíng*, 人迎) 34
ST 12 (*quē pén*, 缺盆) 34
ST 18 (*rǔ gēn*) 261
ST 25 (*tiān shū*) 18, 19, 261
ST 25 (*tiān shū*, 天枢) 35, 320
ST 31 (*bì guān*, 髀关) 35
ST 32 (*fú tù*, 伏兔) 35
ST 34 (*liáng qiū*, 梁丘) 35
ST 35 (*dú bí*, 犊鼻) 35
ST 36 (*zú sān lǐ*) 8, 22, 24
ST 36 (*zú sān lǐ*, 足三里) 35, 320
ST 37 (*shàng jù xū*, 上巨虚) 35
ST 39 (*xià jù xū*, 下巨虚) 35
ST 40 (*fēng long*, 丰隆) 35
ST 41 (*jiě xī*, 解溪) 35
ST 42 (*chōng yang*, 冲阳) 36

T

tài yáng (EX-HN 5, 太阳) 45

Y

yāo yǎn (EX-B 7, 腰眼) 45
yāo yǎn (腰眼) 88
yīn chí (阴池) 280
yìn táng (EX-HN 3, 印堂) 45
yú yāo (EX-HN4, 鱼腰) 45

Index of Point Names—*Pin Yin*

B

ba liao 40
bǎi huì 45
bì guān 35
bǐng fēng 38

C

cháng qiáng 19, 44, 265, 267
chéng jiāng 44
chǐ zé 32
chōng yang 36
cì liáo 22
cuán zhú 38, 258, 288

D

dà cháng shù 40
dà héng 36
dà ling 41
dà zhōng 41
dà zhù 39
dà zhuī 19, 21, 45, 265
dǎn náng xué 46
dǎn shù 21, 39
dàn zhōng 22, 44, 288, 316
dì cāng 34
dì jī 36
dú bí 35

F

fei shù 19, 22, 39
fēng chí 19, 42, 260
fēng fǔ 19, 45
fēng long 35
fēng mén 19, 39
fēng shì 43
fú tù 35

G

gān shù 20, 21, 39
gé shù 39
gōng sūn 36
guān yuán 17, 18, 44, 324
guān yuán shù 40
guāng míng 43

H

hè dǐng 46
hé gǔ 19, 33, 87, 92, 98, 99, 100, 101, 102, 103, 323
hòu xī 37
huán tiào 43
huì zōng 42

J

jí quán 36, 318
jiá chē 34
jiá jǐ 46
jiān jǐng 42
jiān liáo 42
jiān nèi líng 46
jiān wài shù 38
jiān yú 34
jiān zhēn 38
jiān zhōng shù 38
jiāo xìn 41
jiě xī 35
jīn mén 40
jīng gǔ 40
jīng míng 38
jiū wěi 44
jū liáo 42

K

kǒng zuì 32
kūn lún 40

L

lán wěi 46
láo gōng 42, 90, 281
lí gōu 44
liáng qiū 35
liè quē 33

M

mìng mén 17, 18, 45, 323

N

nèi guān 10, 22, 41, 319
nèi láo gōng 255, 277

P

pí shù 7, 8, 18, 20, 23, 39
piān lì 33

Q

qì hǎi 8, 17, 18, 21, 23, 44
qì hǎi shù 40
qī mén 20, 44, 317
qiáo gōng 46
qiū xū 43
qū chí 33
qū zé 41
quán liáo 38
quē pén 34

R

rén yíng 34
rǔ gēn 261

S

sān jiāo shù 39
sān yīn jiāo 36
shàng jù xū 35
shàng liáo 22
shàng wǎn 20
shào hǎi 36
Shào Shāng 114
shào shāng 33
shào zé 37
shēn mài 40
shén mén 37, 319
shén què 19, 44
shèn shù 17, 18, 40
shēn zhù 45
shí mén 44
shí qī zhuī 46
shí xuān 46, 283
shǒu sān lǐ 33
shuǐ gōu 45, 283
shuǐ quán 41
shuǐ tū 34
sì bái 34

T

tài bái 36
tài chōng 43, 316
tài xī 41
tài yáng 45
tài yuān 33
tiān shū 18, 19, 35, 261, 320
tiān tū 21, 22, 44, 86, 322
tiān zhù 38
tiān zōng 38
tōng lǐ 37
tóu wéi 34

W

wài guān 19, 42, 263
wài qiū 43
wàn gǔ 37
wèi shù 7, 8, 18, 20, 22, 23, 39
wēn liū 33

X

xì mén 41
xià guān 34
xià jù xū 35
xià liáo 22
xià wǎn 21
xiǎo hǎi 38
xīn shù 10, 39
xuán zhōng 43
xuè hǎi 21, 36, 318, 321

Y

yáng chí 42, 279
yǎng lǎo 37
yáng líng quán 43, 316
yáng xī 33
yāo yǎn 45, 88
yāo yáng guān 45
yīn chí 280
yīn líng quán 36
yīn mén 40
yìn táng 45
yīn xì 37
yíng xiāng 34, 323
yǒng quán 41, 323
yú jì 33
yú yāo 45

Z

zhāng mén 20, 44, 317
zhào hǎi 41
zhì biān 40
zhì shì 18
zhī zhèng 37
zhōng chōng 318
zhōng dū 44
zhōng fǔ 32, 322
zhōng liáo 22
zhōng wǎn 8, 17, 18, 20, 22, 23, 44, 260, 262, 274, 285, 288
zhōng zhǔ 42
zhù bīn 41
zú lín qì 43
zú sān lǐ 8, 22, 24, 35, 320

Index of Tui Na Manipulations for Adults

B

Back-Carrying 134

C

combing 202
Continuous Pressing Manipulation 124

F

finger-kneading 240
finger-pressing 240, 244
Flicking 129
flicking 145, 152
foulage 121, 183, 186, 219, 222

G

Grasping 126
grasping 19, 22, 152, 155, 159, 176, 198, 206, 214, 218, 221, 222, 240
grasping-kneading 145
Grasping-Kneading Manipulation (*Ná Róu Fă*, 拿揉法) 140

K

kneading 17, 18, 19, 20, 21, 22, 115, 155, 157, 162, 175, 186, 188, 189, 191, 195, 198, 218, 225, 228, 229, 232, 234, 237, 240, 244

M

Mopping 120

O

one-finger pushing 18, 19, 20, 23, 112, 114, 145, 162, 186, 188, 189, 191, 195, 198, 202, 205, 206, 210, 211, 214, 218, 222, 225, 228, 234, 237, 240, 244

P

palm-rubbing 240
palm-vibrating 162
patting 162
Patting Manipulation 128
pinching 25, 125, 159
pinching along the spine 202
plucking 127, 155, 157, 162, 165, 171, 176, 178, 180, 183
pointing 125, 162, 237
pointing-kneading 206, 207
pressing 18, 19, 20, 21, 22, 25, 123, 155, 157, 165, 186, 188, 189, 191, 195, 210, 214, 215, 218, 221, 225, 229, 232, 234, 237, 240
pressing and kneading 218, 237
pressing-kneading 145, 152, 159, 175, 180, 182, 186, 188, 198, 199, 202, 205, 210, 211
pulling 135, 145, 152, 165, 168, 176
pulling-extending 152, 181, 188
pulling-stretching 145, 165
pushing 19, 22, 25, 118, 157, 189, 205, 210, 215, 218

R

rolling 20, 145, 151, 154, 155, 159, 171, 175, 178, 180, 183, 188, 195, 198, 201, 206, 207, 211, 221, 222, 225, 240
rotating 145, 152, 186, 188, 189
Rotation 130
Rubbing 116
rubbing 18, 20, 21, 22, 152, 198, 202, 210, 215, 225, 228, 232, 244

S

scattering 205, 215, 218
Scattering Manipulation 120
scrubbing 17, 18, 22, 117, 145, 155, 157, 159, 162, 165, 168, 171, 173, 176, 181, 183, 186, 192, 198, 199, 202, 207, 211, 215, 218, 222, 225, 229, 232, 237

separating pushing 22
shaking 123, 152
Striking Manipulation 128

T

tapping 176
treading 165
Twiddling 222
twiddling 20, 21, 127, 229

V

vibrating 122, 232, 237

General Index

A

abdominal distending pain 200
aching pain in lumbar region 204
acute lumbar muscular pain 154
acute lumbar sprain 153
ankle twisting 188
Ataxia 149

B

back pain 207
Back-Carrying 134
BL 1 (*jīng míng*, 睛明) 38
BL 2 (*cuán zhú*) 258, 288
BL 2 (*cuán zhú*, 攒竹) 38
BL 10 (*tiān zhù*, 天柱) 38
BL 11 (*dà zhù*, 大杼) 39
BL 12 (*fēng mén*) 19
BL 12 (*fēng mén*, 风门) 39
BL 13 (*fèi shù*) 19, 22
BL 13 (*fèi shù*, 肺俞) 39
BL 15 (*xīn shù*) 10
BL 15 (*xīn shù*, 心俞) 39
BL 17 (*gé shù*, 膈俞) 39
BL 18 (*gān shù*) 20, 21
BL 18 (*gān shù*, 肝俞) 39
BL 19 (*dǎn shù*) 21
BL 19 (*dǎn shù*, 胆俞) 39
BL 20 (*pí shù*) 7, 8, 18, 20, 23
BL 20 (*pí shù*, 脾俞) 39
BL 21 (*wèi shù*) 7, 8, 18, 20, 22, 23
BL 21 (*wèi shù*, 胃俞) 39
BL 22(*sān jiāo shù*, 三焦俞) 39
BL 23 (*shèn shù*) 17, 18
BL 23 (*shèn shù*, 肾俞) 40
BL 24 (*qì hǎi shù*, 气海俞) 40
BL 25 (*dà cháng shù*, 大肠俞) 40
BL 26(*guān yuán shù*, 关元俞) 40
BL 31 (*shàng liáo*) 22
BL 31, 32, 33, 34 (*ba liao*, 八髎) 40
BL 32 (*cì liáo*) 22
BL 33 (*zhōng liáo*) 22
BL 34 (*xià liáo*) 22
BL 37 (*yīn mén*, 殷门) 40
BL 52 (*zhì shì*) 18
BL 54 (*zhì biān*, 秩边) 40
BL 60 (*kūn lún*, 昆仑) 40
BL 62 (*shēn mài*, 申脉) 40
BL 63 (*jīn mén*, 金门) 40
BL 64 (*jīng gǔ*, 京骨) 40
buttock pain 160

C

chest stuffiness 149
Chronic lumbar strain 155
chronic lumbar strain 164
chronic pain of lower back and leg 157
colic pain 193
combing 202
Continuous Pressing Manipulation 124
cramping of neck tendon, neck 147

D

dǎn náng xué (EX-LE 6, 胆囊穴) 46
distending pain in behind the eyeball 150
distending pain in hypochondriac regions 217
dizziness 150
DU 1 (*cháng qiáng*) 19, 265, 267
DU 1 (*cháng qiáng*, 长强) 44
DU 3 (*yāo yáng guān*, 腰阳关) 45
DU 4 (*mìng mén*) 17, 18
DU 4 (*mìng mén*, 命门) 45, 323
DU 12 (*shēn zhù*, 身柱) 45
DU 14 (*dà zhuī*) 19, 21, 265

DU 14 (*dà zhuī*, 大椎) 45
DU 16 (*fēng fǔ* , 风府) 45
DU 16 (*fēng fǔ*) 19
DU 20 (*bǎi huì*, 百会) 45
DU 26 (*shuǐ gōu*) 283
DU 26 (*shuǐ gōu*, 水沟) 45

E

ecchymosis 179
edema 149
elbow pain 312
EN 4 (*guān yuán*, 关元) 44
Epigastric distention or pain 193

F

failure of stretching the body 154
finger-kneading 240
finger-pressing 240, 244
flicking 129, 145, 152
Foulage 121
foulage 183, 186, 219, 222

G

GB 20 (*fēng chí*) 19, 260
GB 20 (*fēng chí*, 风池) 42
GB 21 (*jiān jǐng*, 肩井) 42
GB 29 (*jū liáo*, 居髎) 42
GB 30 (*huán tiào*, 环跳) 43
GB 31 (*fēng shì*, 风市) 43
GB 34 (*yáng líng quán*, 阳陵泉) 43, 316
GB 36 (*wài qiū*, 外丘) 43
GB 37 (*guāng míng*, 光明) 43
GB 39 (*xuán zhōng*, 悬钟) 43
GB 40 (*qiū xū*, 丘墟) 43
GB 41 (*zú lín qì*, 足临泣) 43
grasping 19, 22, 126, 152, 155, 159, 176, 198, 206, 214, 218, 221, 222, 240
Grasping-Kneading Manipulation (*Ná Róu Fǎ*, 拿揉法) 140
grasping-kneading 145

H

hè dǐng (EX-LE 2, 鹤顶) 46
Headache 149
hip pain 160
HT 1 (*jí quán*, 极泉) 36, 318
HT 3 (*shào hǎi* , 少海) 36
HT 5 (*tōng lǐ*, 通里) 37
HT 6 (*yīn xì*, 阴郄) 37
HT 7 (*shén mén*, 神门) 37, 319

I

irregular bowel movement 239

J

jiá jǐ (EX-B 2, 夹脊) 46
jiān nèi líng, 肩内陵 46
joint pain 183

K

KI 1 (*yǒng quán*, 涌泉) 41, 323
KI 3 (*tài xī*, 太溪) 41
KI 4 (*dà zhōng*, 大钟) 41
KI 5 (*shuǐ quán*, 水泉) 41
KI 6 (*zhào hǎi*, 照海) 41
KI 8 (*jiāo xìn*, 交信) 41
KI 9 (*zhù bīn*, 筑宾) 41
kneading 17, 18, 19, 20, 21, 22, 115, 155, 157, 162, 175, 186, 188, 189, 191, 195, 198, 218, 225, 228, 229, 232, 234, 237, 240, 244

L

lán wěi (EX-LE 7, 阑尾穴) 46
lassitude 204
LI 4 (*hé gǔ*) 19, 87, 92, 98, 99, 100, 101, 102, 103
LI 4 (*hé gǔ*, 合谷) 33, 323
LI 5 (*yáng xī*, 阳溪) 33
LI 6 (*piān lì*, 偏历) 33
LI 7 (*wēn liū*, 温溜) 33
LI 10 (*shǒu sān lǐ*, 手三里) 33
LI 11 (*qū chí*, 曲池) 33
LI 15 (*jiān yú*, 肩髃) 34
LI 20 (*yíng xiāng*, 迎香) 34, 323
LU 5 (*chǐ zé*, 尺泽) 32
LU 6 (*kǒng zuì*, 孔最) 32
LU 7 (*liè quē*, 列缺) 33
LU 9 (*tài yuān*,太渊) 33

LU 10 (*yú jì*, 鱼际) 33
LU 11 (*shào shāng*, 少商) 33, 114
lumbago 169
lumbago and leg pain 157
lumbar soreness 217, 227
lumbosacral muscular spasm 160
LV 3 (*tài chōng*, 太冲) 43, 316
LV 5 (*lí gōu*, 蠡沟) 44
LV 6 (*zhōng dū*, 中都) 44
LV 13 (*zhāng mén*) 20
LV 13 (*zhāng mén*, 章门) 44, 317
LV 14 (*qī mén*) 20
LV 14 (*qī mén*, 期门) 44, 317

M

migraine 150
Mopping 120

N

nèi láo gōng (内劳宫) 255, 277
Nodule-like spasm of piriformis 172
numb limbs 149

O

obesity 204
occiput pain 149
one-finger pushing 18, 19, 20, 23, 112, 114, 145, 162, 186, 188, 189, 191, 195, 198, 202, 205, 206, 210, 211, 214, 218, 222, 225, 228, 234, 237, 240, 244

P

pain and numbness of head, neck, shoulder and arm 146
pain in the chest 207
palm-rubbing 240
palm-vibrating 162
palpitation 209
Patting Manipulation 128
patting 162
PC 3 (*qū zé*, 曲泽) 41
PC 4 (*xì mén*, 郄门) 41
PC 6 (*nèi guān*) 10, 22
PC 6 (*nèi guān*, 内关) 41, 319
PC 7 (*dà líng*, 大陵) 41
PC 8 (*láo gōng*) 90, 281
PC 8 (*láo gōng*, 劳宫) 42
PC 9 (*zhōng chōng*, 中冲) 318
pinching along the spine 202
pinching 25, 125, 159
plucking 127, 155, 157, 162, 165, 171, 176, 178, 180, 183
pointing 125, 162, 237
pointing-kneading 206, 207
precordial pain 150, 207
pressing and kneading 218, 237
pressing 18, 19, 20, 21, 22, 25, 123, 155, 157, 165, 186, 188, 189, 191, 195, 210, 214, 215, 218, 221, 225, 229, 232, 234, 237, 240
pressing-Kneading Manipulation 139, 145, 152, 159, 175, 180, 182, 186, 188, 198, 199, 202, 205, 210, 211
pulling 135, 145, 152, 165, 168, 176
pulling-extending 152, 181, 188
Pulling-Stretching Manipulation 132
pulling-stretching 145, 165
pushing 19, 22, 25, 118, 157, 189, 205, 210, 215, 218
Pushing-Rubbing Manipulation 141

Q

qiáo gōng, 桥弓 46

R

RN 4 (*guān yuán*) 17, 18
RN 4 (*guān yuán*, 关元) 324
RN 5 (*shí mén*, 石门) 44
RN 6 (*qì hǎi*) 8, 17, 18, 21, 23
RN 6 (*qì hǎi*, 气海) 44
RN 8 (*shén què*) 19
RN 8 (*shén què*, 神厥) 44
RN 10 (*xià wǎn*) 21
RN 12 (*zhōng wǎn*) 8, 17, 18, 20, 22, 23, 260, 262, 274, 285, 288
RN 12 (*zhōng wǎn*, 中脘) 44
RN 13 (*shàng wǎn*) 20
RN 15 (*jiū wěi*, 鸠尾) 44
RN 17 (*dàn zhōng*) 22, 288

RN 17 (*dàn zhōng*, 膻中) 44, 316
RN 22 (*tiān tū*) 21, 22, 86
RN 22 (*tiān tū*, 天突) 44, 322
RN 24 (*chéng jiāng*, 承浆) 44
rolling 20, 145, 151, 154, 155, 159, 171, 175, 178, 180, 183, 188, 195, 198, 201, 206, 207, 211, 221, 222, 225, 240
rotation 130, 145, 152, 186, 188, 189
rubbing 18, 20, 21, 22, 116, 152, 198, 202, 210, 215, 225, 228, 232, 244

S

Scattering Manipulation 120
scattering 205, 215, 218
sciatica 171
scrubbing 17, 18, 22, 117, 145, 155, 157, 159, 162, 165, 168, 171, 173, 176, 181, 183, 186, 192, 198, 199, 202, 207, 211, 215, 218, 222, 225, 229, 232, 237
separating pushing 22
shaking 123, 152
shí qī zhuī (EX-B8, 十七椎) 46
shí xuān (EX-UE 11, 十宣) 46
shí xuān (十宣) 283
shoulder pain 147
SI 1 (*shào zé*, 少泽) 37
SI 3 (*hòu xī*, 后溪) 37
SI 4 (*wàn gǔ*, 腕骨) 37
SI 6 (*yǎng lǎo*, 养老) 37
SI 7 (*zhī zhèng*, 支正) 37
SI 8 (*xiǎo hǎi*, 小海) 38
SI 9 (*jiān zhēn*, 肩贞) 38
SI 11 (*tiān zōng*, 天宗) 38
SI 12 (*bǐng fēng*, 秉风) 38
SI 14 (*jiān wài shù*, 肩外俞) 38
SI 15 (*jiān zhōng shù*, 肩中俞) 38
SI 18 (*quán liáo*, 颧髎) 38
SJ 3 (*zhōng zhǔ*, 中渚) 42
SJ 4 (*yáng chí*) 279
SJ 4 (*yáng chí*, 阳池) 42
SJ 5 (*wài guān*) 19, 263
SJ 5 (*wài guān*, 外关) 42
SJ 7 (*huì zōng*, 会宗) 42
SJ 14 (*jiān liáo*, 肩髎) 42
SP 3 (*tài bái*, 太白) 36
SP 4 (*gōng sūn*, 公孙) 36
SP 6 (*sān yīn jiāo*, 三阴交) 36
SP 8 (*dì jī*, 地机) 36
SP 9 (*yīn líng quán*, 阴陵泉) 36
SP 10 (*xuè hǎi*) 21
SP 10 (*xuè hǎi*, 血海) 36, 318, 321
SP 15 (*dà héng*, 大横) 36
ST 2 (*sì bái*, 四白) 34
ST 4 (*dì cāng*, 地仓) 34
ST 6 (*jiá chē*, 颊车) 34
ST 7 (*xià guān*, 下关) 34
ST 8 (*tóu wéi*, 头维) 34
ST 9 (*rén yíng*, 人迎) 34
ST 10 (*shuǐ tū*, 水突) 34
ST 12 (*quē pén*, 缺盆) 34
ST 18 (*rǔ gēn*) 261
ST 25 (*tiān shū*) 18, 19, 261
ST 25 (*tiān shū*, 天枢) 35, 320
ST 31 (*bì guān*, 髀关) 35
ST 32 (*fú tù*, 伏兔) 35
ST 34 (*liáng qiū*, 梁丘) 35
ST 35 (*dú bí*, 犊鼻) 35
ST 36 (*zú sān lǐ*) 8, 22, 24
ST 36 (*zú sān lǐ*, 足三里) 35, 320
ST 37 (*shàng jù xū*, 上巨虚) 35
ST 39 (*xià jù xū*, 下巨虚) 35
ST 40 (*fēng long*, 丰隆) 35
ST 41 (*jiě xī*, 解溪) 35
ST 42 (*chōng yang*, 冲阳) 36
stiffness of the back 154
Striking Manipulation 128

T

tài yáng (EX-HN 5, 太阳) 45
tapping 176
tenderness on the area of capitulum radii 312
treading 165
twiddling 127, 222
twisting 20, 21, 229

U

upper abdominal pain 192

V

vibrating 122, 232, 237

Y

yāo yǎn (EX-B 7, 腰眼) 45
yāo yǎn (腰眼) 88
yīn chí (阴池) 280
yìn táng (EX-HN 3, 印堂) 45
yú yāo (EX-HN4, 鱼腰) 45

Notes

Notes

图书在版编目（CIP）数据

推拿学=Tui Na: 英文/金宏柱等主编．—北京：人民卫生出版社，2011.5
国际标准化英文版中医教材
ISBN 978-7-117-14291-5

Ⅰ. ①推… Ⅱ. ①金… Ⅲ. ①推拿-教材-英文
Ⅳ. ①R244.1

中国版本图书馆CIP数据核字（2011）第050764号

推拿学（国际标准化英文版中医教材）（英文版）

主　　编：金宏柱　Secondo Scarsella　丁晓红
出版发行：人民卫生出版社（中继线+8610-5978-7399）
地　　址：中国北京市朝阳区潘家园南里19号
世界医药图书大厦B座
邮　　编：100021
网　　址：http://www.pmph.com
E-mail：pmph @ pmph.com
发　　行：pmphsales@gmail.com
购书热线：+8610-5978 7399/5978 7338（电话及传真）
开　　本：787×1092　1/16
版　　次：2011年5月第1版　2011年5月第1版第1次印刷
标准书号：ISBN 978-7-117-14291-5/R·14292